Computing Concepts
with

JAVA 2

Essentials

Second Edition

Computing Concepts with

JAVA 2

Essentials

Second Edition

Cay S. Horstmann

San Jose State University

John Wiley & Sons, Inc.

New York ◆ Chichester ◆ Weinheim ◆ Brisbane ◆ Singapore ◆ Toronto

ACQUISITIONS EDITOR	Bill Zobrist
MARKETING MANAGER	Katherine Hepburn
SENIOR PRODUCTION EDITOR	Robin Factor
ILLUSTRATION EDITOR	Sigmund Malinowski
COVER DESIGNER	Michael Jung
COVER PHOTO	John Lund/Tony Stone Images
PHOTO EDITOR	Jill Hilycord
PRODUCTION SERVICES	Publication Services

This book was set in Stempel Schneidler by Publication Services, Inc., and printed and bound by Von Hoffmann Printing, Inc. The cover was printed by Phoenix Color.

This book is printed on acid-free paper ∞

ISBN 0-471-34609-8

Printed in the United States of America

10 9 8 7 6 5 4 3 2

Preface

This book gives a traditional introduction to computer science using modern tools. As computer scientists, we have the good fortune of being able to introduce students to an activity that is accessible, satisfying, and deep rather than broad: namely, the activity of *programming*. Like the majority of computer scientists, I believe that programming is a central theme of computer science. Thus this course teaches students how to program.

Although this book remains traditional in outlook, it uses modern techniques in three ways.

First, this book uses a strategic subset of the Java language. Java has many advantages as a teaching language. It has a simpler and more consistent syntax than C or C++. The run-time environment is very strict about enforcing array bounds and valid references. However, Java has many more features than C or Pascal, and an introductory programming course cannot cover them all. This book makes no mention of multithreading, weak references, or reflection, and it necessarily discusses only a small part of the standard library, which has now grown to contain thousands of classes.

The second modern aspect is the early use of objects. Objects are introduced in stages. In Chapters 1 and 2, students learn how to *use* objects. Students become comfortable with the concepts of creating objects and calling methods. In Chapter 3, students learn how to implement classes with *very simple* methods. Chapter 3 introduces just enough object concepts to enable students to write their own graphical programs in Chapter 4. Chapter 7 covers the more technical aspects of the Java syntax, such as static methods and variables. Chapter 9 discusses inheritance and—in preparation for the chapter on event handling—interfaces. Finally, Chapter 14 teaches how to *discover* classes in a systematic way. Some instructors wonder whether "objects early" is a good idea. In C++, the cumbersome syntax and language rules make that approach unattractive, but classes in Java are simple enough to be introduced early. Furthermore, Java programs that use only static methods look very strange, and it is not a good idea to introduce students to a procedural programming style and then teach them to abandon it. Nevertheless, nobody expects students to be able to design complex collections of classes from the outset. This book uses a four-step approach:

1. Use classes.
2. Read the implementations of simple classes.
3. Implement simple classes.
4. Implement collections of classes.

This approach gradually builds up to object-oriented design.

Finally, the book introduces graphics and graphical user interfaces. Students enjoy programming graphics. Starting with the Java 2 release, Java has object-oriented facilities for rendering graphics; I introduce these objects early on. (For example, instead of using the procedural `drawRect` method, students manipulate `Rectangle` objects.) Students also learn how to construct simple user interfaces using the Swing package, which is available with Java 2. The focus is on simplicity, not completeness. For example, I see no sense in spending valuable class time teaching the intricacies of the `GridBagLayout`, when there are so many important *concepts* to cover in CS1. The border, flow, and grid layouts do just fine for simple programs. The first graphics chapter starts with applets to avoid the complexities of window event handling. Graphical applications are introduced in Chapter 10, and user interface construction is the topic of Chapter 12.

One problem for Java textbook authors, instructors, and students is how to deal with the complexity of the Java library. While the language itself is clean and simple, the class library has an annoying amount of clumsiness in text input, date handling, termination of graphics programs, and so on. Java was simply not designed as a teaching language, and no care was given to hide certain implementation details. Furthermore, some library packages were implemented in a hurry, without much regard to good design at all. For the first edition of this book I supplied a "black box" library that shielded students from unimportant details so that more class time could be spent teaching fundamental concepts rather than Java minutiae. That approach turned out not to be as popular as I thought. Students and instructors felt that they were wasting valuable time learning a library that they would never use again. More importantly, they feared that they would be completely lost once they had to go on to the next course, in which the library was no longer available. Some of the most annoying problems in the standard Java library have been fixed in Java 2. These improvements enabled me to drop the graphics library, relying on the standard Java packages for all graphical programs. They also made it possible to encapsulate the complexities of console input in a simple class that students can understand. Students are free to take that class—or just the knowledge of how to implement it—to their next programming course.

When planning a course, you have to make the following decisions:

◆ Do you want to teach graphics and graphical user interfaces? If not, omit Chapters 4, 10, and 12. This has no impact on the remainder of the course.

◆ Do you want to teach classes first, or do you prefer to cover branches and loops before classes? If the latter, cover Chapters 5 and 6 before Chapter 3, with minor adjustments in a couple of sample programs.

◆ Do you want to teach the details of the console reader class? If not, skip sections 2.8 and 3.10.

◆ Which optional chapters do you want to cover? Chapters 8, 14, 15, and 16 on testing and debugging, object-oriented design, algorithms, and data structures stand on their own, and you can include or exclude them as time permits.

Figure 1 shows the dependencies among the chapters.

The material in each chapter is divided into three parts: the essential, the useful, and the optional. To cover the essential material, simply skip over all side notes. It is perfectly reasonable to ignore all side notes completely during lectures and assign them for home reading.

Three of the side note sets are useful for the students, namely those entitled "Common Errors", "Productivity Hints", and "Quality Tips". Students quickly discover the Common Errors and read them on their own. You should encourage students to read the Quality Tips. The Productivity Hints may be challenging to some of the weaker students, but those with more computer experience tend to find them very helpful.

The Random Facts and Advanced Topics are optional. The Random Facts provide historical and social information on computing, as required to fulfill the "historical and social context" requirements of the ACM curriculum guidelines. Most students will read the Random Facts on their own while pretending to follow the lecture. Most of the Advanced Topics cover nonessential or more difficult material, such as alternative syntactical constructions.

In many cases, the book uses one particular language construct but explains alternatives as Advanced Topics. Instructors and students should feel free to use those constructs in their own programs if they prefer them. It has, however, been my experience that many students are grateful for the "keep it simple" approach, because it greatly reduces the number of decisions they have to make.

Appendix A1 contains a style guide for use with this book. I have found it highly beneficial to require a consistent style for all assignments. If this style guide conflicts with instructor sentiment or local customs, it can be modified. The style guide is available in electronic form for this purpose.

Appendix A2 contains a summary of the Java API subset used in this book.

Appendix A3 contains tables of the Basic Latin (also known as ASCII) and Latin-1 subsets of the Unicode.

The book covers the following knowledge units from the ACM curriculum guidelines:

AL1: Basic Data Structures (6 of 13 hours)
AL2: Abstract Data Types (2 of 2 hours)
AL3: Recursion (2 of 3 hours)
AL6: Sorting and Searching (2 of 6 hours)
PL3: Representation of Data Types (2 of 2 hours)
PL4: Sequence Control (2 of 4 hours)
PL5: Data Control, Sharing, and Type Checking (2 of 4 hours)
PR: Introduction to a Programming Language (12 of 12 hours)
SE1: Fundamental Problem Solving Concepts (16 of 16 hours)
SP1: Historical and Social Context of Computing (3 of 3 hours)

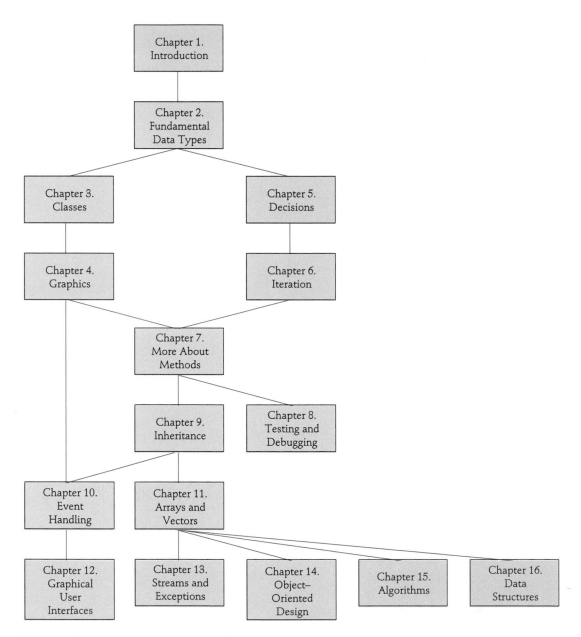

Figure 1

Chapter Dependencies

Acknowledgments

I am very grateful to my acquisitions editors, Regina Brooks and Bill Zobrist, at John Wiley & Sons. Regina had started the "Computing Concepts" series and encouraged me to keep revising it. Bill has taken over rapidly and competently after Regina's departure. Thanks to you both, and also to Jennifer Welter and Robin Factor of John Wiley & Sons.

Once again, I'd like to thank the staff at Publication Services—Jerome Colburn, Jan Fisher, Stephen Beer, Rhonda Ries, Michael Hall, Jason Pankoke—for the excellent production work under a difficult schedule.

Many thanks to Byron Becker of the University of Waterloo, Rick Giles of Acadia University, Tim Kimmet of Seagull Technology, Stuart Reges of the University of Arizona, and Kim Topley, the author of *Core Java Foundation Classes,* for diligently reviewing the manuscript, for finding so many errors and typos, and for your constructive suggestions and encouragement. You made this a better book!

Finally, as always, my love and gratitude goes to my wife Hui-Chen and my children Thomas and Nina for never-ending encouragement and patience.

Contents

Chapter 3 An Introduction to Classes   103

Chapter 4 Applets and Graphics   139

Chapter 5 Decisions   183

Chapter 6 Iteration   223

Chapter 7 More About Methods   269

Chapter 8 Testing and Debugging   313

Chapter 9 Inheritance and Interfaces   341

Chapter 10 Event Handling   395

Chapter 11 Arrays and Vectors   431

Chapter 12 Graphical User Interfaces   479

Chapter 13 Streams and Exceptions

Chapter 14 Object-Oriented Design

Chapter 15 Algorithms

Chapter 16 An Introduction to Data Structures

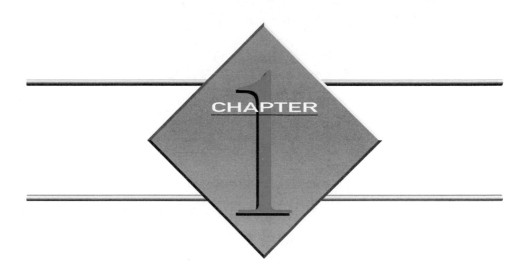

Introduction

Chapter Goals

- ◆ To understand the activity of programming

- ◆ To learn about the architecture of computers

- ◆ To learn about machine languages and higher-level programming languages

- ◆ To become familiar with your compiler

- ◆ To compile and run your first Java program

- ◆ To understand the concepts of classes and objects

- ◆ To recognize syntax and logic errors

1.1   What Is a Computer?

You have probably used a computer for work or fun. Many people use computers for everyday tasks such as balancing a checkbook or writing a term paper. Computers are good for such tasks. They can handle repetitive chores, such as totaling up numbers or placing words on a page, without getting bored or exhausted. More importantly, the computer presents you with the checkbook or the term paper on the screen and lets you fix up mistakes easily. Computers make good game machines because they can play sequences of sounds and pictures, involving the human user in the process.

Actually, what makes all this possible is not just the computer. The computer must be programmed to perform these tasks. One program balances checkbooks; a different program, probably designed and constructed by a different company, processes words; and a third program plays a game. A computer itself is a machine that stores data (numbers, words, pictures), interacts with devices (the monitor screen, the sound system, the printer), and executes programs. Programs are sequences of instructions and decisions that the computer carries out to achieve a task.

Today's computer programs are so sophisticated that it is hard to believe that they are all composed of extremely primitive operations. A typical operation may be one of the following.

- ◆ Put a red dot onto this screen position.
- ◆ Send the letter A to the printer.
- ◆ Get a number from this location in memory.
- ◆ Add up these two numbers.
- ◆ If this value is negative, continue the program at that instruction.

Only because a program contains a huge number of such operations, and because the computer can execute them at great speed, does the computer user have the illusion of smooth interaction.

The flexibility of a computer is quite an amazing phenomenon. The same machine can balance your checkbook, print your term paper, and play a game. In contrast, other machines carry out a much narrower range of tasks; a car drives, and a toaster toasts. Computers can carry out a wide range of tasks because they execute different programs, each of which directs the computer to work on a specific task.

1.2   What Is Programming?

A computer program tells a computer, in minute detail, the sequence of steps that are needed to fulfill a task. The act of designing and implementing these programs is called computer programming. In this course, you will learn how to program a computer—that is, how to direct the computer to execute tasks.

To use a computer you do not need to do any programming. When you write a term paper with a word processor, that program has been programmed by the manufacturer and is ready for you to use. That is only to be expected—you can drive a car without being a mechanic and toast bread without being an electrician. Many people who use computers every day in their careers never need to do any programming.

Of course, a professional computer scientist or software engineer does a great deal of programming. Since you are taking this first course in computer science, it may well be your career goal to become such a professional. Programming is not the only skill required of a computer scientist or software engineer; indeed, programming is not the only skill required to create successful computer programs. Nevertheless, the activity of programming is an important part of computer science. It is also a fascinating and pleasurable activity that continues to attract and motivate students. The discipline of computer science is particularly fortunate that it can make such an interesting activity the foundation of the learning path.

To write a computer game with motion and sound effects or a word processor that supports fancy fonts and pictures is a complex task that requires a team of many highly skilled programmers. Your first programming efforts will be more mundane. The concepts and skills you learn in this course form an important foundation, and you should not be disappointed if your first programs do not rival the sophisticated software that is familiar to you. Actually, you will find that there is an immense thrill even in simple programming tasks. It is an amazing experience to see the computer precisely and quickly carry out a task that would take you hours of drudgery, to make small changes in a program that lead to immediate improvements, and to see the computer become an extension of your mental powers.

1.3   The Anatomy of a Computer

To understand the programming process, you need to have a rudimentary understanding of the building blocks that make up a computer. We will look at a personal computer. Larger computers have faster, larger, or more powerful components, but they have fundamentally the same design.

At the heart of the computer lies the *central processing unit* (CPU) (see Figure 1). It consists of a single *chip* or a small number of chips. A computer chip (integrated circuit) is a component with a plastic or metal housing, metal connectors, and inside wiring made principally from silicon. For a CPU chip, the inside wiring is enormously complicated. For example, the Pentium chip (a popular CPU for personal computers at the time of this writing) is composed of over 3 million structural elements called *transistors*. Figure 2 shows a magnified detail view of a CPU chip. The CPU performs program control, arithmetic, and data movement. That is, the CPU locates and executes the program instructions; it carries out arithmetic operations such as addition, subtraction, multiplication, and division; it fetches data from external memory or devices or stores data back. All data must travel through the CPU whenever it is moved from one location to another. (There are a few technical exceptions to this rule; some devices can interact directly with memory.)

Figure 1

Central Processing Unit

The computer stores data and programs in *memory.* There are two kinds of memory. *Primary storage* is fast but expensive; it is made from memory chips (see Figure 3): so-called *random-access memory* (RAM) and *read-only memory* (ROM). Read-only memory contains certain programs that must always be present—for example, the code needed to start the computer. Random-access memory might have been better called "read-write memory", because the CPU can read data from it and write data back to it. That makes RAM suitable to hold changing data and programs that do not have to be available permanently. RAM memory has two disadvantages. It is comparatively expensive, and it loses all its data when the power is turned off. *Secondary storage,* usually a *hard disk* (see Figure 4), provides less expensive storage that persists without electricity. A hard disk consists of rotating platters, which are coated with a magnetic material, and read/write heads, which can detect and change the magnetic flux on the platters. This is essentially the same storage process that is used in audio or video tapes. Programs and data are typically stored on the hard disk and loaded into RAM when the program starts. The program then updates the data in RAM and writes the modified data back to the hard disk.

You will often use another kind of magnetic storage device: a so-called *floppy disk* or *diskette*. Originally, floppy disks had a fairly low capacity, but recently high-capacity floppies such as the Zip disk and the Superdisk have become popular (see Figure 5). A floppy disk consists of a flexible round base (hence the name "floppy"), covered with a magnetic material, inside a plastic cover (which is usually not flexible). Like a hard disk, a floppy disk can also store data and programs, and the data

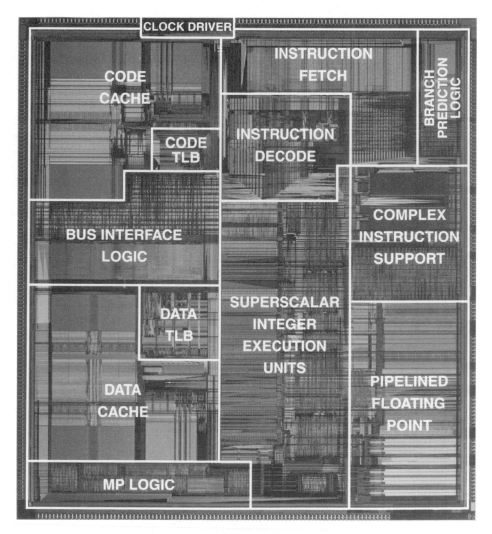

Figure 2

CPU Chip Detail

Figure 3

RAM Chips

Figure 4

A Hard Disk

Figure 5

A High-Capacity
Floppy Disk and Its
Drive

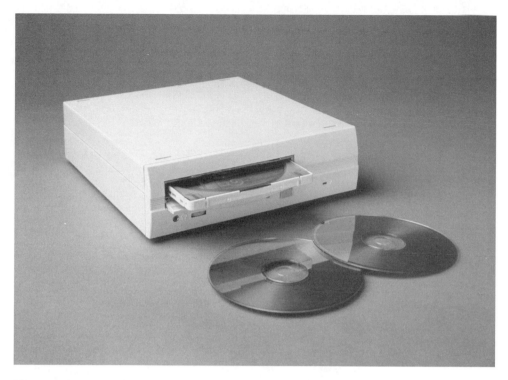

Figure 6

A CD-ROM Drive

are kept without electricity. The most common use for a floppy disk is to move data from one computer to another; you can copy data from your home computer and bring the disk to school to continue working with it, or you can put the disk in the mail. Because a floppy disk is not an integral part of the computer system, it is called an *external storage device*.

Floppy drives are inexpensive, comparatively rugged, and convenient, but they suffer from one disadvantage: One floppy disk cannot hold nearly as much data as a hard disk. That is not so much a problem for your personal data; it is quite likely that all the homework you will produce in this class will easily fit on one floppy. However, audio and video information takes up much more space than a floppy disk provides. That kind of information is typically distributed on a CD-ROM (compact disc read-only memory; see Figure 6) or DVD (digital versatile disk). A CD-ROM looks just like an audio CD and is read by a laser device (in fact, a CD-ROM reader on a personal computer can also play an audio CD). A CD-ROM can hold a large amount of information, and it can be manufactured inexpensively, but it is a read-only device: It can be used only to deliver programs and data from the manufacturer to the user, not by the user to store more data. To store large amounts of user data, *data tapes* (see Figure 7) are commonly used. Like audio and video tape cassettes, data

Figure 7

Tape Backup Drives and Data Tape

Figure 8

A Personal Computer

tapes contain a long strip of magnetic tape for reading and writing data. Data tapes are inexpensive but slow. To locate data in the middle of the tape, the tape must be wound to the portion containing the data—a much slower task than moving a head across a rotating platter.

Some computers are self-contained units, whereas others are interconnected through *networks*. Home computers are usually intermittently connected to the Internet via a modem. The computers in your computer lab are probably permanently connected to a local area network. Through the network cabling, the computer can read programs from central storage locations or send data to other computers. For the user of a networked computer it may not even be obvious which data reside on the computer itself and which are transmitted through the network.

To interact with a human user, a computer requires other peripheral devices. The computer transmits information to the user through a display screen, loudspeakers, and printers. The user can enter information and directions to the computer by using a keyboard or a pointing device such as a mouse. Figure 8 shows a typical personal computer equipped with these devices.

The central processing unit, RAM memory, and the electronics controlling the hard disk and other devices are interconnected through a set of electrical lines called a *bus.* Data travel along the bus from the system memory and peripheral devices to the CPU and back. Figure 9 shows a *motherboard,* which contains the CPU, the

Figure 9

A Motherboard

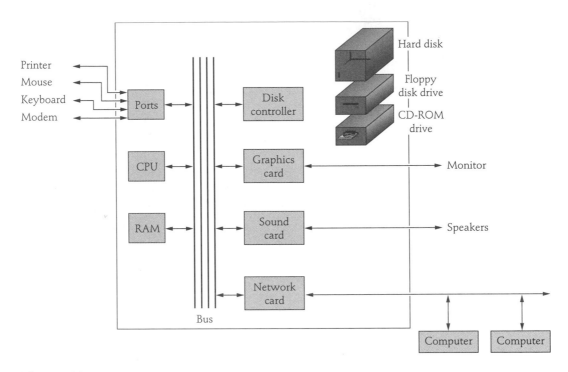

Figure 10

Schematic Diagram of a
Personal Computer

RAM, and card slots, through which cards that control peripheral devices connect to
the bus.

Figure 10 gives a schematic overview of the architecture of a computer. Program instructions and data (such as text, numbers, audio or video) are stored on
the hard disk, on a CD-ROM, or elsewhere on the network. When a program is
started, it is brought into RAM memory, from which the CPU can read it. The
CPU reads the program an instruction at a time. As directed by these instructions, the CPU reads data, modifies them, and writes them back to RAM memory or the hard disk. Some program instructions will cause the CPU to place dots
on the display screen or printer or to vibrate the speaker. As these actions happen
many times over and at great speed, the human user will perceive images and sound.
Some program instructions read user input from the keyboard or mouse. The program analyzes the nature of these inputs and then executes the next appropriate
instructions.

Random Fact 1.1

The ENIAC and the Dawn of Computing

The ENIAC (*electronic numerical integrator and computer*) was the first usable electronic computer. It was designed by J. Presper Eckert and John Mauchly at the University of Pennsylvania and was completed in 1946—two years before transistors were invented. The computer was housed in a large room and consisted of many cabinets containing about 18,000 vacuum tubes (see Figure 11). Vacuum tubes burned out at the rate of several tubes per day. An attendant with a shopping cart full of tubes constantly made the rounds and replaced defective ones. The computer was programmed by connecting wires on panels. Each wiring configuration would set up the computer for a particular problem. To have the computer work on a different problem, the wires had to be replugged.

Work on the ENIAC was supported by the U.S. Navy, which was interested in computations of ballistic tables that would give the trajectory of a projectile, depending on the wind

Figure 11

The ENIAC

resistance, initial velocity, and atmospheric conditions. To compute the trajectories, one must find the numerical solutions of certain differential equations; hence the name "numerical integrator". Before machines like ENIAC were developed, humans did this kind of work, and until the 1950s the word "computer" referred to these people. The ENIAC was later used for peaceful purposes such as the tabulation of U.S. Census data.

1.4   Translating Human–Readable Programs to Machine Code

On the most basic level, computer instructions are extremely primitive. The processor executes *machine instructions.* CPUs from different vendors, such as the Intel Pentium or the Sun SPARC, have different sets of machine instructions. To enable Java programs to run on multiple CPUs without modification, most Java compilers generate a set of machine instructions for a so-called "Java virtual machine", an idealized CPU that is then simulated by a program run on the actual CPU. The difference between actual and virtual machine instructions is not important to us—all you need to know is that machine instructions are very simple and can be executed very quickly. A typical sequence of machine instructions is

1. Load the contents of memory location 40.
2. Load the value 100.
3. If the first value is greater than the second value, continue with the instruction that is stored in memory location 240.

Actually, machine instructions are encoded as numbers so that they can be stored in memory. On the Java virtual machine, this sequence of instruction is encoded as the sequence of numbers

$$21\ 40\ 16\ 100\ 163\ 240$$

On a processor such as an Intel Pentium, the encoding would be quite different. When the virtual machine fetches this sequence of numbers, it decodes them and executes the associated sequence of commands.

How can you communicate the command sequence to the computer? The simplest method is to place the actual numbers into the computer memory. This is, in fact, how the very earliest computers worked. However, a long program is composed of thousands of individual commands, and it is tedious and error-prone to look up the numeric codes for all commands and place the codes manually into memory. As we said before, computers are really good at automating tedious and error-prone activities, and it did not take long for computer programmers to realize that the computers themselves could be harnessed to help in the programming process.

The first step was to assign short names to the commands. For example, `iload` denotes "integer load", `bipush` means "push integer constant", and `if_icmpgt` means "if integers compare greater". Using these commands, the instruction sequence becomes

```
iload      40
bipush     100
if_icmpgt  240
```

That is a lot easier to read for humans. To get the instruction sequences accepted by the computer, though, the names must be translated into the machine codes. Early computers used a computer program called an *assembler* to carry out these translations. An assembler takes the sequence of characters such as `iload`, translates it into the command code 21, and carries out similar operations on the other commands. Assemblers have another feature: They can give names to *memory locations* as well as to instructions. Our program sequence might have checked that some interest rate was greater than 100 percent, and the interest rate was stored in memory location 40. It is usually not important where a value is stored; any available memory location will do. By using symbolic names instead of memory addresses, the program gets even easier to read:

```
iload      intRate
bipush     100
if_icmpgt  intError
```

It is the job of the assembler program to find suitable numeric values for the symbolic names and to put those values into the generated code sequence.

Assembler instructions were a major advance over programming with raw machine codes, but they suffer from two problems. It still takes a great many instructions to achieve even the simplest goals, and the exact instruction sequence differs from one processor to another. For example, the above sequence of machine codes is valid only on the Java virtual machine, not on the Pentium or SPARC processor. That is a real problem for people who invest a lot of time and money producing a software package. If a computer becomes obsolete, the program must be completely rewritten to run on the replacement system.

In the mid-1950s, higher-level programming languages began to appear. In these languages, the programmer expresses the idea behind the task that needs to be performed, and a special computer program, called a *compiler* translates the higher-level description into machine instructions for a particular processor.

For example, in Java, the high-level programming language that you will use in this course, you might give the following instruction:

```
if (intRate > 100) System.out.print("Interest rate error");
```

This means, "If the interest rate is over 100, display an error message." It is then the job of the compiler program to look at the sequence of characters `if (intRate > 100)` and translate that into

```
21 40 16 100 163 240
```

Compilers are quite sophisticated programs. They have to translate logical statements, such as the `if`, into sequences of computations, tests, and jumps, and they must find memory locations for variables like `intRate`. In this course, we will generally take the existence of a compiler for granted. If you become a professional computer scientist, you may well learn more about compiler-writing techniques later in your studies.

Higher-level languages are independent of the underlying hardware. For example, the instruction `if (intRate > 100)` does not rely on particular machine instructions. In fact, it will compile to different code if it is to be run as native code on a Pentium or SPARC processor rather than the Java virtual machine.

1.5   Programming Languages

Programming languages are independent of specific computer architecture, but they are human creations. As such, they follow certain conventions. To ease the translation process, those conventions are much stricter than they are for human languages. When you talk to another person, and you scramble or omit a word or two, your conversation partner will usually still understand what you have to say. Compilers are less forgiving. For example, if you omit the quotation mark close to the end of the instruction,

```
if (intRate > 100) System.out.print("Interest rate error);
```

the Java compiler will get quite confused and complain that it cannot translate an instruction containing this error. That is actually a good thing. If the compiler were to try to guess what you did wrong and tried to fix it, it might not guess your intentions correctly. In that case, the resulting program would do the wrong thing—quite possibly with disastrous effects, if that program controlled a device on whose functions someone's well-being depends. When a compiler reads programming instructions in a programming language, it will translate them into machine code only if the input follows the language conventions exactly.

Just as there are many human languages, there are many programming languages. Consider the instruction

```
if (intRate > 100) System.out.print("Interest rate error");
```

This is how you must format the instruction in Java. Java is a very popular programming language, and it is the one we use in this book. But in Pascal (another programming language that was in common use in the 1970s and 1980s) the same instruction would be written as

```
if intRate > 100 then write('Interest rate error');
```

In this case, the differences between the Java and Pascal versions are slight. For other constructions, there will be far more substantial differences. Compilers are language-specific. The Java compiler will translate only Java code, whereas a Pascal compiler will reject anything but legal Pascal code. For example, if a Java compiler reads the instruction `if intRate > 100 then ...`, it will complain, because the condition of the `if` statement isn't surrounded by parentheses `()` and the compiler doesn't expect the word `then`. The choice of the layout for a language construct like the `if` statement is somewhat arbitrary, and the designers of different languages choose different tradeoffs among readability, easy translation, and consistency with other languages.

1.6 The Java Programming Language

In 1991, a group led by James Gosling and Patrick Naughton at Sun Microsystems designed a language that they code-named "Green" for use in consumer devices such as intelligent television "set-top" boxes. The language was designed to be simple and architecture-neutral, so that it could be executed on a variety of hardware. No customer was ever found for this technology.

Gosling recounts that in 1994 the team realized, "We could write a really cool browser. It was one of the few things in the client/server mainstream that needed some of the weird things we'd done: architecture neutral, real-time, reliable, secure." The HotJava browser, which was shown to an enthusiastic crowd at the SunWorld exhibition in 1995, had one unique property: It could download programs, called *applets,* from the web and run them. Applets, written in the language now called Java, let web developers provide a variety of animation and interaction that can greatly extend the capabilities of a page. (See Figure 12.) In 1996, both Netscape and Microsoft supported Java in their browsers.

Since then, Java has grown at a phenomenal rate. Programmers have embraced the language because it is simpler than its closest rival, C++. In addition to the programming language itself, Java has a rich *library* that makes it possible to write portable programs that can bypass proprietary operating systems—a feature that was eagerly sought by those who wanted to be independent of those proprietary systems and was bitterly fought by their vendors.

Some of the early expectations that were placed on the Java language were overly optimistic, and the slogan "write once, run anywhere" turned into "write once, debug everywhere" for the early adopters of Java, who had to deal with less-than-perfect implementations. Since then, Java has come a long way, and the Java 2 language and library, released in 1998, promises to bring stability to Java development and to fulfill the promise of "write once, run everywhere".

Because Java was designed for the Internet, it has two attributes that make it very suitable for beginners: safety and portability. If you visit a web page that contains applets, those applets automatically start running. It is important that you can trust that applets are inherently safe. If an applet could do something evil, such as damaging data or reading personal information on your computer, then you would be

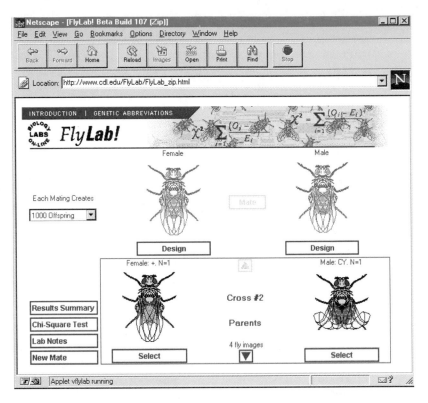

Figure 12

An Applet on a Web Page

in real danger every time you browsed the Web: an unscrupulous designer might put up a Web page containing dangerous code that would execute on your machine as soon as you visited the page. The Java language has an assortment of security features that guarantee that no evil applets can be written. As an added benefit, these features also help you to learn the language faster. The Java virtual machine can catch many kinds of beginners' mistakes and report them accurately. (In contrast, many beginners' mistakes in the C language merely produce programs that act in random and confusing ways).

The other benefit of Java is portability. The same Java program will run, without change, on Windows, UNIX, Linux, or the Macintosh. This too is a requirement for applets. When you visit a web page, the web server that serves up the page contents has no idea what computer you are using to browse the web. It simply returns you the portable code that was generated by the Java compiler. The virtual machine on your computer executes that portable code. Again, there is a benefit for the student. You do not have to learn how to write programs for different computers' operating systems.

At this time, Java has already established itself as one of the most important languages for general-purpose programming as well as for computer science instruction. However, although Java is a good language for beginners, it is not perfect, for two reasons.

Because Java was not specifically designed for students, no thought was given to make it really simple to write basic programs. A certain amount of technical machinery is necessary in Java to write even the simplest programs. To understand what this technical machinery does, you need to know something about programming. This is not a problem for a professional programmer with prior experience in another programming language, but not having a linear learning path is a drawback for the student. As you learn how to program in Java, there will be times when you will be asked to be satisfied with a preliminary explanation and wait for a complete details in a later chapter.

Furthermore, you cannot hope to learn all of Java in one semester. The Java language itself is relatively simple, but Java contains a vast set of *library packages* that are necessary to write useful programs. There are packages for graphics, user interface design, cryptography, networking, sound, database storage, and many other purposes. Even expert Java programmers do not know the contents of all of the packages—they just use those that are needed for particular projects. Using this book, you should expect to learn a good deal about the Java language and about the most important packages. Keep in mind that the central goal of this book is not to make you memorize Java minutiae, but to teach you how to think about programming.

1.7   Becoming Familiar with Your Computer

For many readers this will be your first programming course, and you may well be doing your work on an unfamiliar computer system. You should spend some time making yourself familiar with the computer. Because computer systems vary widely, this book can only give an outline of the steps you need to follow. Using a new and unfamiliar computer system can be frustrating, especially if you are on your own. Look for training courses that your campus offers, or just ask a friend to give you a brief tour.

Step 1. Login

If you use your own home computer, you probably don't need to worry about this step. Computers in a lab, however, are usually not open to everyone. Access is usually restricted to those who have paid the necessary fees and who can be trusted not to mess up the configuration. You will likely need an account number and a password to gain access to the system.

Figure 13

A Startup Screen with Icons

Step 2. Locate the Java Compiler

Computer systems differ greatly in this regard. Some systems let you start the compiler by selecting an icon (see Figure 13) or menu. On other systems you must use the keyboard to type a command to launch the compiler. On most personal computers there is a so-called *integrated environment* in which you can write and test your programs. On other computers you must first launch one program that functions like a word processor, in which you can enter your Java instructions; then launch another program to translate them to virtual machine instructions; and then run the virtual machine interpreter to carry out those instructions.

Step 3. Understand Files and Folders

As a programmer, you will write Java programs, try them out, and improve them. You will be provided a place on the computer to store them, and you need to find out where that place is. You will store your programs in *files*. A Java file is a container of Java instructions. Files have names, and the rules for legal names differ from one

Figure 14

A Directory Hierarchy

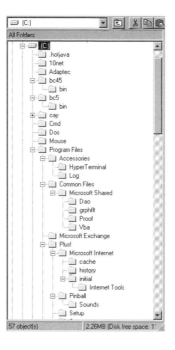

system to another. Some systems allow spaces in file names; others don't. Some distinguish between upper- and lowercase letters; others don't. Most Java compilers require that Java files end in an *extension* .java; for example, test.java. Java file names cannot contain spaces, and the distinction between upper- and lowercase letters is important.

Files are stored in *folders* or *directories*. These file containers can be nested. A folder can contain files as well as other folders, which themselves can contain more files and folders (see Figure 14). This hierarchy can be quite large, especially on networked computers, where some of the files may be on your local disk, others elsewhere on the network. While you need not be concerned with every branch of the hierarchy, you should familiarize yourself with your local environment. Different systems have different ways of showing files and directories. Some use a graphical display and let you move around by clicking the mouse on folder icons. In other systems, you must enter commands to visit or inspect different locations.

Step 4. Write a Simple Program

In the next section, we will introduce a very simple program. You will need to learn how to type it in, how to run it, and how to fix mistakes.

Step 5. Save Your Work

You will spend many hours typing Java programs in and improving them. The resulting program files have some value, and you should treat them as you would other important property. A conscientious safety strategy is particularly important for computer files. They are more fragile than paper documents or other more tangible objects. It is easy to delete a file by accident, and occasionally files are lost because of a computer malfunction. Unless you kept another copy, you must then retype the contents. Because you probably won't remember the entire file, you will likely find yourself spending almost as much time again as you did to enter and improve it in the first place. This costs time, and it may cause you to miss deadlines. It is therefore crucially important that you learn how to safeguard files and get in the habit of doing so *before* disaster strikes. You can make safety or *backup* copies of files by saving copies on a floppy or by saving them into another folder.

Productivity Hint 1.1

Backup Copies

Backing up on floppy disks is the easiest and most convenient method for most people. If you can't back up onto floppies, you can back up into separate folders on your hard disk—but then you need to back up those folders, typically onto data tape, in case the hard disk dies. Here are a few pointers to keep in mind.

◆ *Back up often.* Backing up a file takes only a few seconds, and you will hate yourself if you have to spend many hours recreating work that you could have saved easily. I recommend that you back up your work once every thirty minutes, and every time before you run a program that you wrote.

◆ *Rotate backups.* Use more than one floppy disk for backups, and rotate them. That is, first back up onto the first floppy disk and put it aside. Then back up onto the second floppy disk. Then use the third, and then go back to the first. That way you always have three recent backups. Even if one of the floppy disks has a defect, you can use one of the others. The next day, switch to a new set of three. How many simultaneous backups should you keep? It is a tradeoff between convenience and paranoia. I suggest you keep seven sets of three, one set for each weekday.

◆ *Back up source files only.* The compiler translates the files that you write into files consisting of machine code. There is no need to back up the machine code files, since you can recreate them easily by running the compiler again. Focus your backup activity on those files that represent your effort. That way your backup disks won't fill up with files that you don't need.

◆ *Pay attention to the backup direction.* Backing up involves copying files from one place to another. It is important that you do this right—that is, copy from your work location to the backup location. If you do it the wrong way, you will overwrite a newer file with an older version.

◆ *Check your backups once in a while.* Double-check that your backups are where you think they are. There is nothing more frustrating than to find out that the backups are not there when you need them. This is particularly true if you use a backup program that stores files on an unfamiliar device (such as data tape) or in a compressed format.

◆
◆
◆
◆

◆ *Relax, then restore.* When you lose a file and need to restore it from backup, you are likely to be in an unhappy, nervous state. Take a deep breath and think through the recovery process before you start. It is not uncommon for an agitated computer user to wipe out the last backup when trying to restore a damaged file.

1.8   Compiling a Simple Program

You are now ready to write and run our first Java program. The traditional choice for the very first program in a new programming language is a program that displays a simple greeting: "Hello, World!". We follow that tradition. Here is the "Hello, World!" program in Java.

Program Hello.java

```
public class Hello
{  public static void main(String[] args)
   {  System.out.println("Hello, World!");
   }
}
```

We will explain this program in a minute. For now, you should make a new program file and call it **Hello.java**. Enter the program instructions and compile and run the program, following the procedure that is appropriate for your compiler.

By the way, Java is *case-sensitive*. You must enter upper- and lowercase letters exactly as they appear in the program listing. You cannot type **MAIN** or **PrintLn**. On the other hand, Java has *free-form layout*. Spaces and line breaks are not important, except to separate words. You can cram as many words as possible into each line,

```
public class Hello{public static void main(String[] args){System
.out.println("Hello, World!");}}
```

or write every word and symbol on a separate line,

```
public
class
Hello
{
public
static
void
main
(
String
[
]
args
)
```

```
{
System
.
out
.
println
(
"Hello, World!"
)
;
}
}
```

However, good taste dictates that you lay out your programs in a readable fashion, so you should follow the layout in the program listing.

When you run the program, the message

```
Hello, World!
```

will appear on the screen. On some systems, you may need to switch to a different window to find the message.

Now that you have seen the program working, it is time to understand its makeup. The first line,

```
public class Hello
```

starts a new *class*. Classes are a fundamental concept in Java. Their primary role is as "factories" for *objects*. Objects are another central Java concept, and you will begin to study objects in greater detail in Chapter 3. Right now, think of an object as an item that a program can manipulate.

In our first program, you need not be concerned about classes as object factories. You just want to print a message. Java, like most programming languages, requires that all program statements must be placed inside *methods*. (In many other programming languages, methods are called *functions* or *procedures*, but we will use the Java terminology in this book.) Java, unlike many other languages, further requires that *every* method must be placed inside a class. In Java, classes are the central organizing mechanism for code. That is why we introduce the `Hello` class, as the holder of the `main` method.

The keyword `public` denotes that the class is usable by the "public". You will later encounter `private` features, which are not.

At this point, you should simply regard the

```
public class ClassName
{
    . . .
}
```

as a necessary part of the "plumbing" that is required to write any Java program. In Java, every source file can contain at most one public class, and the name of the public class must match the name of the file containing the class. For example, the class `Hello` *must be* contained in a file Hello.java. It is very important that the names *and the capitalization* match exactly. You can get strange error messages if you call the class `HELLO` or the file `hello.java`.

The construction

```
public static void main(String[] args)
{
}
```

defines a *method* called `main`. A method is a collection of programming instructions that describe how to carry out a particular task. Every Java application must have a `main` method. Most Java programs contain other methods besides `main`, but it will take us until Chapter 3 to learn how to write other methods.

The *parameter* `String[] args` is a required part of the `main` method—it contains the so-called command line arguments (which we will not discuss until Chapter 13). The keyword `static` denotes the fact that the `main` method does not inspect or change objects of the `Hello` class. As you will see in Chapter 3, most methods in Java do operate on objects, and the so-called `static` methods are not common in large Java programs. Nevertheless, `main` must always be `static`.

At this time, simply consider

```
public class ClassName
{  public static void main(String[] args)
   {
       . . .
   }
}
```

as yet another part of the "plumbing". For the time being, simply put all instructions that you want to have executed inside the `main` method of a class.

Java Syntax

1.1 Simple Program

```
public class ClassName
{  public static void main(String[] args)
   {  statements
   }
}
```

Example:

```
public class Greetings
{  public static void main(String[] args)
   {  System.out.println("Greetings, Earthling!");
   }
}
```

Purpose:

To execute a simple program

The instructions or *statements* in the *body* of the `main` method—that is, the statements inside the curly braces {}—are executed one by one. Note that each statement ends in a semicolon ;. Our method has a single statement:

```
System.out.println("Hello, World!");
```

This statement prints a line of text, namely "Hello, World!". However, there are many places where a program can send that string: to a window, to a file, or to a networked computer on the other side of the world. You need to specify that the destination for the string is the *standard output*—that is, a terminal window. The terminal window is represented in Java by an object called `out`. Just as you needed to place the `main` method in a `Hello` class, the designers of the Java library needed to place `out` in a class. They placed it in the `System` class, which contains useful objects and methods to access system resources. To use the `out` object in the `System` class, you must refer to it as `System.out`.

To use an object such as `System.out`, you specify what you want to do to it. In this case, you want to print a line of text. The `println` method (of the `PrintStream` class) carries out this task. You do not have to implement this method—the programmers who wrote the Java library already did that for us—but you do need to *call* the method.

Whenever you call a method in Java, you need to specify three items:

1.   The object that you want to use (in this case, `System.out`)
2.   The name of the method you want to use (in this case, `println`)
3.   A pair of parentheses, containing any other information the method needs (in this case, `("Hello, World!")`)

Note that the two periods in `System.out.println` have two different meanings. The first period means "locate the `out` object in the `System` class". The second period means "apply the `println` method to that object".

A sequence of characters enclosed in quotation marks

```
"Hello, World!"
```

Java Syntax
1.2 Method Call
object. methodName (*parameters*)

Example:
```
System.out.println("Good morning!");
```

Purpose:
To invoke a method of an object and supply any additional parameters

---

is called a *string*. You must enclose the contents of the string inside quotation marks so that the compiler knows you literally mean `"Hello, World!"`. There is a reason for this requirement. Suppose you needed to print the word *main*. By enclosing it in quotation marks, `"main"`, the compiler knows you mean the sequence of characters `m a i n`, not the method named `main`. The rule is simply that you must enclose all text strings in quotation marks, so that the compiler considers them plain text and does not try to interpret them as program instructions.

You can also print numerical values. For example, the statement

```
System.out.println(3 + 4);
```

displays the number 7.

The `println` method prints a string or a number, and then starts a new line. For example, the sequence of statements

```
System.out.println("Hello");
System.out.println("World!");
```

prints two lines of text:

```
Hello
World!
```

There is a second method, called `print`, that you can use to print an item without starting a new line afterwards. For example, the output of the two statements

```
System.out.print("00");
System.out.println(3 + 4);
```

is the single line

```
007
```

◆ Common Error 1.1

Omitting Semicolons

In Java every statement must end in a semicolon. Forgetting to type a semicolon is a common error. It confuses the compiler, because the compiler uses the semicolon to find where one statement ends and the next one starts. The compiler does not use line ends or closing braces to recognize the end of statements. For example, the compiler considers

```
System.out.println("Hello")
System.out.println("World!");
```

a single statement, as if you had written

```
System.out.println("Hello") System.out.println("World!");
```

Then it doesn't understand that statement, because it does not expect the word `System` following the closing parenthesis after `"Hello"`. The remedy is simple. Scan every statement for a terminating semicolon, just as you would check that every English sentence ends in a period.

Advanced Topic 1.1

Escape Sequences

Suppose you want to display a string containing quotation marks, such as

```
Hello, "World"!
```

You can't use

```
System.out.println("Hello, "World"");
```

As soon as the compiler reads `"Hello, "`, it thinks the string is finished, and then it gets all confused about `World` followed by two quotation marks. A human would probably realize that the second and third quotation marks were supposed to be part of the string, but compilers have a one-track mind, and if a simple analysis of the input doesn't make sense to them, they just refuse to go on, and they report an error. Well, how do you then display quotation marks on the screen? You precede the quotation marks inside the string with a *backslash* character. Inside a string, the sequence \" denotes a literal quote, not the end of a string. The correct display statement is therefore

```
System.out.println("Hello, \"World\"!");
```

The backslash character is used as a so-called *escape* character, and the character sequence \" is called an escape sequence. The backslash does not denote itself; instead, it is used to encode other characters that would otherwise be difficult to include in a string.

Now, what do you do if you actually want to print a backslash (for example, to specify a Windows filename)? You must enter two in a row, like this:

```
System.out.println("The secret message is in C:\\Temp\\Secret.txt");
```

This statement prints

```
The secret message is in C:\Temp\Secret.txt
```

Another escape sequence occasionally used is \n, which denotes a newline or line feed character. Printing a newline character causes the start of a new line on the display. For example, the statement

```
System.out.print("*\n**\n***\n");
```

prints the characters

```
*
**
***
```

on three separate lines. Of course, you could have achieved the same effect with three separate calls to `println`.

Finally, escape sequences are useful for including international characters in a string. For example, suppose you want to print `"All the way to San José!"`, with an accented letter é. If you use a U.S. keyboard, you may not have a key to generate that letter. Java uses an encoding scheme called *Unicode* to denote international characters. For example, the é character has Unicode encoding 00E9. You can include that character inside a string by writing \u, followed by its Unicode encoding:

```
System.out.println("All the way to San Jos\u00E9!");
```

You can look up the codes for the U.S. English and Western European characters in Appendix 3, and codes for thousands of characters in reference [1].

1.9   Errors

Experiment a little with the Hello program. What happens if you make a typing error such as

```
System.ouch.println("Hello, World!");
System.out.println("Hello, World!");
System.out.println("Hell, World!");
```

In the first case, the compiler will complain. It will say that it has no clue what you mean by **ouch**. The exact wording of the error message is dependent on the compiler, but it might be something like "Undefined symbol ouch". This is a *compile-time error* or *syntax error*. Something is wrong according to the language rules, and the compiler finds it. When the compiler finds one or more errors, it refuses to translate the program to bytecode, and as a consequence you have no program that you can run. You must fix the error and compile again. In fact, the compiler is quite picky, and it is common to go through several rounds of fixing compile-time errors before compilation succeeds for the first time.

If the compiler finds an error, it will not simply stop and give up. It will try to report as many errors as it can find, so you can fix them all at once. Sometimes, however, one error throws it off track. This is likely to happen with the error in the second line. Because the closing quotation mark is missing, the compiler will think that the) ; are still part of the string. In such cases, it is common for the compiler to emit bogus error reports for neighboring lines. You should fix only those error messages that make sense to you and then recompile.

The error in the third line is of a different kind. The program will compile and run, but its output will be wrong. It will print

```
Hell, World!
```

This is a *run-time error* or *logic error*. The program is syntactically correct and does something, but it doesn't do what it is supposed to do. The compiler cannot find the error. You, the programmer, must flush out this type of error. Run the program, and carefully look at its output.

During program development, errors are unavoidable. Once a program is longer than a few lines, it requires superhuman concentration to enter it correctly without slipping up once. You will find yourself omitting semicolons or quotes more often than you would like, but the compiler will track down these problems for you.

Logic errors are more troublesome. The compiler will not find them—in fact, the compiler will cheerfully translate any program as long as its syntax is correct—but the resulting program will do something wrong. It is the responsibility of the program author to test the program and find any logic errors. Testing programs is an important topic that you will encounter many times in this course. Another important aspect of good craftsmanship is *defensive programming:* structuring programs and development processes in such a way that an error in one place of a program does not trigger a disastrous response.

The error examples that you saw so far were not difficult to diagnose or fix, but as you learn more sophisticated programming techniques, there will also be much more room for error. It is an uncomfortable fact that locating all errors in a program is very difficult. Even if you can observe that a program exhibits faulty behavior, it may not at all be obvious what part of the program caused it and how you can fix it. Special software tools (so-called *debuggers*) let you trace through a program to find *bugs*—that is, logic errors. In this course you will learn how to use a debugger effectively.

Note that all these errors are different from the kind of errors that you are likely to make in calculations. If you total up a column of numbers, you may miss a minus sign or accidentally drop a carry, perhaps because you are bored or tired. Computers do not make these kinds of errors. When a computer adds up numbers, it will get the correct answer. Admittedly, computers can make overflow or roundoff errors, just as pocket calculators do when you ask them to perform computations whose result falls outside their numeric range. An overflow error occurs if the result of a computation is very large or very small. For example, most computers and pocket calculators overflow when you try to compute 10^{1000}. A roundoff error occurs when a value cannot be represented precisely. For example, $\frac{1}{3}$ may be stored in the computer as 0.3333333, a value that is close to, but not exactly equal to $\frac{1}{3}$. If you compute $1 - 3 \times \frac{1}{3}$, you may obtain 0.0000001, not 0, as a result of the roundoff error. We will consider such errors logic errors, because the programmer should have chosen a more appropriate calculation scheme that handles overflow or roundoff correctly.

You will learn a three-part error management strategy in this course. First, you will learn about common errors and how to avoid them. Then you will learn defensive programming strategies to minimize the likelihood and impact of errors. Finally, you will learn debugging strategies to flush out those errors that remain.

◆Common Error 1.2

Misspelling Words

If you accidentally misspell a word, then strange things may happen, and it may not always be completely obvious from the error messages what went wrong. Here is a good example of how simple spelling errors can cause trouble:

```
public class Hello
{  public static void Main(String[] args)
   {  System.out.println("Hello, World!");
   }
}
```

This code defines a method called `Main`. The compiler will not consider this to be the same as the `main` method, because `Main` starts with an uppercase letter and the Java language is *case-sensitive*. Upper- and lowercase letters are considered to be completely different from each other, and to the compiler `Main` is no better match for `main` than `rain`. The compiler will cheerfully compile your `Main` method, but when the Java interpreter is ready to read the compiled file, it will complain about the missing `main` method and refuse to run the program. Of course, the message "missing main method" should give you a clue where to look for the error.

If you get an error message that seems to indicate that the compiler is on the wrong track, it is a good idea to check for spelling and capitalization. All Java keywords use only lowercase letters. Names of classes usually start with an uppercase letter, names of methods and variables with a lowercase letter. If you misspell the name of a symbol (for example, `ouch` instead of `out`), the compiler will complain about an "undefined symbol". That error message is usually a good clue that you made a spelling error.

1.10 The Compilation Process

Some Java development environments are very convenient to use. You just enter the code in one window, click on a button or menu to compile, and click on another button or menu to run your code. Error messages show up in a second window, and the program runs in a third window. Figure 15 shows the screen layout of a popular Java compiler with these features. With such an environment you are completely shielded from the details of the compilation process. On other systems you must carry out every step manually.

Even if you use a convenient Java environment, it is useful to know what goes on behind the scenes, mainly because knowing the process helps you solve problems when something goes wrong.

In many Java environments, you must set up a *project* for every program that you want to write. Instructions for this process vary widely between compiler vendors, and you need to read the documentation of your development environment or ask your instructor.

You enter the program statements into a text editor. The editor stores the text and gives it a name such as `Hello.java`. If the editor window shows a name like `Noname.java`, you should change the name. You should *save* the file to disk frequently, because otherwise the editor stores the text only in the computer's memory. If something goes wrong with the computer and you need to restart it, the contents of the RAM (including your program text) are lost, but anything stored on a hard disk or floppy disk is permanent even if you need to restart the computer.

When you compile your program, the compiler translates the Java *source code* (that is, the statements that you wrote) into so-called *bytecode,* which consists of virtual machine instructions and some other pieces of information on how to load the program into memory prior to execution. The bytecode for a program is stored in a separate file, with extension `.class`. For example, the bytecode for the Hello program will be stored in `Hello.class`.

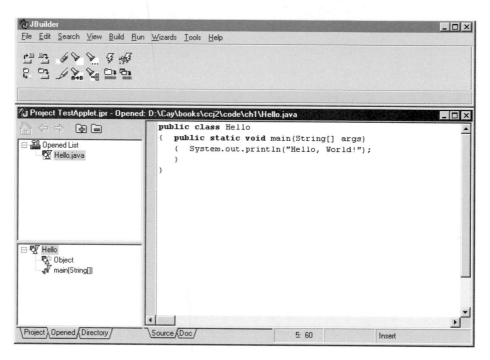

Figure 15

Screen Layout of an Integrated Java
Environment

The bytecode file contains the translation of only the instructions that you wrote.
That is not enough actually to run the program. To display a string on a window, quite
a bit of low-level activity is necessary. The authors of the **System** and **PrintStream**
classes (which define the **out** object and the **println** method) have implemented
all necessary actions and placed the required bytecodes into a *library.* A library is a
collection of code that has been programmed and translated by someone else, ready
for you to use in your program. (More complicated programs are built from more than
one bytecode file and more than one library.)

A *Java interpreter* loads the bytecode of the program that you wrote, starts your
program, and loads the necessary library bytecode files as they are required. These
steps are outlined in Figure 16.

The most basic Java tools require you to invoke the editor, compiler, and loader
manually, by starting these programs from a command line interface. You would type

```
edit Hello.java
javac Hello.java
java Hello
```

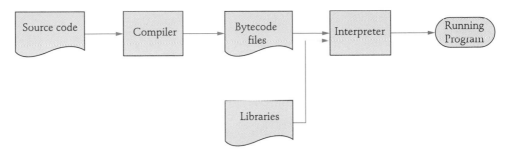

Figure 16

From Source Code to
Running Program

to edit and compile the Hello.java file and to execute the resulting program. In a more
sophisticated environment, you can achieve the same effect by clicking on menus or
toolbar buttons.

Your programming activity centers around these steps. You start in the editor,
writing the source file. You compile the program and look at the error messages. You
go back to the editor and fix the syntax errors. When the compiler succeeds, you run
the executable file. If you find an error, you can run the debugger to execute it a line at
a time. Once you find the cause of the error, you go back to the editor and fix it. You
compile and run again to see whether the error has gone away. If not, you go back to
the editor. This is called the *edit–compile–debug loop* (see Figure 17), and you will spend
a substantial amount of time in this loop in the months and years to come.

1.11 A First Look at Objects and Classes

Objects and classes are central concepts for Java programming. It will take you some
time to master these concepts fully, but since every Java program uses at least a couple
of objects and classes, it is a good idea to have a basic understanding of these concepts
right away.

An *object* is an entity that you can manipulate in your program, generally by calling
methods. For example, `System.out` refers to an object, and you saw how to manipulate
it by calling the `println` method. (Actually, several different methods are available:
all called `println`, one for printing strings, one for printing integers, one for printing
floating-point numbers, and so on.) When you call the `println` method, some activities occur inside the object, and the ultimate effect is that the object causes text to
appear in the console window. For now, you should think of the object as a "black box"
with a public *interface*—the methods you can call—and a hidden *implementation*—the
code and data that are necessary to make these methods work.

Figure 17

Edit–Compile–Debug Loop

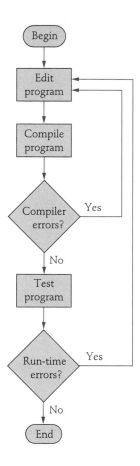

Different objects support different sets of methods. For example, the `println` method can be applied to the `System.out` object, but it cannot be applied to the string object `"Hello, World!"`. That is, it would be an error to call

```
"Hello, World!".println(); // This method call is an error
```

The reason is simple. The `System.out` and `"Hello, World!"` objects belong to different *classes*. The `System.out` object is an object of the class `PrintStream`, and the `"Hello, World!"` object is an object of class `String`. You can apply the `println` method to *any* object of the `PrintStream` class, but the `String` class does not support the `println` method. The `String` class supports a good number of other methods; you will see many of them in Chapter 2. For example, the `length` method counts the number of characters in string. You can apply that method to any object of type `String`. Thus,

```
"Hello, World!".length(); // This method call is ok
```

is a correct method call—it computes the number 13, the number of characters in the string object `"Hello, World!"`. (The quotation marks are not counted.)

A *class* has four purposes:

1. A class specifies the methods that you can use for objects that belong to the class.
2. A class is a factory for objects.
3. A class is a holding place for static methods and objects.
4. A class defines *implementation details*: the data layout of the objects and the code for the methods.

In our first program, you saw the third (and least important) purpose. The `Hello` class holds the static `main` method. The `System` class holds the static `out` object.

To see how a class can be an object factory, let us turn to another class: the `Rectangle` class in the Java class library. Objects of type `Rectangle` describe rectangular shapes—see Figure 18.

Note that a `Rectangle` object isn't a rectangular shape—it is a set of numbers that describe the rectangle (see Figure 19). Each rectangle is described by the *x*- and *y*-coordinates of its top left corner, its width, and its height. To make a new rectangle, you need to specify these four values. For example, you can make a new rectangle with top left corner at (5, 10), width 20 and height 30 as follows:

```
new Rectangle(5, 10, 20, 30)
```

The **new** operator causes the creation of an object of type `Rectangle`. The process of creating a new object is called *construction*. The four values 5, 10, 20, 30 are called the *construction parameters*. Different classes will require different construction parameters. For example, to construct a `Rectangle` object, you supply four numbers that describe the position and size of the rectangle. To construct a `Car` object, you might supply the model name and year.

Actually, some classes let you construct objects in multiple ways. For example, you can also obtain a rectangle object by supplying no construction parameters at all (but you must still supply the parentheses):

```
new Rectangle()
```

This constructs a (rather useless) rectangle with top left corner at the origin (0, 0), width 0 and height 0. Construction without parameters is called *default construction*.

Figure 18
_____

Rectangular Shapes

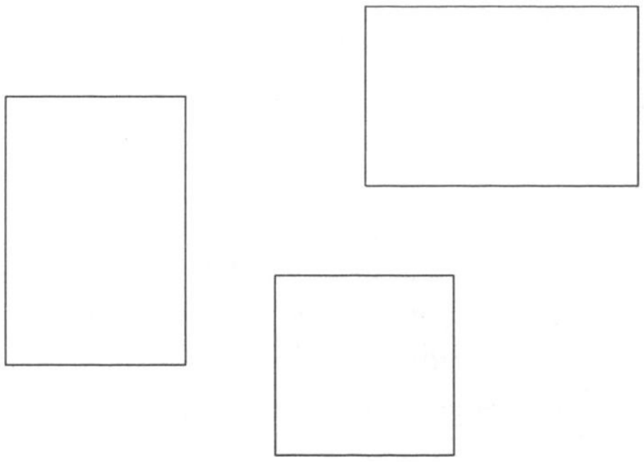

Figure 19

Rectangle Objects

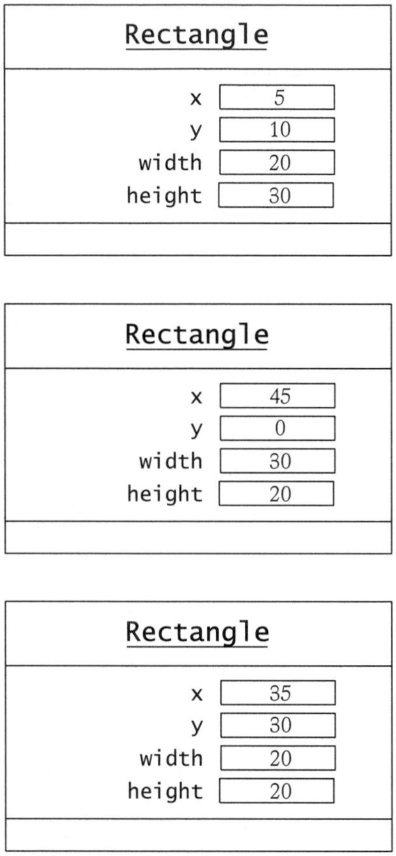

```
                        Rectangle
                  ┌─────────────────────────┐
                  │         x  ┌──── 5 ────┐ │
                  │         y  ┌──── 10 ───┐ │
                  │     width  ┌──── 20 ───┐ │
                  │    height  ┌──── 30 ───┐ │
                  ├─────────────────────────┤
                  └─────────────────────────┘
```

```
                        Rectangle
                  ┌─────────────────────────┐
                  │         x  ┌──── 45 ───┐ │
                  │         y  ┌──── 0 ────┐ │
                  │     width  ┌──── 30 ───┐ │
                  │    height  ┌──── 20 ───┐ │
                  ├─────────────────────────┤
                  └─────────────────────────┘
```

```
                        Rectangle
                  ┌─────────────────────────┐
                  │         x  ┌──── 35 ───┐ │
                  │         y  ┌──── 30 ───┐ │
                  │     width  ┌──── 20 ───┐ │
                  │    height  ┌──── 20 ───┐ │
                  ├─────────────────────────┤
                  └─────────────────────────┘
```

Java Syntax
1.3 Object Construction
new *ClassName* (*parameters*)

Example:
```
new Rectangle(5, 10, 20, 30);
new Car();
```

Purpose:
To construct a new object, initialize it with
the construction parameters, and return a
reference to the constructed object

To construct any object, you do the following:

1. Use the **new** operator
2. Give the name of the class
3. Supply construction parameters (if any) inside parentheses

What can you do with a `Rectangle` object? Not much, for now. In Chapter 4, you will learn how to display rectangles and other shapes in a window. You already know how to print a description of the rectangle object onto the console window—simply call the `System.out.println` method:

```
System.out.println(new Rectangle(5, 10, 20, 30));
```

This code prints the line

```
java.awt.Rectangle[x=5,y=10,width=20,height=30]
```

Or, more specifically, this code creates an object of type `Rectangle`, then passes that object to the `println` method, and finally forgets that object.

Of course, usually you want to do something more to an object than just create it, print it and forget it. To remember an object, you need to hold it in an *object variable*. An object variable is a storage location that stores not the actual object, but information about the object's location—see Figure 20.

You can create an object variable by giving the name of a class, followed by a name for the variable. For example,

```
Rectangle cerealBox;
```

This statement defines an object variable, `cerealBox`. The *type* of this variable is `Rectangle`. In Java, every object variable has a particular type. For example, after the `cerealBox` variable has been defined by the preceding statement, thereafter in the program it must always refer to an object of type `Rectangle`, never to an object of type `Car` or `string`.

However, so far, the `cerealBox` variable doesn't yet refer to any object at all. It is an *uninitialized variable* (see Figure 21). To make `cerealBox` refer to an object, simply set it to another object reference. How do you get another object reference? The **new** operator returns a reference to a newly created object.

Figure 20

An Object Variable That Refers to an Object

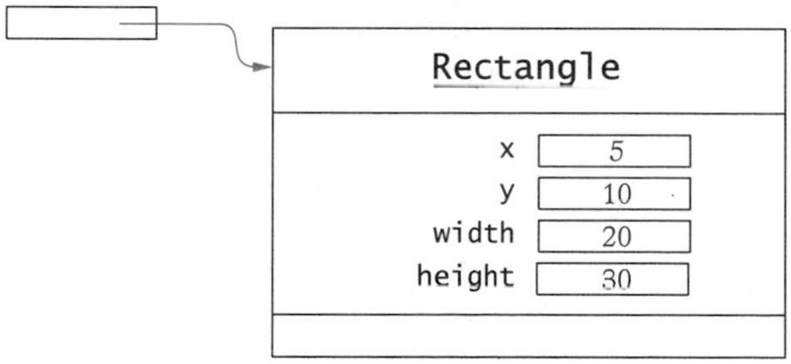

Figure 21

An Uninitialized Object
Variable

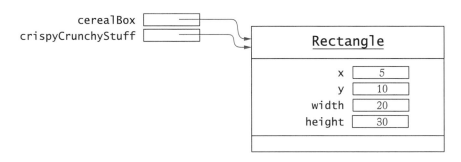

Figure 22

Two Object Variables That Refer to
the Same Object

```
Rectangle cerealBox = new Rectangle(5, 10, 20, 30);
```

It is very important that you remember that the **cerealBox** variable *does not contain* the object. It *refers to* the object. You can have two object variables refer to the same object:

```
Rectangle crispyCrunchyStuff = cerealBox;
```

Now you can access the same **Rectangle** object both as **cerealBox** and as **crispyCrunchyStuff** as shown in Figure 22.

The **Rectangle** class has over 50 methods, some useful, some less so. To give you a flavor of manipulating **Rectangle** objects, let us look at a method of the **Rectangle** class. The **translate** method *moves* a rectangle by a certain distance in the *x*- and *y*-direction. For example,

```
cerealBox.translate(15, 25);
```

moves the rectangle by 15 units in the *x*-direction and 25 units in the *y*-direction. Moving a rectangle doesn't change its width or height, but it changes the top left corner. For example, the code fragment

```
Rectangle cerealBox = new Rectangle(5, 10, 20, 30);
cerealBox.translate(15, 25);
System.out.println(cerealBox);
```

prints

```
java.awt.Rectangle[x=20,y=35,width=20,height=30]
```

Let's turn this code fragment into a complete program. As with the `Hello` program, you need to carry out three steps:

1. Invent a new class, say `MoveRectangle`
2. Supply a `main` method
3. Place instructions inside the `main` method

However, for this program, there is an additional step that you need to carry out: You need to *import* the `Rectangle` class from a *package,* which is a collection of classes with a related purpose. All classes in the standard library are contained in packages. For example, the `System` class and the `String` class are in a package called `java.lang`, and the `Rectangle` class belongs to the package `java.awt`. (The abbreviation `awt` stands for "Abstract Windowing Toolkit"). The `java.awt` package contains many classes for drawing windows and graphical shapes.

To use the `Rectangle` class from the `java.awt` package, simply place the following line at the top of your program:

```
import java.awt.Rectangle;
```

You never need to import classes from the `java.lang` package. All classes from this package are automatically imported. For example, you can use the `System` and `String` classes without importing them.

Java Syntax
1.4 Importing a Class from a Package

`import` *packageName.ClassName*;

Example:
`import java.awt.Rectangle;`

Purpose:
To import a class from a package for use in a program

Thus, the complete program is:

Program MoveRectangle.java

```java
import java.awt.Rectangle;

public class MoveRectangle
{  public static void main(String[] args)
   {  Rectangle cerealBox = new Rectangle(5, 10, 20, 30);
      cerealBox.translate(15, 25);
      System.out.println(cerealBox);
   }
}
```

In this section you have had a first introduction to objects and classes. You saw that each object belongs to a class and that each class defines the set of methods that you can use with all objects of that class. You also learned how to create new objects with the **new** operator, how to store an object reference in an object variable, and how to import a package. In Chapter 2 you will learn how to use objects of the **String** class, and you will also learn about a number of other classes that are necessary to read input from the keyboard. In Chapter 3 you will start implementing your own classes.

Advanced Topic 1.2

Importing Classes

You have seen the simplest and clearest method for importing classes from packages. Simply use an **import** statement that names the package and class for each class that you want to import. For example,

```java
import java.awt.Rectangle;
import java.awt.Point;
```

There is a shortcut that many programmers find convenient. You can import *all* classes from a package name with the construct

```java
import packagename.*;
```

For example, the statement

```java
import java.awt.*;
```

imports all classes from the `java.awt` package. This is less trouble to type, but we won't use this style in this book, for a simple reason. If a program imports multiple packages, and you encounter an unfamiliar class name, then you have to look up all packages to find the class. For example, suppose you see a program that imports

```java
import java.awt.*;
import java.io.*;
```

Furthermore, suppose you see a class name **Image**. You would not know whether the **Image** class is in the **java.awt** package or the **java.io** package. Why do you care in which package it is? You need to know, if you want to use the class in your own programs. You don't have this problem when using an explicit **import** statement:

```
import java.awt.Image;
```

Note that you *cannot* import multiple packages with a single **import** statement. For example,

```
import java.*.*; // Error
```

is a syntax error.

You can avoid all **import** statements by using the *full* name (both package name and class name) whenever you use a class. For example,

```
java.awt.Rectangle cerealBox =
    new java.awt.Rectangle(5, 10, 20, 30);
```

That is pretty tedious, and you won't find many programmers doing it.

1.12 Algorithms

You will soon learn how to program calculations and decision making in Java. But before we look at the mechanics of implementing computations in the next chapter, let us consider the planning process that precedes the implementation.

You may have run across advertisements that encourage you to pay for a computerized service that matches you up with a love partner. Let us think how this might work. You fill out a form and send it in. Others do the same. The data are processed by a computer program. Is it reasonable to assume that the computer can perform the task of finding the best match for you? Suppose your younger brother, not the computer, had all the forms on his desk. What instructions could you give him? You can't say, "Find the best-looking person of the opposite sex who likes inline skating and browsing the Internet". There is no objective standard for good looks, and your brother's opinion (or that of a computer program analyzing the digitized photo) will likely be different from yours. If you can't give instructions for someone to solve the problem by hand, there is no way the computer can magically solve the problem. The computer can do only what you can do by hand. It just does it faster, and it doesn't get bored or exhausted.

Now consider the following investment problem:

You put $10,000 into a bank account that earns 5% interest per year. Interest is compounded annually. How many years does it take for the account balance to be double the original?

Could you solve this problem by hand? Sure, you could. For example, after the first year, you earned $500 (5% of $10,000). The interest gets added to your bank account. Next year, the interest is $525 (5% of $10,500), and your balance is $11,025. You can keep going this way. The following table shows the process:

Year	Balance
0	$10,000.00
1	$10,500.00
2	$11,025.00
3	$11,576.25
4	$12,155.06
. . .	. . .

You keep going until the balance goes over $20,000. Then you look into the Year column, and you have the answer.

Of course, carrying out this computation is intensely boring. You could try to get your younger brother to do it. Seriously, the fact that a computation is boring or tedious is irrelevant to the computer. Computers are very good at carrying out repetitive calculations quickly and flawlessly. What is important to the computer (and your younger brother) is the existence of a systematic approach for finding the solution. The answer can be found just by following a series of steps that involves no guesswork. Here is such a series of steps:

Step 1.   Start with the table

Year	Balance
0	$10,000.00

Step 2.   Repeat steps 2a . . . 2c while the balance is less than $20,000.

    Step 2a.   Add a new row to the table.

    Step 2b.   In column 1 of the new row, put one more than the preceding year value.

    Step 2c.   In column 2 of the new row, place the value of the preceding balance value, multiplied by 1.05 (1 + 5 percent).

Step 3.   Read the last number in the year column and report it as the number of years required to double the investment.

Of course, these steps are not yet in a language that a computer can understand, but you will learn soon how to formulate them in Java. What is important is that the method that we described be

- Unambiguous
- Executable
- Terminating

The method is *unambiguous* because there are precise instructions what to do in every step and where to go next. There is no room for guesswork or creativity. The method is *executable* because each step can be carried out in practice. Had we asked to use a variable rate that depends on economic factors in years to come, not a fixed rate of 5 percent per year, our method would not have been executable, because there is no way for anyone to know what that interest rate will be. Finally, the computation will eventually come to an end. With every step, the balance goes up by at least $500, so eventually it must reach $20,000.

A solution technique that is unambiguous, executable, and terminating is called an *algorithm.* We have found an algorithm to solve our investment problem, and thus we can find the solution with the computer. The existence of an algorithm is an essential prerequisite for programming a task. Sometimes finding an algorithm is very simple. At other times it requires ingenuity or planning. If you cannot find an algorithm, you cannot use the computer to solve your problem. You need to satisfy yourself that an algorithm exists, and that you understand its steps, before you start programming.

Chapter Summary

1. Computers execute very basic operations in rapid succession. The sequence of operations is called a computer program. Different tasks (such as balancing a checkbook, printing a letter, or playing a game) require different programs. Programmers produce computer programs to make the computer solve new tasks.

2. The central processing unit (CPU) of the computer executes one operation at a time. Each operation specifies how data should be processed, how data should be brought into the CPU or out of the CPU, or what operation should be selected next.

3. Data values can be brought into the CPU for processing from storage or from input devices such as the keyboard, the mouse, or a communications link. Processed information is sent back from the CPU to storage or to output devices such as the display or a printer.

4. Storage devices include random-access memory (RAM) and secondary storage. RAM is fast, but it is expensive and loses its information when the power is turned

off. Secondary storage devices use magnetic or optical technology to store information. Access time is slower, but the information is retained without the need for electrical power.

5. Computer programs are stored as machine instructions in a code that depends on the processor type. Writing instruction codes directly is difficult for human programmers. Computer scientists have found ways to make this task easier by using assembly language and higher-level programming languages. The programmer writes the programs in such a "language", and a special computer program translates it into the equivalent sequence of machine instructions. Assembly language instructions are tied to a particular processor or virtual machine type. Higher-level languages are independent of the processor. The same program can be translated to run on many different processor types from different manufacturers.

6. Programming languages are designed by computer scientists for a variety of purposes. Some languages are designed for specific purposes, such as database processing. In this book, we use Java, a general-purpose language that is suited for a wide range of programming tasks.

7. Set aside some time to become familiar with the computer system and the Java compiler that you will use for your class work. Develop a strategy for keeping backup copies of your work before disaster strikes.

8. Java programs contain one or more classes. Classes contain definitions of methods. A method is a sequence of instructions that describes how to carry out a computation. Every Java application contains at least one class with a method called `main`.

9. Classes are factories for objects. You construct a new object of a class with the `new` operator. You store references to objects in object variables. You can have multiple references to the same object.

10. Java classes are grouped into packages. If you use a class from another package (other than the `java.lang` package), you must import the class.

11. Errors are a fact of life for the programmer. Syntax errors are faulty constructs that do not conform to the rules of the programming language. They are detected by the compiler, and no program is generated. Logic errors are constructs that can be translated into a running program, but the resulting program does not perform the action that the programmer intended. The programmer is responsible for inspecting and testing the program to guard against logic errors.

12. Java programs are translated by a program called a compiler into bytecode. In a separate step, a program called an interpreter reads the bytecode of your program as well as previously translated bytecode for input/output and other services used in your program.

13. An algorithm is a description of steps to solve a problem that is unambiguous, executable, and terminating. That is, the description leaves no room for interpretation, the steps can be carried out in practice, and the result is guaranteed to be obtained after a finite amount of time. In order to solve a problem by computer, you must know an algorithm for finding the solution.

Further Reading

[1] The Unicode Consortium, *The Unicode Standard Worldwide Character Encoding, Version 2.0,* Addison-Wesley, 1996.

Classes, Objects, and Methods Introduced in This Chapter

Here is a list of all classes, methods, static variables, and constants introduced in this chapter. Please turn to the documentation in Appendix 2 for more information.

```
java.awt.Rectangle
    translate
java.io.PrintStream
    print
    println
java.lang.String
    length
java.lang.System
    out
```

Review Exercises

Exercise R1.1. Explain the difference between using a computer program and programming a computer.

Exercise R1.2. What distinguishes a computer from a typical household appliance?

Exercise R1.3. Which parts of a computer can store program code? Which can store user data?

Exercise R1.4. Which parts of a computer serve to give information to the user? Which parts take user input?

Exercise R1.5. Rate the storage devices that can be part of a computer system by (*a*) speed, (*b*) cost, and (*c*) storage capacity.

Exercise R1.6. Describe the utility of the computer network in your department's computer lab. To what other computers is a lab computer connected?

Exercise R1.7. What is the Java virtual machine?

Exercise R1.8. What is an applet?

Exercise R1.9. Explain two benefits of higher-level programming languages over assembler code.

Exercise R1.10. List the programming languages mentioned in this chapter.

Exercise R1.11. What is an integrated programming environment?

Exercise R1.12. On your own computer or on your lab computer, find the exact location (folder or directory name) of

- ◆ The sample file `Hello.java`, which you wrote with the editor
- ◆ The Java interpreter `java.exe`
- ◆ The library file `rt.jar` that contains the runtime library

Exercise R1.13. Explain the special role of the \ escape character in Java character strings.

Exercise R1.14. Write three versions of the `Hello.java` program that have different syntax errors. Write a version that has a logic error.

Exercise R1.15. How do you discover syntax errors? How do you discover logic errors?

Exercise R1.16. Write an algorithm to settle the following question: A bank account starts out with $10,000. Interest is compounded at the end of every month at 6 percent per year (0.5 percent per month). At the beginning of every month, $500 is withdrawn to meet college expenses after the interest has been credited. After how many years is the account depleted?

Exercise R1.17. Consider the question of the preceding exercise. Suppose the numbers ($10,000, 6 percent, $500) were user-selectable. Are there values for which the algorithm you developed would not terminate? If so, change the algorithm to make sure it always terminates.

Exercise R1.18. The value of π can be computed according to the following formula:

$$\frac{\pi}{4} = 1 - \frac{1}{3} + \frac{1}{5} - \frac{1}{7} + \frac{1}{9} - \cdots$$

Write an algorithm to compute π. Since the formula is an infinite series and an algorithm must stop after a finite number of steps, you should stop when you have the result determined up to six significant digits.

Exercise R1.19. Suppose you put your younger brother in charge of backing up your work. Write a set of detailed instructions how he should carry out his task. Explain how often he should do it, and what files he needs to copy from which folder to which floppy disk. Explain how he should verify that the backup was carried out correctly.

Exercise R1.20. Explain the difference between an object and an object reference.

Exercise R1.21. Explain the difference between an object and a class.

Exercise R1.22. Explain the difference between an object and a method.

Programming Exercises

Exercise P1.1. Write a program that displays your name inside a box on the terminal screen, like this:

```
+----+
|Dave|
+----+
```

Do your best to approximate lines with characters like | - +.

Exercise P1.2. Write a program that prints a Christmas tree:

Remember to use escape sequences to print the \ and " characters.

Exercise P1.3. Write a program that computes the sum of the first ten positive integers, $1 + 2 + \cdots + 10$. *Hint:* Write a program of the form

```
public class Sum10
{  public static void main(String[] args)
   {  System.out.println(            );
   }
}
```

Exercise P1.4. Write a program that computes the sum of the reciprocals $\frac{1}{1} + \frac{1}{2} + \cdots + \frac{1}{10}$. This is harder than it sounds. Try writing the program, and check the results against a pocket calculator. The program's results aren't likely to be correct. Then write the numbers as *floating-point* numbers, `1.0`, `2.0`, ..., `10.0`, and run the program again. Can you explain the difference in the results? We will explain this phenomenon in Chapter 2.

Exercise P1.5. Write a program that constructs a `Rectangle` object, prints it, and then translates and prints it three more times, so that, if the rectangles were drawn, they would form one large rectangle:

Exercise P1.6. The `intersection` method computes the *intersection* of two rectangles—that is, the rectangle that is formed by two overlapping rectangles:

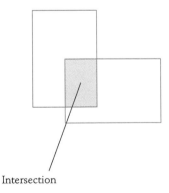

Intersection

You call this method as follows:

```
Rectangle r3 = r1.intersection(r2);
```

Write a program that constructs two rectangle objects, prints them, and then prints their intersection. What happens when the rectangles do not overlap?

Fundamental Data Types

Chapter Goals

- ◆ To understand integer and floating-point numbers

- ◆ To write arithmetic expressions in Java

- ◆ To appreciate the importance of comments and good code layout

- ◆ To be able to define and initialize variables and constants

- ◆ To recognize the limitations of the `int` and `double` types and the overflow and roundoff errors that can result

- ◆ To learn how to read program input and display program output

- ◆ To be able to change the values of variables through assignment

- ◆ To use the `String` type to define and manipulate character strings

In this and the four following chapters you will learn the basic skills needed to write programs in Java. Only in Chapter 7 will you have all necessary tools for actually coding the investment problem at the end of Chapter 1.

This chapter teaches how to manipulate numbers and character strings in Java. The goal of this chapter is to write simple programs using these basic data types.

2.1   Number Types

Consider the following simple problem. I have 8 pennies, 4 dimes, and 3 quarters in my purse. What is the total value of the coins?

Here is a Java program that solves this problem:

Program Coins1.java

```
public class Coins1
{  public static void main(String[] args)
   {  int pennies = 8;   // the purse contains 8 pennies,
      int dimes = 4;      // four dimes,
      int quarters = 3;  // and three quarters

      // compute total value of the coins

      double total = pennies * 0.01 + dimes * 0.10
         + quarters * 0.25;

      // print result

      System.out.print("Total value = ");
      System.out.println(total);
   }
}
```

In this program we manipulate two kinds of numbers. The coin counts (8, 4, 3) are *integers*: whole numbers without a fractional part (including zero and negative whole numbers). The numerical values of the coins (0.01, 0.10, and 0.25), on the other hand, have decimal points. Such numbers are called *floating-point* numbers because they are represented in the computer as a sequence of the significant digits and an indication of the position of the decimal point. For example, the numbers 250, 2.5, 0.25, and 0.025 all have the same digits: 25. When a floating-point number is multiplied or divided by 10, only the position of the decimal point changes; it "floats". This representation corresponds to numbers written in "exponential" or "scientific" notation, such as 2.5×10^2. (Actually, internally the numbers are represented in base 2, as binary numbers, but the principle is the same. See Advanced Topic 2.4 for more information on binary numbers.)

As you have probably guessed, int is the Java name for integers. The **double** type denotes *double-precision* floating-point numbers. There is also a single-precision type, **float**, that denotes *single-precision* floating-point numbers. In general, double-precision floating-point numbers are more useful in Java. All mathematical methods in Java use double-precision floating-point numbers. However, single-precision floating-point numbers are necessary for using the graphics library, as you will see in Chapter 3. See Advanced Topic 2.2 for more information on these two floating-point number types.

Why have both integer and floating-point number types? You could just use

```
double pennies = 8;
```

There are two reasons for having separate types: one philosophical and one pragmatic. By indicating that the number of pennies is an integer, you make explicit an assumption: There can be only a whole number of pennies in the purse. The program would have worked just as well with floating-point numbers to count the coins, but it is generally a good idea to choose programming solutions that document one's intentions. Pragmatically speaking, integers are more efficient than floating-point numbers. They take less storage space and are processed faster.

In Java, multiplication is denoted by an asterisk *, not a raised dot · or a cross ×, because there are no keys for these symbols on most keyboards. For example, $d \cdot 10$ is written as **d * 10**. Do not write commas or spaces in numbers in Java. For example, 10,150.75 must be entered as **10150.75**. To write numbers in exponential notation in Java, use E*n* instead of " ×10*ⁿ*". For example, 5.0×10^{-3} becomes **5.0E-3**.

Note the *comment*

```
// total value of the coins
```

next to the definition of **total**. This comment is purely for the benefit of the human reader, to explain in more detail the meaning of **total**. Anything enclosed between // and the end of the line is completely ignored by the compiler. Comments are used to explain the program to other programmers or to yourself. There is a second comment style, using the /* and */ delimiters, that is also popular. See Advanced Topic 2.3 for details.

The most important feature of our sample program is the introduction of *symbolic names*. You could have just programmed

```
public class Coins1a
{  public static void main(String[] args)
   {  System.out.print("Total value = ");
      System.out.println(8 * 0.01 + 4 * 0.10 + 3 * 0.25);
   }
}
```

This program computes the same answer. Compare it with our first program, though. Which one is easier to read? Which one is easier to update if you need to change the coin counts, such as by adding some nickels? By giving the symbolic names **pennies**, **dimes**, and **quarters** to the counts, you made the program more readable and maintainable. This is an important consideration. You introduce symbolic names to explain what a program does, just as you use variable names such as p, d, and q in algebra.

Java Syntax

2.1 Variable Definition

TypeName variableName;
TypeName variableName = expression;

Example:
```
double total;
int pennies = 8;
```

Purpose:
To define a new variable of a particular type and optionally supply an initial value

---

In Java, each variable has a *type*. By defining `int pennies`, you proclaim that `pennies` can hold only integer values. If you try to put a floating-point value into the `pennies` variable, the compiler will complain.

You define a variable by first giving its type and then its name, such as `int pennies`. You may also add an *initialization value*, such as = 8. Then you end the definition with a semicolon. Even though the initialization is optional, it is a good idea always to initialize variables with a specific value. See Common Error 2.1 for the reason.

Variable names in algebra are usually just one letter long, such as p or A, maybe with a subscript such as p_1. In Java it is common to choose longer and more descriptive names, such as `price` or `area`. You cannot type subscripts, so you just tag an index behind the name: `price1`. You can choose any variable names you like, provided you follow a few simple rules. Names can be made up of letters, digits, the dollar sign $, and the underscore (_) character. They cannot start with a digit, though. You cannot use other symbols such as ? or %. Spaces are not permitted inside names either. Furthermore, you cannot use *reserved words* such as `double` or `return` as names; these words are reserved exclusively for their special Java meanings. Variable names are also *case-sensitive;* that is, `Area` and `area` are *different* names. It would not be a good idea to mix the two in the same program, because it would make that program very confusing to read.

Common Error 2.1

Using Variables without Initial Values

You should always supply an initial value for every variable at the same time you define it. Let us see what happens if you define a variable but leave it uninitialized.

If you just define

```
int nickels;
```

the variable `nickels` comes into existence and memory space is found for it. However, it contains some random value, since you did not initialize the variable. If you mean to initialize the variable to zero, you must do so explicitly:

```
int nickels = 0;
```

Why does an uninitialized variable contain a random value? It would seem less trouble just to put a 0 into a variable than to come up with a random value. Anyway, where does the random value come from? Does the computer roll electronic dice?

When you define a variable in a method, sufficient space is set aside in memory to hold values of the type you specify. For example, when you declare `int nickels`, a block of memory big enough to hold an integer is reserved:

nickels   [   ]

When you initialize the variable, `int nickels = 0`, a zero is placed into the newly acquired memory location:

nickels   [0   ]

If you don't specify the initialization, however, the memory space is found and left as is. There is already *some* value in the memory. After all, you don't get freshly minted transistors—just an area of memory that is currently available and that you give up again when `main` ends. Its uninitialized value is just whatever is left over from prior computations. Thus, it takes no effort at all to give you a random initial value, whereas it does take a tiny effort to initialize a new memory location with zero or another value.

If you don't specify an initialization, the compiler assumes that you are not quite ready to come up with the value that you want to store in the variable. Maybe the value needs to be computed from other variables, like the `total` in our example, and you haven't defined all components yet. It is quite reasonable not to waste time initializing a variable if that initial value is never used before it is overwritten with the truly intended value.

However, suppose you have the following sequence of events:

```
int nickels; // I'll get around to setting it presently
int dimes = 3;
double total = nickels * 0.05 + dimes * 0.10; // Error
nickels = 2 * dimes;
// Now I remember—I have twice as many nickels as dimes
```

This is a problem. The value of `nickels` has been used before it has been set. The Java compiler will refuse to translate this code, but some other programming languages will let you access uninitialized variables. In those languages, uninitialized variables are a common source of errors.

What is the remedy? *Reorder the definitions* so that all of the variables are initialized. This is usually simple to do:

```
int dimes = 3;
int nickels = 2 * dimes;
// I have twice as many nickels as dimes
double total = nickels * 0.05 + dimes * 0.10; // OK
```

Quality Tip 2.1

Choose Descriptive Variable Names

You could save yourself a lot of typing by using shorter variable names, as in

```java
public class Tip2_1
{  public static void main(String[] args)
   {  int p = 8;
      int d = 4;
      int q = 3;
      double t = p * 0.01 + d * 0.10 + q * 0.25;
         // total value of the coins
      System.out.print("Total value = ");
      System.out.println(t);
   }
}
```

Compare this program with the previous one, though. Which one is easier to read? There is no comparison. Just reading pennies is a lot less trouble than reading p and then *figuring out* that it must mean "pennies".

In practical programming, descriptive variable names are particularly important when programs are written by more than one person. It may be obvious to *you* that p must stand for pennies and not percentage (or maybe pressure), but is it obvious to the person who needs to update your code years later, long after you were promoted (or laid off)? For that matter, will you remember yourself what p means when you look at the code six months from now?

Of course, you could use comments:

```java
public class Tip2_2
{  public static void main(String[] args)
   {  int p = 8;    // pennies
      int d = 4;    // dimes
      int q = 3;    // quarters
      double t = p * 0.01 + d * 0.10 + q * 0.25;
         // total value of the coins
      System.out.print("Total value = ");
      System.out.println(t);
   }
}
```

That makes the definitions pretty clear, but the computation p * 0.01 + d * 0.10 + q * 0.25 is still cryptic.

If you have the choice between comments and self-commenting code, choose the latter. It is better to have clear code with no comments than cryptic code with comments. There is a good reason for this. In actual practice, code is not written once, handed to a grader, and subsequently forgotten; programs are modified and enhanced all the time. If the code explains itself, you just have to update it to new code that explains itself. If the code requires explanation, you have to update both the code and the explanation. If you forget to update the explanation, you end up with a comment that is *worse* than useless, because it no longer reflects what is actually going on. The next person reading it must waste time to understand whether the code is wrong or the comment.

Advanced Topic 2.1

Numeric Ranges and Precisions

Unfortunately, `int` and `double` values do suffer from one problem. They cannot represent arbitrarily large integer or floating-point numbers. Integers have a range of −2,147,483,648 (about −2 billion) to +2,147,483,647 (about 2 billion). If you need to refer to these boundaries in your program, use the constants `Integer.MIN_VALUE` and `Integer.MAX_VALUE`, which are defined in a class called `Integer`. If you want to represent the world population, you can't use an `int`. Double-precision floating-point numbers are somewhat less limited; they can go up to 10^{300}. However, `double` floating-point numbers suffer from a different problem: *precision*. They store only about 15 significant digits. Suppose your customers might find the price of three hundred trillion dollars ($300,000,000,000,000) for your product a bit excessive, so you want to reduce it by five cents to a more reasonable-looking $299,999,999,999,999.95. Try running the following program:

```
class Topic2_1
{  public static void main(String[] args)
   {  double originalPrice = 3E14;
      double discountedPrice = originalPrice - 0.05;
      double discount = originalPrice - discountedPrice;
         // should be 0.05;
      System.out.println(discount);
         // prints 0.0625;
   }
}
```

The program prints out `0.0625`, not `0.05`. It is off by more than a penny!

For most of the programming projects in this book, the limited range and precision of `int` and `double` are acceptable. Just bear in mind that overflows or loss of precision can occur.

Advanced Topic 2.2

Other Number Types

If `int` and `double` are not sufficient for your computational needs, there are other data types you can turn to. When the range of integers is not sufficient, the simplest remedy is to use the `long` type. Long integers have a range from −9,223,372,036,854,775,808 to +9,223,372,036,854,775,807.

To specify a long integer constant, you need to append the letter L after the number value. For example,

```
long price = 300000000000000L;
```

There is also an integer type `short` with shorter-than-normal integers, having a range of −32,768 to 32,767. Finally, there is a type `byte` with a range of −128 to 127.

In addition to the `double` type, there is also a single-precision floating-point type called `float`. Values of type `float` take half the storage space of values of type `double`, and computations involving `float` execute a bit faster than those involving `double`, but the precision of float values—23 binary digits, or 7 decimal digits—is insufficient for many programs. For example, you need more than 23 binary digits to store the cost of a $50,000 luxury car in dollars and cents. However, some graphics routines require you to use float values.

If you want to compute with really large numbers, you can use *big number objects*. Big number objects are objects of the BigInteger and BigDecimal classes in the java.math package. Unlike the number types such as int or double, big number objects have essentially no limits on their size and precision. However, computations with big number objects are much slower than those that involve number types. Perhaps more importantly, you can't use the familiar arithmetic operators (+ - * /) with them. Instead, you have to use methods called add, subtract, multiply, and divide. Here is an example of how to create two big numbers and how to multiply them.

```
BigInteger a = new BigInteger("123456789");
BigInteger b = new BigInteger("987654321");
BigInteger c = a.multiply(b);
System.out.println(c); // prints 121932631112635269
```

◆ Advanced Topic 2.3

Alternative Comment Syntax

In Java there are two methods for writing comments. You already learned that the compiler ignores anything that you type between // and the end of the current line. The compiler also ignores any text between a /* and */.

```
double t = p * 0.01 + d * 0.10 + q * 0.25;
    /* total value of the coins */
```

The // comment is easier to type if the comment is only a single line long. If you have a comment that is longer than a line or two, then the /*. . . */ comment is simpler:

```
/*
In this program, we compute the value of a set of coins. The
user enters the count of pennies, nickels, dimes, and quarters.
The program then displays the total value.
*/
```

It would be somewhat tedious to add the // at the beginning of each line and to move them around whenever the text of the comment changes (see Productivity Hint 2.1).

In this book, we use // for comments that will never grow beyond a line or two, and /* . . . */ for longer comments. If you prefer, you can always use the // style. The readers of your code will be grateful for *any* comments, no matter which style you use. (Comments will be discussed further in Chapter 6.)

◆ Random Fact 2.1

The Pentium Floating-Point Bug

In 1994, Intel Corporation released what was then its most powerful processor, the Pentium. Unlike previous generations of Intel's processors, the Pentium had a very fast floating-point unit. Intel's goal was to compete aggressively with the makers of higher-end processors for engineering workstations. The Pentium was an immediate huge success.

In the summer of 1994, Dr. Thomas Nicely of Lynchburg College in Virginia ran an extensive set of computations to analyze the sums of reciprocals of certain sequences of prime numbers. The results were not always what his theory predicted, even after he took into account the inevitable roundoff errors. Then Dr. Nicely noted that the same program did produce the correct results when run on the slower 486 processor, which preceded the Pentium in Intel's lineup. This should not have happened. The optimal roundoff behavior of floating-point calculations has been standardized by the Institute of Electrical and Electronics Engineers (IEEE), and Intel claimed to adhere to the IEEE standard in both the 486 and the Pentium processors. Upon further checking, Dr. Nicely discovered that indeed there was a very small set of numbers for which the product of two numbers was computed differently on the two processors. For example,

$$4,195,835 - ((4,195,835/3,145,727) \times 3,145,727)$$

should of course evaluate to 0, and it did compute as 0 on a 486 processor. On a Pentium processor, however, the result was 256.

As it turned out, Intel had independently discovered the bug in its testing and had started to produce chips that fixed it. The bug was caused by an error in a table that was used to speed up the floating-point multiplication algorithm of the processor. Intel determined that the problem was exceedingly rare. They claimed that under normal use a typical consumer would only notice the problem once every 27,000 years. Unfortunately for Intel, Dr. Nicely had not been a normal user.

Now Intel had a real problem on its hands. It figured that replacing all the Pentium processors that it had already sold would cost it a great deal of money. Intel already had more orders for the chip than it could produce, and it would be particularly galling to have to give out the scarce chips as free replacements instead of selling them. Intel's management decided to punt on the issue and initially offered to replace the processors only for those customers who could prove that their work required absolute precision in mathematical calculations. Naturally, that did not go over well with the hundreds of thousands of customers who had paid retail prices of $700 and more for a Pentium chip and did not want to live with the nagging feeling that perhaps, one day, their income tax program would produce a faulty return.

Ultimately, Intel had to cave in to public demand and replaced all defective chips, at a cost of about 475 million dollars.

What do you think? Intel claims that the probability of the bug occurring in any calculation is extremely small—smaller than many chances you take every day, such as driving to work in an automobile. Indeed, many users had used their Pentium computers for many months without reporting any ill effects, and the computations that Professor Nicely was doing are hardly examples of typical user needs. As a result of its public relations blunder, Intel ended up paying a large amount of money. Undoubtedly, some of that money was added to chip prices and thus actually paid by Intel's customers. Also, a large number of processors, whose manufacture consumed energy and caused some environmental impact, were destroyed without benefiting anyone. Could Intel have been justified in wanting to replace only the processors of those users who could reasonably be expected to suffer an impact from the problem?

Suppose that, instead of stonewalling, Intel had offered you the choice of a free replacement processor or a $200 rebate. What would you have done? Would you have replaced your faulty chip, or would you have taken your chance and pocketed the money?

2.2   Assignment

All but the simplest programs use variables to store values. Variables are locations in memory that can hold values of a particular type. For example, the variable `total` holds values of type `double` because we declared it as `double total`. In our first program, the variables we used were actually not very variable. Once we stored a value in them, that value never varied.

Let us compute the value of the coins in a different way, by keeping a *running total.* First, we set the total to the value of the pennies. Then we set the number of dimes and *add* their value to the total. Then we do the same to the quarters. Here is the program.

Program Coins2.java

```
public class Coins2
{  public static void main(String[] args)
   {   int pennies = 8; // eight pennies in the purse
       double total = pennies * 0.01;

       int dimes = 4; // four dimes in the purse

       // add value of dimes

       total = total + dimes * 0.10;

       int quarters = 3; // three quarters in the purse

       // add value of quarters

       total = total + quarters * 0.25;

       System.out.print("Total value = ");
       System.out.println(total);
   }
}
```

The value of the variable `total` really does vary during program execution. Each time we add another coin value, the total is increased. Let's look carefully how the value of `total` changes. The initialization, `double total = pennies * 0.01`, is straightforward. The second statement is much more interesting:

```
total = total + dimes * 0.10;
```

It means, "Compute the value of the dimes contribution (`dimes * 0.10`), add to it the value of the running total, *and place the result again into the memory location* `total`." (See Figure 1.)

There is a subtle difference between the statements

```
double total = pennies * 0.01;
```

Figure 1

Assignment

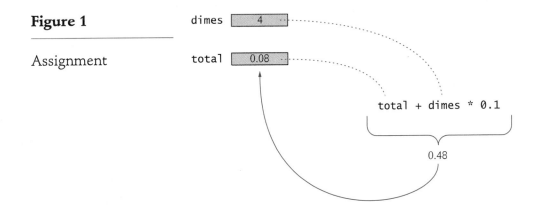

```
Java Syntax
2.2 Assignment
```
variableName = expression;

Example:
```
total = total + quarters * 0.25;
```

Purpose:
To assign a new value to a variable

and

```
total = total + quarters * 0.25;
```

The first statement is the *definition* of **total**. It is a command to create a new variable of type **double**, to give it the name **total**, and to initialize it with the value of the expression **pennies * 0.01**. The second statement is an *assignment statement*: an instruction to replace the contents of the existing variable **total** with another value.

It is not possible to have multiple *definitions* of the same variable. The sequence of statements

```
double total = pennies * 0.01;
...
double total = total + quarters * 0.25; // Error
```

is illegal. The compiler will complain about an attempt to redefine **total**, because it thinks you want to define a new variable in the second statement. On the other hand, it is perfectly legal, and indeed very common, to make multiple *assignments* to the same variable:

```
total = total + dimes * 0.1;
...
total = total + quarters * 0.25;;
```

The = sign doesn't mean that the left-hand side *is* equal to the right-hand side but that the right-hand-side value is copied into the left-hand-side variable. You should not confuse this *assignment operation* with the = used in algebra to denote *equality*. The assignment operator is an instruction to do something, namely place a value into a variable. The mathematical equality states the fact that two values are equal. For example, in Java it is perfectly legal to write

```
month = month + 1;
```

It means to look up the value stored in the variable month, to add 1 to it, and to stuff the sum back into month. (See Figure 2.) The net effect of executing this statement is to increment month by 1. Of course, in mathematics it would make no sense to write that *month* = *month* + 1; no value can equal itself plus 1.

The concepts of assignment and equality have no relationship with each other, and it is a bit unfortunate that the Java language (following C and C++) uses = to denote assignment. Other programming languages use a symbol such as <- or :=, which avoids the confusion.

Consider once more the statement month = month + 1. This statement increments the month counter. For example, if month was 3 before execution of the statement, it is set to 4 afterwards. This increment operation is so common when writing programs that there is a special shorthand for it, namely

```
month++;
```

This statement has exactly the same effect—namely, to add 1 to month—but it is easier to type. As you might have guessed, there is also a decrement operator --. The statement

```
month--;
```

subtracts 1 from month.

Figure 2

Incrementing a
Variable

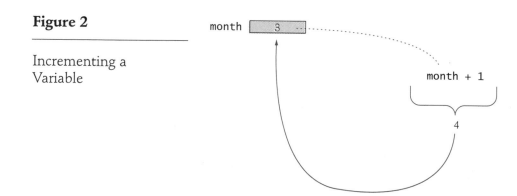

◆◆◆◆◆◆◆◆◆◆◆◆◆◆◆◆◆◆◆◆◆◆◆◆◆◆

Advanced Topic 2.4

Combining Assignment and Arithmetic

In Java you can combine arithmetic and assignment. For example, the instruction

```
total += count * 0.05;
```

is a shortcut for

```
total = total + count * 0.05;
```

Similarly,

```
total -= count * 0.05;
```

means the same as

```
total = total - count * 0.05;
```

and

```
total *= 2;
```

is another way of writing

```
total = total * 2;
```

Many programmers find this a convenient shortcut. If you like it, go ahead and use it in your own code. For simplicity, we won't use it in this book, though.

2.3   Type Conversion

When you make an assignment of an expression into a variable, the *types* of the variable and the expression must be compatible. For example, it is an error to assign

```
double total = "a lot"; // Error
```

because `total` is a floating-point variable and `"a lot"` is a string. It is, however, legal to store an integer expression in a `double` variable:

```
int dollars = 2; // count of dollar coins
double total = dollars; // OK
```

In Java, you cannot assign a floating-point expression to an integer variable. You must convert from floating-point to integer with a *cast*:

```
int dollars = (int)total;
```

The cast (`int`) converts the floating-point value `total` to an integer. The effect of the cast is to discard the fractional part. For example, if `total` is 13.75, then `dollars` is set to 13. If you want to convert the value of a floating-point expression to an integer, you need to enclose the expression in parentheses to ensure that it is computed first:

```
int pennies = (int)(total * 100);
```

This is different from the expression

```
int pennies = (int)total * 100;
```

In the second expression, `total` is *first* converted to an integer, and then the resulting integer is multiplied by 100. For example, if `total` is 13.75, then the first expression computes `total * 100`, or 1375, and then converts that value to the integer 1375. In the second expression, `total` is first cast to the integer 13, and then the integer is multiplied by 100, yielding 1300. Normally, you will want to apply the integer conversion *after* all other computations, so that your computations use the full precision of their input values. That means you should enclose your computation in parentheses and apply the cast to the expression in parentheses.

There is a good reason why you must use a cast in Java when you convert a floating-point number to an integer: The conversion *loses information*. You must confirm that you agree to that information loss. Java is quite strict about this. You must use a cast whenever there is the possibility of information loss. A cast always has the form (*typename*), for example (`int`) or (`float`).

Here is another example. You have seen that you can convert from `int` to `double` without a cast, because no information is lost in the process. However, you must use a cast to convert from integers to the single-precision `float` type, because integers can hold more digits than `float` values can.

```
int a = 23456789;
float f = (float)a; // f is 23456788
```

Java Syntax
2.3 Cast

(*TypeName*)*expression* ;

Example:

```
(int)(x + 0.5);
(int)Math.round(100 * f);
```

Purpose:
To convert an expression to a different type.

Actually, simply using an (int) cast to convert a floating-point number to an integer is not always a good idea. Consider the following example:

```
double price = 44.95;
int dollars = (int)price; // sets dollars to  44
```

What did you want to achieve? Did you want to get the number of dollars in the price? Then dropping the fractional part is the right thing to do. Or did you want to get the approximate dollar amount? Then you really want to *round up* when the fractional part is 0.5 or larger.

One way to round to the nearest integer is to add 0.5, then cast to an integer:

```
double price = 44.95;
int dollars = (int)(price + 0.5); // OK for positive values
System.out.print("The price is approximately $")
System.out.println(dollars); // prints 45
```

Adding 0.5 and casting to the int type works because it turns all values that are between 44.50 and 45.4999... into 45.

Actually, there is a better way. Simply adding 0.5 works fine for positive numbers, but it doesn't work correctly for negative numbers. Instead, use the Math.round method in the standard Java library. It works for both positive and negative numbers. However, that method returns a long integer, because large floating-point numbers cannot be stored in an int. You need to cast the return value to an int:

```
int dollars = (int)Math.round(price); // better
```

This is the first time you have seen the Math class, which contains a collection of helpful methods for carrying out mathematical computations.

There is one important difference between the **round** method (and other methods in the Math class) and methods such as **println**. The **println**, and **print** methods, as you have seen, operate on an object such as System.out. In contrast, the **round** method does not operate on any object. That is, you don't call

```
int dollars = (int)price.round(); // Error
```

Java Syntax
2.4 Static Method Call

ClassName.methodName (parameters)

Example:
```
Math.round(3.14);
```

Purpose:
To invoke a static method (a method that does not operate on an object) and supply its parameters

The reason is that in Java, numbers are not objects, so you can never invoke a method on a number. Instead, you pass a number as a *parameter* to a method, enclosing the number in parentheses after the method name. For example, the number value `price` can be a parameter of the `Math.round` method: `Math.round(price)`.

Beginners might think that the `round` method is applied to an object called `Math`, because `Math.` precedes `round` just as `System.out.` precedes `print`. That·is not true. `Math` is a class, not an object. A method such as `Math.round` that does not operate on any object is known as a *static* method; another example is `main`. Static methods do not operate on objects, but they are still defined inside classes, and you must specify the class to which the `round` method belongs.

How can you tell whether `Math` is a class or an object? It is certainly useful to memorize the names of the more important classes (such as `System` and `Math`). You should also pay attention to capitalization. All classes in the Java library start with an uppercase letter (such as `System`). Objects and methods start with a lowercase letter (such as `out` and `println`). You can tell objects and methods apart because method calls are followed by parentheses. Therefore, `System.out.println()` denotes a call of the `println` method on the `out` object inside the `System` class. On the other hand, `Math.round(price)` denotes a call to the `round` method inside the `Math` class. This use of upper- and lowercase letters is merely a *convention*, not a rule of the Java language. It is, however, a convention that the authors of the Java class libraries follow consistently. You should do the same in your programs. If you give names to objects or methods that start with an uppercase letter, you will likely confuse your fellow programmers. Therefore, we strongly recommend that you follow the standard naming convention.

Common Error 2.2

Roundoff Errors

Roundoff errors are a fact of life when calculating with floating-point numbers. You probably have encountered that phenomenon yourself with manual calculations. If you calculate 1/3 to two decimal places, you get 0.33. Multiplying again by 3, you obtain 0.99, not 1.00.

In the processor hardware, numbers are represented in the binary number system, not in decimal. You still get roundoff errors when binary digits are lost. They just may crop up at different places than you might expect. Here is an example:

```
double f = 4.35;
int n = (int)(100 * f);
System.out.println(n); // prints 434!
```

Of course, one hundred times 4.35 is 435, but the program prints 434.

Computers represent numbers in the binary system (see Advanced Topic 2.5). In the binary system, there is no exact representation for 4.35, just as there is no exact representation for 1/3 in the decimal system. The representation used by the computer is just a little less than 4.35, so 100 times that value is just a little less than 435. When a floating-point value is converted to an integer, the entire fractional part is discarded, even if it is almost 1. As a result, the integer 434 is stored in n. Remedy: Use `Math.round` to convert floating-point numbers to integers:

```
int n = (int)Math.round(100 * f);
```

Note that the wrong result of the first computation is *not* caused by lack of precision. The problem lies with the wrong choice of rounding method. Dropping the fractional part, no matter how close it may be to 1, is not a good rounding method.

Advanced Topic 2.5

Binary Numbers

You are familiar with *decimal* numbers, which use the digits 0, 1, 2, ..., 9. Each digit has a place value of 1, 10, 100 $= 10^2$, 1000 $= 10^3$, and so on. For example,

$$435 = 4 \cdot 10^2 + 3 \cdot 10^1 + 5 \cdot 10^0$$

Fractional digits have place values with negative powers of ten: $0.1 = 10^{-1}$, $0.01 = 10^{-2}$, and so on. For example,

$$4.35 = 4 \cdot 10^0 + 3 \cdot 10^{-1} + 5 \cdot 10^{-2}$$

Computers use *binary* numbers instead, which have just two digits (0 and 1) and place values that are powers of 2. Binary numbers are easier for computers to manipulate, because it is easier to build logic circuits that differentiate between "off" and "on" than it would be to build circuits that can accurately tell apart ten different voltage levels.

It is easy to transform a binary number into a decimal number. Just compute the powers of two that correspond to ones in the binary number. For example,

$$1101 \text{ binary} = 1 \cdot 2^3 + 1 \cdot 2^2 + 0 \cdot 2^1 + 1 \cdot 2^0 = 8 + 4 + 1 = 13$$

Fractional binary numbers use negative powers of two. For example,

$$1.101 \text{ binary} = 1 \cdot 2^0 + 1 \cdot 2^{-1} + 0 \cdot 2^{-2} + 1 \cdot 2^{-3} = 1 + 0.5 + 0.125 = 1.625$$

Converting decimal numbers to binary numbers is a little trickier. Here is an algorithm that converts a decimal integer into its binary equivalent: Keep dividing the integer by 2, keeping track of the remainders. Stop when the number is 0. Then write the remainders as a binary number, starting with the *last* one. For example,

$$100 \div 2 = 50 \text{ R } \mathbf{0}$$
$$50 \div 2 = 25 \text{ R } \mathbf{0}$$
$$25 \div 2 = 12 \text{ R } \mathbf{1}$$
$$12 \div 2 = 6 \text{ R } \mathbf{0}$$
$$6 \div 2 = 3 \text{ R } \mathbf{0}$$
$$3 \div 2 = 1 \text{ R } \mathbf{1}$$
$$1 \div 2 = 0 \text{ R } \mathbf{1}$$

Therefore, 100 in decimal is 1100100 in binary.

Conversely, to convert a fractional number < 1 to its binary format, keep multiplying by 2. If the result is > 1, subtract 1. Stop when the number is 0. Then use the digits before the decimal points as the binary digits of the fractional part, starting with the *first* one. For example,

$$0.35 \cdot 2 = \mathbf{0}.7$$
$$0.7 \cdot 2 = \mathbf{1}.4$$
$$0.4 \cdot 2 = \mathbf{0}.8$$
$$0.8 \cdot 2 = \mathbf{1}.6$$
$$0.6 \cdot 2 = \mathbf{1}.2$$
$$0.2 \cdot 2 = \mathbf{0}.4$$

Here the pattern repeats. That is, the binary representation of 0.35 is 0.01 0110 0110 0110 . . .

To convert any floating-point number into binary, convert the whole part and the fractional part separately. For example, 4.35 is 100.01 0110 0110 0110 . . . in binary.

You don't actually need to know about binary numbers to program in Java, but at times it can be helpful to understand a little about them. For example, knowing that an `int` is represented as a 32-bit binary number explains why the largest integer that you can represent in Java is 0111 1111 1111 1111 1111 1111 1111 1111 binary = 2,147,483,647 decimal. (The first bit is the sign bit. It is off for positive values.)

To convert an integer into its binary representation, you can use the static `toString` method of the `Integer` class. The call `Integer.toString(n, 2)` returns a string with the binary digits of the integer n. Conversely, you can convert a string containing binary digits into an integer with the call `Integer.parseInt(digitString, 2)`. In both of these method calls, the second parameter denotes the base of the number system. It can be any number between 0 and 36. You can use these two methods to convert between decimal and binary *integers*. However, the Java library has no convenient method to do the same for floating-point numbers.

Now you can see why we had to fight with a roundoff error when computing 100 times 4.35 in Common Error 2.2. If you actually carry out the long multiplication, you get:

```
1 1 0 0 1 0 0 * 1 0 0.0 1|0 1 1 0|0 1 1 0|0 1 1 0 . . .
```

```
1 0 0.0 1|0 1 1 0|0 1 1 0|0 1 1 0 . . .
  1 0 0.0 1|0 1 1 0|0 1 1 0|0 1 1 . . .
      0
        0
          1 0 0.0 1|0 1 1 0|0 1 1 0 . . .
              0
                0
```

```
1 1 0 1 1 0 0 1 0.1 1 1 1 1 1 1 1 . . .
```

That is, the result is 434, followed by an infinite number of 1s. The fractional part of the product is the binary equivalent of an infinite decimal fraction 0.999999 . . . , which is equal to 1. But the CPU can only store a finite number of 1s, and it discards them all when converting the result to an integer.

Productivity Hint 2.1

Avoid Unstable Layout

You should arrange program code and comments so that the program is easy to read. For example, you should not cram all statements on a single line, and you should make sure that braces { } line up.

However, you should embark on beautification efforts wisely. Some programmers like to line up the = signs in a series of assignments, like this:

```
pennies = 8;
nickels = 0;
dimes   = 4;
```

This looks very neat, but the layout is not *stable*. Suppose you add a line like the one at the bottom of this:

```
pennies = 8;
nickels = 0;
dimes   = 4;
quarters = 3;
```

Oops, now the = signs no longer line up, and you have the extra work of lining them up *again*.

Here is another example. Some programmers recommend the following style of comments.

```
// In this program, we compute the value of a set of coins. The
// user enters the count of pennies, nickels, dimes, and quarters.
// The program then displays the total value.
```

Suppose the program is extended to work for half-dollar coins as well. Of course, you must modify the comment to reflect that change.

```
// In this program, we compute the value of a set of coins. The
// user enters the count of pennies, nickels, dimes, half dollars
and quarters. // The program then displays the total value.
```

Now you need to rearrange the // to fix up the comment. This scheme is a *disincentive* to keep comments up to date. Don't do it. Instead, for comments that are longer than one or two lines, use the /*...*/ style for comments, and block off the entire comment like this:

```
/*
In this program, we compute the value of a set of coins. The
user enters the count of pennies, nickels, dimes, and quarters.
The program then displays the total value.
*/
```

You may not care about these issues. Perhaps you plan to beautify your program just before it is finished, when you are about to turn in your homework. That is not a particularly useful approach. In practice, programs are never finished. They are continuously maintained and updated. It is better to develop the habit of laying out your programs well from the start and keeping them legible at all times. As a consequence, you should avoid layout schemes that are hard to maintain.

2.4   Constants

We used variables such as `total` for two reasons. By using a name instead of just a formula, you make your programs easier to read. Also, by reserving memory space for the variable, you can change its value during program execution. It is usually a good idea to give symbolic names to constants as well, to make programs easier to read and modify.

Consider the following program:

```
public class Volume
{  public static void main(String[] args)
    {  int bottles = 4; //we have four bottles
       int cans = 10; // and ten cans

       // compute total volume

       double total = bottles * 2 + cans * 0.355; // bad  style

       // print result

       System.out.print("The total volume is ");
       System.out.print(total);
       System.out.println(" liters");
    }
}
```

What is going on here? What is the significance of the **0.355**?

This formula computes the amount of soda in a refrigerator that is filled with two-liter bottles and 12-oz. cans. (See Table 1 for conversion factors between metric and nonmetric units.) Let us make the computation clearer by using constants:

Program Volume.java
```
public class Volume
{  public static void main(String[] args)
    {  final double BOTTLE_VOLUME = 2.0;
       final double CAN_VOLUME = 0.355;
```

Table 1   Conversion between
Metric and Nonmetric
Units

1 *(fluid) ounce (oz)* = 29.586 *milliliter (mL)*
1 *gallon* = 3.785 *liter (L)*
1 *ounce (oz)* = 28.3495 *grams (g)*
1 *pound (lb)* = 453.6 *grams*
1 *inch* = 2.54 *centimeter (cm)*
1 *foot* = 30.5 *centimeter*
1 *mile* = 1.609 *kilometer (km)*

```
int bottles = 4; // we have four bottles
int cans = 10; // and ten cans

// compute total volume

double total = bottles * BOTTLE_VOLUME
    + cans * CAN_VOLUME;

// print result

System.out.print("The total volume is ");
System.out.print(total);
System.out.println(" liters");
    }
}
```

Now `BOTTLE_VOLUME` and `CAN_VOLUME` are named entities. Unlike `total`, they are constant values. Since they are declared as `final`, their values can never change after being initialized. If you try to change the value of a `final` variable, the compiler will report an error and your program will not compile.

Many programmers use all-uppercase names for constants (`final` variables), such as `BOTTLE_VOLUME`. That way, it is easy to distinguish between variables (with mostly lowercase letters) and constants. We will follow this convention in this book. However, this rule is a matter of good style, not a requirement of the Java language. The compiler will not complain if you give a `final` variable a name with lowercase letters.

It is also possible to declare a `final` variable without initializing it right away. Such a `final` variable is sometimes called a *blank final*.

```
final double BOTTLE_VOLUME;
final double CAN_VOLUME;
BOTTLE_VOLUME = 2.0;
// now can't change BOTTLE_VOLUME again
CAN_VOLUME = 0.355;
// now can't change CAN_VOLUME again
```

You can assign to a blank final variable *once*. As soon as you store a value into a final variable, that value is, well, final, and you can't change it any more.

In fact, you can do even better and explain where the value for the can volume came from:

```
final double LITER_PER_OZ = 0.029573529;
final double CAN_VOLUME = 12 * LITER_PER_OZ;
    // 12 oz. cans
```

Sure, it is more trouble to type the constant definitions and use the constant names in the formulas, but it makes the code much more readable. It also makes the code much easier to change. Suppose our program does computations involving volumes in several different places. Then suppose you need to switch from two-liter bottles to half-gallon bottles. If you simply multiply by 2 to get bottle volumes, you must now

---

Java Syntax

2.5 Constant Definition

```
final TypeName variableName
    = expression;
final TypeName  variableName;
```

Example:

```
final double CAN_VOLUME = 0.355;
```

Purpose:

To define a constant of a particular type. If the constant is not immediately initialized, you can assign to it *once*. Once the value is set, it is final.

---

replace every 2 by 1.893 . . . well, not *every* number 2. There may have been other uses of 2 in the program that had nothing to do with bottles. You have to *look* at every number 2 and see whether you need to change it. Did I mention the one formula that multiplied a case count by 36 because there were 18 bottles in every case? That number now needs to be turned into 18×1.893—hopefully you were lucky enough to find it. If, on the other hand, the constant BOTTLE_VOLUME is conscientiously used throughout the program, you need only update it in *one location*. Named constants are very important for program maintenance. See Quality Tip 2.2 for more information.

The Math class defines several useful constants, such as Math.PI and Math.E for the numbers π and e.

Quality Tip 2.2

Do Not Use Magic Numbers

A *magic number* is a numeric constant that appears in your code without explanation. For example,

```
if (col >= 66) ...
```

Why 66? Maybe this program prints in a 12-point font on 8.5×11-inch paper with a 1-inch margin on the left- and right-hand sides? Indeed, then you can fit 65 characters on a line. Once you reach column 66, you are beyond the right margin and must do something special. However, these are awfully fragile assumptions. To make the program work for a different paper size, you must locate all values of 65 (and 66 and 64) and replace them, taking care not to touch those 65s (and 66s and 64s) that have nothing to do with paper size. In a program that is more than a few pages long, that is incredibly tedious and error-prone.

The remedy is to use a named constant instead:

```
final int RIGHT_MARGIN = 65;
if (col > RIGHT_MARGIN) ...
```

You should *never* use magic numbers in your code. Any number that is not completely self-explanatory should be declared as a named constant. We sinned in our sample programs when we used values such as 0.05 and 0.1. We should have used constants NICKEL_VALUE and DIME_VALUE instead.

Even the most reasonable cosmic constant is going to change one day. You think there are 365 days in a year? Your customers on Mars are going to be pretty unhappy about your silly prejudice. Make a constant

```
final int DAYS_PER_YEAR = 365;
```

By the way, the device

```
final int THREE_HUNDRED_AND_SIXTY_FIVE = 365;
```

is counterproductive and frowned upon.

2.5   Arithmetic

You already saw how to add and multiply numbers and values stored in variables:

```
double t = p + d * 0.1 + q * 0.25;
```

You can use all four basic arithmetic operations in Java: addition, subtraction, multiplication, and division. You must write a * b to denote multiplication, not a b or a · b. Division is indicated with a /, not a fraction bar. For example,

$$\frac{a + b}{2}$$

becomes

```
(a + b) / 2
```

Parentheses are used just as in algebra: to indicate in which order the subexpressions should be computed. For example, in the expression (a + b) / 2, the sum a + b is computed first, and then the sum is divided by 2. In contrast, in the expression

```
a + b / 2
```

only b is divided by 2, and then the sum of a and b / 2 is formed. Just as in regular algebraic notation, multiplication and division *bind more strongly* than addition and subtraction. For example, in the expression a + b / 2, the / is carried out first, even though the + operation occurs further to the left.

Division works as you would expect, as long as at least one of the numbers involved is a floating-point number. That is,

```
7.0 / 4.0
7 / 4.0
7.0 / 4
```

all yield 1.75. However, if *both* numbers are integers, then the result of the division is always an integer, with the remainder discarded. That is,

7 / 4

evaluates to 1, because 7 divided by 4 is 1 with a remainder of 3 (which is discarded). This can be a source of subtle programming errors—see Common Error 2.3.

If you are interested only in the remainder, use the % operator:

7 % 4

is 3, the remainder of the integer division of 7 by 4. The % symbol has no analog in algebra. It was chosen because it looks similar to /, and the remainder operation is related to division.

Here is a typical use for the integer / and % operations. Suppose you want to know the value of the coins in a purse in dollars and cents. You can compute the value as an integer, denominated in cents, and then compute the whole dollar amount and the remaining change:

Program Coins3.java

```java
public class Coins3
{  public static void main(String[] args)
   {  final int PENNY_VALUE = 1;
      final int NICKEL_VALUE = 5;
      final int DIME_VALUE = 10;
      final int QUARTER_VALUE = 25;
      final int DOLLAR_VALUE = 100;

      int pennies = 8; // the purse contains 8 pennies,
      int nickels = 0; // no nickels,
      int dimes = 4; // four dimes,
      int quarters = 3; // and three quarters

      // compute total value in pennies

      int total = pennies * PENNY_VALUE
         + nickels * NICKEL_VALUE
         + dimes * DIME_VALUE
         + quarters * QUARTER_VALUE;

      // use integer division to convert to dollars, cents

      int dollar = total / DOLLAR_VALUE;
      int cents = total % DOLLAR_VALUE;
      System.out.print("Total value = ");
      System.out.print(dollar);
      System.out.print(" dollars and ");
```

```
      System.out.print(cents);
      System.out.println(" cents");
   }
}
```

For example, if `total` is 243, then the output statement will display

```
Total value = 2 dollars and 43 cents.
```

To take the square root of a number, you use the `Math.sqrt` method. For example, $\sqrt{x}$ is written as `Math.sqrt(x)`. To compute x^n, you write `Math.pow(x, n)`. However, to compute x^2 it is significantly more efficient simply to write `x * x`. The `sqrt` and `pow` methods are static methods of the `Math` class.

As you can see, the effect of the `/`, `Math.sqrt`, and `Math.pow` operations is to flatten out mathematical terms. In algebra, you use fractions, exponents, and roots to arrange expressions in a compact two-dimensional form. In Java, you have to write all expressions in a linear arrangement. For example, the subexpression

$$\frac{-b + \sqrt{b^2 - 4ac}}{2a}$$

of the quadratic formula becomes

```
(-b + Math.sqrt(b * b - 4 * a * c)) / (2 * a)
```

Figure 3 shows how to analyze such an expression. With complicated expressions like these, it is not always easy to keep the parentheses (...) matched—see Common Error 2.4.

Table 2 shows additional methods of the `Math` class. Inputs and outputs are floating-point numbers.

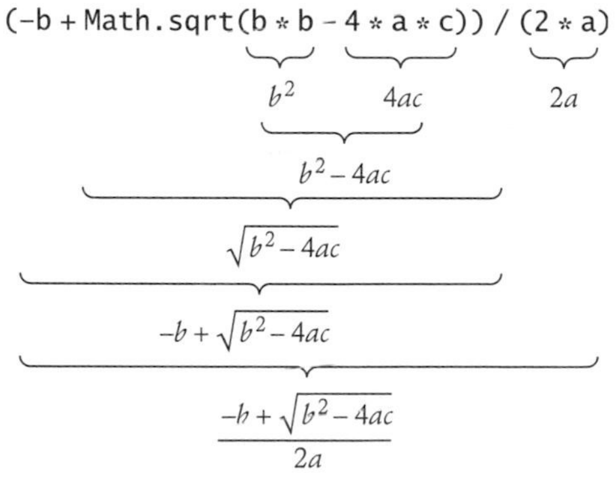

Figure 3

Analyzing an Expression

Table 2 Mathematical Methods

`Math.sqrt(x)`	square root of x $(x \geq 0)$
`Math.pow(x, y)`	x^y ($x > 0$, or $x = 0$ and $y > 0$, or $x < 0$ and y is an integer)
`Math.sin(x)`	sine of x (x in radians)
`Math.cos(x)`	cosine of x
`Math.tan(x)`	tangent of x
`Math.asin(x)`	(arc sine) $\sin^{-1} x \in [-\pi/2, \pi/2]$, $x \in [-1,1]$
`Math.acos(x)`	(arc cosine) $\cos^{-1} x \in [0, \pi]$, $x \in [-1,1]$
`Math.atan(x)`	(arc tangent) $\tan^{-1} x \in (-\pi/2, \pi/2)$
`Math.atan2(y,x)`	(arc tangent) $\tan^{-1}(y/x) \in [-\pi, \pi]$, x may be 0
`Math.toDegrees(x)`	converts x radians to degrees (i.e. returns $x \cdot 180/\pi$)
`Math.toRadians(x)`	converts x degrees to radians (i.e. returns $x \cdot \pi/180$)
`Math.exp(x)`	e^x
`Math.log(x)`	(natural log) $\ln(x)$, $x > 0$
`Math.round(x)`	the closest integer to x (as a `long`)
`Math.ceil(x)`	smallest integer $\geq x$ (as a `double`)
`Math.floor(x)`	largest integer $\leq x$ (as a `double`)
`Math.abs(x)`	absolute value $|x|$

Common Error 2.3

Integer Division

It is unfortunate that Java uses the same symbol, namely /, for both integer and floating-point division. These are really quite different operations. It is a common error to use integer division by accident. Consider this program segment that computes the average of three integers.

```
int s1 = 5; // score of test 1
int s2 = 6; // score of test 2
int s3 = 3; // score of test 3
double average = (s1 + s2 + s3) / 3;   // Error
System.out.print("Your average score is ");
System.out.println(average);
```

What could be wrong with that? Of course, the average of s1, s2, and s3 is

$$\frac{s1 + s2 + s3}{3}$$

Here, however the / does not mean division in the mathematical sense. It denotes integer division, because both s1 + s2 + s3 and 3 are integers. For example, if the scores add up to 14, the average is computed to be 4, the result of the integer division of 14 by 3. That integer 4 is then moved into the floating-point variable **average**. The remedy is to make the numerator or denominator into a floating-point number:

```
double total = s1 + s2 + s3;
double average = total / 3;
```

or

```
double average = (s1 + s2 + s3) / 3.0;
```

Common Error 2.4

Unbalanced Parentheses

Consider the expression

```
1.5 * ((-(b - Math.sqrt(b * b - 4 * a * c)) / (2 * a))
```

What is wrong with it? Count the parentheses. There are five opening parentheses (and four closing parentheses). The parentheses are *unbalanced*. This kind of typing error is very common with complicated expressions. Now consider this expression.

```
1.5 * (Math.sqrt(b * b - 4 * a * c))) - ((b / (2 * a))
```

This expression has five opening parentheses (and five closing parentheses), but it is still not correct. In the middle of the expression,

```
1.5 * (Math.sqrt(b * b - 4 * a * c))) - ((b / (2 * a))
                                     ↑
```

there are only two opening parentheses (but three closing parentheses), which is an error. In the middle of an expression, the count of opening parentheses (must be greater than or equal to the count of closing parentheses), and at the end of the expression the two counts must be the same.

Here is a simple trick to make the counting easier without using pencil and paper. It is difficult for the brain to keep two counts simultaneously, so keep only one count when scanning the expression. Start with 1 at the first opening parenthesis; add 1 whenever you see an opening parenthesis; and subtract 1 whenever you see a closing parenthesis. Say the numbers aloud as you scan the expression. If the count ever drops below zero, or if it is not zero at the end, the parentheses are unbalanced. For example, when scanning the previous expression, you would mutter

```
1.5 * (Math.sqrt(b * b - 4 * a * c) )  ) - ((b / (2 * a))
       1         2                 1 0 -1
```

and you would find the error.

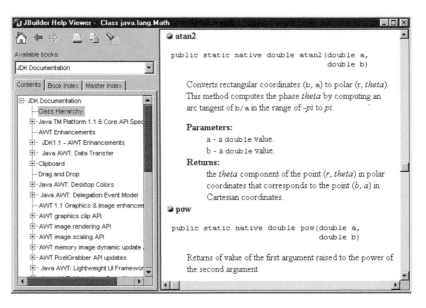

Figure 4

On-Line Help

Productivity Hint 2.2

On–Line Help

Today's integrated Java programming environments contain sophisticated help systems. You should spend some time learning how to use the on-line help in your compiler. Help is available on compiler settings, keyboard shortcuts, and, most importantly, on library methods. If you are not sure how the **pow** method works, or cannot remember whether it was called **pow** or **power**, the on-line help can give you the answer quickly. Figure 4 shows a typical help screen.

Quality Tip 2.3

White Space

The compiler does not care whether you write your entire program onto a single line or place every symbol onto a separate line. The human reader, though, cares very much. You should use blank lines to group your code visually into sections. For example, you can signal to the reader that an output prompt and the corresponding input statement belong together by inserting a blank line before and after the group. You will find many examples in the source code listings in this book.

White space inside expressions is also important. It is easier to read

```
x1 = (-b + Math.sqrt(b * b - 4 * a * c)) / (2 * a);
```

than

```
x1=(-b+Math.sqrt(b*b-4*a*c))/(2*a);
```

Simply put spaces around all operators + - * / % =. However, don't put a space after a *unary* minus: a - used to negate a single quantity, as in -b. That way, it can be easily distinguished from a *binary* minus, as in a - b. Don't put spaces between a method name and the parentheses, but do put a space after every Java keyword. That makes it easy to see that the sqrt in Math.sqrt(x) is a method name, whereas the if in if (x > 0)... is a keyword.

◆Quality Tip 2.4

Factor Out Common Code

Suppose you want to find both solutions of the quadratic equation $ax^2 + bx + c = 0$. The quadratic formula tells us that the solutions are

$$x_{1,2} = \frac{-b \pm \sqrt{b^2 - 4ac}}{2a}$$

In Java, there is no analog to the $\pm$ operation, which indicates how to obtain two solutions simultaneously. Both solutions must be computed separately:

```
x1 = (-b + Math.sqrt(b * b - 4 * a * c)) / (2 * a);
x2 = (-b - Math.sqrt(b * b - 4 * a * c)) / (2 * a);
```

This approach has two problems. First, the computation of Math.sqrt(b * b - 4 * a * c) is carried out twice, which wastes time. Second, whenever the same code is replicated, the possibility of a typing error increases. The remedy is to *factor out* the common code:

```
double root = Math.sqrt(b * b - 4 * a * c);
x1 = (-b + root) / (2 * a);
x2 = (-b - root) / (2 * a);
```

You could go even further and factor out the computation of 2 * a, but the gain from factoring out very simple computations is small, and the resulting code can be hard to read.

2.6   Strings

2.6.1   String Variables

Next to numbers, *strings* are the most important data type that most programs use. A string is a sequence of characters, such as "Hello". In Java, strings are enclosed in quotation marks, which are not themselves part of the string.

You can declare variables that hold strings:

```
String name = "John";
```

Use assignment to place a different string into the variable.

```
name = "Carl";
```

The number of characters in a string is called the *length* of the string. For example, the length of `"Hello, World!"` is 13. You can compute the length of a string with the `length` method.

```
int n = name.length();
```

Note that, unlike numbers, strings are objects. (You can tell that `String` is a class because it starts with an uppercase letter. The basic types `int` and `double` start with a lowercase letter.) Therefore, you can call methods on strings. For example, you compute the length of the string object `name` with the method call `name.length()`, *not* as `String.length(name)`.

A string of length zero, containing no characters, is called the *empty string* and is written as `""`.

2.6.2 Substrings

Once you have a string, what can you do with it? You can extract substrings, and you can glue smaller strings together to form larger ones. To extract a substring, use the `substring` operation:

```
s.substring(start, pastEnd)
```

returns a string that is made up from the characters in the string `s`, starting at character `start`, and containing all characters up to, but not including, the character `pastEnd`. Here is an example:

```
String greeting = "Hello, World!";
String sub = greeting.substring(0, 4);
   // sub is  "Hell"
```

The `substring` operation makes a string that consists of four characters taken from the string `greeting`. A curious aspect of the `substring` operation is the numbering of the starting and ending positions. Starting position 0 means "start at the beginning of the string". For technical reasons that used to be important but are no longer relevant, Java string position numbers start at 0. The first string position is labeled 0, the second one 1, and so on. For example, here are the position numbers in the `greeting` string:

```
┌─┬─┬─┬─┬─┬─┬─┬─┬─┬─┬─┬──┬──┐
│H│e│l│l│o│,│ │W│o│r│l│d │! │
└─┴─┴─┴─┴─┴─┴─┴─┴─┴─┴─┴──┴──┘
 0 1 2 3 4 5 6 7 8 9 10 11 12
```

The position number of the last character (12 for the string `"Hello, World!"`) is always 1 less than the length of the string.

Let us figure out how to extract the substring `"World"`. Count characters starting at 0, not 1. You find that `W`, the 8th character, has position number 7. The first character that you *don't* want, `!`, is the character at position 12. Therefore, the appropriate substring command is

```
String w = greeting.substring(7, 12);
```

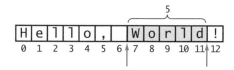

It is curious that you must specify the position of the first character that you do want and then the first character that you don't want. There is one advantage to this setup. You can easily compute the *length* of the substring: it is `pastEnd - start`. For example, the string `"World"` has length $12 - 7 = 5$.

If you omit the second parameter of the `substring` method, then all characters from the starting position to the end of the string are copied. For example,

```
String tail = greeting.substring(7);
    // copies all characters from position 7 on
```

sets `tail` to the string `"World!"`. This is equivalent to the call

```
String tail = greeting.substring(7, greeting.length());
```

2.6.3 Concatenation

Now that you know how to take strings apart, let us see how to put them back together. Given two strings, such as `"Harry"` and `"Hacker"`, you can *concatenate* them to one long string:

```
String fname = "Harry";
String lname = "Hacker";
String name = fname + lname;
```

The + operator concatenates two strings. The resulting string is `"HarryHacker"`. Actually, that isn't really what we are after. We'd like the first and last name separated by a space. No problem:

```
String name = fname + " " + lname;
```

Now we concatenate three strings: `"Harry"`, `" "`, and `"Hacker"`. The result is `"Harry Hacker"`.

The concatenation operator in Java is very powerful. If *one of the expressions,* either to the left or the right of a + operator, is a string, then the other one is automatically forced to become a string as well, and both strings are concatenated.

For example, consider this code:

```
String a = "Agent";
int n = 7;
String bond = a + n;
```

Since `a` is a string, `n` is converted from the integer 7 to the string `"7"`. Then the two strings `"Agent"` and `"7"` are concatenated to form the string `"Agent7"`.

This concatenation is very useful to reduce the number of `System.out.print` instructions. For example, you can combine

```
System.out.print("The total is ");
System.out.println(total);
```

to the single call

```
System.out.println("The total is " + total);
```

The concatenation `"The total is " + total` computes a single string that consists of the string `"The total is "`, followed by the string equivalent of the number `total`.

2.6.4   Converting between Numbers and Strings

Suppose you want to create passwords for user accounts. The password is to be the initials of the user name, converted to lowercase, followed by the age. If Harry J. Hacker is 19 years old, his password will be `hjh19`. (In practice, this would not be a good password. If Carl Cracker is familiar with the scheme, he can break into Harry's account. Even if he isn't sure about Harry's age, he just needs a few tries.)

First, you need to know how to change the initials to lowercase. The `toUpperCase` and `toLowerCase` methods make strings with only upper- or lowercase characters. For example,

```
String greeting = "Hello";
System.out.println(greeting.toUpperCase() + " "
   + greeting.toLowerCase());
```

displays `HELLO hello`. Note that the `toUpperCase` and `toLowerCase` do not change the original `String` object `greeting`. They return new `String` objects that contain the uppercased and lowercased versions of the original string. In fact, *no* `String` methods modify the string object on which they operate. For that reason, strings are called *immutable objects*.

To generate the password, you must extract substrings from the first, middle, and last names. Then you concatenate the substrings and convert the result to lowercase. Now we'd like to combine the initials (such as `"hjh"`) and the age (such as 19) to a string. Here the concatenation operator comes to our help. If you concatenate the string `"hjh"` with the number 19, the latter is forced into a string `"19"`, and then the strings are concatenated to form the string `"hjh19"`. Here is the complete program.

Program MakePassword.java

```
public class MakePassword
{   public static void main(String[] args)
    {   String firstName = "Harold";
        String middleName = "Joseph";
        String lastName = "Hacker";

        // extract initials

        String initials = firstName.substring(0, 1)
            + middleName.substring(0, 1)
            + lastName.substring(0, 1);

        // append age

        int age = 19; // the age of the user
        String password = initials.toLowerCase() + age;

        System.out.println("Your password is " + password);
    }
}
```

In general, if you need to convert a number to a string, you can concatenate with the empty string:

```
String ageString = "" + age;
```

This works very well and is a common idiom. Some programmers prefer to use the **toString** methods of the **Integer** and **Double** classes, because it is more explicit:

```
String ageString = Integer.toString(age);
```

Number conversion does not always work well for floating-point numbers that are meant to denote currency values. For example, consider the following code:

```
int quarters = 2;
int dollars = 3;
double total = dollars + quarters * 0.25; // price is 3.5
final double TAX_RATE = 8.5; // tax rate in percent
double tax = total * TAX_RATE / 100; // tax is 0.2975
System.out.println("Total: $" + total);
System.out.println("Tax:   $" + tax);
```

This code prints

```
Total: $3.5
Tax:   $0.2975
```

We would prefer the numbers to be printed with two digits after the decimal point, with trailing zeroes in the first line, and rounded to the nearest two digits in the second line, like this:

```
Total: $3.50
Tax:   $0.30
```

You can achieve this with the `NumberFormat` class in the `java.text` package. First, you must use the static method `getNumberInstance` to obtain a `NumberFormat` object. Then you set the maximum number of fraction digits to 2:

```
NumberFormat formatter = NumberFormat.getNumberInstance();
formatter.setMaximumFractionDigits(2);
```

Then the numbers are rounded to two digits. For example, 0.2875 will be converted to the string `"0.29"`. But 0.2975 will be converted to `"0.3"`, not `"0.30"`. If you want trailing zeroes, you *also* have to set the minimum number of fraction digits to 2:

```
formatter.setMinimumFractionDigits(2);
```

Then you use the `format` method of that object. The result is a string that you can print.

```
formatter.format(tax)
```

returns the string `"0.30"`. The statement

```
System.out.println("Tax: $" + formatter.format(tax));
```

rounds the value of `tax` to two digits after the decimal point and prints: `Tax: $0.30`.

The "number instance" formatter is useful because it lets you print numbers with as many fraction digits as desired. If you just want to print a currency value, the `getCurrencyInstance` method of the `NumberFormat` class produces a more convenient formatter. The "currency instance" formatter generates currency value strings, with the local currency symbol (such as `$` in the United States) and the appropriate number of digits after the decimal point (for example, two digits in the United States).

```
NumberFormat formatter = NumberFormat.getCurrencyInstance();
System.out.print(formatter.format(tax));
   // prints "$0.30"
```

Occasionally, you have a string containing just digits, and you would like to know its numerical value. For example,

```
String password = "hjh19";
String ageString = password.substring(3); // the string "19"
```

You cannot simply assign the string to an integer:

```
int age = ageString; // ERROR
```

The Java compiler will complain that it is not willing to convert a string to an integer. After all, there is no guarantee that the string contains just digits. Instead, you have to use the static `parseInt` method of the `Integer` class to convert a string containing an integer to its integer value. For example, if `ageString` is the string `"19"`, then `Integer.parseInt(ageString)` is the integer 19:

```
int age = Integer.parseInt(ageString); // age is the number 19
```

To convert a string containing floating-point digits to its floating-point value, use the static `parseDouble` method of the `Double` class. For example,

```
String priceString = "$3.95";
double price = Double.parseDouble(priceString.substring(1));
   // skip  "$" and convert to a number
```

As you will see later in this chapter, these methods are useful for processing input. In Java, you obtain all input as a string. If the input string contains digits, you need to convert it to a number with the `Integer.parseInt` or `Double.parseDouble` method.

2.7   Reading Input with the ConsoleReader Class

The programs of the preceding sections were not very useful. If you have a different collection of coins in your purse, you must change the variable initializations, recompile the program, and run it again. It would be more practical if the program could ask how many coins you have of each kind and then compute the total. In the following sections you will learn how to write programs that accept such user input.

However, as it turns out, accepting user input in Java has some technical complexities. In this book, we will use a special class, called `ConsoleReader`, to make processing keyboard input easier and less tedious. Unlike the other classes discussed in this chapter, `ConsoleReader` is not a standard Java class. Instead, it is a class that was specially written for this book to remove some of the complexity of the standard Java classes for processing input. You will learn how to use that class in this chapter. If you are curious how the class is implemented, you should read the next section on input in standard Java and Section 3.10 in the next chapter.

Just as the `System` class provides an object `System.out` for output, there is an object `System.in` for input. This is an object of type `InputStream`. Unfortunately, the `System.in` object does not directly support convenient methods for reading numbers and strings.

The purpose of the `ConsoleReader` class is to add a friendly interface to an input stream such as `System.in`. First, you need to construct a `ConsoleReader` object, like this:

```
ConsoleReader console = new ConsoleReader(System.in);
```

Next, simply call one of the following three methods:

```
String line = console.readLine(); // read a line of input
int n = console.readInt(); // read an integer
double x = console.readDouble(); // read a floating-point number
```

Here is a typical usage. You want to ask a user a question and read the answer:

```
System.out.println("How many pennies do you have?");
int pennies = console.readInt();
```

The user needs to type a number and hit the Enter key. Immediately afterwards, the **readInt** method returns with the value the user entered, and your program continues.

Here is a complete program that prompts the user for the number of pennies, nickels, dimes, and quarters and then prints the total value of the coins, nicely formatted as a currency string.

Program Coins4.java

```
import java.text.NumberFormat;

public class Coins4
{  public static void main(String[] args)
   {  final double PENNY_VALUE = 0.01;
      final double NICKEL_VALUE = 0.05;
      final double DIME_VALUE = 0.1;
      final double QUARTER_VALUE = 0.25;

      ConsoleReader console = new ConsoleReader(System.in);

      System.out.println("How many pennies do you have?");
      int pennies = console.readInt();

      System.out.println("How many nickels do you have?");
      int nickels = console.readInt();

      System.out.println("How many dimes do you have?");
      int dimes = console.readInt();

      System.out.println("How many quarters do you have?");
      int quarters = console.readInt();

      double total = pennies * PENNY_VALUE
         + nickels * NICKEL_VALUE
         + dimes * DIME_VALUE
         + quarters * QUARTER_VALUE;
            // total value of the coins

      NumberFormat formatter
         = NumberFormat.getCurrencyInstance();

      System.out.println("Total value = "
         + formatter.format(total));
   }
}
```

We recommend that you use the `ConsoleReader` class in your own programs whenever you need to read console input. Simply place the `ConsoleReader.java` file together with your program file, into a common directory. You can find the `ConsoleReader.java` file in the sample code that accompanies this book. If you use an integrated programming environment, add the file to the project that you are building. (Unfortunately, since the way for doing that differs widely between development environments, we cannot give you detailed instructions here.) In Chapter 9 we will go one step further and show you how to place the `ConsoleReader` class in a separate *package*, just like the classes in the standard Java packages.

2.8 Reading Input in Standard Java (Advanced)

If you like the `ConsoleReader` class and have no interest in learning about the more cumbersome support for keyboard input in standard Java, you can safely skip this section. If you want to learn more about programming concepts first, you can come back here later.

Are you still with us? If so, you have decided to stay on for the details of using the standard Java classes for reading keyboard input.

The `System.in` object has the type `InputStream`. The `InputStream` class has no methods for reading numbers or strings. It merely has a `read` method to read a single *byte*. In order actually to read number input, you have to solve three problems.

1. Objects of the `InputStream` class read bytes, but you want to read characters and lines of input. You need to turn `System.in` into an object that can read a line of input. As you will see shortly, that purpose is achieved by creating an object of a class `BufferedReader` and calling its `readLine` method.

2. If the `readLine` method encounters an error while reading input, it generates a so-called *exception*. You must tell the compiler what to do in that case.

3. The `readLine` method always returns a string. If you want to read a number, you have to convert the string to a number.

In the next three sections, we will tackle these issues one by one. Afterwards, you may well agree that you are better off using the `ConsoleReader` class for your own programs so that you are not distracted by technical detail every time you need to process keyboard input.

2.8.1 Converting a Stream to a Reader

Objects of the `InputStream` class read bytes. You want to read characters. In some encoding schemes, such as ASCII, each byte corresponds to a character. Java, however, uses *Unicode* in order to work with many languages. In Unicode, each character is made up of two bytes. In the terminology of Java, *input streams* read sequences of bytes, and *readers* read sequences of characters. Thus, you must turn the `InputStream` object `System.in` into a `Reader` object. There is a class, **InputStreamReader**, that turns an input stream into a reader. You build an input stream reader object that can read characters from `System.in` as follows:

```
InputStreamReader reader = new InputStreamReader(System.in);
```

Objects of the `InputStreamReader` class read characters. However, they can read only single characters. Of course, you can keep reading characters and put them together, but that is tedious. A different class called **BufferedReader** turns any input reader into an input reader with the ability to read entire lines at a time. You build a buffered reader object from **reader**, using the following statement:

```
BufferedReader console = new BufferedReader(reader);
```

Now you are ready to read in a line of text from the keyboard, with the `readLine` method of the `BufferedReader` class.

```
System.out.println("What is your name?");
String name = console.readLine();
```

The whole point of the `InputStreamReader` and `BufferedReader` classes was to turn the somewhat useless `System.in` object into an object that has a `readLine` method. Figure 5 shows how a `BufferedReader` object makes use of an `InputStreamReader` object to read characters, and how the input stream reader uses the input stream object `System.in` to read bytes.

2.8.2 Handling Input/Output Exceptions

In reading input from a stream or reader, things can go wrong. For example, if the input comes from a disk file, there may be a bad sector on the disk. If the input comes from a network connection, there may be network trouble, such as a connection timeout. Whenever the `readLine` method detects such trouble, it uses a special mechanism called an *exception* to notify the program of the problem. In order to compile, your program must be able to handle this notification. Frankly, none of these problems will occur when you read input from the keyboard. But the Java compiler knows that the `readLine` method might generate an exception. Therefore, it insists that you specify what you want to have done when an exception occurs.

As you will see in Chapter 13, there are several ways of dealing with exceptions. Right now, we will just use the simplest way: namely, to *catch* the exception when it occurs. To catch an exception, you must place the statement or statements that can generate an exception into a so-called **try** block. A **try** block starts with the

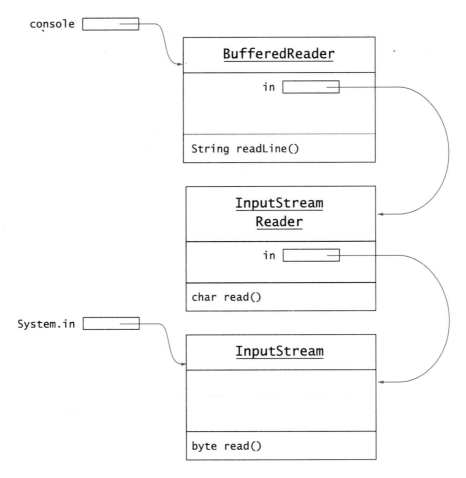

Figure 5

Turning **System.in** into a
BufferedReader Object

keyword **try**, followed by one or more statements enclosed in a pair of braces {},
followed by one or more **catch** clauses. In each **catch** clause, you need to specify
what you want to do when a particular exception occurs.

In this case, you need to catch exceptions whose type is **IOException**. Certain
methods, such as **readLine**, threaten to generate these exceptions whenever there
is a problem with input or output. Until you learn more about exception handling,
you should simply catch all input/output exceptions, print out the exception object,
and terminate the program. Here is the necessary code to achieve this.

```
try
{   statement
    statement
    . . .
}
catch(IOException e)
{   System.out.println(e);
    System.exit(1);
}
```

Now you want to read a line of keyboard input. Since the readLine threatens to throw an IOException, you must place it inside a try block:

```
String input;
try
{   input = console.readLine();
}
catch(IOException e)
{   System.out.println(e);
    System.exit(1);
}
```

If you read multiple input lines, it would be quite tedious to place each of them inside a separate try block. Instead, simply place *all* statements of the main method inside a single try block:

```
import java.io.InputStreamReader;
import java.io.BufferedReader;
import java.io.IOException;

public class MyProgram
{   public static void main(String[] args)
    {   try
        {   InputStreamReader reader = new InputStreamReader(System.in);
            BufferedReader console = new BufferedReader(reader);
            statement
            statement
            . . .
        }
        catch(IOException e)
        {   System.out.println(e);
            System.exit(1);
        }
    }
}
```

The exit method of the System class terminates the current program. The argument of the exit method is 0 if the program exited successfully, or some nonzero value (such as 1 in our case) to indicate program failure.

Java Syntax

2.5 `try` **Block**

```
try
{  statement
   statement
   . . .
}
catch(ExceptionClass exceptionObject)
{  statement
   statement
   . . .
}
```

Example:

```
try
{  System.out.println("What is your name?");
   String name = console.readLine();
   System.out.println("Hello, " + name + "!");
}
catch(IOException e)
{  System.out.println(e);
   System.exit(1);
}
```

Purpose:

To execute one or more statements that may generate exceptions. If an exception of a particular type occurs, then stop executing those statements and instead go to the matching `catch` clause. If no exception occurs, then skip the `catch` clause.

If you know how to read input in another programming language, this Java code may look a bit overwhelming. There are two reasons for this. First, Java is concerned about security. It makes sense to state explicitly what a program should do when things go wrong. Right now, you can simply exit the program. Later, you will learn how to implement more sophisticated error handling. The point is that exiting the program was a *conscious choice*. Other programming languages might have just taken some default action when an error occurred without giving the programmer a choice. Thus, the exception mechanism is a strength of Java, even if it makes some programs a little more complex. Furthermore, the designers of Java were not interested in making keyboard input as simple as possible. Most professional programs don't collect keyboard input in a console window. Instead, they use text fields in a graphical user interface to gather text input. You will learn later in this course how to write such programs.

2.8.3 Reading Numbers

There is one final problem with reading keyboard input. Objects of the
BufferedReader class can read entire lines. However, these lines are *strings*. That is
fine if you are asking for a string input from the user of your program, such as the
user name. If you are asking for a number value, though, such as a dollar amount
or a coin count, you must convert the string value into a number. You do that with
the Integer.parseInt and Double.parseDouble methods that you saw in the
preceding section. Here is an example of how you can read a number:

```
public static void main(String[] args)
{  try
   {  InputStreamReader reader = new InputStreamReader(System.in);
      BufferedReader console = new BufferedReader(reader);

      System.out.println("How many pennies do you have? ");
      String input = console.readLine();
      int pennies = Integer.parseInt(input);
      . . .
   }
   catch(IOException e)
   {  System.out.println(e);
      System.exit(1);
   }
}
```

Here is a complete program, using only the standard Java library, that prompts the
user for the number of pennies, nickels, dimes, and quarters, and then prints the total
value of the coins.

Program Coins5.java

```
import java.io.BufferedReader;
import java.io.InputStreamReader;
import java.io.IOException;

public class Coins5
{  public static void main(String[] args)
   {  try
      {  final double PENNY_VALUE = 0.01;
         final double NICKEL_VALUE = 0.05;
         final double DIME_VALUE = 0.1;
         final double QUARTER_VALUE = 0.25;

         InputStreamReader reader
            = new InputStreamReader(System.in);
         BufferedReader console
            = new BufferedReader(reader);
```

```
        System.out.println("How many pennies do you have?");
        String input = console.readLine();
        int pennies = Integer.parseInt(input);

        System.out.println("How many nickels do you have?");
        input = console.readLine();
        int nickels = Integer.parseInt(input);

        System.out.println("How many dimes do you have?");
        input = console.readLine();
        int dimes = Integer.parseInt(input);

        System.out.println("How many quarters do you have?");
        input = console.readLine();
        int quarters = Integer.parseInt(input);

        double total = pennies * PENNY_VALUE
           + nickels * NICKEL_VALUE
           + dimes * DIME_VALUE
           + quarters * QUARTER_VALUE;
              // total value of the coins
        System.out.println("Total value = " + total);
     }
     catch(IOException e)
     {  System.out.println(e);
        System.exit(1);
     }
  }
}
```

In the interest of full disclosure, we walked through explanations of all the code that is necessary to read input in Java. However, as a practical matter, we recommend that you use the **ConsoleReader** class in your own programs. In the next chapter, you will learn how that class is implemented.

Chapter Summary

1. Java has several data types for numbers. The most common types are **double** and **int**. Floating-point numbers (**double**) can have fractional values; integers (**int**) cannot. Occasionally, other numeric types are required for larger values or higher precision.

2. Numbers, strings, and other values can be stored in *variables*. A variable has a name that indicates its function to the human reader. A variable can hold different values during program execution.

3. When a variable is first filled with a value, it is *initialized*. The initial value can later be replaced with another by a process called *assignment*. In Java, assignment is

denoted by the = operator—a somewhat unfortunate choice, because the Java meaning of = is not the same as mathematical equality.

4. Constants are values with a symbolic name. Constants cannot be changed once they are initialized. Named constants should be used instead of numbers to make programs easier to read and maintain. In Java, constants are declared with the keyword `final`.

5. All common arithmetic operations are provided in Java; however, the symbols are different from mathematical notation. In particular, * denotes multiplication. There is no horizontal fraction bar, and / must be used for division. The % operator computes the remainder of a division. To compute a power a^b or a square root $\sqrt{a}$, use the `Math.pow` and `Math.root` methods. Other methods, such as `Math.sin` and `Math.log`, are available as well. These are *static* methods that do not operate on objects.

6. Strings are sequences of characters. Strings can be *concatenated;* that is, put end to end to yield a new longer string. In Java, string concatenation is denoted by the + operator. The `substring` method extracts substrings. Strings containing digits are not the same as the numbers they represent, but numbers are converted to strings during concatenation. If you want to have more control over the look of the result, use the `NumberFormat` class. Conversely, the `Integer.parseInt` and `Double.parseDouble` methods convert strings to numbers.

7. You use the *cast* notation to convert from one number type to another. For example, if x is a floating-point variable, then `(int)x` is x without its fractional part.

8. We recommend that you use the `ConsoleReader` class for reading input. Its `readLine`, `readInt`, and `readDouble` methods read a string, integer, and floating-point number from an input stream.

Classes, Objects, and Methods Introduced in This Chapter

```
java.io.BufferedReader
java.io.InputStreamReader
java.lang.Double
   parseDouble
   toString
java.lang.Integer
   parseInt
   toString
   MAX_VALUE
   MIN_VALUE
```

```
java.lang.Math
    abs
    acos
    asin
    atan
    atan2
    ceil
    cos
    exp
    floor
    log
    max
    min
    pow
    round
    sin
    sqrt
    tan
    toDegrees
    toRadians
    E
    PI
java.lang.String
    length
    substring
    toLowerCase
    toUpperCase
java.lang.System
    exit
    in
java.math.BigDecimal
    add
    divide
    multiply
    subtract
java.math.BigInteger
    add
    divide
    mod
    multiply
    subtract
java.text.NumberFormat
    format
    getCurrencyInstance
    getNumberInstance
    setMaximumFractionDigits
    setMinimumFractionDigits
```

Review Exercises

Exercise R2.1. Write the following mathematical expressions in Java.

$$s = s_0 + v_0 t + \frac{1}{2} g t^2$$

$$G = 4\pi^2 \frac{a^3}{P^2(m_1 + m_2)}$$

$$FV = PV \cdot \left(1 + \frac{INT}{100}\right)^{YRS}$$

$$c = \sqrt{a^2 + b^2 - 2ab \cos \gamma}$$

Exercise R2.2. Write the following Java expressions in mathematical notation.

```
dm = m * ((Math.sqrt(1 + v / c) / Math.sqrt(1 - v / c)) - 1);
volume = Math.PI * r * r * h;
volume = 4 * Math.PI * Math.pow(r, 3) / 3;
p = Math.atan2(z, Math.sqrt(x * x + y * y));
```

Exercise R2.3. What is wrong with this version of the quadratic formula?

```
x1 = (-b - Math.sqrt(b * b - 4 * a * c)) / 2 * a;
x2 = (-b + Math.sqrt(b * b - 4 * a * c)) / 2 * a;
```

Exercise R2.4. Give an example of integer overflow. Would the same example work correctly if you used floating-point? Give an example of a floating-point roundoff error. Would the same example work correctly if you used integers? When using integers, you would of course need to switch to a smaller unit, such as cents instead of dollars or milliliters instead of liters.

Exercise R2.5. Let n be an integer and x a floating-point number. Explain the difference between

```
n = (int)x;
```

and

```
n = (int)Math.round(x);
```

For what values of x do they give the same result? For what values of x do they give different results? What happens if x is negative?

Exercise R2.6. Find at least five *syntax* errors in the following program.

```
public class ExR2_6
{  public static void main(String[] args)
    {  System.out.print("This program adds two numbers.),
        x = 5;
        int y = 3.5;
        System.out.print("The sum of " + x + " and " + y " is: ");
        System.out.println(x + y)
    }
}
```

Exercise R2.7. Find at least three *logic errors* in the following program.

```
public class ExR2_7
{  public static void main(String[] args)
    {  ConsoleReader console = new ConsoleReader(System.in);
        int total = 1;
        System.out.println("Please enter a number:");
        int x1 = Integer.parseInt(console.readLine());
        total = total + x1;
        System.out.println("Please enter another number:");
        int x2 = Integer.parseInt(console.readLine());
        total = total + x1;
        double average = total / 2;
        System.out.println("The average of the two numbers is "
           + average);
    }
}
```

Exercise R2.8. Explain the differences between 2, 2.0, "2", and "2.0".

Exercise R2.9. Explain what each of the following two program segments computes:

```
x = 2;
y = x + x;
```

and

```
s = "2";
t = s + s;
```

Exercise R2.10. Uninitialized variables can be a serious problem. Should you *always* initialize every variable with zero? Explain the advantages and disadvantages of such a strategy.

Exercise R2.11. True or false? (x is an `int` and s is a `String`)

- ◆ `Integer.parseInt("" + x)` is the same as `x`
- ◆ `"" + Integer.parseInt(s)` is the same as `s`
- ◆ `s.substring(0, s.length())` is the same as `s`

Exercise R2.12. Give two ways for converting a number to a string. What is the advantage of each of these ways?

Exercise R2.13. How do you get the first character of a string? The last character? How do you *remove* the first character? The last character?

Exercise R2.14. How do you get the last digit of a number? The first digit? That is, if n is 23456, how do you find out 2 and 6? Do not convert the number to a string. *Hint:* `%`, `Math.log`.

Exercise R2.15. This chapter contains several recommendations regarding variables and constants that make programs easier to read and maintain. Briefly summarize these recommendations.

Exercise R2.16. What is a `final` variable? Can you define a `final` variable without supplying its value?

Exercise R2.17. What are the values of the following expressions? In each line, assume that

```
double x = 2.5;
double y = -1.5;
int m = 18;
int n = 4;
String s = "Hello";
String t = "World";
```

- ◆ `x + n * y - (x + n) * y`
- ◆ `m / n + m % n`
- ◆ `5 * x - n / 5`
- ◆ `Math.sqrt(Math.sqrt(n))`
- ◆ `(int)Math.round(x)`
- ◆ `(int)Math.round(x) + (int)Math.round(y)`
- ◆ `s + t`
- ◆ `s + n`
- ◆ `1 - (1 - (1 - (1 - (1 - n))))`
- ◆ `s.substring(1, 3)`
- ◆ `s.length() + t.length()`

Programming Exercises

Exercise P2.1. Write a program that prints the values

1

10

100

1000

10000

100000

1000000

10000000

100000000

1000000000

10000000000

100000000000

as integers and as floating-point numbers. Explain the results.

Exercise P2.2. Write a program that displays the squares, cubes, and fourth powers of the numbers 1 through 5.

Exercise P2.3. Write a program that prompts the user for two integers and then prints

- The sum
- The difference
- The product
- The average
- The distance (absolute value of the difference)
- The maximum (the larger of the two)
- The minimum (the smaller of the two)

Exercise P2.4. Write a program that prompts the user for a measurement in meters and then converts it into miles, feet, and inches.

Exercise P2.5. Write a program that prompts the user for a radius and then prints

◆ The area and circumference of the circle with that radius
◆ The volume and surface area of the sphere with that radius

Exercise P2.6. Write a program that asks the user for the lengths of the sides of a rectangle. Then print

◆ The area and perimeter of the rectangle
◆ The length of the diagonal (use the Pythagorean theorem)

Exercise P2.7. Write a program that prompts the user for

◆ The lengths of two sides of a triangle
◆ The size of the angle between the two sides (in degrees)

Then the program displays

◆ The length of the third side
◆ The sizes of the other two angles

Hint: Use the law of cosines.

Exercise P2.8. Write a program that prompts the user for

◆ The length of a side of a triangle
◆ The sizes of the two angles adjacent to that side (in degrees)

Then the program displays

◆ The lengths of the other two sides
◆ The size of the third angle

Hint: Use the law of sines.

Exercise P2.9. *Giving change.* Implement a program that directs a cashier how to give change. The program has two inputs: the amount due and the amount received from the customer. Compute the difference, and compute the dollars, quarters, dimes, nickels, and pennies that the customer should receive in return.

First transform the difference into an integer balance, denominated in pennies. Then compute the whole dollar amount. Subtract it from the balance. Compute the number of quarters needed. Repeat for dimes and nickels. Display the remaining pennies.

Exercise P2.10. Write a program that asks the user to input

◆ The number of gallons of gas in the tank
◆ The fuel efficiency in miles per gallon
◆ The price of gas per gallon

Then print out how far the car can go with the gas in the tank and print the cost per 100 miles.

Exercise P2.11. *DOS file names and extensions.* Write a program that prompts the user for the drive letter (C), the path (\Windows\System), the file name (Readme), and the extension (TXT). Then print the complete file name C:\Windows\System\Readme. TXT. (If you use UNIX or a Macintosh, use / or : instead to separate directories.)

Exercise P2.12. Write a program that reads a number greater than or equal to 1000 from the user and prints it out *with a comma separating the thousands*. Here is a sample dialog; the user input is in color:

```
Please enter an integer >= 1000: 23456
23,456
```

Exercise P2.13. Write a program that reads a number greater than or equal to 1,000 from the user, where the user enters a comma in the input. Then print the number without a comma. Here is a sample dialog; the user input is in color:

```
Please enter an integer between 1,000 and 999,999:   23,456
23456
```

Hint: Read the input as a string. Measure the length of the string. Suppose it contains n characters. Then extract substrings consisting of the first $n - 4$ characters and the last three characters.

Exercise 2.14. *Printing a grid.* Write a program that prints the following grid to play tic-tac-toe.

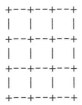

Of course, you could simply write seven statements of the form

```
System.out.println("+--+--+--+");
```

You should do it a smarter way, though. Define string variables to hold two kinds of patterns: a comb-shaped pattern and the bottom line. Print the comb three times and the bottom line once.

Exercise P2.15. Write a program that reads in an integer and breaks it into a sequence of individual digits. For example, the input 16384 is displayed as

```
1 6 3 8 4
```

You may assume that the input has no more than five digits and is not negative. *Hint:* There are two ways of solving this problem. You can use integer arithmetic and repeatedly divide by 10, or you can convert the number into a string and extract the digits from the string.

Exercise P2.16. The following program prints the values of sine and cosine for 0 degrees, 30 degrees, 45 degrees, 60 degrees, and 90 degrees. Rewrite the program for greater clarity by *factoring out common code.*

```java
public class ExP2_16
{  public static void main(String[] args)
   {  System.out.println("0 degrees:   "
           + Math.sin(0) + " " + Math.cos(0));
      System.out.println("30 degrees:   "
           + Math.sin(30 * Math.PI / 180) + " "
           + Math.cos(30 * Math.PI / 180));
      System.out.println("45 degrees:   "
           + Math.sin(45 * Math.PI / 180) + " "
           + Math.cos(45 * Math.PI / 180));
      System.out.println("60 degrees:   "
           + Math.sin(60 * Math.PI / 180) + " "
           + Math.cos(60 * Math.PI / 180));
      System.out.println("90 degrees:   "
           + Math.sin(90 * Math.PI / 180) + " "
           + Math.cos(90 * Math.PI / 180));
   }
}
```

Exercise P2.17. Write a program that prints out a message "Hello, my name is Hal!". Then, on a new line, the program should print the message "What is your name?" Next, the program should read the user's name and print "Hello, *user name*. I am glad to meet you.". Then, on a new line, the program should print the message "What would you like me to do?". Then it is the user's turn to type in an input. Finally, the program should ignore the user input and print the message "I am sorry, *user name*. I cannot do that.".

Here is a typical program run. The user input is printed in color.

```
Hello, my name is Hal!
What is your name?
Dave
Hello, Dave. I am glad to meet you.
What would you like me to do?
Clean up my room
I am sorry, Dave. I cannot do that.
```

Exercise P2.18. (*Hard.*) You don't yet know how to program decisions, but it turns out that there is a way to fake them using `substring`. Write a program that asks the user to input

◆ The number of gallons of gas in the tank
◆ The fuel efficiency in miles per gallon
◆ The distance the user wants to travel

Then print out

```
You will make it
```

or

```
You will not make it
```

The trick here is to subtract the desired distance from the number of miles the user can drive. Suppose that that number is x. Suppose further that you find a way of setting a value n to 1 if x ≥ 0 and to 0 if x < 0. Then you can solve your problem:

```
String answer = " not "; // note the spaces before and after not
System.out.println("You will" + answer.substring(0, 5 - 4 * n)
    + "make it");
```

Hint: Note that x + |x| is 2·x if x ≥ 0, 0 if x < 0. Then divide by x, except that you need to worry about the possibility that x is zero.

Exercise P2.19. Write a program that reads two times in military format (0900, 1730) and prints the number of hours and minutes between the two times. Here is a sample run. User input is in color.

```
Please enter the first time: 0900
Please enter the second time: 1730
8 hours 30 minutes
```

Extra credit if you can deal with the case that the first time is later than the second time:

```
Please enter the first time: 1730
Please enter the second time: 0900
15 hours 30 minutes
```

Exercise P2.20. Run the following program, and explain the output you get.

```
public class ExP2_20
{  public static void main(String[] args)
    {  ConsoleReader console = new ConsoleReader(System.in);
```

```
int total = 0;
System.out.println("Please enter a positive number:");
int x1 = Integer.parseInt(console.readLine());
System.out.println("total = " + total);
total = total + 1 / x1;
System.out.println("total =" + total);
System.out.println("Please enter a positive number:");
int x2 = Integer.parseInt(console.readLine());
total = total + 1 / x1;
System.out.println("total = " + total);
total = total * x1 * x2 / 2;
System.out.println("total = " + total);
System.out.println("The average is " + total);
   }
}
```

Note the *trace messages,* which are inserted to show the current contents of the `total` variable. Then fix up the program, run it with the trace messages in place to verify that it works correctly, and remove the trace messages.

Exercise P2.21. *Writing large letters.* A large letter H can be produced like this:

```
*   *
*   *
*****
*   *
*   *
```

It can be declared as a string constant like this:

```
public static final String LETTER_H =
   "*   *\n*   *\n*****\n*   *\n*   *\n";
```

Do the same for the letters E, L, and O. Then write the message

```
H
E
L
L
O
```

in large letters.

Exercise P2.22. Write a program that transforms numbers 1, 2, 3, . . . , 12 into the corresponding month names `January`, `February`, `March`, . . . , `December`. *Hint:* Make a very long string `"January February March. . ."`, in which you add spaces such that each month name has *the same length.* Then use `substring` to extract the month you want.

Exercise P2.23. Change the password program to make it generate more secure passwords. Use the random number generator Random in the `java.util` package to generate a random number as follows:

```
int r = new Random().nextInt(1000);
```

Multiply the age by the random number. Then concatenate the initials with the *last four digits* of the product.

An Introduction to Classes

Chapter Goals

- ◆ To become familiar with the process of implementing classes

- ◆ To be able to implement simple methods

- ◆ To understand the purpose and use of constructors

- ◆ To understand how to access instance variables

- ◆ To realize how the process of encapsulation helps in structuring a program

- ◆ To understand the copy behavior of object references

- ◆ To write a `Console` class that makes keyboard input more convenient

You have learned about the number and string data types of Java. Although it is possible to write interesting programs using nothing but numbers and strings, most useful programs need to manipulate data items that are more complex and more closely represent entities in the real world. Examples of these data items are bank accounts, employee records, graphical shapes, and so on.

The Java language is ideally suited for designing and manipulating such data items, or *objects*. In Java, you define *classes* that describe the behavior of these objects. In this chapter, you will learn how to define classes that describe objects with very simple behavior. To implement more complex behavior, you will need to know more about control structures in Java, which is the topic of Chapters 5 and 7.

3.1   Determining Object Behavior

In this section, you will learn how to create a simple class that describes the behavior of a *bank account*. First, you will see how to use the class, assuming that someone has already defined it. Next, you will see how to implement the class and its methods.

Before you start programming, you need to understand how the objects of your class behave. Consider what kind of operations you can carry out with a bank account. You can

- Deposit money
- Withdraw money
- Get the current balance

In Java, these operations are expressed as *method calls*. Let's suppose you have an object harrysChecking of type BankAccount. Then you'll want to be able to call methods such as the following:

```
harrysChecking.deposit(2000);
harrysChecking.withdraw(500);
System.out.println("Balance: " + harrysChecking.getBalance());
```

That is, the set of methods

- deposit
- withdraw
- getBalance

forms the *behavior* of the BankAccount class. The behavior is the complete list of methods that you can apply to objects of a given class. (This is also called the *interface* of the class, but in Java, the word *interface* has a more restricted meaning; see Chapter 9.) You can think of an object of type BankAccount as a "black box" that can carry out its methods.

For a more complex class, it takes some amount of skill and practice to discover the appropriate behavior that makes the class useful and is reasonable to implement. You will learn more about this important aspect of class design in Chapter 14. For now, we will work with simple classes for which the behavior is very straightforward.

The behavior of our `BankAccount` class is simple, but it lets you carry out all important operations that commonly occur with bank accounts. For example, here is how you can transfer an amount from one bank account to another:

```
// transfer from one account to another
double transferAmount = 500;
momsSavings.withdraw(transferAmount);
harrysChecking.deposit(transferAmount);
```

And here is how you can add interest to a savings account:

```
double interestRate = 5; // 5% interest
double interestAmount =
    momsSavings.getBalance() * interestRate / 100;
momsSavings.deposit(interestAmount);
```

Finally, we have to discuss how to construct objects of the `BankAccount` class. Recall from chapter 1 that object variables such as `harrysChecking` are *references* to objects. Suppose you declare an object variable:

```
BankAccount harrysChecking;
```

This object variable does not refer to any object at all. If you were to try to invoke a method on this variable, the compiler would tell you that the variable has not been initialized. To initialize the variable, you need to create a new `BankAccount` object. You do this by calling

```
new BankAccount()
```

This call creates a new object and returns a reference to the newly created object (see Figure 1). To use the object, you must assign that reference to an object variable (see Figure 2):

```
BankAccount harrysChecking = new BankAccount();
```

We will implement the `BankAccount` so that a newly created bank account has a zero balance. Here is a scenario to open a new account and to deposit some money:

```
// open a new account
double initialDeposit = 1000;
BankAccount harrysChecking = new BankAccount();
    // constructed with zero balance
harrysChecking.deposit(initialDeposit);
```

Figure 1

Creating a New Object

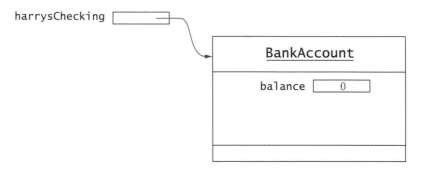

Figure 2

Initializing an Object Variable

As you can see, you can use objects of the **BankAccount** class to carry out meaningful tasks, without knowing how the **BankAccount** objects store their data or how the **BankAccount** methods do their work. This is an important aspect of object-oriented programming.

3.2   Defining Methods

Now that you understand how to use objects of the **BankAccount** class, let's get started designing the Java class that implements this behavior. As you already know, you need to implement a class to describe object behavior:

```
public class BankAccount
{   BankAccount methods
    BankAccount data
}
```

We have identified three methods:

```
public class BankAccount
{   public void deposit(double amount)
    {   method implementation
    }
    public void withdraw(double amount)
    {   method implementation
    }
    public double getBalance()
    {   method implementation
    }
    BankAccount data
}
```

Here we start out with the headers of methods. A method header consists of the following parts:

◆ An *access specifier* (such as `public`)
◆ The *return type* of the method (such as `double` or `void`)
◆ The name of the method (such as `deposit`)
◆ A list of the *parameters* of the method

Let us consider each of these parts in detail.

The access specifier controls which other methods can call this method. Most methods should be declared as `public`. That way, all other methods in your program can call them. (Occasionally, it can be useful to have methods that are not so widely callable—turn to Chapter 9 for more information on this issue.)

The return type is the type of the value that the method computes. For example, the `getBalance` method returns the current account balance, which will be a floating-point number, so its return type is `double`. On the other hand, the `deposit` and `withdraw` methods don't return any value. They just update the current balance but don't return it. That is, you can write

```
harrysChecking.deposit(500); // Ok
```

but you can't write

```
double b = harrysChecking.deposit(500); // Error
```

To indicate that a method does not return a value, use the special type `void`. Both the `deposit` and `withdraw` methods are declared with return type `void`.

The parameters are the inputs to the method. The `deposit` and `withdraw` methods each have one parameter: the amount of money to deposit or withdraw. You need to specify the type of the parameter, such as `double`, and a name for the parameter, such as `amount`. The `getBalance` method has no parameters. In that case, you still need to supply a pair of parentheses () behind the method name.

If a method has more than one parameter, you separate them by commas. For example,

```
public class Rectangle
{   . . .
    public void translate(double x, double y)
    {   method implementation
    }
    . . .
}
```

Once you have specified the method header, you must supply the implementation of the method, in a block that is delimited by braces { . . . }. You will see how to implement the `BankAccount` methods in Section 3.4.

Java Syntax

3.1 Method Implementation

```
public class ClassName
{  . . .
      accessSpecifier returnType methodName
       (parameterType parameterName, ...)
      method implementation
   }
   . . .
}
```

Example:

```
public class BankAccount
{  . . .
   public void deposit(double amount)
   {  balance = balance + amount;
   }
   . . .
}
```

Purpose:
To define the behavior of a method

3.3   Instance Variables

Each object must store its current *state*: the set of values that describe the object and that influence how an object reacts to method calls. In the case of our simple bank account objects, the state is the current balance of the bank account. (A more complex bank account might have a richer state, perhaps the current balance together with the interest rate paid on the current balance.) Each object stores the state in one or more *instance variables*:

```
public class BankAccount
{  . . .
   private double balance;
}
```

An instance variable declaration consists of the following parts:

◆   An *access specifier* (such as **private**)
◆   The *type* of the variable (such as **double**)
◆   The name of the variable (such as **balance**)

Each object of a class has its own copy of the instance variables. For example, if **harrysChecking** and **momsSavings** are two objects of the **BankAccount**

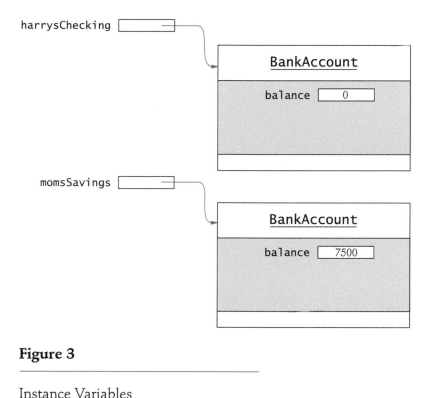

Figure 3

Instance Variables

class, then each object has its own `balance` field, `harrysChecking.balance` and `momsSavings.balance` (see Figure 3).

Instance variables are generally declared with the access specifier `private`. That means, they can be accessed only by the methods of the *same class*, not by any other method. In particular, the `balance` variable can be accessed only by the `deposit`, `withdraw`, and `getBalance` methods.

In other words, if the instance variables are declared private, then all data access must occur through the public methods. Thus, the instance variables of an object are effectively hidden from the programmer who uses a class. They are of concern only to the programmer who implements the class. The process of hiding data is called *encapsulation*. Although it is theoretically possible in Java to leave instance variables unencapsulated (by defining them as `public`), that is very uncommon in practice. We will always make all instance variables private in this book.

For example, because the `balance` instance variable is private, you cannot access the instance variable in other code:

```
double b = harrysChecking.balance; // Error
```

But you can call the public `getBalance` method to inquire about the balance:

```
double b = harrysChecking.getBalance(); // OK
```

Java Syntax

3.2 Instance Variable Declaration

```
class ClassName
{  . . .
      accessSpecifier type variableName;
}
```

Example:

```
public class BankAccount
{  . . .
   private double balance;
}
```

Purpose:

To define a variable that is present in every object of a class

---

Note that there is no equivalent **setBalance** method to set the balance to a particular value. With a real bank account, you cannot simply set the balance to any desired value; you must update the balance the hard way, through withdrawals and deposits. The class behavior captures this not always convenient fact.

The **BankAccount** class is so simple that it is not obvious what benefit you gain from the encapsulation. The primary benefit of the encapsulation mechanism is the guarantee that an object cannot accidentally be put into an incorrect state. For example, suppose you want to make sure that a bank account is never overdrawn. You can simply implement the **withdraw** method so that it refuses to carry out a withdrawal that would result in a negative balance. On the other hand, if any code could freely modify the **balance** instance variable of a **BankAccount** object, then it would be an easy matter to store a negative number in the variable.

We will have more to say about the importance of encapsulation in later chapters. For now, we will simply require that all instance variables be declared private. Hence their values can be examined and set only by the methods of their own class.

3.4   Implementing Methods

You must provide an implementation for every method of the class. Here is the implementation of the three methods of the **BankAccount** class. Note that these methods do not protect the account from being overdrawn. We did not yet introduce the necessary Java statement to carry out that check. You will need to wait until Chapter 5 to see how to implement this enhancement.

```
public class BankAccount
{  public void deposit(double amount)
   {  balance = balance + amount;
   }
```

Java Syntax
3.3 The return Statement

return *expression* ;

or

return;

Example:

```
public class BankAccount
{  public double getBalance()
   {  return balance;
   }
      . . .
}
```

Purpose:
To obtain the value that a method returns, and exit the method immediately. The return value becomes the value of the method call expression.

```
    public void withdraw(double amount)
    {  balance = balance - amount;
    }

    public double getBalance()
    {  return balance;
    }

    private double balance;
}
```

The implementation of the methods is straightforward. When some amount of money is deposited or withdrawn, the balance increases or decreases by that amount. The **getBalance** method simply returns the current balance.

Inside the **getBalance** method, we use a **return** statement to obtain a value, namely the current balance, and return it as the result of the method call.

Consider the definition of the **withdraw** method:

```
public void withdraw(double amount)
{  balance = balance - amount;
}
```

Now look at a particular invocation of this method:

```
momsSavings.withdraw(500);
```

Obviously, the call to the **withdraw** method depends on two values: the object reference **momsSavings** and the value 500. Clearly, when the method executes, the parameter `amount` is set to 500. This parameter is called an *explicit* parameter, because it is explicitly named in the method definition. However, the bank account reference is not explicit in the method definition—it is called the *implicit parameter* of the method. Inside each method, the object reference whose name is the keyword `this` refers to the implicit parameter object. For example, in the preceding method invocation, `this` was set to `momsSavings`.

Every method has one implicit parameter. The type of the implicit parameter is the class that defines the method. You don't give the implicit parameter a name. It is always called `this`. (There is one exception to the rule that every method has an implicit parameter: `static` methods do not. We will discuss them in Chapter 6.)

Methods can have any number of explicit parameters, or no explicit parameter at all. You must give a type and a name for each explicit parameter. When you call a method, you supply the value for the implicit parameter before the method name, separated by a dot (.), and you supply the values for the explicit parameters inside parentheses after the method name:

implicitParameterValue . *methodName* (*explicitParameterValues*) ;

Next, look again closely at the implementation of the `withdraw` method. In the statement

```
balance = balance - amount;
```

it is clear what `amount` means; it is the value of the explicit `amount` parameter. But what is `balance`? There is a `balance` instance variable in the `BankAccount` class, denoting the balance of a particular account. Which account? Java uses a convenient shorthand. When you refer to an instance variable in a method, you automatically refer to the instance variable *of the object for which the method was called (implicit parameter)*. In other words, the `withdraw` method actually executes the statement

```
this.balance = this.balance - amount;
```

For example, when called with

```
momsSavings.withdraw(500);
```

the method call computes

```
momsSavings.balance = momsSavings.balance - 500;
```

3.5   Constructors

There is only one remaining issue with the `BankAccount` class. We need to define the default constructor.

The code for a constructor sets all instance variables of the object. *The purpose of a constructor is to initialize the instance variables of an object.*

```
public class BankAccount
{  public BankAccount()
   {  balance = 0;
   }
   . . .
}
```

Constructors always have the same name as their class. Similar to methods, constructors are generally declared as public to enable any code in a program to construct new objects of the class. Unlike methods, though, constructors do not have return types.

Constructors are always invoked together with the new operator:

```
new BankAccount()
```

The new operator allocates memory for the object, and the constructor initializes it. The value of the new operator is the reference to the newly allocated and constructed object. In most cases, you want to store that object reference in an object variable:

```
BankAccount harrysChecking = new BankAccount();
   // sets  harrysChecking to a new account with zero balance
```

Constructors are not methods. You cannot invoke a constructor on an existing object. For example, the call

```
harrysChecking.BankAccount(); // Error
```

is illegal. You can use a constructor only in combination with the new operator.

The constructor that we just defined is a *default constructor*—it takes no parameters. The BankAccount default constructor sets the bank balance to 0. Some default constructors work harder than that. For example, the default constructor of the Date class in the java.util package constructs an object that stores the current date and time.

If you do not initialize an instance variable that is a number, it is initialized automatically to zero. In this regard, instance variables act differently than local variables! Therefore, you didn't actually have to initialize the balance instance variable to zero. Nevertheless, it is a matter of good style to initialize *every* instance variable explicitly. On the other hand, an object variable is initialized to a special value called null, which indicates that the object variable does not yet refer to an actual object. (See Section 3.9.)

Many classes have more than one constructor. For example, you can supply a second constructor for the BankAccount class that sets the balance instance variable to an initial balance, which is a parameter of the constructor:

```
public class BankAccount
{  public BankAccount()
   {  balance = 0;
   }
```

```
public BankAccount(double initialBalance)
{  balance = initialBalance;
}
   . . .
}
```

The second constructor is used if you supply a number as a construction parameter:

```
BankAccount momsSavings = new BankAccount(5000);
   // sets  momsSavings.balance to 5000
```

Now there are two constructors with the same name. (You have no choice how to name a constructor—it must have the same name as the class.) Whenever you have multiple methods (or constructors) with the same name, the name is said to be *overloaded*. The compiler figures out which one to call by looking at the parameters. For example, if you call

```
new BankAccount()
```

then the compiler picks the first constructor. If you call

```
new BankAccount(5000)
```

then the compiler picks the second constructor. But if you call

```
new BankAccount("lotsa moolah")
```

then the compiler generates an error message—there is no constructor that takes a parameter of type `String`.

We have now completed the implementation of the `BankAccount` class. Here is the complete source code for this class.

Class BankAccount.java

```
public class BankAccount
{  public BankAccount()
   {    balance = 0;
   }

   public BankAccount(double initialBalance)
   {    balance = initialBalance;
   }

   public void deposit(double amount)
   {    balance = balance + amount;
   }

   public void withdraw(double amount)
   {    balance = balance - amount;
   }
```

> **Java Syntax**
> **3.4 Constructor Implementation**
> ```
> class ClassName
> {   . . .
>     accessSpecifier ClassName
>         (parameterType parameterName, . . .)
>     {   constructor implementation
>     }
>     . . .
> }
> ```
>
> Example:
> ```
> public class BankAccount
> {   . . .
>     public BankAccount(double initialBalance)
>     {   balance = initialBalance;
>     }
>     . . .
> }
> ```
>
> Purpose:
> To define the behavior of a constructor. Constructors are used to initialize newly created objects.

```
    public double getBalance()
    {   return balance;
    }

    private double balance;
}
```

Common Error 3.1

Forgetting to Call the Constructor

A very common error for beginners is to allocate an object reference, but not an actual object.

```
BankAccount myAccount;
myAccount.deposit(1000000);
    // Error—myAccount not initialized
```

The myAccount variable holds a *reference* to an object. You still have to make the object. There is only one way to make an object—to construct it with the new operator.

```
BankAccount myAccount = new BankAccount();
```

Common Error 3.2

Trying to Reset an Object by Calling a Constructor

The constructor is invoked only when an object is first created. You cannot call the constructor to reset an object:

```
BankAccount harrysChecking = new BankAccount();
harrysChecking.withdraw(500);
harrysChecking.BankAccount(); // Error—can't reconstruct object
```

The default constructor sets a *new* account object to a zero balance, but you cannot invoke a constructor on an *existing* object. The remedy is simple: Make a new object and overwrite the current one.

```
harrysChecking = new BankAccount(); // OK
```

Common Error 3.3

Trying to Call a Method without an Implicit Parameter

Suppose your main method contains the instruction

```
withdraw(30); // Error
```

The compiler will not know which account to access to withdraw the money. You need to supply an object reference of type BankAccount:

```
BankAccount harrysChecking = new BankAccount();
harrysChecking.withdraw(30);
```

However, there is one situation in which it is legitimate to invoke a method without, seemingly, an implicit parameter. Consider the following modification to the BankAccount class. Add a method to apply the monthly account fee:

```
public class BankAccount
{   . . .
    void monthlyFee()
    {   final double MONTHLY_FEE = 10;
        withdraw(MONTHLY_FEE);
            // OK, withdraw from this account
    }
}
```

That means to withdraw from the *same* account object that is carrying out the monthlyFee operation. In other words, the implicit parameter of the withdraw method is the (invisible) implicit parameter of the monthlyFee method.

If you find it confusing to have an invisible parameter, you can always use the `this` parameter to make the method easier to read:

```
class BankAccount
{  . . .
   public void monthlyFee()
   {  final double MONTHLY_FEE = 10;
      this.withdraw(MONTHLY_FEE);
         //  withdraw from this account
   }
}
```

Advanced Topic 3.1

Overloading

When the same name is used for more than one method or constructor, the name is *overloaded*. This is particularly common for constructors, because all constructors must have the same name—the name of the class. In Java you can overload methods and constructors, provided the parameter types are different. For example, the `PrintStream` class defines many methods, all called `print`, to print various number types and to print objects:

```
class PrintStream
{  public void print(int n) { . . . }
   public void print(double a) { . . . }
   . . .
}
```

When the `print` method is called,

```
print(x);
```

the compiler looks at the type of `x`. If `x` is an `int` value, the first method is called. If `x` is a `double` value, the second method is called. If `x` does not match the parameter type of any of the methods, the compiler generates an error.

For overloading purposes, the type of the *return value* does not matter. You cannot have two methods with identical names and parameter types but different return values.

Advanced Topic 3.2

Calling One Constructor from Another

Consider the `BankAccount` class. It has two constructors: a *default constructor* to initialize the balance with zero, and another constructor to supply an initial balance. In our case, the default constructor is only one line long. In general, though, if the default constructor needs to initialize several instance variables, it can be convenient to have the default constructor call another constructor of the same class instead. There is a shorthand notation to achieve this:

```
class BankAccount
{  public BankAccount (double initialBalance)
   {  balance = initialBalance;
   }
   public BankAccount()
   {  this(0);
   }
   . . .
}
```

The command `this(0);` means "Call another constructor of this class and supply the value 0." Such a constructor call can occur only *as the first line in another constructor.*

This syntax is a minor convenience. We will not use it in this book. Actually, the use of the `this` keyword is a little confusing. Normally, `this` denotes a reference to the implicit parameter, but if `this` is followed by parentheses, it denotes a call to another constructor of this class.

Productivity Hint 3.1

Keyboard Shortcuts for Mouse Operations

Programmers spend a lot of time with the keyboard and the mouse. Programs and documentation are many pages long and require a lot of typing. The constant switching among the editor, compiler, and debugger takes up quite a few mouse clicks. The designers of programs such as a Java integrated development environment have added some features to make your work easier, but it is up to you to discover them.

Just about every program has a user interface with menus and dialog boxes. Click on a menu and click on a submenu to select a task. Click on each field in a dialog box, fill in the requested answer, and click the OK button. These are great user interfaces for the beginner, because they are easy to master, but they are terrible user interfaces for the regular user. The constant switching between the keyboard and the mouse slows you down. You need to move a hand off the keyboard, locate the mouse, move the mouse, click the mouse, and move the hand back onto the keyboard. For that reason, most user interfaces have *keyboard shortcuts:* combinations of keystrokes that allow you to achieve the same tasks without having to switch to the mouse at all.

All Microsoft Windows applications use the following conventions:

◆   The Alt key plus the underlined letter in a menu name (such as the F in "File") pulls down that menu. Inside a menu, just type the underlined character in the name of a submenu to activate it. For example, Alt + F O selects "File" "Open". Once your fingers know about this combination, you can open files faster than the fastest mouse artist.

◆   Inside dialog boxes, the Tab key is important; it moves from one option to the next. The arrow keys move within an option. The Enter key accepts the entire dialog, and Esc cancels it.

♦ In a program with multiple windows, Ctrl + Tab usually toggles through the windows managed by that program, for example between the source and error window.

♦ Alt + Tab toggles between applications, letting you toggle quickly between, for example, the compiler and a folder explorer program.

♦ Hold down the Shift key and press the arrow keys to highlight text. Then use Ctrl + X to cut the text, Ctrl + C to copy it, and Ctrl + V to paste it. These keys are easy to remember. The V looks like an insertion mark that an editor would use to insert text. The X should remind you of crossing out text. The C is just the first letter in "copy". (OK, so it is also the first letter in "Cut"—no mnemonic rule is perfect.) You find these reminders in the Edit menu.

Of course, the mouse has its use in text processing: to locate or select text that is on the same screen but far away from the cursor.

Take a little bit of time to learn about the keyboard shortcuts that the designers of your programs provided for you, and the time investment will be repaid many times during your programming career. When you blaze through your work in the computer lab with keyboard shortcuts, you may find yourself surrounded by amazed onlookers who whisper, "I didn't know you could do *that.*"

3.6 Putting a Class to Work

In the last five sections, you saw how a *class implementer* designs and implements a class: by determining the desired behavior and implementing the methods of the class. Now let's see how a *class user* can make use of the designer's efforts. The class user is still a programmer who wants to solve a particular problem with a class, without necessarily having to think about how the class was implemented. (The class user is not the same as the program user, a nonprogrammer who has no interest at all in how the program is put together.) Of course, as a beginning Java programmer, you are often simultaneously the implementer and user of your own classes. You should nevertheless develop a "split personality". When designing a class, think of the concept that the class represents (such as a bank account), and think of the behavior that you—or any other programmers who might need to write programs involving bank accounts—need to utilize. Conversely, when using a class, whether it is one of your own creation or supplied in a library, you should not think of the internals of the class.

Let's try this out by writing a program that puts the **BankAccount** class to work. We want to study the following scenario:

A savings account is created with a balance of $10,000. For two years in a row, add 5% interest. How much money is in the account after two years?

Now you need *two* classes: the **BankAccount** class that we developed in the preceding sections, and a second class that we will call **BankAccountTest**. The **main** method of the `BankAccountTest` class constructs a `BankAccount` object, adds the interest twice, then prints out the balance.

Program BankAccountTest.java

```java
public class BankAccountTest
{  public static void main(String[] args)
   {  BankAccount account = new BankAccount(10000);

      final double INTEREST_RATE = 5;

      double interest;

      // compute and add interest for one period

interest = account.getBalance() * INTEREST_RATE / 100;
      account.deposit(interest);

      System.out.println("Balance after year 1 is $"
         + account.getBalance());

      // add interest again

      interest = account.getBalance() * INTEREST_RATE / 100;
      account.deposit(interest);

      System.out.println("Balance after year 2 is $"
         + account.getBalance());
   }
}
```

You can distribute your classes over multiple files, or you may find it more convenient to keep all classes of your program together in a single file. If you do the latter, however, there is one caveat. A Java source file can contain only one `public` class. Therefore, you must declare the class with the `main` method as `public`, and you cannot specify the `public` attribute for any other class in the same file. (You do not declare classes as `private`.) Also, you must make sure that the name of the file matches the name of the `public` class. For example, you must store a program file with two classes `BankAccount` and `BankAccountTest` in a file `BankAccountTest.java`, not `BankAccount.java`.

3.7   Discovering Classes

When you have a programming problem, you need to discover one or more classes that help you solve the problem. Discovering useful classes is an important skill that you will practice throughout your first Java programming course. In Chapter 14 we will approach this issue systematically, but for now we just want to give you a useful rule of thumb how to go about discovering classes. That rule of thumb is to look for *nouns* in the description of the problem that you want to solve. *Some* of the nouns may suggest useful classes. Conversely, some of the *verbs* may suggest useful methods of those classes.

Let's try this out with one of the programs of the preceding chapter. Recall that you studied a program that asks a user to specify the number of coins in a purse and then prints out the total amount of money in the purse.

There are three nouns in the problem description: *coin*, *purse*, and *money*. What is a coin? A coin has a name (such as "quarter") and a dollar value (such as $0.25). A purse contains a collection of coins.

We will turn these nouns into classes in a moment. The noun *money* can lead to a useful class, for example, if you want to model different currencies. In a simple example, though, you can just use a floating-point number to store a dollar amount, so we won't make a separate money class now.

A **Coin** object needs to remember its name and dollar value. A constructor sets the name and value, and you need two methods to find out the name and value of a coin. Actually, there is a complexity with coin names. Given a singular name (such as "penny" or "quarter"), the computer has no way of determining the plural form (such as "pennies" and "quarters"). Simply store the plural form. (A better way would be to store both names and pick the correct one, depending on the coin count. However, you don't yet know enough Java to implement this enhancement.)

The **Coin** class is a very simple class, consisting of a constructor, two methods, and two instance variables. Here it is, without much further ado.

```java
class Coin
{   // a constructor for constructing a coin

    public Coin(double aValue, String aName)
    {   value = aValue;
        name = aName;
    }

    // methods to access the value and name

    public double getValue()
    {   return value;
    }

    public String getName()
    {   return name;
    }

    // instance variables to store the value and name

    private double value;
    private String name;
}
```

For example, here is how you construct a quarter:

```
Coin coinType = new Coin(0.25, "quarters");
```

Let's put this class to work. How many coins of that type does a user have?

```
System.out.println("How many " + coinType.getName()
    + " do you have?");
int coinCount = console.readInt();
```

What is that set of coins worth?

```
double value = coinCount * coinType.getValue();
```

Next, let's turn our attention to the concept of a purse. A purse contains a collection of coins. You don't yet know how to implement such a collection, and since we are currently interested in the total value and not the individual coins, we will ignore this aspect of a purse and simply have the purse store the total value. What are useful methods for a purse? We will need to add more coins to the purse and to get the total value of the purse. Here is the **Purse** class with these two methods:

```
class Purse
{   // default constructor makes purse with zero total

    public Purse()
    {  total = 0;
    }

    // methods to add coins and to get the total

    public void addCoins(int coinCount, Coin coinType)
    {   double value = coinCount * coinType.getValue();
        total = total + value;
    }

    public double getTotal()
    {   return total;
    }

    // instance variable to store the total

    private double total;
}
```

This class is also convenient to use. You can add coins to the purse.

```
Coin nickels = new Coin(0.05, "nickels");
thePurse.add(3, nickels);
```

How much money is in the purse after adding a few coins?

```
System.out.println("The total value is $"
    + thePurse.getTotal());
```

Now that you have discovered and implemented these simple classes, the program is easy. First, make a **Purse** object. For each of the four coin types, find out how many coins the user has, and call **addCoins**. Finally, print the total value.

```
public class Coins6
{  public static void main(String[] args)
   {  Purse thePurse = new Purse();
      ConsoleReader console = new ConsoleReader(System.in);

      Coin coin1 = new Coin(0.01, "pennies");
      Coin coin2 = new Coin(0.05, "nickels");
      Coin coin3 = new Coin(0.10, "dimes");
      Coin coin4 = new Coin(0.25, "quarters");

      System.out.println("How many " + coin1.getName()
         + " do you have?");
      int coin1Count = console.readInt();

      System.out.println("How many " + coin2.getName()
         + " do you have?");
      int coin2Count = console.readInt();

      System.out.println("How many " + coin3.getName()
         + " do you have?");
      int coin3Count = console.readInt();

      System.out.println("How many " + coin4.getName()
         + " do you have?");
      int coin4Count = console.readInt();

      thePurse.addCoins(coin1Count, coin1);
      thePurse.addCoins(coin2Count, coin2);
      thePurse.addCoins(coin3Count, coin3);
      thePurse.addCoins(coin4Count, coin4);

      System.out.println("The total value is $"
         + thePurse.getTotal());
   }
}
```

What have you gained? The program composed of the three classes **Coin**, **Purse**, and **Coins6** looks quite a bit longer than the simple program in Chapter 2 that consisted of a single class. That is true, and if you never had to write another program in your life, you should certainly prefer the shorter version. However, the program that is composed of multiple classes has two advantages. Once you have discovered the *concepts* of coins and purses, you may be able to *reuse* these classes in other programs. Further, by splitting the program into different classes, you can *separate the responsibilities* of the various components, making the program easier to understand, easier to implement correctly, and easier to extend. Note that the **Purse** class needs to know nothing about United States coin types (pennies, nickels, dimes, or quarters). You could easily add a few pesos or Zorkmids to the purse.

Designing and implementing appropriate classes is an important part of writing professional Java programs. It takes a bit longer to come up with the classes, and the resulting programs are longer than programs that don't use classes, but experience has shown that such programs are more likely to be correct and are easier to maintain over time. Those considerations are considerably more important in practice than simply trying to write short programs quickly.

Productivity Hint 3.2

Using the Command Line Effectively

If your programming environment lets you accomplish all routine tasks with menus and dialog boxes, you can skip this note. However, if you need to invoke the editor, the compiler, the linker, and the program to test manually, then it is well worth learning about *command line editing.*

Most operating systems (UNIX, DOS, OS/2) have a *command line interface* to interact with the computer. (In Windows, you can use the DOS command line interface by double-clicking the "MS-DOS Prompt" icon.) You launch commands at a *prompt*. The command is executed, and on completion you get another prompt.

When you develop a program, you find yourself executing the same commands over and over. Wouldn't it be nice if you didn't have to type beastly commands like

```
javac MyProg.java
```

more than once? Or if you could fix a mistake rather than having to retype the command in its entirety? Many command line interfaces have an option to do just that, but they don't always make it obvious. If you use DOS/Windows, you need to install a program called DOSKEY. If you use UNIX, try to get the tcsh shell installed for you, not the standard csh shell, and also be sure the history feature is activated—ask a lab assistant or system administrator to help you with the setup. With the proper setup, the up arrow key ↑ is redefined to cycle through your old commands. You can edit lines with the left and right arrow keys. You can also perform *command completion.* For example, to reissue the same `javac` command, type `javac` and press F8 (DOS) or type `!javac` (UNIX).

Random Fact 3.1

Mainframes—When Dinosaurs Ruled the Earth

When the International Business Machines Corporation, a successful manufacturer of punched-card equipment for tabulating data, first turned its attention to designing computers in the early 1950s, its planners assumed that there was a market for perhaps 50 such devices, for installation by the government, the military, and a few of the country's largest corporations.

Figure 4

A Mainframe Computer

Instead, they sold about 1,500 machines of their System 650 model and went on to build and sell more powerful computers.

The so-called *mainframe* computers of the 1950s, 1960s, and 1970s were huge. They filled up whole rooms, which had to be climate-controlled to protect the delicate equipment (see Figure 4). Today, because of miniaturization technology, even mainframes are getting smaller, but they are still very expensive. (At the time of this writing, the cost for a midrange IBM 3090 is approximately 4 million dollars.)

These huge and expensive systems were an immediate success when they first appeared, because they replaced many roomfuls of even more expensive employees, who had previously performed the tasks by hand. Few of these computers do any exciting computations. They keep mundane information, such as billing records or airline reservations; they just keep lots of them.

IBM was not the first company to build mainframe computers; that honor belongs to the Univac Corporation. However, IBM soon became the major player, partially because of technical excellence and attention to customer needs and partially because it exploited its strengths and structured its products and services in a way that made it difficult for customers to mix them with those of other vendors. In the 1960s IBM's competitors, the so-called "Seven Dwarfs"—GE, RCA, Univac, Honeywell, Burroughs, Control Data, and NCR—fell on hard times. Some went out of the computer business altogether, while others tried unsuccessfully to combine their strengths by merging their computer operations. It was generally predicted that they would eventually all fail. It was in this atmosphere that the U.S. government brought an antitrust suit against IBM in 1969. The suit went to trial in 1975 and dragged on until 1982, when the Reagan Administration abandoned it, declaring it "without merit".

Of course, by then the computing landscape had changed completely. Just as the dinosaurs gave way to smaller, nimbler creatures, three new waves of computers had appeared: the minicomputers, workstations, and microcomputers, all engineered by new companies, not the Seven Dwarfs. Today, the importance of mainframes in the marketplace has diminished, and IBM, while still a large and resourceful company, no longer dominates the computer market.

Mainframes are still in use today for two reasons. They still excel at handling large data volumes. More importantly, the programs that control the business data have been refined over the last 20 or more years, fixing one problem at a time. Moving these programs to less expensive computers, with different languages and operating systems, is difficult and error-prone. Sun Microsystems, a leading manufacturer of workstations, was eager to prove that its mainframe system could be "downsized" and replaced by its own equipment. Sun eventually succeeded, but it took over five years—far longer than it expected.

3.8   Copying Object References

Consider the following code that copies a number and then adds an amount to the copy:

```
double balance1 = 1000;
double balance2 = balance1; // see Figure 5
balance2 = balance2 + 500;
```

Of course, now `balance1` is 1000, and `balance2` is 1500.

Now consider the seemingly analogous code with `BankAccount` objects.

```
BankAccount account1 = new BankAccount(1000);
BankAccount account2 = account1; // see Figure 6
account2.deposit(500);
```

Unlike the preceding code, now *both* `account1` and `account2` have a balance of 1500.

In Java, there is a big difference between the assignment of numbers,

```
double balance2 = balance1;
```

and the assignment of objects

```
BankAccount account2 = account1;
```

Each number variable is a memory location that holds a *value*. If you change the contents of either variable, then the other is not affected. Object variables, however, do not hold values; they hold *references* to objects. The actual object is stored elsewhere, and the object variable remembers where it is stored. When you copy an

Figure 5

Copying Numbers

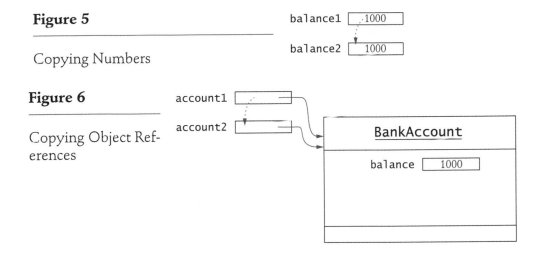

Figure 6

Copying Object References

object variable, you do not make a copy of the object; you merely make a copy of the reference. After the copy, both variables refer to the *same* object. If you use a method that changes the object, then both variables access the changed object.

What can you do if you actually need to make a true copy of an object, that is, a new object whose state is identical to an existing object? As you will see in Chapter 9, you can define a **clone** method for your classes to make such a copy. But in the meantime, you will simply have to construct a new object:

```
BankAccount account2 = new BankAccount(account1.getBalance());
```

3.9   The null Reference

An object variable contains a reference to an object. Unlike a number variable, an object variable may refer to *no object* in particular. This special reference to no object is called **null**. In the following code, **account1** refers first to an object, then to no object; see Figure 7.

Figure 7

A null Reference

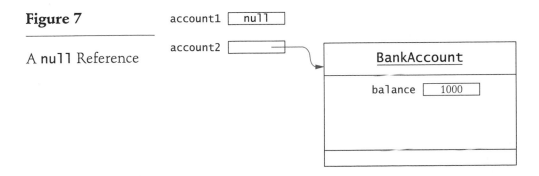

```
BankAccount account1 = new BankAccount(1000);
BankAccount account2 = account1;
account1 = null;
```

If you try to invoke a method on a variable containing a null reference, the program terminates. Clearly you must avoid doing so in your programs.

It is important to note that null is *not the same* as the number 0. The number 0 is a valid number, just like 1000 or −13. A number variable always contains *some* number. However, object variables have the choice between referring to an actual object or referring to no object at all.

Unlike numbers, strings are objects in Java. A String variable can refer either to an actual string or to no string at all:

```
String greeting = "Hello";
String message = ""; // the empty string
String comment = null; // refers to no string at all
int g = greeting.length(); // returns 5
int m = message.length(); // returns 0
int c = comment.length(); // program terminates
```

Note that the empty string and a null reference are *different* (see Figure 8), just as there is a difference between an empty message (say, on an answering machine) and no message at all (such as "no comment" by a spokesman for a politician).

Figure 8

String References

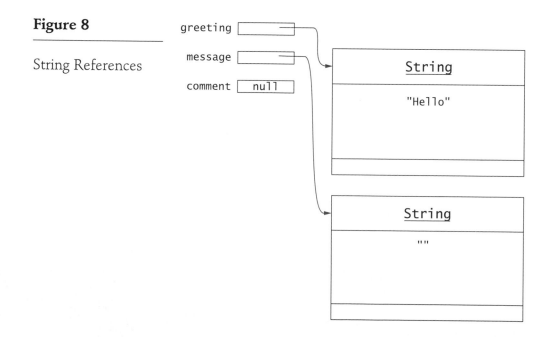

Common Error 3.4

Using a null Reference

If an object variable is set to null, it does not refer to any object, and you cannot call any methods:

```
BankAccount myAccount = null;
myAccount.withdraw(100);
    // Error—cannot call methods on null reference
```

When you execute code such as this, a NullPointerException is thrown, and your program terminates. You will learn in Chapter 5 how to test whether an object reference is null, so that you can avoid this error.

Of course, the remedy is to make sure that the variable points to an actual object, not null, before you make a method call.

```
BankAccount myAccount = new BankAccount();
```

Common Error 3.5

Forgetting to Initialize Object References in a Constructor

Just as it is a common error to forget to initialize a local variable, it is easy to forget about instance variables. Every constructor needs to ensure that all instance variables are set to appropriate values.

If you do not initialize an instance variable, the Java compiler will initialize it for you. Numbers are initialized with 0, but object references—such as string variables—are set to the null reference! Of course, 0 is often a convenient default for numbers. However, null is hardly ever a convenient default for objects. Consider this "lazy" constructor for a modified BankAccount class:

```
public class BankAccount
{  public BankAccount() {} // do nothing
   . . .
   private String accountHolder;
   private double balance;
}
```

The balance field is initialized to zero, a reasonable default. The accountHolder, however, is *not* set to the empty string; it is set to a null reference. If any method accesses that string assuming that it is a real string, the program will terminate with an error.

If you forget to initialize a *local* variable in a *method,* the compiler flags this as an error, and you must fix it before the program runs. If you make the same mistake with an *instance* variable in a *class,* however, the compiler provides a default initialization, and the error becomes apparent only when the program runs and dies with a null-reference error.

To avoid this problem, make it a habit to initialize every instance variable in every constructor.

Random Fact 3.2

Computer Networks and the Internet

Home computers and laptops are usually self-contained units with no permanent connection to other computers. Office and lab computers, however, are usually connected with each other and with larger computers: so-called *servers*. A server can store application programs and make them available on all computers on the network. Servers can also store data, such as schedules and mail messages, that everyone can retrieve. Networks that connect the computers in one building are called *local area networks,* or LANs.

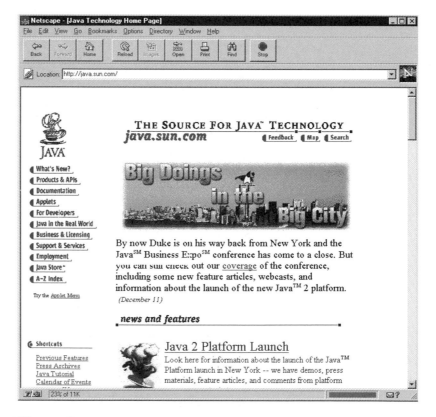

Figure 9

A Web Browser

Other networks connect computers in geographically dispersed locations. Such networks are called *wide area networks* or WANs. The most prominent wide area network is the *Internet*. At the time of this writing, the Internet is in a phase of explosive growth. Nobody knows for certain how many users have access to the Internet, but the user population is estimated in the hundreds of millions. The Internet grew out of the ARPAnet, a network of computers at universities that was funded by the Advanced Research Planning Agency of the U.S. Department of Defense. The original motivation behind the creation of the network was the desire to run programs on remote computers. Using remote execution, a researcher at one institution would be able to access an underutilized computer at a different site. It quickly became apparent, though, that remote execution was not what the network was actually used for. Instead, the "killer application" was *electronic mail:* the transfer of messages between computer users at different locations. To this day, electronic mail is one of the most compelling applications of the Internet.

Over time, more and more *information* became available on the Internet. The information was created by researchers and hobbyists and made freely available to anyone, either out of the goodness of their hearts or for self-promotion. For example, the GNU (GNU's Not UNIX) project is producing a set of high-quality operating system utilities and program development tools that can be used freely by anyone (`ftp://prep.ai.mit.edu/pub/gnu`). The Project Gutenberg makes available the text of important classical books, whose copyright has expired, in computer-readable form (`http://www.gutenberg.org`).

The first interfaces to retrieve this information were clumsy and hard to use. All that changed with the appearance of the *World Wide Web* (WWW). The World Wide Web brought two major advances to Internet information. The information could contain *graphics* and *fonts*—a great improvement over the older text-only format—and it became possible to embed *links* to other information pages. Using a *browser* such as Netscape or Internet Explorer, surfing the Web becomes easy and fun (Figure 9).

Productivity Hint 3.3

Save Your Work before Every Program Run

You now have learned enough about programming that you can write programs that "hang" the computer—that is, run forever without giving you the chance of using the keyboard or the mouse again. Congratulations are in order.

If you don't save your work and your program hangs, you may be in a situation in which you must restart the computer and type it all again.

You should therefore get into the habit of *saving your work* before every program run. Some integrated environments can be configured to do this automatically, but it is not always the default behavior. You can configure your fingers always to issue a "File Save All" command before running a program.

3.10 Implementing the ConsoleReader Class (Advanced)

In this section you will learn how to implement the **ConsoleReader** class that we use for reading keyboard input in this book. If you are interested in the implementation details, you should first read through Section 2.8 to understand the technical issues of reading keyboard input in Java. If you aren't interested in the implementation details of the **ConsoleReader** class, you can safely skip this section.

A central aspect of class design is encapsulation: the hiding of unimportant details from the class user. In Section 2.8 you saw how cumbersome it is in Java to read a number from **System.in**: You must construct a **BufferedReader**, read a line of input as a string, and convert it to a number, being careful about exceptions in the process. That is just the kind of detail that lends itself to encapsulation.

To build the actual **ConsoleReader** class, let us use the same method as with the **BankAccount** class:

1. Discover the behavior
2. Define the methods
3. Determine the instance variables for representing state
4. Implement the methods

Step 1: Let's think of the behavior that you want for reading input. As the user of the class, you are not particularly interested in buffered readers, number conversions, or exceptions. You just want the value that the user is entering, converted to the right type. Here is a set of methods that achieves this goal:

◆ Read an integer
◆ Read a floating-point number
◆ Read a string

Step 2: Translated to Java notation, the method and constructor definitions are as follows:

```
public class ConsoleReader
{  public ConsoleReader(InputStream inStream)
   {  constructor implementation
   }
   public int readInt()
   {  method implementation
   }
   public double readDouble()
   {  method implementation
   }
   public string readLine()
```

```
    {  method implementation
    }

    instance variables
}
```

Step 3: As you know from Section 2.8, you need a `BufferedReader` to read a line of input. We will store that `BufferedReader` object in an instance variable of the `ConsoleReader` class:

```
public class ConsoleReader
{   . . .
    private BufferedReader reader;
}
```

This instance variable is set in the constructor. Recall from Section 2.8 that an input stream can read only individual bytes. To read lines of characters, you must first turn an input stream (such as `system.in`) into an input stream reader and then turn the reader into a buffered reader

```
public class ConsoleReader
{   public ConsoleReader(InputStream inStream)
    {   reader = new BufferedReader(new InputStreamReader(inStream));
    }
    . . .
}
```

Step 4: Now, let us turn to the implementation of the methods. We will first implement the `readLine` method; it calls the `readLine` method of the `reader` object. Now, though, we have to worry about exceptions. As we did in Chapter 2, we will terminate the program when an I/O exception is encountered. Here is the code:

```
public String readLine()
{   String inputLine = "";

    try
    {   inputLine = reader.readLine();
    }
    catch(IOException e)
    {   System.out.println(e);
        System.exit(1);
    }

    return inputLine;
}
```

In other words, the `readLine` method of the `ConsoleReader` class simply calls the `readLine` method of the `BufferedReader` class, and deals with the possibility of the `IOException`, so that you don't have to.

Having implemented this method, the other methods are very simple. To read in an integer, simply read in an input line, using the `readLine` method that we just defined. Then parse the input into an integer and return that value. Floating-point numbers are read in the same fashion.

```
public int readInt()
{  String inputString = readLine();
   int n = Integer.parseInt(inputString);
   return n;
}

public double readDouble()
{  String inputString = readLine();
   double x = Double.parseDouble(inputString);
   return x;
}
```

This completes the implementation of the `ConsoleReader` class.

When you look at the `ConsoleReader.java` file, you will find the method implementations that we just discussed. You will also find *method comments*. Those comments will be explained in Chapter 6.

Chapter Summary

1. You use objects in your program when you need to manipulate data that are more complex than just numbers and strings. Every object belongs to a class. A class determines the behavior of its objects.

2. To define a class, you specify its methods and instance variables.

3. Every instance method has one implicit parameter—the object on which the method is invoked—and zero or more explicit parameters.

4. Objects are constructed with the **new** operator, followed by a constructor.

5. Number variables hold *values*. Object variables hold *references*. When a number is copied into a number variable, the variable gets a copy of the value. When an object is copied into an object variable, the variable gets another reference to the same object.

6. The **null** reference refers to no object. Invoking a method on a **null** reference is a fatal error.

Review Exercises

Exercise R3.1. Explain the difference between an object and a class.

Exercise R3.2. Give the Java code for an *object* of class **BankAccount** and for an *object variable* of class **BankAccount**.

Exercise R3.3. Explain the differences between an instance variable and a local variable.

Exercise R3.4. Explain the difference between

```
new BankAccount(5000);
```

and

```
BankAccount b;
```

Exercise R3.5. What are the construction parameters for a **BankAccount** object?

Exercise R3.6. What is default construction?

Exercise R3.7. Give Java code to construct the following objects:

◆ A square with center (100, 100) and side length 25
◆ A bank account with a balance of $5000
◆ A console reader that reads from **System.in**

Write just objects, not object variables.

Exercise R3.8. Repeat the preceding exercise, but now define object variables that are initialized with the required objects.

Exercise R3.9. Find the errors in the following statements:

```
Rectangle r = (5, 10, 15, 20);

double x = BankAccount(10000).getBalance();

BankAccount b;
b.deposit(10000);
b = new BankAccount(10000);
b.addCoins(new Coin(0.25, "quarters"));

Purse p = null;
p.addCoins(new Coin(0.25, "quarters"));

Purse p = new Purse();
p.addCoins(new Coin());
```

Exercise R3.10. Describe all constructors of the **BankAccount** class. List all methods that can be used to change a **BankAccount** object. List all methods that don't change the **BankAccount** object.

Exercise R3.11. What is the value of **b** after the following operations?

```
BankAccount b = new BankAccount(10);
b.deposit(5000);
b.withdraw(b.getBalance() / 2);
```

Exercise R3.12. If **b1** and **b2** store objects of class **BankAccount**, consider the following instructions.

```
b1.deposit(b2.getBalance());
b2.deposit(b1.getBalance());
```

Are the balances of **b1** and **b2** now identical? Explain.

Exercise R3.13. What is the **this** reference?

Programming Exercises

Exercise P3.1. Write a program that asks for an initial balance amount. Create a **BankAccount** object with that amount. Then ask for a deposit amount and a withdrawal amount. Carry out the deposit and withdrawal, then print the remaining balance.

Exercise P3.2. Implement a class **Employee**. An employee has a name (a string) and a salary (a **double**). Write a default constructor, a constructor with two parameters (name and salary), and methods to return the name and salary. Write a small program that tests your class.

Exercise P3.3. Enhance the class in the preceding exercise by adding a method **raiseSalary(double byPercent)** that raises the employee's salary by a certain percentage. Sample usage:

```
Employee harry = new Employee("Hacker, Harry", 55000);
harry.raiseSalary(10); // Harry gets a 10% raise
```

Exercise P3.4. Implement a class **Car** with the following properties. A car has a certain fuel efficiency (measured in miles/gallon or liters/km—pick one) and a certain amount of fuel in the gas tank. The efficiency is specified in the constructor, and the initial fuel level is 0. Supply a method **drive** that simulates driving the car for a certain distance, reducing the fuel level in the gas tank, and methods **getFuelLevel**, returning the current fuel level, and **tank**, to tank up. Sample usage:

```
Car myBeemer = new Car(29); // 29 miles per gallon
myBeemer.tank(20); // tank 20 gallons
myBeemer.drive(100); // drive 100 miles
System.out.println(myBeemer.getFuelLevel());
// print fuel remaining
```

Exercise P3.5. Change the purse program Coins6 to ask the user to supply coins in a different currency. For example, you can use the following collection of German coins:

```
new Coin(0.01, "Pfennig");
new Coin(0.1, "Groschen");
new Coin(1.0, "Mark");
```

What changes did you have to make? What changes would you have to make to the Coins4 program to change the currency? Which is easier?

Exercise P3.6. Add a method askForCoins(Coin coinType) to the Purse class that asks the user how many coins of that type to add to the purse and that updates the coin count.

Exercise P3.7. Implement a class Student. For the purpose of this exercise, a student has a name and a total quiz score. Supply an appropriate constructor and methods getName(), addQuiz(int score), getTotalScore(), and getAverageScore(). To compute the latter, you also need to store the *number of quizzes* that the student took.

Exercise P3.8. Implement a class Product. A product has a name and a price, for example new Product("Toaster", 29.95). Supply methods printProduct(), getPrice(), and setPrice(). Write in a program that makes two products, prints them, reduces their prices by $5.00, and then prints them again.

Exercise P3.9. Implement a class Circle that has methods getArea() and getCircumference(). In the constructor, supply the radius of the circle.

Exercise P3.10. Implement a class BeerCan with methods getSurfaceArea() and getVolume(). In the constructor, supply the height and radius of the can.

Applets and Graphics

Chapter Goals

- ◆ To be able to write simple applets

- ◆ To display graphical shapes such as lines and ellipses

- ◆ To use colors

- ◆ To display text in multiple fonts

- ◆ To select appropriate units for drawing

- ◆ To develop test cases that validate the correctness of your programs

There are three kinds of Java programs that you will learn to write: *console applications*, *graphical applications*, and *applets*. Console applications run in a single, usually rather plain-looking terminal window (see Figure 1), read input from the keyboard, and display text output in the same window. Graphical applications use one or more windows, usually filled with *user interface components* such as buttons, text input fields, menus, and so on (see Figure 2). Graphical programs can display both text and graph-

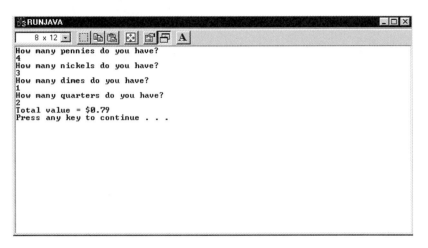

Figure 1

A Console Application

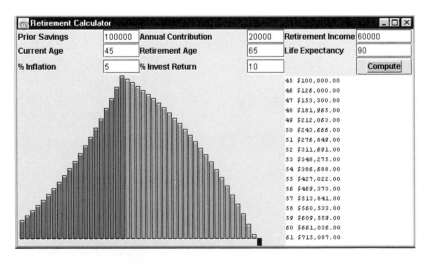

Figure 2

A Graphical Application

ical shapes and images. Most programs that you are familiar with, such as word processors and web browsers, are graphical programs. *Applets* are similar to graphical applications, but they run *inside* a web browser.

Console programs are simpler to write than graphical programs and applets, and we will continue to use console programs frequently in this book to learn about fundamental concepts. Graphical programs and applets can show more interesting output, however, and are often more fun to develop. In this chapter you will learn how to write simple applets that display graphical shapes.

4.1   Why Applets?

The World Wide Web makes a huge amount of information available to anyone with a web browser. When you use a web browser, you connect to a *web server*, which sends *web pages* and images to your browser (see Figure 3). Because the web pages and images have standard formats, your web browser can display them. To retrieve the daily news or your bank balance, you don't have to be at home, in front of your own computer. You can use a browser at school or in an airport terminal or Web café anywhere in the world. This ubiquitous access to information is one reason why the World Wide Web is so hugely popular.

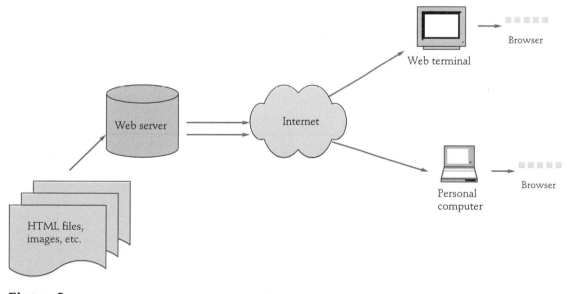

Figure 3

Web Browsers Accessing a Web
Server

Applets are programs that run inside a web browser. The code for an applet is stored on a web server and downloaded into the browser whenever you access a web page that contains the applet. That has one big advantage: You don't have to be at your own computer to run a program that is implemented as an applet. It also has an obvious disadvantage: You have to wait for the applet code to download into the browser, which can take a long time if you have a slow Internet connection. For that reason, complex applets are rare in web pages with a wide audience. Applets work very nicely, however, over a fast connection. For example, employees in a company often have a fast local area network connection. Then the company can deploy applets for schedule planning, health benefit access, product catalog lookup, and so on, and gain a big cost savings over the traditional process of developing corporate applications to be rolled out on the desktop of every user. When the program application changed, a system administrator had to make sure that every desktop was updated—a real hassle. When an applet changes, on the other hand, the code needs to be updated in one location: on the web server.

Web browser programs run on PCs, Macintoshes, UNIX workstations, and special web devices. For this reason, it is important that the applet code be able to execute on multiple platforms. Most traditional programs (such as word processors, computer games, and browsers) are written for a single platform, or perhaps written twice, for the two most popular platforms. Applets are delivered as Java bytecode. Any computer or device that can execute Java bytecode can execute the applet.

Whenever you run a program on your computer, you run a risk that the program might do some kind of damage, because it is poorly written or outright malicious. A poorly written program might accidentally corrupt or erase some of your files. A virus program might do the same intentionally. In the old days, before computers were networked, you had to install every program yourself, and it was a relatively easy matter to check for viruses on the floppy disks that you used to add new programs or data to your computer. Nowadays, programs can come from anywhere— from another machine on a local area network, as email attachments, or as code that is included in a web page. Code that is part of a web page is particularly troublesome, because it starts running immediately when the browser loads the page. It is an easy matter for a malicious person to set up a web page with enticing content, have many people visit the page, and attempt to infect each visitor with a virus. The designers of Java anticipated this problem and came up with two safeguards. Java applets can be *signed*, and they can run at different *security privileges*. The signature tells you where the applet comes from. You can tell the browser that you trust programs from some sources (such as vendors who have delivered quality code to you in the past). Signatures are not limited to applets; some browsers support certificates for machine language code. Once machine language code is allowed to run, however, it is uncontrolled and can create many kinds of problems. In contrast, the Java virtual machine has the ability to control the actions of an applet. By default, an applet runs in a *sandbox*, where it can display information and get user input, but it can't read or touch anything else on the user's computer. Trusted applets can be given more privileges, for example the ability to read and write local files.

4.2   A Brief Introduction to HTML

Applets are embedded inside web pages. Therefore, you need to know a few facts about the structure of web pages. A web page is written in a language called HTML (Hypertext Markup Language). Like Java code, HTML code is made up of text that follows certain strict rules. When a browser reads a web page, the browser *interprets* the code and *renders* the page, displaying characters, fonts, paragraphs, tables, and images.

HTML files are made up of text and *tags*, that tell the browser how to render the text. Nowadays, there are dozens of HTML tags. Fortunately, you need only a few to get started. Here is a typical example of a tag pair:

```
Java is an <I>object-oriented</I> programming language.
```

The tag pair `<I>  </I>` directs the browser to display the text inside the tags as *italics*:

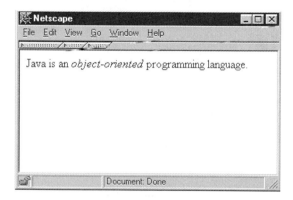

Most HTML tags come in pairs. The closing tag is just like the opening tag, but it is prefixed by a slash (/). For example, bold-faced text is delimited by `<B>  </B>`, and a paragraph is delimited by the tag pair `<P>  </P>`.

```
<P><B>Java</B> is an <I>object-oriented</I>
programming language.</P>
```

Another common construct is a bulleted, or *unnumbered,* list.

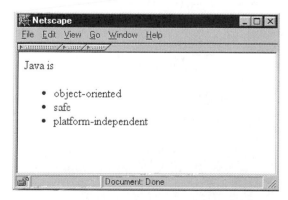

Here is the HTML code to display it:

```
<P>Java is</P>
<UL><LI>object-oriented</LI><LI>safe</LI>
<LI>platform-independent</LI></UL>
```

Each *item* in the list is delimited by <LI> </LI>, and the whole list is surrounded by <UL> </UL>.

As in Java code, you can freely use white space (spaces and line breaks) in HTML code to make it easier to read. For example, you can lay out the code for a list as follows:

```
<P>Java is</P>
<UL>
    <LI>object-oriented</LI>
    <LI>safe</LI>
    <LI>platform-independent</LI>
</UL>
```

The browser ignores the white space.

If you omit a tag (such as a </LI>), most browsers will try to guess the missing tags—sometimes with differing results. It is always best to include all tags.

You can include images in your web pages with the IMG tag. In its simplest form, an image tag has the form

```
<IMG SRC="hamster.jpeg">
```

This tells the browser to load and display the image that is stored in the file hamster.jpeg. Here you see a slightly different tag type. Rather than text inside a tag pair <IMG> </IMG>, the IMG tag uses an *attribute* to specify a file name. Attributes have names and values. For example, the SRC attribute has the value "hamster.jpeg". It is considered polite to use several additional attributes with the IMG tag, namely the *image size* and an *alternate description*:

```
<IMG SRC="hamster.jpeg" WIDTH=640 HEIGHT=480
ALT="A photo of Harry, the Horrible Hamster">
```

These additional attributes help the browser lay out the page and display a temporary description while gathering the data for the image (or if the browser cannot display images, such as a voice browser for blind users). Users with slow network connections really appreciate this extra effort.

The most important tag in web pages is the A tag which makes *links*. It is the links between web pages that make the Web into, well, a web. The browser displays a link in a special way (for example, underlined text in blue color). Here is the code for a typical link:

```
<A HREF="http://java.sun.com">Java</A> is an object-oriented
programming  language.
```

When the viewer of the web page clicks on the word Java, the browser loads the web page located at //java.sun.com. (The prefix http:, for *Hypertext Transfer Protocol*, tells the browser to fetch the file as a web page. Other protocols allow different actions, such as ftp: to download a file and mailto: to send email to a user.)

Finally, the APPLET tag includes an *applet* in a web page. To display an applet, you need first to write and compile a Java file to generate the applet code—you will see how in the next section. Then you tell the browser how to find the code for the applet and how much screen space to reserve for the applet. Here is an example:

```
<APPLET CODE="HamsterApplet.class" WIDTH=400 HEIGHT=300>An
animation of Harry, the Horrible Hamster</APPLET>
```

The text between the <APPLET> and </APPLET> tags is displayed only in lieu of the actual applet by browsers that can't run Java applets.

You have noticed that tags are enclosed in angle brackets (less-than and greater-than signs). What if you want to show an angle bracket in a page? The notations < and > produce the < and > symbols, respectively. Other codes of this kind produce symbols such as accented letters. The & symbol introduces these codes; to get that symbol itself, use &.

You may already have created web pages with a web editor that works like a word processor, giving you a WYSIWYG (what you see is what you get) view of your web page. But the tags are still there, and you can see them when you load the HTML file into a text editor. If you are comfortable using a WYSIWYG web editor, and if your editor can insert applet tags, you don't need to memorize HTML tags at all. But many programmers and professional web designers prefer to work directly with the tags because it gives them more control over their pages.

4.3   A Simple Applet

In our first applet we will simply draw a couple of rectangles (see Figure 4). You'll soon see how to produce more interesting drawings. The purpose of this applet is to show you the basic outline of an applet that creates a drawing.

This applet will be implemented in a single class RectangleApplet. To run this applet, you need an HTML file with an APPLET tag. Here is the simplest possible file

Figure 4

The Rectangle Applet in the Applet Viewer

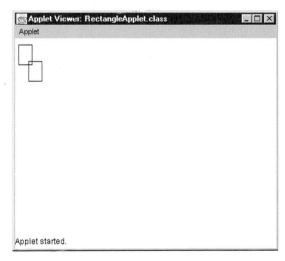

to display the applet:

File RectangleApplet.html

```
<APPLET CODE="RectangleApplet.class" WIDTH=300 HEIGHT=300>
</APPLET>
```

Or you can proudly explain your creation, by adding text and more HTML tags:

File RectangleApplet.html

```
<P>Here is my <I>first applet</I>:</P>
<APPLET CODE="RectangleApplet.class" WIDTH=300 HEIGHT=300>
</APPLET>
```

You can give the file any name you like. In this case, it makes sense to give the HTML file the same name as the applet. An HTML file can have multiple applets, however. For example, you can place all your homework solutions into a single HTML file. Also, some development environments already generate an HTML file with the same name as your project to hold your project notes; then you must give the HTML file containing your applet a different name.

To run the applet, you have two choices. You can use the *applet viewer*, a program that is included with the Java Development Kit from Sun Microsystems. You simply start the applet viewer, giving it the name of the HTML file that contains your applets:

```
appletviewer RectangleApplet.html
```

The applet viewer brings up one window for each applet in the HTML file. It ignores all other HTML tags. Figure 4 shows the applet inside the applet viewer.

You can also show the applet inside any Java 2–enabled web browser. As of April 1999, the major browsers do not yet support Java 2, although it is possible to add Java 2 support by using a browser plug-in (see Advanced Topic 4.1). The Opera browser (http://www.opera.com), however, combined with Sun's Java 2 plug-in, lets you display Java 2 applets. Figure 5 shows the applet, displayed by the Opera browser. As you can see, both the text and the applet are displayed.

An applet is programmed as a class, like any other program in Java. However, the class is declared **public** and it extends **Applet**. That means that our rectangle applet *inherits* the behavior of the **Applet** class. We will discuss inheritance in Chapter 9.

```
public class RectangleApplet extends Applet
{  public void paint(Graphics g)
   {  . . .
   }
}
```

Unlike applications, applets don't have a **main** method. The web browser (or applet viewer) is responsible for starting up the Java virtual machine, for loading the applet code, and for starting the applet. This applet implements only one method: **paint**. There are other methods that you *may* implement; they will be discussed in Section 4.8.

Figure 5

The Rectangle Applet in a Java 2–Enabled Browser

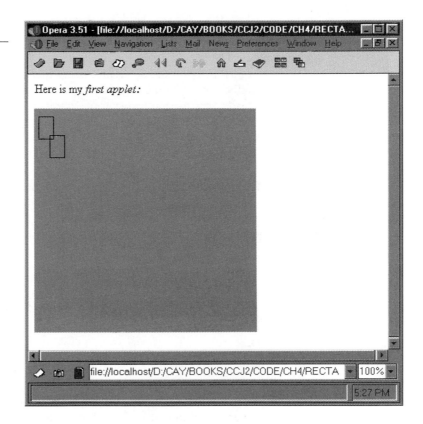

The window manager calls the `paint` method whenever the surface of the applet needs to be filled in. Of course, when the applet is shown for the first time, its contents need to be painted. If the user visits another web page and then goes back to the web page containing the applet, the surface must be painted again, and the window manager calls the `paint` method once more. Thus, you must put all drawing instructions inside the `paint` method, and you must be aware that the window manager can call the `paint` method many times.

The `paint` method receives an object of type `Graphics`. The `Graphics` object stores the *graphics state*: the current color, font, and so on, that are used for the drawing operations. For the drawing programs that we explore in this book, we always convert the `Graphics` object to an object of the `Graphics2D` class:

```
public class RectangleApplet extends Applet
{  public void paint(Graphics g)
   {  // recover Graphics2D
      Graphics2D g2 = (Graphics2D)g;
      . . .
   }
}
```

To understand why, you need to know a little about the history of these classes. The `Graphics` class was included with the first version of Java. It is suitable for very basic drawings, but it does not use an object-oriented approach. After some time, programmers clamored for a more powerful graphics package, and the designers of Java created the `Graphics2D` class. They did not want to inconvenience those programmers who had produced programs that used simple graphics, so they did not change the `paint` method. Instead, they made the `Graphics2D` class *extend* the `Graphics` class, a process that will be discussed in Chapter 9. Whenever the window manager calls the `paint` method, it actually passes a parameter of type `Graphics2D`. Programs with simple graphics needs do not need to know about this, but if you want to use the more sophisticated 2D graphics methods, you recover the `Graphics2D` reference by using a cast.

You use the `draw` method of the `Graphics2D` class to draw shapes such as rectangles, ellipses, line segments, polygons, and arcs. Here we draw a rectangle:

```
public class RectangleApplet extends Applet
{  public void paint(Graphics g)
   {  . . .
      Rectangle cerealBox = new Rectangle(5, 10, 20, 30);
      g2.draw(cerealBox);
      . . .
   }
}
```

The `Graphics`, `Graphics2D`, and `Rectangle` classes are part of the `java.awt` package. The acronym AWT stands for Abstract Windowing Toolkit. This is the original user interface toolkit that Sun supplied for Java. It defines many classes for graphics programming, a mechanism for event handling, and a set of user interface components. In this chapter, we focus on the graphics classes of the AWT.

Here is the complete applet for displaying the rectangle shapes.

Program RectangleApplet.java

```
import java.applet.Applet;
import java.awt.Graphics;
import java.awt.Graphics2D;
import java.awt.Rectangle;

public class RectangleApplet extends Applet
{  public void paint(Graphics g)
   {  // recover Graphics2D

      Graphics2D g2 = (Graphics2D)g;

      // construct a rectangle and draw it

      Rectangle cerealBox = new Rectangle(5, 10, 20, 30);
      g2.draw(cerealBox);
```

```
        // move rectangle 15 units sideways and 25 units down

        cerealBox.translate(15, 25);

        // draw moved rectangle

        g2.draw(cerealBox);
    }
}
```

Advanced Topic 4.1

The Java Runtime Environment and Java Plug-ins

You can run applets inside the applet viewer program, but applets are meant to be executed inside a browser. The first versions of browser programs that supported Java contained a built-in Java virtual machine to execute the downloaded Java applets. That turned out not to be a good idea. New versions of Java appeared rapidly, and the browser manufacturers were unable to keep up. Also, browser manufacturers made minor changes to the Java implementations, causing compatibility problems.

In 1998, Sun Microsystems, the company that invented the Java language, realized that it is best to separate the browser and the virtual machine. Sun now packages the virtual machine as the "Java Runtime Environment", which is to be installed in a standard place on each computer that supports Java. Browser manufacturers are encouraged to use the Java Runtime Environment, and not their own Java implementation, to execute applets. That way, users can update their Java implementations and browsers separately. If your browser uses this approach, then it will be able to execute your Java applets without problems.

However, if you have an older browser, or a browser whose manufacturer insists on supplying its own virtual machine, you may not be able to run your applets inside your browser. To solve this problem, Sun Microsystems provided a second tool, the "Java Plug-in". The Java Plug-in takes advantage of the fact that the two major browsers, Netscape Navigator and Internet Explorer, have an architecture that allows third-party software vendors to extend the capabilities of the browser. The two browser manufacturers use different methods to extend the browser. Netscape uses a proprietary plug-in architecture, and Microsoft uses a component architecture called ActiveX. The Sun Java Plug-in is *both* a Netscape plug-in and an ActiveX component. It interfaces with both browsers, linking them to the Java Runtime Environment. Unfortunately, the HTML required to activate the browser extension is quite a bit more arcane than the simple **APPLET** tag. Sun has developed a program, the "Java Plug-in HTML Converter", that can translate HTML pages containing **APPLET** tags to HTML pages with the appropriate tags to launch the Java Plug-in in either of these browsers. The converter also lets you produce web pages that automatically sense the version of the browser that loads them. If you want to place your applets onto your web site, for anyone to see, then you should use the converter.

However, the best approach may simply be to direct your users to a browser that supports the Java Runtime Environment, such as Opera (http://www.opera.com).

4.4   Graphical Shapes

In Section 4.3 you learned how to write an applet that draws rectangles. In this section, you will learn how to draw other shapes: ellipses and lines. With these graphical elements, you can draw quite a few interesting pictures.

To draw an ellipse, you specify its *bounding box* (see Figure 6) in the same way that you would specify a rectangle, namely by the *x*- and *y*-coordinates of the top-left corner and the width and height of the box.

However, there is no simple `Ellipse` class that you can use. Instead, you must use one of the two classes `Ellipse2D.Float` and `Ellipse2D.Double`, depending on whether you want to store the ellipse coordinates as `float` or as `double` values. Since `double` values are more convenient to use than `float` values in Java, we will always use the `Ellipse2D.Double` class. Here is how you construct an ellipse:

```
Ellipse2D.Double easterEgg = new Ellipse2D.Double(5, 10, 15, 20);
```

The class name `Ellipse2D.Double` looks different from the class names that you have encountered up to now. It consists of two class names `Ellipse2D` and `Double` separated by a period (`.`). This indicates that `Ellipse2D.Double` is a so-called *inner* class inside `Ellipse2D`. When constructing and using ellipses, you don't actually need to worry about the fact that `Ellipse2D.Double` is an inner class—just think of it as a class with a long name. However, in the `import` statement at the top of your

Figure 6

An Ellipse and Its
Bounding Box

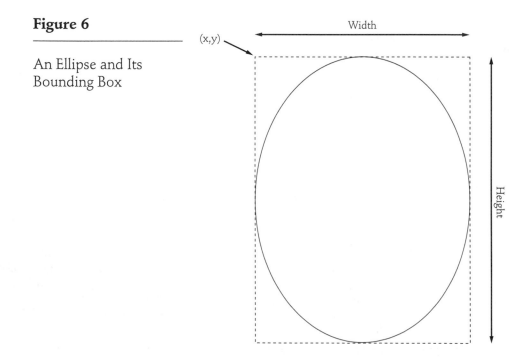

program, you must be careful that you only import the *outer* class:

```
import java.awt.geom.Ellipse;
```

You may wonder why an ellipse would want to store its size as **double** values when the screen coordinates are measured in pixels. As you'll see later in this chapter, working with pixel coordinates can be cumbersome. It is often a good idea to switch to different units, and then it can be handy to use floating-point coordinates. (Note that the **Rectangle** class uses integer coordinates, so you will need to use a separate class called **Rectangle2D.Double** whenever you use rectangles with floating-point coordinates.)

Drawing an ellipse is easy: You use exactly the same **draw** method of the **Graphics2D** class that you used for drawing rectangles.

```
g2.draw(easterEgg);
```

To draw a circle, simply set the width and height to the same value:

```
Ellipse2D.Double circle =
    new Ellipse2D.Double(x, y, diameter, diameter);
g2.draw(circle);
```

Notice that (x, y) is the top-left corner of the bounding box, *not* the center of the circle.

To draw a line, you use an object of the **Line2D.Double** class. You construct a line by specifying its two end points. You can do this in two ways. You can simply give the *x* and *y* coordinates of both end points:

```
Line2D.Double segment = new Line2D.Double(x1, y1, x2, y2);
```

Or you can specify each endpoint as an object of the **Point2D.Double** class:

```
Point2D.Double from = new Point2D.Double(x1, y1);
Point2D.Double to = new Point2D.Double(x2, y2);

Line2D.Double segment = new Line2D.Double(from, to);
```

The latter is more object-oriented, and it is also often more useful, in particular if the point objects can be reused elsewhere in the same drawing.

4.5 Colors

When you first start drawing, all shapes are drawn with a black pen. To change the color, you need to supply an object of type **Color**. Java uses the *RGB color model*. That is, you specify a color by the amounts of the *primary colors*—red, green, and blue— that make up the color. The amounts are given as **float** values and vary from **0.0F** (primary color not present) to **1.0F** (maximum amount present). Note that you must use an F suffix to specify single-precision floating-point numbers. For example,

```
Color magenta = new Color(1.0F, 0.0F, 1.0F);
```

constructs a `Color` object with maximum red, no green, and maximum blue, yielding a bright purple color called magenta.

For your convenience, a number of colors have been predefined in the `Color` class. Table 1 shows those predefined colors and their RGB values. For example, `Color.pink` has been predefined to be the same color as `new Color(1.0F, 0.7F, 0.7F)`.

Once you have an object of type `Color`, you can change the *current color* of the `Graphics2D` object with the `setColor` method. For example, the following code draws a rectangle in black, then switches the color to red, and draws the next rectangle in red:

```
public void paint(Graphics g)
{  Graphics2D g2 = (Graphics2D)g;

   Rectangle cerealBox = new Rectangle(5, 10, 20, 30);
   g2.draw(cerealBox); // draws in black

   cerealBox.translate(15, 25); // move  rectangle

   g2.setColor(Color.red); // set current color to red
   g2.draw(cerealBox); // draws in red
}
```

Table 1   Predefined Colors and
               Their RGB Values

Color	RGB Value
Color.black	0.0F, 0.0F, 0.0F
Color.blue	0.0F, 0.0F, 1.0F
Color.cyan	0.0F, 1.0F, 1.0F
Color.gray	0.5F, 0.5F, 0.5F
Color.darkGray	0.25F, 0.25F, 0.25F
Color.lightGray	0.75F, 0.75F, 0.75F
Color.green	0.0F, 1.0F, 0.0F
Color.magenta	1.0F, 0.0F, 1.0F
Color.orange	1.0F, 0.8F, 0.0F
Color.pink	1.0F, 0.7F, 0.7F
Color.red	1.0F, 0.0F, 0.0F
Color.white	1.0F, 1.0F, 1.0F
Color.yellow	1.0F, 1.0F, 0.0F

If you want to color the inside of the shape, you use the `fill` method instead of the `draw` method. For example,

```
g2.fill(cerealBox);
```

fills the inside of the rectangle with the current color.

4.6 Fonts

You often want to put text inside a drawing, for example to label some of the parts. You use the `drawString` method of the `Graphics2D` class to draw a string anywhere in a window. You must specify the string and the x- and y-coordinates of the *basepoint* of the first character in the string (see Figure 7). For example,

```
g2.drawString("Applet", 50, 100);
```

You can select different fonts. The procedure is similar to setting the drawing color. You create a `Font` object and call the `setFont` method of the `Graphics2D` class. To construct a `Font` object, you specify

- The *font face name*
- The *style* (one of `Font.PLAIN`, `Font.BOLD`, `Font.ITALIC`, or `Font.BOLD + Font.ITALIC`)
- The *point size*

The font face name is either one of the five *logical face names* in Table 2 or a *typeface name*, the name of a typeface that is available on your computer, such as "Times Roman" or "Helvetica". "Times Roman" and "Helvetica" are the names of popular typefaces that were designed many years ago and are in very widespread use

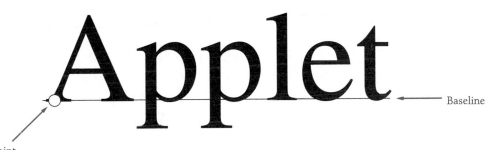

Basepoint

Baseline

Figure 7

Basepoint and Baseline

Table 2   Logical Font Names

Name	Sample	Description
Serif	The quick brown fox	A serif-style font such as Times Roman
SansSerif	The quick brown fox	A sans-serif font such as Helvetica
Monospaced	The quick brown fox	A font in which all characters have the same width, such as Courier
Dialog	The quick brown fox	A screen font suitable for labels in dialogs
DialogIput	The quick brown fox	A screen font suitable for user input in text fields

today. These fonts differ in the shapes of their letters. The most visible difference is that the characters of the Times Roman font are composed of strokes with small cross segments at the ends, so-called *serifs*. The characters of the Helvetica font do not have serifs (see Figure 8). A typeface such as Helvetica is called a *sans-serif* font. It is generally believed that the serifs help make text easier to read. In fact, the Times Roman font was designed specifically for the London *Times* newspaper, to be easy to read on newsprint paper. Most books (including this one) use a serif typeface for the body text. Sans-serif typefaces are appropriate for headlines, figure labels, and so on. Many other typefaces have been designed over the centuries, with and without serifs. For example, Garamond is another popular serif-style typeface. A third kind of typeface that you will commonly see is Courier, a font that was originally designed for typewriters.

Figure 8

Common Fonts

Helvetica

Times Roman

Courier

The design of a good typeface requires artistic judgment and substantial experience. However, in the United States, the shapes of letters are considered industrial design that cannot be protected by copyright. For that reason, typeface designers protect their rights by trademarking the *names* of the fonts. For example, the names "Times Roman" and "Helvetica" are trademarks of the Linotype Corporation. Although other companies can create lookalike fonts (just as certain companies create imitations of famous perfumes), they have to give them different names. That's why you find fonts with names such as "Times New Roman" or "Arial". That makes it bit of a bother to select fonts by their names, especially if you don't know what fonts are available on a particular computer. For that reason, we will specify fonts by their logical face names. There are five logical font names (see Table 2) that are mapped to fonts that exist on every computer system. For example, if you request the "SansSerif" font, then the Java font mapper will go and search for the best general-purpose sans-serif font available. On a computer running the Windows operating system, you will get the "Arial" font. On a Macintosh, you will get "Helvetica".

To create a font, you must specify the *point size*: the height of the font in the typesetter's unit called *points*. The height of a font is measured from the top of the *ascender* (the top part of letters such as b and l) to the bottom of the *descender* (the bottom part of letters such as g and p). There are 72 points per inch. For example, a 12-point font has a height of $\frac{1}{6}$ inch. Actually, the point size of a font is only an approximate measure, and you can't necessarily be sure that two fonts with the same point size have matching character sizes. The actual sizes will in any case depend on the size and resolution of your monitor screen. Without getting into fine points of typography, it is best if you simply remember a few typical point sizes: 8 point ("small"), 12 point ("medium"), 18 point ("large"), and 36 point ("huge").

Here is how you can write "Applet" in huge pink letters:

```
final int HUGE_SIZE = 36;
String message = "Applet";
Font hugeFont = new Font("Serif", Font.BOLD, HUGE_SIZE);
g2.setFont(hugeFont);
g2.setColor(Color.pink);
g2.drawString(message, 50, 100);
```

The *x*- and *y*-positions in the `drawString` method can be specified either as `int` or as `float`.

When drawing strings on the screen, you usually need to position them accurately. For example, if you want to draw two lines of text, one below the other, then you need to know the distance between the two base points. Of course, the size of a string depends on the shapes of the letters, which in turn depends on the font face and point size. You will need to know a few typographical measurements:

- The *ascent* of a font is the height of the largest letter above the baseline.
- The *descent* of a font is the depth of the letter with the lowest descender below the baseline. A descender is the part of a letter such as 'g' or 'j' that extends below the baseline.

◆ The *leading* (pronounced "ledding") of a font is the distance between successive lines of the font. The term "leading" recalls the strips of lead that typesetters inserted between lines of text when metal type was still set by hand.

These values describe the *vertical* extent of strings. The *horizontal* extent depends on the individual letters in a string. In a **monospaced** font, all letters have the same width. Monospaced fonts are still used for computer programs, but for plain text they are as outdated as the typewriter. In a *proportionally spaced font,* different letters have different widths. For example, the letter "l" is much narrower than the letter "m".

To measure the size of a string, you need to construct a **TextLayout** object. The **TextLayout** constructor has three parameters:

◆ The string that you want to measure

◆ The font that you want to use

◆ A **FontRenderContext** object, which you obtain from the **Graphics2D** object by calling **getFontRenderContext**.

The font render context is an object that knows how to transform letter shapes (which are described as curves) into pixels. In general, a "context" object is usually an object that has some specialized knowledge how to carry out complex tasks. You don't have to worry how the context object works; you just create it and pass it along as required. The **Graphics2D** object is another example of a context object—many people call it a "graphics context".

For example, here is how you can create a **TextLayout** object to get typographic measurements of the string **Applet**.

```
String message = "Applet";
Font hugeFont = new Font("Serif", Font.BOLD, HUGE_SIZE);
FontRenderContext context = g2.getFontRenderContext();
TextLayout layout =
    new TextLayout(message, hugeFont, context);
```

Now you can query the ascent, descent, leading, and *advance* of the text (see Figure 9). The advance is the width of the text. The **getAscent**, **getDescent**, **getLeading**, and **getAdvance** methods of the **TextLayout** class return these measurements, as **float** numbers. For example, to compute where to place the next character in the *current* line, you need to query the advance:

```
float xMessageWidth = layout.getAdvance();
```

To compute where to place the *next* line, you compute the total line height:

```
float yMessageHeight
    = layout.getAscent() + layout.getDescent();
```

The following program uses these measurements to center a string precisely in the middle of the applet window (see Figure 10). To center the string, you need to know the size of the applet. (The user might have resized it, so you can't simply use the values of **WIDTH** and **HEIGHT** in the HTML file.) The **getWidth** and **getHeight** methods return the applet size in pixels. To center the string

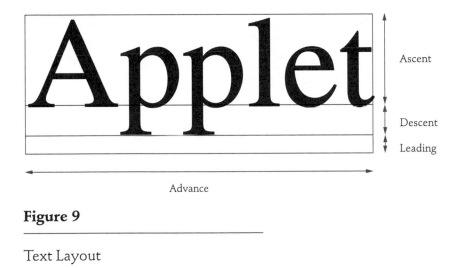

Figure 9

Text Layout

Figure 10

The Font Applet

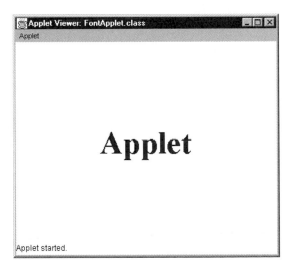

horizontally, think of the amount of blank space that you have available. The width of the applet window is getWidth(). The width of the string is xMessageWidth. Therefore, the blank space is the difference,

```
getWidth() - xMessageWidth
```

Half of that blank space should be distributed on either side. Therefore, the string should start at

```
float xLeft = 0.5F * (getWidth() - xMessageWidth);
```

For the same reason, the top of the string is at

```
float yTop = 0.5F * (getHeight() - yMessageHeight);
```

But the `drawString` method needs the base point of the string. You get to the base position by adding the ascent:

```
float yBase = yTop + layout.getAscent();
```

Here is the complete program. When you run it in the applet viewer, try resizing the applet window and observe that the string always stays centered.

Program FontApplet.java

```java
import java.applet.Applet;
import java.awt.Graphics;
import java.awt.Graphics2D;
import java.awt.Font;
import java.awt.font.FontRenderContext;
import java.awt.font.TextLayout;

public class FontApplet extends Applet
{  public void paint(Graphics g)
   {  Graphics2D g2 = (Graphics2D)g;

      // select the font into the graphics context

      final int HUGE_SIZE = 48;
      Font hugeFont = new Font("Serif", Font.BOLD, HUGE_SIZE);
      g2.setFont(hugeFont);

      String message = "Applet";

      // create a text layout to measure the string

      FontRenderContext context = g2.getFontRenderContext();
      TextLayout layout
         = new TextLayout(message, hugeFont, context);

      // measure the message width and height

      float xMessageWidth = layout.getAdvance();
      float yMessageHeight
         = layout.getAscent() + layout.getDescent();

      // center the message in the window

      float xLeft = 0.5F * (getWidth() - xMessageWidth);
      float yTop = 0.5F * (getHeight() - yMessageHeight);
      float yBase = yTop + layout.getAscent();

      g2.drawString(message, xLeft, yBase);
   }
}
```

Figure 11

A Graphical Applet That
Draws a Sketch of a Car

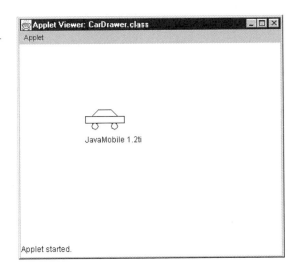

4.7   Simple Drawings

The next program shows how you can put shapes together to draw a simple figure of a car—see Figure 11.

The coordinates of the car parts seem a bit arbitrary. To come up with suitable values, you want to draw the image on graph paper and read off the coordinates—see Figure 12.

Here is the program. Unfortunately, in programs such as these it is difficult to avoid the "magic numbers" for the coordinates of the various shapes.

Program CarDrawer.java

```java
import java.applet.Applet;
import java.awt.Graphics;
import java.awt.Graphics2D;
import java.awt.Rectangle;
import java.awt.geom.Ellipse2D;
import java.awt.geom.Line2D;
import java.awt.geom.Point2D;

public class CarDrawer extends Applet
{  public void paint(Graphics g)
   {  Graphics2D g2 = (Graphics2D)g;

      Rectangle body = new Rectangle(100, 110, 60, 10);

      Ellipse2D.Double frontTire
         = new Ellipse2D.Double(110, 120, 10, 10);
      Ellipse2D.Double rearTire
         = new Ellipse2D.Double(140, 120, 10, 10);
```

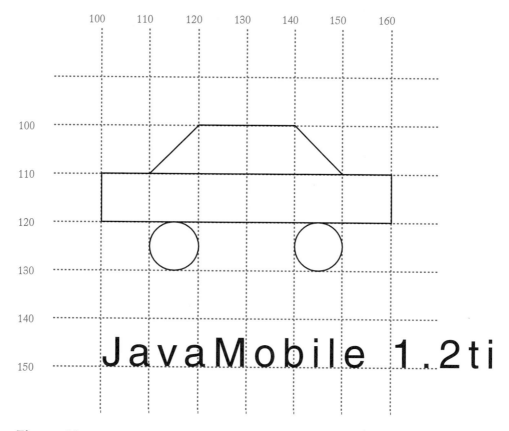

Figure 12

Using Graph Paper to Find Shape
Coordinates

```
Point2D.Double r1 = new Point2D.Double(110, 110);
// the bottom of the front windshield
Point2D.Double r2 = new Point2D.Double(120, 100);
// the front of the roof
Point2D.Double r3 = new Point2D.Double(140, 100);
// the rear of the roof
Point2D.Double r4 = new Point2D.Double(150, 110);
// the bottom of the rear windshield

Line2D.Double frontWindshield
   = new Line2D.Double(r1, r2);
Line2D.Double roofTop = new Line2D.Double(r2, r3);
Line2D.Double rearWindshield
   = new Line2D.Double(r3, r4);
```

```
                g2.draw(body);
                g2.draw(frontTire);
                g2.draw(rearTire);
                g2.draw(frontWindshield);
                g2.draw(roofTop);
                g2.draw(rearWindshield);

                g2.drawString("JavaMobile 1.2ti", 100, 150);
        }
    }
```

Random Fact 4.1

Computer Graphics

The generation and manipulation of visual images is one of the most exciting applications of the computer. We distinguish different kinds of graphics.

Diagrams, such as numeric charts or maps, are artifacts that convey information to the viewer (see Figure 13). They do not directly depict anything that occurs in the natural world but are a tool for visualizing information.

Scenes are computer-generated images that attempt to depict images of the real or an imagined world (see Figure 14). It turns out to be quite challenging to render light and shadows accurately. Special effort must be taken so that the images do not look overly neat and simple; clouds, rocks, leaves, and dust in the real world have a complex and somewhat random appearance. The degree of realism in these images is constantly improving.

Manipulated images are photographs or film footage of actual events that have been converted to digital form and edited by the computer (see Figure 15). For example, film sequences of the movie *Apollo 13* were produced by starting from actual images and changing the perspective, showing the launch of the rocket from a more dramatic viewpoint.

Computer graphics is one of the most challenging fields in computer science. It requires processing of massive amounts of information at very high speed. New algorithms are constantly invented for this purpose. Displaying an overlapping set of three-dimensional objects with curved boundaries requires advanced mathematical tools. Realistic modeling of textures and biological entities requires extensive knowledge of mathematics, physics, and biology.

4.8 Reading Text Input

The applets that you have seen so far are quite nice for drawing, but they aren't interactive—you can't change the positions of the shapes that are drawn on the screen. Interactive input in a graphical program turns out to be more complex than in a console program. In a console program, the programmer dictates the control flow and forces the user to enter input in a predetermined order. A graphical program, however, generally makes available to the program user a large number of controls

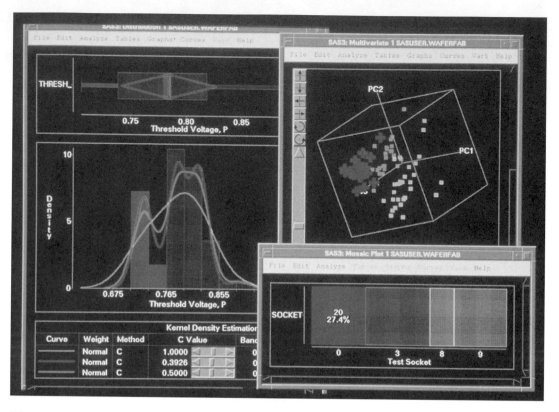

Figure 13

Diagrams

Figure 14

Scene

Figure 15

Manipulated Image

(buttons, input fields, scroll bars, and so on), which users can manipulate in any order they please. Therefore, the program must be prepared to process input from multiple sources in random order. You will learn how to do that in Chapter 10.

In this section you will learn about a simpler input method: a *modal dialog*. A modal dialog stops a program in its tracks and waits until the user has entered a value. Figure 16 shows a typical modal dialog. To display a modal dialog, you use the static `showInputDialog` method of the `JOptionPane` class, which is inside the `javax.swing` package. This is a package for the so-called Swing user interface toolkit, which supersedes the user interface part of the AWT. You will learn more about the Swing toolkit in Chapters 10 and 12.

In the constructor, supply a suitable prompt message:

```
String name
   = JOptionPane.showInputDialog("Please enter your name:");
```

The `showInputDialog` method waits until the user has entered a string and clicks on the "OK" button. Then it returns the string the user entered.

Figure 16

An Input Dialog

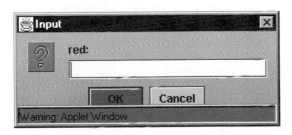

Table 3   The Life Cycle of an Applet

Method	Description
init	Called once, when the browser or applet viewer loads the applet
start	Called every time the user enters the web page containing the applet
paint	Called every time the surface of the applet needs to be repainted
stop	Called every time the user exits the web page containing the applet
destroy	Called once, when the browser or applet viewer exits and unloads the applet

If you ask for a numerical value, you need to convert the string to a number, like this:

```
String input
   = JOptionPane.showInputDialog("Please enter your age:");
int age = Integer.parseInt(input);
```

Next, you need to figure out *when* to ask the user for input. If you place a call to JOptionPane.showInputDialog inside the paint method of your applet, the user is asked to supply the input values again and again, every time the applet needs to repaint itself. Fortunately, the Applet class supplies several other methods that are called at more convenient times. Table 3 shows the methods of the Applet class that determine the life cycle of an applet.

We will use the init method to get user input. That way, the user is prompted for input when the applet is first displayed. If you use the applet viewer, you can get another chance to supply input, namely by selecting "Reload" from the applet viewer menu.

Of course, then your program needs to remember the user input in one or more instance variables of your applet, and refer to these variables in the paint method. Here is a typical example: a program that prompts the user for red, green, and blue values, and then fills a rectangle with the color that the user specified. For example, if you enter 1.0, 0.7, 0.7, then the rectangle is filled with pink color.

Program ColorSelect.java

```
import java.applet.Applet;
import java.awt.Color;
import java.awt.Graphics;
import java.awt.Graphics2D;
import java.awt.Rectangle;
import javax.swing.JOptionPane;

public class ColorSelect extends Applet
{  public void init()
   {  String input;
```

```
      // ask the user for red, green, blue values

      input = JOptionPane.showInputDialog("red:");
      float red = Float.parseFloat(input);

      input = JOptionPane.showInputDialog("green:");
      float green = Float.parseFloat(input);

      input = JOptionPane.showInputDialog("blue:");
      float blue = Float.parseFloat(input);
      fillColor = new Color(red, green, blue);
   }

   public void paint(Graphics g)
   {  final int SQUARE_LENGTH = 100;

      Graphics2D g2 = (Graphics2D)g;

      // select color into graphics context

      g2.setColor(fillColor);

      // construct and fill a square whose center is
      // the center of the window

      Rectangle square = new Rectangle(
         (getWidth() - SQUARE_LENGTH) / 2,
         (getHeight() - SQUARE_LENGTH) / 2,
         SQUARE_LENGTH,
         SQUARE_LENGTH);

      g2.fill(square);
   }

   private color fillColor;
}
```

When you run this program, you will note that the input dialog has a *warning label*. That is an applet security feature. It would be an easy matter for a cracker to write an applet that pops up a dialog "Your password has expired. Please reenter your password." and then sends the password back to the web server. If you should happen to visit the web page containing that applet, you might be confused and reenter the password to your computer account. The yellow warning border tips you off that it is an applet, and not your operating system, that displays the dialog. All windows that pop up from an applet have this warning label.

Obtaining input through a sequence of modal input dialogs is not considered a good user interface design. However, it is easy to program, and it makes sense for you to use it until you learn how to gather input in a more professional way—the topic of Chapter 12.

◆ **Advanced Topic** 4.2

Applet Parameters

You have seen how to use the showInputDialog method of the JOptionPane class to supply user input to an applet. Another way of supplying input is sometimes useful: Use the PARAM tag in the HTML page that loads the applet. The PARAM tag has the form

```
<PARAM NAME="..." VALUE="...">
```

You place one or more PARAM tags between the <APPLET> and </APPLET> tags, like this:

```
<APPLET CODE="ColorApplet" WIDTH=300 HEIGHT=300>
<PARAM NAME="Red" VALUE="1.0">
<PARAM NAME="Green" VALUE="0.7">
<PARAM NAME="Blue" VALUE="0.7">
</APPLET>
```

The applet can read these values with the getParameter method. For example, when the ColorApplet is loaded with the HTML tags given above, then getParameter("Blue") returns the string "0.7". Of course, you then need to convert the string into a number:

```
public class ColorApplet extends Applet
{  public void init()
   {  float r = Float.parseFloat(getParameter("Red"));
      float g = Float.parseFloat(getParameter("Green"));
      float b = Float.parseFloat(getParameter("Blue"));
      fillColor = new Color(r, g, b);
   }

   public void paint(Graphics g)
   {  . . .
   }

   private Color backgroundColor;
}
```

Now you can change the color values simply by editing the HTML page, without having to recompile the applet.

4.9   Comparing Visual and Numerical Information

The next example shows how one can look at the same problem both visually and numerically. You want to figure out the intersection between a circle and a line. The circle has radius 100 and center (100, 100). Ask the user to specify the position of a

Figure 17

Intersection of a Line and
a Circle

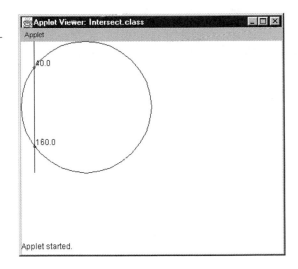

vertical line. Then draw the circle, the line, and the intersection points (see Figure 17). Label them to display the exact locations.

Exactly where do the two shapes intersect? We need a bit of mathematics. The equation of a circle with radius r and center point (a, b) is

$$(x - a)^2 + (y - b)^2 = r^2$$

If you know x, then you can solve for y:

$$(y - b)^2 = r^2 - (x - a)^2$$

or

$$y - b = \pm \sqrt{r^2 - (x - a)^2}$$

hence

$$y = b \pm \sqrt{r^2 - (x - a)^2}$$

That is easy to compute in Java:

```
double root = Math.sqrt(r * r - (x - a) * (x - a));
double y1 = b + root;
double y2 = b - root;
```

But how do you know that you did both the math and the programming right?

If your program is correct, these two points will show up right on top of the actual intersections in the picture. If not, the two points will be at the wrong place.

If you look at Figure 17, you will see that the results match perfectly, which gives us confidence that everything is correct. See Quality Tip 4.1 for more information on verifying that this program works correctly.

Here is the complete program.

Program Intersect.java

```
import java.applet.Applet;
import java.awt.Graphics;
import java.awt.Graphics2D;
import java.awt.geom.Ellipse2D;
import java.awt.geom.Line2D;
import javax.swing.JOptionPane;

public class Intersect extends Applet
{  public void init()
     {  String input
          = JOptionPane.showInputDialog("x:");
        x = Integer.parseInt(input);
}

public void paint(Graphics g)
{  Graphics2D g2 = (Graphics2D)g;

   double r = 100; // the radius of the circle

   // draw the circle

   Ellipse2D.Double circle
      = new Ellipse2D.Double(0, 0, 2 * r, 2 * r);
   g2.draw(circle);

   // draw the vertical line

   Line2D.Double line
      = new Line2D.Double(x, 0, x, 2 * r);
   g2.draw(line);

   // compute the intersection points

   double a = r;
   double b = r;

   double root = Math.sqrt(r * r - (x - a) * (x - a));
   double y1 = b + root;
   double y2 = b - root;

   // draw the intersection points

   final double SMALL_CIRCLE_RADIUS = 2;
```

```
                    Ellipse2D.Double circle1 = new Ellipse2D.Double(
                         x - SMALL_CIRCLE_RADIUS,
                         y1 - SMALL_CIRCLE_RADIUS,
                         2 * SMALL_CIRCLE_RADIUS,
                         2 * SMALL_CIRCLE_RADIUS);
                    Ellipse2D.Double circle2 = new Ellipse2D.Double(
                         x - SMALL_CIRCLE_RADIUS,
                         y2 - SMALL_CIRCLE_RADIUS,
                         2 * SMALL_CIRCLE_RADIUS,
                         2 * SMALL_CIRCLE_RADIUS);

               g2.draw(circle1);
               g2.draw(circle2);

               // label the intersection points

               String label1 = "" + y1;
               String label2 = "" + y2;

               g2.drawString(label1, (float)x, (float)y1);
               g2.drawString(label2, (float)x, (float)y2);

          }

          private double x;

     }
```

At this point you should be careful to specify only lines that intersect the circle. If the line doesn't meet the circle, then the program will attempt to compute a square root of a negative number, and a math error will occur. You do not yet know how to implement a test to protect against this situation. That will be the topic of the next chapter.

Quality Tip 4.1

Calculate Sample Data Manually

It is difficult or impossible to prove that a given program functions correctly in all cases. For gaining confidence in the correctness of a program, or for understanding why it does not function as it should, manually calculated sample data are invaluable. If the program arrives at the same results as the manual calculation, our confidence in it is strengthened. If the manual results differ from the program results, we have a starting point for the debugging process.

Surprisingly, many programmers are reluctant to perform any manual calculations as soon as a program carries out the slightest bit of algebra. Their math phobia kicks in, and they irrationally hope that they can avoid the algebra and beat the program into submission by random tinkering, such as rearranging the + and - signs. Random tinkering is always a great time sink, but it rarely leads to useful results.

It is much smarter to look for test cases that are representative and easy to compute. In our example, let us look for three easy cases that we can compute by hand and then compare against program runs.

First, let the vertical line pass through the center of the circle. That is, x is 100. Then we expect the distance between the center and the intersection point to be the same as the radius of the circle. Now `root = Math.sqrt(100 * 100 - 0 * 0)` which is 100. Therefore, y1 is 0 and y2 is 200. Those are indeed the top and bottom points on the circle. Now, that wasn't so hard.

Next, let the line touch the circle on the right. Then x is 200 and `root = Math.sqrt(100 * 100 - 100 * 100)`, which is 0. Therefore, y1 and y2 are both equal to 100, and indeed (200, 100) is the rightmost point of the circle. That also was pretty easy.

The first two cases were *boundary cases* of the problem. A program may work correctly for several special cases but still fail for more typical input values. Therefore we must come up with an intermediate test case, even if it means a bit more computation. Let us pick a simple value for x, say x = 50. Then `root = Math.sqrt(100 * 100 - 50 * 50) = Math.sqrt(7500)`. Using a calculator, you get approximately 86.6025. That yields y1 = 100 − 86.6025 = 13.3975 and y2 = 100 + 86.6025 = 186.6025. So what? Run the program and enter 50. First, you will find that the program also computes the same *x*- and *y*-values that you computed by hand. That is good—it confirms that you probably typed in the formulas correctly. And the intersection points really do fall on the right place.

4.10 Choosing Useful Units (Advanced)

By default, the `draw` method of the `Graphics2D` class uses *pixels* to measure screen locations. For example, the point (50, 100) is 50 pixels to the right and 100 pixels down from the top left corner of the panel. This default coordinate system is fine for simple test programs, but it is *useless* when dealing with real data. For example, suppose you want to show a graph plotting the average temperature (degrees Celsius) in Phoenix, Arizona, for every month of the year. The temperature ranges from 11 degrees Celsius in January to 33 degrees Celsius in July (see Table 4).

In such a situation, you need to choose coordinates that makes sense for your particular application. Here, the *x*-values range from 1 to 12 and the *y*-values range from 11 to 33. For simplicity, let's say that *x* should go from 0 to 12 and *y* from 0 to 40. Then you need to convert months and temperatures so that the range 0 . . . 12 is mapped to 0 . . . `getWidth()` − 1 and the range 0 . . . 40 is mapped to `getHeight()` − 1 . . . 0 (since you want the largest temperature values on the top).

Here are the instructions to draw one rectangle denoting a temperature measurement of `temp` degrees in a given month:

```
xMonth = month * (getWidth() - 1) / 12;
yTemp = (40 - temp) * (getHeight() - 1) / 40;
xWidth = (getWidth() - 1) / 12;
yHeight = temp * (getHeight() - 1) / 40;
g2.draw(new Rectangle(xMonth, yTemp, xWidth, yHeight));
```

This can get tedious quickly.

Table 4 Average
Temperatures in
Phoenix, Arizona

January	11°C	July	33°C
February	13°C	August	32°C
March	16°C	September	29°C
April	20°C	October	23°C
May	25°C	November	16°C
June	31°C	December	12°C

To encapsulate these computations, we supply a class `UnitConverter`. When you construct a `UnitConverter` object, you supply

◆ The desired x-range (for example $0\ldots12$)

◆ The desired y-range (for example $0\ldots40$)

◆ The window size (`getWidth()` and `getHeight()`)

The unit converter stores these values in instance variables.

```
public class UnitConverter
{  public UnitConverter(double x1, double x2,
      double y1, double y2, double w, double h)
   {  xleft = x1;
      xright = x2;
      ybottom = y1;
      ytop = y2;
      width = w;
      height = h;
   }
   . . .
   private double xleft;
   private double xright;
   private double ytop;
   private double ybottom;
   private double width;
   private double height;
}
```

The following two methods convert x- and y-values into pixels:

```
public double xToPixel(double x)
{  return (x - xleft) * (width - 1) / (xright - xleft);
}

public double yToPixel(double y)
{  return (y - ytop) * (height - 1) / (ybottom - ytop);
}
```

There are also inverses `pixelToX` and `pixelToY` that are useful to translate mouse click positions back to units.

However, you generally don't need to call these methods, because the `UnitConverter` also has three convenience methods called **convert** to convert points, lines, and rectangles. Here is the method for points:

```
public Point2D convert(Point2D p)
{  double x = xToPixel(p.getX());
   double y = yToPixel(p.getY());
   p.setLocation(x, y);
   return p;
}
```

The **convert** methods for lines and rectangles work in the same way, by converting the shape coordinates and setting the object to the new coordinates.

Suppose you have a rectangle in your favorite units:

```
Rectangle rect = new Rectangle(5, 0, 1, MAY_TEMP);
```

And suppose you constructed a converter object:

```
UnitConverter units
    = new UnitConverter(0, 12, 0, 40, getWidth(), getHeight());
```

Now it is really easy to convert and draw the rectangle:

```
units.convert(rect);
g2.draw(rect);
```

Since the **convert** method returns the object that you give it, you can even call

```
g2.draw(units.convert(rect));
```

or

```
g2.draw(units.convert(new Rectangle(5, 0, 1, MAY_TEMP)));
```

Here is the complete program for drawing the temperature bar chart. Figure 18 shows the output.

Program Phoenix.java

```
import java.applet.Applet;
import java.awt.Graphics;
import java.awt.Graphics2D;
import java.awt.Rectangle;

public class Phoenix extends Applet
{  public void paint(Graphics g)
   {  Graphics2D g2 = (Graphics2D)g;
```

Figure 18

Plotting Temperature Data

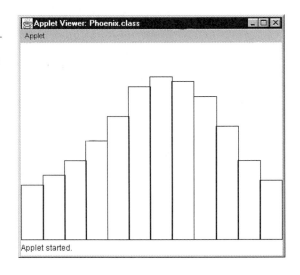

```
month = 0;
units = new UnitConverter(0, 12, 0, 40,
    getWidth(), getHeight());
final int JAN_TEMP = 11;
final int FEB_TEMP = 13;
final int MAR_TEMP = 16;
final int APR_TEMP = 20;
final int MAY_TEMP = 25;
final int JUN_TEMP = 31;
final int JUL_TEMP = 33;
final int AUG_TEMP = 32;
final int SEP_TEMP = 29;
final int OCT_TEMP = 23;
final int NOV_TEMP = 16;
final int DEC_TEMP = 12;

drawBar(g2, JAN_TEMP);
drawBar(g2, FEB_TEMP);
drawBar(g2, MAR_TEMP);
drawBar(g2, APR_TEMP);
drawBar(g2, MAY_TEMP);
drawBar(g2, JUN_TEMP);
drawBar(g2, JUL_TEMP);
drawBar(g2, AUG_TEMP);
drawBar(g2, SEP_TEMP);
drawBar(g2, OCT_TEMP);
drawBar(g2, NOV_TEMP);
drawBar(g2, DEC_TEMP);
    }
```

```
      public void drawBar(Graphics2D g2, int temperature)
      {   // construct rectangle for this month and temperature

         Rectangle rect
            = new Rectangle(month, 0, 1, temperature);

         // convert to pixel coordinates and draw

         units.convert(rect);
         g2.draw(rect);

         month++;
      }

      private int month;
      private UnitConverter units;
   }
```

Productivity Hint 4.1

Choose Convenient Units for Drawing

Whenever you deal with real-world data, you should use units that are matched to the data. Figure out which range of x- and y-coordinates is most convenient for you. For example, suppose you want to display a tic-tac-toe board (see Figure 19) that is supposed to fill the entire applet.

Of course, you could labor mightily and figure out where the lines are in relation to the default pixel coordinate system. Or you can simply set your own units with both x and y going from 0 to 3.

```
   public class TicTacToe extends Applet
   {   public void paint(Graphics g)
      {   Graphics2D g2 = (Graphics2D)g;

         UnitConverter units
            = new UnitConverter(0, 3, 0, 3, getWidth(),
               getHeight());

         g2.draw(units.convert(new Line2D.Double(0, 1, 3, 1)));
         g2.draw(units.convert(new Line2D.Double(0, 2, 3, 2)));
         g2.draw(units.convert(new Line2D.Double(1, 0, 1, 3)));
         g2.draw(units.convert(new Line2D.Double(2, 0, 2, 3)));
      }
   }
```

Some people have horrible memories about coordinate transformations from their high school geometry class and have taken a vow never to think about coordinates again for the

Figure 19

A Tic-Tac-Toe
Board

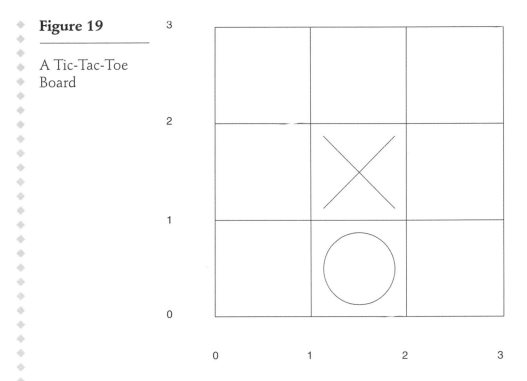

remainder of their lives. If you are among them, you should reconsider. The `UnitConverter` is your friend—it does all the horrible algebra for you, so you don't have to program it by hand.

Chapter Summary

1. There are three types of Java programs: *console applications*, *applets*, and *graphics applications*.

2. Applets are embedded in web pages. To run an applet, you write an HTML page with the **APPLET** tag. You view the applet from a browser or the applet viewer.

3. You draw graphical shapes in an applet by placing the drawing code inside the **paint** method. That method is called whenever the applet needs to be refreshed.

4. The `Rectangle`, `Rectangle2D.Double`, `Ellipse2D.Double`, and `Line2D.Double` classes describe graphical shapes. The `Graphics2D` class has methods to draw and fill graphical shapes and to draw text strings. You need to cast the `Graphics` parameter of the **paint** method to `Graphics2D` to use these methods.

5. You can select different colors and fonts into the graphics context. These colors and fonts are used for subsequent drawing operations.

6. Use the `drawString` method of the `Graphics2D` class to display strings. To position strings accurately, you need to measure their size by using a `TextLayout` object.

7. You can produce many kinds of line drawings with the basic graphics objects. To figure out where to place the graphical shapes, you can make a sketch on graph paper. You can also switch to more convenient units.

8. You can obtain input by displaying a `JOptionPane` in the `init` or `start` method of the applet.

9. You should calculate test cases by hand to double-check that your application computes the correct answers.

Classes, Objects, and Methods Introduced in This Chapter

```
java.applet.Applet
   destroy
   getParameter
   init
   start
   stop
java.awt.Color
java.awt.Container
   getHeight
   getWidth
   paint
java.awt.Font
java.awt.Graphics
   setColor
   setFont
java.awt.Graphics2D
   draw
   drawString
   fill
   getFontRenderContext
java.awt.font.FontRenderContext
java.awt.font.TextLayout
   getAdvance
   getAscent
   getDescent
   getLeading
java.awt.geom.Ellipse2D.Double
java.awt.geom.Line2D
```

```
        getX1
        getX2
        getY1
        getY2
        setLine
java.awt.geom.Line2D.Double
java.awt.geom.Point2D
    getX
    getY
    setLocation
java.awt.geom.Point2D
java.awt.geom.Rectangle2D.Double
java.awt.geom.RectangularShape
    getCenterX
    getCenterY
    getMaxX
    getMaxY
    getMinX
    getMinY
    getWidth
    getHeight
    setFrameFromDiagonal
java.lang.Float
    parseFloat
javax.swing.JOptionPane
    showInputDialog
```

Review Exercises

Exercise R4.1. What is the difference between an applet and an application?

Exercise R4.2. What is the difference between a browser and the applet viewer?

Exercise R4.3. Why do you need an HTML page to run an applet?

Exercise R4.4. Who calls the paint method of an applet? When does the call to the paint method occur?

Exercise R4.5. Why does the parameter of the paint method have type Graphics and not Graphics2D?

Exercise R4.6. What is the purpose of a graphics context?

Exercise R4.7. How do you specify a text color?

Exercise R4.8. What is the difference between a font and a font face?

Exercise R4.9. What is the difference between a monospaced font and a proportionally spaced font?

Exercise R4.10. What are serifs?

Exercise R4.11. What is a logical font?

Exercise R4.12. How do you determine the pixel dimensions of a string in a particular font?

Exercise R4.13. Which classes are used in this chapter for drawing graphical shapes?

Exercise R4.14. What are the three different classes for specifying rectangles in the Java library?

Exercise R4.15. You want to plot a bar chart showing the grade distribution of all students in your class (where A = 4.0, F = 0). What coordinate system would you choose to make the plotting as simple as possible?

Exercise R4.16. Let **e** be any ellipse. Write Java code to plot the ellipse **e** and another ellipse of the same size that touches **e**. *Hint:* You need to look up the accessors that tell you the dimensions of an ellipse.

Exercise R4.17. Write Java instructions to display the letters X and T in a graphics window, by plotting line segments.

Exercise R4.18. Introduce an error in the program `Intersect.java`, by computing `double root = Math.sqrt(r * r + (x - a) * (x - a));`. Run the program. What happens to the intersection points?

Exercise R4.19. Suppose you run the `Intersect` program and give a value of 30 for the *x*-position of the vertical line. Without actually running the program, determine what values you will obtain for the intersection points.

Programming Exercises

Exercise P4.1 Write a graphics program that draws your name in red, centered inside a blue rectangle.

Exercise P4.2 Write a graphics program that draws your name four times, in a large serif font, in plain, bold, italic, and bold italic. The names should be stacked on top of each other, with equal distance between them. Each of them should be centered horizontally, and the entire stack should be centered vertically.

Exercise P4.3. Write a graphics program that draws twelve strings, one each for the 12 standard colors besides `Color.white`, each in its own color.

Exercise P4.4. Write a graphics program that prompts the user to enter a radius. Draw a circle with that radius.

Exercise P4.5. Write a program that draws two solid circles, one in pink and one in purple. Use a standard color for one of them and a custom color for the other.

Exercise P4.6. Draw a "bull's eye"—a set of concentric rings in alternating black and white colors. *Hint:* Fill a black circle, then fill a smaller white circle on top, and so on.

Exercise P4.7. Write a program that fills the applet window with a large ellipse, filled with your favorite color, that touches the window boundaries. The ellipse should resize itself when you resize the window.

Exercise P4.8. Write a program that draws the picture of a house. It could be as simple as the figure below, or if you like, make it more elaborate (3-D, skyscraper, marble columns in the entryway, whatever).

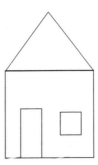

Exercise P4.9. Write a program to plot the following face.

Exercise P4.10. Write a program to plot the string "HELLO", using just lines and circles. Do not call drawString, and do not use System.out.

Exercise P4.11. *Plotting a data set.* Make a bar chart to plot the following data set:

Bridge Name	Longest span (ft)
Golden Gate	4,200
Brooklyn	1,595
Delaware Memorial	2,150
Mackinac	3,800

Make the bars horizontal for easier labeling. *Hint:* Set the window coordinates to 5,000 in the *x*-direction and 4 in the *y*-direction.

```
Golden Gate
Brooklyn
Delaware Memorial
Mackinac
```

Exercise P4.12. Write a graphics program that displays the values of Exercise 4.11 as a *pie chart*.

Exercise P4.13. Write a program that displays the Olympic rings.

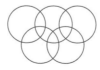

Make the rings colored in the Olympic colors.

Exercise P4.14. Write a graphics program that draws a clock face with a time that the user enters in a text field. (The user must enter the time in the format hh:mm, for example 09:45.)

Hint: You need to find out the angles of the hour hand and the minute hand. The angle of the minute hand is easy: The minute hand travels 360 degrees in 60 minutes. The angle of the hour hand is harder; it travels 360 degrees in 12×60 minutes.

Exercise P4.15. Change the CarDrawer program to make the car appear twice the size of the original example.

Exercise P4.16. Design a class Car whose constructor takes the top left corner point of the car. Supply a method draw(Graphics2D g2) that draws the car. Then populate your screen with a few cars.

Exercise P4.17. Extend Exercise 4.8 by implementing a class House. In the constructor of the House class, supply the bottom left corner of the house and its width and height. Supply a method draw(Graphics2D g2) that draws the house. Then populate your screen with a few houses of different sizes.

Decisions

Chapter Goals

- ◆ To be able to implement decisions using **if** statements
- ◆ To understand how to group statements into blocks
- ◆ To learn how to compare integers, floating-point numbers, strings, and objects
- ◆ To recognize the correct ordering of decisions in multiple branches
- ◆ To program conditions using Boolean operators and variables

The programs we have seen so far were able to do fast computations and render graphs, but they were very inflexible. Except for variations in the input, they worked the same way with every program run. One of the essential features of nontrivial computer programs is the ability to make decisions and to carry out different actions, depending on the nature of the inputs. The goal of this chapter is to learn how to program simple and complex decisions.

5.1   The if Statement

Consider the bank account class of Chapter 3. The withdraw method allows you to withdraw as much money from the account as you like. The balance just moves ever further into the negatives. That is not a realistic model for a bank account. Let's implement the withdraw method so that you cannot withdraw more money than you have in the account. That is, the withdraw method must make a *decision*: whether to allow the withdrawal or not.

The if statement is used to implement a decision. The if statement has two parts: a *test* and a *body*. If the test succeeds, the body of the statement is executed. The body of the if statement consists of a statement:

```
if (amount <= balance)
   balance = balance - amount;
```

The assignment statement is carried out only when the amount to be withdrawn is less than or equal to the balance. (See Figure 1.)

Let us make the withdraw method of the BankAccount even more realistic. Many banks will not only disallow withdrawals that exceed your account balance, but also—adding insult to injury—charge you a penalty for every attempt to do so.

Figure 1

A Decision

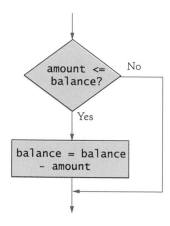

You can't simply program that by providing two complementary if statements:

```
if (amount <= balance)
    balance = balance - amount;
if (amount > balance)
    balance = balance - OVERDRAFT_PENALTY;
```

There are two problems with this approach. First, if you need to modify the condition amount <= balance for some reason, you must remember to update the condition amount > balance as well. If you do not, the logic of the program will no longer be correct. More importantly, if you modify the value of amount in the body of the first if statement (as in this example), then the second condition uses the new value.

To implement a true alternative, use the if/else statement:

```
if (amount <= balance)
    balance = balance - amount;
else
    balance = balance - OVERDRAFT_PENALTY;
```

Now there is only one condition. If it is satisfied, the first block is executed. Otherwise, the second is executed. The flowchart in Figure 2 gives a graphical representation of the branching behavior.

Quite often, however, the body of the if statement consists of multiple statements that must be executed in sequence whenever the test is successful. These statements must be grouped together to form a *block statement* by enclosing them in braces { }. Here is an example.

```
if (amount <= balance)
{   double newBalance = balance - amount;
    balance = newBalance;
}
```

Figure 2

Alternative Conditions

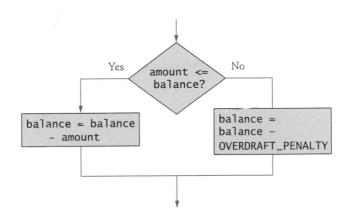

Java Syntax

5.1 The if statement

```
if (condition)
    statement

if (condition)
    statement
else
    statement
```

Example:
```
if (amount <= balance)
    balance = balance - amount;

if (amount <= balance)
    balance = balance - amount;
else
    balance = balance - OVERDRAFT_PENALTY;
```

Purpose:
To execute a statement when a condition is true or false

Java Syntax

5.2 Block Statement

```
{
    statement
    statement
    . . .
}
```

Example:
```
{   double newBalance = balance - amount;
    balance = newBalance;
}
```

Purpose:
To group several statements together to form a single statement

A statement such as

```
    balance = balance - amount;
```

is called a *simple statement*. A conditional statement such as

```
    if (x >= 0) y = x;
```

is called a *compound statement*. In Chapter 6, you will encounter other compound statements: so-called *loops*.

The body of an **if** statement or the **else** alternative must be a statement—that is, a simple statement, a compound statement (such as another **if** statement), or a block statement.

Advanced Topic 5.1

The Selection Operator

Java has a selection operator of the form

test ? *value1* : *value2*

The value of that expression is either *value1* if the test passes or *value2* if it fails. For example, we can compute the absolute value as

```
y = x >= 0 ? x : -x;
```

which is a convenient shorthand for

```
if (x >= 0) y = x;
else y = -x;
```

The selection operator is similar to the **if/else** statement, but it works on a different syntactical level. The selection operator combines *expressions* and yields another expression. The **if/else** statement combines statements and yields another statement.

Expressions have values. For example, **balance + amount** is an expression, as is **x >= 0 ? x : -x**. Any expression can be made into a statement by adding a semicolon. For example, **y = x** is an expression (with value x), but **y = x;** is a statement. Statements do not have values. Since **if/else** forms a statement and does not have a value, you cannot write

```
y = if (x > 0) x; else -x; // Error
```

We don't use the selection operator in this book, but it is a convenient and legitimate construct that you will find in many Java programs.

Quality Tip 5.1

Brace Layout

The compiler doesn't care where you place braces, but we strongly recommend that you follow a simple rule: *Line up* { and }.

```
if (amount <= balance)
{  double newBalance = balance - amount;
   balance = newBalance;
}
```

This scheme makes it easy to spot matching braces.

Some programmers place the opening brace on a line by itself:

```
if (amount <= balance)
{
   double newBalance = balance - amount;
   balance = newBalance;
}
```

That is fine too, but it does take away a line of precious screen real estate.

Some programmers put the opening brace on the same line as the if:

```java
if (amount <= balance) {
   double newBalance = balance - amount;
   balance = newBalance;
}
```

That is an inferior solution that makes it harder to match the braces.

It is important that you pick a layout scheme and stick with it consistently. Which scheme you choose may depend on your personal preference or a coding style guide that you need to follow.

Productivity Hint 5.1

Indentation and Tabs

When writing Java programs, you use *indentation* to indicate nesting levels:

```java
public class BankAccount
{  . . .
|  public void withdraw(double amount)
|  {  if (amount <= balance)
|  |  {  double newBalance = balance - amount;
|  |  |  balance = newBalance;
|  |  }
|  }
|  . . .
}

↑   ↑ ↑ ↑
0   1 2 3
```
Indentation level

How many spaces should you use per indentation level? Some programmers use eight spaces per level, but that isn't a good choice:

```java
public class BankAccount
{         . . .
        public void withdraw(double amount)
        {         if (amount <= balance)
                {         double newBalance = balance - amount;
                        balance = newBalance;
                }
        }
        . . .
}
```

It crowds the code too much to the right side of the screen. As a consequence, long expressions frequently must be broken into separate lines. More common values are two, three, or four spaces per indentation level.

How do you move the cursor from the leftmost column to the appropriate indentation level? A perfectly reasonable strategy is to hit the space bar a sufficient number of times. However, many programmers use the Tab key instead. A tab moves the cursor to the next tab stop. By default, there are tab stops every eight columns, but most editors let you change that value; you should find out how to set your editor's tab stops to, say, every three columns. Note that the Tab key does not simply enter three spaces; it moves the cursor to the next tab column. For example, to enter the lines

```
if (amount <= balance)
{   double newBalance = balance - amount;
    balance = newBalance;
}
```

you type

Some editors actually help you out with an *autoindent* feature. They automatically insert as many tabs or spaces as the preceding line had, because it is quite likely that the new line is supposed to be on the same indentation level. If it isn't, you must add or remove a tab, but that is still faster than tabbing all the way from the left margin.

As nice as tabs are for data entry, they have one disadvantage: They can mess up printouts. If you send a file with tabs to a printer, the printer may either ignore the tabs altogether or set tab stops every eight columns. It is therefore best to save and print your files with spaces instead of tabs. Most editors can convert tabs to spaces for printing.

5.2   Comparing Values

5.2.1   Relational Operators

Every if statement performs a test. In many cases, the test compares two values. For example, in the previous example we tested amount <= balance. Comparison operators such as <= are called *relational operators*. Java has six relational operators:

Java	Math notation	Description
>	>	Greater than
>=	≥	Greater than or equal
<	<	Less than
<=	≤	Less than or equal
==	=	Equal
!=	≠	Not equal

As you can see, only two Java relational operators (> and <) look as you would expect from the mathematical notation. Computer keyboards do not have keys for ≥, ≤, or ≠, but the >=, <=, and != operators are easy to remember because they look similar.

The == operator is initially confusing to most newcomers to Java. In Java, the = symbol already has a meaning, namely assignment. The == operator denotes equality testing:

```
a = 5; // assign 5 to a
if (a == 5) ... // test whether a equals 5
```

You will have to remember to use == for equality testing and to use = for assignment.

5.2.2 Comparing Floating-Point Numbers

Floating-point numbers have only a limited precision, and calculations can introduce roundoff errors. For example, the following code multiplies the square root of 2 by itself.

```
double r = Math.sqrt(2);
if (r * r == 2) System.out.println("sqrt(2) squared is 2");
else System.out.println("sqrt(2) squared is " + r * r);
```

Even though the laws of mathematics tell us that $\sqrt{2} \times \sqrt{2}$ equals 2, this program fragment prints

```
sqrt(2) squared is 2.0000000000000004
```

Unfortunately, such roundoff errors are unavoidable. It plainly does not make sense in most circumstances to compare floating-point numbers exactly. Instead, we should test whether they are *close enough*. That is, the magnitude of their difference should be less than some threshold. Mathematically, we would write that x and y are close enough if

$$|x - y| \leq \epsilon$$

for a very small number, ϵ. ϵ is the Greek letter epsilon, a letter commonly used to denote a very small quantity. It is common to set ϵ to 10^{-14} when comparing **double** numbers.

However, this is not always good enough. Suppose x and y are rather large, say a few billion each. Then one could be a roundoff error for the other even if their difference was quite a bit larger than 10^{-14}. To overcome this problem, you need to divide by the magnitude of the numbers before comparing how close they are. Here is the formula: x and y are close enough if

$$\frac{|x - y|}{\max(|x|, |y|)} \leq \epsilon$$

To avoid division by 0 (in case both x and y are zero), it is better to test

$$|x - y| \leq \epsilon \cdot \max(|x|, |y|)$$

In Java, the code for this test is

```
Math.abs(x-y) <= EPSILON * Math.max(Math.abs(x), Math.abs(y));
```

5.2.3 Comparing Strings

To test whether two strings are equal to each other, you must use the method called **equals**:

```
if (string1.equals(string2)) ...
```

Do not use the **==** *operator to compare strings!* The expression

```
if (string1 == string2) // not useful
```

has an unrelated meaning. It tests whether the two string variables refer to the *identical* string object. You can have strings with identical contents stored in different objects, so this test never makes sense in actual programming; see Common Error 5.1.

In Java, letter case matters. For example, **"Harry"** and **"HARRY"** are not the same string. To ignore the letter case, use the **equalsIgnoreCase** method:

```
if (string1.equalsIgnoreCase(string2)) ...
```

If two strings are not identical to each other, you still may want to know the relationship between them. The **compareTo** method compares strings in dictionary order. If

```
string1.compareTo(string2) < 0
```

then the string **string1** comes before the string **string2** in the dictionary. For example, this is the case if **string1** is **"Harry"**, and **string2** is **"Hell"**. If

```
string1.compareTo(string2) > 0
```

Figure 3

Lexicographic Comparison

Letters   r comes
match   before **t**

then `string1` comes after `string2` in dictionary order. Finally, if

$$string1.compareTo(string2) == 0$$

then `string1` and `string2` are equal.

Actually, the dictionary ordering used by Java is slightly different from that of a normal dictionary. Java is case-sensitive and sorts characters by listing numbers first, then uppercase characters, then lowercase characters. For example, **1** comes before **B**, which comes before **a**. The space character comes before all other characters.

Let us investigate the comparison process closely. When comparing two strings, corresponding letters are compared until one of the strings ends or the first difference is encountered. If one of the strings ends, the longer string is considered the later one. If a character mismatch is found, compare the characters to determine which string comes later in the dictionary sequence. This process is called *lexicographic* comparison. For example, compare `"car"` with `"cargo"`. The first three letters match, and we reach the end of the first string. Therefore `"car"` comes before `"cargo"` in the lexicographic ordering. Now compare `"cathode"` with `"cargo"`. The first two letters match. Since **t** comes after **r**, the string `"cathode"` comes after `"cargo"` in lexicographic ordering. (See Figure 3.)

You can compare numbers only with numbers and strings only with strings. The test

```
String name = "Harry";
if (name > 5)  ... // Error
```

is not valid.

Common Error 5.1

Using == to Compare Strings

It is an extremely common error in Java to write == when `equals` is intended. This is particularly true for strings. If you write

```
if (destination == "Hell")
```

then the test succeeds only if the variable `destination` refers to the exact same string object as the string constant `"Hell"`. For efficiency, Java makes only one string object for every string constant. Therefore, the following test will pass:

```
String destination = "Hell";
...
if (destination == "Hell") // test is true
```

However, if the string with the letters H e l l has been assembled in some other way, then the test will fail:

```
String greeting = "Hello";
String destination = greeting.substring(0, 4);

...

if (destination == "Hell") // test is false
```

This is a particularly distressing situation: The wrong code will sometimes do the right thing, sometimes the wrong thing. Since string objects are always constructed by the compiler, you never have an interest in whether two string objects are shared. You must remember never to use == to compare strings. Always use equals or compareTo to compare strings.

5.2.4 Comparing Objects

If you compare two object references with the == operator, you test whether the references refer to the same *object*. Here is an example:

```
Rectangle cerealBox = new Rectangle(5, 10, 20, 30);
Rectangle crispyCrunchyStuff = cerealBox;
Rectangle oatmealBox = new Rectangle(5, 10, 20, 30);
```

The comparison

```
cerealBox == crispyCrunchyStuff
```

is **true**. Both object variables refer to the same object. But the comparison

```
cerealBox == oatmealBox
```

is **false**. The two object variables refer to *different* objects (see Figure 4). It does not matter that the objects have identical contents.

You can use the equals method to test whether two rectangles have the same *contents*, that is, whether they have the same upper left corner and the same width and height. For example, the test

```
cerealBox.equals(oatmealBox)
```

is **true**.

However, you must be careful when using the equals method. The equals method is defined in the Object class, which all other classes extend (see Chapter 9), and therefore the method can be applied to *every* object. The Object class, however, has no idea what it means for rectangles or other objects to be equal to another, so its equals method takes the easy way out and simply calls ==. Whenever you use equals, you must check whether it has been properly implemented for the objects that you want to compare. For example, the implementers of the Rectangle class provided an equals method that is suitable for comparing rectangles.

For your own classes, you need to supply an appropriate equals method. You will learn how to do that in Chapter 9. Until that point, you should not use the equals method to compare objects of your own classes.

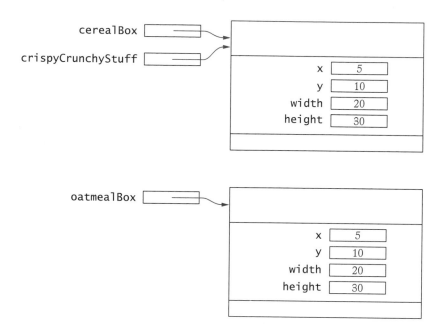

Figure 4

Comparing Objects

Finally, note that you use the == operator (and not **equals**) to test whether an object reference is a **null** reference:

```
if (account == null) . . .
   // account is a null reference
```

Quality Tip 5.2

Avoid Conditions with Side Effects

In Java, it is legal to nest assignment statements inside test conditions:

```
if ((d = b * b - 4 * a * c) >= 0) r = Math.sqrt(d);
```

It is legal to use the increment operator inside other expressions:

```
if (n-- > 0)  ...
```

These are bad programming practice, because they mix a test with another activity. The other activity (setting the variable **d**, decrementing **n**) is called a *side effect* of the test.

As we will see in Advanced Topic 6.2, conditions with side effects can occasionally be helpful to simplify *loops*. For **if** statements they should always be avoided.

5.3   Multiple Alternatives

5.3.1   Sequences of Comparisons

The following program asks for a value describing the magnitude of an earthquake on the Richter scale and prints a description of the likely impact of the quake. The Richter scale is a measurement for the strength of an earthquake. Every step in the scale, for example from 6.0 to 7.0, signifies a tenfold increase in the strength of the quake. The 1989 Loma Prieta earthquake that damaged the Bay Bridge in San Francisco and destroyed many buildings in several Bay Area cities rated 7.1 on the Richter scale.

Program Richter.java

```java
public class Richter
{  public static void main(String[] args)
    {  ConsoleReader console = new ConsoleReader(System.in);
       System.out.println
          ("Enter a magnitude on the Richter scale:");
       double magnitude = console.readDouble();
       Earthquake quake = new Earthquake(magnitude);
       System.out.println(quake.getDescription());
    }
}

class Earthquake
{  public Earthquake(double magnitude)
    {  richter = magnitude;
    }
    public String getDescription()
    {  String r;
       if (richter >= 8.0)
          r = "Most structures fall";
       else if (richter >= 7.0)
          r = "Many buildings destroyed";
       else if (richter >= 6.0)
          r = "Many buildings considerably damaged, some collapse";
       else if (richter >= 4.5)
          r = "Damage to poorly constructed buildings";
       else if (richter >= 3.5)
          r = "Felt by many people, no destruction";
       else if (richter >= 0)
          r = "Generally not felt by people";
       else
          r = "Negative numbers are not valid";
       return r;
    }

    private double richter;
}
```

Here we must sort the conditions and test against the largest cutoff first. Suppose we reverse the order of tests:

```
if (richter >= 0) // Tests in wrong order
   r = "Generally not felt by people";
else if (richter >= 3.5)
   r = "Felt by many people, no destruction";
else if (richter >= 4.5)
   r = "Damage to poorly constructed buildings";
else if (richter >= 6.0)
   r = "Many buildings considerably damaged; some collapse");
else if (richter >= 7.0)
   r = "Many buildings destroyed";
else if (richter >= 8.0)
   r = "Most structures fall";
```

This does not work. All positive values of `richter` fall into the first case, and the other tests will never be attempted.

In this example, it is also important that we use an `if/else/else` test, not just multiple independent `if` statements. Consider this sequence of independent tests:

```
if (richter >= 8.0) // Didn't use else
   r = "Most structures fall";
if (richter >= 7.0)
   r = "Many buildings destroyed";
if (richter >= 6.0)
   r = "Many buildings considerably damaged; some collapse";
if (richter >= 4.5)
   r = "Damage to poorly constructed buildings";
if (richter >= 3.5)
   r = "Felt by many people, no destruction";
if (richter >= 0)
   r = "Generally not felt by people";
```

Now the alternatives are no longer exclusive. If `richter` is 5.0, then the last *four* tests all match, and `r` is set four times.

Advanced Topic 5.2

The switch Statement

A sequence of `if/else/else` that compares a *single integer value* against several *constant* alternatives can be implemented as a `switch` statement. For example,

```
int digit;
...
switch (digit)
```

```
{  case 1: digitName = "one"; break;
   case 2: digitName = "two"; break;
   case 3: digitName = "three"; break;
   case 4: digitName = "four"; break;
   case 5: digitName = "five"; break;
   case 6: digitName = "six"; break;
   case 7: digitName = "seven"; break;
   case 8: digitName = "eight"; break;
   case 9: digitName = "nine"; break;
   default: digitName = ""; break;
}
```

This is a shortcut for

```
int digit;
...
if (digit == 1) digitName = "one";
else if (digit == 2) digitName = "two";
else if (digit == 3) digitName = "three";
else if (digit == 4) digitName = "four";
else if (digit == 5) digitName = "five";
else if (digit == 6) digitName = "six";
else if (digit == 7) digitName = "seven";
else if (digit == 8) digitName = "eight";
else if (digit == 9) digitName = "nine";
else digitName = "";
```

Using the **switch** statement has one advantage. It is obvious that all branches test the *same* value, namely **digit**.

The **switch** statement can be applied only in narrow circumstances. The test cases must be constants, and they must be integers. You cannot use a **switch** to branch on floating-point or string values. For example, the following is an error:

```
switch (name)
{  case "one": ... break; // Error
   ...
}
```

Note how every branch of the switch was terminated by a **break** instruction. If the **break** is missing, execution *falls through* to the next branch, and so on, until finally a **break** or the end of the **switch** is reached. For example, consider the following **switch** statement:

```
switch (digit)
{  case 1: System.out.print("one"); // oops—no break
   case 2: System.out.print("two"); break;
   . . .
}
```

If **digit** has the value 1, then the statement after the **case 1:** label is executed. Since there is no **break**, the statement after the **case 2:** label is executed as well. The program prints "onetwo".

There are a few cases in which this fall-through behavior is actually useful, but they are very rare. Peter van der Linden [1, p. 38] describes an analysis of the switch statements in the Sun C compiler front end. Of the 244 switch statements, each of which had an average of 7 cases, only 3 percent used the fall-through behavior. That is, the default—falling through to the next case unless stopped by a break—is *wrong 97 percent of the time.* Forgetting to type the break is an exceedingly common error, yielding wrong code.

We leave it to you to use the switch statement for your own programs or not. At any rate, you need to have a reading knowledge of switch in case you find it in the code of other programmers.

◆ Productivity Hint 5.2

Copy and Paste in the Editor

When you see code like

```
if (richter >= 8.0)
    r = "Most structures fall";
else if (richter >= 7.0)
    r = "Many buildings destroyed";
else if (richter >= 6.0)
    r = "Many buildings considerably damaged; some collapse";
else if (richter >= 4.5)
    r = "Damage to poorly constructed buildings";
else if (richter >= 3.5)
    r = "Felt by many people, no destruction";
```

you should think "copy and paste".

Make a template

```
else if (richter >= )
    r = "";
```

and copy it. That is usually done by highlighting with the mouse and then selecting Edit and then Copy from the menu bar. (If you follow Productivity Hint 3.1, you are smart and use the keyboard. Hit Shift ↓ to highlight the entire line, then Ctrl+C to copy it. Then paste it multiple times (Ctrl+V) and fill the text into the copy. Of course, your editor may use different commands, but the concept is the same.)

The ability to copy and paste is always useful when you have code from an example or another project that is similar to your current needs. To copy, paste, and modify is faster than to type everything from scratch. You are also less likely to make typing errors.

◆ Random Fact 5.1

Minicomputers and Workstations

Within 20 years after the first computers became operational, they had become indispensable for organizing the customer and financial data of every major corporation in America. Corporate data processing required a centralized computer installation and high staffing levels to ensure the round-the-clock availability of the data. These installations were enormously expensive, but they were vital to running a modern business. Major universities and large research institutions could also afford the installation of these expensive computers, but many scientific and engineering organizations and corporate divisions could not.

In the mid-1960s, when integrated circuits first became available, the cost of computers could be brought down for users who did not require as high a level of support and services (or data storage volume) as corporate data processing installations. Such users included scientists and engineers who had the expertise to operate computers. (At that time, to "operate" a computer did not just mean to turn it on. Computers came with little off-the-shelf software, and most tasks had to be programmed by the computer users.) In 1965 Digital Equipment Corporation introduced the PDP-8 *minicomputer,* housed in a single cabinet (see Figure 5) and thus small enough for departmental use. In 1978, the first 32-bit minicomputer, the VAX, was released, also by DEC. Other companies, such as Data General, brought out competing designs; the book [2] contains a fascinating description of the engineering work at Data General to bring out a machine that could compete with the VAX. Minicomputers were not just used for engineering applications, however. System integration companies would buy these machines, supply software, and resell them to smaller companies for business data processing. Minicomputers such as IBM's successful AS/400 line are still in use today, but they face stiff competition from workstations and personal computers, which are much less expensive and have increasingly powerful software.

In the early 1980s, engineering users became increasingly disenchanted with having to share computers with other users. Computers did divide up their attention among multiple users who were currently logged on, a process known as *time sharing.* However, graphical terminals were becoming available, and the fast processing of graphics was more than could be done in the allotted time slices. The technology had again advanced to the point where an entire computer could be put into a box that would fit on a desk. A new breed of manufacturers, such as Sun Microsystems, started producing *workstations* (Figure 6). These computers are used by individuals with high computing demands—for example, electronic-circuit designers, aerospace engineers, and, more recently, cartoon artists. Workstations typically run an operating system called *UNIX.* Although each workstation manufacturer had its own brand of UNIX, with slight differences in each version, it became economical for software manufacturers to produce programs that could run on several hardware platforms. This was aided by the fact that most workstation manufacturers standardized on the *X Window system* for displaying graphics.

Not all workstation manufacturers were successful. The book [3] tells the story of NeXT, a company that tried to build a workstation and failed, losing over $250 million of its investors' money in the process.

Nowadays workstations are used mainly for two distinct purposes: as fast graphics processors and as *servers* to store data such as electronic mail, sales information, or web pages.

5.3.2 Nested Branches

In the United States, different tax rates are used depending on the taxpayer's marital status. There are two main tax schedules, for single and for married taxpayers. Married taxpayers add their incomes together and pay taxes on the total. (In fact, there are two other schedules, "head of household" and "married filing separately", which we will ignore for simplicity.) Table 1 gives the tax rate computations for each of the filing categories, using the values for the 1992 federal tax return.

Figure 5
_____

A Minicomputer

Figure 6
_____

A Workstation

Table 1. Federal Tax Rate Schedule

If your filing status is Single If the taxable income is over	But not over	The tax is	Of the amount over
$ 0	$ 21,450	15%	$ 0
$ 21,450	$ 51,900	$ 3,217.50+28%	$ 21,450
$ 51,900		$ 11,743.50+31%	$ 51,900
If your filing status is Married **If the taxable income is over**	**But not over**	**The tax is**	**Of the amount over**
$ 0	$ 35,800	15%	$ 0
$ 35,800	$ 86,500	$ 5,370.00+28%	$ 35,800
$ 86,500		$ 19,566.00+31%	$ 86,500

Now let us compute the taxes due, given a filing status and an income figure. The key point is that there are two *levels* of decision making. First, we must branch on the filing status. Then, for each filing status, we must have another branch on income level.

Program Tax.java

```
public class Tax
{  public static void main(String[] args)
   {  ConsoleReader console = new ConsoleReader(System.in);

      System.out.println("Please enter your income:");
      double income = console.readDouble();

      System.out.println("Please enter S for single, "
         + "M for married:");
      String status = console.readLine();

      TaxReturn aTaxReturn = new TaxReturn(income, status);

      System.out.println("The tax is "
         + aTaxReturn.getTax());
   }
}

class TaxReturn
{  public TaxReturn(double anIncome, String aStatus)
   {  income = anIncome;
      status = aStatus;
   }
```

```java
public double getTax()
{   double tax = 0;

    final double RATE1 = 0.15;
    final double RATE2 = 0.28;
    final double RATE3 = 0.31;

    final double SINGLE_CUTOFF1 = 21450;
    final double SINGLE_CUTOFF2 = 51900;

    final double SINGLE_BASE2 = 3217.50;
    final double SINGLE_BASE3 = 11743.50;
    final double MARRIED_CUTOFF1 = 35800;
    final double MARRIED_CUTOFF2 = 86500;

    final double MARRIED_BASE2 = 5370;
    final double MARRIED_BASE3 = 19566;

    if (status.equalsIgnoreCase("S"))
    {   if (income <= SINGLE_CUTOFF1)
            tax = RATE1 * income;
        else if (income <= SINGLE_CUTOFF2)
            tax = SINGLE_BASE2
                + RATE2 * (income - SINGLE_CUTOFF1);
        else
            tax = SINGLE_BASE3
                + RATE3 * (income - SINGLE_CUTOFF2);
    }
    else
    {   if (income <= MARRIED_CUTOFF1)
            tax = RATE1 * income;
        else if (income <= MARRIED_CUTOFF2)
            tax = MARRIED_BASE2
                + RATE2 * (income - MARRIED_CUTOFF1);
        else
            tax = MARRIED_BASE3
                + RATE3 * (income - MARRIED_CUTOFF2);
    }

    return tax;
}

private double income;
private String status;
}
```

The two-level decision process is reflected in two levels of if statements. We say that the income test is *nested* inside the test for filing status. (See Figure 7 for a flowchart.) In theory, nesting can go deeper than two levels. A three-level decision process (first by state, then by status, then by income level) requires three nesting levels.

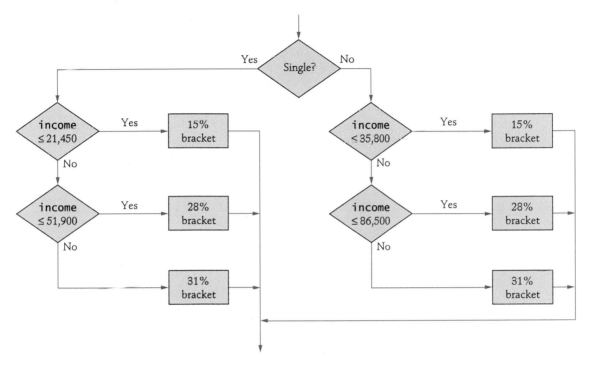

Figure 7

Income Tax Computation

Quality Tip 5.3

Prepare Test Cases Ahead of Time

Let us consider how we can test the tax computation program. Of course, we cannot try out all possible inputs of filing status and income level. Even if we could, there would be no point in trying them all. If the program correctly computes one or two tax amounts in a given bracket, then we have a good reason to believe that all amounts within that bracket will be correct. We want to aim for complete *coverage* of all cases.

There are two possibilities for the filing status and three tax brackets for each status. That makes six test cases. Then we want to test a handful of *error conditions*, such as a negative income. That makes seven test cases. For the first six we need to compute manually what answer we expect. For the remaining one, we need to know what error reports we expect. We write down the test cases and then start coding.

Should you really test seven inputs for this simple program? You certainly should. Furthermore, if you find an error in the program that wasn't covered by one of the test cases, make another test case and add it to your collection. After you fix the known mistakes, *run all test cases again*. Experience has shown that the cases that you just tried to fix are probably working now, but that errors that you fixed two or three iterations ago have a good chance of coming back! If you find that an error keeps coming back, that is usually a reliable sign that you did not fully understand some subtle interaction between features of your program.

It is always a good idea to design test cases *before* starting to code. There are two reasons for this. Working through the test cases gives you a better understanding of the algorithm that you are about to program. Furthermore, it has been noted that programmers instinctively shy away from testing fragile parts of their code. That seems hard to believe, but you will often make that observation about your own work. Watch someone else test your program. There will be times when that person enters input that makes you very nervous because you are not sure that your program can handle it, and you never dared to test it yourself. This is a well-known phenomenon, and making the test plan before writing the code offers some protection.

Productivity Hint 5.3

Make a Schedule and Make Time for Unexpected Problems

Commercial software is notorious for being delivered later than promised. For example, Microsoft originally promised that the successor to its Windows 3 operating system would be available early in 1994, then late in 1994, then in March 1995; it finally was released in August 1995. Some of the early promises might not have been realistic. It was in Microsoft's interest to let prospective customers expect the imminent availability of the product. Had customers known the actual delivery date, they might have switched to a different product in the meantime. Undeniably, though, Microsoft had not anticipated the full complexity of the tasks it had set itself to solve.

Microsoft can delay the delivery of its product, but it is likely that you cannot. As a student or a programmer, you are expected to manage your time wisely and to finish your assignments on time. You can probably do simple programming exercises the night before the due date, but an assignment that looks twice as hard may well take four times as long, because more things can go wrong. You should therefore make a schedule whenever you start a programming project.

First, estimate realistically how much time it will take you to

◆ Design the program logic
◆ Develop test cases
◆ Type the program in and fix syntax errors
◆ Test and debug the program

For example, for the income tax program I might estimate 30 minutes for the design, because it is mostly done; 30 minutes for developing test cases; one hour for data entry and fixing syntax errors; and 2 hours for testing and debugging. That is a total of 4 hours. If I work 2 hours a day on this project, it will take me two days.

Then think of things that can go wrong. Your computer might break down. The lab might be crowded. You might be stumped by a problem with the computer system. (That is a particularly important concern for beginners. It is *very* common to lose a day over a trivial problem just because it takes time to track down a person who knows the magic command to overcome it.) As a rule of thumb, *double* the time of your estimate. That is, you should start four days, not two days, before the due date. If nothing goes wrong, great; you have the program done two days early. When the inevitable problem occurs, you have a cushion of time that protects you from embarrassment and failure.

Common Error 5.2

The Dangling else Problem

When an `if` statement is nested inside another `if` statement, the following error may occur.

```
double shippingCharge = 5.00; // $ 5 inside continental U.S.
if (country.equals("USA"))
   if (state.equals("HI"))
      shippingCharge = 10.00; // Hawaii is more expensive
else // Pitfall!
   shippingCharge = 20.00; // as are foreign shipments
```

The indentation level seems to suggest that the `else` is grouped with the test `country.equals("USA")`. Unfortunately, that is not the case. The compiler ignores all indentation and follows the rule that an `else` always belongs to the closest `if`. That is, the code is actually

```
double shippingCharge = 5.00; // $ 5 inside continental U.S.
if (country.equals("USA"))
   if (state.equals("HI"))
      shippingCharge = 10.00; // Hawaii is more expensive
   else // Pitfall!
      shippingCharge = 20.00;
```

That isn't what we want. We want to group the `else` with the first `if`. For that, we must use braces.

```
double shippingCharge = 5.00; // $ 5 inside continental U.S.
if (country.equals("USA"))
{  if (state.equals("HI"))
      shippingCharge = 10.00; // Hawaii is more expensive
}
else
   shippingCharge = 20.00; // as are foreign shipments
```

To avoid having to think about the pairing of the `else`, we recommend that you *always* use a set of braces when the body of an `if` contains another `if`. In the following example, the braces are not strictly necessary, but they help clarify the code:

```
double shippingCharge = 20.00; // $ 20 for foreign shipments
if (country.equals("USA"))
{  if (state.equals("HI"))
      shippingCharge = 10.00; // Hawaii is more expensive
   else
      shippingCharge = 5.00; // $5 inside continental U.S.
}
```

The ambiguous `else` is called a *dangling* `else`, and it is enough of a syntactical blemish that some programming language designers developed an improved syntax that avoids it altogether. For example, Algol 68 uses the construction

> if *condition* then *statement* else *statement* fi;

The `else` part is optional, but since the end of the `if` statement is clearly marked, the grouping is unambiguous if there are two `if`s and only one `else`. Here are the two possible cases:

> if *c1* then if *c2* then *s1* else *s2* fi fi;

> if *c1* then if *c2* then *s1* fi else *s2* fi;

By the way, `fi` is just `if` backwards. Other languages use `endif`, which has the same purpose but is less fun.

Common Error 5.3

Forgetting to Set a Variable in Some Branches

Consider the following code:

```
double shippingCharge;
if (country.equals("USA"))
{  if (state.equals("HI"))
      shippingCharge = 10.00;
   else if (state.equals("AK"))
      shippingCharge = 8.00;
}
else
   shippingCharge = 20.00;
```

The variable `shippingCharge` is declared but left undefined because its value depends on several circumstances. It is then set in the various branches of the `if` statements. However, if the order is to be delivered inside the United States to a state other than Hawaii or Alaska, then the shipping charge is not set at all.

There are two remedies. Of course, we can check all branches of the `if` statements to make sure that each one of them sets the variable. In this example, we must add one case:

```
if (country.equals("USA"))
{  if (state.equals("HI"))
      shippingCharge = 10.00;
   else if (state.equals("AK"))
      shippingCharge = 8.00;
   else
      shippingCharge = 5.00; // within continental U.S.
}
else
   shippingCharge = 20.00;
```

The safer way is to initialize the variable with the most likely value and then have that value overwritten in the less likely situations:

```
double shippingCharge = 5.00; // within continental U.S.
if (country.equals("USA"))
{  if (state.equals("HI"))
      shippingCharge = 10.00;
   else if (state.equals("AK"))
      shippingCharge = 8.00;
}
else
   shippingCharge = 20.00;
```

That is slightly less efficient, but we are now assured that the variable is never left uninitialized.

5.4   Using Boolean Expressions

5.4.1   The boolean Type

In Java, an expression such as x < 10 has a value, just as the expression x + 10 has a value. The value of a relational expression is either **true** or **false**. For example, if x is 5, then the value of x < 10 is **true**. Try it out: The program fragment

```
int x = 5;
System.out.println(x < 10);
```

prints **true**. The values **true** and **false** are not numbers, nor are they objects of a class. They belong to a separate type, called **boolean**. The Boolean type is named after the mathematician George Boole (1815–1864), a pioneer in the study of logic.

For example, the **equals** method for comparing strings returns a value of type **boolean**.

5.4.2   The Boolean Operators

Suppose you want to test whether today is your brother's birthday. You need to compare the day and month fields of today's date and of the birthday date. Let's store today's date in integer variables **tday** and **tmonth**, and the birthday date in **bday** and **bmonth**. The test passes only if both fields match, that is, if

tday == bday *and* tmonth == bmonth

In Java you use the **&&** operator to represent the *and* to combine test conditions. That is, you can write the test as follows:

```
if (tday == bday && tmonth == bmonth)
   System.out.println("Happy Birthday!");
```

The condition of the test has two parts, joined by the **&&** (*and*) operator. If the days are equal *and* the months are equal, then it is his birthday. If either one of the fields does not match, then the test fails.

The **&&** operator combines several tests into a new test that passes only when all conditions are true. An operator that combines test conditions is called a *logical* operator.

The **||** (*or*) logical operator also combines two or more conditions. The resulting test succeeds if at least one of the conditions is true. For example, in the following test we test whether the month stored in `tmonth` is a 30-day month, that is, April, June, September, or November:

```
if (tmonth == 4 || tmonth == 6 || tmonth == 9 || tmonth == 11)
    lastDay = 30;
```

Figure 8 shows flowcharts for these examples.

You can combine both types of logical operations in one test. Let us test whether your brother's birthday already passed this year. That is the case if we are already past the birthday month, *or* if we are in that month *and* past the day.

The test condition therefore contains both an **&&** and an **||** operator:

```
if (tmonth > bmonth || (tmonth == bmonth && tday > bday))
    System.out.println("Too late to buy a gift");
```

The **&&** and **||** operators are computed using *lazy* (or *short circuit*) evaluation. In other words, logical expressions are evaluated from left to right, and evaluation stops as soon as the truth value is determined. When an *and* is evaluated and the first condition is false, then the second condition is skipped—no matter what it is, the combined

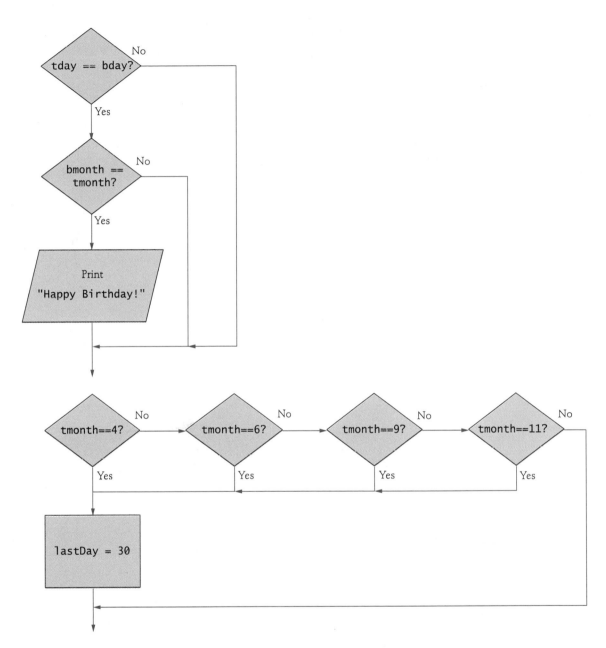

Figure 8

Flowcharts for **&&**
and || Combinations

condition must be false. When an *or* is evaluated and the first condition is true, the second condition is not evaluated, because it does not matter what the outcome of the second test is. Here is an example:

```
if (r >= 0 && -b / 2 + Math.sqrt(r) > 0) ...
```

If r is negative, then the first condition is false, and thus the combined statement is false, no matter what the outcome of the second test is. The second test is never evaluated for negative r, and there is no danger of computing the square root of a negative number.

Sometimes you need to *invert* a condition with the ! (*not*) logical operator. For example, we may want to carry out a certain action only if two strings are *not* equal:

```
if (!country.equals("USA")) shippingCharge = 50;
```

The ! operator takes a single condition and evaluates to **true** if that condition is false and to **false** if the condition is true.

Here is a summary of the three logical operations:

A	B	A && B
true	true	true
true	false	false
false	*Any*	false

A	B	A || B
true	*Any*	true
false	true	true
false	false	false

A	! A
true	false
false	true

Common Error 5.4

Multiple Relational Operators

Consider the expression

```
if (-0.5 <= x <= 0.5) ... // Error
```

This looks just like the mathematical test $-0.5 \leq x \leq 0.5$. Unfortunately, it is not.

Let us dissect the expression `-0.5 <= x <= 0.5`. The first half, `-0.5 <= x`, is a test with outcome `true` or `false`, depending on the value of x. The outcome of that test (`true` or `false`) is then compared against 0.5. This seems to make no sense. Can one compare truth values and floating-point numbers? Is `true` larger than 0.5 or not? In Java, you cannot. The Java compiler rejects this statement.

Instead, use **&&** to combine two separate tests:

```
if (-0.5 <= x && x <= 0.5) ...
```

Another common error, along the same lines, is to write

```
if (x && y > 0) ... // Error
```

to test whether x and y are both positive. Again, the Java compiler flags this construct as an error. You cannot apply the **&&** operator to floating-point numbers such as x. You need to write two Boolean expressions and join them with the **&&** operator:

```
if (x > 0 && y > 0) ...
```

Common Error 5.5

Confusing && and || Conditions

It is a surprisingly common error to confuse *and* and *or* conditions. A value lies between 0 and 100 if it is at least 0 *and* at most 100. It lies outside that range if it is less than 0 *or* greater than 100. There is no golden rule; you just have to think carefully.

Often the *and* or *or* is clearly stated, and then it isn't too hard to implement it. Sometimes, though, the wording isn't as explicit. It is quite common that the individual conditions are nicely set apart in a bulleted list, but with little indication how they should be combined. The instructions for the 1992 tax return say that you can claim single filing status if any one of the following is true:

♦ You were never married.

♦ You were legally separated or divorced on December 31, 1992.

♦ You were widowed before January 1, 1992, and did not remarry in 1992.

Since the test passes if *any one* of the conditions is true, you must combine the conditions with *or*. Elsewhere, the same instructions state that you may use the more advantageous status of married filing jointly if all five of the following conditions are true:

♦ Your spouse died in 1990 or 1991 and you did not remarry in 1992.

♦ You have a child whom you can claim as dependent.

♦ That child lived in your home for all of 1992.

♦ You paid over half the cost of keeping up your home for this child.

♦ You filed (or could have filed) a joint return with your spouse the year he or she died.

Because *all* of the conditions must be true for the test to pass, you must combine them with an *and*.

5.4.3 De Morgan's Law

Suppose we want to charge a higher shipping rate if we don't ship within the continental United States.

```
if (!(country.equals("USA")
        && !state.equals("AK")
        && !state.equals("HI")))
    shippingCharge = 20.00;
```

This test is a little bit complicated, and you have to think carefully through the logic. When it is *not* true that the country is USA *and* the state is not Alaska *and* the state is not Hawaii, then charge $20.00. Huh? It is not true that some people won't be confused by this code.

The computer doesn't care, but humans generally have a hard time comprehending logical conditions with *not* operators applied to *and/or* expressions. De Morgan's law, named after the logician Augustus de Morgan (1806–1871), can be used to simplify these Boolean expressions. De Morgan's law has two forms: one for the negation of an *and* expression and one for the negation of an *or* expression:

$$!(A\ \&\&\ B) \text{ is the same as } !A\ ||\ !\ B$$

$$!(A\ ||\ B) \text{ is the same as } !A\ \&\&!\ B$$

Pay particular attention to the fact that the *and* and *or* operators are *reversed* by moving the *not* inwards. For example, the negation of "the state is Alaska *or* it is Hawaii",

```
!((state.equals("AK") || state.equals("HI"))
```

is "the state is not Alaska *and* it is not Hawaii":

```
!state.equals("AK") && !state.equals("HI")
```

Let us apply the law to our shipping charge computation:

```
if (!(country.equals("USA")
    && !state.equals("AK")
    && !state.equals("HI")))
```

is equivalent to the simpler test

```
if (!country.equals("USA")
        || state.equals("AK")
        || state.equals("HI"))
```

To simplify conditions with negations of *and* or *or* expressions, it is usually a good idea to apply De Morgan's law to move the negations to the innermost level.

5.4.4 Using Boolean Variables

If a condition gets too complicated, it becomes difficult to understand. Because misunderstanding leads to program errors, it is helpful to simplify complex tests by breaking them up into steps. Intermediate steps are the outcomes of tests that can be true or false. Use **boolean** variables to store the outcomes of these tests, and combine those variables to obtain the values of the more complicated conditions.

Here we decide whether we must use air freight or whether we can ship by truck:

```
boolean shipByAir = false;
if (!country.equals("USA")) shipByAir = true;
else if (state.equals("AK") || state.equals("HI"))
    shipByAir = true;

if (shipByAir)
    shippingCharge = 20.00;
else
    shippingCharge = 5.00;
```

Some people like to use a string variable instead:

```
string shippingMethod = "TRUCK";
if (!country.equals("USA")) shippingMethod = "AIR";
```

There is an advantage to using a Boolean variable rather than a string. With a Boolean variable we know with certainty that it holds either **false** or **true**. With a string variable we may intend that it hold either **"AIR"** or **"TRUCK"**, but there isn't an absolute guarantee that an overworked programmer hasn't accidentally set the string to a third value such as **"GROUND"**. It is also far more efficient to use Boolean variables than strings.

Sometimes Boolean variables are called *flags* because they can have just two states: "up" and "down".

It pays to think carefully about the naming of Boolean variables. In our example, it would not be a good idea to give the name **shippingMethod** to the Boolean variable. What does it mean that the shipping method is **true**? With a name like **shipByAir** there is no ambiguity; if **shipByAir** is **true**, the order is shipped by air.

By the way, it is considered gauche to write a test such as

```
if (shipByAir == true) ...// Don't
```

Just use the simpler test

```
if (shipByAir) ...
```

In Chapter 6 we will use Boolean variables to control complex loops.

Random Fact 5.2

Artificial Intelligence

When one uses a sophisticated computer program such as a tax preparation package, one is bound to attribute some intelligence to the computer. The computer asks sensible questions and makes computations that we find a mental challenge. After all, if doing one's taxes were easy, we wouldn't need a computer to do it for us.

As programmers, however, we know that all this apparent intelligence is an illusion. Human programmers have carefully "coached" the software in all possible scenarios, and it simply replays the actions and decisions that were programmed into it.

Would it be possible to write computer programs that are genuinely intelligent in some sense? From the earliest days of computing, there was a sense that the human brain might be nothing but an immense computer, and that it might well be feasible to program computers to imitate some processes of human thought. Serious research into *artificial intelligence* began in the mid-1950s, and the first twenty years brought some impressive successes. Programs that play chess—surely an activity that appears to require remarkable intellectual powers—have become so good that they now routinely beat all but the best human players. In 1975 an *expert-system* program called Mycin gained fame for being better in diagnosing meningitis in patients than the average physician. *Theorem-proving* programs produced logically correct mathematical proofs. *Optical character recognition* software can read pages from a scanner, recognize the character shapes, including those that are blurred or smudged, and reconstruct the original document text, even restoring fonts and layout.

However, there were serious setbacks as well. From the very outset, one of the stated goals of the AI community was to produce software that could translate text from one language to another, for example from English to Russian. That undertaking proved to be enormously complicated. Human language appears to be much more subtle and interwoven with the human experience than had originally been thought. Even the grammar-checking programs that come with many word processors today are more a gimmick than a useful tool, and analyzing grammar is just the first step in translating sentences.

From 1982 to 1992, the Japanese government embarked on a massive research project, funded at over 50 billion Japanese yen. It was known as the *Fifth-Generation Project*. Its goal was to develop new hard- and software to greatly improve the performance of expert systems. At its outset, the project created great fear in other countries that the Japanese computer industry was about to become the undisputed leader in the field. However, the end results were disappointing and did little to bring artificial intelligence applications to market.

One reason that artificial intelligence programs have not performed as well as it was hoped seems to be that they simply don't know as much as humans do. In the early 1990s, Douglas Lenat and his colleagues decided to do something about it and initiated the CYC project (from encyclopedia), an effort to codify the implicit assumptions that underly human speech and writing. The team members started out analyzing news articles and asked themselves what unmentioned facts are necessary to actually understand the sentences. For example, consider the sentence "Last fall she enrolled in Michigan State." The reader automatically realizes that "fall" is not related to falling down in this context, but refers to the season. While there is a State of Michigan, here Michigan State denotes the university. A priori, a computer program has none of this knowledge. The goal of the CYC project was to extract and store the requisite facts—that is, (1) people enroll in universities; (2) Michigan is a state; (3) a state X is likely to have a university named X State University, often abbreviated as X *State*; (4) most people enroll in a university in the fall. In 1995, the project had codified about 100,000 common-sense concepts and about a million facts of knowledge relating them. Even this massive amount of data has not proven sufficient for useful applications.

Successful artificial intelligence programs, such as chess-playing programs, do not actually imitate human thinking. They are just very fast in exploring many scenarios and have been tuned to recognize those cases that do not warrant further investigation. *Neural networks* are interesting exceptions: coarse simulations of the neuron cells in animal and human brains. Suitably interconnected cells appear to be able to "learn". For example, if a network of cells is presented with letter shapes, it can be trained to identify them. After a lengthy training period, the network can recognize letters, even if they are slanted, distorted, or smudged.

When artificial intelligence programs are successful, they can raise serious ethical issues. There are now programs that can scan résumés, select those that look promising, and show only those to a human for further analysis. How would you feel if you knew that your résumé had been rejected by a computer, perhaps on a technicality, and that you never had a chance to be interviewed? When computers are used for credit analysis, and the analysis software has been designed to deny credit systematically to certain groups of people (say, all applicants with certain ZIP codes), is that illegal discrimination? What if the software has not been designed in this fashion, but a neural network has "discovered" a pattern from historical data? These are troubling questions, especially since those that are harmed by such processes have little recourse.

Chapter Summary

1. The **if** statement lets a program carry out different actions depending on the nature of the data to be processed.

2. The **if** statement evaluates a *condition*. Conditions can contain comparisons of numbers or strings, Boolean values, and combinations thereof, using the **&&**, **||**, and **!** Boolean operators.

3. When comparing floating-point numbers, you must usually check whether they are *close enough*, by comparing the absolute value of their difference against a small number.

4. Do not use the **==** operator to compare strings. Use the **equals** and **compareTo** methods instead. The **compareTo** method compares strings in lexicographical order.

5. The **==** operator tests whether two object references are identical. To compare the contents of objects, you need to use the **equals** method.

6. Multiple conditions can be combined to evaluate complex decisions. The correct arrangement depends on the logic of the problem to be solved.

7. Complex combinations of conditions can be simplified by storing intermediate condition outcomes in Boolean variables or by applying De Morgan's law.

Further Reading

[1] Peter van der Linden, *Expert C Programming,* Prentice-Hall, 1994.

[2] Tracy Kidder, *The Soul of a New Machine,* Little, Brown and Co., 1981.

[3] Randall E. Stross, *Steven Jobs and the NeXT Big Thing,* Atheneum, 1993.

[4] William H. Press et al., *Numerical Recipes in C,* Cambridge, 1988.

Classes, Objects, and Methods Introduced in This Chapter

```
java.lang.Object
    equals
java.lang.String
    equalsIgnoreCase
    compareTo
```

Review Exercises

Exercise R5.1. Find the errors in the following `if` statements.

```
if quarters > 0 then System.out.println(quarters + " quarters");

if (1 + x > Math.pow(x, Math.sqrt(2)) y = y + x;

if (x = 1) y++; else if (x = 2) y = y + 2;

if (x && y == 0) p = new Point2D.Double(x, y);

if (1 <= x <= 10)
{  System.out.println("Enter y:");
   y = console.readDouble();
}

if (s != "nickels" || s != "pennies"
   || s != "dimes" || s != "quarters")
   System.out.print("Input error!");

if (input.equalsIgnoreCase("N") || "NO")
   return;

int x = console.readDouble();
if (x != null) y = y + x;

language = "English";
if (country.equals("USA"))
   if (state.equals("PR")) language = "Spanish";
else if (country.equals("China"))
   language = "Chinese";
```

Exercise R5.2. Explain the following terms, and give an example for each construct:

Expression

Condition

Statement

Simple statement

Compound statement

Block

Exercise R5.3. Explain the difference between an if/else /else statement and nested if statements. Give an example for each.

Exercise R5.4. Give an example for an if/else /else statement where the order of the tests does not matter. Give an example where the order of the tests matters.

Exercise R5.5. Of the following pairs of strings, which comes first in lexicographic order?

```
"Tom", "Dick"
"Tom", "Tomato"
"church", "Churchill"
"car manufacturer", "carburetor"
"Harry", "hairy"
"C++", " Car"
"Tom", "Tom"
"Car", "Carl"
"car", "bar"
```

Exercise R5.6. Complete the following truth table by finding the truth values of the Boolean expressions for all combinations of the Boolean inputs p, q, and r.

p	q	r	(p && q) || ! r	! (p && (q || !r))
false	false	false		
false	false	true		
false	true	false		
. . .				
5 more combinations				
. . .				

Exercise R5.7. Before implementing any complex algorithm, it is a good idea to understand and analyze it. The purpose of this exercise is to gain a better understanding of the tax computation algorithm.

Some people object to the fact that the tax rates increase with higher incomes, claiming that certain taxpayers are then better off *not* to work hard and get a raise, since they would then have to pay a higher tax rate and actually end up with less money after taxes. Can you find such an income level, and if not, why not?

Another feature of the tax code is the *marriage penalty.* Under certain circumstances, a married couple pays higher taxes than the sum of what the two partners would pay if they both were single. Find examples for such income levels.

Exercise R5.8. True or false? *A* && *B* is the same as *B* && *A* for any Boolean conditions *A* and *B*.

Exercise R5.9. Explain the difference between

```
s = 0;
if (x > 0) s++;
if (y > 0) s++;
```

and

```
s = 0;
if (x > 0) s++;
else if (y > 0) s++;
```

Exercise R5.10. Use De Morgan's law to simplify the following Boolean expressions.

```
!(x > 0 && y > 0)
```

```
!(x != 0 || y != 0)
```

```
!(country.equals("USA") && !state.equals("HI")
    && !state.equals("AK"))
```

```
!(x % 4 != 0 || !(x % 100 == 0 && x % 400 == 0))
```

Exercise R5.11. Make up another Java code example that shows the dangling-`else` problem, using the following statement. A student with a GPA of at least 1.5, but less than 2, is on probation. With less than 1.5, the student is failing.

Exercise R5.12. Explain the difference between the `==` operator and the `equals` method when comparing strings.

Exercise R5.13. Explain the difference between the tests

```
r == s
```

and

```
r.equals(s)
```

where both `r` and `s` are of type `Rectangle`.

Exercise R5.14. What is wrong with this test to see whether r is `null`? What happens when this code runs?

```
Rectangle r;
. . .
if (r.equals(null))
    r = new Rectangle(5, 10, 20, 30);
```

Exercise R5.15. Explain how the lexicographic ordering of strings differs from the ordering of words in a dictionary or telephone book. *Hint:* Consider strings like `IBM`, `horstmann.com`, `Century 21`, `While-U-Wait`.

Exercise R5.16. Write Java code to test whether two objects of type `Line2D.Double` represent the same line when displayed on the graphics screen. *Do not* use `a.equals(b)`.

```
Line2D.Double a;
Line2D.Double b;

if (your condition goes here)
    g2.drawString("They look the same!", x, y);
```

Hint: If p and q are points, then `Line2D.Double(p, q)` and `Line2D.Double(q, p)` look the same.

Exercise R5.17. Explain why it is more difficult to compare floating-point numbers than integers. Write Java code to test whether an integer n equals 10 and whether a floating-point number x equals 10.

Exercise R5.18. Give an example for two floating-point numbers x and y such that `Math.abs(x - y)` is larger than 1000, but x and y are still identical except for a roundoff error.

Exercise R5.19. Give a set of test cases for the tax program in Section 5.3.2. Compute the expected results manually.

Exercise R5.20. Consider the following test to see whether a point falls inside a rectangle.

```
Point2D.Double p = . . .
boolean xInside = false;
if (x1 <= p.getX() && p.getX() <= x2)
    xInside = true;
boolean yInside = false;
if (y1 <= p.getY() && p.getY() <= y2)
    yInside = true;
if (xInside && yInside)
    g2.drawString("p is inside the rectangle.", x1, y1);
```

Rewrite this code to eliminate the explicit `true` and `false` values, by setting `xInside` and `yInside` to the values of Boolean expressions.

Programming Exercises

Exercise P5.1. Write a program that prints all real solutions to the quadratic equation $ax^2 + bx + c = 0$. Read in a, b, c and use the quadratic formula. If the *discriminant* $b^2 - 4ac$ is negative, display a message stating that there are no real solutions.

Exercise P5.2. Write a program that takes user input describing a playing card in the following shorthand notation:

A	Ace
2...10	Card values
J	Jack
Q	Queen
K	King
D	Diamonds
H	Hearts
S	Spades
C	Clubs

Your program should print the full description of the card. For example,

```
Enter the card notation:
QS
Queen of spades
```

Exercise P5.3. As in the `Intersect` program, compute and plot the intersection of a line and a circle. However, if the line and the circle do not intersect, do not plot the intersection points but display a message instead.

Exercise P5.4. Write a program that reads in three floating-point numbers and prints the largest of the three inputs. For example:

```
Please enter three numbers:
4 9 2.5
The largest number is 9.
```

Exercise P5.5. Write a program that draws a circle with radius 100 and center (110, 120). Ask the user to specify the x- and y- coordinates of a point. If the point lies inside the circle, then show a message "Congratulations." Otherwise, show a message "You missed."

Exercise P5.6. Write a graphics program that asks the user to specify the radii of two circles. The first circle has center (100, 200), and the second circle has center (200, 100). Draw the circles. If they intersect, then display a message "Circles intersect". Otherwise, display "Circles don't intersect". *Hint:* Compute the distance between the centers and compare it to the radii. Your program should draw nothing if the user enters a negative radius.

Exercise P5.7. Write a program that prints the question "Do you want to continue?" and reads a user input. If the user input is "Y," "Yes," "OK," "Sure", or "Why not?", print out "OK." If the user input is "N" or "No," then print out "Terminating." Otherwise, print "Bad input." The case of the user input should not matter. For example, "y" or "yes" are also valid inputs. *Hint:* Convert the user input to lowercase and then compare.

Exercise P5.8. Write a program that translates a letter grade into a number grade. Letter grades are A B C D F, possibly followed by + or –. Their numeric values are

4, 3, 2, 1, and 0. There is no F+ or F-. A + increases the numeric value by 0.3, a – decreases it by 0.3. However, an A+ has value 4.0.

```
Enter a letter grade:
B-
The numeric value is 2.7.
```

Exercise P5.9. Write a program that translates a number between 0 and 4 into the closest letter grade. For example, the number 2.8 (which might have been the average of several grades) would be converted to B-. Break ties in favor of the better grade; for example, 2.85 should be a B.

Exercise P5.10. Write a program that reads in three strings and sorts them lexicographically.

```
Enter three strings:
Charlie Able Baker
Able
Baker
Charlie
```

Exercise P5.11. If you look at the tax tables in Section 4.6, you will note that the percentages 15%, 28%, and 31% are identical for both single and married taxpayers, but the cutoffs for the tax brackets are different. Married people get to pay 15% on their first $35,800, then pay 28% on the next $50,700, and 31% on the remainder. Single people pay 15% on their first $21,450, then pay 28% on the next $30,450, and 31% on the remainder. Write a tax program with the following logic. Set variables `cutoff1` and `cutoff2` that depend on the marital status. Then have a single formula that computes the tax, depending on the incomes and the cutoffs. Verify that your results are identical to that of the Tax.java program.

Exercise P5.12. A year with 366 days is called a leap year. A year is a leap year if it is divisible by 4 (for example, 1980), except that it is not a leap year if it is divisible by 100 (for example, 1900); however, it is a leap year if it is divisible by 400 (for example, 2000). There were no exceptions before the introduction of the Gregorian calendar on October 15, 1582 (for example, 1500 was a leap year). Write a program that asks the user for a year and computes whether that year is a leap year.

Exercise P5.13. Write a program that asks the user to enter a month (1 = January, 2 = February, and so on) and then prints the number of days of the month. For February, print "28 or 29 days."

```
Enter a month:
5
30 days
```

Exercise P5.14. Write a program that reads in two floating-point numbers and tests whether they are the same up to two decimal places. Here are two sample runs.

```
Enter two floating-point numbers:
2.0 1.99998
They are the same up to two decimal places.

Enter two floating-point numbers:
2.0 1.98999
They are different.
```

Exercise P5.15. Enhance the BankAccount class of Chapter 3 by

1. Rejecting negative amounts in the deposit and withdraw methods
2. Rejecting withdrawals that would result in a negative balance

Exercise P5.16. Write a program that reads in the name and hourly wage of an employee. Then ask how many hours the employee worked in the past week. Be sure to accept fractional hours. Compute the pay. Any overtime work (over 40 hours per week) is paid at 150 percent of the regular wage. Print a paycheck for the employee.

Exercise P5.17. Write a unit conversion program using the conversion factors of Table 1 in Chapter 2. Ask the users from which unit they want to convert (fl.oz, gal, oz, lb, in, ft, mi) and which unit they want to convert to (ml, l, g, kg, mm, cm, m, km). Reject incompatible conversions (such as gal to km). Ask for the value to be converted, then display the result:

```
Convert from?
gal
Convert to?
ml
Value?
2.5
2.5 gal = 9462.5 ml
```

Iteration

Chapter Goals

- ◆ To be able to program Loops with the `while`, `for`, and `do` statements
- ◆ To learn how to read input from the console and from a file through redirection
- ◆ To learn how to read string input
- ◆ To implement simulations
- ◆ To avoid infinite loops and off-by-one errors
- ◆ To understand nested loops

6.1   while **Loops**

Recall the investment problem from Chapter 1. You put $10,000 into a bank account that earns 5 percent interest per year. How many years does it take for the account balance to be double the original?

In Java, the `while` statement implements such a repetition. The code

```
while (condition)
     statement
```

keeps executing the statement while the condition is true. Most commonly, the statement is a block statement, that is, a set of statements delimited by { ... }.

Here is the program that solves our investment problem:

Program DoubleInv.java

```
public class DoubleInv
{  public static void main(String[] args)
   {  ConsoleReader console = new ConsoleReader(System.in);

      System.out.println("Interest rate:");
      double rate = console.readDouble();

      System.out.println("Initial balance:");
      double initialBalance = console.readDouble();

      int year = 0;
      double balance = initialBalance;

      // keep accumulating interest until balance doubles

      while (balance < 2 * initialBalance)
      {  year++;
         double interest = balance * rate / 100;
         balance = balance + interest;
      }

      System.out.println("The investment doubled after "
         + year + " years.");
   }
}
```

A `while` statement is often called a *loop*. If you draw a flowchart, you will see that the control loops backwards to the test after every iteration (see Figure 1).

The following loop,

```
while (true)
{  body
}
```

Java Syntax
6.1 The while **Statement**

while (*condition*)
    statement

Example:

```
while (balance < 2 * initialBalance)
{  year++;
   double interest = balance * rate / 100;
   balance = balance + interest;
}
```

Purpose:
To execute a statement while a condition is true

Figure 1

Flowchart of a while Loop

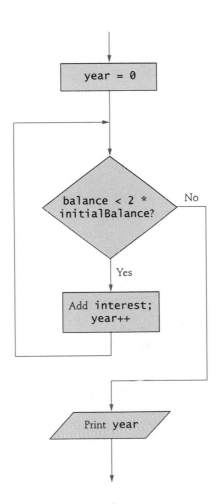

executes the *body* over and over, without ever terminating. Whoa! Why would you want that? The program would never stop. There are two reasons. Some programs indeed never stop; the software controlling an automated teller machine, a telephone switch, or a microwave oven doesn't ever stop (at least not until the device is turned off). Our programs are not usually of that kind, but even if you can't terminate the loop, you can exit from the method that contains it. This can be helpful when the termination test naturally falls into the middle of the loop (see Advanced Topic 6.3).

Common Error 6.1

Infinite Loops

The most annoying loop error is an infinite loop: a loop that runs forever and can be stopped only by killing the program or restarting the computer. If there are output statements in the loop, then reams and reams of output flash by on the screen. Otherwise, the program just sits there and *hangs,* seeming to do nothing. On some systems you can kill a hanging program by hitting Ctrl+Break or Ctrl+C. On others, you can close the window in which the program runs.

A common reason for infinite loops is forgetting to advance the variable that controls the loop:

```
int year = 0;
while (year < 20)
{  double interest = balance * rate / 100;
   balance = balance + interest;
}
```

Here the programmer forgot to add a **year++** command in the loop. As a result, the year always stays 0, and the loop never comes to an end.

Another common reason for an infinite loop is accidentally incrementing a counter that should be decremented (or vice versa). Consider this example:

```
int year = 20;
while (year > 0)
{  year++; // Oops, should have been year--
   double interest = balance * rate / 100;
   balance = balance + interest;
}
```

The **year** variable really should have been decremented, not incremented. This is a common error, because incrementing counters is so much more common than decrementing that your fingers may type the ++ on autopilot. As a consequence, **year** is always larger than 0, and the loop never terminates. (Actually, eventually **year** will exceed the largest representable positive integer and *wrap around* to a negative number. Then the loop exits—of course, that takes a long time, and the result is completely wrong.)

6.2   for Loops

Far and away the most common loop has the form

```
i = start ;
while (i <= end )
{   . . .
    i++;
}
```

Because this loop is so common, there is a special form for it that emphasizes the pattern:

```
for (i = start ; i <= end ; i++)
{   . . .
}
```

You can also *define* the loop counter variable inside the **for** loop header. That is a convenient shorthand. It restricts the use of the variable to the body of the loop.

```
for (int i = start ; i <= end ; i++)
{   . . .
}
```

Here is a program that prints out the growth of an investment over 20 years:

Program Invest.java

```
public class Invest
{   public static void main(String[] args)
    {   ConsoleReader console = new ConsoleReader(System.in);

        System.out.println("Interest rate:");
        double rate = console.readDouble();

        final double INITIAL_BALANCE = 10000;
        final int NYEARS = 20;

        double balance = INITIAL_BALANCE;

        // accumulate interest for NYEARS

        for (int year = 1; year <= NYEARS; year++)
        {   double interest = balance * rate / 100;
            balance = balance + interest;
            System.out.println("year: " + year +
                " balance: " + balance);
        }
    }
}
```

Figure 2 shows the corresponding flowchart.

Java Syntax

6.2 The for Statement

```
for (initialization ; condition ; update)
    statement
```

Example:

```
for (i = 1; i <= 20; i++)
{  double interest = balance * rate / 100;
   balance = balance + interest;
}
```

Purpose:

To execute an initialization, then keep executing
a statement and updating an expression while a
condition is true

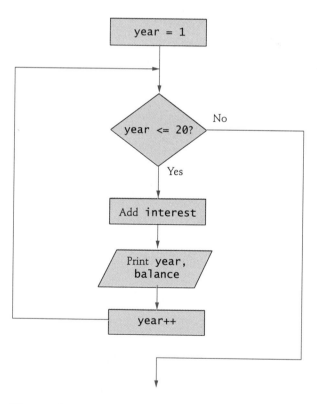

Figure 2

Flowchart of a **for** Loop

The three slots in the **for** header can contain any three expressions. You can count down instead of up:

```
for (year = 20; year > 0; year--)
```

The increment or decrement need not be in steps of 1:

```
for (x = -10; x <= 10; x = x + 0.5) . . .
```

It is possible—but a sign of unbelievably bad taste—to put unrelated conditions into the loop:

```
for (rate = 6; year-- > 0; System.out.println(balance))
     . . . // Bad taste
```

We won't even begin to decipher what that might mean; look in Feuer [1] for puzzles of this kind. You should stick with **for** loops that initialize, test, and update a single variable.

Quality Tip 6.1

Use for Loops for Their Intended Purpose Only

A **for** loop is an *idiom* for a **while** loop of a particular form. A counter runs from the start to the end, with a constant increment:

```
for (set counter to start; test whether counter at end;
        update counter by increment)
{  . . .
     // counter, start, end, increment not changed here
}
```

If your loop doesn't match this pattern, don't use the **for** construction. The compiler won't prevent you from writing idiotic **for** loops:

```
// bad style—unrelated header expressions
for (System.out.println("Inputs:");
        (x = console.readDouble()) > 0;
        sum = sum + x)
    count++;

for (year = 1; year <= 20; year++)
{  // bad style—modifies counter

    if (balance >= 2 * initialBalance)
        year = 20;
    else
    {  double interest = balance * rate / 100;
        balance = balance + interest;
    }
}
```

These loops will work, but they are plainly bad style. Use a **while** loop for iterations that do not fit into the **for** pattern.

Advanced Topic 6.1

Scope of Variables Defined in a for Loop Header

It is legal in Java to declare a variable in the header of a **for** loop. Here is the most common form of this syntax:

```
for (int year = 1; year <= 10; year++)
{  . . .
}
```

```
// year no longer defined here
```

The scope of the variables extends to the end of the **for** loop. That means, **year** is no longer defined after the loop ends. If you need to use the value of the variable beyond the end of the loop, then you need to define it outside the loop. In this loop, you don't need the value of **year**—you know it is 10 when the loop is finished. (Actually, that is not quite true—it is possible to break out of a loop before its end; see Advanced Topic 6.3). When you have two or more exit conditions, though, you may still need the variable. For example, consider the loop

```
for (int year = 1; balance < 2 * initialBalance && year <= 10;
    year++)
{  . . .
}
```

You want the balance to double, but you are only willing to wait ten years. If the balance doubled earlier, you may want to know the value of **year**. Therefore, in this case, it is not appropriate to define the variable in the loop header.

Note that the variables named **i** in the following pair of **for** loops are independent:

```
public static void main(String[] args)
{  for (int i = 1; i <= 10; i++)
      System.out.println(i * i);
   for (int i = 1; i <= 10; i++) // not a redefinition of i
      System.out.println(i * i * i);
}
```

You can declare multiple variables, as long as they are of the same type, and you can include multiple update expressions, separated by commas:

```
for (int i = 0, j = 10; i <= 10; i++, j--)
{  . . .
}
```

However, many people find it confusing if a **for** loop controls more than one variable. We recommend that you don't use this form of the **for** statement (see Quality Tip 6.1). Instead, make the **for** loop control a single counter, and update the other variable explicitly:

```
    int j = 10;
    for (int i = 0; i <= 10; i++) `
    {  . . .
       j--;
    }
```

6.3   do **Loops**

Sometimes you want to execute the body of a loop at least once and perform the loop test after the body was executed. The **do** loop serves that purpose:

> **do**
>> *statement*
> **while** (*condition*);

The *statement* is executed while the *condition* is true. Since the condition is tested after the statement is executed, the statement is executed at least once.

For example, suppose you want to make sure that a user enters a positive number. As long as the user enters a negative number or zero, just keep prompting for a correct input. In this situation, a **do** loop makes sense because you need to get a user input before you can test it.

```
    do
    {  System.out.println("Please enter an interest rate (> 0):");
       rate = console.readDouble();
    } while (rate <= 0);
```

See Figure 3 for a flowchart.

Figure 3

Flowchart of a **do** Loop

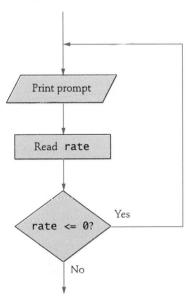

Java Syntax

6.3 The do Statement

```
do
    statement
while (condition );
```

Example:

```
do
{  System.out.println("Please enter an interest rate (> 0):");
   rate = console.readDouble();
} while (rate <= 0);
```

Purpose:

To execute a statement once and then keep executing it as long as a condition is true

Like a **for** loop, a **do** loop can always be replaced by a **while** loop. Here we initialize **rate** with an artificial value to ensure that the test passes the first time around:

```
double rate = -1;
while (rate <= 0)
{  System.out.println("Please enter an interest rate (> 0):");
   rate = console.readDouble();
}
```

This artificial choice is not good style, and it is best to use a **do** loop in this case.

Common Error 6.2

Off–by–1 Errors

Consider our computation of the number of years that are required to double an investment:

```
int year = 0;
while (balance < 2 * initialBalance)
{  year++;
   double interest = balance * rate / 100;
   balance = balance + interest;
}
System.out.println("The investment doubled after "
   + year + " years.");
```

Should **year** start at 0 or at 1? Should you test for **balance < 2 * initialBalance** or for **balance <= 2 * initialBalance**? It is easy to be *off by 1* in these expressions.

Some people try to solve off-by-1 errors by randomly inserting + 1 or – 1 until the program seems to work. That is, of course, a terrible strategy. It can take a long time to compile and test all the various possibilities. Expending a small amount of mental effort is a real time saver.

Fortunately, off-by-1 errors are easy to avoid, simply by thinking through a couple of test cases and using the information from the test cases to come up with a rationale for your decisions.

Should **year** start at 0 or at 1? Look at a scenario with simple values: an initial balance of $100 and an interest rate of 50%. After year 1, the balance is $150, and after year 2 it is $225, or over $200. So the investment doubled after 2 years. The loop executed two times, incrementing **year** each time. Hence **year** must start at 0, not at 1.

In other words, the **balance** variable denotes the balance *after* the end of the year. At the outset, the **balance** variable contains the balance after year 0 and not after year 1.

Next, should you use a < or <= comparison in the test? That is harder to figure out, because it is rare for the balance to be exactly twice the initial balance. Of course, there is one case when this happens, namely when the interest is 100%. The loop executes once. Now **year** is 1, and **balance** is exactly equal to **2 * initialBalance**. Has the investment doubled after one year? It has. Therefore, the loop should *not* execute again. If the test condition is **balance < 2 * initialBalance**, the loop stops, as it should. If the test condition had been **balance <= 2 * initialBalance**, the loop would have executed once more.

In other words, you keep adding interest while the balance *has not yet doubled*.

Common Error 6.3

Forgetting a Semicolon

It occasionally happens that all the work of a loop is already done in the loop header. Suppose you ignored Quality Tip 6.1. Then you could write the investment doubling loop as follows:

```
for (year = 1; (balance = balance
    + balance * rate / 100) < 2 * initialBalance; year++)
    ;
System.out.println("The investment doubled after "
    + year + " years.");
```

The body of the **for** loop is completely empty, containing just one empty statement terminated by a semicolon.

If you do run into a loop without a body, it is important that you really make sure the semicolon is not forgotten. If the semicolon is accidentally omitted, then the code repeats the print statement multiple times.

```
for (year = 1; (balance = balance
    + balance * rate / 100) < 2 * initialBalance; year++)
System.out.println("The investment doubled after "
    + year + " years.");
```

To make the semicolon really stand out, place it on a line all by itself, as shown in the first example.

Common Error 6.4

A Semicolon Too Many

What does the following loop print?

```
sum = 0;
for (i = 1; i <= 10; i++);
    sum = sum + i;
System.out.println(sum);
```

Of course, this loop is supposed to compute $1 + 2 + \cdots + 10 = 55$. But actually, the print statement prints 11!

Why 11? Have another look. Did you spot the semicolon at the end of the **for** loop? This loop really is a loop with an empty body.

```
for (i = 1; i <= 10; i++)
    ;
```

The loop does nothing ten times, and when it is finished, **sum** is still 0 and i is 11. Then the statement

```
sum = sum + i;
```

is executed, and **sum** is 11. The statement was indented, which fools the human reader. But the compiler pays no attention to indentation.

Of course, the semicolon at the end of the statement was a typing error. Someone's fingers were so used to typing a semicolon at the end of every line that a semicolon was added to the **for** loop by accident. The result was a loop with an empty body.

Quality Tip 6.2

Don't Use != to Test the End of a Range

Here is a loop with a hidden danger:

```
for (i = 1; i != nyear; i++)
{ . . .
}
```

The test i != nyear is a poor idea. What would happen if **nyear** happened to be negative? Of course, **nyear** should never be negative, because it makes no sense to have a negative number of years—but the impossible and unthinkable do happen with distressing regularity. If **nyear** is negative, the test i != nyear is never false, because i starts at 1 and increases with every step. The program dies in an infinite loop.

The remedy is simple. Test

```
for (i = 0; i < nyear; i++) . . .
```

For floating-point values, there is another reason not to use !=: Because of roundoff errors, the exact termination point may never be reached.

Of course, you would never write

```
for (rate = 5; rate != 10; rate = rate + 0.3333333) . . .
```

because it is highly unlikely that **rate** would match 10 exactly after 15 steps. But the same problem may happen for the harmless-looking

```
for (rate = 5; rate != 10; rate = rate + 0.1) . . .
```

The number 0.1 is exactly representable in the decimal system, but the computer represents floating-point numbers in binary. There is a slight error in any finite binary representation of 1/10, just as there is a slight error in a decimal representation 0.3333333 of 1/3. Maybe **rate** is exactly 10 after 50 steps; maybe it is off by a tiny amount. There is no point in taking chances. Just use < instead of !=:

```
for (rate = 5; rate < 10; rate = rate + 0.1) . . .
```

Random Fact 6.1

Spaghetti Code

In this chapter we used flowcharts to illustrate the behavior of the loop statements. It used to be common to draw flowcharts for every method, on the theory that flowcharts are easier to read and write than the actual code. Nowadays, flowcharts are no longer routinely used for program development and documentation.

Flowcharts have one fatal flaw. Although it is possible to express the **while**, **for**, and **do** loops with flowcharts, it is also possible to draw flowcharts that cannot be programmed with loops. Consider the chart in Figure 4. The top of the flowchart is simply a statement

```
year = 1;
```

The lower part is a **do** loop:

```
do
{  year++;
   double interest = balance * rate / 100;
   balance = balance + interest;
} while (balance < 2 * initialBalance);
```

But how can you join these two parts? According to the flowchart, you are supposed to jump from the first statement into the middle of the loop, skipping the first statement.

```
year = 1;
goto a; // not an actual Java statement
do
{  year++;
   a:
```

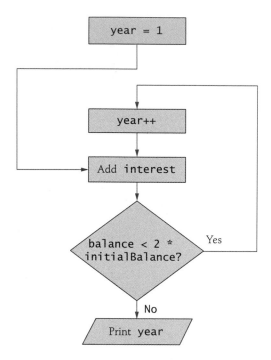

Figure 4

Spaghetti Code

```
    double interest = balance * rate / 100;
    balance = balance + interest;
} while (balance < 2 * initialBalance);
```

In fact, why even bother with the **do** loop? Here is a faithful interpretation of the flowchart:

```
year = 1;
goto a; // not an actual Java statement
b:
year++;
a:
double interest = balance * rate / 100;
balance = balance + interest;
if (balance < 2 * initialBalance) goto b;
```

This *nonlinear* control flow turns out to be extremely hard to read and understand if you have more than one or two **goto** statements. Because the lines denoting the **goto** statements weave back and forth in complex flowcharts, the resulting code is named *spaghetti code*.

In 1968 the influential computer scientist Edsger Dijkstra wrote a famous note, entitled "Goto statements considered harmful" [2], in which he argued for the use of loops instead of unstructured jumps. Initially, many programmers who had been using **goto** for years were mortally insulted and dug out examples where the use of **goto** does lead to clearer or faster

◆
◆   code. Some languages offer weaker forms of **goto** that are less harmful, such as the **break**
◆   statement in Java, discussed in Advanced Topic 6.3. Nowadays, most computer scientists ac-
     cept Dijkstra's argument and fight bigger battles than optimal loop design.

6.4   Nested Loops

Let us print a table that lists the values of the powers x^y for all x between 1 and 10
and y between 1 and 8:

```
 1   1    1     1      1       1        1         1
 2   4    8    16     32      64      128       256
 3   9   27    81    243     729     2187      6561
 4  16   64   256   1024    4096    16384     65536
 5  25  125   625   3125   15625    78125    390625
 6  36  216  1296   7776   46656   279936   1679616
 7  49  343  2401  16807  117649   823543   5764801
 8  64  512  4096  32768  262144  2097152  16777216
 9  81  729  6561  59049  531441  4782969  43046721
10 100 1000 10000 100000 1000000 10000000 100000000
```

The basic idea is simple. You have to print ten rows:

```
for (int x = 1; x <= 10; x++)
{  // print table row
   . . .
}
```

How do you print a table row? You need to print the values $x^1, x^2, \ldots, x^8$. You need
to program another loop:

```
for (int y = 1; y <= 8; y++)
{  int p = (int)Math.pow(x, y);
   System.out.print(p + " ");
}
System.out.println();
```

This loop prints a table row, including the newline at the end. Putting both loops
together yields two *nested loops*:

```
for (int x = 1; x <= 10; x++)
{  // print table row

   for (int y = 1; y <= 8; y++)
   {  int p = (int)Math.pow(x, y);
      System.out.print(p + " ");
   }
   System.out.println();
}
```

The pair of loops prints the following table:

```
1 1 1 1 1 1 1 1
2 4 8 16 32 64 128 256
3 9 27 81 243 729 2187 6561
4 16 64 256 1024 4096 16384 65536
5 25 125 625 3125 15625 78125 390625
6 36 216 1296 7776 46656 279936 1679616
7 49 343 2401 16807 117649 823543 5764801
8 64 512 4096 32768 262144 2097152 16777216
9 81 729 6561 59049 531441 4782969 43046721
10 100 1000 10000 100000 1000000 10000000 100000000
```

Ugh, this looks terrible. The columns don't line up. This is a common problem when printing columns of numbers. To solve it, convert each value into a string and keep adding spaces until the string has the desired length. Then print the padded string.

```java
String pstr = "" + p;
```

```java
// pad with spaces
```

```java
while (pstr.length() < COLUMN_WIDTH)
    pstr = " " + pstr;
```

```java
System.out.print(pstr);
```

Here is the complete program:

Program Table.java

```java
public class Table
{  public static void main(String[] args)
    {   final int COLUMN_WIDTH = 10;

        for (int x = 1; x <= 10; x++)
        {   // print table row

            for (int y = 1; y <= 8; y++)
            {   int p = (int)Math.pow(x, y);

                // convert value to string

                String pstr = "" + p;
                // pad with spaces

                while (pstr.length() < COLUMN_WIDTH)
                    pstr = " " + pstr;

                System.out.print(pstr);
            }
            System.out.println();
        }
    }
}
```

Now you have a total of three nested loops! The outer **for** loop executes 10 times. In each iteration, the inner **for** loop runs 8 times. Therefore, a total of 80 values are computed. For each of these values, the **while** loop is executed to pad the result string.

6.5 Processing Input

6.5.1 Reading a Set of Numbers

Suppose you want to process a set of numbers, for example a set of measurements, to compute some property of the data set such as the average or the maximum value. Let us assume that the numbers are input a line at a time. When reading input in this form, the challenge is to detect the *end* of the input. To solve this problem, you can use the **readLine** method of the **ConsoleReader** class (or the standard **BufferedReader** class). This method returns one line of input, or a **null** string at the end of input.

This loop reads through input data:

```
boolean done = false;
while (!done)
{  String line = console.readLine();
   if (line == null)
      done = true;
   else
   {  process data
   }
}
```

This loop is a little different from the ones you saw before, because the test condition is a variable **done**. That variable stays **false** until you reach the end of the input data; then it is set to **true**. The next time the loop starts at the top, **done** is **true**, and the loop exits.

There is a reason for using a variable. The test for loop termination, **line == null**, occurs in the *middle* of the loop, not at the top or the bottom. You must first try to read a number before you know whether the test succeeds. In Java, there isn't a ready-made control structure for the pattern "do work, then test, then do more work". Therefore, use a combination of a **while** loop and a **boolean** variable. This pattern is sometimes called "loop and a half". Some programmers find it clumsy to introduce a control variable for such a loop. Advanced Topic 6.2 shows a number of alternatives.

Let us put this loop to work to write a simple program that computes the average of a set of measurements. You should read the input values as strings, not as numbers. The reason is that the **readLine** method returns a **null** string at the end of input, allowing us to detect when the end of the data set has been reached. (Note that a **null** string is *not the same* as an empty string "". If the user enters a blank line, then **readLine** returns an empty string.)

You read the input as a string, but you want to interpret it as a number. Therefore, you must use the `Integer.parseInt` or `Double.parseDouble` method to convert the input data from a string to a number. Here is the program to compute the average of a set of input data.

Program Average.java

```
public class Average
{  public static void main(String[] args)
   {  ConsoleReader console = new ConsoleReader(System.in);
      System.out.println("Enter data.");

      double sum = 0;
      int count = 0;

      // compute sum of all input values

      boolean done = false;
      while (!done)
      {  String inputLine = console.readLine();
         if (inputLine == null)
            done = true;
         else
         {  double x = Double.parseDouble(inputLine);
            sum = sum + x;
            count++;
         }
      }
      // compute average

      if (count == 0)
         System.out.println("No data");
      else
         System.out.println("Average = " + sum / count);
   }
}
```

To supply data to the program, you type the input data, a line at a time. When you are done typing, you must indicate to the operating system that all console input for this program has been supplied. The mechanism for this differs from one operating system to the other. For example, in DOS you type Ctrl+Z, and on UNIX, you type Ctrl+D, to indicate the end of console input. This special keystroke combination is a signal to the *operating system* (and not to Java) to end console input. The `System.in` stream never sees this special character. Instead, it just senses the end of the input. The `readLine` method returns a `null` string (and not a string containing a control character) at the end of input.

Of course, typing a long set of numbers at the console is tedious and error-prone. Productivity hint 6.1 shows you how you can prepare the input data in a file and use input redirection to have the `System.in` stream read the characters from that file. In that case you do not terminate the file with a control character, because the operating system knows the size of the file and therefore knows where it ends. But the operating system, not being clairvoyant, cannot know the end of keyboard input—hence the need for the special control character. (Some ancient versions of DOS did terminate text files on disk with a Ctrl+Z, and you will still find some "experts" who tell you that all files have a special end-of-file character at the end. This is plainly not the case—the operating system uses the size of a disk file to determine its end.)

Advanced Topic 6.2

The "Loop and a Half" Problem

When reading data from input, we always used to use a loop like the following, which is somewhat unsightly:

```
boolean done = false;
while (!done)
{  String inputLine = console.readLine();
   if (inputLine == null)
      done = true;
   else
   {  process data
   }
}
```

The true test for loop termination is in the middle of the loop, not at the top. This is called a "loop and a half," because one must go halfway into the loop before knowing whether one needs to terminate.

Some programmers very much dislike the introduction of an additional Boolean variable for loop control. Two Java language features can be used to alleviate the "loop and a half" problem. I don't think either is a superior solution, but since both approaches are fairly common, it is worth knowing about them when reading other people's code.

You can combine an assignment and a test in the loop condition:

```
while ((inputLine = console.readLine()) != null)
{  process data
}
```

The expression `(inputLine = console.readLine()) != null` means, "First read a line; then test whether the end of the input has been reached." This is an expression with a side effect. The primary purpose of the expression is to serve as a test for the `while` loop, but it also actually does some work—namely, reading the input and storing it in the variable `inputLine`. In general, it is always a bad idea to use side effects, because they make a program hard to read and maintain. In this case, however, it is somewhat seductive, because it eliminates the control variable **done**, which also makes the code hard to read and maintain.

The other solution is to exit the loop from the middle, either by a **return** statement or by a **break** statement (see Advanced Topic 6.3). Here is an example. This loop reads input data, and the method containing the loop returns value when the end of input is encountered.

```
double sum = 0;
int count = 0;
while (true)
{  String inputLine = console.readLine();
   if (inputLine == null) // leave loop in the middle
   {  if (count == 0)
          System.out.println("No data");
      else
          System.out.println("Average = " + sum / count);
      return;
   }
   double x = Double.parseDouble(inputLine);
   sum = sum + x;
   count++;
}
```

Advanced Topic 6.3

The break and continue Statements

You already encountered the **break** statement in Advanced Topic 5.2, where it was used to exit a **switch** statement. In addition to breaking out of a **switch** statement, a **break** statement can also be used to exit a **while**, **for**, or **do** loop. For example, the **break** statement in the following loop terminates the loop when the end of input is reached.

```
while (true)
{  String inputLine = console.readLine();
   if (inputLine == null) // leave loop in the middle
      break;
   double x = Double.parseDouble(inputLine);
   sum = sum + x;
   count++;
}
```

In general, a **break** is a very poor way of exiting a loop. Misuse of a **break** caused the failure of an AT&T 4ESS telephone switch on January 15, 1990. The failure propagated through the entire U.S. network, rendering it nearly unusable for about nine hours. A programmer had used a **break** to terminate an **if** statement. Unfortunately, **break** cannot be used with **if**, so the program execution broke out of the enclosing **switch** statement, skipping some variable initializations and running into chaos [3, p. 38]. Using **break** statements also makes it difficult to use *correctness proof* techniques (see Advanced Topic 6.6).

However, when faced with the bother of introducing a separate loop control variable, some programmers find that **break** statements are beneficial in the "loop and a half" case. This issue is often the topic of heated (and quite unproductive) debate. In this book, we won't use the **break** statement, and we leave it to you if you like to use it in your own programs.

In Java, there is a second form of the **break** statement that is used to break out of a nested statement. The statement **break** *label*; immediately jumps to the *end* of the statement that is tagged with a label. Any statement (including **if** and block statements) can be tagged with a label—the syntax is

label : *statement*

The labeled **break** statement was invented to break out of a set of nested loops.

```
outerloop:
while (outer loop condition)
{  . . .
    while (inner loop condition)
    {  . . .
        if (something really bad happened)
            break outerloop;
    }
}
jumps here if something really bad happened
```

Naturally, this situation is quite rare.

Finally, there is another **goto**-like statement, the **continue** statement, which jumps to the end of the *current iteration* of the loop. Here is a possible use for this statement:

```
double sum = 0;
int count = 0;
String inputLine;
do
{  inputLine = console.readLine();
    if (inputLine == null) continue; // jump to the end of the loop body
    double x = Double.parseDouble(inputLine);
    sum = sum + x;
    count++;
    // continue statement jumps here
} while (inputLine != null);
```

By using the **continue** statement, you don't need to place the remainder of the loop code inside an **else** clause. This is a minor benefit. Few programmers use this statement.

6.5.2 Detecting a Sentinel

Suppose you need to read in *two* sets of data from a file. You can't just use the end of the file as the termination criterion. There must be some indication where the first data set ends and the second one begins.

Sometimes you are lucky and no input value can be zero. Then you can prompt the user to keep entering numbers, or 0 to finish that data set. If zero is allowed but negative numbers are not, you can use -1 to indicate termination. Such a value, which is not an actual input but serves as a signal for termination, is called a *sentinel.*

The following program reads in data with a zero value as a sentinel. After reading the input data, this program could continue to read and process a second data set.

Program Sentinel1.java

```
public class Sentinel1
{  public static void main(String[] args)
   {  ConsoleReader console = new ConsoleReader(System.in);
      System.out.println("Enter data (0 to finish):");

      double sum = 0;
      int count = 0;

      // compute sum of all input values

      boolean done = false;
      while (!done)
      {  String inputLine = console.readLine();
         double x = Double.parseDouble(inputLine);
         if (x == 0)
            done = true;
         else
         {  sum = sum + x;
            count++;
         }
      }

      // compute average

      if (count == 0)
         System.out.println("No data");
      else
         System.out.println("Average = " + sum / count);
   }
}
```

Using a special number as a sentinel works if there is some restriction on the input. In many cases, though, there isn't. Suppose you want to compute the average of a data set that may contain 0 or negative values. You can't use -13 as a sentinel, even if it is your lucky number. That number just might occur as a legitimate value in some data set, and you wouldn't be so lucky. In that case, you might prompt the user "Enter a number, Q to finish". But now you must be careful reading the input. If the "Q" is encountered in a call to **readDouble**, then an exception is thrown, and the program terminates. (Alternatively, with the improved behavior described in Advanced Topic 6.4, the program keeps prompting for a number.) Instead, simply read in the input as a string and then convert it to a number if it is not "Q".

Program Sentinel2.java

```java
public class Sentinel2
{  public static void main(String[] args)
   {  ConsoleReader console = new ConsoleReader(System.in);
      System.out.println("Enter data (Q to finish):");

      double sum = 0;
      int count = 0;

      // compute sum of all input values

      boolean done = false;
      while (!done)
      {  String inputLine = console.readLine();
         if (inputLine.equalsIgnoreCase("Q"))
            done = true;
         else
         {  double x = Double.parseDouble(inputLine);
            sum = sum + x;
            count++;
         }
      }
      // compute average

      if (count == 0)
         System.out.println("No data");
      else
         System.out.println("Average = " + sum / count);
   }
}
```

Advanced Topic 6.4

Coping with Number Format Exceptions

The methods `Integer.parseInt` and `Double.parseDouble` throw a `NumberFormat-Exception` if you supply a string that isn't a number. Until now, you have had to live with this fact, and simply had to make sure that the users of your programs (mainly yourself and your instructor or grader) cooperated and supplied properly formatted inputs. If an improperly formatted input was supplied, the program terminated, because no handler for the `NumberFormatException` was provided.

Of course, a robust program should not simply terminate. Instead, it would be preferable to keep prompting the user for the proper input. To do this properly, you need to know about exception handling, a topic that we will cover in detail in Chapter 13. However, if you studied the implementation of the `ConsoleReader` class in Chapter 3, you already saw how to catch an `IOException`. To handle a formatting error, you need to catch a `NumberFormatException` instead. The following loop keeps reading an integer until the user has typed a properly formatted number. (We use the `trim` method to remove leading or trailing white space from the input string. For example, if the user enters " 3", then the `Integer.parseInt` method complains that the leading space is not a legal part of a number. The `trim` method returns a string with that space removed.)

```
int n = 0;
boolean inputOk = false;
do
{ try
    { String inputString = console.readLine();
        n = Integer.parseInt(inputString.trim());
        inputOk = true;
    }
    catch(NumberFormatException e)
    { System.out.println("Input error. Try again.");
    }
} while (!inputOk);
```

If the call to `parseInt` succeeds, then the assignment `inputOk = true` is carried out, and the loop exits. Otherwise, the `catch` clause for the `NumberFormatException` is executed. An error message is printed, and the loop is repeated because `inputOk` is still false.

6.5.3 String Tokenization

In the last examples, input data were provided a line at a time. However, sometimes it is convenient if an input line can contain several items of input data. Suppose an input line contains two numbers:

5.5 10000

You can't convert the string "5.5 10000" to a number, because the parse method would complain that this string is not a legal number and throw an exception. Instead, you need to break the input line into a sequence of strings, each of which represents a separate input item. There is a special class, the `StringTokenizer`, that can break up a string into items or, as they are sometimes called, *tokens*. By default, the string tokenizer uses white space (spaces, tabs, and newlines) as delimiters. For example, the string "5.5 10000" will be decomposed into two tokens: "5.5" and "10000". The delimiting white space is discarded.

Here is how you break up a string. Construct a `StringTokenizer` object and supply the string to be broken up in the constructor:

```
StringTokenizer tokenizer = new StringTokenizer(inputLine);
```

Then keep calling the `nextToken` method to get the next token.

However, if the entire string has been consumed and there are no more tokens, the `nextToken` method is a bit hostile and throws an exception rather than returning a `null` string. Therefore, you need to call the `hasMoreTokens` method to ensure that there still are tokens to be processed. The following loop traverses all tokens in a string:

```
while (tokenizer.hasMoreTokens())
{   String token = tokenizer.nextToken();
    process token
}
```

Alternatively, you can use the **countTokens** method to find out how many tokens are in the string. Then you get the tokens as follows:

```
int tokenCount = tokenizer.countTokens();
for (int i = 0; i < tokenCount; i++)
{   String token = tokenizer.nextToken();
    process token
}
```

By the way, note that it would not be a good idea to write the seemingly simpler loop

```
for (int i = 0; i < tokenizer.countTokens(); i++) // Inefficient
{   String token = tokenizer.nextToken();
    process token
}
```

This loop would call the **countTokens** method at the end of every loop iteration. That is not a good idea, because **countTokens** is a relatively slow method—it needs to process the entire input string to determine the number of tokens.

Here is a program that simply counts the number of words in an input file. This program is useful if you are a writer who is paid by the word. Note that the loop that breaks up each input line is *nested* inside the loop that reads the lines.

Program Words.java

```
import java.util.StringTokenizer;

public class Words
{   public static void main(String[] args)
    {   ConsoleReader console = new ConsoleReader(System.in);
        System.out.println("Enter Words:");

        int count = 0;

        boolean done = false;
        while (!done)
        {   String inputLine = console.readLine();
            if (inputLine == null)
                done = true;
            else
            {   // break up input line into words

                StringTokenizer tokenizer
                    = new StringTokenizer(inputLine);
```

```
        while (tokenizer.hasMoreTokens())
        {  tokenizer.nextToken(); // read and discard
           count++; // count each word
        }
     }
   }

   System.out.println(count + " words");
}
}
```

Productivity Hint 6.1

Redirection of Input and Output

Consider the word-counting program of Section 6.3.2. How would you use it? You would type text in, and at the end of the input the program would tell you how many words you typed. However, none of the words would be saved for posterity. That is truly dumb—you would never want to use such a program. Such programs are not intended for keyboard input.

The program does make a lot of sense if input is read from a *file*. The command line interfaces of most operating systems provide a way to link a file to the input of a program, as if all the characters in the file had actually been typed by a user. If you type

```
java Words < article.txt
```

the word-counting program is executed. Its input instructions no longer expect input from the keyboard. The `readLine` method gets the input from the file article.txt.

This mechanism works for any program that reads its input from the standard input stream `System.in`. By default, the standard input is tied to the keyboard, but it can be tied to any file by specifying *input redirection* on the command line.

If you have always launched your program from the integrated environment, you need to find out whether your environment supports input redirection. If it does not, you need to learn how to open a command window (often called a *shell*) and launch the program in the command window by typing its name and redirection instructions.

You can also redirect output. In this program, that is not terribly useful. If you run

```
java Words < article.txt > output.txt
```

the file output.txt contains two lines ("Enter words:" and something like "513 words"). However, redirecting output is obviously useful for programs that produce lots of it. You can print the file containing the output or edit it before you turn it in for grading.

Advanced Topic 6.5

Pipes

Output of one program can become the input of another program. Here is a simple program that writes each word of the input file onto a separate line:

Program Split.java

```
import java.util.StringTokenizer;

public class Split
{  public static void main(String[] args)
   {  ConsoleReader console = new ConsoleReader(System.in);

      boolean done = false;
      while (!done)
      {  String inputLine = console.readLine();
         if (inputLine == null)
            done = true;
         else
         {  // break input line into words

            StringTokenizer tokenizer
               = new StringTokenizer(inputLine);
            while (tokenizer.hasMoreTokens())
            {  // print each word
               String word = tokenizer.nextToken();
               System.out.println(word);
            }
         }
      }
   }
}
```

Then

```
java Split < article.txt
```

lists the words in the file article.txt, one on each line. That isn't too exciting, but it becomes useful when combined with another program: *sort*. You don't yet know how to write a program that sorts strings, but most operating systems have a sort program. A sorted list of the words in a file would be quite useful—for example, for making an index.

You can save the unsorted words in a temporary file:

```
java Split < article.txt > temp.txt
sort < temp.txt > sorted.txt
```

Now the sorted words are in the file sorted.txt.

Because this operation is so common, there is a command line shorthand for it.

```
java Split < article.txt | sort > sorted.txt
```

The split program runs first, reading input from article.txt. Its output becomes the input of the sort program. The output of sort is saved in the file sorted.txt. The | operator instructs the operating system to construct a *pipe* linking the output of the first program to the input of the second.

◆ **Figure 5**
◆
◆

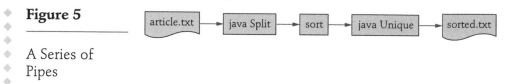

◆
◆ A Series of
◆ Pipes
◆
◆
◆
◆
◆
◆   The file sorted.txt has one blemish. It is likely to contain runs of repeated words, like
◆
◆   ```
◆   a
◆   a
◆   a
◆   an
◆   an
◆   anteater
◆   asia
◆   ```
◆
◆   This is easy to fix with another program that removes *adjacent* duplicates. Removing duplicates
◆   in arbitrary positions is quite hard, but adjacent duplicates are easy to handle:
◆
◆
◆   **Program Unique.java**
◆
◆   ```java
◆   public class Unique
◆   { public static void main(String[] args)
◆   { ConsoleReader console = new ConsoleReader(System.in);
◆
◆   String lastLine = "";
◆
◆   boolean done = false;
◆
◆   while(!done)
◆   { String inputLine = console.readLine();
◆   if (inputLine == null)
◆   done = true;
◆   else if (!inputLine.equals(lastLine))
◆   { // it's a different line from its predecessor
◆   System.out.println(inputLine);
◆   lastLine = inputLine;
◆   }
◆   }
◆   }
◆   }
◆   ```
◆
◆   The sorted word list, with duplicates removed, is obtained as the series of pipes (see Figure 5).
◆
◆   ```
◆   java Split < article.txt | sort | java Unique > sorted.txt
◆   ```
◆
◆   Redirection and pipes make it possible to combine simple programs to do useful work.
◆ This approach was pioneered in the UNIX operating system, which comes with dozens of
◆ commands that perform common tasks and are designed to be combined with each other.

6.5.4 Traversing the Characters in a String

In the last section, you learned how to decompose a string into tokens. Sometimes, you need to go further and analyze the individual characters of a string. The `charAt` method of the `String` class returns an individual character as a value of the `char` type: `s.charAt(i)` is the character at position `i` of the string `s`. As with the `substring` method, the positions in a string are counted starting from 0. That is, the parameter `i` in the call `s.charAt(i)` must be a value between 0 and `s.length() - 1`.

Therefore, the general pattern to traverse all characters in a string is

```
for (int i = 0; i < s.length(); i++)
{  char ch = s.charAt(i);
   do something with ch
}
```

This is the first time you have encountered the `char` type. A variable of type `char` can hold a single character. There isn't a lot you can do with a single character. You can concatenate it with a string, such as

```
String s;
String t = s + ch;
```

You can compare it against a character constant. Character constants look like string constants, except that character constants are delimited by single quotes: `'A'` is a character, `"A"` is a string containing a single character. You can use escape sequences (see Advanced Topic 1.1) inside character constants. For example, `'\n'` is the newline character, and `'\u00E9'` is the character é.

Let us use the string traversal pattern to write a method that computes the *reverse* of a string. For example, the reverse of `"Hello"` is `"olleH"`. To compute the reverse, stick each new character *before* the other characters that you already found. For example, the reverse of `"Hello"` is built up as

```
""
"H"
"eH"
"leH"
"lleH"
"olleH"
```

Program Reverse.java

```
public class Reverse
{  public static void main(String[] args)
   {  ConsoleReader console = new ConsoleReader(System.in);
      System.out.println("Please enter a string:");
      String s = console.readLine();
      String r = "";
      for (int i = 0; i < s.length(); i++)
```

```
      { char ch = s.charAt(i);
         r = ch + r; // add ch in front
      }
      System.out.println(s + " reversed is " + r);
   }
}
```

Quality Tip 6.3

Symmetric and Asymmetric Bounds

It is easy to write a loop with i going from 1 to n:

```
for (i = 1; i <= n; i++) . . .
```

The values for i are bounded by the relation $1 \leq i \leq n$. Because there are $\leq$ comparisons on both bounds, the bounds are called *symmetric*.

When traversing the characters in a string, the bounds are *asymmetric*.

```
for (i = 0; i < s.length(); i++) . . .
```

The values for i are bounded by $0 \leq i < s.length()$, with a $\leq$ comparison to the left and a $<$ comparison to the right. That is appropriate, because s.length() is not a valid position.

It is not a good idea to force symmetry artificially:

```
for (i = 0; i <= s.length() - 1; i++) . . .
```

That is more difficult to read and understand.

For every loop, consider which form is most natural according to the needs of the problem and use that.

Quality Tip 6.4

Count Iterations

Finding the correct lower and upper bounds for an iteration can be confusing. Should I start at 0? Should I use <= b or < b as a termination condition?

Counting the number of iterations is a very useful device for better understanding a loop. Counting is easier for loops with asymmetric bounds. The loop

```
for (i = a; i < b; i++) . . .
```

is executed b - a times. For example, the loop traversing the characters in a string,

```
for (i = 0; i < s.length(); i++) . . .
```

runs s.length() times. That makes perfect sense, since there are s.length() characters in a string.

The loop with symmetric bounds,

```
for (i = a; i <= b; i++)
```

is executed $b - a + 1$ times. That "+1" is the source of many programming errors. For example,

```
for (x = 0; x <= 10; x++)
```

runs 11 times. Maybe that is what you want; if not, start at 1 or use < 10.

One way to visualize this "+1" error is to think of the posts and sections of a fence. Suppose the fence has ten sections (=). How many posts (|) does it have?

|=|=|=|=|=|=|=|=|=|=|

A fence with ten sections has *eleven* posts. Each section has one post to the left, *and* there is one more post after the last section. Forgetting to count the last iteration of a "<=" loop is often called a "fence post error".

If the increment is a value c other than 1, then the counts are

$$(b - a)/c \qquad \text{for the asymmetric loop}$$
$$(b - a)/c + 1 \quad \text{for the symmetric loop}$$

For example, the loop for (i = 10; i <= 40; i += 5) executes $(40 - 10)/5 + 1 = 7$ times.

6.6 Random Numbers and Simulations

In a simulation you generate random events and evaluate their outcomes. Here is a typical problem that can be decided by running a simulation: the *Buffon needle experiment,* devised by Comte Georges-Louis Leclerc de Buffon (1707–1788), a French naturalist. A needle of length 1 inch is dropped onto paper that is ruled with lines 2 inches apart. If the needle drops onto a line, count it as a *hit.* Buffon conjectured that the quotient *tries/hits* approximates π. (See Figure 6.)

Now, how can you run this experiment in the computer? You don't actually want to build a robot that drops needles on paper. The Random class of the Java library implements a *random number generator,* which produces numbers that appear to be completely random. To generate random numbers, you construct an object of the Random class, and then apply one of the following methods:

nextInt(n)   returns a random integer between the integers 0 (inclusive) and n (exclusive)

nextDouble()   returns a random floating-point number between 0 (inclusive) and 1 (exclusive)

Figure 6

The Buffon Needle Experiment

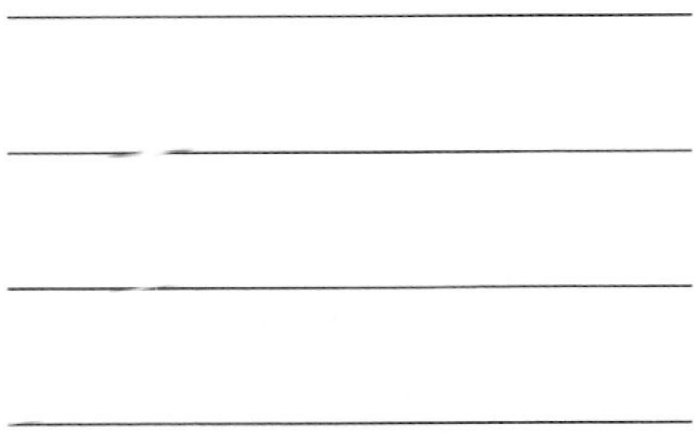

For example, you can simulate the throwing of a die as follows:

```
Random generator = new Random();
int d = 1 + generator.nextInt(6);
```

The call `generator.nextInt(6)` gives you a random number between 0 and 5 (inclusive). Add 1 to obtain a number between 1 and 6.

To give you a feeling for the random numbers, run the following program a few times:

Program Dice.java

```
import java.util.Random;

public class Dice
{  public static void main(String[] args)
   {  Random generator = new Random();
      // roll dice ten times

      for (int i = 1; i <= 10; i++)
      {  int d = 1 + generator.nextInt(6);
         System.out.print(d + " ");
      }
      System.out.println();
   }
}
```

Here are a few typical program runs.

```
6 5 6 3 2 6 3 4 4 1
3 2 2 1 6 5 3 4 1 2
4 1 3 2 6 2 4 3 3 5
```

As you can see, this program produces a different stream of simulated dice throws every time it is run. Actually, the numbers are not completely random. They are drawn from very long sequences of numbers that don't repeat for a long time. These sequences are actually computed from fairly simple formulas; they just behave like random numbers. For that reason, they are often called *pseudorandom* numbers. How to generate good sequences of numbers that behave like truly random sequences is an important and well-studied problem in computer science. We won't investigate this issue further, though; we'll just use the random numbers produced by the **Random** class.

To run the Buffon needle experiment, we have to work a little harder. When you throw a die, it has to come up with one of six faces. When throwing a needle, however, there are many possible outcomes. You must generate *two* random numbers: one to describe the starting position and one to describe the angle of the needle with the x-axis. Then you need to test whether the needle touches a grid line. Stop after 10,000 tries.

Let us agree to generate the *lower* point of the needle. Its x-coordinate is irrelevant, and you may assume its y-coordinate y_{low} to be any random number between 0 and 2. However, since it can be a random *floating-point* number, we use the `nextDouble` method of the **Random** class. It returns a random floating-point number between 0 and 1. Multiply by 2 to get a random number between 0 and 2.

Figure 7

Variables in a Trial of
the Buffon Needle
Experiment

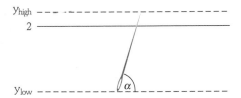

The angle α between the needle and the x-axis can be any value between 0 degrees and 180 degrees. The upper end of the needle has y-coordinate

$$y_{high} = y_{low} + \sin \alpha$$

The needle is a hit if y_{high} is at least 2. See Figure 7.

Here is the program to carry out the simulation of the needle experiment.

Program Buffon.java

```java
import java.util.Random;

public class Buffon
{  public static void main(String[] args)
   {  Random generator = new Random();
      int hits = 0;
      final int NTRIES = 10000;

      for (int i = 1; i <= NTRIES; i++)
      {  // simulate needle throw

         double ylow = 2 * generator.nextDouble();
         double angle = 180 * generator.nextDouble();

         // compute high point of needle

         double yhigh = ylow + Math.sin(Math.toRadians(angle));
         if (yhigh >= 2) hits++;
      }

      // print approximation of PI

      System.out.println("Tries / Hits = "
         + (NTRIES * 1.0) / hits);
   }
}
```

On one computer I obtained the result 3.10 when running 10,000 iterations and 3.1429 when running 100,000 iterations.

The point of this program is *not* to compute π—there are far more efficient ways for that purpose. Rather, the point is to show how a physical experiment can be simulated on the computer. Buffon had to drop the needle physically thousands of times and record the results, which must have been a rather dull activity. You can have the computer execute the experiment quickly and accurately.

Simulations are very common computer applications. All simulations use essentially the same pattern as the code of this example: In a loop, a large number of sample values are generated; the values of certain observations are recorded for each sample; when the simulation is completed, the averages of the observed values are printed out.

A typical example of a simulation is the modeling of customer queues at a bank or a supermarket. Rather than observing real customers, one simulates their arrival and their transactions at the teller window or checkout stand in the computer. One can try out different staffing or building layout patterns in the computer simply by making changes in the program. In the real world, making many such changes and measuring their effect would be impossible, or at least very expensive.

Advanced Topic 6.6

Loop Invariants

Consider the task of computing a^n, where a is a floating-point number and n is a positive integer. Of course, you can multiply $a \times a \times \cdots \times a$, n times, but if n is large, you'll end up doing a lot of multiplications. The following loop computes a^n in far fewer steps:

```
double a = . . .;
int n = . . .;
double r = 1;
double b = a;
int i = n;
while (i > 0)
{  if (i % 2 == 0) // i is even
   {  b = b * b;
      i = i / 2;
   }
   else
   {  r = r * b;
      i--;
   }
}
// now r equals  Math.pow(a, n);
```

Consider the case n = 100. The method performs the following steps.

b	i	r
a	100	1
a^2	50	
a^4	25	
	24	a^4
a^8	12	a^4
a^{16}	6	
a^{32}	3	
	2	a^{36}
a^{64}	1	
	0	a^{100}

Amazingly enough, the algorithm yields exactly a^{100}. Do you understand why? Are you convinced it will work for all values of n? Here is a clever argument to show that the method always computes the correct result. We will demonstrate that whenever the program reaches the top of the `while` loop, it is true that

$$r \cdot b^i = a^n \quad (I)$$

Certainly, it is true the first time around, because $r = 1$, $b = a$, and $i = n$. Suppose that (I) holds at the beginning of the loop. We label the values of r, b, and i as "old" when entering the loop and as "new" when exiting the loop. We assume that upon entry

$$r_{old} \cdot b_{old}^{i_{old}} = a^n$$

In the loop we have to distinguish two cases: i even and i odd. If i is even, the loop performs the following transformations:

$r_{new} = r_{old}$

$b_{new} = b_{old}^2$

$i_{new} = i_{old}/2$

Therefore,

$$r_{new} \cdot b_{new}^{i_{new}} = r_{old} \cdot b_{old}^{2 \cdot i_{old}/2}$$

$$= r_{old} \cdot b_{old}^{i_{old}}$$

$$= a^n$$

On the other hand, if i is odd, then

$r_{new} = r_{old} \cdot b_{old}$

$b_{new} = b_{old}$

$i_{new} = i_{old} - 1$

Therefore,

$$r_{new} \cdot b_{new}^{i_{new}} = r_{old} \cdot b_{old} + bi_{old}^{i_{old}-1}$$

$$= r_{old} \cdot b_{old}^{i_{old}}$$

$$= a^n$$

In either case, the new values for r, b, and i fulfill the *loop invariant* (I). So what? When the loop finally exits, (I) holds again:

$$r \cdot b^i = a^n$$

Furthermore, we know that $i = 0$, since the loop is terminating. But because $i = 0$, $r \cdot b^i = r \cdot b^0 = r$. Hence $r = a^n$, and the method really does compute the nth power of a.

This technique is quite useful, because it can explain an algorithm that is not at all obvious. The condition (I) is called a loop invariant because it is true when the loop is entered, at the top of each pass, and when the loop is exited. If a loop invariant is chosen skillfully, you may be able to deduce correctness of a computation. See [4] for another nice example.

Random Fact 6.2

Correctness Proofs

In Advanced Topic 6.6 we introduced the technique of loop invariants. If you skipped that note, have a glance at it now. That technique can be used to prove rigorously that a loop computes exactly the value that it is supposed to compute. Such a proof is far more valuable than any testing. No matter how many test cases you try, you always worry whether another case that you haven't tried yet might show a bug. A proof settles the correctness for *all* possible inputs.

For some time, programmers were very hopeful that proof techniques such as loop invariants would greatly reduce the need of testing. You would prove that each simple method is correct, and then put the proven components together and prove that they work together as they should. Once it is proved that `main` works correctly, no testing is required at all! Some researchers were so excited about these techniques that they tried to omit the programming step altogether. The designer would write down the program requirements, using the notation of formal logic. An automatic prover would prove that such a program could be written and generate the program as part of its proof.

Unfortunately, in practice these methods never worked very well. The logical notation to describe program behavior is complex. Even simple scenarios require many formulas. It is easy enough to express the idea that a method is supposed to compute a^n, but the logical formulas describing all methods in a program that controls an airplane, for instance, would fill many pages. These formulas are created by humans, and humans make errors when they deal with difficult and tedious tasks. Experiments showed that instead of buggy programs, programmers wrote buggy logic specifications and buggy program proofs.

Van der Linden [3], p. 287, gives some examples of complicated proofs that are much harder to verify than the programs they are trying to prove.

Program proof techniques are valuable for proving the correctness of individual methods that make computations in nonobvious ways. At this time, though, there is no hope to prove any but the most trivial programs correct in such a way that the specification and the proof can be trusted more than the program. There is hope that correctness proofs will become more applicable to real-life programming situations in the future. At this point, however, engineering and management are at least as important as mathematics and logic for the successful completion of large software projects.

Chapter Summary

1. Loops execute a block of code repeatedly. A termination condition controls how many times the loop is executed.

2. There are three kinds of loops: `while`, `for`, and `do` loops. You use a `for` loop when a number runs from a starting to an ending value with a constant increment or decrement; `do` loops are appropriate when the loop body must be executed at least once.

3. An off-by-one error is a common error when programming loops. You should count the number of iterations of a `for` loop and make a choice between symmetric and asymmetric bounds.

4. Loops can be nested. A typical example for nested loops is printing a table.

5. When reading input, you can detect the end of the input by checking for the end of the file, or you can use a sentinel value.

6. You can break an input line into words by using a string tokenizer, or you can access the individual characters.

7. In a simulation, you repeatedly generate random numbers and use them to simulate an activity.

8. With simple loops, you can use correctness proofs to show that the loop is correct. Correctness proofs, as well as informal reasoning about correctness, work best if you exit from a loop only when the loop condition fails. Therefore, it is best to avoid breaking out from the middle of a loop.

Further Reading

[1] Alan Feuer, *The C Puzzle Book,* Prentice-Hall, 1989.

[2] E. W. Dijkstra, "Goto Statements Considered Harmful", *Communications of the ACM,* vol. 11, no. 3 (March 1968), pp. 147–148.

[3] Peter van der Linden, *Expert C Programming,* Prentice-Hall, 1994.

[4] Jon Bentley, *Programming Pearls,* Addison-Wesley, 1986, Chapter 4, "Writing Correct Programs".

[5] Kai Lai Chung, *Elementary Probability Theory with Stochastic Processes,* Undergraduate Texts in Mathematics, Springer-Verlag, 1974.

[6] Rudolf Flesch, *How to Write Plain English,* Barnes & Noble Books, 1979.

Classes, Objects, and Methods Introduced in This Chapter

```
java.util.Random
   nextDouble
   nextInt
java.util.StringTokenizer
   countTokens
   hasMoreTokens
   nextToken
```

Review Exercises

Exercise R6.1. Which loop statements does Java support? Give simple rules when to use each loop type.

Exercise R6.2. What does the following code print?

```
for (int i = 0; i < 10; i++)
{  for (int j = 0; j < 10; j++)
      System.out.print(i * j % 10);
   System.out.println();
}
```

Exercise R6.3. How often do the following loops execute? Assume that i is not changed in the loop body.

```
for (i = 1; i <= 10; i++) . . .
for (i = 0; i < 10; i++) . . .
for (i = 10; i > 0; i--) . . .
for (i = -10; i <= 10; i++) . . .
for (i = 10; i >= 0; i++) . . .
for (i = -10; i <= 10; i = i + 2) . . .
for (i = -10; i <= 10; i = i + 3) . . .
```

Exercise R6.4. Rewrite the following `for` loop into a `while` loop.

```
int s = 0;
for (int i = 1; i <= 10; i++) s = s + i;
```

Exercise R6.5. Rewrite the following `do` loop into a `while` loop.

```
int n = 1;
double x = 0;
double s;
do
{   s = 1.0 / (n * n);
    x = x + s;
    n++;
}  while (s > 0.01);
```

Exercise R6.6. What is an infinite loop? On your computer, how can you terminate a program that executes an infinite loop?

Exercise R6.7. There are two ways to supply input to `System.in`. Describe both methods. Explain how the "end of file" is signaled in both cases.

Exercise R6.8. In DOS/Windows and UNIX, there is no special "end of file" character stored in a file. Verify that statement by producing a file with known character count—for example, a file consisting of the following three lines

```
Hello
cruel
world
```

Then look at the directory listing. How many characters does the file contain? Remember to count the newline characters. (In DOS, you may be surprised that the count is not what you expect. DOS text files store each newline as a two-character sequence. The input readers and output streams automatically translate between this carriage return/line feed sequence used by files and the '\n' character used by Java programs, so you don't need to worry about it.) Why does this prove that there is no "end of file" character? Why do you nevertheless need to type Ctrl+Z/Ctrl+D to end console input?

Exercise R6.9. How can you read input from `System.in` (1) a character at a time, (2) a word at a time, and (3) a line at a time?

Exercise R6.10. Show how to use a string tokenizer to break up the string `"Hello, cruel world!"` into tokens. What are the resulting tokens?

Exercise R6.11. Give a strategy for reading input of the form

name of bridge   length of bridge

Here the name of the bridge can be a single word ("Brooklyn") or consist of several words ("Golden Gate"). The length is a floating-point number.

Exercise R6.12. What is a "loop and a half"? Give three strategies to implement the following "loop and a half":

```
loop
{   read employee name
    if not OK, exit loop
    read employee salary
    if not OK, exit loop
    give employee 5 percent raise
    print employee data
}
```

Use a Boolean variable, a **break** statement, and a method with multiple **return** statements. Which of these three approaches do you find clearest?

Exercise R6.13. What is a sentinel value? Give simple rules when it is better to use a sentinel value and when it is better to use the end of the input file to denote the end of a data sequence. *Hint:* Consider the number of data sets and the origin of the data (keyboard input vs. file input).

Exercise R6.14. How would you use a random number generator to simulate the drawing of a playing card?

Exercise R6.15. What is an "off by one" error? Give an example from your own programming experience.

Exercise R6.16. Give an example of a **for** loop in which symmetric bounds are more natural. Give an example of a **for** loop in which asymmetric bounds are more natural.

Exercise R6.17. What are nested loops? Give an example where a nested loop is typically used.

Programming Exercises

Exercise P6.1. The series of pipes in Advanced Topic 6.5 has one final problem: The output file contains upper- and lowercase versions of the same word, such as "The" and "the". Modify the procedure, either by changing one of the programs or, in the true spirit of piping, by writing another short program and adding it to the series.

Exercise P6.2. *Currency conversion.* Write a program that asks the user to enter today's exchange rate between U.S. dollars and the Euro. Then the program reads U.S. dollar values and converts each to Euro values. Use 0 as a sentinel to denote the end of inputs.

Exercise P6.3. Write a program that asks the user to enter today's exchange rate between U.S. dollars and the Euro. Then the program reads U.S. dollar values and converts each to Euro values. Use 0 as the sentinel value to denote the end of dollar inputs. Then the program reads a sequence of Euro amounts and converts them to dollars. The second sequence is terminated by the end of the input file.

Exercise P6.4. *Random walk.* Simulate the wandering of an intoxicated person in a square street grid. Draw a grid of 10 streets horizontally and 10 streets vertically. Represent the simulated drunkard by a dot, placed in the middle of the grid to start. For 100 times, have the simulated drunkard randomly pick a direction (east, west, north, south), move one block in the chosen direction, and redraw the dot. After the iterations, display the distance that the drunkard has covered. (One might expect that on average the person might not get anywhere because the moves to different directions cancel another out in the long run, but in fact it can be shown that with probability 1 the person eventually moves outside any finite region. See, for example, [5], chapter 8, for more details.)

Exercise P6.5. *Projectile flight.* Suppose a cannonball is propelled vertically into the air with a starting velocity v_0. Any calculus book will tell us that the position of the ball after t seconds is $s(t) = -0.5 \cdot g \cdot t^2 + v_0 \cdot t$, where $g = 9.81$ m/sec^2 is the gravitational force of the earth. No calculus book ever mentions why someone would want to carry out such an obviously dangerous experiment, so we will do it in the safety of the computer.

In fact, we will confirm the theorem from calculus by a simulation. In our simulation, we will consider how the ball moves in very short time intervals Δt. In a short time interval the velocity v is nearly constant, and we can compute the distance the ball moves as $\Delta s = v \cdot \Delta t$. In our program, we will simply set

```
double deltaT = 0.01;
```

and update the position by

```
s = s + v * deltaT;
```

The velocity changes constantly—in fact, it is reduced by the gravitational force of the earth. In a short time interval, $v = -g \cdot \Delta t$, and we must keep the velocity updated as

```
v = v - g * deltaT;
```

In the next iteration the new velocity is used to update the distance.

Now run the simulation until the cannonball falls back onto the earth. Get the initial velocity as an input (100 m/sec is a good value). Update the position and velocity 100 times per second, but print out the position only every full second. Also print out the values from the exact formula $s(t) = -0.5 \cdot g \cdot t^2 + v_0 \cdot t$ for comparison.

What is the benefit of this kind of simulation when an exact formula is available? Well, the formula from the calculus book is *not* exact. Actually, the gravitational force diminishes the further the cannonball is away from the surface of the earth. This complicates the algebra sufficiently that it is not possible to give an exact formula for the actual motion, but the computer simulation can simply be extended to apply a variable gravitational force. For cannonballs, the calculus-book formula is actually good enough, but computers are necessary to compute accurate trajectories for higher-flying objects such as ballistic missiles.

Exercise P6.6. Most cannonballs are not shot upright but at an angle. If the starting velocity has magnitude v and the starting angle is α, then the velocity is actually a vector with components $v_x = v \cos \alpha$, $v_y = v \sin \alpha$. In the x-direction the velocity does not change. In the y-direction the gravitational force takes its toll. Repeat the simulation from the previous exercise, but store the position of the cannonball as a Point2D variable. Update the x and y positions separately, and also update the x and y components of the velocity separately. Every full second, plot the location of the cannonball on the graphics display. Repeat until the cannonball has reached the earth again.

This kind of problem is of historical interest. The first computers were designed to carry out just such ballistic calculations, taking into account the diminishing gravity for high-flying projectiles and wind speeds.

Exercise P6.7. The *Fibonacci sequence* is defined by the following rule. The first two values in the sequence are 1 and 1. Every subsequent value is the sum of the two values preceding it. For example, the third value is $1 + 1 = 2$, the fourth value is $1 + 2 = 3$, and the fifth is $2 + 3 = 5$. If f_n denotes the nth value in the Fibonacci sequence, then

$$f_1 = 1$$
$$f_2 = 1$$
$$f_n = f_{n-1} + f_{n-2} \text{ if } n > 2$$

Write a program that prompts the user for n and prints the nth value in the Fibonacci sequence.

Hint: There is no need to store all values for f_n. You only need the last two values to compute the next one in the series:

```
fold1 = 1;
fold2 = 1;
fnew = fold1 + fold2;
```

After that, discard fold2, which is no longer needed, and set fold2 to fold1 and fold1 to fnew. Repeat computing fnew for an appropriate number of times.

Exercise P6.8. Write a program that prints a *bar chart* from a data set. The program should be a graphics applet that prompts the user for the values, all to be entered into a single option dialog, separated by spaces (for example, **40 60 50**). Assume all values are between 0 and 100. Then draw a bar chart like this:

Exercise P6.9. *Mean and standard deviation.* Write a program that reads a set of floating-point data values from the input. When the end of file is reached, print out the count of the values, the average, and the standard deviation. The average of a data set $\{x_1, \ldots, x_n\}$ is $\bar{x} = \sum x_i / n$, where $\sum x_i = x_1 + \cdots + x_n$ is the sum of the input values. The standard deviation is

$$S = \sqrt{\frac{\sum (x_i - \bar{x})^2}{n - 1}}$$

However, that formula is not suitable for our task. By the time you have computed the mean, the individual x_i are long gone. Until you know how to save these values, use the numerically less stable formula

$$S = \sqrt{\frac{\sum x_i^2 - \frac{1}{n} \sum x_i}{n - 1}}$$

You can compute this quantity by keeping track of the count, the sum, and the sum of squares as you process the input values.

Exercise P6.10. Write a graphical applet that prompts a user to enter a number n and that draws n circles with random center and random radius.

Exercise P6.11. *Flesch Readability Index.* The following index [6] was invented by Flesch as a simple tool to gauge the legibility of a document without linguistic analysis.

◆ Count all words in the file. A *word* is any sequence of characters delimited by white space, whether or not it is an actual English word.

◆ Count all syllables in each word. To make this simple, use the following rules: Each *group* of adjacent vowels (a,e,i,o,u,y) counts as one syllable (for example, the "ea" in "real" contributes one syllable, but the "e..a" in "regal" count as two syllables). However, an "e" at the end of a word doesn't count as a syllable. Also, each word has at least one syllable, even if the previous rules give a count of 0.

◆   Count all sentences. A sentence is ended by a period, colon, semicolon, question mark, or exclamation mark.

◆   The index is computed by

$$\text{Index} = 206.835 - 84.6 \times (\text{Number of syllables / Number of words})$$

$$- 1.015 \times (\text{Number of words / Number of sentences})$$

rounded to the nearest integer.

This index is a number, usually between 0 and 100, indicating how difficult the text is to read. Some examples for random material for various publications are

Comics	95
Consumer ads	82
Sports Illustrated	65
Time	57
New York Times	39
Auto insurance policy	10
Internal Revenue Code	−6

Translated into educational levels, the indices are

91–100	5th grader
81–90	6th grader
71–80	7th grader
66–70	8th grader
61–66	9th grader
51–60	High school student
31–50	College student
0–30	College graduate
Less than 0	Law school graduate

The purpose of the index is to force authors to rewrite their text until the index is high enough. This is achieved by reducing the length of sentences and by removing long words. For example, the sentence

> The following index was invented by Flesch as a simple tool to estimate the legibility of a document without linguistic analysis.

can be rewritten as

> Flesch invented an index to check whether a text is easy to read. To compute the index, you need not look at the meaning of the words.

His book [7] contains delightful examples of translating government regulations into "plain English".

Your program should read in a text file, compute the legibility index, and print out the equivalent educational level.

Exercise P6.12. *Factoring of integers.* Write a program that asks the user for an integer and then prints out all its factors. For example, when the user enters 150, the program should print

```
2
3
5
5
```

Exercise P6.13. *Prime numbers.* Write a program that prompts the user for an integer and then prints out all prime numbers up to that integer. For example, when the user enters 20, the program should print

```
2
3
5
7
11
13
17
19
```

Recall that a number is a prime number if it is not divisible by any number except 1 and itself.

Exercise P6.14. The best known iterative method for computing the *roots* of a function f (that is, the x-values for which $f(x)$ is 0) is *Newton–Raphson approximation.* To find the zero of a function whose derivative is also known, compute

$$x_{new} = x_{old} - f(x_{old})/f'(x_{old}).$$

For this exercise, write a program to compute nth roots of floating-point numbers. Prompt the user for a and n, then obtain $\sqrt[n]{a}$ by computing a zero of the function $f(x) = x^n - a$.

Exercise P6.15. Write a graphical applet that displays a checkerboard with 64 squares, alternating white and black.

Exercise P6.16. Write a program that reads a series of floating-point numbers and prints

- The maximum value
- The minimum value
- The average value

Exercise P6.17. *The game of Nim.* This is a well-known game with a number of variants. We will consider the following variant, which has an interesting winning strategy. Two players alternately take marbles from a pile. In each move, a player chooses how many marbles to take. The player must take at least one but at most half of the marbles. Then the other player takes a turn. The player who takes the last marble loses.

You will write a program in which the computer plays against a human opponent. Generate a random integer between 10 and 100 to denote the initial size of the pile. Generate a random integer between 0 and 1 to decide whether the computer or the human takes the first turn. Generate a random integer between 0 and 1 to decide whether the computer plays *smart* or *stupid*. In stupid mode, the computer simply takes a random legal value (between 1 and $n/2$) from the pile whenever it has a turn. In smart mode the computer takes off enough marbles to make the size of the pile a power of two minus 1—that is, 3, 7, 15, 31, or 63. That is always a legal move, except if the size of the pile is currently one less than a power of two. In that case, the computer makes a random legal move.

You will note that the computer cannot be beaten in smart mode when it has the first move, unless the pile size happens to be 15, 31, or 63. Of course, a human player who has the first turn and knows the winning strategy can win against the computer.

Exercise P6.18. The value of e^x can be computed as the power series

$$e^x = \sum_{n=0}^{\infty} \frac{x^n}{n!} = 1 + x + \frac{x^2}{2!} + \frac{x^3}{3!} + \cdots$$

Write a program that computes e^x using this formula. Of course, you can't compute an infinite sum. Just keep adding values until an individual summand (term) is less than a certain threshold. At each step, you need to compute the new term and add it to the total. Update these terms as follows:

```
term = term * x / n;
```

Exercise P6.19. Program the following simulation: Darts are thrown at random points onto the square with corners $(1, 1)$ and $(-1, -1)$. If the dart lands inside the unit circle (that is, the circle with center $(0, 0)$ and radius 1), it is a hit. Otherwise it is a miss. Run this simulation and use it to determine an approximate value for π. Explain why this is a better method for estimating π than the Buffon needle program.

Exercise P6.20. It is easy and fun to draw graphs of curves with the Java graphics library. Simply draw a hundred line segments joining the points $(x, f(x))$ and $(x + d, f(x + d))$, where x ranges from x_{min} to x_{max} and $d = (x_{max} - x_{min})/100$. Draw the curve $f(x) = x^3/100 - x + 10$, where x ranges from -10 to 10 in this fashion.

Exercise P6.21. Draw a picture of the "four-leaved rose" whose equation in polar coordinates is $r = \cos 2\theta, 0 \le \theta \le 2\pi$. Let θ go from 0 to 2π in 100 steps. Each time, compute r and then compute the (x, y) coordinates from the polar coordinates by using the formula

$$x = r \cos \theta, \quad y = r \sin \theta$$

You can get extra credit if you can vary the number of petals.

More about Methods

Chapter Goals

◆ To understand how parameters are passed into methods and how return values are returned from methods

◆ To minimize the use of side effects

◆ To understand the difference between instance methods and static methods

◆ To introduce the concept of static variables

◆ To be able to determine the scope of variables

◆ To appreciate the importance of method comments

◆ To document the responsibilities of methods and their callers with preconditions

◆ To be able to program recursive methods

In this chapter you will learn more about methods. You have already implemented several simple methods and are familiar with the basic concepts. We will go over parameters, return values, and variable scope in a more systematic fashion. You will also learn about several more technical issues, such as static methods and variables. Finally, we will discuss several concepts that will enable you to implement methods correctly.

7.1   Method Parameters

In the implementation of a method you define the *parameters* of the method. For example, consider the deposit method of the BankAccount class:

```
public class BankAccount
{  . . .
   public void deposit(double amount)
   {  . . .
   }
   . . .
}
```

This method has two parameters:

1. The implicit parameter this, the bank account to which money is deposited
2. An explicit parameter amount, the amount of the deposit

These values are sometimes called the *formal* parameters.

In each method call, you supply a set of *actual parameters* or *arguments*, the values that you use for a particular call. For example, consider the call

```
harrysChecking.deposit(allowance - 200);
```

This method call has two actual parameters:

1. The object reference stored in the object variable harrysChecking
2. The value of the expression allowance - 200

When a method is called, the actual parameter values are computed and copied into the formal parameter variables (see Figure 1).

```
this = harrysChecking;
amount = allowance - 200;
```

When the method returns, the formal parameter variables are abandoned, and their values are lost.

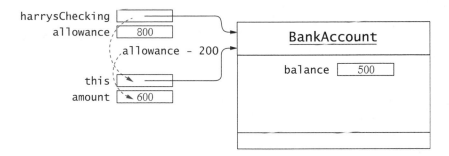

Figure 1

Parameter Passing

Explicit parameter variables are no different from other variables. You can modify them during the execution of the method:

```
public void deposit(double amount)
{  amount = amount + balance; // bad style
   balance = amount;
}
```

However, it is considered bad style to modify the contents of a parameter variable.

In the preceding example, the explicit parameter of the method was a number value. Let's consider a slightly more complex example, with a parameter that is an object reference. The following method can be used to transfer money from one account to another:

```
public class BankAccount
{  . . .
   public void transfer(BankAccount other, double amount)
   {  withdraw(amount);
      other.deposit(amount);
   }
   . . .
}
```

For example,

```
double allowance = 800;
momsSavings.transfer(harrysChecking, allowance);
```

Now there are three formal parameter variables: **this**, **other**, and **amount**. Figure 2 shows how they are initialized. Note that both the object references and the numbers are *copied* into the method. After the method exits, the two bank account balances

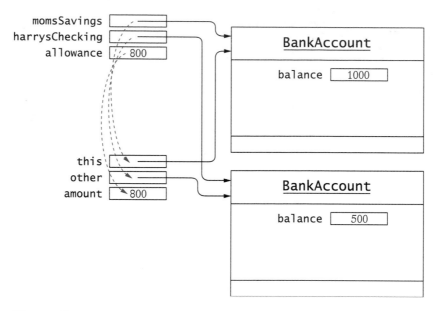

Figure 2

Object References and
Number Parameters

have changed. The method was able to change the accounts because it received
copies of the object references. Of course the contents of the **allowance** variable
was not changed. In Java, no method can modify the contents of a *number* variable
that is passed as a parameter.

Quality Tip 7.1

Use Meaningful Names for Parameters

You can give any name you like to method parameters. Choose explicit names for parameters
that have specific roles; choose simple names for those that are completely generic. The goal
is to make the reader understand the purpose of the parameter without having to read the
description.

For example, **double sin(double x)** is not as good as **double sin(double radian)**.
Naming the parameter **radian** gives additional information: namely, that the angle cannot be
given in degrees.

The **Math** class contains a method that is declared as

```
double atan2(double a, double b)
```

I can never remember where to put the *x*-value and where to put the *y*-value, or whether it computes $\tan^{-1}(a/b)$ or $\tan^{-1}(b/a)$. I wish they had named the parameters more sensibly:

```
double atan2(double yNumerator, double xDenominator)
```

Common Error 7.1

Type Mismatch

The compiler takes the types of the method parameters and return values very seriously. It is an error to call a method with a value of an incompatible type. The compiler automatically converts from `int` to `double` and from ordinary classes to superclasses (see Chapter 9). It does not convert, however, when there is a possibility of information loss, and it doesn't convert between numbers and strings or objects. For this reason, Java is called a *strongly typed* language. This is a useful feature, because it lets the compiler find programming errors before they create havoc when the program runs.

For example, you cannot give a string to a numerical method, even if the string contains only digits:

```
String num = "100";
double x = Math.sqrt(num); // Error
```

You cannot store a numerical return value in a string variable:

```
String root = Math.sqrt(2); // Error
```

7.2   Accessor Methods, Mutator Methods, and Side Effects

A method that accesses an object and returns some information about it, without changing the object, is called an *accessor* method. In contrast, a method that modifies the state of an object is called a *mutator* method. For example, in the `BankAccount` class, `getBalance` is an accessor method and the `deposit/withdraw` methods are mutator methods.

In other words, an accessor method does not modify the object to which the `this` parameter refers, whereas a mutator method does.

You can call an accessor method as many times as you like—you always get the same answer, and it does not change the state of your object. That is clearly a desirable property, because it makes the behavior of such a method very predictable.

As a rule of thumb, it is best to separate accessors and mutators. If a method returns a value, then it should not modify the object. Conversely, mutators should have a return type of `void`. This is not a rule of the Java language, but just a recommendation to make it easy to differentiate between mutators and accessors.

Some classes have been designed to have only accessor methods and no mutator methods at all. Such classes are called *immutable*. An example is the `String` class. Once a string has been constructed, its contents never change. No method in the `String` class can modify the contents of a string. For example, the `substring` method does not remove characters from the original string. Instead, it constructs a *new* string that contains the substring characters.

An immutable class has a major advantage: It is safe to give out references to its objects freely. If no method can change the object's value, then no code can modify the object at an unexpected time. In contrast, if you give out a `BankAccount` reference to any other method, you have to be aware that the state of your object may change—the other method can call the `deposit` and `withdraw` methods on the reference that you gave it.

Even though an accessor method can change parameter objects, you generally don't expect it to. Here is an `equals` method that compares whether two bank accounts have the same balance.

```
public class BankAccount
{   public boolean equals(BankAccount other)
    {   . . .
    }
}
```

Consider the comparison

```
if (account1.equals(account2)) . . .
```

You would be, to say the least, surprised if this call withdrew some money from either `account1` or `account2`. Although we all have come to expect unreasonable bank charges, an "equality testing charge" would be disturbing.

In other words, there is the expectation that accessor methods do not modify any parameters, and that mutator methods do not modify any parameters beyond `this`. That ideal situation is not always the case. For example, the `transfer` method that we discussed in the last section does update the `other` account. Such a method is said to have a *side effect*. A side effect of a method is any kind of *observable behavior* outside the object.

Consider this example. You want to print the balance of a bank account.

```
System.out.println("The balance is now $" +
    momsSavings.getBalance());
```

Why don't you simply have the `getBalance` method *print* the value as it is getting it?

```
public double getBalance()
{   System.out.println("The balance is now $" + balance);
    return balance();
}
```

That would be more convenient when you actually want to print the value. But of course there are cases when you want the value for some other purpose. You don't want to have the output littered with balance reports every time the balance is accessed. Therefore, a method that computes a value and, "while it is at it", has the side effect of printing output, is undesirable.

One particularly reprehensible practice is printing error messages inside methods. You should never do that:

```
public void deposit(double amount)
{  if (amount <= 0)
       System.out.println("Bad value of amount"); // bad style
   else
       balance = balance + amount;
}
```

Printing an error message severely limits the reusability of a method. Such a method can be used only in programs that can print to System.out—eliminating applets and embedded systems such as the computer inside an automatic teller machine. The method can be used only in applications where the user can understand an error message in the English language—eliminating the majority of your potential customers. Let the methods do just the computation, not the error report to the user. You will learn later in this chapter and in Chapter 13 how a method can use *exceptions* to indicate problems.

Quality Tip 7.2

Minimize Side Effects

In an ideal world, all methods would be accessors that simply return an answer without changing any value at all. (In fact, programs that are written in so-called *functional* programming languages such as Scheme and ML come close to this ideal.) Of course, in an object-oriented programming language, we use objects to remember state changes. Therefore, a method that just changes the state of its implicit parameter is certainly acceptable. A method that does anything else is said to have a side effect. While side effects cannot be completely eliminated, they can be the cause of surprises and problems and should be minimized. Here is a classification of method behavior.

- ◆ Best: Accessor methods with no changes to any explicit parameters—no side effects. Example: getBalance.

- ◆ Good: Mutator methods with no changes to any explicit parameters, no side effects: Example: withdraw.

- ◆ Fair: Methods that change an explicit parameter. Example: transfer.

- ◆ Poor: Methods that change a static variable (see Section 7.4) or print messages to System.out.

7.3   Static Methods

Sometimes you write methods that don't need an implicit parameter. Such a method is called a **static** method or a *class method*. In contrast, the methods that you saw in the preceding sections are often called *instance methods* because they operate on a particular instance of an object. You have seen static method calls in Chapter 2. For example, the `sqrt` method in the `Math` class is a static method. When you call `Math.sqrt(x)`, you don't supply any implicit parameter. (Recall that `Math` is the name of a class, not an object.) And, of course, every application has a static `main` method (however, applets do not).

Why would you want to write a method without an implicit parameter? The most common reason is that you want to encapsulate some computations that involve only numbers. Since numbers aren't objects, you can't pass them as implicit parameters.

Here is a typical example of a static method that carries out some simple algebra. Recall from Chapter 5 that two floating-point numbers x and y are approximately equal if

$$\frac{|x - y|}{max(|x|, |y|)} \le \epsilon$$

where ϵ is a small number, typically chosen to be 10^{-14}.

Of course, this formula is just complex enough that it makes a lot of sense to encapsulate it in a method. Since the parameters are numbers, the method doesn't operate on any objects at all, and we make it into a **static** method:

```
public static boolean approxEqual(double x, double y)
{  final double EPSILON = 1E-14;
   double xymax = Math.max(Math.abs(x), Math.abs(y));
   return Math.abs(x - y) <= EPSILON * xymax;
}
```

You need to find a home for this method. You have two choices. You can simply add this method to a class whose methods need to call it. Or you can come up with a new class (similar to the `Math` class of the standard Java library) to contain this method. In this book, we will generally use the latter approach. Since this method has to do with numbers, we'll design a class `Numeric` to hold the `approxEqual` method. Here is the class:

```
class Numeric
{  public static boolean approxEqual(double x, double y)
   {  final double EPSILON = 1E-14;
      double xymax = Math.max(Math.abs(x), Math.abs(y));
      return Math.abs(x - y) <= EPSILON * xymax;
   }
   // more numeric methods can be added here
}
```

When calling the static method, you supply the name of the class containing the method so that the compiler can find it. For example,

```
double r = Math.sqrt(2);
if (Numeric.approxEqual(r * r, 2))
    System.out.println("Math.sqrt(2) squared is approximately 2");
```

Note that you do not supply an object of type `Numeric` when you call the method. Static methods have no implicit parameter—in other words, they don't have a `this` parameter.

Now we can tell you why the `main` method is static. When the program starts, there aren't any objects yet. Therefore, the *first* method in the program must be a static method.

You may well wonder why these methods are called `static` methods. The normal meaning of the word *static* ("staying fixed at one place") does not seem to have anything to do with what static methods do. That is indeed the case. Java uses the `static` keyword because C++ uses it in the same context. C++ uses `static` to denote class methods because the inventors of C++ did not want to invent another keyword. Someone noted that there was a relatively rarely used keyword, `static`, that denotes certain variables that stay in a fixed location for multiple method calls. (Java does not have this feature, nor does it need it.) It turned out that the keyword could be reused to denote class methods without confusing the compiler. The fact that it can confuse humans was apparently not a big concern. You'll just have to live with the fact that "`static` method" means "class method": a method that does not operate on an object and that has only explicit parameters.

◆ Common Error 7.2

Trying to Modify Numeric Parameters

Let us try to write a method that updates a number, representing the balance of a bank account, by applying an interest rate.

```
public static void updateBalance(double balance,
    double interestRate)
{   double interest = balance * interestRate / 100;
    balance = balance + interest;
}
public static void main(String[] args)
{   double savings = 10000;
    double rate = 5;
    updateBalance(savings, rate);
    // savings is not updated
    . . .
}
```

This doesn't work. Let's walk through the method call. As the method starts, the parameter variable `balance` is set to the same value as `savings`, and `interestRate` is set to `rate`. Then

Figure 3

A Method Cannot Modify
Numeric Parameters

Figure 4

A Method Can
Modify the
State of Object
Parameters

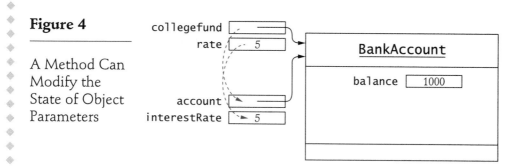

balance is modified, but that modification had no effect on savings, because balance is a separate variable (see Figure 3). When the method exits, balance is forgotten, and savings isn't increased.

In Java, a method can *never* modify the values of numbers that are passed to it. It is therefore plainly impossible to write a method updateBalance that actually updates a **double** parameter passed to it.

This sounds like a serious limitation, but in practice it is not a big problem. You already know the solution. If the bank balance is contained inside an *object*, you can pass an object reference to a method, and the method can modify the bank balance.

```
public static void updateBalance(BankAccount account,
   double interestRate)
{  double interest = account.getBalance * interestRate / 100;
   account.deposit(interest);
}

public static void main(String[] args)
{  BankAccount collegeFund = new BankAccount(10000);
   double rate = 5;
   updateBalance(collegeFund, rate);
   . . .
}
```

This method does update the balance of collegeFund. Figure 4 shows the reason. The object reference account is a copy of the object reference collegeFund, and both refer to the same object.

Advanced Topic 7.1

Call by Value and Call by Reference

In Java, method parameters are *copied* into the parameter variables when a method starts. Computer scientists call this call mechanism "call by value". There are some limitations to the "call by value" mechanism. As you saw in Common Error 7.2, it is not possible to implement methods that modify the contents of number variables. Other programming languages such as C++ support an alternate mechanism, called "call by reference". For example, in C++ it would be an easy matter to write a method that modifies a number, by using a so-called *reference parameter*. Here is the C++ code, for those of you who know C++:

```cpp
// this is C++
void updateBalance(double& balance, double interestRate)
   // balance is a double&, a reference to a double
{  double interest = balance * interestRate / 100;
   balance = balance + interest;
}

int main()
{  double savings = 10000;
   double rate = 5;
   updateBalance(savings, rate);
   // in C++, savings is updated
   . . .
}
```

You will sometimes read in Java books that "numbers are passed by value, objects are passed by reference". That is technically not quite correct. In Java, both numbers and object references are copied by value. To see this clearly, let us consider another scenario. This method tries to set the `betterAccount` parameter to the account with the better balance:

```java
public static void chooseAccount(BankAccount betterAccount,
   BankAccount candidate1, BankAccount candidate2)
{  if (candidate1.getBalance() > candidate2.getBalance())
      betterAccount = candidate1;
   else
      betterAccount = candidate2;
}

public static void main(String[] args)
{  BankAccount collegeFund = new BankAccount(10000);
   BankAccount momsSavings = new BankAccount(8000);
   BankAccount myAccount = null;

   chooseAccount(myAccount, momsSavings, collegeFund); // NO
   . . .
}
```

In this situation, we are not trying to change the state of the object to which the parameter variable **betterAccount** refers; We are trying to replace the object with a different one (see Figure 5). Now the parameter variable **betterAccount** is replaced with a reference to **collegeFund**, but that change does not affect the **myAccount** variable that is supplied in the call.

As you can see, a Java method can update an object's state, but it cannot *replace* the contents of an object reference. This shows that object references are passed by value in Java.

Of course, there is a simple remedy: Make the method return the better account:

```java
public static BankAccount chooseAccount(BankAccount candidate1,
    BankAccount candidate2);
{  BankAccount betterAccount;
   if (candidate1.getBalance() > candidate2.getBalance())
      betterAccount = candidate1;
   else
      betterAccount = candidate2;
   return betterAccount;
}
```

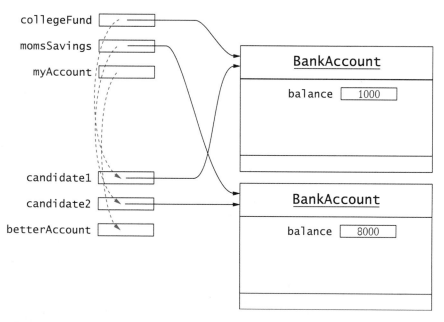

Figure 5

A Method Cannot Replace
Object Parameters

```
public static void main(String[] args)
{   BankAccount collegeFund = new BankAccount(10000);
    BankAccount momsSavings = new BankAccount(8000);
    BankAccount myAccount;

    myAccount = chooseAccount(momsSavings, collegeFund);
    . . .
}
```

7.4   The return Statement

A method that has a return type other than **void** must return a value, by executing a statement of the form

> **return** *expression* ;

Note that you can return the value of any expression. For example, consider the following method, a simplified version of the **getTax** method from the preceding chapter:

```
public double getTax()
{   double tax;

    if (income <= CUTOFF1)
        tax = RATE1 * income;
    else if (income <= CUTOFF2)
        tax = BASE2 + RATE2 * (income - CUTOFF1);
    else
        tax = BASE3 + RATE3 * (income - CUTOFF2);
    return tax;
}
```

You don't need to store the result in a variable and then return the variable. If you like, you can simply return the value of an expression:

```
public double getTax()
{   if (income <= CUTOFF1)
        return RATE1 * income;
    else if (income <= CUTOFF2)
        return BASE2 + RATE2 * (income - CUTOFF1);
    else
        return BASE3 + RATE3 * (income - CUTOFF2);
}
```

When the **return** statement is processed, the method exits *immediately*. This is convenient for handling exceptional cases at the beginning:

```
public double getTax()
{   if (income < 0) return 0;
    // never gets here if income < 0
    double tax;

    if (income <= CUTOFF1)
       tax = RATE1 * income;
    else if (income <= CUTOFF2)
       tax = BASE2 + RATE2 * (income - CUTOFF1);
    else
       tax = BASE3 + RATE3 * (income - CUTOFF2);
    return tax;
}
```

If the method is called when income is less than zero, the method returns 0 and the
remainder of the method is not executed.

It is important that every branch of a method return a value. Consider the following incorrect version of the getTax method:

```
public double getTax()
{   if (income > CUTOFF2)
       return BASE3 + RATE3 * (income - CUTOFF2);
    else if (income > CUTOFF1)
       return BASE2 + RATE2 * (income - CUTOFF1);
    else if (income >= 0)
       return RATE1 * income;
    // Error
}
```

If income is less than zero, no return value is specified. The Java compiler will flag
this as an error. The remedy is, of course, to return a value in every case.

Common Error 7.3

Missing Return Value

A method whose return type is not void always needs to return something. If the code of the
method contains several if/else branches, make sure that each one of them returns a value:

```
public static int sign(double x)
{   if (x < 0) return -1;
    if (x > 0) return +1;
    // Error: missing return value if x equals 0
}
```

This method computes the sign of a number: −1 for negative numbers and +1 for positive
numbers. If the parameter x is zero, however, no value is returned. The Java compiler will
refuse to compile a method that does not return a value under some circumstances.

7.5   Static Variables

Consider a slight variation of our **BankAccount** class: a bank account has both a balance and an *account number*:

```
public class BankAccount
{  . . .
   private double balance;
   private int accountNumber;
}
```

We want to assign account numbers sequentially. That is, we want the bank account constructor to construct the first account with number 1, the next with number 2, and so on. Therefore, we must store the last assigned account number somewhere. It makes no sense, though, to make this value into an instance variable:

```
public class BankAccount
{  . . .
   private double balance;
   private int accountNumber;
   private int lastAssignedNumber; // NO—won't work
}
```

In that case each *instance* of the **BankAccount** class would have its own value of **lastAssignedNumber**. Instead, we need to have a single value of **lastAssigned-Number** that is the same for the entire *class*. Such a variable is called a *class variable* or, in Java, a **static** variable, because you declare it using the **static** keyword.

```
public class BankAccount
{  . . .
   private double balance;
   private int accountNumber;
   private static int lastAssignedNumber;
}
```

Every **BankAccount** object has its own **balance** and **accountNumber** instance variables, but there is only a single copy of the **lastAssignedNumber** variable (see Figure 6).

Every method of a class can access its static variables. Here is the constructor of the **BankAccount** class, which increments the last assigned number and then uses it to initialize the account number of the object to be constructed:

```
class BankAccount
{  public BankAccount()
   {  // generate next account number to be assigned

      lastAssignedNumber++;
         // updates the class variable
      // assign to account number of this bank account

      accountNumber = lastAssignedNumber;
         // updates the instance variable
   }
   . . .
}
```

How do you initialize static variables? You can't initialize them in the class constructor:

```
public BankAccount()
{   lastAssignedNumber = 0; // NO—would reset to 0 each time
    . . .
}
```

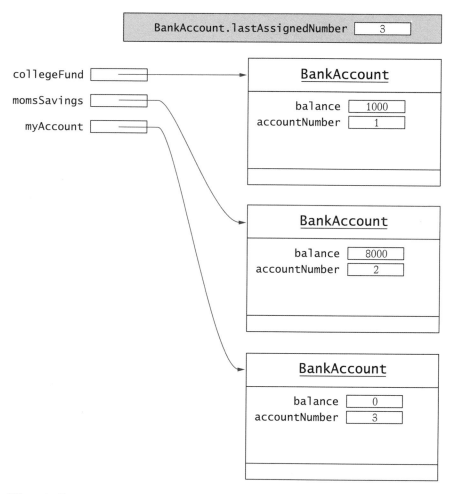

Figure 6

Instance Variables and a
Static Variable

Then the initialization would occur each time a new instance is constructed. There are three ways to initialize a static variable:

1. Do nothing. The static variable is then initialized with 0 (for numbers), `false` (for `boolean` values) or `null` (for objects).

2. Use an explicit initializer:

    ```
    public class BankAccount
    {  . . .
       private static lastAssignedNumber = 0;
    }
    ```

    The initialization is executed once before the first object of the class is constructed.

3. Use a static initialization block:

    ```
    public class BankAccount
    {  . . .
       private static lastAssignedNumber;
       static
       {  lastAssignedNumber = 0;
       }
    }
    ```

    All statements in the static initialization block are executed once before the first object of the class is constructed. This construct is rarely used in practice.

In general, static variables are considered undesirable. Methods that read and modify static variables have *side effects*. That is, the behavior of such methods does not simply depend on their inputs. If you call such a method twice, with the exact same inputs, it may still act differently, because the settings of the static variables are different. In fact, if you call the `BankAccount` constructor in the preceding example twice in a row, you will get two different results—that was the point of introducing the static `lastAssignedNumber` variable. However, in practical programs, static variables are rarely useful. If your program relies on a static variable, you should think carefully whether you merely used that static variable as a momentary convenience to "park" a value so that it can be picked up by another method. That is a bad strategy, because many other methods can also access and change that static variable.

Like instance variables, static variables, when used at all, should always be declared as `private` to ensure that methods of other classes do not change their values. However, static *constants* are often declared public. For example, the `Math` class defines several constant values, such as

```
public class Math
{  . . .
   public static final double PI = 3.14159265358979323846;
}
```

You can refer to such a constant in any method as `Math.PI`.

Why are these class variables called `static` variables? As with static methods, the `static` keyword itself is just a meaningless holdover from C++. But static variables and static methods have much in common: they apply to the entire *class*, not to specific instances of the class.

Quality Tip 7.3

Do Not Abuse Static Variables

We have purposefully not covered static variables earlier in this book. They make it possible to write programs that are hard to understand and maintain. Consider the following bad example. We want to sort three numbers in increasing order and print them. The `setMinMax` "helper" method sorts two numbers by setting the static variables `min` and `max` to hold the smaller and the larger values.

```
class Sort // bad code
{ public static void setMinMax(double a, double b)
   { if (a < b) { min = a; max = b; }
     else { min = b; max = a; }
   }

   public static void sortAndPrint3(double a, double b, double c)
   { setMinMax(a, b);
     if (c < min)
        System.out.println(c); // c is the smallest of the three
     else
     { System.out.print(min); // min is the smallest of the three
       setMinMax(c, max); //sort c and max
     }
     System.out.println(" " + min + " " + max);
        //print the other two
   }

   private static double min;
   private static double max;
}
```

The writer of this class had a problem. The `setMinMax` method computes both the smaller and the larger of its input values, but it can't return both. Therefore, the programmer chose to return neither value and instead stored them in static variables. In this example, the code will work correctly, but there is a danger. If you don't *immediately* retrieve the answers from the static variables, some other part of the program may overwrite them. Accidental overwriting happens with distressing regularity when static variables are used in larger programs, and therefore they are best avoided.

7.6 Variable Lifetime, Initialization, and Scope

You have now encountered the four kinds of variables that Java supports:

1. Instance variables
2. Static variables
3. Local variables
4. Parameter variables

The *lifetime* of a variable defines when the variable is created and how long it stays around.

When an object is constructed, all its instance variables are created. As long as any part of the program can access the object, it stays alive. Once the *garbage collector* has determined that no part of the program can access the object any more, it is recycled. That is, as long as you can reach an object, its instance variables stay intact.

A static variable is created when its class is first loaded, and it lives until the class is unloaded.

A local variable is created when the program enters the statement that defines it. It stays alive until the *block* that encloses the variable definition is exited. For example, consider the following method:

```java
public void withdraw(double amount)
{  if (amount <= balance)
   {  double newBalance = balance - amount;
         // local variable newBalance created
      balance = newBalance;
   } // end of lifetime of local variable newBalance
}
```

The newBalance variable is created when the declaration

```java
double newBalance = balance - amount;
```

is executed. It stays alive until the end of the enclosing block.

Finally, when a method is called, its parameter variables are created. They stay alive until the method returns to its caller:

```java
public void deposit(double amount)
      // parameter variable amount created
{  balance = balance + amount;
} // end of lifetime of parameter variable amount
```

Next, let us summarize what we know about the *initialization* of these four types of variables. Instance variables and static variables are automatically initialized with a default value (0 for numbers, false for boolean, null for objects) unless you specify another initial value. Parameter variables are initialized with copies of the actual parameters. Local variables are not initialized by default; you must supply an initial value, and the compiler complains if you try to use a local variable that you never initialized.

The *scope* of a variable is the part of the program in which you can access it. As you know, instance and static variables are usually declared as `private`, and you can access them only in the methods of their own class. The scope of a local variable extends from the point of its definition to the end of the enclosing block. The scope of a parameter variable is the entire body of its method.

It sometimes happens that the same variable name is used in two methods. Consider the variables r in the following example:

```java
public static double area(Rectangle rect)
{  double r = rect.getWidth() * rect.getHeight();
   return r;
}

public static void main(String[] args)
{  Rectangle r = new Rectangle(5, 10, 20, 30);
   double a = area(r);
   . . .
}
```

These variables are independent from each other. You can have variables with the same name r in different methods, just as you can have different motels with the same name "Bates Motel" in different cities.

In this situation, the scopes of the two variables named r are disjoint. Problems arise, however, if you have two or more variable names with overlapping scope. There are Java language rules that tell you which of the variables is accessed when you use the ambiguous name. The other variables are then *shadowed*. Here is a purposefully bad example. Suppose you use the same name for an instance variable and a local variable:

```java
public class Coin
{  . . .
   public void draw(Graphics2D g2)
   {  String name = "SansSerif"; // local variable
      int size = 18;
      g2.setFont(new Font(name, Font.BOLD, size));
      . . .
   }
   private String name; // instance variable
   private double value;
}
```

Inside the `draw` method, the variable name **name** could potentially have two meanings: the local variable or the instance variable. The Java language specifies that in this situation the *local* variable wins out. This sounds pretty arbitrary, but there is actually a good reason: You can still refer to the instance variable as `this.name`. Some people use this trick on purpose so that they don't have to come up with new variable names:

```java
public Coin(String name, double value)
{  this.name = name;
```

```
            this.value = value;
      }
```

It isn't actually a good idea to write code like this. You can easily change the name of the local variable to something else, such as fontName or aName. Then you, and the other readers of your code, don't have to remember the arcane language rule that local variables shadow instance variables.

Common Error 7.4

Shadowing

Using the same name accidentally for a local variable and an instance variable is a surprisingly common error. As you saw in the preceding section, the local variable then *shadows* the instance variable. Even though you may have meant to access the instance variable, the local variable is quietly accessed. For some reason, this problem is most common in constructors. Look at this example of a wrong constructor:

```
public class Coin
{   public Coin(double aValue, String aName)
    {   value = aValue;
        String name = aName; // oops...
    }

    . . .

    private double value;
    private String name;
}
```

The programmer declared a local variable name in the constructor. In all likelihood, that was just a typo—the programmer's fingers were on autopilot and typed the keyword String, even though the programmer all the time intended to access the instance variable. Unfortunately, the compiler gives no warning in this situation and quietly sets the local variable to the value of aName. The instance variable of the object that is being constructed is never touched, and remains null.

Advanced Topic 7.2

Alternative Forms of Instance Variable Initializations

As you have seen, instance variables are initialized with a default value (0, false, or null, depending on their type). You can then set them to any desired value in a constructor, and that is the style that we prefer in this book.

However, there are two other mechanisms to specify an initial value for instance variables. Just as with local variables, you can specify initialization values for instance variables. For example,

```
public class Coin
{   . . .
    private double value = 1;
    private String name = "Dollar";
}
```

These default values are used for *every* object that is being constructed.

There is also another, much less common, syntax, which is analogous to the static initialization blocks that you saw in Section 7.5. You can place one or more *initialization blocks* inside the class definition. All statements in that block are executed whenever an object is being constructed. Here is an example:

```
public class Coin
{   . . .
    {   value = 1;
        name = "Dollar";
    }
    private double value;
    private String name;
}
```

Since the rules for the alternative initialization mechanisms are somewhat complex, we recommend that you simply use constructors to do the job of construction.

Advanced Topic 7.3

Calling One Constructor from Another

Consider the **BankAccount** class. It has two constructors: a *default constructor* to initialize the balance with zero, and another constructor to supply an initial balance. In our case, the default constructor is only one line long. But in general, if the default constructor needs to initialize several instance variables, it can be convenient to have the default constructor call another constructor of the same class instead. There is a shorthand notation to achieve this:

```
public class BankAccount
{   public BankAccount(double initialBalance)
    {   balance = initialBalance;
    }

    public BankAccount()
    {   this(0);
    }
    . . .
}
```

The command `this(0);` means "Call another constructor of this class and supply the value 0." Such a constructor call can occur only *as the first line in another constructor*.

This syntax is a minor convenience, and we will not use it in this book. Actually, the use of the `this` keyword is a little confusing, because normally `this` denotes a reference to the implicit parameter. However, if `this` is followed by parentheses, it denotes a call to another constructor of this class.

7.7 Comments

As you progress to implementing more complex classes and methods, you must get into the habit of thoroughly *commenting* their behavior. In Java there is a very useful standard form for *documentation* comments, and there are tools to extract class and method documentation automatically. In fact, the online class library documentation has been automatically extracted from the class library code.

A documentation comment starts with a `/**`, a special comment delimiter used by the `javadoc` utility, which automatically extracts and formats documentation comments. (See Productivity Hint 7.1 for a description of this utility.) Then you describe the method's *purpose*. Then, for each method parameter, you supply a line that starts with `@param`, followed by the parameter name and a short explanation. Finally, you supply a line that starts with `@return`, describing the return value.

Here is a typical example.

```
/**
    Tests whether two floating-point numbers are
    equal, except for a roundoff error.
    @param x a floating-point number
    @param y a floating-point number
    @return true if x and y are approximately equal
*/
public static boolean approxEqual(double x, double y)
{  final double EPSILON = 1E-14;
   double xymax = Math.max(Math.abs(x), Math.abs(y));
   return Math.abs(x - y) <= EPSILON * xymax;
}
```

Whoa! The comment is longer than the method! Indeed it is, but that is irrelevant. We were just lucky this particular method was easy to compute. The method comment documents not the implementation but the idea—ultimately a more valuable property.

According to the standard Java documentation style, every method (except `main`) should have a comment explaining its purpose. If a method doesn't have parameters, you omit the `@param` tag. If the return type is `void`, omit the `@return` tag.

Occasionally, you will find that these comments are silly to write. That is particularly true for general-purpose methods:

```
/**
    Computes the maximum of two integers.
    @param x an integer
    @param y another integer
    @return the larger of the two inputs
*/
public static int max(int x, int y)
{  if (x > y)
        return x;
    else
        return y;
}
```

It should be pretty clear that max computes the maximum, and it is perfectly obvious that the method receives two integers x and y. Indeed, *in this case* the comment is somewhat overblown. We nevertheless strongly recommend writing the comment for every method. It is easy to spend more time pondering whether the comment is too trivial to write than it takes just to write it. In practical programming, very simple methods are rare. It is harmless to have a trivial method overcommented, whereas a complicated method without any comment can cause real grief to future maintenance programmers.

If you override a method of the class that your class extends (see Chapter 9), and you do not do any more than that method's comment already indicates, you do not have to add a comment. For example, if you override the paint method of Applet, then you don't have to explain what the paint method does. However, if your paint method does something interesting, of which the people who read and maintain your code should be aware, then by all means add the comment.

It is always a good idea to write the method comment *first,* before writing the method code. This is an excellent test to see that you firmly understand what you need to program. If you can't explain the method's inputs and outputs, you aren't ready to implement it.

The comments you have just seen explain individual *methods.* As you begin to write programs that are composed of multiple *classes,* you should also get into the habit of supplying a brief comment for each class, explaining its purpose.

The comment syntax for class comments is very simple: Just place the documentation comment above the class.

```
/**
    A bank account for depositing and withdrawing money.
*/
public class BankAccount
{  . . .
}
```

The javadoc utility, described in Productivity Hint 7.1, copies the *first* sentence of each class and method comment to summary tables. Therefore, it is best to write that first sentence with some care. It should start with an uppercase letter and end with a period. It does not have to be a grammatically complete sentence, but it should be meaningful when it is pulled out of the comment and displayed in a summary.

Quality Tip 7.4

Keep Methods Short

There is a certain cost for writing a method. You need to write the documentation; you need to pass parameters when you call the method; you should test the method in isolation; you should think how to make the method reusable. To avoid this cost, it is always tempting just to stuff more and more code in one place rather than going through the trouble of breaking up the code into separate methods. It is quite common to see inexperienced programmers produce methods that are several hundred lines long.

Ideally, each method should contain no more than one screenful of text. That makes it easy to read the code in the text editor. As a rule of thumb, a method longer than 30 lines (not counting comments) is usually suspect and should probably be broken up. Of course, there are exceptions to this rule, but they are surprisingly rare. Most programmers, when forced to break up long methods into smaller ones, find the result superior to their original version.

Productivity Hint 7.1

The javadoc Utility

The Java Development Kit from Sun Microsystems provides a utility called **javadoc** to generate documentation that can be inspected by a Web browser for your programs (see Figure 7). You must use the *exact* format for method comments that was described in the preceding section. That is, you must write comments of the form

```
/**
    purpose
    @param name  description
    @param name  description
    @return description
*/
```

Every comment must come immediately before the class or method to which it applies. The first line must be /**. (In early versions of the **javadoc** program, each subsequent line had to start with a *; the designers of those versions apparently were unaware of Productivity Hint 2.1. That requirement has now been removed.)

From a command shell, you invoke the **javadoc** utility with the command

```
javadoc MyProg.java
```

The **javadoc** utility then produces a file `MyProg.html` in HTML format, which you can inspect in a browser. If you know HTML (see Chapter 4), you can embed HTML tags into the comments to specify fonts or add images. Perhaps most importantly, **javadoc** automatically provides *hyperlinks* to other classes and methods.

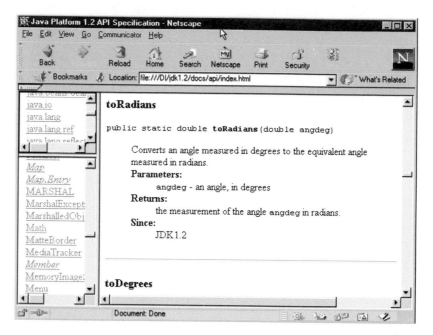

Figure 7

An HTML Page Produced by the
javadoc Utility

The **javadoc** tool is wonderful because it does one thing right: it lets you put the documentation *together with your code*. That way, when you update your programs, you can see right away which documentation needs to be updated. Hopefully, you will then update it right then and there. Afterwards, run **javadoc** again and get a nicely formatted HTML page.

Productivity Hint 7.2

Global Search and Replace

Suppose you chose an unfortunate name for a method—say **ae** instead of **approxEqual**—and you regret your choice. Of course, you can locate all occurrences of **ae** in your code and replace them manually. However, most programming editors have a command to search for the **ae**'s automatically and replace them with **approxEqual**.

You need to specify some details about the search:

◆   Do you want it to ignore case? That is, should **Ae** be a match? In Java you usually don't want that.

◆ Do you want it to match whole words only? If not, the `ae` in `maelstrom` is also a match. In Java you usually want to match whole words.

◆ Is this a regular-expression search? No, but regular expressions can make searches even more powerful—see Productivity Hint 7.3.

◆ Do you want to confirm each replace, or simply go ahead and replace all matches? I usually confirm the first three or four, and when I see that it works as expected, I give the go-ahead to replace the rest. (By the way, a *global* replace means to replace all occurrences in the document.) Good text editors can undo a global replace that has gone awry. Find out whether yours will.

◆ Do you want the search to go from the cursor to the rest of the program file, or should it search the currently selected text? Restricting replacement to a portion of the file can be very useful, but in this example you would want to move the cursor to the top of the file and then replace until the end of the file.

Not every editor has all these options. You should investigate what your editor offers.

Productivity Hint 7.3

Regular Expressions

Regular expressions describe character patterns. For example, numbers have a simple form. They contain one or more digits. The regular expression describing numbers is `[0-9]+`. The set `[0-9]` denotes any digit between 0 and 9, and the + means "one or more".

What good is it? Several utility programs use regular expressions to locate matching text. Also, the search commands of some programming editors understand regular expressions. The most popular program that uses regular expressions is *grep* (which stands for "generalized regular expression pattern"). You can run grep from a command prompt or from inside some compilation environments. It needs a regular expression and one or more files to search. When grep runs, it displays a set of lines that match the regular expression.

Suppose you want to look for all magic numbers (see Quality Tip 2.2) in a file. The command

```
grep [0-9]+ Homework.java
```

lists all lines in the file Homework.java that contain sequences of digits. That isn't terribly useful; lines with variable names `x1` will be listed. OK, you want sequences of digits that do *not* immediately follow letters:

```
grep [^A-Za-z][0-9]+ Homework.java
```

The set `[^A-Za-z]` denotes any characters that are *not* in the ranges A ro Z and a to z. This works much better, and it shows only lines that contain actual numbers.

There are a bewildering number of symbols (sometimes called *wildcards*) with special meanings in the regular expression syntax, and unfortunately, different programs use different styles of regular expressions. It is best to consult the program documentation for details.

◆ ◆

◆ **Productivity Hint** 7.4

Empty Stubs

Some people first write all code and then start compiling and testing. Others prefer to see some results quickly. If you are among the impatient, you will like the technique of *stubs*.

A stub is a method that is completely empty and returns a trivial value. The stub can be used to test that the code compiles and to debug the logic of other parts of the program.

```
/**
    Gives a description of the
    effects of an earthquake.
    @return the description
*/
public getDescription String ()
{  return "mumble";
}
```

If you combine the stub with the remainder of the program and test it, you may get an output of "**Effect of earthquake:**", which shows you that you are on the right track. You can then flesh out one stub at a time.

This method is particularly helpful if you like composing your programs directly on the computer. Of course, the initial planning requires thought, not typing, and is best done at a desk. Once you know what methods you need, however, you can enter their interface descriptions and stubs, compile, implement one method, compile and test, implement the next method, compile and test, until you are done.

7.8   Preconditions

What should a method do when it is called with inappropriate inputs? For example, how should `Math.sqrt(-1)` react? What should `account.deposit(-1000)` do? There are two choices.

◆ A method can fail safely and return to its caller. For example, the `deposit` method can simply do nothing when called with an unexpected input.

◆ A method can terminate the program. For example, the `deposit` method can call
`System.exit(1)` when called with an unexpected method.

Java has a third, very sophisticated mechanism that allows a method to terminate and send an *exception*, which signals to an appropriate receiver that something has gone very wrong. As long as such a receiver is in place, it can handle the problem and avoid termination of the program. Right now, we'll show you how to terminate a method by *throwing* an exception.

```
public double deposit(double amount)
{  if (amount <= 0)
      throw new IllegalArgumentException();
   balance = balance + amount;
}
```

When the method is called with an illegal argument, the program aborts with an error message

```
java.lang.IllegalArgumentException
      at BankAccount.deposit(BankAccount.java:14)
```

Of course, for realistic programs, aborting the program is not desirable. The Java exception-handling mechanism allows programmers to *catch* the exception and take corrective action, as we saw in Section 2.7.2. Turn to Chapter 13 for more information on this topic.

When writing a method, how should you handle bad inputs? Should you terminate the method or should you fail safely? Consider `Math.sqrt`. It would be an easy matter to implement a square root method that returns 0 for negative values and the actual square root for positive values. Suppose you use that method to compute the intersection points of a circle and a line. Suppose they don't intersect, but you forgot to take that possibility into account. Now the square root of a negative number will return a wrong value, namely 0, and you will obtain two bogus intersection points. (Actually, you will get the same point twice.) You may miss that during testing, and the faulty program may make it into production. This isn't a big deal for our graphics program, but suppose the program directs a dental drill robot. It would start drilling somewhere outside the tooth. This makes termination an attractive alternative. It is hard to overlook termination during testing, and it is better if the drill stops rather than boring through the patient's gums.

In general, it is best if you don't fudge a return value, or quietly do nothing, when presented with an improper input value. Thus, you should expect that some methods have conditions that describe what is a valid input and what is not. Such a condition is called a *precondition* of a method.

Here is what you should do when writing a method:

- Establish clear *preconditions* for all inputs. Write in the `@param` comment what values you are not willing to handle.
- Throw an exception if a precondition is not satisfied.
- Be sure to supply correct results for all inputs that fulfill the precondition.

Let us apply that strategy to the `deposit` method:

```
/**
   Deposits money into this account.
   @param amount  the amount of money to deposit; must be > 0
*/
```

```
public void deposit(double amount)
{  if (amount <= 0)
      throw new IllegalArgumentException();
   balance = balance + amount;
}
```

We advertised that **amount** must be greater than 0. This is a precondition of the **deposit** method. The method is responsible only for handling inputs that conform to the precondition. It is free to do *anything* if the precondition is not fulfilled. It would be perfectly legal if the method reformatted the hard disk every time it was called with a wrong input. Naturally, that isn't reasonable. Instead, we check the precondition and throw an exception if it is not fulfilled. In the absence of a handler for this exception, the program terminates. That may not be "nice", but it is legal. Remember that the method can do anything if the precondition is not fulfilled.

Another alternative is to let the method fail safely by doing nothing when called with improper arguments:

```
/**
    Deposits money into this account.
    @param amount  the amount of money to deposit; must be > 0
*/
public void deposit(double amount)
{  if (amount <= 0)
      return;
   balance = balance + amount;
}
```

That is not as good. If the program calling the **deposit** method has a few bugs that cause it to pass a negative amount as an input value, then the version that throws the exception will make the bugs very obvious during testing—it is hard to ignore when the program aborts. The fail-safe version, on the other hand, will quietly do nothing, and you may not notice that it performs some wrong calculations as a consequence.

Bertrand Meyer [1] compares preconditions to contracts. The method promises to compute the correct answer for all inputs that fulfill the precondition. The caller promises never to call the method with illegal inputs. If the caller fulfills its promise and gets a wrong answer, it can take the method to programmer's court. If the caller doesn't fulfill its promise and something terrible happens as a consequence, it has no recourse.

7.9   Recursion

An important mathematical function is the *factorial*. The value $n!$ (read n factorial) is defined to be the product $1 \times 2 \times 3 \times \cdots \times n$. Also, by convention, $0! = 1$. Factorials for negative numbers are not defined. Here are the first few values of the factorial function:

n	$n!$
0	1
1	1
2	2
3	6
4	24
5	120
6	720
7	5040
8	40320

As you can see, these values get large very quickly. The factorial function is interesting, because it describes how many ways one can scramble or *permute* n distinct objects. For example, there are 3! = 6 rearrangements of the letters in the string "rum": namely mur, mru, umr, urm, rmu, and rum itself. There are 24 permutations of the string "drum".

How can you program a method that computes the factorial function? Of course you can't write

```
public static int factorial(int n)
{   return 1 * 2 * 3 * ... * n;
}
```

There is no magic "..." operation in Java that fills in the details.

Consider how I filled in the table of factorials. When I computed 6! for the table, I did not multiply $1 \times 2 \times 3 \times 4 \times 5 \times 6$. I took the preceding entry, 120, and multiplied that by 6. That is, $6! = 6 \times 5!$. In general, $n! = n \times (n-1)!$ You can implement that.

```
public static int factorial(int n)
{   int result = n * factorial(n - 1);
    return result;
}
```

In Java, a method can call itself, as long as it calls itself with a simpler value. Let us walk through this method, computing factorial(6). The first line asks to compute 6 * factorial(5). You don't know what that is, so you temporarily suspend that thought and walk through the computation of factorial(5). It needs to compute 5 * factorial(4). You don't know what that is either, so you temporarily suspend *that* thought and work out factorial(4), which needs factorial(3). Eventually you are down to factorial(2), factorial(1), and factorial(0). Now you should be getting nervous. That call returns 0 * factorial(-1), so something must be wrong. You really must handle 0! separately and have it return 1.

Program Fac.java

```java
public class Fac
{   public static void main(String[] args)
    {   ConsoleReader console = new ConsoleReader(System.in);
        System.out.println("Please enter a number:");
        int n = console.readInt();
        System.out.println(n + "! = " + factorial(n));
    }

    /**
        Computes the factorial of an integer.
        @param n an integer >= 0
        @return n!
    */
    public static int factorial(int n)
    {   if (n == 0)
            return 1;
        else
        {   int result = n * factorial(n - 1);
            return result;
        }
    }
}
```

With that fix, everything goes well. (It helps that 1! $= 1 \times 0! = 1 \times 1$.) Here is an illustration of the sequence of calls and return values.

```
factorial(6) calls  factorial(5)
    factorial(5) calls  factorial(4)
        factorial(4) calls  factorial(3)
            factorial(3) calls  factorial(2)
                factorial(2) calls  factorial(1)
                    factorial(1) calls  factorial(0)
                        factorial(0) returns  1
                    factorial(1) returns 1 (1×1)
                factorial(2) returns 2 (2×1)
            factorial(3) returns 6 (3×2)
        factorial(4) returns 24 (4×6)
    factorial(5) returns 120 (5×24)
factorial(6) returns 720 (6×120)
```

The process of having a method call itself over and over is called *recursion*. The call pattern of a recursive method looks complicated, and the key to the successful design of a recursive method is *not to think about it*.

Instead, let us look at the `factorial` method again. The first part is utterly reasonable.

```
if (n == 0)
   return 1;
```

That just sets 0! to 1. The next part is actually also reasonable,

```
else
{  int result = n * factorial(n - 1);
   return result;
}
```

as long as you are willing to believe that the method works for simpler inputs. If `factorial` works as advertised, then `factorial(n - 1)` is $1 \times 2 \times 3 \times \cdots \times (n-1)$. Multiplying that number by n yields $n \times 1 \times 2 \times 3 \times \cdots \times (n-1) = n!$.

There are two key requirements to make sure that the recursion is successful:

◆ Every recursive call must simplify the computation in some way.

◆ There must be special cases to handle the simplest computations.

For the `factorial` method, "simpler" means "smaller parameter". In general, though, "simpler" does not necessarily mean smaller. It might mean shorter strings, or curves with fewer wiggles.

The `factorial` method calls itself again with smaller and smaller integers. Eventually the parameter value must reach 0, and there is a special case for computing 0!. Thus, the `factorial` method always succeeds.

Actually, you have to be careful. What happens when you call `factorial(-1)`? It calls `-1 * factorial(-2)`, so the parameter value gets bigger in magnitude. We never wanted to permit this case in the first place. Now is a good time to apply the lesson from Section 7.7 and spell out the precondition of the method:

```
/**
   Computes the factorial of an integer.
   @param n an integer ≥ 0
   @return n!
*/
public static int factorial(int n)
{  if (n < 0) throw new IllegalArgumentException();

   if (n == 0)
      return 1;
   else
   {  int result = n * factorial(n - 1);
      return result;
   }
}
```

Common Error 7.5

Infinite Recursion

A common programming error is an infinite recursion: a method calling itself over and over with no end in sight. The computer needs some amount of memory for bookkeeping for each call. After some number of calls, all memory that is available for this purpose is exhausted. Your program shuts down and reports a "stack fault".

Infinite recursion happens either because the parameter values don't get simpler or because a special terminating case is missing.

Random Fact 7.1

The Explosive Growth of Personal Computers

In 1971, Marcian E. "Ted" Hoff, an engineer at Intel Corporation, was working on a chip for a manufacturer of electronic calculators. He realized that it would be a better idea to develop a *general-purpose* chip that could be *programmed* to interface with the keys and display of a calculator, rather than to do yet another custom design. Thus, the *microprocessor* was born. At the time, its primary application was as a controller for calculators, washing machines, and the like. It took years for the computer industry to notice that a genuine central processing unit was now available as a single chip.

Hobbyists were the first to catch on. In 1974 the first computer *kit,* the Altair 8800, was available from MITS Electronics for about $350. The kit consisted of the microprocessor, a circuit board, a very small amount of memory, toggle switches, and a row of display lights. Purchasers had to solder and assemble it, then program it in machine language through the toggle switches. It was not a big hit.

The first big hit was the Apple II. It was a real computer with a keyboard, a monitor, and a floppy disk drive. When it was first released, users had a $3000 machine that could play Space Invaders, run a primitive bookkeeping program, or let users program it in BASIC. The original Apple II did not even support lowercase letters, making it worthless for word processing. The breakthrough came in 1979 with a new *spreadsheet* program, VisiCalc. In a spreadsheet, you enter financial data and their relationships into a grid of rows and columns (see Figure 8). Then you modify some of the data and watch in real time how the others change. For example, you can see how changing the mix of widgets in a manufacturing plant might affect estimated costs and profits. Middle managers in companies, who understood computers and were fed up with having to wait for hours or days to get their data runs back from the computing center, snapped up VisiCalc and the computer that was needed to run it. For them, the computer was a spreadsheet machine.

The next big hit was the IBM Personal Computer, ever after known as the PC. It was the first widely available personal computer that used Intel's 16-bit processor, the 8086, whose successors are still being used in personal computers today. The success of the PC was based not on any engineering breakthroughs but on the fact that it was easy to *clone*. IBM published specifications for plug-in cards, and it went one step further. It published the exact source code of the so-called BIOS (Basic Input/Output System), which controls the keyboard, monitor, ports, and disk drives and must be installed in ROM form in every PC. This allowed

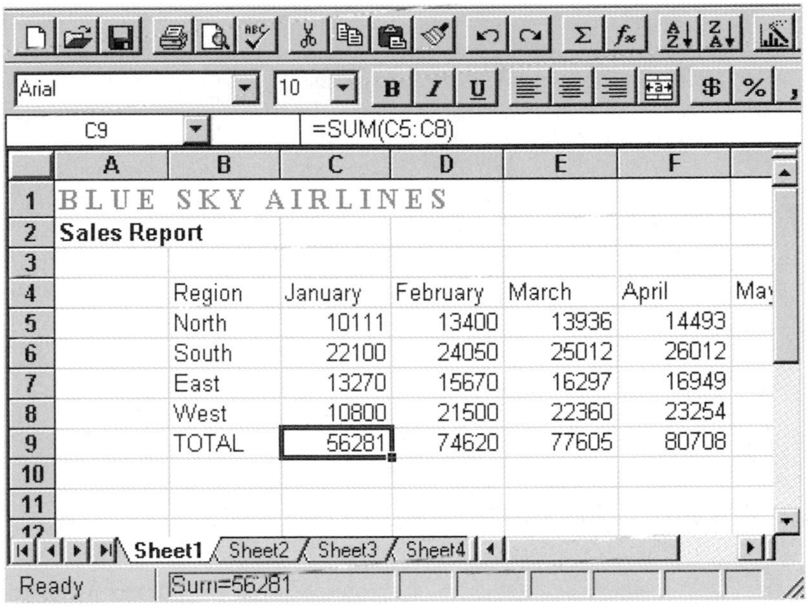

Figure 8

A Spreadsheet

third-party vendors of plug-in cards to ensure that the BIOS code, and third-party extensions of it, interacted correctly with the equipment. Of course, the code itself was the property of IBM and could not be copied legally. Perhaps IBM did not foresee that functionally equivalent versions of the BIOS nevertheless could be recreated by others. Compaq, one of the first clone vendors, had fifteen engineers, who certified that they had never seen the original IBM code, write a new version that conformed precisely to the IBM specifications. Other companies did the same, and soon there were a number of vendors selling computers that ran the same software as IBM's PC but distinguished themselves by a lower price, increased portability, or better performance. In time, IBM lost its dominant position in the PC market. It is now one of many companies producing IBM PC–compatible computers.

IBM never produced an *operating system* for its PCs—that is, the software that organizes the interaction between the user and the computer, starts application programs, and manages disk storage and other resources. Instead, IBM offered customers the option of three separate operating systems. Most customers couldn't care less about the operating system. They chose the system that was able to launch most of the few applications that existed at the time. It happened to be DOS (Disk Operating System) by Microsoft. Microsoft cheerfully licensed the same operating system to other hardware vendors and encouraged software companies to write DOS applications. A huge number of useful application programs for PC-compatible machines was the result.

PC applications were certainly useful, but they were not easy to learn. Every vendor developed a different *user interface:* the collection of keystrokes, menu options, and settings that a user needed to master to use a software package effectively. Data exchange between applications was difficult, because each program used a different data format. The Apple Macintosh changed all that in 1984. The designers of the Macintosh had the vision to supply an intuitive user interface with the computer and to force software developers to adhere to it. It took Microsoft and PC–compatible manufacturers years to catch up.

The book [2] is highly recommended for an amusing and irreverent account of the emergence of personal computers.

At the time of this writing, it is estimated that one in two U.S. households owns a personal computer and that one in four uses the Internet at least occasionally. Most personal computers are used for word processing, home finance (banking, budgeting, taxes), accessing information from CD-ROM and online sources, and entertainment. Some analysts predict that the personal computer will merge with the television set and cable network into an entertainment and *information appliance.*

Chapter Summary

1. A *method* receives input parameters and computes a result that depends on those inputs.

2. *Actual parameters* are supplied in the method call. They are stored in the *formal parameter* variables of the method. The types of the actual and formal parameters must match.

3. Once the method result has been computed, the `return` statement terminates the method and sends the result to the caller.

4. Method comments explain the purpose of the method and the meaning of the parameters and return value, as well as any special requirements.

5. Side effects are externally observable results outside the implicit parameter caused by a method call, for example, modifying a static variable or displaying a message. Generally, side effects should be avoided.

6. In Java, methods can never change number parameters. Object parameters can be modified but not replaced.

7. *Preconditions* are restrictions on the method parameters. If a method is called in violation of a precondition, the method is not responsible for computing the right result. To protect against violations of preconditions, you can throw an exception.

8. A method can call itself *recursively,* but it must provide a simpler parameter to itself in successive recursive calls. There must be special cases to handle the simplest parameter values.

Further Reading

[1] Bertrand Meyer, *Object-Oriented Software Construction,* Prentice-Hall, 1989, chapter 7.

[2] Robert X. Cringely, *Accidental Empires,* Addison-Wesley, 1992.

Classes, Objects, and Methods Introduced in This Chapter

```
java.lang.IllegalArgumentException
```

Review Exercises

Exercise R7.1. Give realistic examples of the following:

- ◆ A method with a `double` parameter and a `double` return value
- ◆ A method with an `int` parameter and a `double` return value
- ◆ A method with an `int` parameter and a `String` return value
- ◆ A method with two `double` parameters and a `boolean` return value
- ◆ A method with no parameter and an `int` return value
- ◆ A method with an `Ellipse2D.Double` parameter and a `double` return value
- ◆ A method with a `Line2D.Double` parameter and a `Point2D.Double` return value

Just describe what these methods do. Do not program them. For example, some answers to the first question are "sine" and "square root".

Exercise R7.2. True or false?

- ◆ A method has exactly one `return` statement.
- ◆ A method has at least one `return` statement.
- ◆ A method has at most one return value.
- ◆ A method with return value `void` never has a `return` statement.
- ◆ When executing a `return` statement, the method exits immediately.
- ◆ A method without parameters always has a side effect.
- ◆ A method with return value `void` always has a side effect.
- ◆ A method without side effects always returns the same value when called with the same parameters.

Exercise R7.3. Write detailed method comments for the following methods. Be sure to describe those conditions under which the method cannot compute its result. Just write the comments, not the methods.

```
public static double sqrt(double x)
public static Point2D.Double midpoint(Point2D.Double a,
    Point2D.Double b)
public static double area(Ellipse2D.Double c)
public static String romanNumeral(int n)
public static double slope(Line2D.Double a)
public static boolean isLeapYear(int year)
public static String weekday(int day)
```

Exercise R7.4. Consider these methods:

```
public static double f(double x)
{  return g(x) + Math.sqrt(h(x));
}

public static double g(double x) { return 4 * h(x); }

public static double h(double x) { return x * x + k(x) - 1; }

public static double k(double x) { return 2 * (x + 1); }
```

Without actually compiling and running a program, determine the results of the following method calls:

```
double x1 = f(2);
double x2 = g(h(2));
double x3 = k(g(2) + h(2));
double x4 = f(0) + f(1) + f(2);
double x5 = f(-1) + g(-1) + h(-1) + k(-1);
```

Exercise R7.5. A *predicate* method is a method with return type `boolean`. Give an example of a predicate method and an example of how to use it.

Exercise R7.6. What is the difference between a parameter value and a return value? What is the difference between a parameter value and a parameter variable? What is the difference between a parameter value and a value parameter?

Exercise R7.7. Ideally, a method should have no side effect. Can you write a program in which no method has a side effect? Would such a program be useful?

Exercise R7.8. What is the difference between a method and a program? The `main` method and a program?

Exercise R7.9. What preconditions do the following methods from the standard Java library have?

```
Math.sqrt
Math.tan
```

```
Math.log

Math.exp

Math.pow

Math.abs
```

Exercise R7.10. When a method is called with parameters that violate its precondition, it can terminate, or it can fail safely. Give two examples of library methods (standard or the library methods used in this book) that fail safely when called with invalid parameters, and give two examples of library methods that terminate.

Exercise R7.11. Consider the following method that is intended to swap the values of two floating-point numbers:

```java
public static void falseSwap(double a, double b)
{   double temp = a;
    a = b;
    b = temp;
}

public static void main(String[] args)
{   double x = 3;
    double y = 4;
    falseSwap(x, y);
    System.out.println(x + " " + y);
}
```

Why doesn't the method swap the contents of x and y?

Exercise R7.12. How *can* you write a method that swaps two floating-point numbers? *Hint:* Point2D.Double.

Programming Exercises

Exercise P7.1. Implement the BankAccount.equals method described in Section 7.2.

Exercise P7.2. Write a method printSorted(int a, int b, int c) that prints its three inputs in sorted order.

Exercise P7.3. Write static methods

```java
public static double sphereVolume(double r)
public static double sphereSurface(double r)
public static double cylinderVolume(double r, double h)
public static double cylinderSurface(double r, double h)
public static double coneVolume(double r, double h)
public static double coneSurface(double r, double h)
```

that compute the volume and surface area of a sphere with radius r, a cylinder with circular base with radius r and height h, and a cone with circular base with radius r and height h. Place them into an appropriate class. Then write a program that prompts the user for the values of r and h, calls the six methods, and prints the results.

Exercise P7.4. Write methods

```
public static double perimeter(Ellipse2D.Double c);
public static double area(Ellipse2D.Double c);
```

that compute the area and the perimeter of the ellipse e. Use these methods in a graphics program that prompts the user to specify an ellipse. Then display messages with the perimeter and area of the ellipse.

Exercise P7.5. Write a method

```
public static double distance(Point2D.Double p, Point2D.Double q)
```

that computes the distance between two points. Write a test program that asks the user to select two points. Then display the distance.

Exercise P7.6. Write the method

```
public static boolean isInside(Point2D.Double p, Ellipse2D.Double e)
```

that tests whether a point is inside an ellipse.

Exercise P7.7. Write a method

```
public static double readDouble(String prompt)
```

that displays the prompt string, followed by a space, reads a floating-point number in, and returns it. Here is a typical usage:

```
salary = readDouble("Please enter your salary:");
percRaise =
    readDouble("What percentage raise would you like?");
```

Exercise P7.8. Write methods

```
public static displayH(Graphics2D g2, Point2D.Double p);
public static displayE(Graphics2D g2, Point2D.Double p);
public static displayL(Graphics2D g2, Point2D.Double p);
public static displayO(Graphics2D g2, Point2D.Double p);
```

that show the letters H, E, L, O on the graphics window, where the point p is the top left corner of the letter. Fit the letter in a 1 × 1 square. Then call the methods to draw the words "HELLO" and "HOLE" on the graphics display. Draw lines and circles. Do not use the **drawString** method. Do not use **System.out**.

Exercise P7.9. *Leap years.* Write a predicate method

```
public static boolean isLeapYear(int year)
```

that tests whether a year is a leap year: that is, a year with 366 days. Leap years are necessary to keep the calendar synchronized with the sun, because the earth revolves around the sun once every 365.25 days. Actually, that figure is not entirely precise, and for all dates after 1582 the *Gregorian correction* applies. Usually years that are divisible by 4 are leap years, for example 1996. However, years that are divisible by 100 (for example, 1900) are not leap years, but years that are divisible by 400 are leap years (for example, 2000).

Exercise P7.10. *Postal bar codes.* For faster sorting of letters, the United States Postal Service encourages companies that send large volumes of mail to use a bar code denoting the ZIP code (see Figure 9).

The encoding scheme for a five-digit ZIP code is shown in Figure 10. There are full-height frame bars on each side. The five encoded digits are followed by a correction digit, which is computed as follows: Add up all digits, and choose the correction digit to make the sum a multiple of 10. For example, the ZIP code 95014 has sum of digits 19, so the correction digit is 1 to make the sum equal to 20.

Each digit of the ZIP code, and the correction digit, is encoded according to the following table:

	7	4	2	1	0
1	0	0	0	1	1
2	0	0	1	0	1
3	0	0	1	1	0
4	0	1	0	0	1
5	0	1	0	1	0
6	0	1	1	0	0
7	1	0	0	0	1
8	1	0	0	1	0
9	1	0	1	0	0
0	1	1	0	0	0

where 0 denotes a half bar and 1 a full bar. Note that they represent all combinations of two full and three half bars. The digit can be easily computed from the bar code

Figure 9

A Postal Bar Code

```
*************** ECRLOT ** CO57

CODE  C671RTS2
JOHN DOE                                    CO57
1009 FRANKLIN BLVD
SUNNYVALE      CA 95014 – 5143
```

IlIluuI.I.IIIuuuIIIuIuIIIuuIIIuIuIIIuIuI

Figure 10

Encoding for
Five-Digit Bar Codes

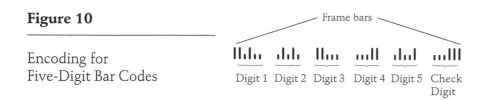

using the column weights 7, 4, 2, 1, 0. For example, 01100 is $0 \times 7 + 1 \times 4 + 1 \times 2 + 0 \times 1 + 0 \times 0 = 6$. The only exception is 0, which would yield 11 according to the weight formula.

Write a program that asks the user for a ZIP code and prints the bar code. Use : for half bars, | for full bars. For example, 95014 becomes

||:|:::|:|:||:::::::||:|::|:::|||

Exercise P7.11. Write a program that displays the bar code, using actual bars, on your graphic screen. *Hint:* Write methods `halfBar(Point2D.Double start)` and `fullBar(Point2D.Double start)`.

Exercise P7.12. Write a program that reads in a bar code (with : denoting half bars and | denoting full bars) and prints out the ZIP code it represents. Print an error message if the bar code is not correct.

Exercise P7.13. Consider the following algorithm for computing x^n for integer n. If $n < 0$, x^n is $1/x^{-n}$. x^0 is 1. If n is positive and even, then $x^n = (x^{n/2})^2$. If n is positive and odd, then $x^n = x^{n-1} \cdot x$. Implement a method `intPower(double x, int n)` that uses this algorithm.

Exercise P7.14. *Towers of Hanoi.* This is a well-known puzzle. A stack of disks of decreasing size is to be transported from the leftmost peg to the rightmost peg. The middle peg can be used as a temporary storage. (See Figure 11.) One disk can be moved at one time, from any peg to any other peg. You can only place smaller disks on top of larger ones, not the other way around. Write a method that prints the moves necessary to solve the puzzle for n disks. (Ask the user for n at the beginning of the program.) Print moves in the form

```
Move disk from peg 1 to peg 3
```

Hint: Rather than writing a method `hanoi()` without parameters, write a method

```
public static void hanoi(int from, int to, int n)
```

that moves the top n disks from the peg `from` to the peg `to`. Then figure out how you can achieve that by first moving the pile of the top $n - 1$ disks to the third peg, moving the nth disk to the destination, and then moving the pile from the third peg to the destination peg, this time using the original peg as the temporary storage.

Exercise P7.15. Write a method

```
public static int find(String s, String t)
```

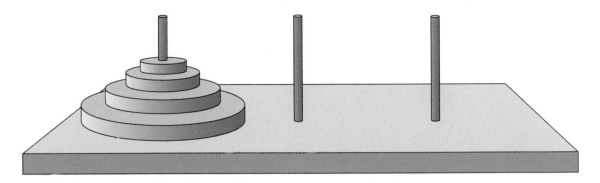

Figure 11

Towers of Hanoi

that tests whether the string **t** is contained in the string **s**. If so, it returns the offset of the first match. If not, it returns −1. For example,

```
find("Mississippi", "is") returns 1.
find("Mississippi", "Miss") returns 0.
find("Mississippi", "pi")returns 9.
find("Mississippi", "hip") returns −1.
```

Hint: If **t** is longer than **s**, you can return −1 with confidence. Otherwise, compare **t** and the initial substring of **s** with **t.length()** characters. If those are the same strings, then return 0. Otherwise call the method recursively with the tail of **s** (that is, **s** without the first character).

Exercise P7.16. A *palindrome* is a string that is identical to its reverse, ignoring upper- and lowercase, spaces, and punctuation marks. Examples are "Radar", "A man, a plan, a canal: Panama", and of course, the world's first palindrome: "Madam, I'm Adam". Write a predicate method

```
public static boolean isPalindrome(String s)
```

Use the following logic: If the first character of **s** (that is, **s.substring(0, 1)**) is not a letter, simply ignore it by calling **isPalindrome(s.substring(1, s.length()))**. Do the same for the last character. If both the first and last characters are letters, check whether they match. If they don't, the string is not a palindrome. If they do, it might be one. In that case remove both the first character and the last and call the method again. When should the recursion stop?

Testing and Debugging

Chapter Goals

- ◆ To learn how to design test harnesses for testing components of your programs in isolation

- ◆ To understand the principles of test case selection and evaluation

- ◆ To learn how to use assertions

- ◆ To become familiar with the debugger

- ◆ To learn strategies for effective debugging

A complex program never works right the first time; it will contain errors, commonly called *bugs,* and will need to be tested. It is easier to test a program if it has been designed with testing in mind. This is a common engineering practice: On television circuit boards or in the wiring of an automobile, you will find lights and wire connectors that serve no direct purpose for the TV or car but are put in place for the repair person in case something goes wrong. In the first part of this chapter you will learn how to instrument your programs in a similar way. It is a little more work up-front, but that work is amply repaid by shortened debugging times.

In the second part of this chapter you will learn how to run the debugger to cope with programs that don't do the right thing.

8.1   Unit Tests

The single most important testing tool is the unit test of a method or a set of co-operating methods. For this test, the methods are compiled outside the program in which they will be used, together with a *test harness* that feeds parameters to the methods.

The test arguments can come from one of three sources: from user input, by running through a range of values in a loop, and as random values.

In the following sections, we will use a simple example for a method to test, namely an approximation algorithm to compute square roots that was known to the ancient Greeks. The algorithm starts by guessing a value x that might be somewhat close to the desired square root $\sqrt{a}$. The initial value doesn't have to be very close; $x = a$ is a perfectly good choice. Now consider the quantities x and a/x. If $x < \sqrt{a}$, then $a/x > a/\sqrt{a} = \sqrt{a}$. Similarly, if $x > \sqrt{a}$, then $a/x < a/\sqrt{a} = \sqrt{a}$. That is, $\sqrt{a}$ lies between x and a/x. Make the *midpoint* of that interval our improved guess of the square root, as shown in Figure 1. Therefore set $x_{new} = (x + a/x)/2$ and repeat the procedure—that is, compute the average of x_{new} and a/x_{new}. Stop when two successive approximations differ from each other by a very small amount.

This method converges very rapidly. To compute $\sqrt{400}$, only 10 steps are required:

```
400
200.5
101.24750623441396
52.599110411804922
30.101900881222353
21.695049123587058
20.06621767747577
20.000109257780434
20.000000000298428
20
```

Figure 1

Approximation of the Square
Root

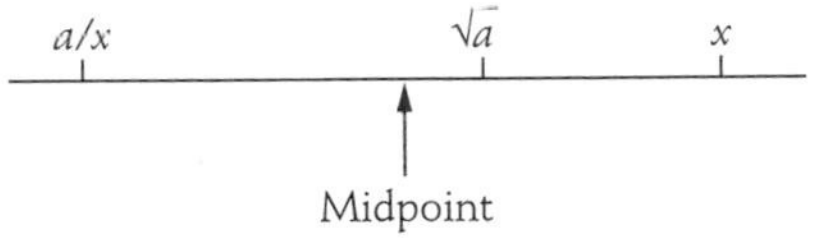

Here is a static method sqrt in a class MathAlgs that implements this algorithm.

```
class MathAlgs
{  public static double sqrt(double a)
   {  if (a <= 0) return 0;
      double xnew = a;
      double xold;
      do
      {  xold = xnew;
         xnew = (xold + a / xold) / 2;
      } while (!Numeric.approxEqual(xnew, xold));
      return xnew;
   }
}
```

Does this method work correctly? Let us approach this question systematically. First, let us write a test harness to supply individual values to the method to be tested.

Program SqrtTest1.java

```
public class SqrtTest1
{  public static void main(String[] args)
   {  ConsoleReader console = new ConsoleReader(System.in);
      boolean done = false;
      while (!done)
      {  String inputLine = console.readLine();
         if (inputLine == null) done = true;
         else
         {  double x = Double.parseDouble(inputLine);
            double y = MathAlgs.sqrt(x);

            System.out.println("square root of " + x
               + " = " + y);
         }
      }
   }
}
```

When you run this test harness, you need to enter inputs and to force an end of input when you are done, by typing a key such as Ctrl+Z or Ctrl+D (see Section 6.5.1). You can store the test data in a file and use redirection (see Productivity Hint 6.1):

```
java SqrtTest1 < test1.in
```

For each test case, the harness code calls the `MathAlgs.sqrt` method and prints the result. You can then manually check the computations. Once you have confidence that the method works correctly, you can plug it into your program.

It is also possible to generate test cases automatically. If there are few possible inputs, it is feasible to run through a representative number of them with a loop:

Program SqrtTest2.java

```java
public class SqrtTest2
{   public static void main(String[] args)
    {   for (double x = 0; x <= 10; x = x + 0.5)
        {   double y = MathAlgs.sqrt(x);
            System.out.println("square root of " + x
                + " = " + y);
        }
    }
}
```

Note that we purposefully test boundary cases (zero) and fractional numbers.

Unfortunately, this test is restricted to only a small subset of values. To overcome that limitation, random generation of test cases can be useful:

Program SqrtTest3.java

```java
import java.util.Random;

public class SqrtTest3
{   public static void main(String[] args)
    {   Random generator = new Random();
        for (int i = 1; i <= 100; i++)
        {   // generate random test value

            double x = 1.0E6 * generator.nextDouble();
            double y = MathAlgs.sqrt(x);

            System.out.println("square root of " + x
                + " = " + y);
        }
    }
}
```

No matter how you generate the test cases, the important point is that you test the method thoroughly before you put it into the program. If you ever put together a computer or fixed a car, you probably followed a similar process. Rather than simply throwing all the parts together and hoping for the best, you probably first tested each part in isolation. It takes a little longer, but it greatly reduces the possibility of complete failure once the parts are put together.

8.2 Selecting Test Cases

Selecting good test cases is an important skill for debugging programs. Of course, you want to test your program with inputs that a typical user might supply.

You should test all program features. In the program that prints English names of numbers, you should check typical test cases such as 5, 19, 29, 1093, 1728, 30000. These tests are *positive* tests. They consist of legitimate inputs, and you expect the program to handle them correctly.

Next, you should include *boundary cases*. Test what happens if the input is 0 or -1. Boundary cases are still legitimate inputs, and you expect that the program will handle them correctly—usually in some trivial way.

Finally, gather *negative* test cases. These are inputs that you expect the program to reject. Examples are inputs in the wrong format, such as five.

How should you collect test cases? This is easy for programs that get all their input from standard input. Just make each test case into a file—say, test1.in, test2.in, test3.in. These files contain the keystrokes that you would normally type at the keyboard when the program runs. Feed the files into the program to be tested, using redirection:

```
java Program < test1.in > test1.out
java Program < test2.in > test2.out
java Program < test3.in > test3.out
```

Then study the outputs and see whether they are correct.

Keeping a test case in a file is smart, because you can then use it to test every version of the program. In fact, it is a common and useful practice to make a test file whenever you find a program bug. You can use that file to verify that your bug fix really works. Don't throw it away; feed it to the next version after that and all subsequent versions. Such a collection of test cases is called a *test suite*.

You will be surprised how often a bug that you fixed will reappear in a future version. This is a phenomenon known as *cycling*. Sometimes you don't quite understand the reason for a bug and apply a quick fix that appears to work. Later, you apply a different quick fix that solves a second problem but makes the first problem appear again. Of course, it is always best to really think through what causes a bug and fix the root cause instead of doing a sequence of "Band-Aid" solutions. If you don't succeed in doing that, however, at least you want to have an honest appraisal of how well the program works. By keeping all old test cases around and testing them all against every new version, you get that feedback. The process of testing against a set of past failures is called *regression testing*.

Testing the functionality of the program without consideration of its internal structure is called *black-box testing*. That is an important part of testing, because, after all, the users of a program do not know its internal structure. If a program works perfectly on all positive inputs and fails gracefully on all negative ones, then it does its job.

However, it is impossible to ensure absolutely that a program will work correctly on all inputs just by supplying a finite number of test cases. As the famous computer scientist Edsger Dijkstra pointed out, testing can show only the presence of bugs—not their absence. To gain more confidence in the correctness of a program, it is useful to consider its internal structure. Testing strategies that look inside a program are called *white-box testing*. Performing unit tests of each method is a part of white-box testing.

You want to make sure that each part of your program is exercised at least once by one of your test cases. This is called *test coverage*. If some code is never executed by any of your test cases, you have no way of knowing whether that code would perform correctly if it ever were executed by user input. That means that you need to look at every if/else branch to see that each of them is reached by some test case. Many conditional branches are in the code only to take care of strange and abnormal inputs, but they still do something. It is a common phenomenon that they end up doing something incorrect, but that those faults are never discovered during testing, because nobody supplied the strange and abnormal inputs. Of course, these flaws become immediately apparent when the program is released and the first user types in a bad input and is incensed when the program crashes. A test suite should ensure that each part of the code is covered by some input.

For example, in testing the getTax method of the tax program in Chapter 5, you want to make sure that every if statement is entered for at least one test case. You should test both single and married taxpayers, with incomes in each of the three tax brackets.

It is a good idea to write the first test cases *before* the program is written completely. Designing a few test cases can give you insight into what the program should do, which is valuable for implementing it. You will also have something to throw at the program when it compiles for the first time. Of course, the initial set of test cases will be augmented as the debugging process progresses.

Modern programs can be quite challenging to test. In a program with a graphical user interface, the user can click random buttons with a mouse and supply input in random order. Programs that receive their data through a network connection need to be tested by simulating occasional network delays and failures. All this is much harder, since you cannot simply place keystrokes in a file. You need not worry about these complexities as you study this book, and there are tools to automate testing in these scenarios. The basic principles of regression testing (never throwing a test case away) and complete coverage (executing all code at least once) still hold.

8.3 Test Case Evaluation

In the last section we worried about how to get test *inputs*. Now let us consider what to do with the *outputs*. How do you know whether the output is correct?

Sometimes you can verify the output by calculating the correct values by hand. For example, for a payroll program you can compute taxes manually.

Sometimes a computation does a lot of work, and it is not practical to do the computation manually. That is the case with many approximation algorithms, which may run through dozens or hundreds of iterations before they arrive at the final answer. The square root method of Section 8.1 is an example of such an approximation.

How can you test that the square root method works correctly? You can supply test inputs for which you know the answer, such as 4 and 900, and also $\frac{25}{4}$, so that you don't just restrict the inputs to integers.

Alternatively, you can write a test harness that verifies that the output values fulfill certain properties. For the square root program you can compute the square root, compute the square of the result, and verify that you obtain the original input:

Program SqrtTest4.java

```
import java.util.Random;

public class SqrtTest4
{  public static void main(String[] args)
   {  Random generator = new Random();
      for (int i = 1; i <= 100; i++)
      {  // generate random test value

         double x = 1.0E6 * generator.nextDouble();
         double y = MathAlgs.sqrt(x);

         // check that test value fulfills square property

         if (Numeric.approxEqual(y * y, x))
            System.out.println("Test passed.");
         else
            System.out.println("Test failed.");
         System.out.println("square root of " + x + " = " + y);
      }
   }
}
```

Finally, there may be a less efficient way of computing the same value that a method produces. You can then run a test harness that computes the method to be tested, together with the slower process, and compares the answers. For example, $\sqrt{x} = x^{1/2}$, so you can use the slower Math.pow method to generate the same value. Such a slower but reliable method is called an *oracle*.

Program SqrtTest5.java

```
import java.util.Random;

public class SqrtTest5
{  public static void main(String[] args)
   {  Random generator = new Random();
      for (int i = 1; i <= 100; i++)
      {  // generate random test value
```

```
double x = 1.0E6 * generator.nextDouble();
double y = MathAlgs.sqrt(x);

// compare against oracle

if (Numeric.approxEqual(y, Math.pow(x, 0.5)))
    System.out.println("Test passed. ");
else
    System.out.println("Test failed. ");
System.out.println("square root of " + x + " = " + y);
    }
  }
}
```

Productivity Hint 8.1

Batch Files and Shell Scripts

If you need to perform the same tasks repeatedly on the command line, then it is worth learning about the automation features offered by your operating system.

Under DOS, you use *batch files* to execute a number of commands automatically. For example, suppose you need to test a program with three inputs:

```
java Program < test1.in
java Program < test2.in
java Program < test3.in
```

Then you find a bug, fix it, and run the tests again. Now you need to type the three commands once more. There has to be a better way. Under DOS, put the commands in a text file and call it test.bat:

File test.bat

```
java Program < test1.in
java Program < test2.in
java Program < test3.in
```

Then you just type

```
test
```

and the three commands in the batch file execute automatically.

It is easy to make the batch file more useful. If you are done with Program and start working on Program2, you can of course write a batch file test2.bat, but you can do better than that. Give the test batch file a *parameter*. That is, call it with

```
test Program
```

or

```
test Program2
```

You need to change the batch file to make this work. In a batch file, %1 denotes the first string that you type after the name of the batch file, %2 the second string, and so on:

File test.bat

```
java %1 < test1.in
java %1 < test2.in
java %1 < test3.in
```

What if you have more than three test files? DOS batch files have a very primitive **for** loop:

File test.bat

```
for %%f in (test*.in) do java %1 < %%f
```

If you work in a computer lab, you will want a batch file that copies all your files onto a floppy disk when you are ready to go home. Put the following lines in a file gohome.bat:

File gohome.bat

```
copy *.java a:
copy *.txt a:
copy *.in a:
```

There are lots of uses for batch files, and it is well worth it to learn more about them.

Batch files are a feature of the DOS operating system, not of Java. On a UNIX system, *shell scripts* are used for the same purpose.

8.4   Program Traces

Sometimes you run a program and you are not sure where it spends its time. To get a printout of the program flow, you can insert trace messages into the beginning and end of every method:

```
public static double sqrt(double a)
{  System.out.println("Entering MathAlgs.sqrt. a = " + a);

   . . .
   System.out.println
      ("Leaving MathAlgs.sqrt. Return value = " + xnew);
   return xnew;
}
```

To get a proper trace, you must locate *each* method exit point. Place a trace message before every **return** statement and at the end of the method:

```
public static int factorial(int n)
{  System.out.println("Entering factorial. n = " + n);
   if (n < 0) throw new IllegalArgumentException();

   if (n == 0)
```

```
    {  System.out.println
          ("Exiting factorial. Return value = " + 1);
       return 1;
    }
    else
    {  int result = n * factorial(n-1);
       System.out.println
          ("Leaving factorial. Return value = " + result);
       return result;
    }
}
```

You aren't restricted to "enter/exit" messages. You can report on progress inside a method:

```
public static double sqrt(double a)
{  . . .

   do
   {  xold = xnew;
      xnew = (xold + a / xold) / 2;
      System.out.println("MathAlgs.sqrt. xold = " + xold +
         ", xnew = " + xnew);
   } while (!Numeric.approxEqual(xnew, xold));
      . . .
}
```

Program traces can be useful to analyze the behavior of a program, but they have some definite disadvantages. It can be quite time-consuming to find out which trace messages to insert. If you insert too many messages, you produce a flurry of output that is hard to analyze; if you insert too few, you may not have enough information to spot the cause of the error. When you are done with the program, you need to remove all trace messages. If you find another error, however, you need to stick the print statements back in. If you find that a hassle, you are not alone. Most professional programmers use a *debugger*, not trace messages, to locate errors in their code. The debugger is covered later in this chapter.

8.5   Asserting Conditions

Programs often contain implicit assumptions. For example, denominators need to be nonzero; salaries should not be negative. Sometimes the iron force of logic ensures that these conditions are satisfied. If you divide by 1 + x * x, then that value will never be zero, and you need not worry. Negative interest rates on savings accounts, however, are not necessarily ruled out by logic but merely by convention. Surely nobody would ever deposit money in an account that earns negative interest, but such a value might creep into a program due to an input or processing error. In practice the "impossible" happens with distressing regularity.

An assumption that you believe to be true is called an *assertion*. Testing for assertions is a powerful quality control mechanism. It is useful to build a special class for testing assertions. Here is an example of such a class:

```
public class Assertion
{  public static void check(boolean b)
   {  if (!b)
      {  System.out.println("Assertion failed.");
         // construct a Throwable object to get a stack trace
         new Throwable().printStackTrace();
         System.exit(1);
      }
   }
}
```

This particular implementation prints a *stack trace*, a printout of all pending methods, if it finds the assertion has been violated. Here is a typical stack trace:

```
java.lang.Exception
        at Assertion.check(Assertion.java:6)
        at DentalRobot.computeIntersection(DentalRobot.java:37)
        at RobotTest.testDrill(RobotTest.java:93)
        at RobotTest.main(RobotTest.java:10)
```

The line just below `Assertion.check` indicates the culprit.

Here is a typical assertion check:

```
public void computeIntersection()
{  . . .
   double y = r * r - (x - a) * (x - a);
   Assertion.check(y >= 0);

   . . .

   root = Math.sqrt(y);
   . . .
}
```

In this program excerpt, the programmer expects that the quantity y can never be negative. When the assertion is correct, no harm is done, and the program works in the normal way. If, for some reason, the assertion fails, then the programmer would rather have the program terminate than go on, compute the square root of a negative number, and cause greater harm later.

Assertions are different from trace messages in one important respect. You can leave them in your code when testing is complete.

8.6 The Debugger

As you have undoubtedly realized by now, computer programs rarely run perfectly the first time. At times, it can be quite frustrating to find the bugs. Of course, you can insert trace messages to show the program flow as well as the values of key variables, run the program, and try to analyze the printout. If the printout does not clearly point to the problem, you may need to add and remove print commands and run the program again. That can be a time-consuming process.

Modern development environments contain special programs, called *debuggers,* that help you locate bugs by letting you follow the execution of a program. You can stop and restart your program and see the contents of variables whenever your program is temporarily stopped. At each stop, you have the choice of what variables to inspect and how many program steps to run until the next stop.

Some people feel that debuggers are just a tool to make programmers lazy. Admittedly some people write sloppy programs and then fix them up with the debugger, but the majority of programmers make an honest effort to write the best program they can before trying to run it through the debugger. These programmers realize that the debugger, while more convenient than print statements, is not cost-free. It does take time to set up and carry out an effective debugging session.

In actual practice, you cannot avoid using the debugger. The larger your programs get, the harder it is to debug them simply by inserting print statements. You will find that the time investment to learn about the debugger is amply repaid in your programming career.

Random Fact 8.1

The First Bug

According to legend, the first bug was one found in 1947 in the Mark II, a huge electromechanical computer at Harvard University. It really was caused by a bug—a moth was trapped in a relay switch. Actually, from the note that the operator left in the log book next to the moth (see Figure 2), it appears as if the term "bug" had already been in active use at the time.

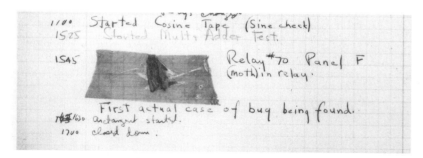

Figure 2

The First Bug

◆
◆
◆
◆
　　The pioneering computer scientist Maurice Wilkes wrote: "Somehow, at the Moore School and afterwards, one had always assumed there would be no particular difficulty in getting programs right. I can remember the exact instant in time at which it dawned on me that a great part of my future life would be spent finding mistakes in my own programs."

8.6.1　Using a Debugger

Like compilers, debuggers vary widely from one system to another. On some systems they are quite primitive and require you to memorize a small set of arcane commands; on others they have an intuitive window interface.

You will have to find out how to prepare a program for debugging and how to start the debugger on your system. If you use an integrated development environment, which contains an editor, compiler, and debugger, this step is usually very easy. You just build the program in the usual way and pick a menu command to start debugging. On many UNIX systems, you must manually build a debug version of your program and invoke the debugger.

Once you have started the debugger, you can go a long way with just three debugging commands: "run until this line", "step to next line", and "inspect variable". The names and keystrokes or mouse clicks for these commands differ widely between debuggers, but all debuggers support these basic commands. You can find out how, either from the documentation or a lab manual, or by asking someone who has used the debugger before.

The "run until this line" command is the most important. Many debuggers show you the source code of the current program in a window. Select a line with the mouse or cursor keys. Then hit a key or select a menu command to run the program to the selected line. On other debuggers, you have to type in a command or a line number. In either case, the program starts execution and stops as soon as it reaches the line you selected (see Figure 3). Of course, you may have selected a line that will not be reached at all during a particular program run. Then the program terminates in the normal way. The very fact that the program has or has not reached a particular line can be valuable information.

The "step to next line" command executes the current line and stops at the next program line. Once the program has stopped, you can look at the current values of variables. Again, the method for selecting the variables differs among debuggers. Some debuggers always show you a window with the current local variables (see Figure 4). On other debuggers you issue a command such as "inspect variable" and type in or click on the variable. The debugger then displays the contents of the variable. If all variables contain what you expected, you can run the program until the next point where you want to stop.

When inspecting objects, you often need to give a command to "open up" the object, for example by clicking on a tree node. Once the object is opened up, you see its instance variables.

Finally, when the program has completed running, the debug session is also finished. You can no longer inspect variables. To run the program again, you may be

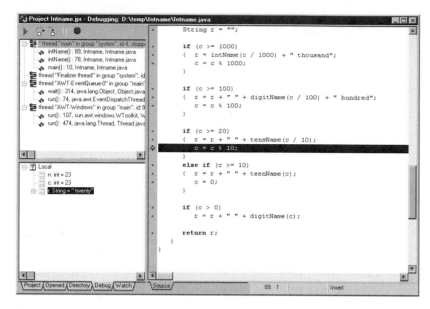

```
                  String r = "";

          if (c >= 1000)
          {   r = intName(c / 1000) + " thousand";
              c = c % 1000;
          }

          if (c >= 100)
          {   r = r + " " + digitName(c / 100) + " hundred";
              c = c % 100;
          }

          if (c >= 20)
          {   r = r + " " + tensName(c / 10);
              c = c % 10;
          }
          else if (c >= 10)
          {   r = r + " " + teenName(c);
              c = 0;
          }

          if (c > 0)
              r = r + " " + digitName(c);

          return r;
      }
  }
```

Figure 3

Debugger Stopped at Selected Line

Figure 4

Inspecting Variables

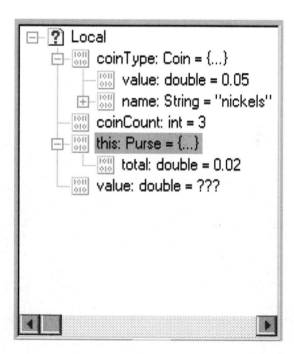

able to reset the debugger, or you may need to exit the debugging program and start over. Details depend on the particular debugger.

◆ Productivity Hint 8.2

◆
◆
◆
◆
◆

Inspect this in the Debugger

It is a good idea to inspect the this object frequently. Then you know the state of the implicit parameter of the method through which you are currently tracing. If your debugger has a "watch" window where you can place values that you always want to have displayed, add this to the watch window!

8.6.2   A Sample Debugging Session

Consider the following program, whose purpose is to compute all prime numbers up to a number n. An integer is defined to be prime if it is not evenly divisible by any number except by 1 and itself. Also, mathematicians find it convenient not to call 1 a prime. Thus, the first few prime numbers are 2, 3, 5, 7, 11, 13, 17, 19.

Program PrimeBug.java

```
public class PrimeBug                                  // 1
{   /**                                                // 2
        Tests whether an integer is prime              // 3
        @param n any positive integer                  // 4
        @return true iff n is a prime                  // 5
    **/                                                // 6
                                                       // 7
    public static boolean isPrime(int n)               // 8
    {   if (n == 2) return true;                       // 9
        if (n % 2 == 0) return false;                  // 10
        int k = 3;                                     // 11
        while (k * k < n)                              // 12
        {   if (n % k == 0) return false;              // 13
            k = k + 2;                                 // 14
        }                                              // 15
        return true;                                   // 16
    }                                                  // 17
                                                       // 18
    public static void main(String[] args)             // 19
    {   ConsoleReader console                          // 20
            = new ConsoleReader(System.in);            // 21
        System.out.println                             // 22
            ("Please enter the upper bound:");         // 23
        int n = console.readInt();                     // 24
```

```
      for (int i = 1; i <= n; i = i + 2)                // 25
      {  if (isPrime(i))                                 // 26
            System.out.println(i);                       // 27
      }                                                  // 28
                                                         // 29
   }                                                     // 30
}                                                        // 31
```

We numbered the lines so that we can refer to them in this example. Probably your debugger won't actually number them.

When you run this program with an input of 10, then the output is

```
1
3
5
7
9
```

That is not very promising; it looks as if the program just prints all odd numbers. Let us find out what it does wrong, by using the debugger. (Actually, for such a simple program, it is easy to correct mistakes simply by looking at the faulty output and the program code. However, we want to learn to use the debugger.)

Let us first go to line 27. On the way, the program will stop to read the input into n. Supply the input value 10.

```
      int n = console.readInt();                         // 24
                                                         // 25
      for (int i = 1; i <= n; i = i + 2)                // 26
      {  if (isPrime(i))                                 // 27
            System.out.println(i);                       // 28
      }                                                  // 29
```

Now we wonder why the program treats 1 as a prime. Go to line 9.

```
   public static boolean isPrime(int n)                  //  8
   {  if (n == 2) return true;                           //  9
      if (n % 2 == 0) return false;                      // 10
      int k = 3;                                         // 11
      while (k * k < n)                                  // 12
      {  if (n % k == 0) return false;                   // 13
         k = k + 2;                                      // 14
      }                                                  // 15
      return true;                                       // 16
   }                                                     // 17
```

Convince yourself that the parameter n of isPrime is currently 1, by inspecting its value in the debugger. Then execute the "run to next line" command. You will notice that the program goes to lines 10 and 11 and then directly to line 16.

```
   public static boolean isPrime(int n)                  //  8
   {  if (n == 2) return true;                           //  9
      if (n % 2 == 0) return false;                      // 10
```

```
    int k = 3;                              // 11
    while (k * k < n)                       // 12
    {  if (n % k == 0) return false;        // 13
       k = k + 2;                           // 14
    }                                       // 15
    return true;                            // 16
}                                           // 17
```

Inspect the value of k. It is 3, and therefore the while loop was never entered. It looks as though the isPrime method needs to be rewritten to treat 1 as a special case.

Next, we would like to know why the program doesn't print 2 as a prime even though the isPrime method does recognize that 2 is a prime, whereas all other even numbers are not. Go again to line 9, the next call of isPrime. Inspect n; you will note that n is 3. Now it becomes clear: The for loop in main tests only odd numbers. The main should either test both odd and even numbers or, better, just handle 2 as a special case.

Finally, we would like to find out why the program believes 9 is a prime. Go again to line 9 and inspect n; it should be 5. Repeat that step twice until n is 9. (With some debuggers, you may need to go from line 9 to line 10 before you can go back to line 9.) Now use the "run to next line" command repeatedly. You will notice that the program again skips past the while loop; inspect k to find out why. You will find that k is 3. Look at the condition in the while loop. It tests whether k * k < n. Now k * k is 9 and n is also 9, so the test fails. Actually, it does make sense to test divisors only up to $\sqrt{n}$; if n has any divisors except 1 and itself, at least one of them must be less than $\sqrt{n}$. However, actually that isn't quite true; if n is a perfect square of a prime, then its sole nontrivial divisor is *equal* to $\sqrt{n}$. That is exactly the case for $9 = 3^2$.

By running the debugger, we have now discovered three bugs in the program:

◆ isPrime falsely claims 1 to be a prime.

◆ main doesn't handle 2.

◆ The test in isPrime should be while (k * k <= n).

Here is the improved program:

Program GoodPrime.java

```
public class GoodPrime
{  /**
      Tests whether an integer is a prime
      @param n  any positive integer
      @return true iff n is a prime
   */
```

```
public static boolean isPrime(int n)
{  if (n == 1) return false;
   if (n == 2) return true;
   if (n % 2 == 0) return false;
   int k = 3;
   while (k * k <= n)
   {  if (n % k == 0) return false;
      k = k + 2;
   }
   return true;
}

public static void main(String[] args)
{  ConsoleReader console
      = new ConsoleReader(System.in);
   System.out.println
      ("Please enter the upper bound:");
   int n = console.readInt();

   if (n >= 2) System.out.println(2);
   for (int i = 1; i <= n; i = i + 2)
   {  if (isPrime(i))
         System.out.println(i);
   }
}
}
```

Is our program now free from bugs? That is not a question the debugger can answer.
Remember: Testing can show only the presence of bugs, not their absence.

8.6.3 Stepping through a Program

You have learned how to run a program until it reaches a particular line. Variations
of this strategy are often useful.

There are two methods of running the program in the debugger. You can tell it to
run to a particular line; then it gets speedily to that line, but you don't know how
it got there. You can also *single-step* with the "run to next line" command. Then you
know how the program flows, but it can take a long time to step through it.

Actually, there are two kinds of single-stepping commands, often called "step
over" and "step into". The "step over" command always goes to the next program
line. The "step into" command steps into method calls. For example, suppose the
current line is

```
String name = console.readLine();
System.out.println("Hello " + name + "! I'm glad to meet you.");
```

When you "step over" method calls, you get to the next line:

```
String name = console.readLine();
System.out.println("Hello " + name + "! I'm glad to meet you.");
```

However, if you "step into" method calls, you enter the first line of the readLine method.

```
public String readLine()
{  String inputLine = "";
     . . .
}
```

You should step into a method to check whether it carries out its job correctly. You should step over a method if you know it works correctly.

If you single-step past the last line of a method, either with the "step over" or the "step into" command, you return to the line in which the method was called.

You should not step into system methods like println. It is easy to get lost in them, and there is no benefit in stepping through system code. If you do get lost, there are three ways out. You can just choose "step over" until you are finally again in familiar territory. Many debuggers have a command "run until method return" that executes to the end of the current method, and then you can select "step over" to get out of the method. Finally, most debuggers can show you a *call stack:* a listing of all currently pending method calls. On the one end of the call stack is main, on the other the method that is currently executing (see Figure 5). Sometimes, the debugger shows you multiple *threads*—you should ignore those threads that don't have the methods that you are debugging. By selecting another method in the middle of the call stack, you can jump to the code line containing that method call. Then move the cursor to the next line and choose "run until this line". That way, you get out of any nested morass of method calls.

The techniques you saw so far let you trace through the code in various increments. All debuggers support a second navigational approach: You can set so-called *breakpoints* in the code. Breakpoints are set at specific code lines, with a command "add breakpoint here"; again, the exact command depends on the debugger. You can set as many breakpoints as you like. When the program reaches any one of them, execution stops and the breakpoint that causes the stop is displayed. Breakpoints stay active until you remove them.

Breakpoints are particularly useful when you know the point at which your program starts doing the wrong thing. You can set a breakpoint, have the program run at full speed to the breakpoint, and then start tracing slowly to observe the program's behavior.

Figure 5

Call Stack Display

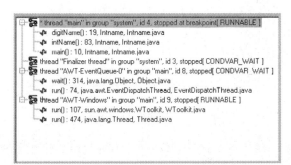

Some debuggers let you set *conditional breakpoints*. A conditional breakpoint stops the program only when a certain condition is met. You could stop at a particular line only if a variable n has reached 0, or if that line has been executed for the twentieth time. Conditional breakpoints are an advanced feature that can be indispensable in knotty debugging problems.

Common Error 8.1

Tracing through Recursive Methods

When you set a breakpoint in a recursive method, the program stops as soon as that program line is encountered in *any* call to the recursive method. Suppose you want to debug the `factorial` method:

```
public static int factorial(int n)                              // 1
{  if (n < 0) throw new IllegalArgumentException();             // 2
   if (n == 0)                                                  // 3
      return 1;                                                 // 4
   else                                                         // 5
   {  int f = factorial(n - 1);                                 // 6
      int result = n * f;                                       // 7
      return result;                                            // 8
   }                                                            // 9
}                                                               //10
```

Suppose you inspect n in line 2, and it is 4. You tell the debugger to run until line 7. When you inspect n again, its value is 1! That makes no sense. There was no instruction that changed the value of n! Is that a bug with the debugger?

No. The program stopped in the first *recursive* call to `factorial` that reached line 7. If you are confused, try this and look at the *call stack*. You will see that four calls to `factorial` are pending.

You can debug recursive methods with the debugger. You just need to be particularly careful, and watch the call stack frequently.

8.7   Debugging Strategies

Now you know about the mechanics of debugging, but all that knowledge may still leave you helpless when you fire up the debugger to look at a sick program. There are a number of strategies that you can use to recognize bugs and their causes.

8.7.1 Reproduce the Error

As you test your program, you notice that your program sometimes does something wrong. It gives the wrong output, it seems to print something completely random, it goes in an infinite loop, or it crashes. Find out exactly how to *reproduce* that behavior. What numbers did you enter? Where did you click with the mouse?

Run the program again; type in exactly the same answers and click with the mouse on the same spots (or as close as you can get). Does the program exhibit the same behavior? If so, then you are ready to fire up the debugger to study this particular problem. Debuggers are good for analyzing particular failures. They aren't terribly useful for studying a program in general.

8.7.2 Divide and Conquer

Now that you have a particular failure, you want to get as close to the failure as possible. Suppose your program dies with a division by 0. Since there are many division operations in a typical program, it is often not feasible to set breakpoints to all of them. Instead, use a technique of *divide and conquer*. Step over the methods in `main`, but don't step inside them. Eventually, the failure will happen again. Now you know which method contains the bug: It is the last method that was called from `main` before the program died. Restart the debugger and go back to that line in `main`, then step inside that method. Repeat the process.

Eventually, you will have pinpointed the line that contains the bad division. Maybe it is completely obvious from the code why the denominator is not correct. If not, you need to find the location where it is computed. Unfortunately, you can't go *back* in the debugger. You need to restart the program and move to the point where the denominator computation happens.

8.7.3 Know What Your Program Should Do

The debugger shows you what the program *does* do. You must know what the program *should* do, or you will not be able to find bugs. Before you trace through a loop, ask yourself how many iterations you *expect* the program to make. Before you inspect a variable, ask yourself what you expect to see. If you have no clue, set aside some time and think first. Have a calculator handy to make independent computations. When you know what the value should be, inspect the variable. This is the moment of truth. If the program is still on the right track, then that value is what you expected, and you must look further for the bug. If the value is different, you may be on to something. Double-check your computation. If you are sure your value is correct, find out why your program comes up with a different value.

In many cases, program bugs are the result of simple errors such as loop termination conditions that are off by 1. Quite often, however, programs make computational errors. Maybe they are supposed to add two numbers, but by accident the code was written to subtract them. Unlike your calculus instructor, programs don't make a special effort to ensure that everything is a simple integer. You will need to make some calculations with large integers or nasty floating-point numbers. Sometimes these calculations can be avoided if you just ask yourself, "Should this quantity be positive? Should it be larger than that value?" Then inspect variables to verify those theories.

8.7.4 Look at All Details

When you debug a program, you often have a theory about what the problem is. Nevertheless, keep an open mind and look around at all details. What strange messages are displayed? Why does the program take another unexpected action? These details count. When you run a debugging session, you really are a detective who needs to look at every clue available.

If you notice another failure on the way to the problem that you are about to pin down, don't just say, "I'll come back to it later". That very failure may be the original cause for your current problem. It is better to make a note of the current problem, fix what you just found, and then return to the original mission.

8.7.5 Understand Each Error Before You Fix It

Once you find that a loop makes too many iterations, it is very tempting to apply a "Band-Aid" solution and subtract 1 from a variable so that the particular problem doesn't appear again. Such a quick fix has an overwhelming probability of creating trouble elsewhere. You really need to have a thorough understanding of how the program should be written before you apply a fix.

It does occasionally happen that you find bug after bug and apply fix after fix, and the problem just moves around. That usually is a symptom of a larger problem with the program logic. There is little you can do with the debugger. You must rethink the program design and reorganize it.

Random Fact 8.2

The Therac-25 Incidents

The Therac-25 is a computerized device to deliver radiation treatment to cancer patients (see Figure 6). Between June 1985 and January 1987, several of these machines delivered serious overdoses to at least six patients, killing some of them and seriously maiming the others.

The machines were controlled by a computer program. Bugs in the program were directly responsible for the overdoses. According to [1], the program was written by a single programmer, who had since left the manufacturing company producing the device and could not be located. None of the company employees interviewed could say anything about the educational level or qualifications of the programmer.

The investigation by the federal Food and Drug Administration (FDA) found that the program was poorly documented and that there was neither a specification document nor a formal test plan. (This should make you think. Do you have a formal test plan for your programs?)

The overdoses were caused by an amateurish design of the software that had to control different devices concurrently, namely the keyboard, the display, the printer, and of course the radiation device itself. Synchronization and data sharing between the tasks were done in an ad hoc way, even though safe multitasking techniques were known at the time. Had the programmer enjoyed a formal education that involved these techniques, or taken the effort to study the literature, a safer machine could have been built. Such a machine would have

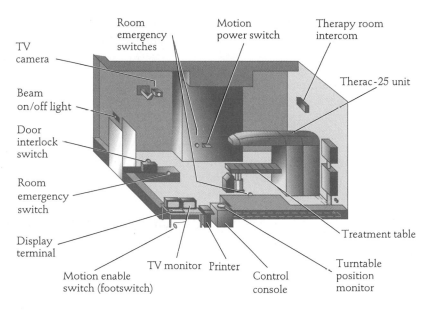

Figure 6

Typical Therac-25 Facility

probably involved a commercial multitasking system, which might have required a more expensive computer.

The same flaws were present in the software controlling the predecessor model, the Therac-20, but that machine had hardware interlocks that mechanically prevented overdoses. The hardware safety devices were removed in the Therac-25 and replaced by checks in the software, presumably to save cost.

Frank Houston of the FDA wrote in 1985 [1]: "A significant amount of software for life-critical systems comes from small firms, especially in the medical device industry; firms that fit the profile of those resistant to or uninformed of the principles of either system safety or software engineering."

Who is to blame? The programmer? The manager who not only failed to ensure that the programmer was up to the task but also didn't insist on comprehensive testing? The hospitals that installed the device, or the FDA, for not reviewing the design process? Unfortunately, even today there are no firm standards of what constitutes a safe software design process.

Chapter Summary

1. Use *unit tests* to test each key method in isolation. Write a *test harness* to feed test data to the method being tested. Select test cases that cover each branch of the method.

2. Use assertions to document assumptions that you are making in your programs.

3. You can debug a program by inserting trace printouts, but that gets quite tedious for even moderately complex debugging situations. You should learn to use the debugger.

4. You can make effective use of the debugger by mastering just three commands: "run until this line", "step to next line", and "inspect variable". The names and keystrokes or mouse clicks for these commands differ between debuggers.

5. There are three windows in the debugger to which you should pay attention: the window that shows your source code and, in particular, the currently executed instruction; the window that shows the values of program variables; and the call stack, which shows which method calls are currently "stacked up".

6. Use the "divide-and-conquer" technique to locate the point of failure of a program. Inspect variables and compare their actual contents against the values that you know they should have.

7. The debugger can be used only to analyze the presence of bugs, not to show that a program is bug-free.

Further Reading

[1] Nancy G. Leveson and Clark S. Turner, "An Investigation of the Therac-25 Accidents," *IEEE Computer,* July 1993, pp. 18–41.

Classes, Objects, and Methods Introduced in This Chapter

```
java.lang.Throwable
    printStackTrace
```

Review Exercises

Exercise R8.1. Define the terms *unit test* and *test harness.*

Exercise R8.2. If you want to test a program that is made up of four different methods, one of which is `main`, how many test harness programs do you need?

Exercise R8.3. What is an oracle?

Exercise R8.4. Define the terms *regression testing* and *test suite.*

Exercise R8.5. What is the debugging phenomenon known as "cycling"? What can you do to avoid it?

Exercise R8.6. The arc sine function is the inverse of the sine function. That is, $y = \arcsin x$ if $x = \sin y$. It is defined only if $-1 \le x \le 1$. Suppose you need to write a Java method to compute the arc sine. List five positive test cases with their expected return values and two negative test cases with their expected outcomes.

Exercise R8.7. What is a program trace? When does it make sense to use a program trace, and when does it make more sense to use a debugger?

Exercise R8.8. Explain the differences between these debugger operations:

◆ Stepping into a method

◆ Stepping over a method

Exercise R8.9. Explain the differences between these debugger operations:

◆ Running until the current line

◆ Setting a breakpoint to the current line

Exercise R8.10. Explain the differences between these debugger operations:

◆ Inspecting a variable

◆ Watching a variable

Exercise R8.11. What is a call stack display in the debugger? Give two debugging scenarios in which the call stack display is useful.

Exercise R8.12. Explain in detail how to inspect the information stored in a `Point2D.Double` object in your debugger.

Exercise R8.13. Explain in detail how to inspect the string stored in a `String` object in your debugger.

Exercise R8.14. Explain in detail how to use your debugger to inspect a string stored in a `BankAccount` object.

Exercise R8.15. Explain the "divide-and-conquer" strategy to get close to a bug in the debugger.

Exercise R8.16. True or false:

◆ If a program has passed all tests in the test suite, it has no more bugs.

◆ If a program has a bug, that bug always shows up when running the program through the debugger.

◆ If all methods in a program were proven correct, then the program has no bugs.

Programming Exercises

Exercise P8.1. The arc sine function is the inverse of the sine function. That is,

$$y = \arcsin x$$

if

$$x = \sin y$$

For example,

$$\arcsin(0) = 0$$
$$\arcsin(0.5) = \pi/6$$
$$\arcsin(\sqrt{2}/2) = \pi/4$$
$$\arcsin(\sqrt{3}/2) = \pi/3$$
$$\arcsin(1) = \pi/2$$
$$\arcsin(-1) = \pi/2$$

The arc sine is defined only for values between -1 and 1. This function is also often called $\sin^{-1}x$. Note, however, that it is not at all the same as $1/\sin x$. There is a Java standard library method to compute the arc sine, but you should not use it for this exercise. Write a Java method that computes the arc sine from its Taylor series expansion

$$\arcsin x = x + x^3/3! + x^5 \cdot 3^2/5! + x^7 \cdot 3^2 \cdot 5^2/7! + x^9 \cdot 3^2 \cdot 5^2 \cdot 7^2/9! + \cdots$$

You should compute the sum until a new term is $< 10^{-6}$. This method will be used in subsequent exercises.

Exercise P8.2. Write a simple test harness for the `arcsin` method that reads floating-point numbers from standard input and computes their arc sines, until the end of the input is reached. Then run that program and verify its outputs against the arc sine function of a scientific calculator.

Exercise P8.3. Write a test harness that automatically generates test cases for the `arcsin` method, namely numbers between -1 and 1 in a step size of 0.1.

Exercise P8.4. Write a test harness that generates 10 random floating-point numbers between -1 and 1 and feeds them to `arcsin`.

Exercise P8.5. Write a test harness that automatically tests the validity of the `arcsin` method by verifying that `Math.sin(arcsin(x))` is approximately equal to x. Test with 100 random inputs.

Exercise P8.6. The arc sine function can be computed from the arc tangent function, according to the formula

$$\arcsin x = \arctan\left(x/\sqrt{1 - x^2}\right)$$

Use that expression as an *oracle* to test that your arc sine method works correctly. Test your method with 100 random inputs and verify against the oracle.

Exercise P8.7. The domain of the arc sine function is $-1 \le x \le 1$. Supply an exception to your `arcsin` method that ensures that the input is valid. Test your method by computing `arcsin(1.1)`. What happens?

Exercise P8.8. Place trace messages into the loop of the arc sine method that computes the power series. Print the value of `n`, the value of the current term, and the current approximation to the result. What trace output do you get when you compute `arcsin(0.5)`?

Exercise P8.9. Add trace messages to the beginning and end of the `isPrime` method in the buggy prime program. Also put a trace message as the first statement of the `while` loop in the `isPrime` method. Print relevant values such as method parameters, return values, and loop counters. What trace do you get when you compute all primes up to 20? Are the messages informative enough to spot the bug?

Exercise P8.10. Run a test harness of the `arcsin` method through the debugger. Step inside the computation of `arcsin(0.5)`. Step through the computation until the x^7 term has been computed and added to the sum. What is the value of the current term and of the sum at this point?

Exercise P8.11. Run a test harness of the `arcsin` method through the debugger. Step inside the computation of `arcsin(0.5)`. Step through the computation until the x^n term has become smaller than 10^{-6}. Then inspect `n`. How large is it?

Exercise P8.12. The following method has a subtle bug:

```
class MathAlgs
{  public static double sqrt(double a)
   {  if (a < 0) return 0;
      double xnew = a / 2;
      double xold;
      do
      {  xold = xnew;
         xnew = (xold + a / xold) / 2;
      }
      while (!Numeric.approxEqual(xnew, xold));
      return xnew;
   }
}
```

Create a series of test cases to flush out the bug. Then run a debugging session to find it. Run the debugger to the line in which the bug manifests itself. What are the values of all local variables at that point?

Exercise P8.13. Write a program that tests the recursive factorial method from Chapter 7. Compute `factorial(6)`. Step inside recursive calls until you arrive at `factorial(3)`. Then display the call stack. Which calls are currently pending?

Exercise P8.14. Find all bugs in the following version of a `factorial` method. Describe how you found the bugs.

```
class Numeric
{  public int factorial(int n)
   {  int p = 1;
      int i = n;

      // compute  p = n * (n-1) * (n-2) * . . . * 2

      while (i >= 2);
      {  i--;
         p = p * i;
      }

      return i;
   }
}
```

Inheritance and Interfaces

Chapter Goals

- To learn about inheritance

- To be able to convert between supertype and subtype references

- To understand how to inherit and override superclass methods

- To understand the concept of polymorphism

- To design and use abstract classes and interfaces

- To understand the common superclass `Object` and to override its `toString`, `equals`, and `clone` methods

- To learn about packages and Java access control

9.1   An Introduction to Inheritance

Inheritance is a mechanism for enhancing existing, working classes. If you need to implement a new class and a class representing a more general concept is already available, then the new class can inherit from the existing class. For example, suppose you need to define a class `SavingsAccount` to model an account that pays a fixed interest rate on deposits. You already have a class `BankAccount`, and a savings account is a special case of a bank account. In this case, it makes sense to use the language construct of inheritance. Here is the syntax for the class definition:

```
class SavingsAccount extends BankAccount
{   new methods
    new instance variables
}
```

In the `SavingsAccount` class definition you specify only new methods and instance variables. All methods and instance variables of the `BankAccount` class are *automatically inherited* by the `SavingsAccount` class. For example, the `deposit` method automatically applies to savings accounts:

```
SavingsAccount collegeFund = new SavingsAccount(10);
collegeFund.deposit(500);
    // OK to use BankAccount method with SavingsAccount object
```

We must introduce some more terminology here. The more general class that forms the basis for inheritance is called the *superclass*. The more specialized class that inherits from the superclass is called the *subclass*. In our example, `BankAccount` is the superclass and `SavingsAccount` is the subclass.

In Java, every class that does not specifically extend another class is a subclass of the class `Object`. For example, the `BankAccount` class extends the class `Object`. The `Object` class has a small number of methods that make sense for all objects, such as the `toString` method that you can use to obtain a string that describes the state of an object.

Figure 1 is a *class diagram* showing the relationship between the three classes `Object`, `BankAccount`, and `SavingsAccount`. In this book, we use the UML notation for objects and classes. (UML, for "Unified Modeling Language", is a notation for object-oriented analysis and design, invented by Grady Booch, Ivar Jacobson, and James Rumbaugh, three leading researchers in object-oriented software development.) The UML notation distinguishes between *object diagrams* and class diagrams. In an object diagram the class names are <u>underlined</u>; in a class diagram the class names are not underlined. In a class diagram, you denote inheritance by an arrow with a "hollow triangle" tip that points to the superclass.

One important reason for inheritance is *code reuse*. By inheriting from an existing class, you do not have to replicate the effort that went into designing and perfecting that class. For example, when implementing the `SavingsAccount` class, you can rely on the `withdraw`, `deposit`, and `getBalance` methods of the `BankAccount` class without touching them.

Figure 1

Inheritance Diagram

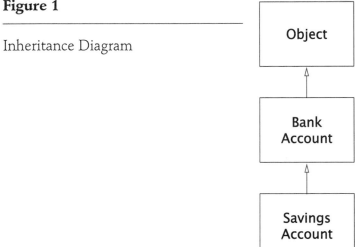

Let us see how our savings account objects are different from `BankAccount` objects. We will set an interest rate in the constructor, and then we need a method to apply that interest periodically. That is, in addition to the three methods that can be applied to every account, there is an additional method `addInterest`. These new methods and instance variables must be defined in the subclass.

```
public class SavingsAccount extends BankAccount
{  public SavingsAccount(double rate)
   {  constructor implementation
   }


   public void addInterest()
   {  method implementation
   }

   private double interestRate;
}
```

Figure 2 shows the layout of a `SavingsAccount` object. It inherits the `balance` instance variable from the `BankAccount` superclass, and it gains one additional instance variable: `interestRate`.

Next, you need to implement the new `addInterest` method. This method computes the interest due on the current balance and deposits that interest to the account.

```
public class SavingsAccount extends BankAccount
{  public SavingsAccount(double rate)
   {  interestRate = rate;
   }
```

Java Syntax

9.1 Inheritance

```
class SubclassName   extends SuperclassName
{  methods
     instance  variables
}
```

Example:

```java
public class SavingsAccount extends BankAccount
{  public SavingsAccount(double rate)
   {  interestRate = rate;
   }

   public void addInterest()
   {  double interest = getBalance() * interestRate / 100;
      deposit(interest);
   }

   private double interestRate;
}
```

Purpose:
To define a new class that inherits from an existing class, and
define the methods and instance variables that are added in the
new class

Figure 2

Layout of a
Subclass Object

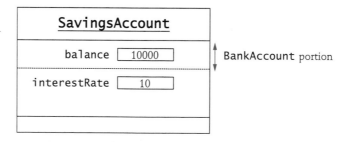

```java
   public void addInterest()
   {  double interest = getBalance() * interestRate / 100;
      deposit(interest);
   }

   private double interestRate;
}
```

Note how the **addInterest** method calls the **getBalance** and **deposit** methods of the superclass. Because no object is specified for the calls to **getBalance** and deposit, the calls apply to the implicit parameter of the addInterest method. In other words, the following statements are executed:

```
double interest = this.getBalance() * this.interestRate / 100;
this.deposit(interest);
```

For example, if you call

```
collegeFund.addInterest();
```

then the following instructions are executed:

```
double interest = collegeFund.getBalance() *
    collegeFund.interestRate / 100;
collegeFund.deposit(interest);
```

Common Error 9.1

Confusing Super- and Subclasses

If you compare an object of type SavingsAccount with an object of type BankAccount, then you find that

- The keyword extends suggests that the SavingsAccount object is an extended version of a BankAccount.
- The SavingsAccount object is larger; it has an added instance variable interestRate.
- The SavingsAccount object is more capable; it has an addInterest method.

It seems a superior object in every way. So why is SavingsAccount called the *subclass* and BankAccount the *superclass*?

The *super/sub* terminology comes from set theory. Look at the set of all bank accounts. Some of them are plain bank accounts, and some of them are SavingsAccount objects. Therefore, the set of BankAccount objects is a *superset* of the set of SavingsAccount objects, and the set of SavingsAccount objects is a *subset* of the set of all BankAccount objects. The more specialized objects in the subset have richer state and more capabilities.

9.2 Converting between Class Types

The class SavingsAccount extends the class BankAccount. In other words, a SavingsAccount object is a special case of a BankAccount object. Therefore, you can store a reference to a `SavingsAccount` object into an object variable of type BankAccount:

```
SavingsAccount collegeFund = new SavingsAccount(10);
BankAccount anAccount = collegeFund;
Object anObject = collegeFund;
```

Now the three object references stored in `collegeFund`, `anAccount`, and `anObject` all refer to the same object of type `SavingsAccount` (see Figure 3).

However, the object variable **anAccount** knows less than the full story about the object to which it refers. Because **anAccount** is an object of type **BankAccount**, you can use the **deposit** and **withdraw** methods to change the balance of the savings account. You cannot use the **addInterest** method, though—it is not a method of the **BankAccount** superclass:

```
anAccount.deposit(1000); // OK
anAccount.addInterest();
    // No—not a method of the class to which anAccount belongs
```

And, of course, the variable **anObject** knows even less. You can't even apply the **deposit** method to it—**deposit** is not a method of the **Object** class.

Why would anyone *want* to know less about an object and store a reference in an object variable of a superclass? This can happen if you want to reuse code that knows about the superclass but not the subclass. Here is a typical example. Consider the **transfer** method that we discussed in Section 7.1, which transfers money from one account to another:

```
void transfer(BankAccount other, double amount)
{  withdraw(amount);
   other.deposit(amount);
}
```

You can use this method to transfer money from one bank account to another:

```
BankAccount momsChecking = . . . ;
BankAccount harrysChecking = . . . ;
momsChecking.transfer(harrysChecking, 1000);
```

Figure 3

Object Variables of Different Types Refer to the Same Object

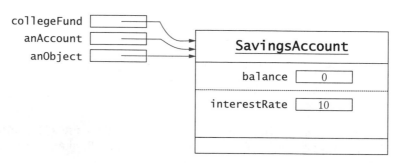

You can *also* use the method to transfer money into a SavingsAccount:

```
SavingsAccount collegeFund = . . . ;
momsChecking.transfer(collegeFund, 1000);
    // OK to pass a SavingsAccount reference to a
    // method expecting a BankAccount
```

The transfer method expects a reference to a BankAccount, and it gets a reference to the subclass SavingsAccount. Fortunately, rather than complaining about a type mismatch, the compiler simply copies the subclass reference collegeFund to the superclass reference other. The transfer method doesn't actually know that, in this case, other refers to a SavingsAccount reference. It knows only that other is a BankAccount, and it doesn't need to know anything else. All it cares about is that the other object can carry out the deposit method.

However, while you can convert an object reference into a superclass reference, you *cannot* convert between unrelated classes:

```
Rectangle r = collegeFund; // Error—unrelated classes
```

The compiler knows that Rectangle is not a superclass of SavingsAccount, and it refuses to compile this statement.

Occasionally, it happens that you convert an object to a superclass reference and you need to convert it back. Suppose you captured a reference to a savings account in a variable of type Object:

```
Object anObject = collegeFund;
```

Much later, you want to add interest to the account, but you no longer have access to the original object variable. You cannot simply assign a supertype reference to a subtype reference. However, as long as you are absolutely sure that anObject really refers to a SavingsAccount object, you can use the *cast* notation to convert it back:

```
SavingsAccount aSavingsAccount = (SavingsAccount)anObject;
```

If you are wrong, and the object doesn't actually refer to a savings account, your program will throw an exception and terminate.

This cast notation is the same notation that you saw in Chapter 2 to convert between number types. For example, if x is a floating-point number, then (int)x is the integer part of the number. The intent is similar—to convert from one type to another. However, there is one big difference between casting of number types and casting of class types. When casting number types, you *lose information*, and you use the cast to tell the compiler that you agree to the information loss. When casting object types, on the other hand, you *take a risk*—namely, that the object type wasn't actually of the type that you thought it was and that the program will be terminated as a result, and you tell the compiler that you agree to that risk.

You saw one example of using casts in graphics programs, when you had to cast the Graphics object to a Graphics2D object. That cast is really not a sign of good programming; the library designers used the cast as a quick fix for a compatibility

> **Java Syntax**
> **9.2 The `instanceof` Operator**
> *object* `instanceof` *ClassName*
>
> Example:
> ```
> Rectangle r;
> if (x instanceof Rectangle)
>    r = (Rectangle)x;
> ```
>
> Purpose:
> To return `true` if the *object* is an instance of *ClassName* (or one of its subclasses), and `false` otherwise

problem. At any rate, situations for casts occasionally arise. When they do, it is best to play it safe and test whether a cast will succeed before carrying out the cast. For that purpose, you use the `instanceof` operator. It tests whether an object belongs to a particular class. For example,

```
anObject instanceof SavingsAccount
```

returns `true` if the type of `anObject` is `SavingsAccount` (or a subclass of `Savings-Account`), `false` if it is not. Therefore, a safe cast can be programmed as follows:

```
SavingsAccount aSavingsAccount;
if (anObject instanceof SavingsAccount)
   aSavingsAccount = (SavingsAccount)anObject;
else
   aSavingsAccount = null;
```

9.3   Inheritance Hierarchies

In the real world, you often categorize concepts into *hierarchies*. Hierarchies are frequently represented as trees, with the most general concepts at the root of the hierarchy and more specialized ones towards the branches. Figure 4 shows a typical example.

In Java it is equally common to group classes in complex *inheritance hierarchies*. The classes representing the most general concepts are near the root, more specialized classes towards the branches. For example, Figure 5 shows part of the hierarchy of Swing user interface components in Java.

When designing a hierarchy of classes, you ask yourself which features and behavior are common to all the classes that you are designing. Those common properties are collected in a superclass. For example, all user interface components have a width and height, and the `getWidth` and `getHeight` methods of the `JComponent` class return the component's dimensions. More specialized properties can be found in subclasses. For example, buttons can have text and icon labels.

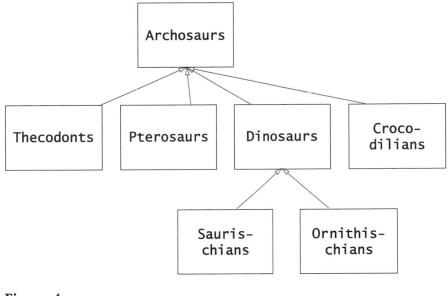

Figure 4

A Part of the Hierarchy of
Ancient Reptiles

The class `AbstractButton`, but not the superclass `JComponent`, has methods to set
and get the button text and icon, and instance variables to store them. The individual button classes (such as `JButton`, `JRadioButton`, and `JCheckBox`) inherit these
properties. In fact, the `AbstractButton` class was created to express the common-
ality between these buttons.

We will use a simpler example of a hierarchy in our study of inheritance concepts.
Consider a bank that offers its customers three kinds of accounts:

1. The checking account has no interest, gives you a small number of free transactions per month, and charges a transaction fee for each additional transaction.
2. The savings account compounds interest monthly. (In our implementation,
   the interest is compounded using the balance of the last day of the month,
   which is somewhat unrealistic. Typically, banks use either the average or the
   minimum daily balance. Exercise P9.1 asks you to implement this enhancement.)
3. The time deposit account is just like a savings account, but you promise to
   leave the money in the account for a particular number of months, and there
   is a penalty for early withdrawal.

Let us construct an inheritance hierarchy for these account classes. All accounts have
something in common—they are bank accounts with a balance and the ability to
deposit money and (within limits) to withdraw money. They also differ in important

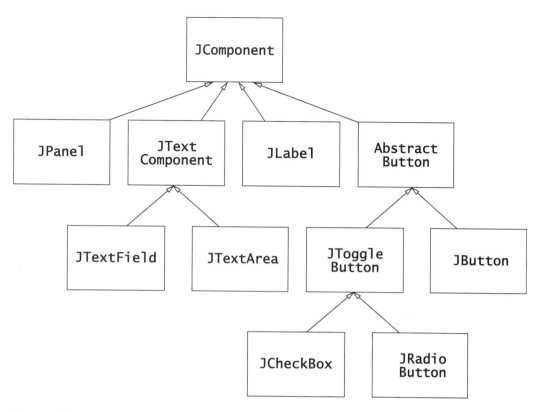

Figure 5

A Part of the Hierarchy of Swing
User Interface Components

respects. The passbook savings and time deposit accounts are *savings accounts*, the
checking account is not. That leads us to the inheritance hierarchy of Figure 6.

Next, let us determine the behavior of these classes. All bank accounts support the
`getBalance` method, which simply reports the current balance. They also support
the `deposit` and `withdraw` methods, although the details of the implementation
differ. For example, a checking account must keep track of the number of transactions
to account for the transaction fees. A time deposit account must reject withdrawals
for other than the full balance.

The checking account needs a method `deductFees` to deduct the monthly fees
and to reset the transaction counter. The `deposit` and `withdraw` methods must be
redefined to count the transactions.

The savings accounts need a method `addInterest` to add interest.

Finally, the `TimeDepositAccount` class redefines the `addInterest` method,
to keep track of the number of months that the account has been open, and the
`withdraw` method, to collect the early withdrawal penalty when appropriate.

Figure 6

Inheritance
Hierarchy for
Bank Account
Classes

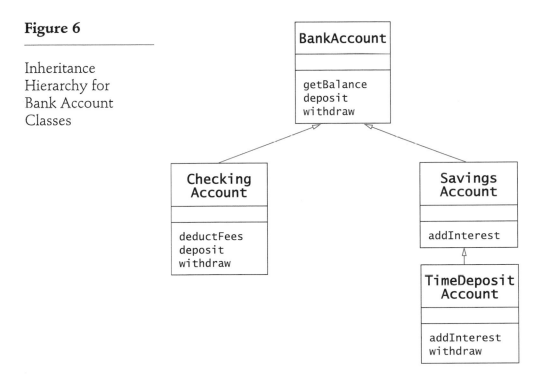

Figure 6 shows which methods are implemented in each class. Following the UML notation, methods are listed in the third compartment of the class rectangles. You will see the details in the next section.

9.4   Inheriting Instance Variables and Methods

When you form a subclass of a given class, you can specify additional instance variables and methods. In this section, we will discuss this process in detail.

Let us look at methods first. When defining the methods for a subclass, there are three possibilities.

1. You can *override* methods from the superclass. If you specify a method with the same *signature* (that is, the same name and the same parameter types), it overrides the method of the same name in the superclass. Whenever the method is applied to an object of the subclass type, the overridden method, and not the original method, is executed. For example, `CheckingAccount.deposit` overrides `BankAccount.deposit`.

2. You can *inherit* methods from the superclass. If you do not explicitly override a superclass method, you automatically inherit it. The superclass method can

be applied to the subclass objects. For example, the `CheckingAccount` class inherits the `BankAccount.getBalance` method.

3. You can define new methods. If you define a method that did not exist in the superclass, then the new method can be applied only to subclass objects. For Example, `CheckingAccount.deductFees` is a new method that does not exist in the superclass `BankAccount`.

The situation for instance variables is quite different. You can never override instance variables. When defining instance variables for a subclass, there are only two cases:

1. You can inherit variables from the superclass. All instance variables from the superclass are automatically inherited. For example, all subclasses of the `BankAccount` class inherit the instance variable `balance`.

2. You can define new variables. Any new instance variables that you define in the subclass are only present in subclass objects. For example, the subclass `SavingsAccount` defines a new instance variable `interestRate`.

What happens if you define a new variable with the same name as a superclass variable? For example, what happens if you define another variable named `balance` in the `SavingsAccount` class? Then each `SavingsAccount` object has *two* instance variables of the same name (see Figure 7). The newly defined subclass variable *shadows* the superclass variable. That is, the superclass variable is still present, but it cannot be accessed. Whenever you refer to `balance` in a `SavingsAccount` method, you access the new instance variable. Of course, if the superclass instance variable is private (as all instance variables should be), the subclass methods aren't able to access it anyway. Shadowing instance variables is harmless, but it can be a source of confusion (see Common Error 9.2).

We already implemented the `BankAccount` and `SavingsAccount` classes. Now we will implement the subclass `CheckingAccount` so that you can see in detail how methods and instance variables are inherited. Recall that the `BankAccount` class has three methods and one instance variable:

```
public class BankAccount
{  public double getBalance() { . . . }
   public void deposit(double d) { . . . }
   public void withdraw(double d) { . . . }
```

Figure 7

Shadowing Instance
Variables

```
private double balance;
}
```

The `CheckingAccount` has an added method `deductFees` and an added instance variable `transactionCount`, and it overrides the `deposit` and `withdraw` methods to increment the transaction count:

```
public class CheckingAccount extends BankAccount
{  public void deposit(double d) { . . . }
   public void withdraw(double d) { . . . }
   public void deductFees() { . . . }

   private int transactionCount;
}
```

Each object of class `CheckingAccount` has two instance variables:

`balance` (inherited from `BankAccount`)

`transactionCount` (new to `CheckingAccount`)

You can apply four methods to `CheckingAccount` objects:

`getBalance()` (inherited from `BankAccount`)

`deposit(double)` (overrides `BankAccount` method)

`withdraw(double)` (overrides `BankAccount` method)

`deductFees()` (new to `CheckingAccount`)

Next, let us implement these methods. The `deposit` method increments the transaction count and deposits the money:

```
public class CheckingAccount extends BankAccount
{  public void deposit(double amount)
   {  transactionCount++;
      // now add amount to balance
      . . .
   }
   . . .
}
```

Now we have a problem. We can't simply add `amount` to `balance`:

```
public class CheckingAccount extends BankAccount
{  public void deposit(double amount)
   {  transactionCount++;
      // now add amount to balance
      balance = balance + amount; // ERROR
   }
   . . .
}
```

Although every `CheckingAccount` object has a `balance` instance variable, that instance variable is *private* to the superclass `BankAccount`. Subclass methods have no more access rights to the private data of the superclass than any other methods. If you want to modify a private superclass variable, you must use a public method of the superclass, just like everyone else.

How can we add the deposit amount to the balance, using the public interface of the BankAccount class? There is a perfectly good method for just that purpose—namely, the deposit method of the BankAccount class. So we have to invoke the deposit on some object. On which object? The checking account into which the money is deposited—that is, the implicit parameter of the deposit method of the CheckingAccount class. As you saw in Chapter 3, to invoke another method on the implicit parameter, you don't specify the parameter but just write the method name:

```
public class CheckingAccount extends BankAccount
{  public void deposit(double amount)
   {  transactionCount++;
      // now add amount to balance
      deposit(amount); // not complete
   }
   . . .
}
```

But this won't quite work. The compiler interprets

```
deposit(amount);
```

as

```
this.deposit(amount);
```

The this parameter is of type CheckingAccount. There is a method called deposit in the CheckingAccount class. Therefore, that method will be called—but that is just the method we are currently writing! The method will call itself over and over, and the program will die in an infinite recursion.

Instead, we must be more specific that we want to invoke only the *superclass's* deposit method. There is a special keyword super for this purpose:

```
public class CheckingAccount extends BankAccount
{  public void deposit(double amount)
   {  transactionCount++;
      // now add amount to balance
      super.deposit(amount);
   }
   . . .
}
```

This version of the deposit method is correct. To deposit money into a checking account, update the transaction count and then call the deposit method of the superclass.

The remaining methods are now straightforward.

```
Java Syntax
9.3 Calling a Superclass
Method
```

returnType *methodName*(*parameters*)
```
{   . . .
    super.methodName (parameters);
    . . .
}
```

Example:
```
public void deposit(double amount)
{   transactionCount++;
    super.deposit(amount);
}
```

Purpose:
To call a method of the superclass instead of the method of the current class

```
public class CheckingAccount extends BankAccount
{   . . .

    public void withdraw(double amount)
    {   transactionCount++;
        // now subtract amount from balance
        super.withdraw(amount);
    }

    public void deductFees()
    {   if (transactionCount > FREE_TRANSACTIONS)
        {   double fees = TRANSACTION_FEE
                * (transactionCount - FREE_TRANSACTIONS);
            super.withdraw(fees);
        }
        transactionCount = 0;
    }
    . . .
    private static final int FREE_TRANSACTIONS = 3;
    private static final double TRANSACTION_FEE = 2.0;
}
```

Next, we will turn to the implementation of the `TimeDepositAccount`, a subclass of the `SavingsAccount` class. In a time deposit account, the account holder promises to leave the money in the account for some number of months, presumably in exchange for a higher interest rate. We store this number as the *maturity* of the account. The value is set in the constructor—see the next section for the constructor implementation. Once the account has matured, there is no withdrawal penalty.

```
public class TimeDepositAccount extends SavingsAccount
{  . . .
   public void addInterest()
   {  periodsToMaturity--;
      super.addInterest();
   }

   public void withdraw(double amount)
   { if (periodsToMaturity > 0)
        super.withdraw(EARLY_WITHDRAWAL_PENALTY);
     super.withdraw(amount);
   }

   private int periodsToMaturity;
   private static final double EARLY_WITHDRAWAL_PENALTY = 20.0;
}
```

Note that the TimeDepositAccount is *two* levels removed from the BankAccount class. The BankAccount class is a superclass, but not the immediate superclass. The TimeDepositAccount class still inherits two methods from the BankAccount class, namely getBalance and deposit (see Figure 6). Methods can be inherited from an indirect superclass as long as none of the intermediate superclasses overrides them.

Consider the method calls super.addInterest and super.withdraw in the addInterest and withdraw methods of the TimeDepositAccount class. Which methods do they call? The keyword super indicates that they call the methods of the superclass—that is, SavingsAccount. In the case of the addInterest method that is true, because the SavingsAccount class actually has an addInterest method. The SavingsAccount class doesn't have a withdraw method, though; it inherits that method from the BankAccount class (again, see Figure 6). Therefore, super. withdraw actually calls BankAccount.withdraw. In general, the *closest* method in the inheritance hierarchy is called.

Common Error 9.2

Shadowing Instance Variables

A subclass has no access to the private instance variables of the superclass. For example, the methods of the CheckingAccount class cannot access the balance variable:

```
public class CheckingAccount extends BankAccount
{  public void deposit(double amount)
   {  transactionCount++;
      balance = balance + amount; // ERROR
   }
   . . .
}
```

It is a common beginner's error to "solve" this problem by adding *another* instance variable with the same name.

```
public class CheckingAccount extends BankAccount
{  public void deposit(double amount)
   {  transactionCount++;
      balance = balance + amount;
   }
   . . .
   private double balance;
}
```

Sure, now the `deposit` method compiles, but it doesn't update the correct balance! Such a `CheckingAccount` object has two instance variables, both named `balance` (see Figure 7). The `getBalance` method of the superclass retrieves one of them, and the `deposit` method of the subclass updates the other.

Common Error 9.3

Overriding Superclass Methods

A common error in extending the functionality of a superclass method is to forget the `super.` qualifier. For example, to withdraw money from a checking account, update the transaction count and then withdraw the amount:

```
public void withdraw(double amount)
{  transactionCount++;
   withdraw(amount); // Error—should be super.withdraw(amount)
}
```

Here `withdraw(amount)` refers to the `withdraw` method applied to the implicit parameter of the method. The implicit parameter is of type `CheckingAccount`, and the `CheckingAccount` class has a `withdraw` method, so that method is called. Of course, that is a recursive call to the current method. Instead, you must be precise which `withdraw` method you want to call.

Another common error is to forget to call the superclass method altogether. Then the functionality of the superclass mysteriously vanishes.

9.5   Subclass Construction

Let us define a constructor to set the initial balance of a checking account.

```
public class CheckingAccount extends BankAccount
{  public CheckingAccount(double initialBalance)
   {  // construct superclass
      . . .
      // initialize transaction count
      transactionCount = 0;
   }
   . . .
}
```

We want to invoke the BankAccount constructor to set the balance to the initial balance. There is a special instruction to call the superclass constructor from a subclass constructor. You use the keyword super, followed by the construction parameters in parentheses:

```
public class CheckingAccount extends BankAccount
{  public CheckingAccount(double initialBalance)
   {  // construct superclass
      super(initialBalance);
      // initialize transaction count
      transactionCount = 0;
   }
   . . .
}
```

When the keyword super is followed by a parenthesis, it indicates a call to the superclass constructor. When used in this way, the constructor call must be *the first statement of the subclass constructor*. If super is followed by a period and a method name, on the other hand, it indicates a call to a superclass method as you saw in the preceding section. Such a call can be made anywhere in any subclass method. The dual use of the super keyword is analogous to the dual use of the this keyword (see Advanced Topic 7.3).

If a subclass constructor does not call the superclass constructor, the superclass is constructed with its default constructor. If the superclass does not have a default constructor, then the compiler reports an error.

For example, you can implement the CheckingAccount constructor without calling the superclass constructor. Then the BankAccount class is constructed with its default constructor, which sets the balance to zero. Of course, then the CheckingAccount constructor must explicitly deposit the initial balance.

```
public class CheckingAccount extends BankAccount
{  public CheckingAccount(double initialBalance)
   {  // superclass has been constructed with its default constructor
      // now set initial balance
      super.deposit(initialBalance); // initialize transaction count
      transactionCount = 0;
   }
   . . .
}
```

However, in the case of the TimeDepositAccount we have no choice. The superclass, SavingsAccount, has no default constructor. Therefore, we must call the superclass constructor explicitly.

```
public class TimeDepositAccount extends SavingsAccount
{  public TimeDepositAccount(double rate, int maturity)
   {  super(rate);
      periodsToMaturity = maturity;
   }
   . . .
}
```

9.6   Polymorphism

The inheritance relationship is often called the "is-a" relationship. Every object of the subclass is also a superclass object, but with special properties. For example, every checking account is a bank account.

Therefore, it is always possible to use a subclass object in place of a superclass object. For example, consider again the `transfer` method that can be used to transfer money from another account:

```
public void transfer(BankAccount other, double amount)
{   withdraw(amount);
    other.deposit(amount);
}
```

Because all our account classes extend the `BankAccount` class, you can pass objects of any account class to this method:

```
BankAccount collegeFund = . . . ;
CheckingAccount harrysChecking = . . . ;
collegeFund.transfer(harrysChecking, 1000);
```

Now let us follow the method call more precisely. Inside the method call, there are two variables of type `BankAccount`, but they refer to a `TimeDepositAccount` and a `CheckingAccount` object (see Figure 8).

Consider the call to the `deposit` method. *Which* `deposit` method? The `other` parameter has type `BankAccount`, so it would appear as if `BankAccount.deposit`

Figure 8

Polymorphism

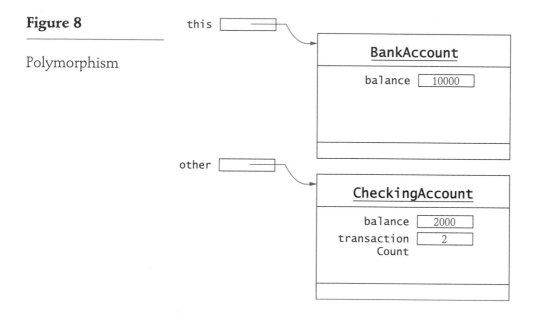

is called. On the other hand, the CheckingAccount class provides its own deposit method that updates the transaction count. Since the other variable actually refers to an object of the subclass CheckingAccount, it would be appropriate if the CheckingAccount.deposit method was called instead.

In Java, method calls *are always determined by the type of the actual object*, not the type of the object reference. That is, if the actual object has the type CheckingAccount, then the CheckingAccount.deposit method is called. It does not matter that the object reference is stored in a variable of type BankAccount.

That means that the same statement

```
other.deposit(amount);
```

can call different methods. If the transfer method is called with a CheckingAccount object for the other parameter, the CheckingAccount.deposit method is called.

The principle that the actual type of the object determines the method to be called is called *polymorphism*. The term "polymorphism" comes from the Greek words for "many shapes". The same computation works for objects of many shapes, and adapts itself to the nature of the objects. In Java, all instance methods are polymorphic.

The following program calls the polymorphic withdraw and deposit methods. You should manually calculate what the program should print for each account balance, and confirm that the correct methods have in fact been called.

Program AccountTest.java

```
public class AccountTest
{  public static void main(String[] args)
```

```
    {  SavingsAccount momsSavings
          = new SavingsAccount(0.5);

       TimeDepositAccount collegeFund
          = new TimeDepositAccount(1, 3);

       CheckingAccount harrysChecking
          = new CheckingAccount(0);

       momsSavings.deposit(10000);
       collegeFund.deposit(10000);

       momsSavings.transfer.(harrysChecking, 2000);
       collegeFund.transfer.(harrysChecking, 980);

       harrysChecking.withdraw(500);
       harrysChecking.withdraw(80);
       harrysChecking.withdraw(400);

       endOfMonth(momsSavings);
       endOfMonth(collegeFund);
       endOfMonth(harrysChecking);

       printBalance("mom's savings", momsSavings);
          // $10000 – $2000 + 0.5% interest = $8040
       printBalance("the college fund", collegeFund);
          // $10000 – $980 – $20 penalty + 1% interest
          // = $9090
       printBalance("Harry's checking", harrysChecking);
          // $2000 + $980 – $500 – $80 – $400 – $4 fees
          // = $1996
    }

    public static void endOfMonth(SavingsAccount savings)
    {  savings.addInterest();
    }

    public static void endOfMonth(CheckingAccount checking)
    {  checking.deductFees();
    }

    public static void printBalance(String name,
       BankAccount account)
    {  System.out.println("The balance of " + name
          + " account is $" + account.getBalance());
    }
}
```

When you see a polymorphic method call, such as `other.deposit(amount)`, there are several possible `deposit` methods that can be called. You have already seen another case in which the same method name can refer to different methods, namely when a method name is *overloaded*: that is, when a single class has several methods with the same name but different parameter types. For example, you can have two constructors BankAccount() and BankAccount(double). Then the compiler selects the appropriate method when compiling the program, simply by looking at the types of the parameters:

```
account = new BankAccount();
    // compiler selects BankAccount()
account = new BankAccount(10000);
    // compiler selects BankAccount(double)
```

For another example of overloading, consider the static endOfMonth methods in the AccountTest class. The compiler uses the type of the explicit parameter to pick the appropriate method.

There is an important difference between polymorphism and overloading. The compiler picks an overloaded method when translating the program, before the program ever runs. This method selection is called *early binding*. However, when selecting the method matching the type of the *implicit* parameter, as in the case of the deposit method that we just analyzed, the compiler does not make any decision when translating the method. The program has to run before anyone can know what is stored in other. Therefore, the virtual machine, and not the compiler, selects the appropriate method. This method selection is called *late binding*.

9.7   Interfaces

Several useful Java methods in effect tell you: "If only your objects were of the Comparable type, I would be happy to sort them for you", or, "If you just gave me a MouseListener, I would tell it about every mouse click." These methods accept parameters of type Comparable or MouseListener. If you care about sorting or mouse listening, you have a powerful incentive to create objects that you can pass to these methods.

For example, suppose you want to sort a collection of savings accounts by increasing interest rates, to find out the best place to put your money. Normally, you would just make the SavingsAccount class extend whatever class the sorting method expects. But wait. The SavingsAccount class already extends another class, BankAccount. In Java, a class cannot have two direct superclasses. In other words, you cannot write

```
public class SavingsAccount
    extends BankAccount, Comparable // ERROR
{ public int compareTo(Object other)
    { . . .
```

```
    }
        . . .
}
```

There is nothing wrong in principle with having more than one superclass—many object-oriented programming languages have this capability, often called *multiple inheritance*. In those languages, though, multiple inheritance is the cause of some technical difficulties. The Java designers decided to keep the language simple and therefore did not allow full-fledged multiple inheritance.

It turns out that one can avoid the complexities of multiple inheritance, and still keep most of the benefits, if one limits all but one of the superclasses to a very restricted form. To enable this form of inheritance, you use *interfaces* instead of superclasses.

An interface is similar to a class, but there are several important restrictions:

◆ An interface does not have instance variables.

◆ All methods in an interface are *abstract*; that is, they have a name, parameters, and a return type, but they don't have an implementation.

◆ All methods in an interface are automatically public.

For example, the `java.lang` package defines a `Comparable` interface as follows:

```
public interface Comparable
{   int compareTo(Object other); // no implementation
}
```

You don't extend interfaces; you *implement* them, using the special `implements` keyword:

```
public class SavingsAccount extends BankAccount
    implements Comparable
{   . . .
}
```

Any class that implements the `Comparable` interface *must* supply the `compareTo` method.

```
public class SavingsAccount extends BankAccount
    implements Comparable
{   . . .
    public int compareTo(Object other)
    {   // supply implementation
        . . .
    }
}
```

Note that the class must declare the method as `public`, whereas the interface does not—all methods in an interface are public.

The `compareTo` method is intended for sorting collections of objects. A sorting method will repeatedly call

```
first.compareTo(second)
```

and decide, depending on the return value, whether the objects are in the correct order or whether they need to be rearranged. (You will see in Chapter 15 how to implement such a sorting method.) Of course, when sorting numbers, the sorting method can just see which number is larger. But how can it sort bank accounts or rectangles? The sorting method itself has no knowledge of these objects and their meaning. The sorting method therefore declares, "I am willing to sort a collection of objects, *provided* they implement the `Comparable` interface."

Why doesn't *every* class have a `compareTo` method? Comparison doesn't make sense for all objects. You can sort savings accounts by their interest rates, but there is no natural way for sorting `PrintStream` or `Graphics2D` objects. Thus, by default, objects of arbitrary classes are not comparable. A developer must *want* a class to be comparable and demonstrate that desire by implementing the `Comparable` interface.

Let us finally provide the code for the `compareTo` method of the `SavingsAccount` class. The `compareTo` method should return zero if two objects are identical, a negative number if the first one should come before the second when the objects are sorted, and a positive number if the first one should come after the second. The exact value of the returned integer does not matter; only the sign (+ or -) counts.

```java
public class SavingsAccount
    extends BankAccount implements Comparable
{  public int compareTo(Object other)
   {  SavingsAccount otherAccount = (SavingsAccount)other;
      if (interestRate < otherAccount.interestRate) return -1;
      if (interestRate > otherAccount.interestRate) return 1;
      return 0;
   }
   . . .
}
```

Once a class implements an interface, you can convert a class reference to an interface reference:

```java
SavingsAccount harrysSavings = new SavingsAccount();
Comparable first = harrysSavings;
```

In particular, you can give `SavingsAccount` objects to methods that don't know or care about savings accounts but that accept parameters of type `Comparable`, such as the searching and sorting methods that you will see in Chapter 15.

However, you can *never* construct an interface:

```java
Comparable second; // OK
second = new Comparable(); // ERROR
```

> ## Java Syntax
> ### 9.5 Defining an Interface
> ```
> public interface InterfaceName
> {  method signatures
> }
> ```
>
> Example:
> ```
> public interface Comparable
> {  int compareTo(Object other);
> }
> ```
>
> Purpose:
> To define an interface and its method signatures. The methods are automatically public.

> ## Java Syntax
> ### 9.6 Implementing an Interface
> ```
> class SubclassName implements InterfaceName, InterfaceName, ...
> {  methods
>    instance variables
> }
> ```
>
> Example:
> ```
> public class SavingsAccount
>    extends BankAccount
>    implements Comparable
> {  // other SavingsAccount methods
>    public int compareTo(Object other)
>    {  // method implementation
>    }
> }
> ```
>
> Purpose:
> To define a new class that implements the methods of an interface

Interfaces aren't classes, so you can't construct interface *objects*. However, it is perfectly legal to have interface *references*. All interface references refer to objects of other classes—classes that implement the interface.

A class can have only one superclass, but it can implement any number of interfaces. For example, there is an interface `Cloneable` that we will discuss in the next section. The `SavingsAccount` can implement both the `Comparable` and the

`Cloneable` interfaces. Simply supply the names of all interfaces, separated by commas, after the `implements` keyword:

```
public class SavingsAccount extends BankAccount
    implements Comparable, Cloneable
{  . . .
}
```

Another common interface is the `Shape` interface. The `draw` and `fill` methods of the `Graphics2D` class take a parameter of type `Shape`. You can draw and fill objects of *any* class that implements the `Shape` interface, such as `Line2D` and `Rectangle`. You will encounter more interfaces in the next chapter—they play an important role for implementing *event listeners* in graphical applications.

Advanced Topic 9.1

Constants in Interfaces

Interfaces cannot have variables, but you can specify *constants*, which will be inherited by all classes that implement the interface.

For example, the `SwingConstants` interface defines various constants such as `SwingConstants.NORTH`, `SwingConstants.EAST`, and so on. Several classes implement this interface. For example, since `JLabel` implements the `SwingConstants` interface, users can refer to them as `JLabel.NORTH`, `JLabel.EAST`, and so on, when using these constants in conjunction with `JLabel` objects.

When defining a constant in an interface, you can (and should) omit the keywords `public static final`, because all variables in an interface are automatically `public static final`. For example,

```
public interface SwingConstants
{  int NORTH = 1;
   int NORTH_EAST = 2;
   int EAST = 3;
   . . .
}
```

Advanced Topic 9.2

Abstract Classes

When you extend an existing class, you have the *choice* whether or not to redefine the methods of the superclass. Sometimes, it is desirable to *force* programmers to redefine a method. That happens when there is no good default for the superclass, and only the subclass programmer can know how to implement the method properly.

Here is an example. Suppose the First National Bank of Java decides that every account type must have some monthly fees. Therefore, a `deductFees` method should be added to the BankAccount class:

```
public class BankAccount
{  public void deductFees() { . . . }
   . . .
}
```

But what should this method do? Of course, we could have the method do nothing. But then a programmer implementing a new subclass might simply forget to implement the `deductFees` method, and the new account would inherit the do-nothing method of the superclass. There is a better way: namely, to declare the `deductFees` method as an *abstract method*:

```
public abstract void deductFees();
```

An abstract method has no implementation. This forces the implementors of subclasses to specify concrete implementations of this method. (Of course, some subclasses might decide to implement a do-nothing method, but then that is their choice—not a silently inherited default.)

You cannot construct objects of classes with abstract methods. For example, once the BankAccount class has an abstract method, the compiler will flag an attempt to create a new `BankAccount()` as an error. Of course, if the `CheckingAccount` subclass overrides the `deductFees` method and supplies an implementation, then you can create `CheckingAccount` objects. A class for which you cannot create objects is called an *abstract class*. A class for which you can create objects is sometimes called a *concrete class*.

In Java, you must declare all abstract classes with the keyword **abstract**:

```
public abstract class BankAccount
{  public abstract void deductFees();
   . . .
}
```

A class that defines an abstract method, or that inherits an abstract method without overriding it, *must* be declared as abstract. You can also declare classes with no abstract methods as abstract. Doing so prevents programmers from creating instances of that class but allows them to create their own subclasses.

Note that you cannot construct an *object* of an abstract class, but you can still have an *object reference* whose type is an abstract class. Of course, the actual object to which it refers must be an instance of a concrete subclass:

```
BankAccount anAccount; // OK
anAccount = new BankAccount(); // Error—BankAccount is abstract
anAccount = new SavingsAccount(); // OK
anAccount = null; // OK
```

The reason for using abstract classes is to force programmers to create subclasses. The reason for abstract methods is to avoid the trouble of coming up with useless default methods and to avoid inheriting them by accident.

Abstract classes differ from interfaces in an important way—they can have instance variables, and they can have some concrete methods.

Advanced Topic 9.3

Final Methods and Classes

In Advanced Topic 9.2 you have seen how you can force other programmers to create subclasses of abstract classes and override abstract methods. Occasionally, you may want to do the opposite and *prevent* other programmers from creating subclasses or from overriding certain methods. In these situations, you use the `final` keyword. For example, the `String` class in the standard Java library has been declared as

```
public final class String { . . . }
```

That means that nobody can extend the `String` class. The reason is twofold. The compiler can generate more efficient method calls if it knows that it doesn't have to worry about late binding. Also, the `String` class is meant to be *immutable*—string objects can't be modified by any of their methods. Since the Java language does not enforce this, the class designers did. Nobody can create subclasses of `String`; therefore, you know that all `String` references can be copied without the risk of mutation.

You can also declare individual methods as final:

```
public class MyApplet extends Applet
{  . . .
    public final boolean checkPassword(String password)
    {  . . .
    }
}
```

This way, nobody can override the `checkPassword` method with another method that simply returns `true`.

9.8   Access Control

Java has four levels of controlling access to variables, methods, and classes:

- ◆ `public` access
- ◆ `private` access
- ◆ `protected` access (see Advanced Topic 9.4)
- ◆ Package access (the default, when no access modifier is given)

We have already used the `private` and `public` modifiers extensively. Private features can be accessed only by the methods of their own class. Public features can be accessed by methods of all classes. We will discuss protected access in Advanced Topic 9.4—we will not need it in this book.

If you do not supply an access control modifier, then the default is *package access*. That is, all methods of classes in the same package can access the feature. For example, if a class is declared as `public`, then all other classes in all packages can use it. But if a class is declared without an access modifier, then only the other classes in the same package can use it. For that reason, the compiler must look inside all source files of the current package, but it only needs to look for source files with the same name as the class when locating classes from other packages. (Recall that a source file can have at most one public class, and that it must have the same name as the file.)

Package access is a good default for classes, but it is extremely unfortunate for variables. Instance and static variables of classes should always be `private`. There are a small number of exceptions:

◆ Public constants (`public static final` variables) are useful and safe.

◆ Some objects, such as `System.out`, need to be accessible to all programs and therefore should be public.

◆ Very occasionally, several classes in a package must collaborate very closely. In that case, it may make sense to give some variables package access. But inner classes are usually a better solution—you will see examples in Chapter 16.

However, it is a common error to *forget* the keyword `private`, thereby opening up a potential security hole. For example, at the time of this writing, the `Window` class in the `java.awt` package contained the following declaration:

```
public class Window extends Container
{  String warningString;
   . . .
}
```

The programmer was careless and didn't make the variable private. There actually was no good reason to grant package access to the `warningString` variable—*no other class accesses it*. It is a security risk. Packages are not closed entities—any programmer can make a new class, add it to the `java.awt` package, and gain access to the `warningString` variables of all `Window` objects!

Package access is very rarely useful, and most variables are given package access by accident because the programmer simply forgot the `private` keyword and the compiler didn't complain—see Common Error 9.4

Methods should generally be `public` or `private`. Public methods are the norm. Private methods make sense for implementation-dependent tasks that should be carried out only by methods of the same class. Methods with package access can be called by any other method in the same package. That can occasionally make sense if a package consists of a small number of closely collaborating classes, but more often than not, it is simply an accident—the programmer forgot the `public` modifier. We recommend that you do not use package-visible methods.

Classes and interfaces can have public or package access. Classes that are generally useful should have public access. Classes that are used for implementation reasons should have package access. You can hide them even better by turning them into inner classes; you will see examples of inner classes in Chapters 10 and 16. Inner classes can be declared as **public**, **private**, or **protected**. They too have package access if no modifier is given. There are a few examples of public inner classes, such as the familiar `Ellipse.Float` and `Ellipse.Double` classes. However, in general, inner classes should be private.

Common Error 9.4

Accidental Package Access

It is very easy to forget the **private** modifier for instance variables.

```
public class BankAccount
{   . . .
    double balance; // Package access really intended?
}
```

Most likely, this was just an oversight. Probably the programmer never intended to grant access to this variable to other classes in the same package. The compiler won't complain, of course. Much later, some other programmer may take advantage of the access privilege, either out of convenience or out of evil intent. This is a serious problem, and you must get into the habit of scanning your variable declarations for missing **private** modifiers.

Common Error 9.5

Making Inherited Methods Less Accessible

If a superclass declares a method to be publicly accessible, you cannot override it to be more private. For example,

```
public class BankAccount
{   public void withdraw(double amount) { . . . }
    . . .
}

public TimeDepositAccount
{   private void withdraw(double amount) { . . . }
        // Error—subclass method cannot be more private
    . . .
}
```

The compiler does not allow this, because the increased privacy would be an *illusion*. Anyone can still call the method through a superclass reference:

```
BankAccount account = new TimeDepositAccount();
account.withdraw(100000); // calls  TimeDepositAccount.withdraw
```

◆
◆   Because of late binding, the subclass method is called.
◆   These errors are usually an oversight. If you forget the `public` modifier, your subclass
◆   method has package access, which is more restrictive. Simply restore the `public` modifier,
◆   and the error will go away.

◆
◆   ## Advanced Topic 9.4
◆
◆   ### Protected Access
◆
◆   We ran into some degree of grief when trying to implement the `deposit` method of the
◆   `CheckingAccount` class. That method needed access to the `balance` instance variable of the
◆   superclass. Our remedy was to use the appropriate methods of the superclass to set the bal-
◆   ance.
◆   Java offers another solution to this problem. The superclass can declare an instance variable
◆   as *protected*:
◆
◆   ```
◆   public class BankAccount
◆   { . . .
◆   protected double balance;
◆   }
◆   ```
◆
◆   Protected data can be accessed by the methods of a class and all its subclasses. For example,
◆   `CheckingAccount` inherits from `BankAccount`, so its methods can access the protected in-
◆   stance variables of the `BankAccount` class. Furthermore, protected data can be accessed by all
◆   methods of classes in the same package.
◆   Some programmers like the `protected` access feature because it seems to strike a balance
◆   between absolute protection (making all variables private) and no protection at all (making
◆   all variables public). However, experience has shown that protected variables are subject to
◆   the same kind of problems as public variables. The designer of the superclass has no control
◆   over the authors of subclasses. Any of the subclass methods can corrupt the superclass data.
◆   Furthermore, classes with protected variables are hard to modify. Even if the author of the
◆   superclass would like to change the data implementation, the protected variables cannot be
◆   changed, because someone somewhere out there might have written a subclass whose code
◆   depends on them.
◆   It is best to leave all data private. If you want to grant access to the data only to subclass
◆   methods, consider making the *accessor* method protected.

9.9   Object: The Cosmic Superclass

In Java, every class that does not extend another class automatically extends the class
`Object`. That is, the class `Object` is the direct or indirect superclass of *every* class in
Java (see Figure 9)

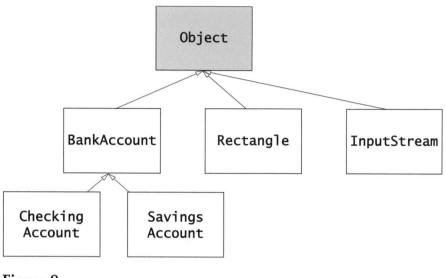

Figure 9

The `Object` Class Is the Superclass of
Every Java Class

Of course, the methods of the `Object` class are very general. Here are the most
useful ones:

`String toString()`	Returns a string representation of the object
`boolean equals(Object other)`	Tests whether the object equals another object
`Object clone()`	Makes a full copy of an object

It is a good idea for you to override these in your classes.

9.9.1　Overriding the `toString` Method

The `toString` method returns a string representation for each object. It is used for
debugging. For example,

```
Rectangle cerealBox = new Rectangle(5, 10, 20, 30);
String s = cerealBox.toString();
   // sets s to "java.awt.Rectangle[x=5,y=10,width=20,height=30]"
```

In fact, this `toString` method is called whenever you concatenate a string with an
object. Consider the concatenation

```
"cerealBox means " + cerealBox;
```

On one side of the + concatenation operator is a string, but on the other side is an object reference. The Java compiler automatically invokes the toString method to turn the object into a string. Then both strings are concatenated. In this case, the result is the string

```
"cerealBox means java.awt.Rectangle[x=5,y=10,width=20,height=30]"
```

This works only if one of the objects is already a string. If you try to apply the + operator to two objects, neither of which is a string, then the compiler reports an error.

The compiler can invoke the toString method because it knows that *every* object has a toString method: Every class extends the Object class, and that class defines toString.

As you know, even numbers are converted to strings when they are concatenated with other strings. For example,

```
int age = 18;
String s = "Harry's age is " + age;
    // sets s to "Harry's age is 18"
```

In this case, the toString method is not involved. Numbers are not objects, and there is no toString method for them. There is only a small set of number types, however, and the compiler knows how to convert them to strings.

Let's try the toString method for the BankAccount class:

```
BankAccount momsSavings = new BankAccount(5000);
String s = momsSavings.toString();
    // sets s to something like "BankAccount@d24606bf"
```

That's disappointing—all that's printed is the name of the class, followed by the address of the object in memory. We don't care *where* the object is in memory. We want to know what is inside the object, but, of course, the toString method of the Object class does not know what is inside our BankAccount class. Therefore, we have to override the method and supply our own version in the BankAccount class. We'll follow the same format that the toString method of the Rectangle class uses: first print the name of the class, and then the values of the instance variables inside brackets.

```
public class BankAccount
{  . . .
   public String toString()
   {  return "BankAccount[balance=" + balance + "]";
   }
}
```

This works better:

```
BankAccount momsSavings = new BankAccount(5000);
String s = momsSavings.toString();
    // sets s to "BankAccount[balance=5000]"
```

9.9.2 Overriding the equals Method

The **equals** method is called whenever you want to compare whether two objects have the same contents:

```
if (account1.equals(account2)) . . .
    // contents are the same
```

That is different from the test with the == operator. That operator tests whether the two references are to the *same* object:

```
if (account1 == account2) . . .
    // objects are the same
```

Let us implement the **equals** method for the **BankAccount** class. You need to override the **equals** method of the **Object** class:

```
public class BankAccount
{   . . .
    public boolean equals(Object otherObject)
    {  . . .
    }
    . . .
}
```

Now you have a slight problem. The **Object** class knows nothing about bank accounts, so it defines the **otherObject** parameter of the **equals** method to have the type **Object**. When redefining the method, you are not allowed to change the object signature. Of course, you can cast the parameter to the class **BankAccount**:

```
BankAccount other = (BankAccount)otherObject;
```

But what if someone called **account.equals(x)** where x wasn't a **BankAccount** object? Then the bad cast would generate an exception, and the program would die. Therefore, you first want to test whether **otherObject** really is an instance of the **BankAccount** class. For such a test, you use the **instanceof** operator. Of course, if the test returns **false**, then the implicit parameter and **otherObject** can't be equal to each other, since we know that the implicit parameter has type **BankAccount**. Therefore, we can formulate our test as follows:

```
public class BankAccount
{   . . .
    public boolean equals(Object otherObject)
    {  if (otherObject instanceof BankAccount)
       {  BankAccount other = (BankAccount)otherObject;
          return balance == other.balance;
       }
       else
          return false;
    }
    . . .
}
```

9.9.3. Overriding the clone Method

You know that copying an object reference simply gives you two references to the same object:

```
BankAccount account1 = new BankAccount(1000);
BankAccount account2 = account1;
account2.deposit(500);
    // now both account1 and account2 have a balance of 1500
```

What can you do if you actually want to make a copy of an object? That is the purpose of the clone method. The clone method must return a *new* object that has identical state to the existing object (see Figure 10). Here is a clone method for the BankAccount class.

```
public class BankAccount
{   . . .
    public Object clone()
    {   // make an account with the identical balance
        BankAccount clonedAccount = new BankAccount(balance);
        return clonedAccount;
    }
}
```

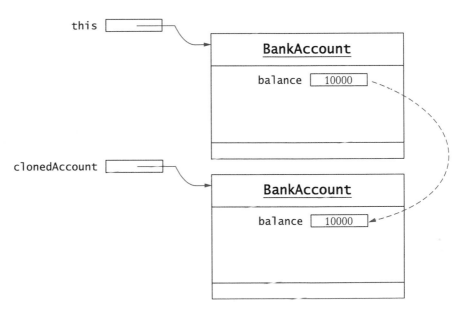

Figure 10

Cloning Objects

Since the `clone` method is defined in the `Object` class, it cannot know the *type* of the object to be returned. Therefore, its return type is `Object`. That is not a problem when implementing the `clone` method. But when you call the method, you must use a cast to convince the compiler that `account1.clone()` really has the same type as `account1`. Here is an example:

```
BankAccount account2 = (BankAccount)account1.clone();
```

The approach to cloning that was described here works for simple classes. For more complex classes, there is a better way to clone an object. You can use the `Object.clone` method to make a new object whose instance variables are copies of the original. See Advanced Topic 9.5 for details.

Productivity Hint 9.1

Supply toString in All Classes

If you have a class whose `toString()` method returns a string that describes the object state, then you can simply call `System.out.println(x)` whenever you need to inspect the current state of an object `x`. This works because the `println` method of the `PrintStream` class invokes `x.toString()` when it needs to print an object. That is extremely helpful if there is an error in your program and your objects don't behave the way you think they should. You can simply insert a few print statements and peek inside the object state during the program run. Some debuggers can even invoke the `toString` method on objects that you inspect.

Sure, it is a bit more trouble to write a `toString` method when you aren't sure your program ever needs one—after all, it might just work correctly on first try. Then again, many programs don't work on first try. As soon as you find out that yours doesn't, consider adding those `toString` methods so that you can easily print out objects.

Common Error 9.6

Forgetting to Clone

In Java, object variables contain references to objects, not actual objects. This can be convenient for giving *two names to the same object*:

```
BankAccount harrysChecking = new BankAccount();
BankAccount slushFund = harrysChecking;
    // Use Harry's checking account for the slush fund
slushFund.deposit(80000)
    // a lot of money ends up in Harry's checking account
```

However, if you don't intend two references to refer to the same object, then this is a problem. In that case, you should use the `clone` method:

```
BankAccount slushFund = (BankAccount)harrysChecking.clone();
```

Quality Tip 9.1

Clone Mutable Instance Variables

Consider the following class:

```
public class Customer
{   public Customer(String aName)
    {   name = aName;
        account = new BankAccount();
    }

    public String getName()
    {   return name;
    }

    public BankAccount getAccount();
    {   return account;
    }

    private String name;
    private BankAccount account;
}
```

This class looks very boring and normal, but the **getAccount** method has a curious property. It *breaks encapsulation*, because anyone can modify the object state without going through the public interface:

```
Customer harry = new Customer("Harry Handsome");
BankAccount account = harry.getAccount();
    // anyone can withdraw money!
account.withdraw(100000);
```

Maybe that wasn't what the designers of the class had in mind? Maybe they only wanted class users to inspect the account? In such a situation, you should *clone* the object reference:

```
public BankAccount getAccount();
{   return (BankAccount)account.clone();
}
```

Do you also need to clone in the **getName** method? No—that method returns a string, and strings are immutable. It is safe to give out a reference to an immutable object.

The rule of thumb is that a class should clone all references to mutable objects that it gives out.

The converse is true as well—a class should ideally clone references that it receives.

```
public Customer(String aName, BankAccount anAccount)
{   name = aName;
    account = (BankAccount)anAccount.clone();
}
```

Otherwise, someone else can continue withdrawing from the account object that they give to the constructor.

◆ Advanced Topic 9.5

Using Object.clone

You saw how to clone an object by constructing a new object with the same state:

```
public class BankAccount
{  . . .
   public Object clone()
   {  // make an account with the identical balance
      BankAccount clonedAccount = new BankAccount(balance);
      return clonedAccount;
   }
}
```

But if you have an object with many instance variables, it can be tedious to copy them all into a new object. The Object.clone method automates that task. It simply creates a new object whose instance variables are copies of the original.

However, this Object.clone method must be used with care. It only shifts the problem of cloning by one level and does not completely solve it. Specifically, if an object contains a reference to another object, then the Object.clone method makes a copy, not another clone,

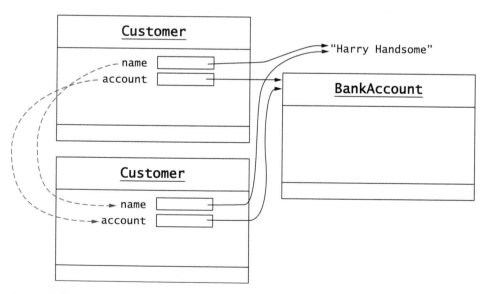

Figure 11

The Object.clone Method Makes a
Shallow Copy

of that object reference. Figure 11 shows how the `Object.clone` method works if a `Customer` object has a reference to a `BankAccount` object. As you can see, the `Object.clone` method copies the reference to the `Customer` object and does not clone it. Such a copy is called a *shallow copy*.

There is a reason why the `Object.clone` method does not systematically clone all sub-objects. In some situations, it is unnecessary. For example, if an object contains a reference to a string, there is no harm in copying the string reference, since Java string objects can never change their contents. The `Object.clone` method does the right thing if an object contains only numbers, truth values, and strings. But it must be used with caution when an object contains references to other objects.

For that reason, there are two safeguards built into the `Object.clone` method to ensure that it is not used accidentally. First, the method is declared **protected** (see Advanced Topic 9.4). This prevents you from accidentally calling `x.clone()` if the class to which `x` belongs hasn't redefined `clone` to be public. However, when defining a `clone` method, you can call `Object.clone`. And of course you will want to make your `clone` method public.

```
public class BankAccount
{  . . .
   public Object clone()
   {  // not complete
      Object clonedAccount = super.clone();
      return clonedAccount;
   }
}
```

As a second precaution, `Object.clone` checks that the object being cloned implements the `Cloneable` interface. If not, it throws an exception. That is, the `Object.clone` method looks like this:

```
public class Object
{  protected Object clone() throws CloneNotSupportedException
   {  if (this instanceof Cloneable)
      {  // copy the instance variables
         . . .
      }
      else
         throw new CloneNotSupportedException();
   }
}
```

Unfortunately, all that safeguarding means that the legitimate callers of `Object.clone()` pay a price—they must catch that exception *even if their class implements* `Cloneable`.

```
public class BankAccount implements Cloneable
{  . . .
   public Object clone()
   {  try
      {  // clones all instance variables
         Object clonedAccount = super.clone();
         return clonedAccount;
      }
```

```
            catch(CloneNotSupportedException e)
            {   // can't happen because we implement Cloneable
                // but we still must catch it
                return null;
            }
        }
    }
```

If an object contains a reference to another mutable object, then you need to call `clone` for that reference. For example, suppose the `Customer` class has an instance variable of class `BankAccount`. Then you can implement `Customer.clone` as follows:

```
    public class Customer implements Cloneable
    {   . . .
        public Object clone()
        {   try
            {   Customer clonedCustomer = (Customer)super.clone();
                clonedCustomer.account = (BankAccount)account.clone();
                return clonedCustomer;
            }
            catch(CloneNotSupportedException e)
            {   // can't ever happen because we implement Cloneable
                return null;
            }
        }

        private String name;
        private BankAccount account;
    }
```

9.10 Packages

9.10.1 Organizing Related Classes into Packages

A Java program consists of a collection of classes. So far, most of your programs have consisted of a single class or a small number of classes that were placed into a single file. When your programs get larger or you work in a team, that situation changes; you will need to split your code into separate source files. There are two primary reasons why this split-up is necessary. First, it takes time to compile a file, and it seems silly to wait for the compiler to translate code over and over that doesn't change. If your code is distributed over several source files, then only those files that you changed need to be recompiled. The second reason becomes apparent when you work with other programmers in a team. It would be very difficult for multiple programmers to edit a single source file simultaneously. Therefore, the program code is broken up so that each programmer is solely responsible for one or more files.

As programs get even larger, however, simply distributing the classes over multiple files isn't enough. An additional structuring mechanism is needed. In Java, packages provide this structuring mechanism. A Java package is a set of related classes. For example, the Java library consists of dozens of packages, some of which are listed in Table 1.

To put classes in a package, you must place a line

```
package packagename;
```

as the first instruction in the source file containing the classes. As you can see from the examples in the Java library, a package name consists of one or more identifiers separated by periods.

For example, consider the **ConsoleReader** and **Numeric** classes that you used for many of the programs in this book. For simplicity, you have simply included these classes together with your own programs. However, it would be much more professional to place these classes into a separate package. That way, your own programs are clearly separated from the book classes.

Let us place the book classes into a package named **com.horstmann.ccj**. (See Section 9.10.3 for an explanation of how to construct package names.) Each source file in that package must start with the instruction

```
package com.horstmann.ccj;
```

For example, the **ConsoleReader.java** file starts out as follows:

```
package com.horstmann.ccj;

import java.io.InputStream;
import java.io.InputStreamReader;
```

Table 1. Important Packages in the Java Library

Package	Purpose	Sample classes
java.lang	Language support	Math
java.util	Utilities	Random
java.io	Input and output	PrintStream
java.awt	Abstract Windowing Toolkit	Color
java.applet	Applets	Applet
java.net	Networking	Socket
java.sql	Database access through Structured Query Language	ResultSet
javax.swing	Swing user interface	JButton
omg.org.CORBA	Common Object Request Broker Architecture for distributed objects	ORB

```
import java.io.BufferedReader;
import java.io.IOException;

public class ConsoleReader
{  . . .
}
```

Not only must the package name be placed into the source file; the source file itself must be placed in a special location. The next section describes where to place the file.

In addition to the named packages (such as `java.util`), there is a special package, called the *default package*, which has no name. If you did not include any `package` statement at the top of your source file, its classes are placed in the default package.

9.10.2 Importing Packages

If you want to use a class from a package, you can refer to it by its full name (package name plus class name). For example, `java.awt.Color` refers to the `Color` class in the `java.awt` package, and `com.horstmann.ccj.ConsoleReader` refers to the `ConsoleReader` class in the `com.horstmann.ccj` package:

```
java.awt.Color backgroundColor = new java.awt.Color(1.0, 0.7, 0.7);
```

Naturally, that is somewhat inconvenient. You can instead *import* a name with an `import` statement:

```
import java.awt.Color;
import com.horstmann.ccj.ConsoleReader;
```

Then you can refer to the classes as `Color` and `ConsoleReader` without the package prefixes.

You can import *all classes* of a package with an `import` statement that ends in `.*`. For example, you can use the statement

```
import java.awt.*;
```

Java Syntax
9.7 Package Specification
package *packageName* ;

Example:
package com.horstmann.ccj ;

Purpose:
To declare that all classes in this file
belong to a particular package

---

to import all classes from the `java.awt` package. That statement lets you refer to classes like `Graphics2D` or `Color` without a `java.awt` prefix. This is the most convenient method for importing classes, but if a program starts with multiple imports of this form, it can be harder to guess to which package a class belongs. Suppose for example a program imports

```
import java.awt.*;
import java.io.*;
```

Then suppose you see a class name `Image`. You would not know whether the `Image` class is in the `java.awt` package or the `java.io` package. For that reason, we prefer to use an explicit `import` statement for each class, though many programmers like the convenience of importing all classes in a package.

However, you never need to import the classes in the `java.lang` package explicitly. That is the package containing the most basic Java classes, such as `Math` and `Object`. These classes are always available to you. In effect, an automatic `import java.lang.*;` statement has been placed into every source file.

Common Error 9.7

Confusing Dots

In Java, the dot symbol (`.`) is used as a separator in the following situations:

◆ Between package names (`java.util`)

◆ Between package and class names (`java.util.Random`)

◆ Between class and inner class names (`Ellipse2D.Double`)

◆ Between class and instance variable names (`Math.PI`)

◆ Between objects and methods (`position.move(10, -10)`)

When you see a long chain of dot-separated names, it can be a challenge to find out which part is a package name, a class name, an instance variable name, and a method name. Consider

```
java.lang.System.out.println(x);
```

Since the `println` is followed by an opening parenthesis, it must be a method name. Therefore, `out` must be either an object or a class with a `static println` method. (Of course, we know that `out` is an object reference of type `PrintStream`.) Again, it is not at all clear, without context, whether `System` is another object, with a public variable `out`, or a class with a `static` variable. Judging from the number of pages that the Java reference manual [1] devotes to this issue, even the compiler has trouble interpreting these dot-separated sequences of strings.

To avoid problems, it is helpful to adopt a strict coding style. If class names always start with an uppercase letter, while variable, method, and package names always start with a lowercase letter then confusion can be avoided.

9.10.3 Package Names

Placing related classes into a package is clearly a convenient mechanism to organize classes. However, there is a more important reason for packages: to avoid *name clashes*. In a large project, it is inevitable that two people will come up with the same name for the same concept. This even happens in the standard Java class library (which has now grown to thousands of classes). There is a class `Object` in the `java.lang` package and an interface, also called `Object`, in the `org.omg.CORBA` package. Fortunately, you never needed to import both packages. If you did, then the name `Object` would be *ambiguous*. However, thanks to the package concept, not all is lost. You can still tell the Java compiler exactly which `Object` class you need, simply by referring to them as `java.lang.Object` and `org.omg.CORBA.Object`.

Of course, for the package-naming convention to work, there must be some way to ensure that package names are unique. It wouldn't be good if the car maker BMW placed all its Java code into the package `bmw`, and some other programmer (perhaps Bertha M. Walters) had the same bright idea. To avoid this problem, the inventors of Java recommend that you use a package-naming scheme that takes advantage of the uniqueness of Internet domain names.

If your company or organization has an Internet domain name, then you have an identifier that is guaranteed to be unique—the organizations who assign domain names take care of that. For example, I have a domain name `horstmann.com`, and there is nobody else on the planet with the same domain name. (I was lucky that the domain name `horstmann.com` had not been taken by anyone else when I applied. Bertha M. Walters won't be so lucky—`bmw.com` has already been assigned to someone else, namely the car company.) To get a package name, turn the domain name around, to produce a package name prefix:

```
org.omg
com.horstmann
```

Then it is up to the owner of the domain name to subdivide package names further. For example, the Object Management Group, the holder of the `omg.org` domain name, decided to use the package name `org.omg.CORBA` for the Java classes that implement their Common Object Request Broker Architecture (a mechanism for communication between objects that are distributed on different computers).

If you don't have your own domain name, you can still create a package name that has a high probability of being unique, by writing your email address backwards. For example, if Bertha M. Walters has email address `bmw@cs.sjsu.edu`, then she can use a package name `edu.sjsu.cs.bmw` for her own classes.

9.10.4 How Classes Are Located

If the Java compiler has been properly set up on your system, and you use only the standard classes, you ordinarily need not worry about the location of class files and can safely skip this section. If you want to add your own packages, however, or if the compiler cannot locate a particular class or package, you need to understand the mechanism.

A package is located in a subfolder that matches the package name. The parts of the name between periods represent successively nested folders. For example, the package com.horstmann.ccj would be placed in a subfolder com/horstmann/ccj. If the package is only to be used in conjunction with a single program, then you can place the subfolder inside the folder holding that program's files. For example, if you do your homework assignments in a folder ~/cs1hw, then you can place the class files for the com.horstmann.ccj package into the folder ~/cs1hw/com/horstmann /ccj. However, if you want to place your programs into many different folders, such as ~/cs1hw/hw1, ~/cs1hw/hw2, ..., then you probably don't want to have lots of identical subfolders ~/cs1hw/hw1/com/horstmann/ccj, ~/cs1hw/hw2/ com/ horstmann/ccj, and so on. In that case, you want to make a single folder with a name such as ~/ccjbook/com/horstmann/ccj, place all class files for the package in that directory, and tell the Java compiler once and for all how to locate the class files.

You need to add the folders that might contain packages to the *class path*. If you place the com.horstmann.ccj package into a folder ~/ccjbook/com/horstmann/ ccj, you need to add the ~/ccjbook directory to that class path. The details for doing this depend on your compilation environment. You need to consult the documentation for your compiler, or your instructor, for detailed instructions how to perform that. If you use the Sun JDK, you may need to set the class path. The exact command depends on the operating system. In UNIX, the command might be

```
setenv CLASSPATH $(HOME)/ccjbook:.
```

A typical example for Windows would be

```
set CLASSPATH=c:\ccjbook;.
```

Note that the class path contains the base folders that may contain package folders. For example, if ~/ccjbook is listed in the class path, then the compiler will look for the com.horstmann.ccj package in the folder ~/ccjbook/com/horstmann/ccj. It is a common error to place the complete package address in the class path. If the class path mistakenly contains ~/ccjbook/com/horstmann/ccj, then the compiler will attempt to locate the com.horstmann.ccj package in ~/ccjbook/com/horstmann/ccj/ com/horstmann/ccj and won't find the files.

As you can see, it is a bit tricky to place class files in packages, and to set the class path. It is a common beginner's error to place the files in the wrong directory or to forget setting the class path. For that reason, the classes in this book (such as ConsoleReader) were not actually placed into packages.

To complicate matters more, sets of class files can be packaged into a single file for efficiency. For example, you may not be able to find a /jdk/jre/lib/java/util/ Random.class file on your system. That file may be contained inside a *Java archive,* called rt.jar in some systems, that is located in the /jdk/jre/lib folder. When you place your own packages, you don't need to worry about archives.

Now that you have seen how packages are located, let us see how the compiler finds a particular class. Suppose the compiler needs to locate the class `com.horstmann-`. `ccj.ConsoleReader`. Then the compiler looks for the file com/horstmann/ccj / ConsoleReader.class inside all directories on the class path. On the other hand, if you have an unqualified name, such as `BankAccount`, then the compiler first looks for a class `BankAccount.class`, but if it does not find it, it will look through *all source files in the default package* to see whether any of them contains the class `BankAccount` as a non-`public` class.

After finding a named class, the compiler checks whether the matching compiled class file is newer than the source file. If not, it is automatically recompiled. That way, the compiler automatically uses the most up-to-date program code.

Random Fact 9.1

Operating Systems

Without an operating system, a computer would not be useful. Minimally, you need an operating system to locate files and to start programs. The programs that you run need services from the operating system to access devices and to interact with other programs. Operating systems on large computers need to provide more services than those on personal computers. Here are some typical services:

◆ *Program loading.* Every operating system provides some way of launching application programs. The user indicates what program should be run, usually by typing the name of the program in or by clicking on an icon. The operating system locates the program code, loads it in memory, and starts it.

◆ *Managing files.* A storage device such as a hard disk is, electronically, simply a device capable of storing a huge sequence of zeroes and ones. It is up to the operating system to bring some structure to the storage layout and organize it into files, folders, and so on. The operating system also needs to impose some amount of security and re dundancy into the file system so that a power outage does not jeopardize the con tents of an entire hard disk. Some operating systems do a better job in this regard than others.

◆ *Virtual memory.* RAM is expensive, and few computers have enough RAM to hold all programs and their data that a user would like to run simultaneously. Most operating systems extend the available memory by storing some data on the hard disk. The application programs do not realize what is happening. When a program accesses a data item that is currently not in RAM, the processor senses this and notifies the operating system. The operating system swaps the needed data from the hard disk into RAM, simultaneously swapping out a memory block of equal size that had not been accessed for some time.

◆ *Handling multiple users.* The operating systems of large and powerful computers allow simultaneous access by multiple users. Each user is connected to the computer through a separate terminal. The operating system authenticates users by checking that they have a valid account and password. It gives each user a small *slice* of processor time, then serves the next user.

- *Multitasking.* Even if you are the sole user of a computer, you may want to run multiple applications—for example, to read your email in one window and run the Java compiler in another. The operating system is responsible for dividing processor time between the applications you are running, so that each can make progress.

- *Printing.* The operating system queues up the print requests that are sent by multiple applications. This is necessary to make sure that the printed pages do not contain a mixture of words sent simultaneously from separate programs.

- *Windows.* Many operating systems present their users with a desktop made up of multiple windows. The operating system manages the location and appearance of the window frames; the applications are responsible for the interior.

- *Fonts.* To render text on the screen and the printer, the shapes of characters must be defined. This is especially important for programs that can display multiple type styles and sizes. Modern operating systems contain a central font repository.

- *Communicating between programs.* The operating system can facilitate the transfer of information between programs. That transfer can happen through *cut and paste* or *interprocess communication.* Cut and paste is a user-initiated data transfer in which the user copies data from one application into a transfer buffer (often called a "clipboard") managed by the operating system and inserts the buffer's contents into another application. Interprocess communication is initiated by applications that transfer data without direct user involvement.

- *Networking.* The operating system provides protocols and services for enabling applications to reach information on other computers attached to the network.

Today, the most popular operating systems are UNIX and its variants (such as Linux), Windows, and the MacOS.

Chapter Summary

1. When defining a subclass, you specify added instance variables, added methods, and changed or *overridden* methods.

2. When overriding a method in a subclass, you may need to call the overridden method in the superclass. Use the **super** keyword.

3. Subclass references are automatically converted to superclass references. The opposite conversion requires a cast. If the reference is not actually a reference to the desired subclass, an exception is thrown.

4. The **instanceof** operator tests whether an object belongs to a particular class.

5. To call the superclass constructor, you use the **super** keyword in the first statement of the subclass constructor.

6. When you call a method, the type of the object to which the implicit parameter refers determines which actual method is called. This selection process is called *polymorphism*.

7. Polymorphism and overloading are both mechanisms to select among methods with the same name, but they have one essential difference. Overloading is resolved at compile time and is therefore called *early binding*. Polymorphism is resolved at run time and is therefore called *late binding*.

8. An *interface* is equivalent to a class with no data and no method implementations. A class can only have one superclass, but it can implement arbitrarily many interfaces.You can have references whose type is an interface, but you cannot have instances of an interface.

9. Every class inherits from the **Object** class. You should redefine the **toString**, **equals**, and **clone** methods in classes that you create for general use.

10. The **clone** method makes a new object with the same value as an existing object.

11. Java packages are used to organize classes and to avoid name clashes.

12. Variables should be declared **private**, and methods should be declared **public** or **private**. If the access specifier is omitted, the variable or method is accessible by all methods of classes in the same package, which is usually not desirable.

Further Reading

[1] James Gosling, Bill Joy, and Guy Steele, *The Java Language Specification,* Addison-Wesley, 1996.

Classes, Objects, and Methods Introduced in This Chapter

```
java.lang.Cloneable
java.lang.Comparable
    compareTo
java.lang.Object
    clone
    toString
java.awt.Shape
```

Review Exercises

Exercise R9.1. What is the balance of **b** after the following operations?

```
SavingsAccount b = new SavingsAccount(10);
b.deposit(5000);
b.withdraw(b.getBalance() / 2);
b.addInterest();
```

Exercise R9.2. Describe all constructors of the SavingsAccount class. List all methods that are inherited from the BankAccount class. List all methods that are added to the SavingsAccount class.

Exercise R9.3. Can you convert a superclass reference into a subclass reference? A subclass reference into a superclass reference? If so, give an example. If not, explain why.

Exercise R9.4. How does a cast of class references such as (SavingsAccount)b differ from a cast of number values such as (int)x?

Exercise R9.5. In the following pairs of classes, identify the superclass and the subclass:

```
Employee, Manager
Polygon, Triangle
GraduateStudent, Student
Person, Student
Employee, GraduateStudent
BankAccount, CheckingAccount
Vehicle, Car
Vehicle, Minivan
Car, Minivan
Truck, Vehicle
```

Exercise R9.6. Suppose the class Sub extends the class Sandwich. Which of the following assignments are legal?

```
Sandwich x = new Sandwich();
Sub y = new Sub();
x = y;
y = x;
y = new Sandwich();
x = new Sub();
```

Exercise R9.7. Draw an inheritance diagram that shows the inheritance relationships between the classes

```
Person
Employee
```

```
Student
Instructor
Classroom
Object
```

Exercise R9.8. In an object-oriented traffic simulation system, we have the following classes:

```
Vehicle
Car
Truck
Sedan
Coupe
PickupTruck
SportUtilityVehicle
Minivan
Bicycle
Motorcycle
```

Draw an inheritance diagram that shows the relationships between these classes.

Exercise R9.9. What inheritance relationships would you establish among the following classes?

```
Student
Professor
TeachingAssistant
Employee
Secretary
DepartmentChair
Janitor
SeminarSpeaker
Person
Course
Seminar
Lecture
ComputerLab
```

Exercise R9.10. Which of these conditions returns **true**? Check the Java documentation for the inheritance patterns.

```
Rectangle r = new Rectangle(5, 10, 20, 30);
if (r instanceof Rectangle) . . .
if (r instanceof Point) . . .
if (r instanceof Rectangle2D.Double) . . .
if (r instanceof RectangularShape) . . .
if (r instanceof Object) . . .
if (r instanceof Shape) . . .
```

Exercise R9.11. Explain the two meanings of the **super** keyword. Explain the two meanings of the **this** keyword. How are they related?

Exercise R9.12. (Tricky.) Consider the two calls

```
public class D extends B
{  public void f()
   {  this.g(); // 1
   }
   public void g()
   {  super.g(); // 2
   }
   . . .
}
```

Which of them is an example of early binding? Which of them is an example of late binding?

Exercise R9.13. In the `AccountTest` program of Section 9.4, are the calls to the `endOfMonth` methods resolved by early binding or late binding? Inside the `endOfMonth(SavingsAccount)` method, is the call to `addInterest` resolved by early binding or late binding?

Exercise R9.14. Explain the terms *shallow copy* and *deep copy*.

Exercise R9.15. Make a trivial change to the ConsoleReader.java file, by adding a comment. Save it and note the *exact* time you modified it. Don't recompile the `ConsoleReader` class. Recompile any program that uses the `ConsoleReader` class. Then check the file date of ConsoleReader.class file. Explain.

Exercise R9.16. What happens if you have two `public` classes in a Java source file? If you have no `public` classes? Try it out and explain the results.

Exercise R9.17. What happens if the name of the `public` class in a Java source file doesn't match the name of the file? Try it out and explain the results.

Exercise R9.18. Every Java program can be rewritten to avoid `import` statements. Explain how, and rewrite Intersect.java from Chapter 4 to avoid import statements.

Exercise R9.19. What is the default package? Have you used it before this chapter in your programming?

Exercise R9.20. What access attribute should instance variables have? What access attribute should static variables have?

Exercise R9.21. What access attribute should instance methods have? Does the same hold for static methods?

Exercise R9.22. The variables `System.in` and `System.out` are static public variables. Is it possible to overwrite them? If so, how?

Exercise R9.23. Why are public variables dangerous? Are public static variables more dangerous than public instance variables?

Programming Exercises

Exercise P9.1. Enhance the `addInterest` method of the `SavingsAccount` class to compute the interest on the *minimum* balance since the last call to `addInterest`. *Hint*: You need to modify the `withdraw` method as well, and you need to add an instance variable to remember the minimum balance.

Exercise P9.2. Implement a subclass `Square` that extends the `Rectangle` class. In the constructor, accept the *x*- and *y*-positions of the *center* and the side length of the square. Call the `setLocation` and `setSize` methods of the `Rectangle` class. Look up these methods in the documentation for the `Rectangle` class. Also supply a method `getArea` that computes and returns the area of the square. Write a sample program that asks for the center and side length, then prints out the square (using the `toString` method that you inherit from `Rectangle`) and the area of the square.

Exercise P9.3. Implement a superclass `Person`. Make two classes, `Student` and `Instructor`, inherit from `Person`. A person has a name and a year of birth. A student has a major, and an instructor has a salary. Write the class definitions, the constructors, and the methods `toString` for all classes. Supply a test program that tests these classes and methods.

Exercise P9.4. Make a class `Employee` with a name and salary. Make a class `Manager` inherit from `Employee`. Add an instance variable, named `department`, of type `String`. Supply a method `toString` that prints the manager's name, department, and salary. Make a class `Executive` inherit from `Manager`. Supply a method `toString` that prints the string `"Executive"`, followed by the information stored in the `Manager` superclass object. Supply a test program that tests these classes and methods.

Exercise P9.5. Write a superclass `Worker` and subclasses `HourlyWorker` and `SalariedWorker`. Every worker has a name and a salary rate. Write a method `computePay(int hours)` that computes the weekly pay for every worker. An hourly worker gets paid the hourly wage for the actual number of hours worked, if `hours` is at most 40. If the hourly worker worked more than 40 hours, the excess is paid at time and a half. The salaried worker gets paid the hourly wage for 40 hours, no matter what the actual number of hours is. Write a static method that uses polymorphism to compute the pay of any `Worker`. Supply a test program that tests these classes and methods.

Exercise P9.6. Implement a superclass `Vehicle` and subclasses `Car` and `Truck`. A vehicle has a position on the screen. Write methods `draw` that draw cars and trucks as follows:

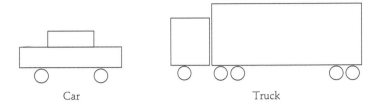

Car   Truck

Then write a method `randomVehicle` that randomly generates `Vehicle` references, half of them cars and half of them trucks, with random positions. Call it ten times and draw all of them.

Exercise P9.7. Write a method `randomShape` that randomly generates objects implementing the `Shape` interface, some mixture of rectangles, ellipses, and lines, with random positions. Call it ten times and draw all of them.

Exercise P9.8. Implement the `toString`, `equals`, and `clone` methods for all four bank account classes used in this chapter.

Exercise P9.9. Implement the `toString`, `equals`, and `clone` methods for the `Coin` and `Purse` classes introduced in Chapter 3.

Exercise P9.10. Reorganize the bank account classes as follows. In the `BankAccount` class, introduce an abstract method `endOfMonth` with no implementation. Rename the `addInterest` and `deductFees` methods into `endOfMonth` in the subclasses. Which classes are now abstract and which are concrete? Write a static method `void test(BankAccount account)` that makes five random transactions, prints out the balance after each of them, then calls `endOfMonth` and prints the balance once again. Test it with instances of all concrete account classes.

Exercise P9.11. Modify the `Coin` and `Purse` classes introduced in Chapter 3 to have them implement the `Comparable` interface.

Exercise P9.12. Supply a class `Person` that implements the `Comparable` interface. Compare persons by their names. Ask the user to input ten names and generate ten `Person` objects. Using the `compareTo` method, determine the first and last person among them and print them.

Exercise P9.13. This exercise assumes that you have an email address. Write a `Hello` class in a package whose name is derived from your email address, as described in Section 9.7.

Exercise P9.14. Reorganize the bank account classes used in this chapter by placing them into the package `com.horstmann.accounts`. Leave the `AccountTest` program in the default package.

Event Handling

Chapter Goals

- ◆ To understand the Java event model

- ◆ To install window, mouse, and action event handlers

- ◆ To accept mouse and text input in applets and applications

- ◆ To display frame windows

- ◆ To understand how user interface components are added to a frame window

In the console applications and applets you have written so far, user input was under control of the *program*. The program asked the user for input in a specific order. For example, a program might ask the user to supply first a name, then some dollar amount. But the programs that you use every day on your computer don't work like that. In a program with a modern graphical user interface, the *user* is in control. The user can use both the mouse and the keyboard and can manipulate many parts of the user interface in any desired order. For example, the user can enter information into text fields, pull down menus, click buttons, drag scroll bars, and close windows, in any order. The program must react to the user commands, in whatever order they arrive. Having to deal with many possible inputs in random order is quite a bit harder than simply forcing the user to supply input in a fixed order.

In this chapter you will learn how to write Java programs that can react to user interface events such as keystrokes, mouse clicks, and button pushes. The Java window toolkit has a very sophisticated mechanism that allows a program to specify the events in which it is interested and which objects to notify when one of these events occurs.

10.1 Events, Event Listeners, and Event Sources

Whenever the user of a graphical program types characters or uses the mouse anywhere inside one of the windows of the program, the Java window manager sends a notification to the program that an *event* has occurred. The window manager can generate huge numbers of events. For example, whenever the mouse moves a tiny interval over a window, a "mouse move" event is generated. Most programs have no interest in many of these events. In order not to be flooded by boring events, every program must indicate which events it likes to receive. It does that by installing *event listener* objects. Furthermore, there are different *kinds* of events, such as keyboard events, mouse move events, and mouse click events. To make event listening more organized, you use different event listener classes to listen to different kinds of events.

To install a listener, you need to know the *event source*. The event source is the user interface component that generates a particular event. For example, a button is the event source for button click events; a menu item is the event source for a menu selection event; and a scrollbar is the event source for a scrollbar adjustment event. You tell the event source which event listeners you want to install.

This sounds somewhat complex, so let's run through an example. We will listen to mouse clicks in an applet. There are three classes involved:

1. *The event class.* In the case of mouse clicks, this is the class MouseEvent. A mouse event object can tell you the *x*- and *y*-position of the mouse pointer and which mouse button the user clicked.

2. *The listener class.* In the case of mouse clicks, this must be a class that implements the `MouseListener` interface. The mouse listener interface has several methods, which we will discuss below. These methods are called when the mouse button is depressed, when it is released, and so on. Each of these methods has a `MouseEvent` parameter.

3. *The event source.* This is the component that generates the mouse event and that manages the listeners. In our case, the event source is the applet in whose area on the screen the user may click with the mouse. We must tell the applet which mouse listeners should be notified when a mouse event occurs.

All event classes are subclasses of the `EventObject` class. Figure 1 shows an inheritance diagram of the most common event classes. The `EventObject` class has an important method, `getSource`, that returns the object that generated this event. Subclasses have their own methods that describe the event further. For example, the

Figure 1

Event Classes

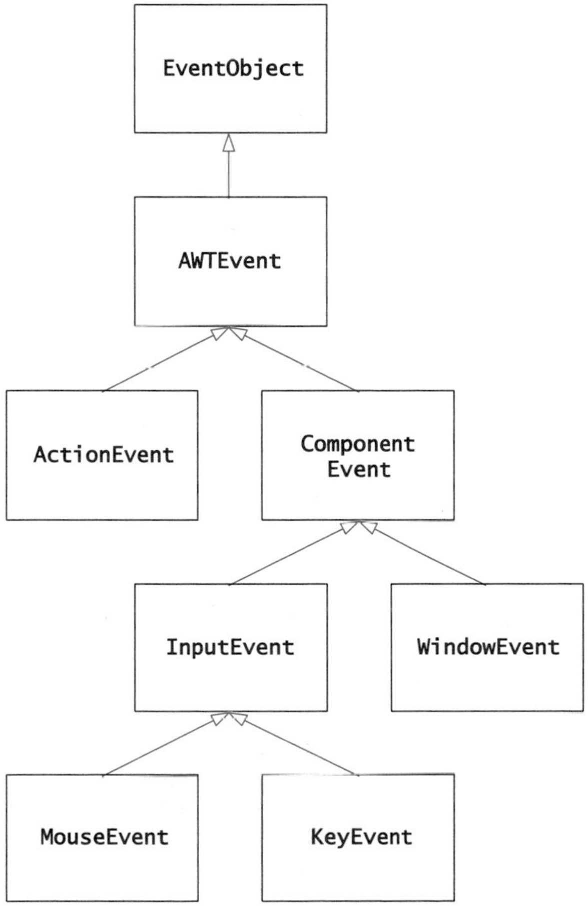

MouseEvent class has methods getX and getY that tell you the position of the mouse at the time the event was generated.

The most complex part of Java event handling is to come up with the listener. A mouse listener must implement the MouseListener interface and implement the following five methods:

```
public interface MouseListener
{   void mouseClicked(MouseEvent event);
        // Called when the mouse has been clicked on a component
    void mouseEntered(MouseEvent event);
        // Called when the mouse enters a component
    void mouseExited(MouseEvent event);
        // Called when the mouse exits a component
    void mousePressed(MouseEvent event);
        // Called when a mouse button has been pressed on a component
    void mouseReleased(MouseEvent event);
        // Called when a mouse button has been released on a component
}
```

Right now, we just want to "spy" on the mouse events and print them out as they occur. For that purpose, we'll implement a particular listener:

```
class MouseSpy implements MouseListener
{   public void mouseClicked(MouseEvent event)
    {   System.out.println("Mouse clicked. x = "
            + event.getX() + " y = " + event.getY());
    }

    public void mouseEntered(MouseEvent event)
    {   System.out.println("Mouse entered. x = "
            + event.getX() + " y = " + event.getY());
    }

    public void mouseExited(MouseEvent event)
    {   System.out.println("Mouse exited. x = "
            + event.getX() + " y = " + event.getY());
    }

    public void mousePressed(MouseEvent event)
    {   System.out.println("Mouse pressed. x = "
            + event.getX() + " y = " + event.getY());
    }

    public void mouseReleased(MouseEvent event)
    {   System.out.println("Mouse released. x = "
            + event.getX() + " y = " + event.getY());
    }
}
```

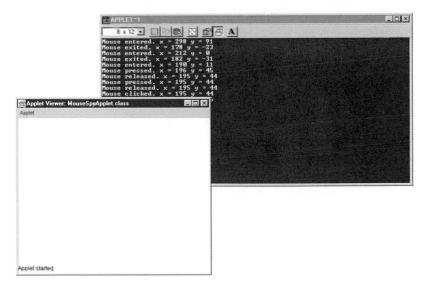

Figure 2

Spying on Mouse Events

The listener methods simply print out the cause of the event and the x- and y-positions of the mouse.

Now let's install the listener. You need to call the `addMouseListener` method of the event source. In our case, that is the applet that receives the mouse clicks. Construct a mouse spy object and pass it as the parameter to the `addMouseListener` method.

```
public class MouseSpyApplet extends Applet
{  public MouseSpyApplet()
   {  MouseSpy listener = new MouseSpy();
      addMouseListener(listener);
   }
}
```

As the applet senses mouse events, it calls the appropriate methods of the listener object. For example, when the user clicks with the mouse in the applet area, the applet calls `listener.mousePressed(event1)` and `listener.mouseReleased(event2)`, where `event1` and `event2` are mouse event objects that describe the mouse position at the time of the mouse button press and release. If the press and release were in quick succession, the applet also calls `listener.mouseClicked(event3)`. You can try this out by opening a console window, starting the applet viewer from that console window, clicking with the mouse in the applet, and watching the messages in the console window (see Figure 2).

10.2 Event Adapters

In the preceding section you saw how to install a mouse listener into a mouse event source and how the listener methods are called when an event occurs. Usually, a program is not interested in all listener notifications. For example, a program may only be interested in mouse clicks and may not care that these mouse clicks are composed of "mouse pressed" and "mouse released" events. Of course, the program could supply a listener that defines all those methods in which it has no interest as "do nothing" methods, for example:

```
public class MouseClickListener implements MouseListener
{  public void mouseClicked(MouseEvent event)
   {  // mouse click action here
   }

   public void mouseEntered(MouseEvent event)
   {  // do nothing
   }

   public void mouseExited(MouseEvent event)
   {  // do nothing
   }

   public void mousePressed(MouseEvent event)
   {  // do nothing
   }

   public void mouseReleased(MouseEvent event)
   {  // do nothing
   }
}
```

This is boring. Fortunately, some friendly soul has created an *adapter* class that implements the MouseListener interface such that all methods do nothing:

```
public class MouseAdapter implements MouseListener
// This class is defined in the java.awt.event package
{  public void mouseClicked(MouseEvent event)
   {  // do nothing
   }

   public void mouseEntered(MouseEvent event)
   {  // do nothing
   }

   public void mouseExited(MouseEvent event)
   {  // do nothing
   }

   public void mousePressed(MouseEvent event)
   {  // do nothing
   }
```

```
public void mouseReleased(MouseEvent event)
{ // do nothing
}
}
```

Then you can define a listener by extending the `MouseAdapter` class and overriding just the methods that you care about, like this:

```
class MouseClickListener extends MouseAdapter
{ public void mouseClicked(MouseEvent event)
   { // mouse click action here
   }
}
```

Several listener interfaces, such as the `ActionListener` interface that you will encounter later in this chapter, have only a single method. In that case, there is no corresponding adapter class, since it is just as easy to implement the interface as it would be to extend the adapter. However, the `java.awt.event` package contains an adapter class for all event listener interfaces that have at least two methods. For example, the `WindowListener`, a class with seven methods, has a corresponding `WindowAdapter` that defines all seven methods to do nothing. We will use that adapter later in this chapter.

10.3 Implementing Listeners as Inner Classes

In the preceding example, our mouse listener simply printed all mouse events to `System.out`. In practice, you want something more interesting to happen when the user clicks the mouse. For example, suppose we want to write a program that moves an ellipse to the mouse click position.

Here is a program that draws an ellipse on the screen. The ellipse is stored as an instance variable so that we can later modify it:

```
import java.applet.Applet;
import java.awt.Graphics;
import java.awt.Graphics2D;
import java.awt.geom.Ellipse2D;

public class EggApplet extends Applet
{ public EggApplet()
   { egg = new Ellipse2D.Double(0, 0, EGG_WIDTH, EGG_HEIGHT);
   }

   public void paint(Graphics g)
   { Graphics2D g2 = (Graphics2D)g;
      g2.draw(egg);
   }
```

```
      private Ellipse2D.Double egg;
      private static final double EGG_WIDTH = 15;
      private static final double EGG_HEIGHT = 25;
   }
```

Now, let us add a mouse listener that listens to a mouse click and moves the ellipse.

```
   public class EggApplet extends Applet
   {  public EggApplet()
      {  egg = new Ellipse2D.Double(0, 0, EGG_WIDTH, EGG_HEIGHT);

         // add mouse click listener
         MouseClickListener listener = new MouseClickListener();
         addMouseListener(listener);
      }
      . . .
   }

   class MouseClickListener extends MouseAdapter
   {  public void mouseClicked(MouseEvent event)
      {  int mouseX = event.getX();
         int mouseY = event.getY();
         // now move the ellipse to (mouseX, mouseY)
         . . .
      }
   }
```

Unfortunately, now we have a problem: The MouseClickListener class has no access to the private egg instance variable of the EggApplet class.

This situation is typical for event listeners. Usually, the event methods need to access the variables in another class. There is, fortunately, a simple remedy. We can make the listener into an *inner* class. An inner class is defined inside another class. It acts just like a regular class; that is, you can construct objects and invoke methods in the usual way. There is just one exception: The methods of the inner class are allowed to access the private instance variables of the outer class. Let us turn the MouseClickListener into an inner class:

```
   public class EggApplet extends Applet
   {  public EggApplet()
      {  egg = new Ellipse2D.Double(0, 0, EGG_WIDTH, EGG_HEIGHT);

         // add mouse click listener
         MouseClickListener listener = new MouseClickListener();
         addMouseListener(listener);
      }

      . . .
      private Ellipse2D.Double egg;

      // inner class definition
```

Java Syntax
10.1 Inner Classes
```
class OuterClassName
{   . . .
    accessSpecifier class InnerClassName
    {  methods
       variables
    }
    . . .
}
```

Example:
```
public class MyApplet extends Applet
{   . . .
    private class MouseClickListener
        extends MouseAdapter
    {  . . .
    }
}
```

Purpose:
To define an inner class whose methods are allowed to access the private variables and methods of the outer class

```
private class MouseClickListener extends MouseAdapter
   {  public void mouseClicked(MouseEvent event)
      {  int mouseX = event.getX();
         int mouseY = event.getY();
         // now move the ellipse to (mouseX, mouseY)
         egg.setFrame(mouseX - EGG_WIDTH / 2,
            mouseY - EGG_HEIGHT / 2,
            EGG_WIDTH, EGG_HEIGHT);
         repaint();
      }
   }
}
```

As you can see, the `mouseClicked` method of the inner class accesses the `egg` instance variable. Since the inner class has no instance variable called `egg` (in fact, it has no instance variables at all), the compiler interprets `egg` to mean "the `egg` instance variable of the outer-class object that constructed this inner-class object".

If you look inside the constructor of the outer applet class, you will see that it constructs an inner-class object `listener` and adds it as a mouse listener. That inner-class listener object *remembers the applet object that constructed it* (see Figure 3). Whenever

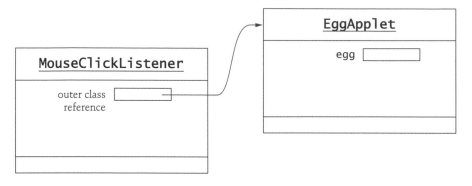

Figure 3

An Inner-Class Object Remembers
the Outer-Class Object That
Constructed It

you refer to an instance variable of an outer class inside an inner-class method, then
the following process occurs:

1. The inner-class object retrieves the reference to the object that created it.
2. The instance variable of that object is accessed.

Remarkably, the inner-class method has the privilege of accessing the private data
of the outer class. That sounds dangerous, but it really isn't. The problem with a
public instance variable is that *any* method can access it. You have no way of knowing
which other methods actually take advantage of that privilege. But since the inner
classes are contained inside the outer classes, you can still control exactly which
methods can access the private data.

When a mouse click occurs, we call `setFrame` on the ellipse object. However,
that call has no effect on the screen display. The `setFrame` method merely updates
the Java object that stores the ellipse's position. We need to redraw the ellipse. We
could call the `paint` method, but then we would need a `Graphics` object, which we
don't have. It is possible to get such an object, but that is actually not a good idea.
You should never call `paint` directly—it can interfere with the window manager.
Instead, you should *tell the applet to repaint itself* at the next convenient moment. You
do that by calling the `repaint` method, which causes the `paint` method to be called,
at an opportune moment, with an appropriate `Graphics` object.

Let us have another look at the call to `repaint` in the `mouseClicked` method of
the `MouseClickListener` class. Of course, the inner class doesn't have a method
called `repaint`. Therefore, the compiler looks in the outer applet class, where it
does find a `repaint` method (which is inherited from its superclass `Component`). It

invokes the method. On which object? Again, on the outer-class object that created the inner-class object—namely, the applet that constructed the listener.

Inner classes are a fairly specialized tool. They are very useful for event listeners, but you will rarely need them for other purposes. You may simply want to recognize and reuse the programming *pattern*. Whenever an event listener needs to access variables or methods in a particular class, use the following outline:

```
class MyClass
{  public MyClass()
   {  . . .
      MyListener listener = new MyListener();
      anEventSource.addAListener(listener);
   }

   // outer-class methods
   . . .

   // outer-class instance variables
   . . .

   // inner-class  definition
   private class MyListener extends AnEventAdapter
   {  public void anEventOccurred(AnEvent event)
      {   // event action goes here
         . . .
         // OK to access outer-class instance variables
         // OK to invoke outer-class methods
      }
   }
}
```

Finally, we are ready to put all the pieces together. Note how the use of inner classes makes the program easy to read—the rather specialized event listener class is placed out of the way and hidden inside the applet class. (See Advanced Topic 10.1 on how you can hide it even further.)

By the way, when you compile the source file, have a look at the class files on your disk—you will find that the inner classes are stored in files with curious names, such as `EggApplet$MouseClickListener.class`. The $ sign separates the outer- and inner-class names.

Go ahead and run the program. Whenever you click the mouse on the applet, the center of the ellipse moves to the mouse pointer (see Figure 4). While perhaps not the most eggsciting program that you have ever used, it does demonstrate how to provide mouse input to a graphical application.

Program EggApplet.java

```
import java.applet.Applet;
import java.awt.Graphics;
import java.awt.Graphics2D;
```

Figure 4

Handling Mouse Events

```
import java.awt.event.MouseAdapter;
import java.awt.event.MouseEvent;
import java.awt.geom.Ellipse2D;

public class EggApplet extends Applet
{  public EggApplet()
   {  egg = new Ellipse2D.Double(0, 0, EGG_WIDTH, EGG_HEIGHT);

      // add mouse click listener
      MouseClickListener listener = new MouseClickListener();
      addMouseListener(listener);
   }

   public void paint(Graphics g)
   {  Graphics2D g2 = (Graphics2D)g;
      g2.draw(egg);
   }

   private Ellipse2D.Double egg;
   private static final double EGG_WIDTH = 30;
   private static final double EGG_HEIGHT = 50;

   // inner class definition

   private class MouseClickListener extends MouseAdapter
   {  public void mouseClicked(MouseEvent event)
      {  int mouseX = event.getX();
         int mouseY = event.getY();

         // now move the ellipse to (mouseX, mouseY)
```

```
        egg.setFrame(mouseX - EGG_WIDTH / 2,
          mouseY - EGG_HEIGHT / 2, EGG_WIDTH, EGG_HEIGHT);
        repaint();
      }
    }
  }
```

Common Error 10.1

Forgetting to Repaint

A drawing program stores the data that are necessary to repaint the window. The `paint` method retrieves the data, generates geometric shapes such as lines, ellipses, and rectangles, and draws them. When you make a change to the data, your drawing is *not* automatically updated. You must tell the window manager that the data has changed, by calling the `repaint` method. However, do not call the `paint` method directly. Only the window manager should call `paint`.

Advanced Topic 10.1

Anonymous Inner Classes

An entity is *anonymous* if it does not have a name. In a program, something that is only used once doesn't usually need a name. For example, you can replace

```
Rectangle rect = new Rectangle(100, 100, 100, 100);
g2.fill(rect);
```

with

```
g2.fill(new Rectangle(100, 100, 100, 100));
```

if the rectangle is not used elsewhere in the same method. The object `new Rectangle(100, 100, 100, 100)` is an *anonymous object*. Programmers like anonymous objects, because they don't have to go through the trouble of coming up with a name. If you have struggled with the decision whether to call a rectangle r, `rect`, `rectangle`, or `aRectangle`, you'll understand this sentiment.

Listener classes give rise to a similar situation. After a single object of the mouse click listener has been installed, the class `MouseClickListener` is never used again:

```
public class MyApplet extends Applet
{  public MyApplet()
   {   . . .
       addMouseListener(new MouseClickListener());
   }
```

```
        . . .

    private class MouseClickListener extends MouseAdapter
    {  public void mouseClicked(MouseEvent event)
       {  // mouse click action goes here
          . . .
       }
    }
}
```

In Java, it is possible to define *anonymous classes* if all you ever need is a single object of the class. This mechanism lets you simplify the listener installation:

```
public class MyApplet extends Applet
{  public MyApplet()
   {  . . .
      addMouseListener(new MouseAdapter() // name of superclass
         {  public void mouseClicked(MouseEvent event)
            // methods of anonymous subclass
            {  // mouse click action goes here
               . . .
            }
         });

   }
   . . .
}
```

This means: Construct an object of a class that extends MouseAdapter and define a new mouseClicked method.

Some programmers like this style, but many newcomers find it quite bewildering. We will not cover it further in this book—you can find more information in reference [1].

Random Fact 10.1

Programming Languages

There are many hundreds of programming languages in existence today. That is actually quite surprising. The idea behind a high-level programming language is to provide a medium for programming that is independent from the instruction set of a particular processor, so that one can move programs from one computer to another without rewriting them. Moving a program from one programming language to another is a difficult process, however, and it is rarely done. Thus, it seems that there would be little use for so many programming languages.

Unlike human languages, programming languages are created with specific purposes. Some programming languages make it particularly easy to express tasks from a particular problem domain. Some languages specialize in database processing; others in "artificial intelligence" programs that try to infer new facts from a given base of knowledge; others in multimedia programming. The Pascal language was purposefully kept simple because it was designed as a teaching language. The C language was developed to be translated efficiently into fast machine code, with a minimum of housekeeping overhead. The C++ language builds on C by adding features for object-oriented programming. The Java language was designed for deploying programs across the Internet.

In the early 1970s the U.S. Department of Defense (DoD) was seriously concerned about the high cost of the software components of its weapons equipment. It was estimated that more than half of the total DoD budget was spent on the development of this *embedded-systems* software—that is, the software that is embedded in some machinery, such as an airplane or missile, to control it. One of the perceived problems was the great diversity of programming languages that were used to produce that software. Many of these languages, such as TACPOL, CMS-2, SPL/1, and JOVIAL, were virtually unknown outside the defense sector.

In 1976 a committee of computer scientists and defense industry representatives was asked to evaluate existing programming languages. The committee was to determine whether any of them could be made the DoD standard for all future military programming. To nobody's surprise, the committee decided that a new language would need to be created. Contractors were then invited to submit designs for such a new language. Of 17 initial proposals, four were chosen to develop their languages. To ensure an unbiased evaluation, the languages received code names: Red (by Intermetics), Green (by CII Honeywell Bull), Blue (by Softech), and Yellow (by SRI International). All four languages were based on Pascal. The Green language emerged as the winner in 1979. It was named Ada in honor of the world's first programmer, Ada Lovelace (see Random Fact 15.1).

The Ada language was roundly derided by academics as a typical bloated Defense Department product. Military contractors routinely sought, and obtained, exemptions from the requirement that they had to use Ada on their projects. Outside the defense industry, few companies used Ada. Perhaps that is unfair. Ada had been *designed* to be complex enough to be useful for many applications, whereas other, more popular languages, notably C++, have *grown* to be just as complex and ended up being unmanageable.

The initial version of the C language was designed about 1972. Unlike Ada, C is a simple language that lets you program "close to the machine". It is also quite unsafe. Because different compiler writers added different features, the language actually sprouted various dialects. Some programming instructions were understood by one compiler but rejected by another. Such divergence is an immense pain to a programmer who wants to move code from one computer to another, and an effort got underway to iron out the differences and come up with a standard version of C. The design process ended in 1989 with the completion of the ANSI (American National Standards Institute) Standard. In the meantime, Bjarne Stroustrup of AT&T added features of the language Simula (an object-oriented language designed for carrying out simulations) to C. The resulting language was called C++. From 1985 until today, C++ has grown by the addition of many features, and a standardization process was completed in 1998. C++ has been enormously popular because programmers could take their existing C code and move it to C++, with only minimal changes. In order to keep compatibility with existing code, every innovation in C++ had to work around the existing language constructs, yielding a language that is powerful but somewhat cumbersome to use.

In 1995, Java was designed to be conceptually simpler and more internally consistent than C++, while retaining the syntax that is familiar to millions of C and C++ programmers. The Java *language* was a great design success. It is indeed clean and simple. As for the Java *library*, you know from your own experience that it is neither.

10.4 Frame Windows

Up to now, all the graphical programs that you wrote have been *applets*, programs that run inside a browser or the applet viewer. You can also write regular graphical programs in Java that do not run inside another program. In this section, you will learn how to write such *graphical applications*.

Every graphical program puts up one or more *frame windows* (see Figure 5). A frame window has a *border* and a *title bar*. (An applet does not have a title bar, as you can see when you run the applet inside a browser. When you run an applet inside the applet viewer, you see the title bar of the applet viewer, not the applet.)

To show a frame, you use the JFrame class in the `javax.swing` package. The JFrame class is a fundamental class in the *Swing* toolkit, the most advanced user interface toolkit that Sun Microsystems has created for Java. Before the creation of Swing, Java used components in the AWT (Abstract Windowing Toolkit) for graphical applications. Both AWT and Swing components are *multiplatform*—that is, programs can run on Windows, the Macintosh, UNIX, and other platforms without modification. This behavior is often described as "write once, run anywhere". However, the toolkits achieved this goal in different ways. AWT uses the *native* user interface elements (buttons, text fields, menus, and so on) of the host platform. This turned out not to work very well. There are slight differences in behavior on each platform, and programmers soon began complaining about "write once, debug everywhere". Swing takes a different approach—it *paints* the shapes for buttons, text fields, menus, and so on. That is slower but more consistent. The user interface components of the AWT toolkit are now obsolete, and we will use Swing for all graphical user interfaces in this book. However, Swing uses other parts of the AWT, such as the parts for drawing

Figure 5

A Frame Window

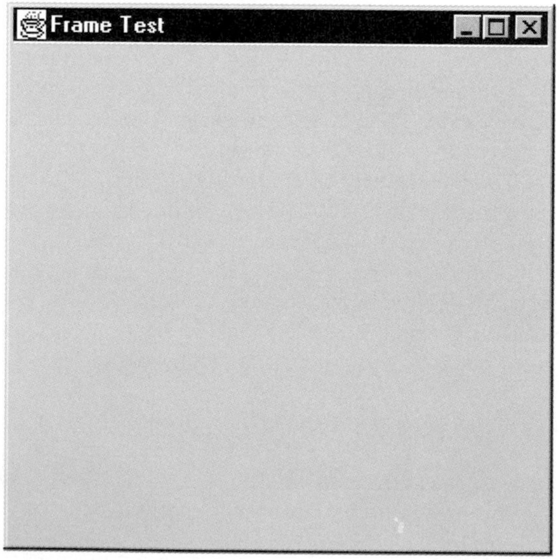

graphical shapes and handling events, so you will continue to use some classes from the `java.awt` package. The Swing classes are placed in the `javax.swing` package, where the `javax` package name denotes a *standard extension* of Java. Swing was first released as a standard extension to Java 1.1, and it became a standard part of Java 2. For compatibility reasons, the package name was not changed from `javax` to `java`, however.

To get started, let's simply put up a frame window with nothing inside. With applets, you specify the window size in the HTML file. Applications do not use an HTML file. Instead, you specify the size with the `setSize` method of the `JFrame` class. By default, frames have a (rather useless) size of 0×0 pixels, so it is important that you call the `setSize` method before you show the frame. If you like, you can call the `setTitle` method to set the title. Finally, invoke the `show` method, which causes the window manager to display the frame. Here is the complete program:

Program FrameTest1.java

```
import javax.swing.JFrame;

public class FrameTest1
{  public static void main(String[] args)
    {  EmptyFrame frame = new EmptyFrame();
       frame.setTitle("Frame Test");
       frame.show();
    }
}

class EmptyFrame extends JFrame
{  public EmptyFrame()
    {  final int DEFAULT_FRAME_WIDTH = 300;
       final int DEFAULT_FRAME_HEIGHT = 300;
       setSize(DEFAULT_FRAME_WIDTH, DEFAULT_FRAME_HEIGHT);
    }
}
```

Unlike applets, graphical applications have a `main` method. The `main` method of the `FrameTest1` program constructs an `EmptyFrame` object, calls `show`, and then exits. But even though the `main` method exits, the program is still running. The frame window stays on the screen, and you can move it around, resize it, and so on. This is an important difference between console programs and graphical programs. Once you show a frame window, the program starts a new *thread of execution* that displays the graphical user interface. When the `main` method is finished, the *main thread* is completed, but the Java program does not yet terminate, because the user interface thread is still running.

As a result, this program suffers from an annoying problem. Even when you close the frame window (by clicking on the "close" icon in the title bar), the program keeps running. The program just sits there and does nothing. You must manually kill the program. The method for killing a program differs from one operating system to the next. In Windows and UNIX, you can hit Ctrl+C in the console window that started the Java interpreter. If you use another operating system, or if you use an integrated development environment, you'll need to find out how to kill a wayward program.

Of course, this is not satisfactory. We want the program to terminate when the user closes the frame window. To terminate the program, you must execute the statement

```
System.exit(0);
```

The problem is *when* to execute this statement. You can't put it at the end of the main method:

```
public class FrameTest1
{  public static void main(String[] args)
   {  EmptyFrame frame = new EmptyFrame();
      frame.setTitle("Frame Test");
      frame.show();
      System.exit(0); // Error
   }
}
```

This program would show the window for a very brief moment, then exit immediately.

Instead, we want to exit the program when the user clicks the "close" icon in the title bar. But we don't know when that happens. The user is in control of the program and can do many things in any order, such as moving and resizing the window, clicking on the close icon, and so on. The solution is the same as in the preceding section—we must install an event handler that is called when the user clicks on the close icon. In reaction to that event, we will exit the program.

To find out when the user closes a window, you must listen to *window* events. Seven kinds of window events can occur in a Java program:

1. A window has just opened for the first time.

2. A window has just closed as a result of the dispose method.

3. A window has just been *activated* (typically because the user clicked inside it).

4. A window has just been *deactivated* (typically because the user clicked inside another window).

5. A window is being *iconified* (typically because the user clicked on the "minimize" icon in the title bar).

6. A window is being *deiconified* (typically because the user clicked on the icon of the minimized window).

7. A window is being closed by the user (typically because the user clicked on the "close" icon in the title bar).

To listen to these events, you must add a *window listener* object to the frame. A window listener object must implement the `WindowListener` interface, which has seven methods:

```
public interface WindowListener
{   void windowOpened(WindowEvent e);
    void windowClosed(WindowEvent e);
    void windowActivated(WindowEvent e);
    void windowDeactivated(WindowEvent e);
    void windowIconified(WindowEvent e);
    void windowDeiconified(WindowEvent e);
    void windowClosing(WindowEvent e);
}
```

Of course, our simple program doesn't care about the first six events. The `JFrame` superclass already listens to them and knows how to deal with them. More sophisticated graphics programs do need to know about some of these events. For example, a program that displays an animation may want to stop the animation when a window is iconified and restart it when the window is displayed again.

You may well wonder why a `JFrame` object won't simply call `System.exit` when it is being closed. There is a simple reason. A program can have multiple frame windows; it would not be a good idea if the entire program terminated if the user closed only one of its windows. Therefore, we have to teach our particular frame window to exit the program when the user closes it. We achieve that by installing a window listener object whose `windowClosing` method terminates the program.

The `WindowListener` is another event listener interface with many methods, and again there is a convenience class called `WindowAdapter` with all seven methods implemented to do nothing. We simply extend the `WindowAdapter` class to a class that we call `WindowCloser`:

```
class WindowCloser extends WindowAdapter
{   public void windowClosing(WindowEvent event)
    {   System.exit(0);
    }
}
```

Finally, you need to add an object of the `WindowCloser` class as a window listener to the frame, by calling the `addWindowListener` method.

Program FrameTest2.java

```
import java.awt.event.WindowAdapter;
import java.awt.event.WindowEvent;
import javax.swing.JFrame;

public class FrameTest2
{   public static void main(String[] args)
    {   EmptyFrame frame = new EmptyFrame();
        frame.setTitle("Close me!");
```

```
            frame.show();
      }
}

class EmptyFrame extends JFrame
{  public EmptyFrame()
    {  final int DEFAULT_FRAME_WIDTH = 300;
       final int DEFAULT_FRAME_HEIGHT = 300;
       setSize(DEFAULT_FRAME_WIDTH, DEFAULT_FRAME_HEIGHT);

       WindowCloser listener = new WindowCloser();
       addWindowListener(listener);
    }

    private class WindowCloser extends WindowAdapter
    {  public void windowClosing(WindowEvent event)
        {  System.exit(0);
        }
    }
}
```

Now the application will close properly when the user closes the frame window.

10.5 Adding User Interface Components to a Frame

You should not directly draw onto the surface of a frame. Frames have been designed to arrange *user interface components* such as buttons, menus, scroll bars, and so on. (You will learn more about these components in Chapter 12.) Drawing directly on the frame interferes with the display of the user interface components. If you want to show graphics in a frame, you draw the graphics onto a separate component and add that component to the frame. The Swing user interface toolkit provides a special component, called JPanel, just for this purpose. A JPanel is completely blank, and you can draw onto it what you like.

Drawing on a panel is a bit different from drawing on an applet. To draw on an applet, you override the paint method. To draw on a JPanel, you instead override the paintComponent method. There is a second important difference. When implementing your own paintComponent method, you *must* call the paintComponent method of the superclass. This gives the superclass method a chance to erase the old contents of the panel.

Here is an outline of the paintComponent method

```
public class MyPanel extends JPanel
{  public void paintComponent(Graphics g)
    {  super.paintComponent(g);
       Graphics2D g2 = (Graphics2D)g;
```

```
            // your drawing instructions go here
            . . .
      }
}
```

Once you have called `super.paintComponent` and obtained a `Graphics2D` object, you are ready to draw graphical shapes in the usual way.

To add the panel to a `JFrame`, you need to know more about the structure of the frame surface. The surface of a Swing frame is covered with four *panes* (see Figure 6). Three of them, namely the root pane, the layered pane, and the glass pane, are of no interest to most Java programmers. You need to know about the *content pane*, which holds the components that you want to display in the window. (Just in case you are curious what the other three panes are good for: The glass pane is transparent, and its principal purpose is to capture mouse events. The layered pane holds the menu bar and the content pane together. Finally, the root pane holds the glass pane and the layered pane together.)

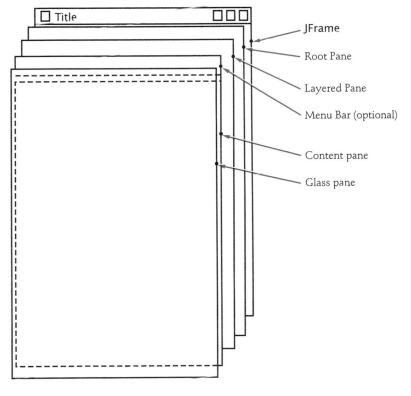

Figure 6

Anatomy of a Swing Frame

Figure 7

_____

Component Areas of a Border Layout

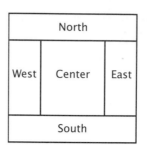

To add a component (such as a panel or button) to the content pane of a frame, you must first get a reference to the content pane object by calling the **getContentPane** method. This method returns a reference of type **Container**. A container is a window object that can contain other components. Then you use the **add** method of the **Container** class to add your component. You need to specify both the component that you want to add (such as the panel) and the location where you want to add the component. The content pane uses a *border layout* to arrange its components. You specify locations in a border layout as one of the five strings **"Center"**, **"North"**, **"South"**, **"East"**, or **"West"** (see Figure 7). In Chapter 12, you will see how to use other layouts. For now, let's see how to put a panel into the **"Center"** area of the content pane.

```
class MyFrame extends JFrame
{  public MyFrame()
   {  MyPanel panel = new MyPanel();
      Container contentPane = getContentPane();
      contentPane.add(panel, "Center");
         . . .
   }
      . . .
}
```

In the next section you will put these techniques to work by building a frame with a panel in the center and a text field below it.

_____

Common Error 10.2

Forgetting to Call the paintComponent Method of the Superclass

The **paintComponent** method of every subclass of a Swing component must call **super. paintComponent** in order to give the superclass **paintComponent** method a chance to draw the background, draw borders and decorations, and set the attributes of the **Graphics** object. If you forget to call **super.paintComponent**, then parts of the border decoration may be missing, or your drawing instructions may not work properly. Even if you spot no ill effects when testing your programs, someone else who uses your program with a different *look and feel* may experience problems, because the behavior of **super.paintComponent** depends on the chosen look and feel.

Figure 8

A Frame with a Text Field

10.6 Reading Text Input

In Section 10.2 you saw how to obtain input from the mouse. Let us next turn to text input. So far, your applets received text input by calling the `showInputDialog` method of the `JOptionPane` class, but that was not a very natural user interface. Most graphical programs collect text input through *text fields* (see Figure 8). In this section, you will learn how to add a text field to a frame and how to read what the user types into it.

Adding the text field to a frame is simple. Create a `JTextField` object and add it to the `"South"` location of the content pane:

```
class MyFrame extends JFrame
{  public MyFrame()
   {  textField = new JTextField();
      Container contentPane = getContentPane();
      contentPane.add(textField, "South");
      . . .
   }
   . . .
   private JTextField textField;
}
```

When the user hits the Enter key inside a text field, the text field generates an *action event*. Listening to an action event is a simpler task than listening to a mouse event, because the `ActionListener` interface has a single method:

```
public interface ActionListener
{  public void actionPerformed(ActionEvent event);
}
```

The action event tells you which component sent the event and what kind of action the user wants to have carried out. You will see many examples of action events in Chapter 12. Right now, we can ignore the contents of the **event** object, since we know that they must come from a single component, namely the text field, that sends out action events.

As before, we need to install a listener. The listener is added to the source of the action event (that is, the text field).

```
class MyFrame extends JFrame
{  public MyFrame()
   {  textField = new JTextField();
      textField.addActionListener(new TextFieldListener());

      Container contentPane = getContentPane();
      contentPane.add(textField, "South");
   }
   . . .
   private JTextField textField;
   . . .
   private class TextFieldListener implements ActionListener
   {  public void actionPerformed(ActionEvent event)
      {   // This method is called when the user
          // hits Enter in the text field
      }
   }
}
```

When the user hits Enter, you will want to know what has been typed into the text field. The **getText** method returns the contents. The **actionPerformed** method retrieves the contents of the text field and processes it. Afterwards, you will want to clear the text field so that the user has a visual indication that the input has been processed. You clear the text field by setting its text to the empty string with the **setText** method. Here is the outline of the event-processing method:

```
private class TextFieldListener implements ActionListener
{  public void actionPerformed(ActionEvent event)
   {   // get user input
       String input = textField.getText();
       // now process input
       . . .
       // clear text field
       textField.setText("");
   }
}
```

Let us now write a test program in which the user can type a number, and then we paint as many random eggs as the user requested (see Figure 9).

Figure 9

Drawing Random Eggs

We paint the eggs in an EggPanel, which we also add to the content pane of the frame:

```
class EggPanel extends JPanel
{  . . .
}

public class EggFrame extends JFrame
{  public EggPanel()
   {  panel = new EggPanel();
      textField = new JTextField();
      Container contentPane = getContentPane();
      contentPane.add(panel, "Center");
      contentPane.add(textField, "South");
   }
   . . .
}
```

When implementing a new component such as the EggPanel, you need to think about minimizing the interrelationship between the component and the rest of your program. If you store information in the wrong place, you keep handing it back and forth all the time. A good rule of thumb is: *A component should store the data that it needs to repaint itself.* In our case, the information is simple—just the number of eggs to be drawn:

```
public class EggPanel extends JPanel
{  public void paintComponent(Graphics g)
   {  super.paintComponent(g);
      Graphics2D g2 = (Graphics2D)g;
```

```
        // draw eggCount random ellipses
        . . .
    }
// data needed for painting

    private int eggCount;
}
```

Furthermore, the EggPanel needs to be notified whenever the user enters a new value. We supply a setEggCount method that passes the user input to the EggPanel. That method updates the egg count and repaints the panel:

```
public class EggPanel extends JPanel
{   . . .
    public void setEggCount(int count)
    {   eggCount = count;
        repaint();
    }
    . . .
}
```

In general, since changing the data affects how the component looks, you should always call **repaint** after updating the data.

Now we almost have all the pieces together. The actionPerformed method must call the setEggCount method to pass the text on to the panel:

```
private class TextFieldListener implements ActionListener
{   public void actionPerformed(ActionEvent event)
    {   // get user input
        String input = textField.getText();
        // now process input
        panel.setEggCount(Integer.parseInt(input));
        // clear text field
        textField.setText("");
    }
}
```

That way, every time the user types a number and hits the Enter key, the panel is repainted with the requested number of eggs.

Program Eggs.java

```
import java.awt.Container;
import java.awt.Graphics;
import java.awt.Graphics2D;
import java.awt.event.ActionEvent;
import java.awt.event.ActionListener;
import java.awt.event.WindowAdapter;
import java.awt.event.WindowEvent;
import java.awt.geom.Ellipse2D;
import java.util.Random;
```

```
import javax.swing.JFrame;
import javax.swing.JPanel;
import javax.swing.JTextField;

public class Eggs
{  public static void main(String[] args)
   {  EggFrame frame = new EggFrame();
      frame.setTitle("Enter number of eggs");
      frame.show();
   }
}

class EggFrame extends JFrame
{  public EggFrame()
   {  final int DEFAULT_FRAME_WIDTH = 300;
      final int DEFAULT_FRAME_HEIGHT = 300;
      setSize(DEFAULT_FRAME_WIDTH, DEFAULT_FRAME_HEIGHT);

      addWindowListener(new WindowCloser());

      // construct components

      panel = new EggPanel();

      textField = new JTextField();
      textField.addActionListener(new TextFieldListener());

      // add components to content pane

      Container contentPane = getContentPane();
      contentPane.add(panel, "Center");
      contentPane.add(textField, "South");
   }

   private JTextField textField;
   private EggPanel panel;

   private class TextFieldListener implements ActionListener
   {  public void actionPerformed(ActionEvent event)
      {  // get user input

         String input = textField.getText();

         // process user input

         panel.setEggCount(Integer.parseInt(input));

         // clear text field

         textField.setText("");
```

```
         }
      }

      private class WindowCloser extends WindowAdapter
      {  public void windowClosing(WindowEvent event)
         {  System.exit(0);
         }
      }
   }

   class EggPanel extends JPanel
   {  public void paintComponent(Graphics g)
      {  super.paintComponent(g);
         Graphics2D g2 = (Graphics2D)g;

         // draw  eggCount ellipses with random centers

         Random generator = new Random();
         for (int i = 0; i < eggCount; i++)
         {  double x = getWidth() * generator.nextDouble();
            double y = getHeight() * generator.nextDouble();
            Ellipse2D.Double egg = new Ellipse2D.Double(x, y,
               EGG_WIDTH, EGG_HEIGHT);
            g2.draw(egg);
         }
      }

      /**
         Sets the number of eggs to be drawn and repaints
         the panel.
         @param count the new number of eggs
      */
      public void setEggCount(int count)
      {  eggCount = count;
         repaint();
      }

      private int eggCount;
      private static final double EGG_WIDTH = 30;
      private static final double EGG_HEIGHT = 50;
   }
```

Advanced Topic 10.2

Using a Component as a Listener

In this book, we use inner classes for interface listeners. That approach works for many different event types, and once you master the technique, you don't have to think about it anymore.

It is also similar to the technique that is used by many development environments that have a tool to generate user interface source code.

However, many programmers bypass the event listener classes for listeners that have a *single* method, such as the `ActionListener` interface. Since any class can implement another interface, it is simple to add the `actionPerformed` method to any convenient class. Here is a typical example:

```java
public class EggFrame extends JFrame
    implements ActionListener
{  public EggFrame()
   {  // construct components

      panel = new EggPanel();

      textField = new JTextField();
      textField.addActionListener(this);

      // add components to content pane

      Container contentPane = getContentPane();
      contentPane.add(panel, "Center");
      contentPane.add(textField, "South");
   }

   public void actionPerformed(ActionEvent event)
   {  String input = textField.getText();
      panel.setEggCount(Integer.parseInt(input));
      textField.setText("");
   }

   private JTextField textField;
   private EggPanel panel;
}
```

Now the `actionPerformed` method is a part of the `EggFrame` class rather than in a separate listener class. The listener is installed as `this`.

However, this technique does not work as well for mouse or window listeners. Consider the `EggApplet` class. It cannot simultaneously extend the `Applet` and `MouseAdapter` classes. It could implement the `MouseListener` interface, but then it would have to implement four do-nothing methods.

Advanced Topic 10.3

Adding the main Method to the Frame Class

Have another look at the `Eggs` program. We had two classes: `Eggs`, a class with only a main method that constructed and showed the frame, and the class `EggFrame`, which contained the frame's constructor, instance variables, and event listeners. Some programmers prefer to combine these two classes, simply by adding the `main` method to the frame class:

```
public class EggFrame extends JFrame
{  public static void main(String[] args)
   {  EggFrame frame = new EggFrame();
      frame.setTitle("Enter number of eggs");
      frame.show();
   }

   public EggFrame()
   {  . . .
   }
   . . .
}
```

This is a convenient shortcut that you will find in many programs, but it does muddle the responsibilities between the frame class and the program. Therefore, we do not use this approach in this book.

Advanced Topic 10.4

Converting a Frame to an Applet

If you enjoyed placing your applets onto a web page, then you will want to know how to convert a graphical application into an applet. The `javax.swing` package supplies a class `JApplet` that is very similar to a `JFrame`. Unlike a plain `Applet`, a `JApplet` also has a content pane whose default is the border layout. Therefore, laying out components in a `JApplet` works exactly the same as for a `JFrame`.

Thus, there are only a few steps to convert from a frame to an applet:

1. Drop the class with the `main` method that shows the frame.
2. Inherit from `JApplet`, not `JFrame`.
3. Remove the window listener.
4. Remove the call to `setSize` and instead set the size in the applet's HTML page.
5. Remove the call to `setTitle`

Productivity Hint 10.1

Code Reuse

Suppose you are given the task to write another graphical program that reads input from a text field and draws some set of shapes. You don't have to start from scratch. Instead, you can—and often should—*reuse* the outline of an existing program, such as the **Eggs** program above.

To reuse program code, simply make a copy of a program file and give the copy a new name. For example, you may want to copy Eggs.java to a file MyProg.java. Then remove the

◆
◆
◆
◆
◆
◆
◆
◆
◆
◆

code that is clearly specific to the old problem, but leave the outline in place. That is, keep the panel, text field, event handler, and so on. Fill in the code for drawing your new shapes. Finally, rename classes (such as `EggPanel`), frame titles, and so on.

Once you understand the principles behind layout managers, event listeners, and panels, there is no need to rethink them every time. Reusing the structure of a working program makes your work more efficient.

However, reuse by "copy and rename" is still a mechanical and somewhat error-prone approach. It is even better to package reusable program structures into a set of common classes. You have seen several examples in this book. The `ConsoleReader` and `UnitConverter` classes were designed to reuse repetitive code efficently, without copy and paste.

Chapter Summary

1. *Event* classes contain detailed information about various kinds of events.

2. Event notifications happen in *event listener* classes. An event listener class implements an *event listener interface*. The interface lists all possible notifications for a particular event category.

3. Events are generated from *event source* classes. You install listeners with the event sources.

4. To make it easy to define listeners that implement only one or a few listener interface methods, many interfaces have matching *adapter* classes that have all interface methods implemented as do-nothing methods.

5. You use a *mouse listener* to capture mouse events.

6. You often install event listeners as *inner classes*. An object of an inner class can access the outer-class object that created it, including its private instance variables.

7. A graphical application displays output in one or more windows. The `JFrame` class implements a *top-level* window with a border.

8. To find out when a window is being closed, you must install a *window listener*. In particular, this is required to have a graphical application exit automatically when the user closes the frame window.

9. You draw graphical shapes in a *panel* by overriding its `paintComponent` method. That method is called whenever the panel contents need to be refreshed. You can force repainting by calling the `repaint` method.

10. You add components to the content pane of a frame or JApplet. The content pane uses a *border layout*. When adding components, you have to specify the "North", "East", "South", "West", or "Center" position.

11. To be notified when the user hits Enter in a text field, you install an *action listener*.

Further Reading

[1] Cay S. Horstmann and Gary Cornell, *Core Java 1.2 Volume 1: Fundamentals*, Prentice Hall, 1999.

Classes, Objects, and Methods Introduced in This Chapter

```
java.awt.Component
   addActionListener
   repaint
   setSize
java.awt.Container
   add
java.awt.Frame
   setTitle
java.awt.Window
   addWindowListener
   show
java.awt.event.ActionListener
   actionPerformed
java.awt.event.ActionEvent
java.awt.event.MouseAdapter
   mouseClicked
java.awt.event.MouseEvent
   getX
   getY
java.awt.event.MouseListener
   mouseClicked
java.awt.event.WindowAdapter
   windowClosing
java.awt.event.WindowEvent
java.awt.event.WindowListener
   windowClosing
java.awt.event.WindowEvent
java.util.EventObject
   getSource
javax.swing.JApplet
   getContentPane
```

```
javax.swing.JComponent
    paintComponent
javax.swing.JFrame
    getContentPane
javax.swing.JPanel
javax.swing.JTextField
javax.swing.text.JTextComponent
    getText
    setText
```

Review Exercises

Exercise R10.1. What is an event? An event source? An event handler? An event listener? An event adapter?

Exercise R10.2. From a programmer's perspective, what is the most important difference between the user interfaces of a console application and a graphical application?

Exercise R10.3. What is the difference between an ActionEvent and a MouseEvent?

Exercise R10.4. Why does the ActionListener interface have only one method, whereas the MouseListener has five methods?

Exercise R10.5. Why isn't there an ActionAdapter class that implements the ActionListener interface?

Exercise R10.6. Can an event source be its own listener?

Exercise R10.7. Can a class be an event source for multiple event types?

Exercise R10.8. What information does every event object carry? What additional information does a mouse event object carry?

Exercise R10.9. Why are we using inner classes for event listeners? If Java did not have inner classes, could we still implement event listeners? How?

Exercise R10.10. How can you tell that the inner-class listener object has a reference to the outer-class object that created it?

Exercise R10.11. How are inner classes stored on disk?

Exercise R10.12. What is the difference between the paint and repaint methods?

Exercise R10.13. What is the difference between the paint and paintComponent methods?

Exercise R10.14. What happens if you don't call `super.paintComponent` in a class that extends `JPanel`? Try it out with the `Eggs` program. Can you find out how the program misbehaves when you comment out that call?

Exercise R10.15. What is the difference between an `Applet` and a `JApplet`?

Exercise R10.16. What happens when you paint directly on a frame? Try it out—rewrite the `Eggs` application and move the `paintComponent` method directly into the `EggFrame` class.

Exercise R10.17. What happens when you close a frame that doesn't have a window listener installed? Why doesn't Java supply a more useful default behavior?

Exercise R10.18. If a program adds two `JTextField` components to a frame, one north and one south, how can you tell which action events are generated by which text field?

Exercise R10.19. What happens when you try to add a component directly to a `JFrame` and not the content pane? Try it out and explain.

Exercise R10.20. What happens when you add a text field to the content pane and misspell the position (for example, `contentPane.add(textField, "Centre")`)? What happens if you omit the position? Try it out and explain.

Programming Exercises

Exercise P10.1. Implement a `WindowEventSpy` program that spies on all window events. Describe what you have to do to make the various events happen.

Exercise P10.2. Write a program that adds two `JTextField` components to a frame, one north and one south. The user enters the x-coordinate of the egg's center in the northern text field and the y-component in the southern text field. Update the egg position whenever the user hits Enter in either text field. (Never mind that this is a strange user interface—you'll learn how to develop a better one in Chapter 12.)

Exercise P10.3. Write a graphics program that prompts the user to enter a radius. Draw a circle with that radius.

Exercise P10.4. Implement the `MouseClickListener` in the `EggApplet` as a regular class (that is, not an inner-class). *Hint:* Store a reference to the applet object in the listener, and add a public method for moving the egg position to the applet.

Exercise P10.5. Write a program that lets a user type the four parameters of an ellipse (x, y, width, and height), separated by spaces, into the text field and then draws the ellipse when the user hits Enter. *Hint:* Use a string tokenizer to parse the input.

Exercise P10.6. Write a program that lets a user specify a triangle with three mouse clicks. *Hint:* In the mouse click handler, you must keep track of how many corners you already received. When the user clicks for the first time, draw a small circle to mark the position. When the user clicks for the second time, draw a line joining the two points. Finally, after the third click, draw the entire triangle.

Exercise P10.7. Write a graphics program that prompts the user to click on the center of a circle, then on one of the points on the boundary of the circle. Draw the circle that the user specified. *Hint:* The radius of the circle is the distance between the two points, which is computed as

$$\sqrt{(a_x - b_x)^2 + (a_y - b_y)^2}$$

Exercise P10.8. Write a graphics program that prompts the user to click on two points. Then draw a line joining the points and write a message displaying the *slope* of the line; that is, the "rise over run" ratio. The message should be displayed at the *midpoint* of the line.

Exercise P10.9. Write a graphics program that prompts the user to click on two points. Then draw a line joining the points and write a message displaying the *length* of the line, as computed by the Pythagorean formula. The message should be displayed at the *midpoint* of the line.

Exercise P10.10. Write a graphics program that prompts the user to click on three points. Then draw a circle passing through the three points.

Exercise P10.11. Write a graphics program that asks the user to enter four data values. Then draw a pie chart showing the data values.

Exercise P10.12. Write a program that plots a *regression line*: that is, the line with the best fit through a collection of points. The regression line is the line with equation

$$y = \bar{y} + m(x - \bar{x}), \quad \text{where } m = \frac{\sum x_i y_i - n\bar{x}\bar{y}}{\sum x_i^2 - n\bar{x}^2}$$

$\bar{x}$ is the mean of the x-values and $\bar{y}$ is the mean of the y-values.

The user keeps clicking on points. You don't need to store the individual points, but you need to keep track of

- The count of input values
- The sum of x, y, x^2, and xy values

To draw the regression line, compute its endpoints at the left and right edges of the screen and draw a segment. Each time the user clicks on another point, you update the screen again.

Exercise P10.13. Write a graphics program that draws a clock face with a time that the user enters in the text field. (The user must enter the time in the format hh:mm, for example 09:45.)

Hint: You need to find out the angles of the hour hand and the minute hand. The angle of the minute hand is easy: The minute hand travels 360 degrees in 60 minutes. The angle of the hour hand is harder; it travels 360 degrees in 12 × 60 *minutes*.

Exercise P10.14. Write an application that asks the user to enter an integer *n*, and then draw an *n* by *n* grid on the panel. Whenever the user clicks inside one of the grid squares on the panel, color that grid square in black.

Exercise P10.15. Write a program that asks the user for a number of bars, and then generate a random bar chart (similar to the chart in the **Phoenix** program in Chapter 4) with the given number of bars.

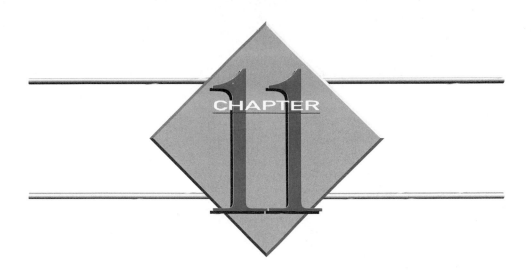

Arrays and Vectors

Chapter Goals

- ◆ To become familiar with using arrays and vectors to collect objects

- ◆ To be able to access array and vector elements

- ◆ To implement partially filled arrays

- ◆ To be able to pass arrays to methods

- ◆ To learn about common array algorithms

- ◆ To be able to build classes containing arrays and vectors

- ◆ To learn how to use two-dimensional collections

11.1 Using Arrays to Store Data

11.1.1 Accessing Array Elements

Suppose you want to write a program that reads a set of prices offered by ten vendors for a particular product and then prints them, marking the lowest one.

```
19.95
23.95
24.95
18.95 <-- lowest price
29.95
19.95
20.00
22.99
24.95
19.95
```

Of course, you need to read in *all* data items first before you can tell which one is the lowest one.

If you knew that there were always ten data items, then you could store the data in ten variables **data1, data2, data3, ... , data10**. But such a sequence of variables is not very practical to use. You would have to write quite a bit of code ten times, once for each of the variables. There might also be a hundred data items. In Java there is a better way of storing a sequence of data items: the array construct.

An *array* is a collection of data items of the same type. Every element of the collection can be accessed separately. Here is how you define an array of ten floating-point numbers:

```
double[] data = new double[10];
```

This is the definition of a variable **data** whose type is **double[]**. That is, **data** is a reference to an array of floating-point numbers. The call **new double[10]** creates the actual array of 10 numbers. (See Figure 1.)

Figure 1

An Array Reference and an Array

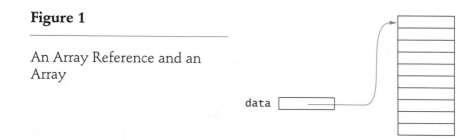

Java Syntax
11.1 Array Construction
new *typeName[length]*

Example:
`new double[10]`

Purpose:
To construct an array with a given
number of elements

When the array is first created, all values are initialized with 0 (for an array of numbers such as `int[]` or `double[]`), `false` (for a `boolean[]` array), or `null` (for an array of objects).

To get some values into the **data** array, you need to specify which slot in the array you want to use. That is done with the `[]` operator, which follows the name of the array and encloses an integer-valued expression called an *index* or *subscript*:

`data[4] = 29.95;`

Now the slot with index 4 of **data** is filled with the value 29.95. (See Figure 2.)

To read out the data value at index 4, you simply use the expression `data[4]` as you would any variable of type **double**:

`System.out.println("The price of this item is $" + data[4]);`

Before going on, we must take care of one unpleasant detail of Java arrays. If you look carefully at Figure 2, you will find that the *fifth* slot was filled with data when `data[4]` was changed. Unfortunately, in Java, the slots of arrays are numbered *starting at 0*.

Figure 2

Filling an Array
Element

Java Syntax
11.2 Array Element Access
arrayReference [*index*]

Example:
```
a[4] = 29.95;
```

Purpose:
To access an element in an array

That is, the legal slots for the **data** array are

> **data[0]**, the first slot
>
> **data[1]**, the second slot
>
> **data[2]**, the third slot
>
> **data[3]**, the fourth slot
>
> **data[4]**, the fifth slot
>
> . . .
>
> **data[9]**, the tenth slot

In "ancient" times there was a technical reason why this setup was a good idea, and so many programmers got used to it in C and C++ that Java arrays follow it too. It is, however, a major source of grief for the newcomer.

The index in an array reference has an important restriction: Trying to access a slot that does not exist in the array is an error. For example, if **data** holds ten employees, then the statement

```
int i = 20;
System.out.println("The price of this item is $" + data[i]);
```

is an error. There is no **data[20]**. The compiler does not catch this error. Generally, it is too difficult for the compiler to follow the current contents of **data** and **i**. However, when an invalid index is detected during the execution of a program, the program terminates with an **ArrayIndexOutOfBoundsException**.

The most common bounds error is the following:

```
double[] data = new double[10];
data[10] = 29.95;
```

There is no **data[10]** in an array with ten elements. Because the first element has index 0, the legal subscripts are 0 through 9.

Another common error is to forget to initialize the array:

```
double[] data; // not initialized
data[0] = 29.95;
```

When an array variable is defined, it must be initialized with an array such as **new double[10]** before any array elements can be accessed.

A Java array has an instance variable **length**, which you can access to find out the size of the array. For example, here is how you can find out the lowest price in an array of prices:

```
double lowest = data[0];
for (int i = 1; i < data.length; i++)
    if (data[i] < lowest)
        lowest = data[i];
```

Note that there are *no parentheses* following **length**—it is an instance variable of the array object, not a method. However, you cannot assign a new value to this instance variable. In other words, **length** is a final public instance variable. This is quite an anomaly. Normally, Java programmers use a method to inquire about the properties of an object. You just have to remember to omit the parentheses in this case.

Using **length** is a much better idea than using a number such as 10, even if you know that the array has ten elements. If the program changes later, and there are now 20 data items, then the loop automatically stays valid. This principle is another case of avoiding magic numbers, as discussed in Quality Tip 2.2.

Note that i is a legal index for the array a if $0 \le i$ and $i < a.length$. Therefore the **for** loop

```
for (int i = 0; i < a.length; i++)
    do something with a[i];
```

is extremely common for visiting all elements in an array. By the way, don't write it as

```
for (int i = 0; i <= a.length - 1; i++)
```

The condition i <= a.length - 1 means the same thing as i < a.length, but it is harder to read (see Quality Tip 6.3).

Common Error 11.1

Bounds Errors

The most common array error is accessing a nonexistent slot.

```
double[] data = new double[10];
data[10] = 5.4;
    // Error—data has 10 elements with subscripts 0 to 9
```

When the program runs, an out-of-bounds subscript generates an exception and terminates the program. This is a great improvement over languages such as C and C++. With those languages there is no error message; instead, the program will quietly (or not so quietly) corrupt some memory. Except for very short programs, in which the problem may go unnoticed, that corruption will make the program act flaky or cause a horrible death many instructions later. These are serious errors that can be difficult to detect.

Common Error 11.2

Uninitialized Arrays

A common error is to allocate an array reference, but not an actual array.

```
double[] data;
if (data[0] == 0) . . .  // Error—data not  initialized
```

Array variables work exactly like object variables—they are only references to the actual array. To construct the actual array, you must use the **new** operator:

```
double[] data = new double[10];
```

Quality Tip 11.1

Don't Combine Array Access and Index Increment

It is possible to increment a variable that is used as an array index, for example

```
x = v[i++];
```

That is a shortcut for

```
x = v[i];
i++;
```

Many years ago, when compilers were not very powerful, the v[i++] shortcut was useful, because it made the compiler generate faster code. Nowadays, the compiler generates the same efficient code for both versions. You should therefore use the second version, because it is clearer and less confusing.

Advanced Topic 11.1

Array Initialization

You can initialize an array by allocating it and then filling each entry:

```
int[] primes = new int[5];
primes[0] = 2;
primes[1] = 3;
primes[2] = 5;
primes[3] = 7;
primes[4] = 11;
```

However, if you already know all the elements that you want to place in the array, there is an easier way. You can list all elements that you want to include in the array, enclosed in braces and separated by commas:

```
int[] primes = { 2, 3, 5, 7, 11 };
```

The Java compiler counts how many elements you want to place in the array, allocates an array of the correct size, and fills it with the elements that you specify.

If you want to construct an array and pass it on to a method that expects an array parameter, you can initialize an *anonymous array* as follows:

```
new int[] { 2, 3, 5, 7, 11 }
```

11.1.2 Copying Arrays

Array variables work just like object variables—they hold a *reference* to the actual array. If you copy the reference, you get another reference to the same array (see Figure 3):

```
double[] data = new double[10];
. . . // fill array
double[] prices;
prices = data;
```

If you want to make a true copy of an array, you must make a new array of the same length as the original and copy over all values:

```
double[] prices = new double[data.length];
for (int i = 0; i < data.length; i++)
    prices[i] = data[i];
```

Instead of the for loop, you can also use the static System.arrayCopy method. That method can be used to copy any portion of an array into another array (see Figure 4):

```
System.arrayCopy(from, fromStart, to, toStart, count);
```

To copy the entire data array into the prices array, you use the call

```
System.arrayCopy(data, 0, prices, 0, data.length);
```

Figure 3

Copying an Array Reference

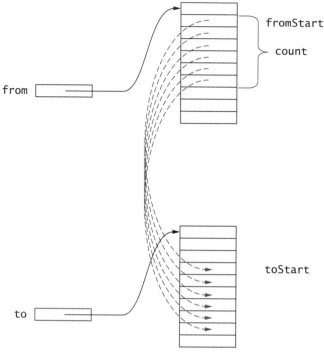

Figure 4

The `System.arrayCopy` Method

11.1.3 Partially Filled Arrays

Let us go back to our price check program. How many data items will the user enter? You can't very well ask the user to count the items for us before entering them—that is just the kind of work that the user expects the computer to do. Unfortunately, you now run into a problem. You need to set the size of the array before you know how many elements you need. Once the array size is set, it cannot be changed. Other programming languages have smarter arrays that can grow on demand, and Java also has a `Vector` class that can overcome this problem. Unfortunately the `Vector` class is not as easy to use as an array. We will discuss vectors in Section 11.6.

To solve this problem, you can sometimes make an array that is guaranteed to be larger than the largest possible number of entries, and *partially fill it*. For example, you can decide that the user will never enter more than 1000 data points. Then allocate an array of size 1000:

```
final int DATA_LENGTH = 1000;
double[] data = new double[DATA_LENGTH];
```

Then keep a *companion variable* that tells how many elements in the array are actually used. It is an excellent idea *always* to name this companion variable by adding the suffix `Size` to the name of the array.

```
int dataSize = 0;
```

Now `data.length` is the *capacity* of the array `data`, and `dataSize` is the *current size* of the array (see Figure 5). Keep adding elements into the array, incrementing the size variable each time.

```
double price = console.readDouble();
data[dataSize] = price;
dataSize++;
```

This way, `dataSize` always contains the correct element count. When inspecting the array elements, you must be careful to stop at `dataSize`, not at `data.length`:

```
for (int i = 0; i < dataSize; i++)
    System.out.println(data[i]);
```

You must be careful not to overfill the array. Insert elements only if there is still room for them!

```
if (dataSize < data.length)
{   data[dataSize] = price;
    dataSize++;
}
```

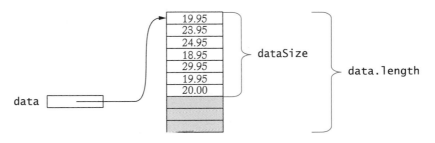

Figure 5

Size of a Partially Filled Array

If the array fills up, there are two approaches you can take. The simple way out is to refuse additional entries:

```
if (dataSize >= data.length)
   System.out.println("Sorry, the array is full.");
```

Of course, refusing to accept all input is often unreasonable. Users routinely use software on larger data sets than the original developers ever dreamt of. In Java, there is another approach to cope with data sets whose size cannot be estimated in advance. When you run out of space in an array, you can create a new, larger array; copy all elements into the new array; and then attach the new array to the old array variable:

```
if (dataSize >= data.length)
{  // make a new array of twice the size
   double[] newData = new double[2 * data.length];
   // copy over all elements from data to newData
   System.arrayCopy(data, 0, newData, 0, data.length);
   // abandon the old array and store in data
   // a reference to the new array
   data = newData;
}
```

An array that grows on demand is often called a *dynamic array* (see Figure 6). If you find that growing an array on demand is too tedious, you can use vectors (see Section 11.6).

We now have all the pieces together to implement the program outlined at the beginning of the chapter. This program reads data values and prints them out, marking those entries with the lowest price. For simplicity, this program uses an array with a fixed size and refuses to accept inputs that exceed the array's capacity.

Program BestPrice.java

```
public class BestPrice
{  public static void main(String[] args)
   {  final int DATA_LENGTH = 1000;
      double[] data = new double[DATA_LENGTH];
      int dataSize = 0;

      // read data

      ConsoleReader console = new ConsoleReader(System.in);

      boolean done = false;
      while (!done)
      {  System.out.println("Enter price, 0 to quit:");
         double price = console.readDouble();
         if (price ++ 0) // end of input
            done = true;
```

Figure 6

Growing a Dynamic Array

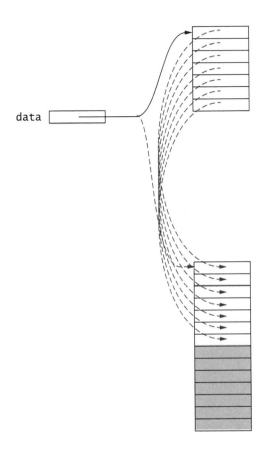

```
    else if (dataSize < data.length)
    {   // add price to data array
        data[dataSize] = price;
        dataSize++;
    }
    else // array is full
    {   System.out.println("Sorry, the array is full.");
        done = true;
    }
}

// compute lowest price

if (dataSize == 0) return; // no data
double lowest = data[0];
for (int i = 1; i < dataSize; i++)
    if (data[i] < lowest) lowest = data[i];
// print out prices, marking the lowest one
```

```
        for (int i = 0; i < dataSize; i++)
        {  System.out.print(data[i]);
           if (data[i] == lowest)
              System.out.print(" <--lowest price");
           System.out.println();
        }
     }
   }
```

Common Error 11.3

Underestimating the Size of a Data Set

It is a common programming error to underestimate the amount of input data that a user will pour into an unsuspecting program. The most common reason for underestimating input data is the use of fixed-sized arrays. Suppose you write a program to search for text in a file. You store each line in a string, and keep an array of strings. How big do you make the array? Surely nobody is going to test your program with an input that is more than 1,000 lines. Really? A smart grader can easily feed in the entire text of *Alice in Wonderland* or *War and Peace* (which are available on the Internet). All of a sudden, your program has to deal with tens or hundreds of thousands of lines. What will it do? Will it handle the input? Will it politely reject the excess input? Will it crash and burn?

A famous article [1] analyzed how several UNIX programs reacted when they were fed large or random data sets. Sadly, about a quarter didn't do well at all, crashing or hanging without a reasonable error message. For example, in some versions of UNIX the tape backup program *tar* cannot handle file names that are longer than 100 characters, which is a pretty unreasonable limitation. Many of these shortcomings are caused by features of the C language that, unlike Java, makes it difficult to store strings of arbitrary size.

Random Fact 11.1

The Internet Worm

In November 1988, a college student from Cornell University launched a virus program that infected about 6,000 computers connected to the Internet across the United States. Tens of thousands of computer users were unable to read their email or otherwise use their computers. All major universities and many high-tech companies were affected. (The Internet was much smaller then than it is now.)

The particular kind of virus used in this attack is called a *worm*. The virus program crawled from one computer on the Internet to the next. The entire program is quite complex; its major parts are explained in [2]. However, one of the methods used in the attack is of interest here. The worm would attempt to connect to the *finger* program on its remote victim. The C language has the same problem as Java. When you construct an array, you have to make up your mind how many elements you need—arrays don't grow on demand. The *finger* program (which expects only a user login name) allocated an array of 512 characters to hold a line of input, since it was assumed that nobody would ever provide such a long input. Unfortunately,

C, unlike Java, does not check that an array index is less than the length of the array. If you write into an array, using an index that is too large, you simply overwrite memory locations that belong to some other objects. In some versions of the *finger* program, the programmer was lazy and did not check whether the array holding the input characters was large enough to hold the input. The worm program purposefully filled the 512-character array with 536 bytes. The purpose of this was not to fill the line, but to overwrite a return address that the attacker knew was stored just after the line buffer. When that function was finished, it didn't return to its caller but to code supplied by the worm. That code ran under the same super-user privileges as *finger*, allowing the worm to gain entry into the remote system.

Had the programmer who wrote *finger* been more conscientious, this particular attack would not be possible. In C++ and C, all programmers must be especially careful not to over-run array boundaries.

One may well wonder what would possess a skilled programmer to spend many weeks or months to plan the antisocial act of breaking into thousands of computers and disabling them. It appears that the break-in was fully intended by the author, but the disabling of the computers was a side effect of continuous reinfection and efforts by the worm to avoid being killed. It is not clear whether the author was aware that these moves would cripple the attacked machines.

In recent years, the novelty of vandalizing other people's computers has worn off, and there are fewer jerks with programming skills who write new viruses. Other attacks by individuals with more criminal energy, whose intent has been to steal information or money, have surfaced. Reference [3] gives a very readable account of the discovery and apprehension of one such person.

11.2 Array Parameters and Return Values

Methods often have array parameters. This method computes the average of an array of floating-point numbers:

```
public static double average(double[] data)
{  if (data.length == 0) return 0;
   double sum = 0;
   for (int i = 0; i < data.length; i++)
      sum = sum + data[i];
   return sum / data.length;
}
```

To visit each element of the array data, the method needs to determine the length of data. It inspects all elements, with index starting at 0 and going up to, but not including, data.length.

When an array is passed to a method, the array parameter contains a copy of the *reference* to the argument array. Figure 7 shows what happens when this method is called as average(prices).

Figure 7

Passing an Array to a Method

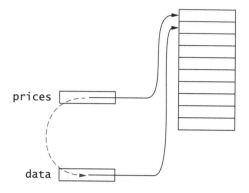

Because an array parameter is just another reference to the array, a method can actually modify the entries of any array that you give it.

A method can *return* an array. This is useful if a method computes a result that consists of a collection of values of the same type. Here is a method that returns a random data set, perhaps to test a chart-plotting program:

```
public static int[] randomData(int length, int n)
{  Random generator = new Random();
   int[] data = new int[length];
   for (int i = 0; i < data.length; i++)
      data[i] = generator.nextInt(n);
   return data;
}
```

11.3 Simple Array Algorithms

In this section we discuss several very common and important array algorithms. More complex algorithms will be the topic of Chapter 15.

11.3.1 Finding a Value

Suppose you have an array of prices for computers and want to find the first price ≤ $1,000. You can simply inspect each element until you find a match or reach the end of the array. Note that the loop might fail to find an answer, namely if all prices are above $1,000.

```
double[] prices;
double targetPrice = 1000;
   . . .
```

```
int i = 0;
boolean found = false;
while (i < prices.length && !found)
{  if (prices[i] <= targetPrice)
       found = true;
   else
       i++;
}
if (found)
   System.out.println("Item " + i + " has a price of "
       + prices[i]);
```

At the end of this loop, either **found** is true, in which case **prices[i]** is the first computer fulfilling our requirements, or **i** is **prices.length**, which means that you searched the entire list without finding a match. Note that you should *not* increment **i** if you had a match—you want to have the correct value of **i** after exiting the loop.

11.3.2 Counting

Suppose you want to find *how many* computers have a price $\leq$ \$1,000.

```
double[] prices;
double targetPrice = 1000;
. . .
int count = 0;
for (int i = 0; i < prices.length; i++)
{  if (prices[i] <= targetPrice)
       count++;
}
System.out.println(count + " computers.");
```

Now you don't stop on the first match but keep going to the end of the list, counting how many entries match.

11.3.3 Removing an Element

Suppose you want to *remove* an element from an array. If the elements in the array are not in any particular order, that task is easy to accomplish. Simply overwrite the element to be removed with the *last* element of the array. (See Figure 8.) Unfortunately, an array cannot be shrunk to get rid of the last element. In this case, you can use the technique of a partially filled array together with a companion variable (see Section 11.1.3).

Program Remove1.java

```
public class Remove1
{  public static void main(String[] args)
    {  ConsoleReader console = new ConsoleReader(System.in);
        String[] staff = new String[5];
```

Figure 8

Removing an Element from an Array

Element to be removed

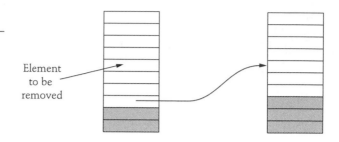

```
staff[0] = "Harry";
staff[1] = "Romeo";
staff[2] = "Dick";
staff[3] = "Juliet";
staff[4] = "Tom";
int staffSize = staff.length;

print(staff, staffSize);

System.out.println("Remove which element? (0 - 4)");
int pos = console.readInt();

// overwrite the removed element with the last element

staff[pos] = staff[staffSize - 1];
staffSize--;

print(staff, staffSize);
}

/**
   Prints an array of strings
   @param s the string array
   @param sSize the number of strings in the array
*/
public static void print(String[] s, int sSize)
{  for (int i = 0; i < sSize; i++)
      System.out.println(i + ": " + s[i]);
}
}
```

The situation is more complex if the order of the elements matters. Then you must move all elements beyond the element to be removed by one slot. (See Figure 9.)

Program Remove2.java

```
public class Remove2
{  public static void main(String[] args)
   {  ConsoleReader console = new ConsoleReader(System.in);
```

Figure 9

Removing an Element
from an
Ordered Array

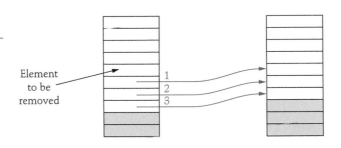

Element
to be
removed

```
String[] staff = new String[5];
staff[0] = "Dick";
staff[1] = "Harry";
staff[2] = "Juliet";
staff[3] = "Romeo";
staff[4] = "Tom";
int staffSize = staff.length;

print(staff, staffSize);

System.out.println("Remove which element? (0 - 4)");
int pos = console.readInt();

// shift all elements above pos down

for (int i = pos; i < staffSize - 1; i++)
   staff[i] = staff[i + 1];

staffSize--;

print(staff, staffSize);
}

/**
   Prints an array of strings
   @param s the string array
   @param sSize the number of strings in the array
*/
public static void print(String[] s, int sSize)
{  for (int i = 0; i < sSize; i++)
      System.out.println(i + ": " + s[i]);
}
}
```

11.3.4 Inserting an Element

Conversely, suppose you want to insert an element in the middle of an array. Then
you must move all elements beyond the insertion location by one slot. Note that
the order of the movement is different: When you remove an element, you first move

Figure 10

Inserting an Element in
an Ordered Array

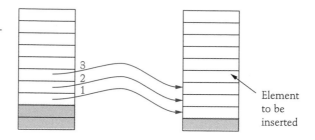

Element
to be
inserted

the next element, then the one after that, until you finally get to the end of the array. When you insert an element, you start at the end of the array, move that element, then go to the one before that, until you finally get to the insertion location (see Figure 10).

Program Insert.java

```java
public class Insert
{  public static void main(String[] args)
   {  ConsoleReader console = new ConsoleReader(System.in);
      String[] staff = new String[6];
      staff[0] = "Dick";
      staff[1] = "Harry";
      staff[2] = "Juliet";
      staff[3] = "Romeo";
      staff[4] = "Tom";
      int staffSize = staff.length - 1;

      print(staff, staffSize);

      System.out.print
         ("Insert before which element? (0 - 4)");
      int pos = console.readInt();

      // shift all element after pos up by one

      for (int i = staffSize; i > pos; i--)
         staff[i] = staff[i - 1];

      // insert new element into freed slot

      staff[pos] = "New, Nina";

      staffSize++;

      print(staff, staffSize);
   }
```

```
/**
    Prints an array of strings
    @param s the string array
    @param sSize the number of strings in the array
*/
public static void print(String[] s, int sSize)
{   for (int i = 0; i < sSize; i++)
        System.out.println(i + ": " + s[i]);
}
}
```

11.4 Parallel Arrays

The first program in this chapter showed how to find the lowest price in a data set. Of course, simply picking the lowest price may not be the best bargain. You also want to know how about performance. In this section, we will analyze a data set that contains the names, prices, and performance scores of a collection of products.

The product with the highest score may be very expensive and thus not a good buy. Savvy buyers will look for products that give good performance at a low price; those that have the best score / price ratio. We need a program that reads the product data in and prints them back out, marking the best buy:

```
AceAcro 750                   $3499.0 score = 71
ACMA P500                     $3195.0 score = 64
AMS Infogold P500             $2595.0 score = 58
Comtrade Tornado              $2495.0 score = 60
Cornell P500                  $2295.0 score = 57
Digital 500                   $4021.0 score = 59
DTK QUIN-35                   $2250.0 score = 50
Everex Step SP/500            $3479.0 score = 57
HP VL 5/500                   $2923.0 score = 62
Insight P500 MM               $3299.0 score = 66
Intelesys Star 500            $2099.0 score = 30
Maximus Magna Media           $2195.0 score = 72 <-- best buy
Micro Express MicroFLEX       $2499.0 score = 23
MidWest Micro P500            $2999.0 score = 55
Polywell Poly 450IP           $2338.0 score = 64
Reason Square 5-LXP/IP-500    $2495.0 score = 76
Summit Mount Brooks           $2995.0 score = 48
Tagram P500                   $2195.0 score = 68
Tangent AGI-450               $2475.0 score = 53
Tri-CAD P-500                 $2999.0 score = 79
USA Flex PT-500               $2595.0 score = 80
ZEOS Pentium-III/500          $2545.0 score = 70
```

Program BestData.java

```java
public class BestData
{  public static void main(String[] args)
   {  final int DATA_LENGTH = 1000;
      String[] names = new String[DATA_LENGTH];
      double[] prices = new double[DATA_LENGTH];
      int[] scores = new int[DATA_LENGTH];

      int dataSize = 0;

      // read data

      ConsoleReader console = new ConsoleReader(System.in);

      boolean done = false;
      while (!done)
      {  System.out.println
            ("Enter name or leave blank when done:");
         String inputLine = console.readLine();
         if (inputLine == null || inputLine.equals(""))
            done = true;
         else if (dataSize < DATA_LENGTH)

         {  names[dataSize] = inputLine;
            System.out.println("Enter price:");
            inputLine = console.readLine();
            prices[dataSize] = Double.parseDouble(inputLine);
            System.out.println("Enter score:");
            inputLine = console.readLine();
            scores[dataSize] = Integer.parseInt(inputLine);
            dataSize++;
         }
         else // array is full
         {  System.out.println("Sorry, the array is full.");
            done = true;
         }
      }

      // compute best buy

      if (dataSize == 0) return; // no data
      double best = scores[0] / prices[0];
      for (int i = 1; i < dataSize; i++)
         if (scores[i] / prices[i] > best)
            best = scores[i] / prices[i];

      // print out products, marking the best buys

      final int COLUMN_WIDTH = 30;
```

```
        for (int i = 0; i < dataSize; i++)
        {  System.out.print(names[i]);

            // pad with spaces to fill column

            int pad = COLUMN_WIDTH - names[i].length();
            for (int j = 1; j <= pad; j++)
                System.out.print(" ");

            // print price and score

            System.out.print("  $" + prices[i]
                + " score = " + scores[i]);

            // mark if best buy

            if (scores[i] / prices[i] == best)
                System.out.print("  <-- best buy");
            System.out.println();
        }
    }
}
```

The problem with this program is that it contains three arrays (`names`, `prices`, `scores`) of the same length, where the `i`th *slice* `names[i]`, `prices[i]`, `scores[i]`, contains data that needs to be processed together. These arrays are called *parallel arrays* (Figure 11).

Parallel arrays become a headache in larger programs. The programmer must ensure that the arrays always have the same length and that each slice is filled with values that actually belong together. Most importantly, any method that operates on a slice must get all arrays as parameters, which is tedious to program.

The remedy is simple. Look at the slice and find the *concept* that it represents. Then make the concept into a class. In our example each slice contains a name, a price, and a score, describing a *product*. Let's turn this into a class.

Figure 11

Parallel Arrays

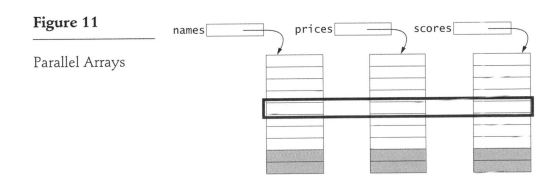

```
class Product
{  . . .
   private String name;
   private double price;
   private int score;
}
```

The program now has a single array of **Product** objects. This shows that the process of eliminating parallel arrays was successful. The set of parallel arrays is replaced by a single array. Each element in the resulting array corresponds to a slice in the set of parallel arrays (see Figure 12). Once you have this single concept available, it suddenly becomes much easier to give the program a better structure. Note how the following program can easily factor out methods for reading and printing objects:

Program BestProduct.java

```
public class BestProduct
{  public static void main(String[] args)
   {  final int DATA_LENGTH = 1000;
      Product[] data = new Product[DATA_LENGTH];
      int dataSize = 0;

      // read data

      ConsoleReader console = new ConsoleReader(System.in);

      boolean done = false;
```

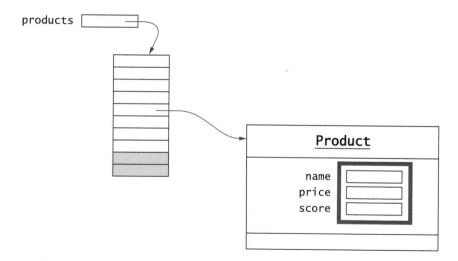

Figure 12

Eliminating Parallel Arrays

```
      while (!done)
      {  Product p = readProduct(console);
         if (p == null)
            done = true;
         else if (dataSize < DATA_LENGTH)
         {  data[dataSize] = p;
            dataSize++;
         }
         else // array is full
         {  System.out.println("Sorry, the array is full.");
            done = true;
         }
      }

      // compute best buy

      if (dataSize == 0) return; // no data

      double best
         = data[0].getScore() / data[0].getPrice();

      for (int i = 1; i < dataSize; i++)
      {  double ratio
            = data[i].getScore() / data[i].getPrice();
         if (ratio > best)
            best = ratio;
      }

      // print out data, marking the best buys

      for (int i = 0; i < dataSize; i++)
      {  printProduct(data[i]);
         if (data[i].getScore() / data[i].getPrice() == best)
            System.out.print(" <-- best buy");
         System.out.println();
      }
   }

   /**
      Reads a product from a console reader.
      @param in the reader
      @return the product read if a product was successfully
      read, null if end of input was detected
   */

   public static Product readProduct(ConsoleReader in)
   {  System.out.println
         ("Enter name or leave blank when done:");
      String name = in.readLine();
      if (name == null || name.equals("")) return null;
      System.out.println("Enter price:");
```

```
                    String inputLine = in.readLine();
                    double price = Double.parseDouble(inputLine);
                    System.out.println("Enter score:");
                    inputLine = in.readLine();
                    int score = Integer.parseInt(inputLine);
                    return new Product(name, price, score);
                }

                /**
                    Prints a product description.
                    @param p the product to print
                */
                public static void printProduct(Product p)
                {  final int COLUMN_WIDTH = 30;

                    System.out.print(p.getName());

                    // pad with spaces to fill column

                    int pad = COLUMN_WIDTH - p.getName().length();
                    for (int i = 1; i <= pad; i++)
                        System.out.print(" ");

                    System.out.print("  $" + p.getPrice()
                        + "  score = " + p.getScore());
                }
            }
```

To really see the advantage of using objects instead of parallel arrays, consider the **readProduct** method in the second program. How *would* you implement that method if you didn't have a product object? You would have to return three values: the name, price, and score of the next product. In Java, though, you can't return three values in a method. Of course, you could have made the three arrays into static variables so that your read method could deposit the values there instead of returning them. But that would have been an inferior programming practice (see Quality Tip 7.3).

Quality Tip 11.2

Make Parallel Arrays into Arrays of Objects

If you find yourself using two arrays that have the same length, ask yourself whether you couldn't replace them with a single array of a class type. For example,

```
String[] name;
double[] salary;
```

◆
◆
◆
◆
◆
◆
◆

could become

```
Employee[] staff;
```

Why is this beneficial? Think ahead. Maybe your program will change and you will need to store the job title of the employees as well. It is a simple matter to update the **Employee** class. It may well be quite complicated to add a new array and make sure that all methods that accessed the original two arrays now also correctly access the third one.

11.5 Arrays as Object Data

A *polygon* is a closed sequence of lines (Figure 13). To describe a polygon, you need to store the sequence of its corner points. Because the number of points is variable, you should use an array.

```
class Polygon
{  public Polygon(int n)
   {  corners = new Point2D.Double[n];
      cornersSize = 0;
   }

   public void add(int i, Point2D.Double p)
   {  if (cornersSize < corners.length)
      {  corners[cornersSize] = p;
         cornersSize++;
   }
   public void draw(Graphics2D g2) { . . . }
   private Point2D.Double[] corners;
}
```

Here are two examples of polygons. First, a triangle:

```
Polygon triangle = new Polygon(3);
triangle.add(new Point2D.Double(40, 40));
```

Figure 13

A Polygon

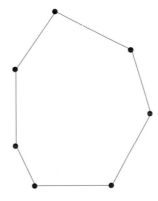

```
triangle.add(new Point2D.Double(120, 160));
triangle.add(new Point2D.Double(20, 120));
```

A *regular* polygon has all sides of the same length. It is easy to generate a regular polygon. A regular n-gon with center (x, y) and radius r has n corners, $c_0, \ldots, c_{n-1}$, where

$$c_i = (x + r \cdot \cos(2\pi i/n), y + r \cdot \sin(2\pi i/n))$$

Here is a fragment of code that generates a regular pentagon:

```
Polygon pentagon = new Polygon(5);
for (int i = 0; i < 5; i++)
   pentagon.add(new Point2D.Double(
      x + r * Math.cos(2 * Math.PI * i / 5),
      y + r * Math.sin(2 * Math.PI * i / 5)));
```

Of course, it would be good to see what the polygon looks like. To plot a polygon, you need to draw the lines joining adjacent corners and then close up the path by joining the last and first corners:

```
public void draw(Graphics2D g2)
{  for (int i = 0; i < cornersSize; i++)
   {  Point2D.Double from = corners[i];
      Point2D.Double to = corners[(i + 1) % corners.length];
      g2.draw(new Line2D.Double(from, to));
   }
}
```

Here is a complete program. Figure 14 shows the plot.

Program PolygonTest.java

```
import java.applet.Applet;
import java.awt.Graphics;
```

Figure 14

The Output of the PolygonTest program

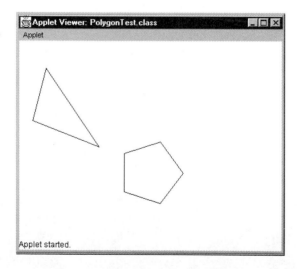

```
import java.awt.Graphics2D;
import java.awt.geom.Line2D;
import java.awt.geom.Point2D;

public class PolygonTest extends Applet
{  public void paint(Graphics g)
   {  Graphics2D g2 = (Graphics2D)g;

      Polygon triangle = new Polygon(3);
      triangle.add(new Point2D.Double(40, 40));
      triangle.add(new Point2D.Double(120, 160));
      triangle.add(new Point2D.Double(20, 120));

      double x = 200;
      double y = 200;
      double r = 50;
      Polygon pentagon = new Polygon(5);
      for (int i = 0; i < 5; i++)
         pentagon.add(new Point2D.Double(
            x + r * Math.cos(2 * Math.PI * i / 5),
            y + r * Math.sin(2 * Math.PI * i / 5)));

      triangle.draw(g2);
      pentagon.draw(g2);
   }
}

/**
    A polygon is a closed curve made up from line segment
    that join the corner points.
*/

class Polygon
{  /**
       Constructs a polygon with a given number of corner
       points.
       @param n the number of corner points.
    */
   public Polygon(int n)
   {  corners = new Point2D.Double[n];
      cornersSize = 0;
   }

   /**
       Adds a corner point of the polygon. The point is
       ignored if the maximum number of points has been added.
       @param p the corner point
    */
   public void add(Point2D.Double p)
   {  if (cornersSize < corners.length)
```

```
    {  corners[cornersSize] = p;
       cornersSize++;
    }
  }

  /**
     Draws the polygon.
     @param g2 the graphics context
  */
  public void draw(Graphics2D g2)
  {  for (int i = 0; i < cornersSize; i++)
     {  Point2D.Double from = corners[i];
        Point2D.Double to
           = corners[(i + 1) % corners.length];
        g2.draw(new Line2D.Double(from, to));
     }
  }

  private Point2D.Double[] corners;
  private int cornersSize;
}
```

We modeled a polygon as a class containing an array of points. It is a certain amount of trouble to define a new class. Why didn't we just write a polygon plot method with a `Point2D.Double[]` parameter?

```
  public static void drawPolygon(Graphics2D g2, Point2D.Double[] a)
  {  for (int i = 0; i < a.length; i++)
     {  Point2D.Double from = a[i];
        Point2D.Double to = a[(i + 1) % a.length];
        g2.draw(new Line2D.Double(from, to));
     }
  }
```

Indeed, this is simpler than defining a new class to represent polygons. Conceptually, however, it is wrong to say that an array of points and a polygon are one and the same thing.

Consider another geometric configuration: a *cloud* of points, as in Figure 15. A cloud is a set of dots that are not connected by lines. Like a polygon, it too is described by a collection of points, but, of course, the code for plotting a cloud is completely different from the code for plotting a polygon:

Program CloudTest.java

```
import java.applet.Applet;
import java.awt.Graphics;
import java.awt.Graphics2D;
import java.awt.geom.Ellipse2D;
import java.awt.geom.Point2D;
import java.util.Random;
```

Figure 15

The Output of the
CloudTest Program

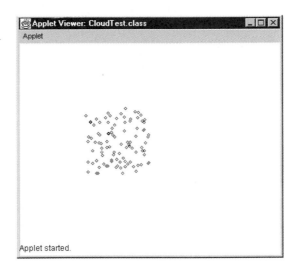

```java
public class CloudTest extends Applet
{  public void paint(Graphics g)
   {  Graphics2D g2 = (Graphics2D)g;

      Random generator = new Random();

      final int CLOUD_SIZE = 100;
      Cloud randomCloud = new Cloud(CLOUD_SIZE);

      for (int i = 0; i < CLOUD_SIZE; i++)
      {  // generate two random numbers between 100 and 200

         double x = 100 + 100 * generator.nextDouble();
         double y = 100 + 100 * generator.nextDouble();

         randomCloud.add(new Point2D.Double(x, y));
      }

      randomCloud.draw(g2);
   }
}

/**
   A cloud is a collection of dots.
*/

class Cloud
{  /**
      Constructs a cloud with a given number of dots.
      @param n the number of dots.
   */
```

```
    public Cloud(int n)
    {  dots = new Point2D.Double[n];
       dotsSize = 0;
    }

    /**
        Sets a dot point of the cloud. The point is
        ignored if the maximum number of points has been added.
        @param p the dot point
    */
    public void add(Point2D.Double p)
    {  if (dotsSize < dots.length)
       {  dots[dotsSize] = p;
          dotsSize++;
       }
    }

    /**
        Draws the cloud.
        @param g2 the graphics context
    */
    public void draw(Graphics2D g2)
    {  final double SMALL_CIRCLE_RADIUS = 2;

       for (int i = 0; i < dotsSize; i++)
       {  Ellipse2D.Double smallCircle
             = new Ellipse2D.Double(
             dots[i].getX() - SMALL_CIRCLE_RADIUS,
             dots[i].getY() - SMALL_CIRCLE_RADIUS,
             2 * SMALL_CIRCLE_RADIUS,
             2 * SMALL_CIRCLE_RADIUS);

          g2.draw(smallCircle);
       }
    }

    private Point2D.Double[] dots;
    private int dotsSize;
}
```

Again, it would be simpler to omit the **Cloud** class and pass the array of points directly to a **drawCloud** method:

```
public static void drawCloud(Graphics2D g2, Point2D.Double[] a)
{  final double SMALL_CIRCLE_RADIUS = 2;
   for (int i = 0; i < a.length; i++)
   {  Ellipse2D.Double smallCircle = new Ellipse2D.Double(
          a[i].getX() - SMALL_CIRCLE_RADIUS,
          a[i].getY() - SMALL_CIRCLE_RADIUS,
          2 * SMALL_CIRCLE_RADIUS,
```

```
          2 * SMALL_CIRCLE_RADIUS);
      g2.draw(smallCircle);
   }
}
```

Then you have two methods to plot a `Point2D.Double[]` array, namely `drawPolygon` and `drawCloud`. For a given array of points, you have to know which one is appropriate.

`Point2D.Double[] a; //` Is it a polygon or a cloud?

Making separate classes for polygons and clouds clarifies the code using the geometric objects.

`Cloud a; //` It is a cloud

As a beginning programmer you usually spend a lot of effort implementing methods that operate on simple data types, such as plotting clouds or computing the area of a polygon, and you would naturally like to simplify your life as much as possible. In most larger programs, however, where the focus is on using these methods on actual data, it is not so important that the data type is a little more complicated to define. After all, the type only needs to be written once, but if it is at all useful, it will be used many times. It is important to see at a glance what every variable stands for.

There is a second reason why we like to declare a polygon class that contains an array of points rather than just equating polygons with arrays of points. As you will learn in Chapter 16, there is more than one way of collecting points. An *array* of points may or may not be the most efficient container. Perhaps a *list* of points is more appropriate. When the concept of a polygon is made explicit, it is easy to carry out a change to a more useful container structure.

11.6 Vectors

We discussed that Java requires the programmer to specify the size of an array when the array is allocated, even though the actual size may not be known at that time. If you know that the array can never hold more than a certain number of elements, you can allocate a large array and partially fill it, using a companion variable to remember how many elements are actually in the array. You can also dynamically grow an array by allocating a larger array, shoveling the contents from the smaller to the larger array, and then attaching the larger array to the array variable. This is tedious and repetitive code. The `Vector` class automates this process.

11.6.1 Adding, Setting, and Getting Vector Elements

A vector is a container of objects that grows automatically. You add new elements at the end of the vector with the **add** method:

```
Vector products = new Vector();
boolean done = false;
while (!done)
{  Product p = readProduct();
   if (p == null) // last product read
      done = true;
   else
      products.add(p);
         // add the object to the end of the vector
}
```

You don't have to come up with a length for the vector, and there is *no limit* to the number of elements that you can add. Internally, the Vector class keeps an Object[] array, and it keeps constructing longer Object[] arrays as you add more elements to the Vector.

You can also replace an existing element with another element. However, since vectors are objects of a class and not arrays, you cannot use the [] operator. Instead, you use the **set** method to write an element, and the **get** method to read an element. For example, the call

```
Product toaster = . . .;
products.set(0, toaster);
```

stores the object **toaster** in the 0 position of the **products** vector.

As with arrays, vector positions start at 0. The number of elements currently stored in a vector is obtained by the **size** method:

```
int n = products.size();
```

Reading an element from a vector, however, is considerably more complicated. Whereas every array type has a distinct element type, so that anything read from a Product[] array is certain to be a product, a Vector can hold objects of *any* type at all. The reason is that a vector collects values of type Object and all Java classes are subclasses of the generic class Object. When you insert an element into a vector with the **add** or **set** method, the object reference is automatically converted to a plain Object reference. That means, though, that you get only Object references when you retrieve objects from a vector, no matter what you put in.

To read a value in a vector, you use the **get** method: products.get(i) is the ith element in the vector **products**. However, because the return type of the **get** method is the class Object, you must cast the return value of the **get** method to the correct type. In particular, you must *remember* what elements you added to your vector:

```
Product p = (Product)products.get(i);
```

Here is a typical loop that traverses the elements of a vector:

```
for (int i = 0; i < products.size(); i++)
{  Product p = (Product)products.get(i);
   do something with p;
}
```

You can also insert an object in the middle of a vector. The call `v.add(i, p)` adds the object `p` at position `i` and moves all elements by one position, from the current element at position `i` to the last element in the vector. Afterwards, the size of the vector is increased by 1. Conversely, the call `v.remove(i)` removes the element at position `i`, moves all elements after the removed element down by one position, and reduces the size of the vector by 1. These methods carry out the algorithms described in Sections 11.3.3 and 11.3.4.

11.6.2 Storing Numbers in Vectors

You can use vectors to store objects of any class. However, since numbers are not objects in Java, you cannot have vectors of numbers. To store sequences of integers, floating-point numbers, or `boolean` values, in a vector, you must use *wrapper classes*. The classes `Integer`, `Double`, and `Boolean` wrap numbers and truth values inside objects. These wrapper objects can be stored inside vectors.

The `Double` class is a typical number wrapper. There is a constructor that makes a `Double` object out of a `double` value:

```
Double d = new Double(29.95);
```

Conversely, the `doubleValue` method retrieves the `double` value that is stored inside the `Double` object.

```
double x = d.doubleValue();
```

Here is how you can add a number into a vector. First construct a wrapper object, then add the object to the vector:

```
Vector data = new Vector();
data.add(new Double(29.95));
```

To retrieve the number, you need to cast the return value of the `get` method to `Double`, then call the `doubleValue` method:

```
double x = ((Double)data.get(0)).doubleValue();
```

As you can see, using wrapper classes to store numbers in a vector is also a considerable hassle, maybe more so than storing a partially filled array of numbers and growing the array when necessary.

By the way, the `Integer` and `Double` classes should look familiar. You have used their `parseInt` and `parseDouble` method many times. These static methods really have nothing to do with wrapper objects for numbers; they were just put inside these classes because it seemed to be a convenient place.

11.6.3 Converting Vectors to Arrays

Now you have seen the advantages and drawbacks of vectors. The advantage of vectors is the dynamic growth. You need not know the final size of the vector, and you need not use a companion variable to denote the size of a partially full vector. The disadvantage is the cumbersome access syntax. Rather than accessing elements with the convenient v[i] syntax, you need to use the awkward v.set(i, x) and (*Type*)v.get(i) method calls and casts.

There is one common programming situation where you can combine the best of both worlds—dynamic growth and convenient syntax. Quite often, your program code naturally falls into two parts: first to fill an array, then to process its contents. In this case, you can start out with a vector and then convert it to an array with the copyInto method:

```
// read values into a vector
Vector productVector = new Vector();
boolean done = false;
while (!done)
{  Product p = readProduct();
   if (p == null) // last product read
      done = true;
   else
      productVector.add(p);
         // add the object to the end of the vector
}

// now all values are read and the final size is known

// allocate an array of the correct size
Product[] products = new Product[productVector.size()];

// copy the elements from the vector to the array
productVector.copyInto(products);

for (int i = 0; i < products.length, i++)
   do something with products[i];
      // access values with the convenient  [] syntax
```

This strategy is highly recommended whenever you need to read in a set of objects, you don't know how many to expect, and no objects will be added or removed afterwards.

Common Error 11.4

Length and Size

Unfortunately, the Java syntax for determining the number of elements in an array, a vector, and a string is not at all consistent.

Data type	Number of elements
Array	a.length
Vector	a.size()
String	a.length()

It is a common error to confuse these. You just have to remember the correct syntax for every data type.

Common Error 11.5

Inserting Objects of the Wrong Type in a Vector

Vectors are very convenient for collecting an arbitrary number of elements. However, using vectors can be more error-prone than using arrays. A vector is a container of objects, and therefore it is legal to put a mixture of objects into a vector:

```
Vector products = new Vector();
Product toaster = new Product(...);
products.add(toaster);
Rectangle cerealBox = new Rectangle(5, 10, 20, 30);
products.add(cerealBox);
```

The second call to **add** is technically correct—a Rectangle value can be converted to **Object**, and therefore it can be inserted into the vector. For that reason, the compiler will not complain. But this was still a programming error. The programmer's intention is that **products** contain products. In fact, the code for looking up an element in the **products** vector looks like this:

```
Product p = (Product)products.get(i);
```

If **i** is 1, then **products.get(i)** is a reference to a **Rectangle** object, not a **Product** object. When the program attempts to retrieve that object, the cast **(Product)** fails, because it is not possible to convert a **Rectangle** reference to a **Product** reference. As a result, an exception is thrown.

11.7 Two-Dimensional Arrays

Arrays and vectors can store linear sequences. It often happens that you want to store collections that have a two-dimensional layout. For example, in Section 6.4 we wrote a program that produces a table of values:

1	1	1	1	1	1	1	1
2	4	8	16	32	64	128	256
3	9	27	81	243	729	2187	6561
4	16	64	256	1024	4096	16384	65536
5	25	125	625	3125	15625	78125	390625
6	36	216	1296	7776	46656	279936	1679616
7	49	343	2401	16807	117649	823543	5764801
8	64	512	4096	32768	262144	2097152	16777216
9	81	729	6561	59049	531441	4782969	43046721
10	100	1000	10000	100000	1000000	10000000	100000000

Such an arrangement, consisting of rows and columns of values, is called a *two-dimensional array* or *matrix*. When constructing a two-dimensional array, you specify how many rows and columns you need. In this case, ask for 10 rows and 8 columns:

```
int[][] powers = new int[10][8];
```

To access a particular element in the matrix, specify two subscripts in separate brackets:

```
powers[3][4] = Math.pow(4, 5);
```

In Java, two-dimensional arrays are stored as arrays of arrays. For example, **powers** is an array of 10 objects, each of which is an `int[]` array of length 8 (see Figure 16).

Because a two-dimensional array is really an array of the row arrays, the number of rows is

```
int nrows = powers.length;
```

As described in Advanced Topic 11.2, it is possible for the row lengths to vary. However, as long as you know that all rows have the same length, you can find the number of columns, which is the same as the length of a row, as

```
int ncols = powers[0].length;
```

The following program fills a two-dimensional array with numbers and then prints its contents as a table:

Program Table2.java

```
public class Table2
{  public static void main(String[] args)
   {  final int COLUMN_WIDTH = 10;

      int[][] powers = new int[10][8];
      for (int i = 0; i < powers.length; i++)
         for (int j = 0; j < powers[i].length; j++)
            powers[i][j] = (int)Math.pow(i + 1, j + 1);

      printTable(powers, COLUMN_WIDTH);
   }

   /**
      Prints a two-dimensional array of integers
      @param table the values to be printed
      @param width the column width
   */
   public static void printTable(int[][] table, int width)
   {  for (int i = 0; i < table.length; i++)
      {  for (int j = 0; j < table[i].length; j++)
         {  System.out.print(format(table[i][j], width));
         }
```

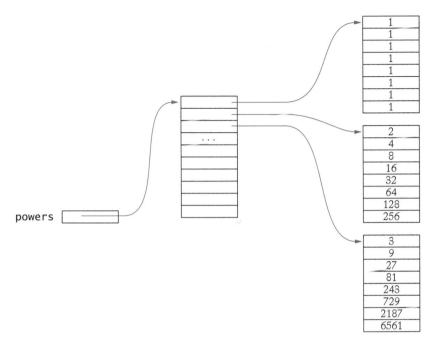

Figure 16

A Two-Dimensional Array

```
        System.out.println();
    }
}
/**
    Formats an integer to fit in a field of constant width.
    @param n the integer to format
    @param width the field width
    @return a string of length width, consisting of
    leading spaces followed by the number n
*/
public static String format(int n, int width)
{   String nstr = "" + n;

    // pad with spaces

    while (nstr.length() < width)
        nstr = " " + nstr;

    return nstr;
    }
}
```

◢dvanced Topic 11.2

Two-Dimensional Arrays with Variable Row Lengths

When you declare a two-dimensional array with the command

```
int[][] a = new int[5][5];
```

then you get a 5-by-5 matrix that can store 25 elements:

```
a[0][0] a[0][1] a[0][2] a[0][3] a[0][4]
a[1][0] a[1][1] a[1][2] a[1][3] a[1][4]
a[2][0] a[2][1] a[2][2] a[2][3] a[2][4]
a[3][0] a[3][1] a[3][2] a[3][3] a[3][4]
a[4][0] a[4][1] a[4][2] a[4][3] a[4][4]
```

In this matrix, all rows have the same length. In Java it is possible to declare arrays in which the row length varies. For example, you can store an array that has triangular shape, such as this one:

```
b[0][0]
b[1][0] b[1][1]
b[2][0] b[2][1] b[2][2]
b[3][0] b[3][1] b[3][2] b[3][3]
b[4][0] b[4][1] b[4][2] b[4][3] b[4][4]
```

To allocate such an array, you must work harder. First, you allocate space to hold five rows. You indicate that you will manually set each row by leaving the second array index empty:

```
int[][] b = new int[5][];
```

Then you need to allocate each row separately.

```
for (int i = 0; i < b.length; i++)
    b[i] = new int[i + 1];
```

You can access each array element as b[i][j], but you must now be careful that j is less than b[i].length.

Naturally, such "ragged" arrays are not very common.

Chapter Summary

1. Use an array to collect multiple values of the same type. Individual values are accessed by an integer index: a[i]. Valid values for the index range from 0 to one less than the length of the array. Supplying an invalid index is a common programming error that results in an exception.

2. When creating an array, you must supply the number of elements you want the array to hold. Use the length data member to find the number of elements in an

array. Arrays are often *partially filled*. Then you need to remember the number of elements that you actually placed in the array.

3. Arrays can occur as the parameters and return values of methods. Classes can have instance variables that are arrays of values.

4. Avoid parallel arrays by changing them into arrays of objects.

5. Many common algorithms on arrays traverse the elements from 0 either to the end of the array or until a specific element has been found. Common algorithms include finding elements and counting elements with a certain property.

6. You can use vectors instead of arrays of objects. Vectors automatically grow on demand. However, since vectors hold generic `Object` references, element access is a bit cumbersome.

7. Two-dimensional arrays form a tabular, two-dimensional arrangement. Individual elements in two-dimensional arrays are accessed by an index pair `a[i][j]`.

Further Reading

[1] Barton P. Miller, Louis Fericksen, and Bryan So, "An Empirical Study of the Reliability of Unix Utilities", *Communications of the ACM,* vol. 33, no. 12 (December 1990), pp. 32–44.

[2] Peter J. Denning, *Computers under Attack,* Addison-Wesley, 1990.

[3] Cliff Stoll, *The Cuckoo's Egg,* Doubleday, 1989.

Classes, Objects, and Methods Introduced in This Chapter

```
java.lang.Boolean
    booleanValue
java.lang.Double
    doubleValue
java.lang.Integer
    intValue
java.lang.System
    arrayCopy
java.util.Vector
    add
    copyInto
    get
    remove
    set
    size
```

Review Exercises

Exercise R11.1. For each of the following sets of values, write code that fills an array a with the values.

- ◆   1 2 3 4 5 6 7 8 9 10
- ◆   0 2 4 6 8 10 12 14 16 18 20
- ◆   1 4 9 16 25 36 49 64 81 100
- ◆   0 0 0 0 0 0 0 0 0 0
- ◆   1 4 9 16 9 7 4 9 11

Use a loop when appropriate.

Exercise R11.2. Write a loop that fills an array a with ten random numbers between 1 and 100. Write code for two nested loops that fill a with ten *different* sequences of ten random numbers between 1 and 100.

Exercise R11.3. Write Java code for a loop that simultaneously computes the maximum and minimum of an array.

Exercise R11.4. What is wrong with the following loop?

```
int[] v = new int[10];
for (int i = 1; i <= 10; i++) v[i] = i * i;
```

Explain two ways of fixing the error.

Exercise R11.5. What is an array index? What are the bounds of an array? What is a bounds error?

Exercise R11.6. Write a program that contains a bounds error. Run the program. What happens on your computer? How does the error message help you locate the error?

Exercise R11.7. Write a program that fills an array with the numbers 1, 4, 9, . . . , 100. Compile it and launch the debugger. After the array has been filled with three numbers, *inspect it.* What are the contents of the elements in the array beyond those that you filled?

Exercise R11.8. Write a loop that reads ten numbers and a second loop that prints them out in the opposite order from which they were entered.

Exercise R11.9. Give an example of

- ◆   A useful method that has an array of integers as a parameter that is not modified

◆ A useful method that has an array of integers as a parameter that is modified
◆ A useful method that has an array of integers as a return value

Just describe each method. Don't implement the methods.

Exercise R11.10. A method that has an array as a parameter can change the array in two ways. It can change the contents of individual array elements, or it can rearrange the elements. Describe two useful methods with `Product[]` parameters that change an array of products in each of the two ways just described.

Exercise R11.11. What are parallel arrays? Why are parallel arrays indications of poor programming? How can they be avoided?

Exercise R11.12. Design a class `Catalog` that stores a collection of products. What public methods should you support? What advantages and disadvantages does a `Catalog` class have over a `Product[]` array?

Exercise R11.13. Suppose v is a *sorted* vector of products. Describe how a new product can be inserted in its proper position so that the resulting vector stays sorted.

Exercise R11.14. How do you perform the following tasks with arrays in Java?

◆ Test that two arrays contain the same elements in the same order.
◆ Copy one array to another.
◆ Fill an array with zeroes, overwriting all elements in it.
◆ Remove all elements from an array.

Exercise R11.15. True or false?

◆ All elements of an array are of the same type.
◆ Array subscripts must be integers.
◆ Arrays cannot contain strings as elements.
◆ Arrays cannot use strings as subscripts.
◆ Parallel arrays must have equal length.
◆ Two-dimensional arrays always have the same numbers of rows and columns.
◆ Two parallel arrays can be replaced by a two-dimensional array.
◆ Elements of different columns in a two-dimensional array can have different types.
◆ Elements in a vector can have different types.

Exercise R11.16. True or false?

◆ A method cannot return a two-dimensional array.
◆ A method can change the length of an array parameter.

- ◆ A method cannot change the dimensions of a two-dimensional array parameter.
- ◆ A method cannot change the length of a vector that is passed as a parameter.
- ◆ A method can only reorder the elements of an array parameter, not change the elements.

Programming Exercises

Exercise P11.1. Write a method

```
static double scalarProduct(double[] a, double[] b)
```

that computes the scalar product of two mathematical vectors (represented as arrays). The scalar product is

$$a_0 b_0 + a_1 b_1 + \cdots + a_{n-1} b_{n-1}$$

Exercise P11.2. Write a method that computes the *alternating sum* of all elements in an array. For example, if `alternatingSum` is called with an array containing

$$1 \quad 4 \quad 9 \quad 16 \quad 9 \quad 7 \quad 4 \quad 9 \quad 11$$

then it computes

$$1 - 4 + 9 - 16 + 9 - 7 + 4 - 9 + 11 = -2$$

Exercise P11.3. Write a method `reverse` that reverses the sequence of elements in an array. For example, if `reverse` is called with an array containing

$$1 \quad 4 \quad 9 \quad 16 \quad 9 \quad 7 \quad 4 \quad 9 \quad 11$$

then the array is changed to

$$11 \quad 9 \quad 4 \quad 7 \quad 9 \quad 16 \quad 9 \quad 4 \quad 1$$

Exercise P11.4. Write a method

```
public static int[] append(int[] a, int[] b)
```

that appends one array after another. For example, if **a** is

$$1 \quad 4 \quad 9 \quad 16$$

and **b** is

$$9 \quad 7 \quad 4 \quad 9 \quad 11$$

then **append** returns the array

$$1 \quad 4 \quad 9 \quad 16 \quad 9 \quad 7 \quad 4 \quad 9 \quad 11$$

Exercise P11.5. Write a predicate method

```
public static boolean equals(int[] a, int[] b)
```

that checks whether two arrays have the same elements in the same order.

Exercise P11.6. Write a predicate method

```
public static boolean sameSet(int[] a, int[] b)
```

that checks whether two arrays have the same elements in some order, ignoring multiplicities. For example, the two arrays

$$1 \quad 4 \quad 9 \quad 16 \quad 9 \quad 7 \quad 4 \quad 9 \quad 11$$

and

$$11 \quad 11 \quad 7 \quad 9 \quad 16 \quad 4 \quad 1$$

would be considered to have the same set. You will probably need one or more helper methods.

Exercise P11.7. Write a predicate method

```
public static boolean sameElements(int[] a, int[] b)
```

that checks whether two arrays have the same elements in some order, with the same multiplicities. For example,

$$1 \quad 4 \quad 9 \quad 16 \quad 9 \quad 7 \quad 4 \quad 9 \quad 11$$

and

$$11 \quad 1 \quad 4 \quad 9 \quad 16 \quad 9 \quad 7 \quad 4 \quad 9$$

would be considered to have the same elements, but

$$1 \quad 4 \quad 9 \quad 16 \quad 9 \quad 7 \quad 4 \quad 9 \quad 11$$

and

$$11 \quad 11 \quad 7 \quad 9 \quad 16 \quad 4 \quad 1$$

would not. You will probably need one or more helper methods.

Exercise P11.8. Write methods of the `Polygon` class

```
public double perimeter()
```

and

```
public double area()
```

that compute the circumference and the area of a polygon. To compute the perimeter, compute the distance between adjacent points, and total up the distances. The area of a polygon with corners $(x_0, y_0), \ldots, (x_{n-1}, y_{n-1})$ is

$$\frac{1}{2}|x_1y_2 + x_2y_3 + \cdots + x_{n-1}y_0 - y_1x_2 - y_2x_3 - \cdots - y_{n-1}x_0|$$

As test cases, compute the perimeter and area of a rectangle and of a regular hexagon.

Exercise P11.9. Write a program that asks the user to input a number n and prints all permutations of the sequence of numbers $1, 2, 3, \ldots, n$. For example, if n is 3, the program should print

```
1   2   3
1   3   2
2   1   3
2   3   1
3   1   2
3   2   1
```

Hint: Write a method

```
public static void permutationHelper(int[] prefix,
    int[] toPermute)
```

that computes all the permutations in the array `toPermute` and prints each permutation, prefixed by all numbers in the array `prefix`. For example, if `prefix` contains the number 2 and `toPermute` the numbers 1 and 3, then `permutationHelper` prints

```
2   1   3
2   3   1
```

The `permutationHelper` method does the following: If `toPermute` has no elements, print the elements in `prefix`. Otherwise, for each element e in `toPermute`, make an array `toPermute2`, which is equal to `permute` except for e, and an array `prefix2`, consisting of `prefix` and e. Then call `permutationHelper` with `prefix2` and `toPermute2`.

Exercise P11.10. Write a program that produces 10 random permutations of the numbers 1 to 10. To generate a random permutation, you need to fill an array with the numbers 1 to 10 so that no two entries of the array have the same contents. You can do it by brute force, by calling `Random.nextInt` until it produces a value that is not yet in the array. Instead, you should implement a smart method. Make a second array and fill it with the numbers 1 to 10. Then pick one of those at random, *remove it,* and append it to the permutation array. Repeat ten times.

Exercise P11.11. Write a method

```
public static void barChart(double[] data)
```

that displays a bar chart of the values in **data**. You may assume that all values in **data** are positive. *Hint:* You must figure out the maximum of the values in **data**. Set the coordinate system so that the x-range equals the number of bars and the y-range goes from 0 to the maximum.

Exercise P11.12. Improve the **barChart** method of the preceding exercise to work correctly when **data** contains negative values.

Exercise P11.13. Write a method

```
static void pieChart(double[] data)
```

that displays a pie chart of the values in **data**. You may assume that all values in **data** are positive.

Exercise P11.14. Write a program that plays tic-tac-toe. The tic-tac-toe game is played on a 3 × 3 grid as in

The game is played by two players, who take turns. The first player marks moves with a circle, the second with a cross. The player who has formed a horizontal, vertical, or diagonal sequence of three marks wins. Your program should draw the game board, accept mouse clicks into empty squares, change the players after every successful move, and pronounce the winner.

Exercise P11.15. *Magic squares.* An $n \times n$ matrix that is filled with the numbers 1, 2, 3, ..., n^2 is a magic square if the sum of the elements in each row, in each column, and in the two diagonals is the same value. For example,

$$
\begin{array}{cccc}
16 & 3 & 2 & 13 \\
5 & 10 & 11 & 8 \\
9 & 6 & 7 & 12 \\
4 & 15 & 14 & 1 \\
\end{array}
$$

Write a program that reads in n^2 values from the keyboard and tests whether they form a magic square when put into array form. You need to test three features:

◆ Did the user enter n^2 numbers for some n?

◆ Does each of the numbers 1, 2, ..., n^2 occur exactly once in the user input?

◆ When the numbers are put into a square, are the sums of the rows, columns, and diagonals equal to each other?

If the size of the input is a square, test whether all numbers between 1 and *n* are present. Then compute the row, column, and diagonal sums.

Exercise P11.16. Implement the following algorithm to construct magic *n*-by-*n* squares; it works only if *n* is odd. Place a 1 in the middle of the bottom row. After *k* has been placed in the (i, j) square, place $k + 1$ into the square to the right and down, wrapping around the borders. However, if the square to the right and down has already been filled, or if you are in the lower right corner, then you must move to the square straight up instead. Here is the 5×5 square that you get if you follow this method:

11	18	25	2	9
10	12	19	21	3
4	6	13	20	22
23	5	7	14	16
17	24	1	8	15

Write a program whose input is the number *n* and whose output is the magic square of order *n* if *n* is odd.

Exercise P11.17. The *Game of Life* is a well-known mathematical game that gives rise to amazingly complex behavior, although it can be specified by a few simple rules. (It is not actually a game in the traditional sense, with players competing for a win.) Here are the rules. The game is played on a rectangular board. Each square can be either empty or occupied. At the beginning, you can specify empty and full cells in some way; then the game runs automatically. In each *generation,* the next generation is computed. A new cell is born on an empty square if it is surrounded by exactly three neighbor cells. A cell dies of overcrowding if it is surrounded by four or more neighbors, and it dies of loneliness if it is surrounded by zero or one neighbors. A neighbor is an inhabitant of an adjacent square to the left, right, top, or bottom or in a diagonal direction. The following shows a cell and its neighbors.

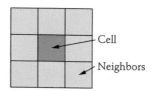

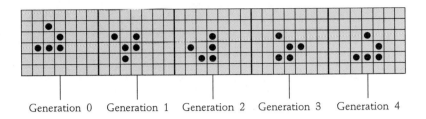

Generation 0   Generation 1   Generation 2   Generation 3   Generation 4

Figure 17

Glider

Many configurations show interesting behavior when subjected to these rules. Figure 17 shows a *glider,* observed over five generations. Note how it moves. After four generations, it is transformed into the identical shape, but located one square to the right and below.

One of the more amazing configurations is the *glider gun:* a complex collection of cells that, after 30 moves, turns back into itself and a glider. (See Figure 18.)

Program the game to eliminate the drudgery of computing successive generations by hand. Use a matrix to store the rectangular configuration. Write a program that shows successive generations of the game on the graphics screen. You get extra credit if you let the user add or remove cells by clicking with the mouse.

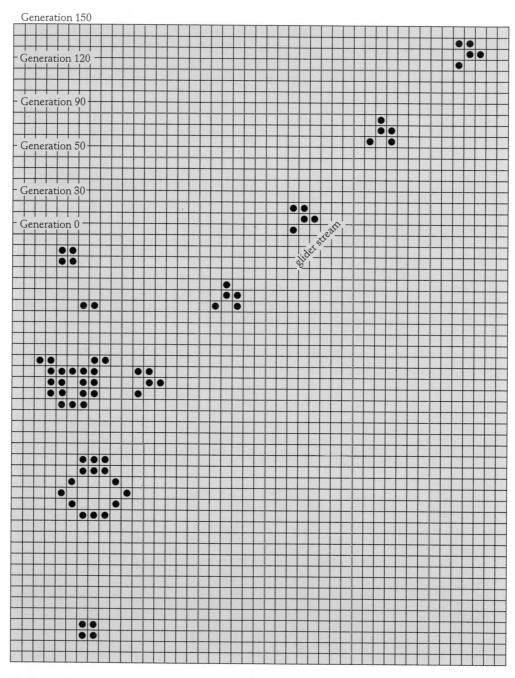

Figure 18

Glider Gun

CHAPTER

Graphical User Interfaces

Chapter Goals

- ◆ To become familiar with common user interface components such as buttons, text components, combo boxes, and menus

- ◆ To understand the use of layout managers to arrange user interface components in a container

- ◆ To build programs that handle events from user interface components

- ◆ To learn how to browse the Java documentation

Up to now, your graphical programs received user input from an input dialog, a text field, or a mouse. However, the graphical applications you are familiar with have a large number of visual gadgets for information entry: buttons, scroll bars, menus, and so on. In this chapter, you will learn how to use the most common user interface components in the Java Swing user interface toolkit. However, Swing has many more components than you can master in a first course, and even the basic components have many advanced options that we cannot cover here. In fact, few programmers ever try to learn everything about a particular user interface component. It is much better to understand the concepts and to search the Java documentation for the details. This chapter walks you through one example to show you how the Java documentation is organized and how you can rely on it for your own programming.

12.1 Layout Management

Consider a frame that has multiple buttons, such as the one in Figure 1. How can you add the buttons to the frame? The buttons appear in the southern area of the frame. However, you can't simply add them all:

```
contentPane.add(upButton, "South");
contentPane.add(downButton, "South"); // Error
```

If you add multiple buttons to the same area in a border layout, they are just put on top of each other. Instead, you need to put the buttons inside a new panel:

```
JPanel buttonPanel = new JPanel();
buttonPanel.add(upButton);
```

Figure 1

A Program with
Four Buttons

```
buttonPanel.add(downButton);
buttonPanel.add(leftButton);
buttonPanel.add(rightButton);
```

Then you add the entire panel to the South area of the content pane:

```
contentPane.add(buttonPanel, "South");
```

Now the user interface is composed of two containers, each of which has its own layout manager (see Figure 2).

Unlike the content pane, a panel uses a *flow layout*. A flow layout simply arranges its components in a row and starts a new row when there is no more room in the current row.

In Java, you build up user interfaces by adding components into containers. The content pane is a container, and you can use JPanel objects if you need additional containers. Each container has its own layout manager, which determines how the components are laid out. With the border layout, you have to tell where a component should be added, by specifying a location ("South", "Center", and so on). With the flow layout, the components are arranged in the order in which you add them.

By default, the content pane has a border layout and a panel has a flow layout. You can change the layout manager of a container with the setLayout method. For example, you can make a panel with a border layout:

```
JPanel panel = new JPanel();
panel.setLayout(new BorderLayout());
```

There is one important difference between the border layout and the flow layout. The border layout grows each component to fill all available space in its area. For example, Figure 3 shows how a button looks when it is placed in the South area of a

Figure 2

Containers with
Separate Layout
Managers

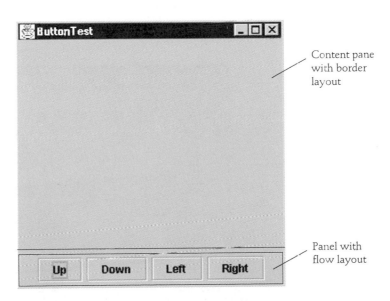

Content pane
with border
layout

Panel with
flow layout

border layout. In contrast, the flow layout leaves each component at its *preferred* size. That is why the buttons in Figure 2 stay at their natural size. Therefore, even if you have a single button, if you want to protect it from being resized, place it inside a new panel.

There is a third layout that is sometimes useful: the *grid layout*. The grid layout arranges components in a grid with a fixed number of rows and columns, resizing each of the components so that they all have the same size. Like the border layout, it also grows each component to fill the entire allotted area. (If that is not desirable, you need to place each component inside a panel, as described previously.) Figure 4

Figure 3

The Border Layout Grows
Components

Figure 4

Grid Layout

shows a number pad panel that uses a grid layout. To create a grid layout, you supply the number of rows and columns in the constructor. Then you add the components, row by row, left to right:

```
JPanel numberPanel = new JPanel();
numberPanel.setLayout(new GridLayout(4, 3));
numberPanel.add(button7);
numberPanel.add(button8);
numberPanel.add(button9);
numberPanel.add(button4);

. . .
```

Sometimes you want to have a tabular arrangement of the components where columns have different sizes or one component spans multiple columns. There is a more complex layout manager, the grid bag layout, that can handle these situations. However, the grid bag layout is quite complex to use, and we do not cover it in this book; see, for example, [1] for more information. Using the border layout, flow layout, and grid layout, along with panels, it is possible to create acceptable-looking layouts in nearly all situations. If you want more control over component layout, you can check out the grid bag layout, or you can use a development environment with a layout tool that lets you place the components visually and then generates the appropriate Java code.

12.2 Buttons

You construct a button by supplying a label string, an icon, or both. Here are the alternatives:

Figure 5

Buttons with Labels and Icons

```
leftButton = new JButton("Left");
leftButton = new JButton(new ImageIcon("left.gif"));
leftButton = new JButton("Left", new ImageIcon("left.gif"));
```

See Figure 5 for two buttons with label strings and icons.

When a button is clicked, it sends an action event. To capture it, you need to install an action listener. You already saw action listeners in Chapter 10, where they were used to trap the Enter key in a text field. Action events are used by several user interface components in Java.

Here is how you can install a listener for a button:

```
class MyFrame
{  public MyFrame()
   {  . . .
      upButton = new JButton("Up");
      ActionListener listener = new UpListener();
      upButton.addActionListener(listener);
      . . .
   }
   . . .
   JButton upButton;
   . . .
   private class UpListener implements ActionListener
   {  public void actionPerformed(ActionEvent event)
      {  // this method is called when upButton is clicked
      }
   }
}
```

If you install a separate action listener for each button, you can ignore the action event parameter of the `actionPerformed` method. However, sometimes you have buttons that carry out similar tasks, and you may not want to come up with a separate listener for each of them. You can share one listener among multiple buttons. Of course, then the `actionPerformed` method needs to know which button was clicked. Use the `getSource` method of the `ActionEvent` parameter. It returns a reference to the button that was clicked. Here is an example:

```
class ButtonFrame
{  public ButtonFrame()
   {  . . .
      upButton = new JButton("Up");
      downButton = new JButton("Down");
      leftButton = new JButton("Left");
      rightButton = new JButton("Right");
      ActionListener listener = new DirectionListener();

      // add the same listener to all four buttons
      upButton.addActionListener(listener);
      downButton.addActionListener(listener);
      leftButton.addActionListener(listener);
```

```
        rightButton.addActionListener(listener);
        . . .
   }
   . . .
   private JButton upButton;
   private JButton downButton;
   private JButton leftButton;
   private JButton rightButton;
   . . .
   private class DirectionListener implements ActionListener
   {  public void actionPerformed(ActionEvent event)
      {   // this method is called when any of the
          // direction buttons is clicked
          // find the button that was clicked
          Object source = event.getSource();
          if (source == upButton)
            panel.moveRectangle(0, -1);
          else if (source == downButton)
            panel.moveRectangle(0, 1);
          else if (source == leftButton)
            panel.moveRectangle(-1, 0);
          else if (source == rightButton)
            panel.moveRectangle(1, 0);
      }
   }
}
```

The same `DirectionListener` object listens to all four buttons. Hence it must find out the source of each button click.

Here is the whole program:

Program ButtonTest.java

```
import java.awt.Container;
import java.awt.Graphics;
import java.awt.Graphics2D;
import java.awt.Rectangle;
import java.awt.event.ActionEvent;
import java.awt.event.ActionListener;
import java.awt.event.WindowAdapter;
import java.awt.event.WindowEvent;
import javax.swing.JButton;
import javax.swing.JFrame;
import javax.swing.JPanel;

public class ButtonTest
{  public static void main(String[] args)
   {  ButtonFrame frame = new ButtonFrame();
      frame.setTitle("ButtonTest");
      frame.show();
   }
}
```

```
class ButtonFrame extends JFrame
{  public ButtonFrame()
   {  final int DEFAULT_FRAME_WIDTH = 300;
      final int DEFAULT_FRAME_HEIGHT = 300;
      setSize(DEFAULT_FRAME_WIDTH, DEFAULT_FRAME_HEIGHT);

      addWindowListener(new WindowCloser());

      // construct components

      panel = new RectanglePanel();
      JPanel buttonPanel = new JPanel();

      ActionListener listener = new DirectionListener();

      upButton = new JButton("Up");
      upButton.addActionListener(listener);

      downButton = new JButton("Down");
      downButton.addActionListener(listener);

      leftButton = new JButton("Left");
      leftButton.addActionListener(listener);

      rightButton = new JButton("Right");
      rightButton.addActionListener(listener);

      // add components to content pane

      Container contentPane = getContentPane();
      contentPane.add(panel, "Center");

      buttonPanel.add(upButton);
      buttonPanel.add(downButton);
      buttonPanel.add(leftButton);
      buttonPanel.add(rightButton);

      contentPane.add(buttonPanel, "South");
   }

   private RectanglePanel panel;
   private JButton upButton;
   private JButton downButton;
   private JButton leftButton;
   private JButton rightButton;

   // inner class definition
```

```
        private class DirectionListener implements ActionListener
        {  public void actionPerformed(ActionEvent event)
            {  // find the button that was clicked

               Object source = event.getSource();

               if (source == upButton)
                  panel.moveRectangle(0, -1);
               else if (source == downButton)
                  panel.moveRectangle(0, 1);
               else if (source == leftButton)
                  panel.moveRectangle(-1, 0);
               else if (source == rightButton)
                  panel.moveRectangle(1, 0);
            }
        }

        private class WindowCloser extends WindowAdapter
        {  public void windowClosing(WindowEvent event)
            {  System.exit(0);
            }
        }
}

class RectanglePanel extends JPanel
{  public RectanglePanel()
    {  rect = new Rectangle(0, 0, RECT_WIDTH, RECT_HEIGHT);
    }

    public void paintComponent(Graphics g)
    {  super.paintComponent(g);
       Graphics2D g2 = (Graphics2D)g;
       g2.draw(rect);
    }

    /**
        Moves the rectangle and repaints it. The rectangle
        is moved by multiples of its full width or height.
        @param dx the number of width units
        @param dy the number of height units
    */
    public void moveRectangle(int dx, int dy)
    {  rect.translate(dx * RECT_WIDTH, dy * RECT_HEIGHT);
       repaint();
    }

    private Rectangle rect;
    private static final int RECT_WIDTH = 20;
    private static final int RECT_HEIGHT = 30;
}
```

Quality Tip 12.1

Do Not Identify Components by Their Label Text

If you have several event sources with the same listener, the listener needs to tell them apart. Do not use the label text to distinguish between them.

```
public void actionPerformed(ActionEvent event)
{  JButton source = (JButton)event.getSource();
   String label = source.getText();
   if (label.equals("Right")) . . . // Don't!
   else . . .
}
```

Your program will fail mysteriously if the label of the button is being changed, say, to

```
rightButton = new JButton("East");
```

or

```
rightButton = new JButton("Rechts"); // German version
```

The button label no longer matches the condition, and the button becomes inactive. Always use the object reference to identify the event source:

```
public void actionPerformed(ActionEvent event)
{  JButton source = (JButton)event.getSource();
   if (source == rightButton) . . . // OK
   else . . .
}
```

Common Error 12.1

Forgetting to Attach a Listener

If you run your program and find that your buttons seem to be dead, double-check that you attached the button listener. The same holds for other user interface components. It is a surprisingly common error to program the listener class and the event handler action without actually attaching it to the event source.

Another common error is to use the wrong signature when overriding an adapter method. The effect is to add a new method rather than to override the do-nothing adapter method.

12.3 Text Components

You already saw in Chapter 10 how to construct text fields. A text field holds a single line of text. To display multiple lines of text, you use the **JTextArea** class. Both **JTextField** and **JTextArea** are subclasses of the **JTextComponent** class.

When constructing a text field, you can specify the desired number of characters in the constructor.

```
JTextField interestRateField = new JTextField(5);
```

Of course, since character widths are variable, this is only an approximate measurement. With a text area, you can specify the number of rows and columns:

```
JTextArea resultArea = new JTextArea(10, 40);
```

If the user hits the Enter key in a `JTextArea` component, no `ActionEvent` is generated—the Enter key just starts a new line. Thus, there is no easy way to find out when a user is done entering text into a text area. User interface designers solve that problem by adding a button at the bottom of each form with a text area (see Figure 6). When the user clicks the button, the handler for the button click calls the `getText` method of the `JTextComponent` class to retrieve the text that the user entered.

You can use the `setText` method to set the text of a text field. If you want to use a text component for display purposes only, then you can use the `setEditable` method:

```
JTextField result = new JTextField();
result.setEditable(false);
```

Now the user can no longer edit the contents of the field, but your program can still call `setText` to change it.

You can set the font of a text component with the `setFont` method.

If you have a form with several text components, you need to label them so that the user can see which text field is used for which purpose. Unlike a button, you cannot place the label inside the text component—after all, that is where the user is

Figure 6

A Frame with a Text Area and a Text Field

supposed to type text. Instead, you construct yet another component, an object of type JLabel, and position it next to the text field. You specify the text or icon image of the label in the constructor. You can specify how you want the label text to be aligned by using one of the values SwingConstants.LEFT, SwingConstants.CENTER, and SwingConstants.RIGHT. Right alignment is the most useful setting, because then the label is closest to the item that it labels. Here is an example of how to construct a label:

```
JLabel resultLabel = new JLabel("Average:",SwingConstants.RIGHT);
```

The following sample program puts these concepts together. A user can enter numbers into the text area and then click on the "Calculate" button. The average is then displayed in the text field with the label "Average". That text field is not editable.

Program TextTest.java

```
import java.awt.Container;
import java.awt.GridLayout;
import java.awt.event.ActionEvent;
import java.awt.event.ActionListener;
import java.awt.event.WindowAdapter;
import java.awt.event.WindowEvent;
import java.util.StringTokenizer;
import javax.swing.JButton;
import javax.swing.JFrame;
import javax.swing.JLabel;
import javax.swing.JPanel;
import javax.swing.JTextArea;
import javax.swing.JTextField;

public class TextTest
{  public static void main(String[] args)
   {  TextFrame frame = new TextFrame();
      frame.setTitle("TextTest");
      frame.show();
   }
}

class TextFrame extends JFrame
{  public TextFrame()
   {  final int DEFAULT_FRAME_WIDTH = 300;
      final int DEFAULT_FRAME_HEIGHT = 300;
      setSize(DEFAULT_FRAME_WIDTH, DEFAULT_FRAME_HEIGHT);
      addWindowListener(new WindowCloser());

      // construct components

      inputArea = new JTextArea();
```

```
      resultField = new JTextField(20);
      resultField.setEditable(false);

      calcButton = new JButton("Calculate");
      calcButton.addActionListener(new ButtonListener());

      // add components to content pane

      Container contentPane = getContentPane();
      contentPane.add(inputArea, "Center");

      // arrange the label and text field in a panel

      JPanel resultPanel = new JPanel();
      resultPanel.add(new JLabel("Average:"));
      resultPanel.add(resultField);

      // place the button in a panel

      JPanel buttonPanel = new JPanel();
      buttonPanel.add(calcButton);

      // stack up these two panels in another panel

      JPanel southPanel = new JPanel();
      southPanel.setLayout(new GridLayout(2, 1));
      southPanel.add(resultPanel);
      southPanel.add(buttonPanel);

      contentPane.add(southPanel, "South");
   }

   /**
      Reads numbers from a string that contains a sequence
      of floating-point numbers separated by white space.
      @param input the string containing the numbers
      @return the numbers that were found in the string
   */
   public static double[] getData(String input)
   {  StringTokenizer tokenizer = new StringTokenizer(input);
      double[] data = new double[tokenizer.countTokens()];
      for (int i = 0; i < data.length; i++)
         data[i] = Double.parseDouble(tokenizer.nextToken());
      return data;
   }

   /**
      Computes the average of an array of floating-point numbers.
      @param data the numbers to average
      @return the average, or 0 if the array was empty
   */
```

```
      public static double average(double[] data)
      {  if (data.length == 0) return 0;
         double sum = 0;
         for (int i = 0; i < data.length; i++)
            sum = sum + data[i];
         return sum / data.length;
      }

      private JTextArea inputArea;
      private JTextField resultField;
      private JButton calcButton;

      private class ButtonListener implements ActionListener
      {  public void actionPerformed(ActionEvent event)
         {   // get user input from text area

            double[] data = getData(inputArea.getText());

            // compute average and display in result field

            double avg = average(data);
            resultField.setText("" + avg);
         }
      }

      private class WindowCloser extends WindowAdapter
      {  public void windowClosing(WindowEvent event)
         {  System.exit(0);
         }
      }
   }
```

12.4 Choices

12.4.1 Radio Buttons

In this section you will see how to present a finite set of choices to the user. If the choices are mutually exclusive, you use a set of *radio buttons*. In a radio button set, only one button can be selected at one time. When the user selects another button in the same set, the old selection is automatically turned off. (These buttons are called radio buttons because they work like the station selector buttons on a car radio: if you select a new station, the old station is automatically deselected.) For example, in Figure 7, the font sizes are mutually exclusive. You can select small, medium, or large, but not a combination of them.

To create a set of radio buttons, you first create each button individually, and then you add all buttons of the set to a ButtonGroup object:

```
JRadioButton smallButton = new JRadioButton("Small");
JRadioButton mediumButton = new JRadioButton("Medium");
JRadioButton largeButton = new JRadioButton("Large");

ButtonGroup sizeGroup = new ButtonGroup();
sizeGroup.add(smallButton);
sizeGroup.add(mediumButton);
sizeGroup.add(largeButton);
```

Note that the button group does *not* place the buttons close to each other on the container. The purpose of the button group is simply to find out which buttons to turn off when one of them is turned on. It is still your job to arrange the buttons on the screen.

Your program can turn a button on or off, without the user clicking on it, by calling the setSelected method. If you have a reference to a button, you can call the isSelected method to find out whether the button is currently selected or not. For example,

```
if (largeButton.isSelected()) size = LARGE_SIZE;
```

You should call setSelected(true) on one of the radio buttons in each radio button group before showing the container.

If you have multiple button groups in a container, it is a good idea to group them together visually. You probably use panels to build up your user interface, but the panels themselves are invisible. You can add a border to a panel to make it visible. Figure 7 has an example; the panels containing the radio buttons and check boxes each have a border.

Figure 7

A Combo Box, Radio Buttons, and Check Boxes

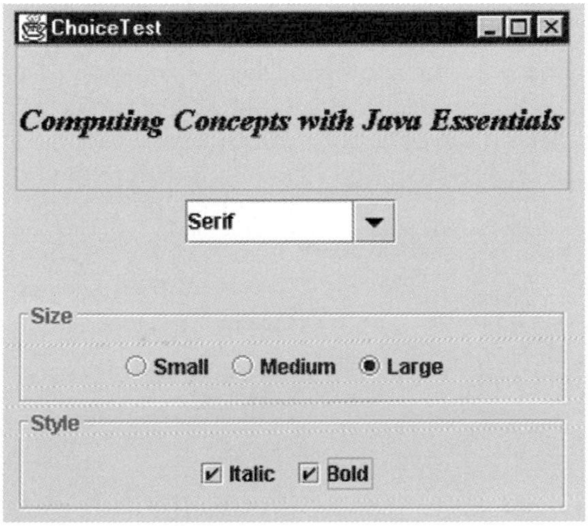

There is a large number of border types. We will show only one variation and leave it to the border enthusiasts to look up the others in the Swing documentation. The `EtchedBorder` class yields a border with a 3-D "etched" effect. You can add a border to any component, but most commonly you apply it to a panel:

```
JPanel sizeGroupPanel = new JPanel();
sizeGroupPanel.setBorder(new EtchedBorder());
```

If you want to add a title to the border, you need to construct a `TitledBorder`. Swing borders can be layered, similar to stream objects (discussed in Chapter 13). You make a titled border by supplying a basic border and then the title you want. Here is a typical example:

```
sizeGroupPanel.setBorder(new TitledBorder(new EtchedBorder(),
    "Size"));
```

12.4.2 Check Boxes

The choices for "Bold" and "Italic" in Figure 7 are *not* exclusive. You can choose either, both, or neither. Therefore, they are implemented as a set of separate *check boxes*. Radio buttons and check boxes have different visual appearances. Radio buttons are round and have a black dot when selected. Check boxes are square and have a check mark when selected. (Strictly speaking, the appearance depends on the chosen look and feel. It is possible to create a different look and feel in which check boxes have a different shape or in which they give off a particular sound when selected.)

You construct a check box by giving the name in the constructor:

```
JCheckBox italicCheckBox = new JCheckBox("Italic");
```

Do not place check boxes inside a button group.

12.4.3 Combo Boxes

If you have a large number of choices, you don't want to make a set of radio buttons, because that would take up a lot of space. Instead, you can use a *combo box*. When you click on the arrow of a combo box, a list of selections is displayed, and you can choose one of them (see Figure 8). If the combo box is *editable*, you can also type in

Figure 8

An Opened Combo Box

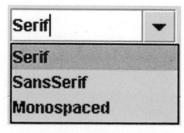

your own selection. To make a combo box editable, call the **setEditable** method. This component is called a combo box because it is a combination of a list and a text field.

You add strings to a combo box with the **addItem** method.

```
JComboBox facenameCombo = new JComboBox();
facenameCombo.addItem("Serif");
facenameCombo.addItem("SansSerif");
. . .
```

You get the item that the user has selected by calling the **getSelectedItem** method. However, since combo boxes can store other objects besides strings, the **getSelectedItem** method has return type **Object**. Hence you must cast the returned value back to **String**.

```
String selectedString = (String)facenameCombo.getSelectedItem();
```

You can select an item for the user with the **setSelectedItem** method.

Radio buttons, check boxes, and combo boxes generate an **ActionEvent** whenever the user selects an item. If you share a listener among components, you can then call the **getSource** method to find out which component caused the event. In the following program, we don't even care which component was clicked. Whenever the user clicks on any one of them, we simply ask each component for its current content, using the **isSelected** and **getSelectedItem** methods. We then redraw the text sample with the new font.

Program ChoiceTest.java

```
import java.awt.Container;
import java.awt.Font;
import java.awt.GridLayout;
import java.awt.event.ActionEvent;
import java.awt.event.ActionListener;
import java.awt.event.WindowAdapter;
import java.awt.event.WindowEvent;
import javax.swing.ButtonGroup;
import javax.swing.JButton;
import javax.swing.JCheckBox;
import javax.swing.JComboBox;
import javax.swing.JFrame;
import javax.swing.JLabel;
import javax.swing.JPanel;
import javax.swing.JRadioButton;
import javax.swing.JTextField;
import javax.swing.border.EtchedBorder;
import javax.swing.border.TitledBorder;
```

```java
public class ChoiceTest
{  public static void main(String[] args)
   {  ChoiceFrame frame = new ChoiceFrame();
      frame.setTitle("ChoiceTest");
      frame.show();
   }
}

class ChoiceFrame extends JFrame
{  public ChoiceFrame()
   {  final int DEFAULT_FRAME_WIDTH = 300;
      final int DEFAULT_FRAME_HEIGHT = 300;
      setSize(DEFAULT_FRAME_WIDTH, DEFAULT_FRAME_HEIGHT);

      addWindowListener(new WindowCloser());

      // construct components

      sampleField = new JTextField
         ("Computing Concepts with Java Essentials");
      sampleField.setEditable(false);

      ChoiceListener listener = new ChoiceListener();

      facenameCombo = new JComboBox();
      facenameCombo.addItem("Serif");
      facenameCombo.addItem("SansSerif");
      facenameCombo.addItem("Monospaced");
      facenameCombo.setEditable(true);
      facenameCombo.addActionListener(listener);

      italicCheckBox = new JCheckBox("Italic");
      italicCheckBox.addActionListener(listener);

      boldCheckBox = new JCheckBox("Bold");
      boldCheckBox.addActionListener(listener);

      smallButton = new JRadioButton("Small");
      smallButton.setSelected(true);
      smallButton.addActionListener(listener);

      mediumButton = new JRadioButton("Medium");
      mediumButton.addActionListener(listener);

      largeButton = new JRadioButton("Large");
      largeButton.addActionListener(listener);

      // add radio buttons to button group
```

```
ButtonGroup sizeGroup = new ButtonGroup();
sizeGroup.add(smallButton);
sizeGroup.add(mediumButton);
sizeGroup.add(largeButton);

// add components to panels

JPanel facenamePanel = new JPanel();
facenamePanel.add(facenameCombo);

JPanel sizeGroupPanel = new JPanel();
sizeGroupPanel.add(smallButton);
sizeGroupPanel.add(mediumButton);
sizeGroupPanel.add(largeButton);
sizeGroupPanel.setBorder
   (new TitledBorder(new EtchedBorder(), "Size"));

JPanel styleGroupPanel = new JPanel();
styleGroupPanel.add(italicCheckBox);
styleGroupPanel.add(boldCheckBox);
styleGroupPanel.setBorder
   (new TitledBorder(new EtchedBorder(), "Style"));

// line up component panels

JPanel southPanel = new JPanel();
southPanel.setLayout(new GridLayout(3, 1));
southPanel.add(facenamePanel);
southPanel.add(sizeGroupPanel);
southPanel.add(styleGroupPanel);

// add panels to content pane

Container contentPane = getContentPane();
contentPane.add(sampleField, "Center");
contentPane.add(southPanel, "South");

setSampleFont();
}

/**
   Gets user choice for font name, style, and size
   and sets the font of the text field.
*/
public void setSampleFont()
{  // get font name

   String facename
      = (String)facenameCombo.getSelectedItem();
```

```
      // get font style

      int style = 0;
      if (italicCheckBox.isSelected())
         style = style + Font.ITALIC;
      if (boldCheckBox.isSelected())
         style = style + Font.BOLD;

      // get font size

      final int SMALL_SIZE = 12;
      final int MEDIUM_SIZE = 16;
      final int LARGE_SIZE = 24;

      int size = 0;
      if (smallButton.isSelected())
         size = SMALL_SIZE;
      else if (mediumButton.isSelected())
         size = MEDIUM_SIZE;
      else if (largeButton.isSelected())
         size = LARGE_SIZE;

      // set font of text field

      sampleField.setFont(new Font(facename, style, size));
      sampleField.repaint();
   }

   private JTextField sampleField;
   private JCheckBox italicCheckBox;
   private JCheckBox boldCheckBox;
   private JRadioButton smallButton;
   private JRadioButton mediumButton;
   private JRadioButton largeButton;
   private JComboBox facenameCombo;

   private class ChoiceListener implements ActionListener
   {  public void actionPerformed(ActionEvent event)
      {  setSampleFont();
      }
   }

   private class WindowCloser extends WindowAdapter
   {  public void windowClosing(WindowEvent event)
      {  System.exit(0);
      }
   }
}
```

12.5 Menus

Everyone who has ever used a graphical user interface is familiar with pulldown menus (see Figure 9). In Java, it is easy to create these menus. The container for the top-level menu items is called a *menu bar* in the Java world. You create a menu bar and attach it to the frame:

```
public class MyFrame extends JFrame
{  public MyFrame()
   {  JMenuBar menuBar = new JMenuBar();
      setJMenuBar(menuBar);
      . . .
   }
}
```

Then you add menus to the menu bar:

```
JMenu fileMenu = new JMenu("File");
menuBar.add(fileMenu);
```

A *menu* is a collection of *menu items* and more menus. You add menu items and submenus with the **add** method:

```
JMenuItem fileNewMenuItem = new JMenuItem("New");
fileMenu.add(fileNewMenuItem);
```

Figure 9

Pulldown Menus

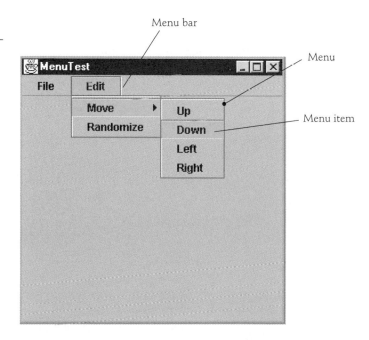

A menu item has no further submenus. When the user selects a menu item, the menu item sends an action event. Therefore, you want to add a listener to each menu item:

```
fileNewMenuItem.addActionListener(fileNewListener);
```

You add action listeners only to menu items, not to menus or the menu bar. When the user clicks on a menu name and a submenu opens, no action event is sent.

The following program builds up a small but typical menu and traps the action events from the menu items.

Program MenuTest.java

```java
import java.awt.Container;
import java.awt.Graphics;
import java.awt.Graphics2D;
import java.awt.Rectangle;
import java.awt.event.ActionEvent;
import java.awt.event.ActionListener;
import java.awt.event.WindowAdapter;
import java.awt.event.WindowEvent;
import java.util.Random;
import javax.swing.JFrame;
import javax.swing.JMenu;
import javax.swing.JMenuBar;
import javax.swing.JMenuItem;
import javax.swing.JPanel;

public class MenuTest
{  public static void main(String[] args)
   {  MenuFrame frame = new MenuFrame();
      frame.setTitle("MenuTest");
      frame.show();
   }
}

class MenuFrame extends JFrame
{  public MenuFrame()
   {  final int DEFAULT_FRAME_WIDTH = 300;
      final int DEFAULT_FRAME_HEIGHT = 300;
      setSize(DEFAULT_FRAME_WIDTH, DEFAULT_FRAME_HEIGHT);

      addWindowListener(new WindowCloser());

      // add drawing panel to content pane

      panel = new RectanglePanel();
      Container contentPane = getContentPane();
      contentPane.add(panel, "Center");

      // construct menu
```

```java
            JMenuBar menuBar = new JMenuBar();
            setJMenuBar(menuBar);

            JMenu fileMenu = new JMenu("File");
            menuBar.add(fileMenu);

            MenuListener listener = new MenuListener();

            newMenuItem = new JMenuItem("New");
            fileMenu.add(newMenuItem);
            newMenuItem.addActionListener(listener);

            exitMenuItem = new JMenuItem("Exit");
            fileMenu.add(exitMenuItem);
            exitMenuItem.addActionListener(listener);

            JMenu editMenu = new JMenu("Edit");
            menuBar.add(editMenu);

            JMenuItem moveMenu = new JMenu("Move");
            editMenu.add(moveMenu);

            upMenuItem = new JMenuItem("Up");
            moveMenu.add(upMenuItem);
            upMenuItem.addActionListener(listener);

            downMenuItem = new JMenuItem("Down");
            moveMenu.add(downMenuItem);
            downMenuItem.addActionListener(listener);

            leftMenuItem = new JMenuItem("Left");
            moveMenu.add(leftMenuItem);
            leftMenuItem.addActionListener(listener);

            rightMenuItem = new JMenuItem("Right");
            moveMenu.add(rightMenuItem);
            rightMenuItem.addActionListener(listener);

            randomizeMenuItem = new JMenuItem("Randomize");
            editMenu.add(randomizeMenuItem);
            randomizeMenuItem.addActionListener(listener);
        }

        private JMenuItem exitMenuItem;
        private JMenuItem newMenuItem;
        private JMenuItem upMenuItem;
        private JMenuItem downMenuItem;
        private JMenuItem leftMenuItem;
        private JMenuItem rightMenuItem;
```

```java
      private JMenuItem randomizeMenuItem;
      private RectanglePanel panel;

      private class MenuListener implements ActionListener
      {  public void actionPerformed(ActionEvent event)
         {  // find the menu that was selected

            Object source = event.getSource();

            if (source == exitMenuItem)
               System.exit(0);
            else if (source == newMenuItem)
               panel.reset();
            else if (source == upMenuItem)
               panel.moveRectangle(0, -1);
            else if (source == downMenuItem)
               panel.moveRectangle(0, 1);
            else if (source == leftMenuItem)
               panel.moveRectangle(-1, 0);
            else if (source == rightMenuItem)
               panel.moveRectangle(1, 0);
            else if (source == randomizeMenuItem)
               panel.randomize();
         }
      }

      private class WindowCloser extends WindowAdapter
      {  public void windowClosing(WindowEvent event)
         {  System.exit(0);
         }
      }
}

class RectanglePanel extends JPanel
{  public RectanglePanel()
   {  rect = new Rectangle(0, 0, RECT_WIDTH, RECT_HEIGHT);
   }

   public void paintComponent(Graphics g)
   {  super.paintComponent(g);
      Graphics2D g2 = (Graphics2D)g;
      g2.draw(rect);
   }

   /**
      Resets the rectangle to the top left corner.
   */
   public void reset()
   {  rect.setLocation(0, 0);
      repaint();
   }
```

```
/**
    Moves the rectangle to a random position.
*/
public void randomize()
{  Random generator = new Random();
   rect.setLocation(generator.nextInt(getWidth()),
      generator.nextInt(getHeight()));
   repaint();
}

/**
    Moves the rectangle and repaints it. The rectangle
    is moved by multiples of its full width or height.
    @param dx the number of width units
    @param dy the number of height units
*/
public void moveRectangle(int dx, int dy)
{  rect.translate(dx * RECT_WIDTH, dy * RECT_HEIGHT);
   repaint();
}

private Rectangle rect;
private static int RECT_WIDTH = 20;
private static int RECT_HEIGHT = 30;
}
```

12.6 Example: Exploring the Swing Documentation

In the preceding sections, you saw the basic properties of the most common user interface components. We purposefully omitted many options and variations to simplify the discussion. You can go a long way by using only the simplest properties of these components. If you want to implement a more sophisticated effect, you can look inside the Swing documentation. However, you will probably find the documentation quite intimidating at first glance. The purpose of this section is to show you how you can use the documentation to your advantage without becoming overwhelmed.

Recall the **Color** class that was introduced in Chapter 4. Every combination of red, green, and blue values represents a different color. It should be fun to mix your own colors, with a slider for the red, green, and blue values (see Figure 10).

The Swing user interface toolkit has a large set of user interface components. How do you know whether there is a slider? You can buy a book that illustrates all Swing components, such as [2]. Or you can run the sample application included in the Java Development Kit that shows off all Swing components (see Figure 11). Or you can look at the names of all of the classes that start with J and decide that JSlider may be a good candidate.

Next, you need to ask yourself a few questions:

◆ How do I construct a JSlider?
◆ How can I get notified when the user has moved it?
◆ How can I tell to which value the user has set it?

If you can answer these questions, then you can put a slider to good use. Once you achieve that, you can fritter away more time and find out how to set tick marks or otherwise enhance the visual beauty of your creation.

When you look at the documentation of the JSlider class, you will probably not be happy. There are over 50 methods in the JSlider class and over 250 inherited methods, and some of the method descriptions look downright scary, such as the one in Figure 12. Apparently some folks out there are concerned about the valueIsAdjusting property, whatever that may be, and the designers of this class felt it necessary to supply a method to tweak that property. Until you too feel that need, your best bet is to ignore this method. As the author of an introductory book, it pains me to tell you to ignore certain facts. But the truth of the matter is that the Java library is so large and complex that nobody understands it in its entirety, not even the designers of Java themselves. You need to develop the ability to separate fundamental concepts from ephemeral minutiae. For example, it is important that you understand the concept of event handling. Once you understand the concept, you can ask the question, "What event does the slider send when the user moves it?" But it is not important that you memorize how to set tick marks or that you know how to implement a slider with a custom look and feel.

Figure 10

A Color Mixer

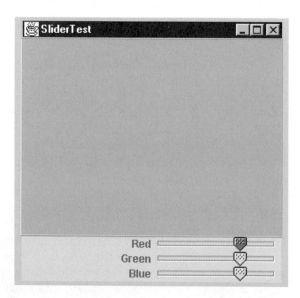

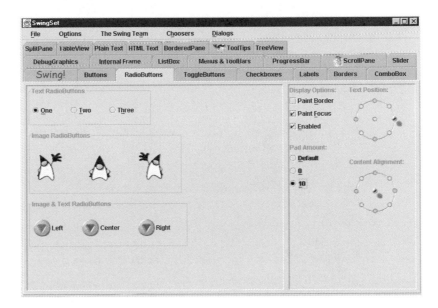

Figure 11

A Demonstration Application from
the Java Development Kit

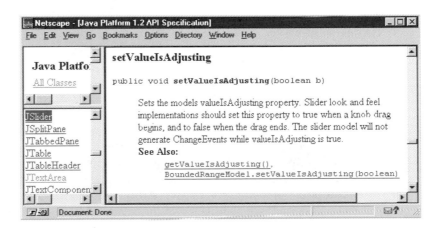

Figure 12

A Mysterious Entry in the JSlider
Documentation

Let us go back to our fundamental questions. In Java 2, there are six constructors for the `JSlider` class. (There may well be more by the time you read this.) You want to learn about one or two of them. You need to strike a balance somewhere between the trivial and the bizarre. Consider

`public JSlider()`
    Creates a horizontal slider with the range 0 to 100 and an initial value of 50.

Maybe that is good enough for now, but what if you want another range or initial value? It seems too limited.

On the other side of the spectrum, there is

`public JSlider(BoundedRangeModel brm)`
    Creates a horizontal slider using the specified <u>BoundedRangeModel</u>.

Whoa! What is that? You can click on the **BoundedRangeModel** link to get a long explanation of this class. This appears to be some internal mechanism for the Swing implementors. Let's try to avoid this constructor if we can. Looking further, we find

`public JSlider(int min, int max, int value)`
    Creates a horizontal slider using the specified min, max, and value.

This sounds general enough to be useful and simple enough to be usable. You might want to stash away the fact that you can have vertical sliders as well.

Next, you want to know what events a slider generates. There is no **addAction-Listener** method. That makes sense. Adjusting a slider seems different from clicking a button, and Swing uses a different event type for these events. There is a method

`public void addChangeListener(ChangeListener l)`

Click on the **ChangeListener** link to find out more about this interface. It has a single method

`void stateChanged(ChangeEvent e)`

Apparently, that method is called whenever the user moves the slider. What is a **ChangeEvent**? Once again, click on the link, to find out that this event class has *no* methods of its own, but it inherits the **getSource** method from its superclass **EventObject**. Now we have a plan: Add a change event listener to each slider. When the slider is changed, the **stateChanged** method is called. Find out the new value of the slider. Recompute the color value and repaint the color panel. That way, the color panel is continually repainted as the user moves one of the sliders.

To compute the color value, you will still need to get the current value of the slider. Look at all the methods that start with **get**. Sure enough, you find

`public int getValue()`
    Returns the slider's value.

Now you know everything to write the program. The program uses one new constructor, two new methods, and one event listener of a new type. Of course, now that you have "tasted blood", you may want to add those tick marks—see Exercise P12.15.

Program SliderTest.java

```java
import java.awt.Color;
import java.awt.Container;
import java.awt.GridLayout;
import java.awt.event.WindowAdapter;
import java.awt.event.WindowEvent;
import javax.swing.JFrame;
import javax.swing.JLabel;
import javax.swing.JPanel;
import javax.swing.JSlider;
import javax.swing.SwingConstants;
import javax.swing.event.ChangeListener;
import javax.swing.event.ChangeEvent;

public class SliderTest
{  public static void main(String[] args)
    {  SliderFrame frame = new SliderFrame();
        frame.setTitle("SliderTest");
        frame.show();
    }
}

class SliderFrame extends JFrame
{  public SliderFrame()
    {  final int DEFAULT_FRAME_WIDTH = 300;
        final int DEFAULT_FRAME_HEIGHT = 300;
        setSize(DEFAULT_FRAME_WIDTH, DEFAULT_FRAME_HEIGHT);

        addWindowListener(new WindowCloser());

        // construct components

        colorPanel = new JPanel();

        ColorListener listener = new ColorListener();

        redSlider = new JSlider(0, 100, 100);
        redSlider.addChangeListener(listener);

        greenSlider = new JSlider(0, 100, 70);
        greenSlider.addChangeListener(listener);

        blueSlider = new JSlider(0, 100, 70);
        blueSlider.addChangeListener(listener);
```

```
      // fill content pane

      JPanel southPanel = new JPanel();
      southPanel.setLayout(new GridLayout(3, 2));
      southPanel.add(new JLabel("Red",
         SwingConstants.RIGHT));
      southPanel.add(redSlider);
      southPanel.add(new JLabel("Green",
         SwingConstants.RIGHT));
      southPanel.add(greenSlider);
      southPanel.add(new JLabel("Blue",
         SwingConstants.RIGHT));
      southPanel.add(blueSlider);

      Container contentPane = getContentPane();
      contentPane.add(colorPanel, "Center");
      contentPane.add(southPanel, "South");

      setSampleColor();
   }

   /**
      Reads the slider values and sets the panel to
      the selected color.
   */
   public void setSampleColor()
   {  // read slider values

      float red = 0.01F * redSlider.getValue();
      float green = 0.01F * greenSlider.getValue();
      float blue = 0.01F * blueSlider.getValue();

      // set panel background to selected color

      colorPanel.setBackground(new Color(red, green, blue));
      colorPanel.repaint();
   }

   private JPanel colorPanel;
   private JSlider redSlider;
   private JSlider greenSlider;
   private JSlider blueSlider;

   private class ColorListener implements ChangeListener
   {  public void stateChanged(ChangeEvent event)
      {  setSampleColor();
      }
   }
```

```
        private class WindowCloser extends WindowAdapter
        {  public void windowClosing(WindowEvent event)
           {  System.exit(0);
           }
        }
    }
}
```

Random Fact 12.1

Visual Programming

Programming as you know it involves typing code into a text editor and then running it. A programmer must be familiar with the programming language to write even the simplest of programs. When programming in graphics, one must compute every screen position.

A new *visual* style of programming makes this much easier. When you use a visual programming environment, such as Visual Café or JBuilder, you use your mouse to specify where text, buttons, and other fields should appear on the screen (see Figure 13). You still need to do some programming. You need to write code for every event. For example, you can drag a button to its desired location, but you still need to specify what should happen when the user clicks on it.

Visual programming offers two benefits. It is much easier to lay out a screen by dragging buttons and images with the mouse than it is to compute the coordinates in a program. The

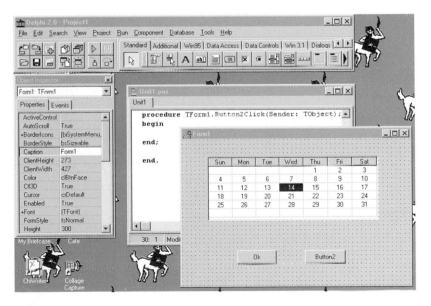

Figure 13

Visual Programming Environment

visual programming environment also makes it easy to place objects with sophisticated behavior onto the screen. For example, a calendar object can show the current month's calendar, with buttons to move to the next or previous month; all of that has been preprogrammed by someone (usually the hard way, using a traditional programming language), but you can add a fully working calendar to your program simply by dragging it off a toolbar and dropping it into your program.

A prebuilt component such as a calendar chooser usually has a large number of *properties* that you can simply choose from a table. For example, you can simply check whether you want the calendar to be weekly or monthly. The provider of the calendar component had to work hard to include both cases in the code, but the programmer using the component does not have to care. When written in Java, these prepackaged components are called *Java Beans*.

User interface design in a visual environment is *much* easier than writing the equivalent code in Java. In days a programmer can design an attractive user interface that would take weeks to complete by writing code. These systems are highly recommended for user interface programming.

Chapter Summary

1. You arrange user interface components by placing them inside containers. Containers can be placed inside larger containers. Each container has a *layout manager* that directs the arrangement of its components.

2. Three useful layout managers are the border layout, flow layout, and grid layout.

3. The content pane of a frame or applet has a border layout by default. A panel has a flow layout by default. However, you can set another layout manager in place of the default.

4. By default, panels use a flow layout. With that layout the individual components of a panel stay at their preferred size. If you like, you can place a border around the panel to group its contents visually.

5. Buttons and menu items can have string labels and icons. They generate action events. You can have the same listener listen to multiple buttons or menu items. If you do, you should use the button references, not use the string labels, to identify the buttons.

6. You can display text in text fields and multiline text areas.

7. To let a user select from a finite set of choices, you can use a set of radio buttons or a combo box if the choices are mutually exclusive, or a set of check boxes if they can be combined.

8. You should learn to navigate the Java documentation to find out more about user interface components.

Further Reading

[1] Cay S. Horstmann and Gary Cornell, *Core Java 1.2 Volume 1: Fundamentals,* Prentice Hall, 1999.

[2] Kim Topley, *Core Java Foundation Classes,* Prentice Hall, 1998.

Classes. Objects. and Methods Introduced in This Chapter

```
java.awt.BorderLayout
java.awt.Container
    setLayout
java.awt.FlowLayout
java.awt.Frame
    setMenuBar
java.awt.GridLayout
javax.swing.AbstractButton
    addActionListener
    isSelected
    setSelected
javax.swing.ButtonGroup
    add
javax.swing.EtchedBorder
javax.swing.ImageIcon
javax.swing.JCheckBox
javax.swing.JComboBox
    addItem
    getSelectedItem
    isEditable
    setEditable
javax.swing.JComponent
    setBorder
    setFont
javax.swing.JLabel
javax.swing.JMenu
    add
javax.swing.JMenuBar
    add
javax.swing.JMenuItem
javax.swing.JRadioButton
javax.swing.JSlider
    addChangeListener
    getValue
javax.swing.JTextArea
javax.swing.border.TitledBorder
```

```
javax.swing.event.ChangeEvent
 javax.swing.event.ChangeListener
   stateChanged
javax.swing.text.JTextComponent
  isEditable
  setEditable
```

Review Exercises

Exercise R12.1. What is a layout manager? What is the advantage of a layout manager over telling the container "place this component at position (x,y)"?

Exercise R12.2. In Figure 7, indicate how the content pane has been subdivided into containers, and indicate the layout manager for each container.

Exercise R12.3. In Figure 10, indicate how the content pane has been subdivided into containers, and indicate the layout manager for each container.

Exercise R12.4. The SliderTest program uses a grid layout manager. Explain a drawback of the grid that is apparent from Figure 10. What could you do to overcome this drawback?

Exercise R12.5. What happens when you place a single button into the "Center" area of a container that uses a border layout? What happens if you place multiple buttons into the "South" area? Try it out, by writing a small sample program, if you aren't sure about the answer.

Exercise R12.6. Can you add icons to check boxes, radio buttons, and combo boxes? Browse the Java documentation to find out.

Exercise R12.7. Why is it not a good idea to identify buttons and menus by their label text in a listener method? Give *two* better alternatives.

Exercise R12.8. What events does a **JTextArea** generate? How can you tell when a user is done entering text into it?

Exercise R12.9. What is the difference between radio buttons and check boxes?

Exercise R12.10. Why do you need a button group for radio buttons but not for check boxes?

Exercise R12.11. What is the difference between a menu bar, a menu, and a menu item?

Exercise R12.12. When browsing through the Java documentation for more information about sliders, we ignored the `JSlider` default constructor. Why? Would it have worked in our sample program?

Exercise R12.13. How do you construct a vertical slider? Consult the Swing documentation for an answer.

Exercise R12.14. Why doesn't a slider send out action events?

Exercise R12.15. What component would you use to show a set of choices, just as in a combo box, but so that several items are visible at the same time? Run the Swing demo app or look at a book with Swing example programs to find the answer.

Exercise R12.16. How many Swing user interface components are there? Look at the Java documentation to get an approximate answer.

Exercise R12.17. How many methods does the `JProgressBar` component have? Be sure to count inherited methods. Look at the Java documentation.

Programming Exercises

Exercise P12.1. Write an application with three buttons labeled "Red", "Green", and "Blue" that changes the background color of a panel in the center of the content pane to red, green, or blue.

Exercise P12.2. Add icons to the buttons of the preceding Exercise.

Exercise P12.3. Write a calculator application. Use a grid layout to arrange buttons for the digits and for the $+ - \times \div$ operations. Add a text field to display the result.

Exercise P12.4. Write an application with three radio buttons labeled "Red", "Green", and "Blue" that changes the background color of a panel in the center of the content pane to red, green, or blue.

Exercise P12.5. Write an application with three check boxes labeled "Red", "Green", and "Blue" that adds a red, green, or blue component to the the background color of a panel in the center of the content pane. This application can display a total of eight color combinations.

Exercise P12.6. Write an application with a combo box containing three items labeled "Red", "Green", and "Blue" that changes the background color of a panel in the center of the content pane to red, green, or blue.

Exercise P12.7. Modify the Eggs application of Chapter 10 to replace the text field with buttons "Fewer" and "More" that generate fewer or more random eggs. Each time the user clicks on "Fewer", the egg count should be halved. Each time the user clicks on "More", the count should be doubled.

Exercise P12.8. Modify the Eggs application of Chapter 10 to replace the text field with a slider to generate fewer or more random eggs.

Exercise P12.9. Write an application with three labeled text fields, one each for the initial amount of a savings account, the annual interest rate, and the number of years. Add a button "Calculate" and a read-only text field to display the result, namely the balance of the savings account after the given number of years.

Exercise P12.10. Add a bar graph to the preceding exercise that shows the balance after the end of each year.

Exercise P12.11. Write a program that contains a text area, a button "Draw Graph", and a panel that draws a bar chart of the numbers that a user typed into the text area. Use a string tokenizer to break up the text in the text area.

Exercise P12.12. Write a program that lets users design charts such as the following:

```
┌──────────────────────────────────────────┐
│ Golden Gate                              │
└──────────────────────────────────────────┘
┌──────────────────────┐
│ Brooklyn             │
└──────────────────────┘
┌──────────────────────────────┐
│ Delaware Memorial            │
└──────────────────────────────┘
┌──────────────────────────────────────┐
│ Mackinac                             │
└──────────────────────────────────────┘
```

Use appropriate components to ask for the length, label, and color, then apply them when the user clicks an "Add Bar" button.

Exercise P12.13. Write a program that lets users create pie charts. Design your own user interface.

Exercise P12.14. Write a program that lets users manipulate a set of cars on the screen. The screen contains multiple cars at different positions. When the user clicks on a car, that car becomes active. Have menu items to move the active car up, down, left, and right and to remove it. Have a menu item to add a new car in a random position. The newly added car becomes the active one. Finally, have a menu item to exit the program.

Exercise P12.15. In the slider test program, add a set of tick marks to each slider that show the exact slider position.

Streams and Exceptions

Chapter Goals

- ◆ To learn how to throw and catch exceptions

- ◆ To be able to read and write files

- ◆ To become familiar with the concepts of text and binary streams

- ◆ To be able to process the command line

- ◆ To learn about encryption

- ◆ To be able to read and write objects using serialization

All of the programs we have discussed until now read their input from the keyboard and mouse and displayed their output on the screen. For console programs, you are able to read from a file or write to a file, by using redirection (see Productivity Hint 6.1). That method for accessing files is useful but still limited. In this chapter you will learn how to write Java programs that interact with disk files and other sources of bytes and characters.

13.1 Streams, Readers, and Writers

There are two fundamentally different ways to store data. Data can be encoded in *text* or *binary* format. In text format, data items are represented in human-readable form, as a sequence of *characters*. For example, the integer 12,345 is stored as the sequence of five characters:

'1' '2' '3' '4' '5'

In binary form, data items are represented in *bytes*. A byte is composed of 8 bits and can denote one of 256 values. For example, in binary format, the integer 12345 is stored as a sequence of four *bytes*:

0 0 48 57

(because $12345 = 48 \cdot 256 + 57$).

If you store information in text form, as a sequence of characters, you need to use the `Reader` and `Writer` class and their subclasses to process input and output. If you store information in binary form, as a sequence of bytes, you use the `InputStream` and `OutputStream` classes and their subclasses.

Text input and output are more convenient for humans because it is easier to produce input (just by using a text editor) and it is easier to check that output is correct (just by looking at the output file in an editor). However, binary storage is more compact and more efficient.

To read text data from a disk file, you create a `FileReader` object:

```
FileReader reader = new FileReader("input.txt");
```

To read binary data from a disk file, you create a `FileInputStream` object instead:

```
FileInputStream inputStream = new FileInputStream("input.dat");
```

Similarly, you use `FileWriter` and `FileOutputStream` objects to write data to a disk file in text or binary form:

```
FileWriter writer = new FileWriter("output.txt");
FileOutputStream outputStream =
    new FileOutputStream("output.dat");
```

All these classes are defined in the `java.io` package.

The `Reader` class has a method `read` to read a single character at a time. (The `FileReader` class uses an overridden method to obtain the characters from a disk file.) However, the `read` method actually returns an `int` so that it can signal either that a character has been read or that the end of input has been reached. At the end of input, **read** returns -1. Otherwise, it returns the character (as an integer between 0 and 65535). You should test the return value, and if it is not -1, cast it to a **char**:

```
Reader reader = . . .;
int next = reader.read();
char c;
if (next != -1)
    c = (char)next;
```

The **InputStream** class also has a method **read** to read a single byte. The method also returns an **int**, namely either the byte that was input (as an integer between 0 and 255) or the integer -1 if the end of the input stream has been reached. You should test the return value, and if it is not -1, cast it to a **byte**:

```
InputStream in = . . .;
int next = in.read();
byte b;
if (next != -1)
    b = (byte)next;
```

Similarly, the **Writer** and **FileOutputStream** classes have a **write** method to write a single character or byte.

These basic methods are the only input and output methods that the file input and output classes provide. The Java stream package is built upon the principle that each class should have a very focused responsibility. The job of a **FileInputStream** is to interact with files. Its job is to *get* data, not to analyze it. If you want to read numbers, strings, or other objects, you have to combine the class with other classes whose responsibility is to group individual bytes or characters together into numbers, strings, and objects. You will see those classes later in this chapter.

Common Error 13.1

Backslashes in File Names

When you specify a file name as a constant string, and the name contains backslash characters (as in a Windows filename), you must supply each backslash *twice:*

```
in = new FileReader("c:\\homework\\input.dat");
```

Recall that a single backslash inside quoted strings is an *escape character* that is combined with another character to form a special meaning, such as \n for a newline character. The \\ combination denotes a single backslash.

When a user enters a file name into a string variable, however, the user should not type the backslash twice.

Common Error 13.2

Negative byte Values

In Java, the **byte** type is a *signed* type. There are 256 values of the **byte** type, from -128 to 127. The top bit of the byte is the *sign bit*. If it is on, the number is negative. In converting an integer into a byte, only the least significant byte of the integer is taken, and the remaining bytes are ignored. The result can be negative even though the integer was positive. For example,

```
int n = 233; // binary 00000000 00000000 00000000 11101001
byte b = (byte)n; // binary   11101001, sign bit is on
if (b == n) . . . // not true! b is negative, n is positive
```

When the byte is converted back to an integer, then the result is still negative. In particular, it is *different* from the original.

Here is an even trickier case. Consider this test:

```
int next = in.read();
byte b = (byte)next;
if (b == 'é') . . .
```

This test is *never* true, *even if* next was equal to the Unicode value for the 'é' character. That Unicode value happens to be 233, but a single byte is always a value between −128 and 127. American readers won't be too concerned, because all characters and symbols used in American English have Unicode values in the "safe" range between 1 and 127, but Western European programmers who use characters with Unicode values between 128 and 255 find this a source of continual frustration.

Random Fact 13.1

International Alphabets

The English alphabet is pretty simple: upper- and lowercase *a* to *z*. Other European languages have accent marks and special characters. For example, German has three so-called *umlaut* characters (ä, ö, ü) and a *double-s* character ß. These are not optional frills; you couldn't write a page of German text without using these characters a few times. German computer keyboards have keys for these characters (see Figure 1).

Figure 1

A German Keyboard

This poses a problem for computer users and designers. The American standard character encoding (called ASCII, for American Standard Code for Information Interchange) specifies 128 codes: 52 upper- and lowercase characters, 10 digits, 32 typographical symbols, and 34 control characters (such as space, newline, and 32 others for controlling printers and other devices). The umlaut and double-s are not among them. Some German data processing systems replace seldom-used ASCII characters with German letters: [\ ] { | } are replaced with Ä Ö Ü ä ö ü ß. While most people can live without these characters, programmers using Java definitely cannot. Other encoding schemes take advantage of the fact that one byte can encode 256 different characters, of which only 128 are standardized by ASCII. Unfortunately, there are multiple incompatible standards for such encodings, resulting in a certain amount of aggravation among European computer users (and their American email penpals).

Many countries don't use the Roman script at all. Russian, Greek, Hebrew, Arabic, and Thai letters, to name just a few, have completely different shapes (see Figure 2). To complicate matters, Hebrew and Arabic are typed from right to left. Each of these alphabets has between 30 and 100 letters, and the countries using them have established encoding standards for them.

The situation is much more dramatic in languages that use the Chinese script: the Chinese dialects, Japanese, and Korean. The Chinese script is not alphabetic but *ideographic*—a character represents an idea or thing rather than a single sound. (See Figure 3; can you identify the characters for soup, chicken, and wonton?) Most words are made up of one, two, or three of these ideographic characters. Over 50,000 ideographs are known, of which about 20,000 are in active use. Therefore, two bytes are needed to encode them. China, Taiwan, Japan, and Korea have incompatible encoding standards for them. (Japanese and Korean writing use a mixture of native syllabic and Chinese ideographic characters.)

The inconsistencies among character encodings have been a major nuisance for international electronic communication and for software manufacturers vying for a global market. Between 1988 and 1991 a consortium of hardware and software manufacturers developed a uniform 16-bit encoding scheme called *Unicode* that is capable of encoding text in essentially all written languages of the world [1]. About 39,000 characters have been given codes, including 21,000 Chinese ideographs. Since a 16-bit code can incorporate 65,000 codes, there is ample space for expansion. Future versions of the standard will be able to encode such scripts as the Cherokee syllabary and the ancient Javanese script.

All Unicode characters can be stored in Java strings, but which ones can actually be displayed depends on your computer system.

13.2 Reading and Writing Text Files

In the previous section you learned how to write data to a text file. You construct a `FileWriter` object from the file name:

```
FileWriter writer = new FileWriter("output.txt");
```

Now you can send your output to the file, a character at a time, by calling the `write` method. Of course, you don't have the output available a character at a time. You have the output in the form of numbers or strings. For that reason, you need another class whose task it is to break up numbers and strings into individual characters

Figure 2

The Thai Script

	ฐ	ภ	ะ	เ	๐		เ◌
ก	ฑ	ม	◌ั	แ	๑		แ◌
ข	ฒ	ย	า	โ	๒		โ◌
ฃ	ณ	ร	◌ำ	ใ	๓		ใ◌
ค	ด	ฤ	◌ิ	ไ	๔		ไ◌
ฅ	ต	ล	◌ี	ๅ	๕		
ฆ	ถ	ฦ	◌ึ	ๆ	๖		
ง	ท	ว	◌ื	◌ุ	๗		
จ	ธ	ศ	◌ฺ	◌่	๘		
ฉ	น	ษ	◌ุ	◌๎	๙		
ช	บ	ส	◌.	◌๚	๚		
ซ	ป	ห		◌๛	๛		
ฌ	ผ	ฬ		◌์			
ญ	ฝ	อ		◌ํ			
ฎ	พ	ฮ		◌ฯ			
ฏ	ฟ	ฯ					

CLASSIC SOUPS

		Sm.	Lg.
清燉雞湯	57. House Chicken Soup (Chicken, Celery, Potato, Onion, Carrot)	1.50	2.75
雞　飯　湯	58. Chicken Rice Soup	1.85	3.25
雞　麵　湯	59. Chicken Noodle Soup	1.85	3.25
廣東雲吞	60. Cantonese Wonton Soup	1.50	2.75
蕃茄蛋湯	61. Tomato Clear Egg Drop Soup	1.65	2.95
雲　吞　湯	62. Regular Wonton Soup	1.10	2.10
酸　辣　湯	63. ≥ Hot & Sour Soup	1.10	2.10
蛋　花　湯	64. Egg Drop Soup	1.10	2.10
雲　蛋　湯	65. Egg Drop Wonton Mix	1.10	2.10
豆腐菜湯	66. Tofu Vegetable Soup	NA	3.50
雞玉米湯	67. Chicken Corn Cream Soup	NA	3.50
蟹肉玉米湯	68. Crab Meat Corn Cream Soup	NA	3.50
海　鮮　湯	69. Seafood Soup	NA	3.50

Figure 3

The Chinese Script

and send them to a writer. That class is called a `PrintWriter`. You construct a `PrintWriter` from any `Writer` object:

```
PrintWriter out = new PrintWriter(writer);
```

Now you can use the familiar `print` and `println` methods to print numbers, objects, and strings:

```
out.println(29.95);
out.println(new Rectangle(5, 10, 15, 25));
out.println("Hello, World!");
```

The `print` and `println` methods convert numbers to their decimal string representations and use the `toString` method to convert objects to strings. Strings are broken up into individual characters, and each character is given to the writer. The writer then sends them off to a file, a network connection, or some other destination. Reading text files is unfortunately much less convenient. The Java library supplies no classes to read numbers directly. The best you can do is use the `BufferedReader` class, which has a `readLine` method that lets you read a line at a time. The `readLine` method keeps calling the `read` method of the reader object that you supplied in the constructor, until it has collected an entire input line. Then it returns that line. When all input has been consumed, the `readLine` method returns `null`.

After reading a line of input, you can use the `Integer.parseInt` and `Double.parseDouble` methods to convert the strings you find in the input to numbers.

```
FileReader reader = new FileReader("input.txt");
BufferedReader in = new BufferedReader(reader);
String inputLine = in.readLine();
double x = Double.parseDouble(inputLine);
```

If there are several items in a single input line, you can use the `StringTokenizer` class to break up the input line into multiple strings.

When you are done reading from a file or writing to a file, you should *close* the reader or writer:

```
reader.close();
writer.close();
```

Before you can put these classes to work, you need to know about exception handling. Whenever you deal with input and output, you can run into a great deal of problems that are not of your own making. There may be read errors due to bad network connections, or you may try to write to a disk that has completely filled up. Rather than having each method return an error code (which you might easily forget to check), most methods in the `java.io` package use exceptions to indicate that a failure has occurred. We mentioned exception handling briefly in Chapter 2; will take it up in more detail in the next section.

13.3 An Introduction to Exception Handling

13.3.1 Throwing Exceptions

When a method detects a problematic situation, what should it do? The traditional solution is that the method returns an indicator whether it succeeded or failed. For example, the `readLine` method returns either a string or `null` at the end of input. However, this approach has two problems.

1. The caller may forget to check the return value.
2. The caller may not be able to do anything about the failure.

If the caller forgets to check the return value, a failure notification may go completely undetected. Then the program keeps going, processing faulty information.

If the caller knows about the failure but it cannot do anything about it, it can fail too and let *its* caller worry about it. That would be a real hassle for the programmer, because many method calls would need to be checked for failure. Instead of programming for success,

```
x.doStuff();
```

you would always be programming for failure:

```
if (!x.doStuff()) return false;
```

That is fine when done occasionally, but if you have to check *every* method call, then your programs become very hard to read.

The exception-handling mechanism has been designed to solve these two problems:

1. Exceptions can't be overlooked.
2. Exceptions can be handled by a *competent* handler—not just the caller of the failed method.

Let us look into the details of this mechanism.

First, the good news. When you detect an error condition, your job is really easy. You just throw an appropriate exception object, and you are done. For example, suppose you write a method that reads a product in from a reader:

```
public class Product
{  public void read(BufferedReader in)
      {  // read product name
         name = in.readLine();
         // read product price
         String inputLine = in.readLine();
         price = Double.parseDouble(inputLine);
         // read product score
         inputLine = in.readLine();
         score = Integer.parseInt(inputLine);
      }
      . . .
      private String name;
      private double price;
      private int score;
}
```

What if you reach the end of input?

```
String inputLine = in.readLine();
if (inputLine == null)
   // now what?
```

You can return **false**, but then your method is at the mercy of its caller. The caller might forget to check the return value, and much later some other part of your program will process this faulty **Product** object. Or you can throw an exception.

Throwing an exception is simple. You first need to look for an appropriate exception class. The Java library provides many classes to signal all sorts of exceptional conditions. To signal an unexpected end of file, you can use the **EOFException**, a subclass of the **IOException** class, which denotes input/output errors. You make an object of the exception class, and you *throw* it:

```
String inputLine = readLine();
if (inputLine == null)
{  EOFException exception
      = new EOFException("EOF when reading price");
   throw exception;
}
```

Actually, you don't have to store the exception object in a variable. You can just throw the object that the **new** operator returns:

```
String inputLine = in.readLine();
if (inputLine == null)
    throw new EOFException("EOF when reading price");
```

When you throw an exception, the method exits immediately, just as with a **return** statement. Execution does not continue with the method's caller but with an *exception handler*. That is the topic of the next section.

13.3.2 Catching Exceptions

When an exception is thrown, an exception handler needs to *catch* it. If the exception is not caught, your program terminates. Of course, you don't want your program to die just because some method detected an unexpected error. Therefore, you must install exception handlers for all exceptions that your program might throw.

You install an exception handler with the **try** statement. Each **try** block contains one or more method calls that may cause an exception, and **catch** clauses for all possible exception types that the **try** block is willing to handle. Here is an example:

```
try
{   BufferedReader in
        = new BufferedReader(new InputStreamReader(System.in));
    System.out.println("How old are you?");
    String inputLine = in.readLine();
    int age = Integer.parseInt(inputLine);
    age++;
    System.out.println("Next year, you'll be " + age);
}
catch(IOException e)
{   System.out.println("Input/output error " + e);
}
catch(NumberFormatException e)
{   System.out.println("Input was not a number");
}
```

Java Syntax

13.1 Throwing an Exception

throw *exceptionObject*;

Example:

throw new IllegalArgumentException();

Purpose:
To throw an exception and transfer control to the closest matching **catch** clause

---

In this example, the `try` block contains six statements. There are two potential exceptions that can be thrown in this code. The `readLine` method can throw an `IOException`, and `Integer.parseInt` can throw a `NumberFormatException`. If either of these exceptions is actually thrown, then the rest of the instructions in the `try` block are skipped, and the appropriate `catch` clause is executed. In that case, we inform the user of the source of the problem. In practice, a better way of dealing with the exception would be to give the user another chance to provide a correct input.

When the `catch(IOException e)` block is executed, then some method in the `try` block has failed with an `IOException`, and that exception object is stored in the variable `e`. The `catch` clause can analyze that object to find out more details about the failure. Note that the caught object may belong to a *subclass* of `IOException` (such as `EOFException`). Since all exceptions are subclasses of the class `Throwable`, that means that you can catch all exceptions with a `catch(Throwable e)` clause. However, that is actually not a good idea (see Quality Tip 13.1).

Occasionally, you need to take some action whether or not an exception is thrown. The `finally` construct is used to handle this situation. Here is a typical situation. Suppose a method opens a file, calls one or more methods, and then closes the file:

```
BufferedReader in;
in = new BufferedReader(new FileReader("input.txt"));
readProducts(in);
in.close();
```

Now suppose that one of the methods throws an exception. Then the call to `close` is never executed! You solve this problem by placing the call to `close` inside a `finally` clause:

```
BufferedReader in = null;
try
{  in = new BufferedReader(new FileReader("input.txt"));
   readProducts(in);
}
// optional catch clauses here
finally
{  if (in != null)
      in.close();
}
```

In the normal case, there will be no problem. When the `try` block is completed, the `finally` clause is executed, and the file is closed. However, if an exception occurs, the `finally` clause is also executed before the exception is passed to its handler.

Notice that the `finally` clause closes the file only when `in` is not `null`. Of course, if `readProducts` throws an exception, then `in` is not `null`. If the `FileReader` constructor throws an exception, however (usually because there is no file with the given name), then `in` has not yet been set, and you cannot close it.

Use the `finally` clause whenever you need to do some cleanup, such as closing a file, to ensure that the cleanup happens no matter how the method exits. (Actually, there is a problem with closing a file in a `finally` clause. The `close` method can again throw an `IOException`, and you need a second `try` block to handle that.)

Java Syntax
13.2 General Try Block

```
try
{   statement
    statement
      . . .
}
catch(ExceptionClass exceptionObject)
{   statement
    statement
      . . .
}
catch(ExceptionClass exceptionObject)
{   statement
    statement
      . . .
}
  . . .
finally
{   . . .
}
```

Example:

```
try
{   System.out.println("What is your name?");
    String name = console.readLine();
    System.out.println("Hello, " + name + "!");
}
catch(IOException e)
{   System.out.println(e);
    System.exit(1);
}
```

Purpose:
To execute one or more statements that may generate exceptions. If an exception of a particular type occurs, then stop executing those statements and instead go to the matching `catch` clause. If no exception occurs, then skip the `catch` clauses. In all cases, execute the `finally` clause if one is present.

13.3.3 Checked Exceptions

Java exceptions fall into two categories, called *checked* and *unchecked* exceptions. When you call a method that throws a checked exception, you *must* tell the compiler what you are going to do about the exception if it is ever thrown. For example, all subclasses of `IOException` are checked exceptions. However, the compiler does not require you to keep track of unchecked exceptions. Exceptions such as `NumberFormatException`, `IllegalArgumentException`, and `NullPointer-`

Exception are unchecked exceptions. In general, all exceptions that belong to sub-classes of **RuntimeException** are unchecked, and all other subclasses of the class **Exception** are checked by the compiler (see Figure 4). There is a second category of internal errors that are reported by throwing objects of type **Error**.

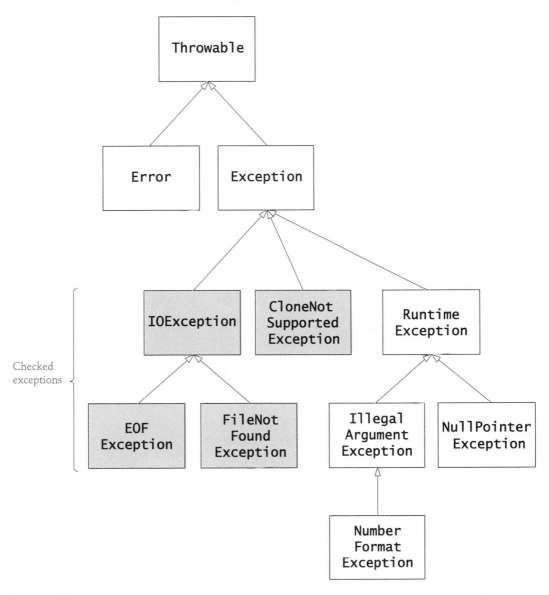

Figure 4

A Part of the Exception Class Hierarchy

These are fatal errors that are beyond your control, and you can ignore them. They too are unchecked.

Why have two kinds of exceptions? The checked exceptions are the ones that *aren't your fault*. The unchecked exceptions are your fault. For example, an unexpected end of file can be caused by forces beyond your control, such as a disk error or a broken network connection. But you are to blame for a `NullPointerException`, since your code was wrong when it tried to use a `null` reference.

The compiler doesn't check whether you handle a `NullPointerException`, because you should test your references for `null` before using them instead of installing a handler for that exception. The compiler does insist that your program be able to *deal with* error conditions it cannot *prevent*. (Actually, those categories aren't perfect. For example, it isn't your fault if a user enters an incorrect number, but `Integer.parseInt` throws an unchecked `NumberFormatException`. In that case, you need to take the initiative and catch the exception anyway.)

Suppose you write a method that calls `BufferedReader.readLine`, which can throw an `IOException`. The `IOException` is a checked exception, so you need to tell the compiler what you are going to do about it. You have two choices. You can place the call to `readLine` inside a `try` block and supply a `catch` clause for the `IOException` class or one of its superclasses `Exception` or `Throwable`. Or you can simply tell the compiler that you are aware of this exception and that you want your method to be terminated when it occurs. You do the latter by tagging the method with a `throws` clause:

```
public class Product
{  public void read(BufferedReader in) throws IOException
   {  . . .
   }
}
```

The `throws` clause in turn signals the caller of your method that it may encounter an `IOException`. Then it needs to make the same decision—catch the exception, or tell its caller that the exception may be thrown.

If your method can throw multiple checked exceptions, you separate them by commas:

```
public void read(BufferedReader in)
   throws EOFException, FileNotFoundException
```

It sounds somehow irresponsible not to catch an exception when you know that it happened. But actually, it is usually best not to catch an exception. After all, what can you do when you catch it? Can you tell the user? How? By sending a message to `System.out`? You don't know whether this method is called in an applet or maybe an embedded system such as a vending machine, where the user may never see `System.out`. And even if your users can see your error message, how do you know that they can understand English? Your class may be used to build an application for users in another country. Of course, *some* classes in the program know how to communicate with the user. Let them worry about reporting the error.

Or can you perhaps fix up the object and keep going? How? If you set a variable to `null` or an empty string, that may just cause the program to break later, with much

> **Java Syntax**
> **13.3 Exception Specifications**
> *accessSpecifier returnType methodName*
>   *(parameterType parameterName, . . .)*
>   throws *ExceptionClass, ExceptionClass, ...*
>
> Example:
> ```
> public void read(BufferedReader in)
>    throws IOException
> ```
>
> Purpose:
> To indicate the checked exceptions that this
> method can throw

greater mystery. If you encountered a genuine error, it is better to report it than to squelch it.

Every checked exception should be caught *somewhere* in your program. It is technically legal to have even the `main` method leak out exceptions:

```
public static void main(String[] args)
    throws Exception // bad style
{  . . .
}
```

But that is considered extremely bad style.

Let us implement a `Product.read` method that follows these guidelines. The method reads in a single record, consisting of three lines containing the name, price, and score, such as

```
Silverstar 686XL
829.95
85
```

We pass along all exceptions of type `IOException` that `readLine` may throw. When we encounter an unexpected end of file, we report it as an `EOFException`.

Note that we differentiate between an *expected* end of file and an *unexpected* end of file. All files must come to an end. We are prepared for the case that the end of the file has been reached before the *start* of a record. In that case, the method simply returns `false`. However, if the file ends in the *middle* of a record, then we throw an exception.

```
public class Product
{  public boolean read(BufferedReader in)
      throws IOException
   {  // read product name
      name = in.readLine();
      if (name == null) return false;
```

```
            // read product price
            String inputLine = in.readLine();
            if (inputLine == null)
               throw new EOFException
                  ("EOF when reading price");
            price = Double.parseDouble(inputLine);
            // read product score
            inputLine = in.readLine();
            if (inputLine == null)
               throw new EOFException
                  ("EOF when reading score");
            score = Integer.parseInt(inputLine);
            return true;
         }
         . . .
         private String name;
         private double price;
         private int score;
      }
```

Now let us put this method to use. The following method reads product records and puts them into a panel. It is completely unconcerned with any exceptions. If there is a problem with the input file, it simply passes the exception to its caller.

```
      public void readProducts(BufferedReader in)
         throws IOException
      {  boolean done = false;
         while (!done)
         {  Product p = new Product();
            if (p.read(in))
               panel.addProduct(p);
            else // last product read
               done = true;
         }
      }
```

Next, let's implement the user interaction. We ask the user for a file name and read the product file. If there is a problem, we report the nature of the problem. The program is not terminated, and the user has a chance to open a different file.

```
      public void openFile()
      {  BufferedReader in = null;
         try
         {  // select file name
            . . .
            in = new BufferedReader
               (new FileReader(selectedFile));

            readProducts(in);
         }
```

```
        catch(FileNotFoundException e)
        {   JOptionPane.showMessageDialog
                (null, "Bad filename. Try again.");
        }
        catch(IOException e)
        {   JOptionPane.showMessageDialog
                (null, "Corrupted file. Try again.");
        }
        finally
        {   if (in != null)
                try
                {   in.close();
                }
                catch(IOException e)
                {   JOptionPane.showMessageDialog
                        (null, "Error closing file.");
                }
        }
}
```

This example shows the separation between error detection (in the `Product.read` method) and error handling (in the `openFile` method). In between the two is the `readProducts` method, which just passes exceptions along.

Quality Tip 13.1

Do Not Squelch Exceptions

When you call a method that throws a checked exception, the compiler complains. In your eagerness to continue your work, it is an understandable impulse to shut the compiler up by *squelching* the exception:

```
try
{   in.close(); // compiler complained about IOException
} catch (Exception e) {} // so there!
```

The do-nothing exception handler fools the compiler into thinking that the exception has been handled. In the long run, this is clearly a bad idea. Exceptions were designed to transmit problem reports to a *competent* handler. Installing an incompetent handler simply hides an error condition that could be serious.

Quality Tip 13.2

Use Exceptions Only for Exceptional Cases

Consider the `readLine` method of the `BufferedReader` class. It returns `null` at the end of the input. Why doesn't it throw an `EOFException`?

The designers of this method did the right thing. Every file must come to an end. In other words, the end of a file is a normal condition, not an exceptional one. Whenever you read a line of input, you must be prepared to deal with the possibility that you reached the end. However, if the end of input occurs inside a data record that should be complete, then you can throw an EOFException to indicate that the file came to an *unexpected* end. This must have been caused by some exceptional event, such as a corrupted file. In particular, you should *never* use exceptions as a "break statement on steroids". Of course, you can throw an exception to exit a deeply nested loop or a set of recursive method calls. But that is considered an abuse of the exception mechanism.

13.4 Example: Reading Input Data in a Graphics Program

Recall the BestProduct program in Section 11.4, which reads product data from the keyboard and then marks the best buys. If the user makes a single mistake in a data value, there is no going back, and all data values must be entered again.

It makes more sense for the user to place the data values into a file using a text editor and then to specify the name of that file when the data values are to be used.

Our example program displays its results in a graph (see Figure 5). It shows data points of prices and performance scores of computers. Prices grow in the x-direction, performance in the y-direction. Such a graph is useful to get a quick visual impression of the data set. The product with the highest score may be very expensive and thus not a good buy. Savvy buyers will look for products that give good performance at a low price; those are the ones in the upper left corner of the diagram. On the other hand, the products in the lower right corner of the diagram have a comparatively high price for the performance they offer. Unless there are other factors, such as exceptional service, one would be less inclined to choose those models.

In this program, we will add another improvement. We will supply a *file dialog* that lets users choose files on their computers. Figure 6 shows a typical file dialog.

The JFileChooser class implements a file dialog for the Swing user interface toolkit. The JFileChooser class relies on another class, File, which describes disk files and directories. For example,

```
File inputFile = new File("input.txt");
```

describes the file input.txt in the current directory. The File class has methods to delete or rename the file. However, you cannot directly read data from a File object. You still need to construct a FileReader or FileInputStream from the File object:

```
FileReader in = new FileReader(inputFile);
```

The JFileChooser class has many options to fine-tune the display of the dialog, but in its most basic form it is quite simple: Construct a file chooser object; then call the showOpenDialog or showSaveDialog method. Both methods show the same dialog, but the button for selecting a file is labeled "Open" or "Save", depending on which method you call. For better placement of the dialog on the screen,

Figure 5

Plotting Product
Performance
against Price

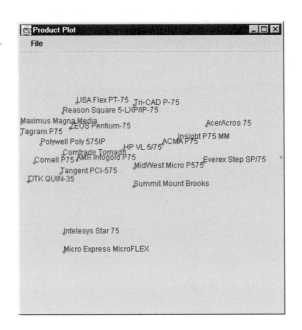

Figure 6

A File Chooser Dialog

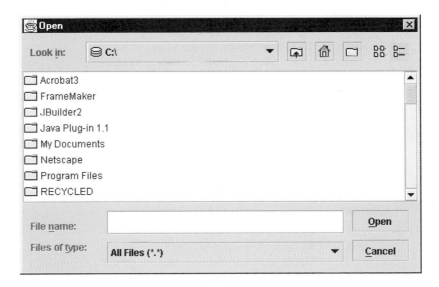

you can specify the user interface component over which to pop up the dialog. If you don't care where the dialog pops up, you can simply pass **null**. These methods return either **JFileChooser.APPROVE_OPTION** if the user has chosen a file, or **JFileChooser.CANCEL_OPTION** if the user canceled the selection. If a file was chosen, then you call the **getSelectedFile** method to obtain a **File** object that describes the file. Here is a complete example:

```
JFileChooser chooser = new JFileChooser();
FileReader in = null;
if (chooser.showOpenDialog(null) == JFileChooser.APPROVE_OPTION)
{  File selectedFile = chooser.getSelectedFile();
   in = new FileReader(selectedFile);
}
```

Here is the complete program that reads the computer data in and plots the graph. As you can see, a program can get quite lengthy once you add good error handling and a user interface.

Program PlotProducts.java

```
import java.awt.Container;
import java.awt.Graphics;
import java.awt.Graphics2D;
import java.awt.event.ActionEvent;
import java.awt.event.ActionListener;
import java.awt.event.WindowEvent;
import java.awt.event.WindowAdapter;
import java.awt.geom.Ellipse2D;
import java.io.BufferedReader;
import java.io.File;
import java.io.FileNotFoundException;
import java.io.FileReader;
import java.io.IOException;
import javax.swing.JFileChooser;
import javax.swing.JFrame;
import javax.swing.JMenu;
import javax.swing.JMenuBar;
import javax.swing.JMenuItem;
import javax.swing.JPanel;
import javax.swing.JOptionPane;
import javax.swing.JTextField;

public class PlotProducts
{  public static void main(String[] args)
   {  PlotProductsFrame frame = new PlotProductsFrame();
      frame.setTitle("Product Plot");
      frame.show();
   }
}
```

```java
class PlotProductsFrame extends JFrame
{  public PlotProductsFrame()
   {  final int DEFAULT_FRAME_WIDTH = 300;
      final int DEFAULT_FRAME_HEIGHT = 300;
      setSize(DEFAULT_FRAME_WIDTH, DEFAULT_FRAME_HEIGHT);

      addWindowListener(new WindowCloser());

      // add panel to content pane

      Container contentPane = getContentPane();

      panel = new ProductPanel();
      contentPane.add(panel, "Center");

      // set menu items

      JMenuBar menuBar = new JMenuBar();
      setJMenuBar(menuBar);

      JMenu fileMenu = new JMenu("File");
      menuBar.add(fileMenu);

      MenuListener listener = new MenuListener();

      openMenuItem = new JMenuItem("Open");
      fileMenu.add(openMenuItem);
      openMenuItem.addActionListener(listener);

      exitMenuItem = new JMenuItem("Exit");
      fileMenu.add(exitMenuItem);
      exitMenuItem.addActionListener(listener);
   }

   /**
      Handles the open file menu. Prompts user for file
      name and reads products from file.
   */
   public void openFile()
   {  BufferedReader in = null;
      try
      {  // show file chooser dialog
         JFileChooser chooser = new JFileChooser();
         if (chooser.showOpenDialog(null)
            == JFileChooser.APPROVE_OPTION)
         {  // construct reader and read products
```

```
            File selectedFile = chooser.getSelectedFile();
            in = new BufferedReader
               (new FileReader(selectedFile));

            plotProducts(in);
         }
      }
      catch(FileNotFoundException e)
      {  JOptionPane.showMessageDialog
            (null, "Bad filename. Try again.");
      }
      catch(IOException e)
      {  JOptionPane.showMessageDialog
            (null, "Corrupted file. Try again.");
      }
      finally
      {  if (in != null)
            try
            {   in.close();
            }
            catch(IOException e)
            {  JOptionPane.showMessageDialog
                  (null, "Error closing file.");
            }
      }
   }


   /**
      Reads products and adds them to the product panel.
      @param in the buffered reader to read from
   */
   public void plotProducts(BufferedReader in)
      throws IOException
   {  panel.clearProducts();
      boolean done = false;
      while (!done)
      {  Product p = new Product();
         if (p.read(in))
            panel.addProduct(p);
         else
            // last product read
            done = true;
      }
   }


   private JMenuItem openMenuItem;
   private JMenuItem exitMenuItem;
   private ProductPanel panel;
```

```java
        private class MenuListener implements ActionListener
        {  public void actionPerformed(ActionEvent event)
           {  Object source = event.getSource();
              if (source == openMenuItem) openFile();
              else if (source == exitMenuItem) System.exit(0);
           }
        }

        private class WindowCloser extends WindowAdapter
        {  public void windowClosing(WindowEvent event)
           {  System.exit(0);
           }
        }
   }

   class ProductPanel extends JPanel
   {  public ProductPanel()
      {  final int PRODUCTS_LENGTH = 100;
         products = new Product[PRODUCTS_LENGTH];
         productsSize = 0;
      }

      public void paintComponent(Graphics g)
      {  super.paintComponent(g);
         Graphics2D g2 = (Graphics2D)g;

         // compute price range

         if (productsSize == 0) return; // nothing to plot
         double minPrice = products[0].getPrice();
         double maxPrice = products[0].getPrice();

         for (int i = 1; i < productsSize; i++)
         {  double price = products[i].getPrice();
            if (price < minPrice) minPrice = price;
            if (price > maxPrice) maxPrice = price;
         }

         final int MAX_SCORE = 100;
         UnitConverter units
            = new UnitConverter(minPrice, maxPrice,
               0, MAX_SCORE, getWidth(), getHeight());

         // draw a labeled point for each product

         for (int i = 0; i < productsSize; i++)
         {  Product p = products[i];

            double x = units.xToPixel(p.getPrice());
            double y = units.yToPixel(p.getScore());
```

```
        final double SMALL_CIRCLE_RADIUS = 2;
           Ellipse2D.Double circle = new Ellipse2D.Double(
              x - SMALL_CIRCLE_RADIUS,
              y - SMALL_CIRCLE_RADIUS,
              2 * SMALL_CIRCLE_RADIUS,
              2 * SMALL_CIRCLE_RADIUS);

        g2.draw(circle);
        g2.drawString(p.getName(), (float)x, (float)y);
     }
  }

  /**
     Clears all products from the graph and repaints it.
  */
  public void clearProducts()
  {  productsSize = 0;
     repaint();
  }

  /**
     Adds a new product to the graph and repaints it.
     @param p the product to add
  */
  public void addProduct(Product p)
  {  if (productsSize < products.length)
     {  products[productsSize] = p;
        productsSize++;
     }
     repaint();
  }

  private Product[] products;
  private int productsSize;
}
```

13.5 Command Line Arguments

Depending on the operating system and Java development system used, there are
different methods of starting a program—for example, by selecting "Run" in the compilation environment, by clicking on an icon, or by typing the name of the program
at a prompt in a terminal or shell window. The latter method is called "invoking the
program from the command line". When you use this method, you must of course
type the name of the program, but you can also type in additional information that

the program can use. These additional strings are called *command line arguments*. For example, if you start a program with the command line

```
java Prog -v input.dat
```

then the program receives two command line arguments: the strings "-v" and "input.dat". It is entirely up to the program what to do with these strings. It is customary to interpret strings starting with a - as options and other strings as file names.

Only application programs receive command line arguments; you cannot pass a command line to an applet. (The corresponding mechanism for applets is the HTML <PARAM> tag; see Advanced Topic 4.3.)

Command line arguments are placed in the args parameter of the main method:

```
public static void main(String[] args)
{ . . .
}
```

Now you finally know the use of the args array that you have seen in so many programs. In our example, args contains the two strings

```
args[0]   "-v"
args[1]   "input.dat"
```

Let us write a program that *encrypts* a file—that is, scrambles it so that it is unreadable except to those who know the decryption method and the secret keyword. Ignoring 2000 years of progress in the field of encryption, we will use a method familiar to Julius Caesar. The person performing any encryption chooses an *encryption key;* here the key is a number between 1 and 25 that indicates the shift to be used in encrypting each letter. For example, if the key is 3, replace A with a D, B with an E, and so on (see Figure 7).

The program takes the following command line arguments:

♦ An optional -d flag to indicate decryption instead of encryption
♦ An optional encryption key, specified with a -k flag
♦ The input file name
♦ The output file name

If no key is specified, then 3 is used. For example,

```
java Crypt input.txt encrypt.txt
```

encrypts the file input.txt with a key of 3 and places the result into encrypt.txt.

Figure 7

The Caesar Cipher

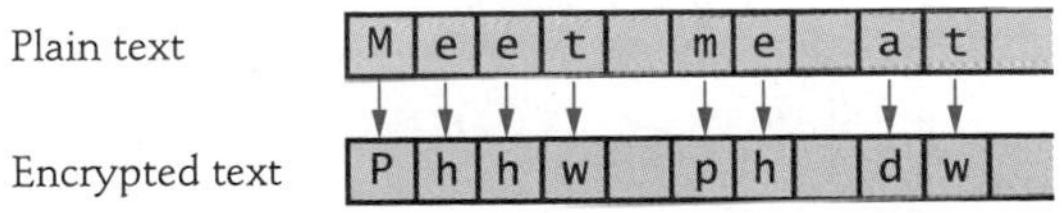

Plain text

M	e	e	t		m	e		a	t	

Encrypted text

P	h	h	w		p	h		d	w	

```
java Crypt -d -k11 encrypt.txt output.txt
```

decrypts the file encrypt.txt with a key of 11 and places the result into output.txt.
Here is the program:

Program Crypt.java

```java
import java.io.FileReader;
import java.io.FileWriter;
import java.io.IOException;

public class Crypt
{   public static void main(String[] args)
    {   boolean decrypt = false;
        int key = DEFAULT_KEY;
        FileReader infile = null;
        FileWriter outfile = null;

        if (args.length < 2 || args.length > 4) usage();

        // gather command line arguments and open files

        try
        {   for (int i = 0; i < args.length; i++)
            {   if (args[i].substring(0, 1).equals("-"))
                // it is a command line option
                {   String option = args[i].substring(1, 2);
                    if (option.equals("d"))
                        decrypt = true;
                    else if (option.equals("k"))
                    {   key = Integer.parseInt
                            (args[i].substring(2));
                        if (key < 1 || key >= NLETTERS)
                            usage();
                    }
                }
                else
                {   if (infile == null)
                        infile = new FileReader(args[i]);
                    else if (outfile == null)
                        outfile = new FileWriter(args[i]);
                }
            }
        }
        catch(IOException e)
        {   System.out.println("Error opening file");
            System.exit(0);
        }
```

```
        if (infile == null || outfile == null) usage();

        // encrypt or decrypt the input

        if (decrypt) key = NLETTERS - key;

        try
        {  encryptFile(infile, outfile, key);
           infile.close();
           outfile.close();
        }
        catch(IOException e)
        {  System.out.println("Error processing file");
           System.exit(0);
        }
    }

    /**
        Prints a message describing proper usage and exits.
    */
    public static void usage()
    {  System.out.println
            ("Usage: java Crypt [-d] [-kn] infile outfile");
        System.exit(1);
    }

    /**
        Encrypts a character with the Caesar cipher. Only
        upper- and lowercase letters are encrypted.
        @param c the character to encrypt
        @param k the encryption key
        @return the encrypted character
    */
    public static char encrypt(char c, int k)
    {  if ('a' <= c && c <= 'z')
            return (char)('a' + (c - 'a' + k) % NLETTERS);
        if ('A' <= c && c <= 'Z')
            return (char)('A' + (c - 'A' + k) % NLETTERS);

        return c;
    }

    /**
        Encrypts all characters in a file.
        @param in the plaintext file
        @param out the file to store the encrypted characters
        @param k the encryption key
    */
```

```
public static void encryptFile(FileReader in,
    FileWriter out, int k) throws IOException
{  while (true)
   {  int next = in.read();
      if (next == -1) return; // end of file
      char c = (char)next;
      out.write(encrypt(c, k));
   }
}

public static final int DEFAULT_KEY = 3;
public static final int NLETTERS = 'z' - 'a' + 1;
}
```

Random Fact 13.2

Encryption Algorithms

The exercises at the end of this chapter give a few algorithms to encrypt text. Don't actually use any of those methods to send secret messages to your lover. Any skilled cryptographer can *break* these schemes in a very short time—that is, reconstruct the original text without knowing the secret keyword.

In 1978 Ron Rivest, Adi Shamir, and Leonard Adleman introduced an encryption method that is much more powerful. The method is called *RSA* encryption, after the last names of its inventors. The exact scheme is too complicated to present here, but it is not actually difficult to follow. You can find the details in [2].

RSA is a remarkable encryption method. There are two keys: a public key and a private key. (See Figure 8.) You can print the public key on your business card (or in your email signature block) and give it to anyone. Then anyone can send you messages that only you can decrypt.

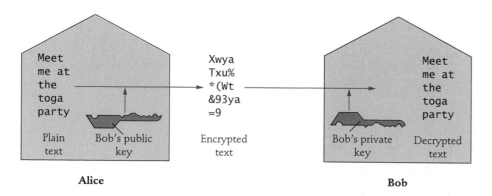

Alice   Bob

Figure 8

Public Key Encryption

Even though everyone else knows the public key, and even if they intercept all the messages coming to you, they cannot break the scheme and actually read the messages. In 1994, hundreds of researchers, collaborating over the Internet, cracked an RSA message encrypted with a 129-digit key. Messages encrypted with a key of 230 digits or more are expected to be secure.

The inventors of the algorithm obtained a *patent* for it. That means that anyone using it must seek a license from the inventors. They have given permission for most noncommercial usage, but if you implement RSA in a product that you sell, you must get their permission and probably pay them some amount of money.

A patent is a deal that society makes with an inventor. For a period of 20 years after the filing date, the inventor has an exclusive right for its commercialization, may collect royalties from others wishing to manufacture the invention, and may even stop competitors from marketing it altogether. In return, the inventor must publish the invention, so that others may learn from it, and must relinquish all claim to it after the protection period ends. The presumption is that in the absence of patent law, inventors would be reluctant to go through the trouble of inventing, or they would try to cloak their techniques to prevent others from copying their devices. The RSA patent expires on September 20, 2000.

What do you think? Are patents a fair deal? Unquestionably, some companies have chosen not to implement RSA, and instead chose a less capable method, because they could not or would not pay the royalties. Thus, it seems that the patent may have hindered, rather than advanced, commerce. Had there not been patent protection, would the inventors have published the method anyway, thereby giving the benefit for society without the cost of the 20-year monopoly? In this case, the answer is probably yes; the inventors were academic researchers, who live on salaries rather than sales receipts and are usually rewarded for their discoveries by a boost in their reputation and careers. Would their followers have been as active in discovering (and patenting) improvements? There is no way of knowing, of course. Is an algorithm even patentable, or is it a mathematical fact that belongs to nobody? The patent office did take the latter attitude for a long time. The RSA inventors and many others described their inventions in terms of imaginary electronic devices, rather than algorithms, to circumvent that restriction. Nowadays, the patent office will award software patents.

There is another fascinating aspect to the RSA story. A programmer named Phil Zimmermann, developed a program called PGP (for *Pretty Good Privacy*) [3]. PGP implements RSA. That is, you can have it generate a pair of public and private keys, publish the public key, receive encrypted messages from others who use their copy of PGP and your public key, and decrypt them with your private key. Even though the encryption can be performed on any personal computer, decryption is not feasible even with the most powerful computers. You can get a copy of PGP by anonymous ftp (Internet file transfer protocol) from `net-dist.mit.edu` in the directory `/pub/PGP`. As long as it is for personal use, there is no charge, courtesy of Phil Zimmermann and the folks at RSA.

The existence of PGP bothers the government to no end. They worry that criminals use the package to correspond by email and that the police cannot tap those "conversations". Foreign governments can send communications that the National Security Agency (the premier electronic spy organization of the United States) cannot decipher. Recently, the U.S. government attempted to standardize on a different encryption scheme, called *Skipjack*, to which government organizations hold a decryption key that—of course—they promise not to use without a court order. There have been serious proposals to make it illegal to use any other encryption method in the United States. At one time, the government considered charging Mr. Zimmermann with breaching another law that forbids the unauthorized export of munitions as a crime and defines cryptographic technology as "munitions". They made the argument that, even though Mr. Zimmermann never exported the program, he should have known that it would immediately spread through the Internet when he released it in the United States.

What do you think? Will criminals and terrorists be harder to detect and convict once encryption of email and phone conversations is widely available? Should the government therefore have a backdoor key to any legal encryption method? Or is this a gross violation of our civil liberties? Is it even possible to put the genie back into the bottle at this time?

13.6 Random Access

Consider a file that contains a set of product data. We want to change the prices of some of the products. Of course, we can read all data into an array, update the information that has changed, and save the data out again. If the data set in the file is very large, we may end up doing a lot of reading and writing just to update a handful of records. It would be better if we could locate the changed information in the file and just replace it.

This is quite different from the file access you have programmed up to now. In the past, you read from a file an item at a time and wrote to a file an item at a time. That access pattern is called *sequential access*. Now we would like to access specific locations in a file and change just those locations. This access pattern is called *random access* (see Figure 9). There is nothing "random" about random access—the term just means that you can read and modify any byte stored at any location in the file.

Only disk files support random access; the System.in and System.out streams, which are attached to the keyboard and the terminal, do not. Each disk file has a special *file pointer* position (see Figure 10). Normally, the file pointer is at the end of the file, and any output is appended to the end. However, if you move the file pointer to the middle of the file and write to the file, the output overwrites what is already

Figure 9

Sequential and Random Access

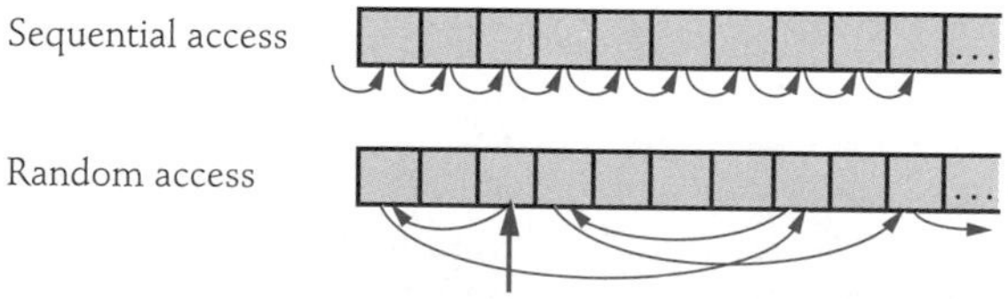

Sequential access

Random access

Figure 10

The File Pointer

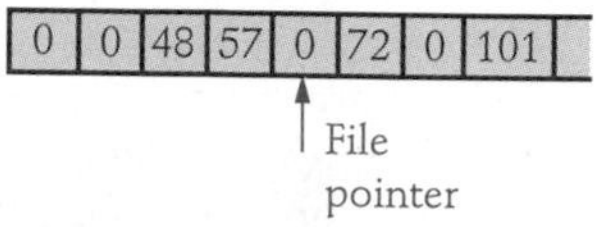

| 0 | 0 | 48 | 57 | 0 | 72 | 0 | 101 | |

File pointer

there. The next read command starts reading input at the file pointer location. You can move the file pointer just beyond the last byte currently in the file but no further.

In Java, you use a `RandomAccessFile` object to access a file and move a file pointer. To open a random-access file, you supply a file name and a string to specify the *open mode*. You can open a file either for reading only ("r") or for reading and writing ("rw"). For example, the following command opens the file `products.dat` for both reading and writing:

```
RandomAccessFile f = new RandomAccessFile("products.dat", "rw");
```

The method call

```
f.seek(n);
```

moves the file pointer to byte n counted from the beginning of the file. To find out the current position of the file pointer (counted from the beginning of the file), use

```
n = f.getFilePointer();
```

Because files can be very large, the file pointer values are long integers. To find out the number of bytes in a file, use the `length` method:

```
long fileLength = f.length();
```

If you want to manipulate a data set in a file, you have to pay special attention to the formatting of the data. Suppose you just store the data as text:

| i | M | a | r | k | P | l | u | s | \n | 9 | 9 | 5 | . | 0 | \n | 8 | 5 | \n |

If the price is increased by $50, the new price has more digits. If one places the file pointer to the first character of the old value and simply writes out the new value, the result is

| i | M | a | r | k | P | l | u | s | \n | 1 | 0 | 4 | 5 | . | 0 | 8 | 5 | \n |

That is not working too well. The update is overwriting the newline that separates the fields.

In order to be able to update a file, you must give each field a *fixed* size that is sufficiently large. As a result, every record in the file has the same size. That has another advantage: It is then easy to skip quickly to, say, the 50th record, without having to read in the first 49 records. (See Figure 11.)

When storing numbers in a file with fixed record sizes, it is easier to store them in binary format, not in text format. For that reason, the `RandomAccessFile` class

Variable-size records

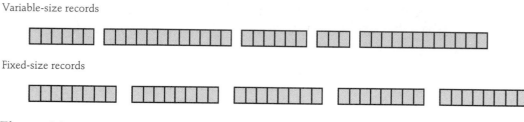

Fixed-size records

Figure 11

Variable-Size and Fixed-Size Records

stores data in binary. The **readInt** and **writeInt** methods read and write integers as four-byte quantities. The **readDouble** and **writeDouble** methods process double-precision floating-point numbers as eight-byte quantities.

```
int n = f.readInt();
f.writeInt(n);
double x = f.readDouble();
f.writeDouble(x);
```

In addition, we must store strings in a fixed size. In the sample product database program, we will store each product name as a string of 30 characters. Java uses Unicode characters to store strings, so each character occupies two bytes.

Unfortunately, there are no convenient methods in the **RandomAccessFile** class to read and write a string of a fixed size such as 30 characters. The sample program contains two methods **readFixedString** and **writeFixedString** to solve this problem. The **readFixedString** method keeps calling **readChar** and assembles the characters into a string. The **writeFixedString** method calls **writeChars** to print either the entire string, followed by spaces if necessary, or the substring consisting of the first **n** characters.

To structure the data file in our example for random access, we set the field lengths to the following dimensions:

◆ Name: 30 characters at two bytes each = 60 bytes

◆ Price: one **double** = 8 bytes

◆ Score: one **int** = 4 bytes

Now that we have determined the file layout, we can implement our random-access file methods. The following program asks the user to enter the position of the record that should be updated, and the new price. The user can also add new records to the database.

Program Database.java

```
import java.io.IOException;
import java.io.RandomAccessFile;
public class Database
{  public static void main(String[] args)
   {  ConsoleReader console = new ConsoleReader(System.in);
      System.out.println
         ("Please enter the data file name:");
      String filename = console.readLine();
      try
      {  RandomAccessFile file
            = new RandomAccessFile(filename, "rw");
         long nrecord = file.length() / RECORD_SIZE;
         boolean done = false;
         while (!done)
         {  System.out.println
               ("Please enter the record to update (1 - "
               + nrecord + "), new record (0), quit (-1)");
            int pos = console.readInt();

            if (1 <= pos && pos <= nrecord) // update record
            {  file.seek((pos - 1) * RECORD_SIZE);
               Product p = readProduct(file);
               System.out.println("Found " + p.getName()
                  + " " + p.getPrice() + " " + p.getScore());
               System.out.println
                  ("Enter the new price:");
               double newPrice = console.readDouble();
               p.setPrice(newPrice);
               file.seek((pos - 1) * RECORD_SIZE);
               writeProduct(file, p);
            }
            else if (pos == 0) // add record
            {  System.out.println("Enter new product:");
               String name = console.readLine();
               System.out.println("Enter price:");
               double price = console.readDouble();
               System.out.println("Enter score:");
               int score = console.readInt();
               Product p = new Product(name, price, score);
               file.seek(nrecord * RECORD_SIZE);
               writeProduct(file, p);
               nrecord++;
            }
            else if (pos == -1)
               done = true;
         }
         file.close();
      }
```

```
      catch(IOException e)
      { System.out.println("Input/Output Exception " + e);
      }
   }

   /**
      Reads a fixed-width string.
      @param f the file to read from
      @param size the number of characters to read
      @return the string with leading and trailing spaces removed
   */
   public static String readFixedString(RandomAccessFile f,
      int size) throws IOException
   { String b = "";
      for (int i = 0; i < size; i++)
         b += f.readChar();
      return b.trim();
   }

   /**
      Writes a fixed-width string.
      @param f the file to write to
      @param size the number of characters to write
   */
   public static void writeFixedString(RandomAccessFile f,
      String s, int size) throws IOException
   { if (s.length() <= size)
      { f.writeChars(s);
         for (int i = s.length(); i < size; i++)
            f.writeChar(' ');
      }
      else
         f.writeChars(s.substring(0, size));
   }

   /**
      Reads a product record.
      @param f the file to read from
      @return the next product stored in the file.
   */
   public static Product readProduct(RandomAccessFile f)
      throws IOException
   { String name = readFixedString(f, NAME_SIZE);
      double price = f.readDouble();
      int score = f.readInt();
      return new Product(name, price, score);
   }
   /**
      Writes a product record.
      @param f the file to write to
   */
```

```
    public static void writeProduct(RandomAccessFile f,
        Product p) throws IOException
    {   writeFixedString(f, p.getName(), NAME_SIZE);
        f.writeDouble(p.getPrice());
        f.writeInt(p.getScore());
    }

    public static final int NAME_SIZE = 30;

    public static final int CHAR_SIZE = 2;
    public static final int INT_SIZE = 4;
    public static final int DOUBLE_SIZE = 8;

    public static final int RECORD_SIZE
        = CHAR_SIZE * NAME_SIZE + DOUBLE_SIZE + INT_SIZE;
}
```

Random Fact 13.3

Databases and Privacy

Most companies use computers to keep huge data files of customer records and other business information. Special *database* programs are used to search and update that information rapidly. This sounds like a straightforward extension of the techniques you learned in this chapter, but it does take special skills to handle truly massive amounts of data. You will likely take a course in database programming as part of your computer science education.

Databases not only lower the cost of doing business; they improve the quality of service that companies can offer. Nowadays it is almost unimaginable how time-consuming it used to be to withdraw money from a bank branch or to make travel reservations.

Today most databases are organized according to the *relational model.* Suppose a company stores your orders and payments. They will probably not repeat your name and address on every order; that would take unnecessary space. Instead, they will keep one file of all their customer names and identify each customer by a unique customer number. Only that customer number, not the entire customer information, is kept with an order record. (See Figure 12.)

To print an invoice, the database program must issue a *query* against both the customer and order files and pull the necessary information (name, address, articles ordered) from both. Frequently, queries involve more than two files. For example, the company may have a file of addresses of car owners and a file of people with good payment history and may want to find all of its customers who placed an order in the last month, drive an expensive car, and pay their bills, to send them another catalog. This kind of query is, of course, much faster if all customer files use the *same* key, which is why so many organizations in the United States try to collect the Social Security numbers of their customers.

The Social Security Act of 1935 provided that each contributor be assigned a Social Security number to track contributions into the Social Security Fund. These numbers have a distinctive format, such as 078-05-1120. (This particular number is not actually a Social Security number belonging to any person. It was printed on sample cards that were inserted in wallets in the 1940s and 1950s.) Figure 13 shows a Social Security card.

Although they had not originally been intended for use as a universal identification number, Social Security numbers have become just that in the last 60 years. The tax authorities

Customers   Orders

Cust. #:	Name
11439	Hacker, Harry

Order #:	Cust. #:	Item	
59673	11439	DOS for idiots	
59897	11439	Computing concepts	
61013	11439	Core Java	

Figure 12

Relational Database Files

Figure 13

A Social Security
Card

and many other government agencies are required to collect the numbers, as are banks (for the reporting of interest income) and, of course, employers. Many other organizations find it convenient to use the number as well.

From a technical standpoint, Social Security numbers are a lousy method for indexing a database. There is a risk of having two records with the same number, because many illegal immigrants use fake numbers. Not everyone has a number—in particular, foreign customers. Because there is no checksum, a clerical error (such as transposing two digits) cannot be detected. (Credit card numbers have a checksum.) For the same reason, it is easy for anyone to make up a number.

Some people are very concerned about the fact that just about every organization wants to store their Social Security number. Unless there is a legal requirement, such as for banks, one can usually fight it or take one's business elsewhere. Even when an organization is required to collect the number, such as an employer, one can insist that the number be used only on tax and Social Security paperwork, not on the face of an ID card. Unfortunately, it usually takes near-superhuman effort to climb the organizational ladder to find someone with the authority to process paperwork with no Social Security number or to assign another identification number.

As the Internet becomes a more pervasive part of our lives, you can witness first-hand the voracious appetite for personal information by marketers of products and services. There are many opportunities to obtain free services (such as free email), if you are willing to divulge some personal information, and if you agree to the monitoring of your browsing and purchasing habits.

The discomfort that many people have about the computerization of their personal information is understandable. There is the possibility that companies and the government can merge multiple databases and derive information about us that we may wish they did not have or that simply may be untrue. An insurance company may deny coverage, or charge a higher premium, if it finds that you have too many relatives with a certain disease. You may be denied a job because of an inaccurate credit or medical report, and you may not even know the reason. These are very disturbing developments that have had a very negative impact for a small but growing number of people. See [4] for more information.

13.7 Object Streams

In the preceding programs you saved **Product** objects by breaking them up into strings and numbers. When reading them back in, you put the strings and numbers back into objects. Actually, in Java, there is an easier way. The **ObjectOutputStream** class can save entire objects out to disk, and the **ObjectInputStream** class can read them back in. Objects are saved in binary format; hence, you use streams and not writers.

For example, you can write a **Product** object to a file as follows:

```
Product p = . . .;
ObjectOutputStream out = new ObjectOutputStream
   (new FileOutputStream("products.dat"));
out.writeObject(p);
```

The object output stream automatically saves all instance variables of the object to the stream. When reading the object back in, you use the **readObject** method of the `ObjectInputStream` class. That method returns an `Object` reference, so you need to remember the types of the objects that you saved and use a cast:

```
ObjectInputStream in = new ObjectInputStream
    (new FileInputStream("products.dat"));
Product p = (Product)in.readObject();
```

You can do even better than that, though. You can store a whole bunch of objects in an array or vector, or inside another object, and then save that object:

```
Vector v = new Vector();
// now add many Product objects into v
out.writeObject(v);
```

With one instruction, you can save the vector and *all the objects that it contains*. You can read all of them back with one instruction:

```
Vector v = (Vector)in.readObject();
```

This is a truly amazing capability that is highly recommended (see Productivity Hint 13.1).

To place objects of a particular class into an object stream, that object must implement the `Serializable` interface. That interface has no methods, so there is no effort involved in implementing it:

```
class Product implements Serializable
{   . . .
}
```

The process of saving objects to a stream is called *serialization* because each object is assigned a serial number on the stream. If the same object is saved twice, the second time only the serial number is written out. Conversely, when the objects are read back in, duplicate serial numbers are restored as references to the same object.

Why don't all classes implement `Serializable`? For security reasons, some programmers may not want to serialize classes with confidential contents. Once a class is serializable, anyone can write its objects to disk and analyze the disk file. There are also some classes that contain values that are meaningless once a program exits, such as window handles. These values should not be serialized.

Serialization is suitable for many programs—it is safe and convenient. However, files that contain serialized objects do not allow random access. Therefore, the `RandomAccessFile` is useful when access speed is more important than convenience.

Productivity Hint 13.1

Use Object Streams

Object streams have a huge advantage over other data file formats. You don't have to come up with a way of breaking objects up into numbers and strings when writing a file. You don't have to come up with a way of combining numbers and strings back into objects when reading a file. The serialization mechanism takes care of this automatically. You simply write and read objects. For this to work, you need to have each of your classes implement the `Serializable` interface, which is trivial to do.

To save your data to disk, it is best to put them all into one large object (such as a vector or an object that describes your entire program state) and save that object. When you need to read the data back, read that object back in. It is easier for you to retrieve data from an object than it is to search for them in a file. For example, consider the program for drawing product records. If the user can add or remove records (by clicking with the mouse or through menus and dialogs), then you want to save your products. Put them all in a catalog object:

```
class Catalog implements Serializable
{  public void addProduct(Product p) { . . . }
   . . .
   private Vector products;
}
```

Then load and save the entire catalog:

```
class ProductEditor
{  . . .
   public void saveFile()
   {  ObjectOutputStream out = . . .;
      out.writeObject(productCatalog);
      out.close();
   }

   public void loadFile()
   {  ObjectInputStream in = . . .;
      productCatalog = (Catalog)readObject();
      in.close();
   }

   private Catalog productCatalog;
}
```

Chapter Summary

1. You use streams to process binary data and readers and writers for data in text format.

2. Use `FileInputStream`, `FileOutputStream`, `FileReader`, and `FileWriter` objects to access disk files. When you are done using the file, you should close the file object.

3. The basic streams only process one byte at a time. The basic readers and writers process only single characters. You use *filters* to adapt these classes to read and write numbers and strings. The `PrintWriter` can print numbers and strings. The `BufferedReader` can read whole lines, but you must still parse their contents.

4. When a method detects a problem it cannot handle, it should throw an exception. You can throw any instance of a subclass of `Throwable`.

5. A `try` block is used to install exception handlers. Each `catch` clause specifies a handler for a particular exception type. An optional `finally` clause contains statements that must be executed no matter how the `try` block exits.

6. Java distinguishes *checked* and *unchecked* exceptions. Checked exceptions are caused by events beyond your control. A method needs to declare all checked exceptions that can occur when it is executed, using the `throws` keyword.

7. In a graphical program, you can use a file chooser dialog to select file names.

8. Programs that start from the command line can retrieve the command line arguments in the `args` parameter of the `main` method.

9. You can access any position in a random-access file by moving the *file pointer* prior to a read or write operation. That is particularly useful if all records in a file have the same size.

10. You can read and write complete objects with the `ObjectInputStream` and `ObjectOutputStream` classes. The objects must belong to classes that implement the `Serializable` interface.

Further Reading

[1] The Unicode Consortium, *The Unicode Standard Worldwide Character Encoding, Version 2.0,* Addison-Wesley, 1996.

[2] Bruce Schneier, *Applied Cryptography,* John Wiley & Sons, 1994.

[3] Phillip R. Zimmermann, *The Official PGP User's Guide,* MIT Press, 1995.

[4] David F. Linowes, *Privacy in America,* University of Illinois Press, 1989.

[5] Abraham Sinkov, *Elementary Cryptanalysis,* Mathematical Association of America, 1966.

[6] Don Libes, *Obfuscated C and Other Mysteries,* John Wiley & Sons, 1993.

Classes, Objects, and Methods Introduced in This Chapter

```
java.io.EOFException
java.io.File
java.io.FileInputStream
java.io.FileNotFoundException
java.io.FileOutputStream
```

```
java.io.FileReader
java.io.FileWriter
java.io.InputStream
   read
   close
java.io.ObjectInputStream
   readObject
java.io.ObjectOutputStream
   writeObject
java.io.OutputStream
   write
   close
java.io.PrintWriter
   print
   println
java.io.RandomAccessFile
   getFilePointer
   length
   readChar
   readDouble
   readInt
   seek
   writeChar
   writeChars
   writeDouble
   writeInt
java.io.Reader
   read
   close
java.io.Writer
   write
   close
java.lang.NullPointerException
java.lang.NumberFormatException
java.lang.RuntimeException
java.lang.Serializable
javax.swing.JFileChooser
   getSelectedFile
   showOpenDialog
   showSaveDialog
javax.swing.JOptionPane
   showMessageDialog
```

Review Exercises

Exercise R13.1. What is the difference between a stream and a reader?

Exercise R13.2. How can you open a file both for reading and writing in Java?

Exercise R13.3. What happens if you try to write to a file reader? What happens if you try to write to a random-access file that you opened only for reading? Try it out if you don't know.

Exercise R13.4. What happens if you try to open a file for reading that doesn't exist? What happens if you try to open a file for writing that doesn't exist?

Exercise R13.5. What happens if you try to open a file for writing, but the file or device is write-protected (sometimes called read-only)? Try it out with a short test program!

Exercise R13.6. Some operating systems have a limit on the number of files that an application can open at the same time. Find out whether your operating system has such a limitation, by opening output streams for files file1.txt, file2.txt, . . . , file1000.txt, until the call to the `FileInputStream` constructor fails.

Exercise R13.7. How do you open a file whose name contains a backslash, like temp\output.dat?

Exercise R13.8. What is the difference between throwing and catching an exception?

Exercise R13.9. What is the purpose of the `finally` clause? Give an example how it can be used.

Exercise R13.10. What is a checked exception? What is an unchecked exception? Is a `NullPointerException` checked or unchecked? Which exceptions do you need to declare with the `throws` keyword?

Exercise R13.11. What happens if an exception does not have a matching `catch` clause?

Exercise R13.12. What is a command line? How can a program read its command line arguments?

Exercise R13.13. If a program Woozle is started with the command

```
java Woozle -DNAME=Piglet -I\eeyore -v heff.txt a.txt lump.txt
```

what are the values of `args[0]`, `args[1]`, and so on?

Exercise R13.14. How can you break the Caesar cipher? That is, how can you read a document that was encrypted with the Caesar cipher, even though you don't know the key?

Exercise R13.15. What is the difference between sequential access and random access?

Exercise R13.16. What is the file pointer in a file? How do you move it? How do you tell the current position? Why is it a long integer?

Exercise R13.17. How do you move the file pointer to the first byte of a file? To the last byte? To the exact middle of the file?

Exercise R13.18. What happens if you try to move the file pointer past the end of a file? Can you move the file pointer of `System.in`? Try it out and report your results.

Exercise R13.19. What happens if you try to save an object that is not serializable in an object stream? Try it out and report your results.

Exercise R13.20. Why is it better to save an entire array or `Vector` to an object stream instead of programming a loop that writes each element?

Programming Exercises

Exercise P13.1. Write a program that asks the user for a file name and that prints the number of characters, words, and lines in that file. Then the program asks for the name of the next file. When the user enters a file that doesn't exist (such as the empty string), the program exits.

Exercise P13.2. *Random monoalphabet cipher.* The Caesar cipher, to shift all letters by a fixed amount, is ridiculously easy to crack—just try out all 25 possible keys. Here is a better idea. For the key, don't use numbers but words. Suppose the key word is FEATHER. Then first remove duplicate letters, yielding FEATHR, and append the other letters of the alphabet in reverse order:

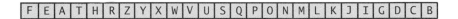

Now encrypt the letters as follows:

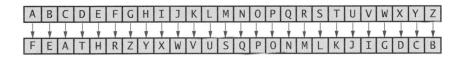

Write a program that encrypts or decrypts a file using this cipher. For example,

```
java Crypt -d -kFEATHER encrypt.txt output.txt
```

decrypts a file using the keyword FEATHER. It is an error not to supply a keyword.

Exercise P13.3. *Letter frequencies.* If you encrypt a file using the cipher of the preceding exercise, it will have all of its letters jumbled up, and it doesn't look as if there was any hope of decrypting it without knowing the keyword. Guessing the keyword seems hopeless too. There are just too many possible keywords. However, someone who is trained in decryption will be able to break this cipher in no time at all. The average letter frequencies of English letters are well known. The most common letter is E, which occurs about 13% of the time. Here are the average frequencies of the letters (see [5]).

A	8%	N	8%
B	1%	O	7%
C	3%	P	3%
D	4%	Q	1%
E	12%	R	8%
F	3%	S	6%
G	2%	T	9%
H	4%	U	3%
I	7%	V	1%
J	1%	W	2%
K	1%	X	1%
L	4%	Y	2%
M	3%	Z	1%

Write a program that reads an input file and prints the letter frequencies in that file. Such a tool will help a code breaker. If the most frequent letters in an encrypted file are H and K, then there is an excellent chance that they are the encryptions of E and T.

Exercise P13.4. *Vigenère cipher.* The trouble with a monoalphabetic cipher is that it can be easily broken by frequency analysis. The so-called Vigenère cipher overcomes this problem by encoding a letter into one of several cipher letters, depending on its position in the input document. Choose a keyword, for example **TIGER**. Then encode the first letter of the input text like this:

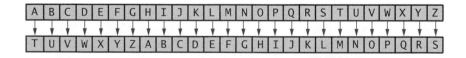

That is the encoded alphabet is just the regular alphabet shifted to start at T, the first letter of the keyword **TIGER**. The second letter is encrypted according to the map

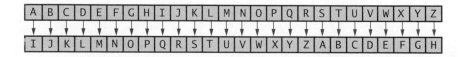

The third, fourth, and fifth letters in the input text are encrypted using the alphabet sequences beginning with characters G, E, and R, and so on. Because the key is only five letters long, the sixth letter of the input text is encrypted in the same way as the first.

Write a program that encrypts or decrypts an input text according to this cipher.

Exercise P13.5. *Playfair cipher.* Another way of thwarting a simple letter frequency analysis of an encrypted text is to encrypt *pairs* of letters together. A simple scheme to do this is the Playfair cipher. You pick a keyword and remove duplicate letters from it. Then you fill the keyword, and the remaining letters of the alphabet, into a 5×5 square. (Since there are only 25 squares, I and J are considered the same letter.) Here is such an arrangement with the keyword PLAYFAIR:

```
P L A Y F
I R B C D
E G H K M
N O Q S T
U V W X Z
```

To encrypt a letter pair, say AT, look at the rectangle with corners A and T:

```
P L A Y F
I R B C D
E G H K M
N O Q S T
U V W X Z
```

The encoding of this pair is formed by looking at the other two corners of the rectangle—in this case, FQ. If both letters happen to be in the same row or column, such as GO, simply swap the two letters. Decryption is done in the same way.

Write a program that encrypts or decrypts an input text according to this cipher.

Exercise P13.6. The program in Section 13.6 only locates one record and updates the price. Write a program that raises or lowers the prices of all products by a given percentage.

Exercise P13.7. The program in Section 13.6 asks the user to specify the record number. More likely than not, a user has no way of knowing the record number. Write a program that asks the user for the name of a product, finds the record with that name, and displays the record. Then the program should give the following options to the user:

- Change the price of this record
- View the next record
- Find another product
- Quit

For extra credit, supply a graphical user interface.

Exercise P13.8. To find a particular product in a database file, the program needs to search one record at a time. If the records are *sorted,* there is a faster way. Count the number of records in the file, by dividing the length of the file by the length of each record. Set a variable `first` to 1, `last` to `nrecords`. Compute `mid = (first + last)/2`. Read the record at `mid`. Maybe you are lucky, and you actually found the record you wanted. If so, print it and exit. Is its name before or after the name that you are searching? Adjust either `last` to `mid - 1` or `first` to `mid + 1` and repeat the search. This searching method is called a *binary* search, and it is much faster than a sequential search through all records. Implement this searching method.

Exercise P13.9. Write a program that keeps a product database in a random-access file. Implement methods for adding and removing products. You need not keep products in sorted order. To remove a product, just fill the entire record with a blank record (spaces for strings, 0 for numbers). When adding a product, try to add it into one of those empty spots first before appending it to the end of the file.

Exercise P13.10. Write a program that manipulates three database files. The first file contains the names and telephone numbers of a group of people. The second file contains the names and Social Security numbers of a group of people. The third file contains the Social Security numbers and annual salaries of a group of people. The groups of people should overlap but need not be completely identical. Your program should ask the user for a telephone number and then print the name, Social Security number, and annual income, if it can determine that information.

Exercise P13.11. A bank keeps all bank accounts in a random-access file in which each line has the format

accountNumber balance

Write a program that simulates an automatic teller machine. A user can deposit money to an account by specifying the account number and amount, withdraw money, query the account balance, or transfer money from one account to another.

Exercise P13.12. Write a program `CopyFile` that copies one file to another. The file names are specified on the command line. For example,

```
java CopyFile report.txt report.sav
```

Exercise P13.13. Write a program that *concatenates* the contents of several files into one file. For example,

```
java CatFiles chapter1.txt chapter2.txt chapter3.txt book.txt
```

makes a long file book.txt that contains the contents of the files chapter1.txt, chapter2.txt, and chapter3.txt. The target file is always the last file specified on the command line.

Exercise P13.14. Write a program `Find` that searches all files specified on the command line and prints out all lines containing a keyword. For example, if you call

```
java Find Buff report.txt address.txt Homework.java
```

then the program might print

```
report.txt: Buffet style lunch will be available at the
address.txt: Buffet, Warren|11801 Trenton Court|Dallas|TX
address.txt: Walters, Winnie|59 Timothy Circle|Buffalo|MI
Homework.java: BufferedReader in;
```

The keyword is always the first command line argument.

Exercise P13.15. Write a program that checks the spelling of all words in a file. It should read each word of a file and check whether it is contained in a word list. A word list is available on most UNIX systems in the file /usr/dict/words. (If you don't have access to a UNIX system, your instructor should be able to get you a copy.) The program should print out all words that it cannot find in the word list.

Exercise P13.16. Write a program that opens a file for reading and writing, and replaces each line with its reverse. For example, if you run

```
java Reverse Hello.java
```

then the contents of Hello.java are changed to

```
olleH ssalc cilbup
)sgra ][gnirtS(niam diov citats cilbup  {
;"n\!dlroW, olleH" = gniteerg gnirtS  {
;)gniteerg(tnirp.tuo.metsyS
}
}
```

Of course, if you run `Reverse` twice on the same file, you get back the original file.

Exercise P13.17. The preceding exercise shows a limitation of the Hello.java program. If you reverse every line, it no longer is a legal Java program. You may not think that this is much to worry about, but there are people who try hard to write programs that can be scrambled in various ways. For example, a winner of the 1989 Obfuscated C Contest wrote a program that can be reversed and still does something useful. The grand prize winner of the 1990 contest wrote a C program that can be sorted! The unsorted version solves a differential equation, whereas the version in which the lines are sorted in alphabetical order prints Fibonacci numbers. Look at [6] for a highly entertaining account of these contests.

Your task is to write a Java program that turns into another legal Java program when you reverse each line.

Exercise P13.18. Write a program that reads a file from standard input and rewrites the file to standard output, replacing all tab characters `'\t'` with the *appropriate* number of spaces. Make the distance between tab columns a constant and set it to 3, the value we use in this book for Java programs. Then expand tabs to the number of spaces necessary to move to the next tab column. *That may be less than three spaces.* For example, the line

must be converted to

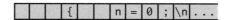

Exercise P13.19. Implement the `ReadProducts` program by using an object input stream. You will also need to write a program that writes an object stream with a number of product records.

Object-Oriented Design

Chapter Goals

- ◆ To learn about the software life cycle

- ◆ To learn how to discover new classes and methods

- ◆ To understand the use of CRC cards for class discovery

- ◆ To be able to identify inheritance, aggregation, and dependency relationships between classes

- ◆ To master the use of UML class diagrams to describe class relationships

- ◆ To learn how to use object-oriented design to build complex programs

To implement a software system successfully, be it as simple as your next home-work project or as complex as the next air traffic monitoring system, some amount of planning, design, and testing is required. In fact, for larger projects, the amount of time spent on planning is much higher than the amount of time spent on program-ming and testing. If you find that most of your homework time is spent in front of the computer, keying in code and fixing bugs, you are probably spending more time on your homework than you should. You could cut down your total time by spend-ing more on the planning and design phase. This chapter tells you how to approach these tasks in a systematic manner.

14.1 The Software Life Cycle

In this section we will discuss the *software life cycle*: the activities that take place be-tween the time a software program is first conceived and that it is finally retired.

A software project usually starts because some customer has some problem and is willing to pay money to have it solved. The Department of Defense, the customer of many programming projects, was an early proponent of a *formal process* for software development. A formal process identifies and describes different phases and gives guidelines how to carry out the phases and when to move from one phase to the next.

Many software engineers break down the development process into the following five phases:

- Analysis
- Design
- Implementation
- Testing
- Deployment

In the *analysis* phase you decide *what* the project is supposed to accomplish; you do not think about *how* the program will accomplish its tasks. The output of the analysis phase is a *requirements document*, which describes in complete detail what the program will be able to do once it is completed. A part of this requirements document can be a user manual that tells how the user will operate the program to derive the promised benefits. Another part sets performance criteria—how many inputs the program must be able to handle in what time, or what its maximum memory and disk storage requirements are.

In the *design* phase you develop a plan for how you will implement the sys-tem. You discover the structures that underlie the problem to be solved. When you use object-oriented design, you decide what classes you need and what their most important methods are. The output of this phase is a description of the classes and methods, with diagrams that show the relationships among the classes.

In the *implementation* phase you write and compile program code to implement the classes and methods that were discovered in the design phase. The output of this phase is the completed program.

In the *testing* phase you run tests to verify that the program works correctly. The output of this phase is a report describing the tests that you carried out and their results.

In the *deployment* phase the users of the program install it and use it for its intended purpose.

When formal development processes were first established in the early 1970s, software engineers had a very simple visual model of these phases. They postulated that one phase would run to completion, its output would spill over to the next phase, and the next phase would begin. This model is called the *waterfall model* of software development (see Figure 1).

In an ideal world the waterfall model has a lot of appeal: You figure out what to do; then you figure out how to do it; then you do it; then you verify that you did it right; then you hand the product to the customer. But when rigidly applied, the waterfall model simply did not work. It was very difficult to come up with a perfect requirement specification. It was quite common to discover in the design phase that the requirements were not consistent or that a small change in the requirements would lead to a system that was both easier to design and more useful for the customer, but since the analysis phase was over, the designers had no choice—they had to take the existing requirements, errors and all. This problem would repeat itself during implementation. The designers may have thought they knew how best to solve the problem, but when the design was actually implemented, it turned out that the resulting program was not as fast as the designers had thought. The next transition is one with which you are surely familiar. When the program was handed to the quality assurance department for testing, many bugs were found that would

Figure 1

The Waterfall
Model

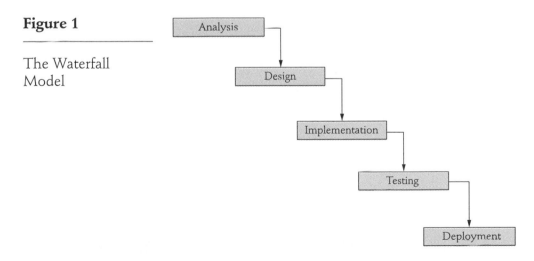

best be fixed by reimplementing, or maybe even redesigning, the program, but the waterfall model did not allow for this. Finally, when the customers received the finished product, they were often not at all happy with it. Even though the customers typically were very involved in the analysis phase, they themselves often were not sure exactly what they needed. After all, it can be very difficult to describe how you want to use a product that you have never seen before. But when the customers started using the program, they began to realize what they would have liked. Of course, then it was too late and they had to live with what they got.

Clearly, the model needs to be modified to permit *iterations* between the phases. Figure 2 shows such a model.

Having some level of iteration is clearly necessary. There simply must be a mechanism to deal with errors from the preceding phase. However, there is also a danger. If engineers believe that they don't have to do a good job because they can always do another iteration, then there will be many iterations and it will take a very long time for the process to complete. Going backwards to fix problems is a good thing, but it only works when there is good quality control and scheduling in the entire project. More complex "spiral" models to describe when and how to do the iterations have been proposed by a number of researchers.

Another useful approach is to go a small step forward into the next phase, before completing a phase. You are already familiar with one aspect of this principle from Chapter 8, where we recommended *unit tests* of methods and classes. In a unit test, the programmer tests that the individual classes work correctly. After all, there is no point in letting the quality assurance department find errors if the developer can find them much more quickly. Another "limited forward" technique is *beta testing*—deploying the product with selected customers before general deployment. In the analysis and design phase, you can feel your way toward a solution by *prototyping*. A prototype is a small system that shows some aspects of the final system. Because prototypes model only a part of a system and do not need to withstand customer

Figure 2

The Waterfall Model with Iterations

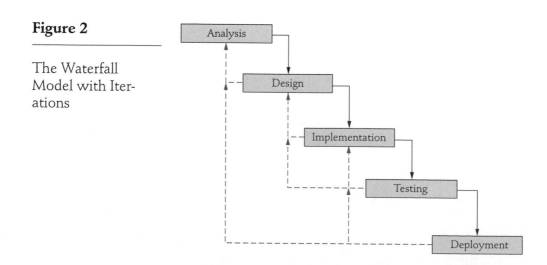

Figure 3

A Software
Development
Model with
Iterations and
Limited Forward-
Looking Steps

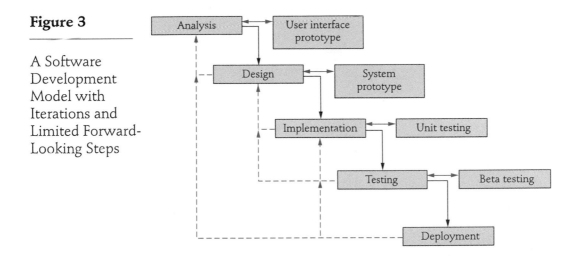

abuse, they can be implemented quickly. In the analysis phase, it is common to build a *user interface prototype* that shows the user interface in action. This gives customers an early chance to become more familiar with the system and to suggest improvements before the analysis is complete. In the design phase, *system prototypes* can be helpful to verify that a particular design plan can in fact be efficiently implemented, and that the design did not omit any important parts. Figure 3 shows a software development model that employs both iterations and limited forward-looking steps.

In the remainder of this chapter we will have a closer look at the *design phase* of the software development process.

Random Fact 14.1

Programmer Productivity

If you talk to your friends in this programming class, you will find that some of them consistently complete their assignments much more quickly than others. Perhaps they have more experience. Even when comparing programmers with the same education and experience, however, wide variations in competence are routinely observed and measured. It is not uncommon to have the best programmer in a team be five to ten times as productive as the worst, using any of a number of reasonable measures of productivity [1].

That is a staggering range of performance among trained professionals. In a marathon race, the best runner will not run five to ten times faster than the slowest one. Software product managers are acutely aware of these disparities. The obvious solution is, of course, to hire only the best programmers, but even in recent periods of economic slowdown the demand for good programmers has greatly outstripped the supply.

Fortunately for all of us, joining the rank of the best is not necessarily a question of raw intellectual power. Good judgment, experience, broad knowledge, attention to detail, and superior planning are at least as important as mental brilliance. These skills can be acquired by individuals who are genuinely interested in improving themselves.

Even the most gifted programmer can deal with only a finite number of details in a given time period. Suppose a programmer can implement and debug one method every two hours, or one hundred methods per month. (This is a generous estimate. Few programmers are this productive.) If a task requires 10,000 methods (which is typical for a medium-sized program), then a single programmer would need 100 months to complete the job. Such a project is sometimes expressed as a "100-man-month" project. But as F. Brooks explains in his famous book [2], the concept of "man-month" is a myth. One cannot trade months for programmers. One hundred programmers cannot finish the task in one month. In fact, 10 programmers probably couldn't finish it in 10 months. First of all, the 10 programmers need to learn about the project before they can get productive. Whenever there is a problem with a particular method, both the author and its users need to meet and discuss it, taking time away from all of them. A bug in one method may have all of its users twiddling their thumbs until it is fixed.

It is difficult to estimate these inevitable delays. They are one reason why software is often released later than originally promised. What is a manager to do when the delays mount? As Brooks points out, adding more personnel will make a late project even later, because the productive people have to stop working and train the newcomers.

You will experience these problems when you work on your first team project with other students. Be prepared for a major drop in productivity, and be sure to set ample time aside for team communications.

There is, however, no alternative to teamwork. Most important and worthwhile projects transcend the ability of one single individual. Learning to function well in a team is as important for your education as it is to be a competent programmer.

14.2 Discovering Classes

In the design phase of software development, your task is to discover structures that make it possible to implement a set of tasks on a computer. When you use the object-oriented design process, you carry out the following tasks:

1. Discover classes

2. Determine the behavior of each class

3. Describe the relationships between the classes

A class represents some useful concept. You have seen classes for concrete entities such as bank accounts, ellipses, and products. Other classes represent abstract concepts such as streams and windows. A simple rule for finding classes is to look for *nouns* in the task description. For example, suppose your job is to print an invoice such as the one in Figure 4. Obvious classes that come to mind are `Invoice`, `Item`, and `Customer`. It is a good idea to keep a list of *candidate classes* on a whiteboard or a

Figure 4

An Invoice

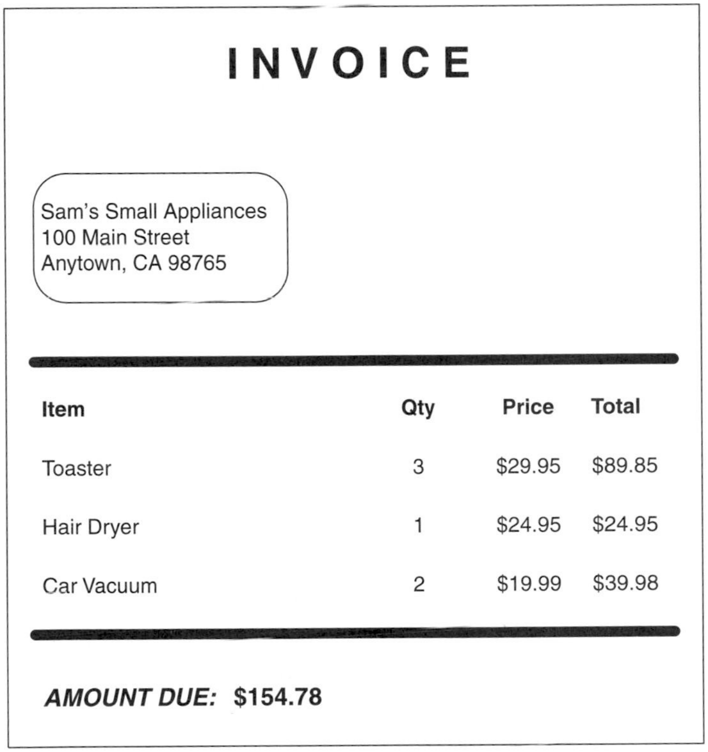

INVOICE

Sam's Small Appliances
100 Main Street
Anytown, CA 98765

Item	Qty	Price	Total
Toaster	3	$29.95	$89.85
Hair Dryer	1	$24.95	$24.95
Car Vacuum	2	$19.99	$39.98

AMOUNT DUE: $154.78

sheet of paper. As you brainstorm, simply put all ideas for classes onto the list. You can always cross out the ones that weren't useful after all.

Once a set of classes has been identified, you need to define the behavior for each class. That is, you need to find out what methods each object needs to carry out to solve the programming problem. A simple rule for finding these methods is to look for *verbs* in the task description, and then match the verbs to the appropriate objects. For example, in the invoice program, some class needs to compute the amount due. Now you need to figure out *which class* is responsible for this method. Do customers compute what they owe? Do invoices total up the amount due? Do the items total themselves up? The best choice is to make `compute amount due` the responsibility of the `Invoice` class.

An excellent way to carry out this task is the so-called *CRC* card method. (CRC stands for *classes, responsibilities, collaborators*.) In its simplest form, the method works as follows. Use an index card for each class (see Figure 5). As you think about verbs in the task description that indicate methods, you pick the card of the class that you think should be responsible, and write the responsibility onto the card. For each responsibility, you record which other classes are needed to fulfill it. Those classes are the *collaborators*.

For example, suppose you decide that an invoice should compute the amount due. Then you write `compute amount due` on an index card with the title `Invoice`.

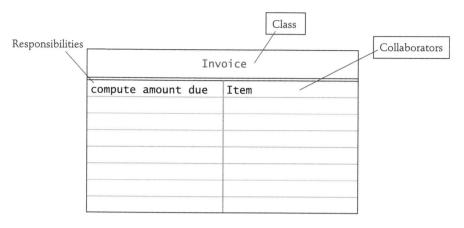

Figure 5

A CRC Card

Invoice	
compute amount due	

If a class can carry out that responsibility all by itself, you do nothing further. But if the class needs the help of other classes, you write the names of these collaborators on the right-hand side of the card.

To compute the total, the invoice needs to ask each item about its price. Therefore, the Item class is a collaborator:

Invoice	
compute amount due	Item

This is a good time to look up the index card for the Item class. Does it have a get total price method? If not, add one:

Item	
get total price	

How do you know that you are on the right track? For each responsibility, ask yourself how it can actually be done, using just the responsibilities written on the various cards. Many people find it helpful to group the cards on a table so that the collaborators are close to each other, and to simulate tasks by moving a token (such as a coin) from one card to the next to indicate which object is currently active.

The CRC card method is informal on purpose, so that you can be creative and discover classes and their properties. Once you find that you have settled on a good set of classes, then you want to know how they are related to each other. Can you find classes with common properties so that some responsibilities can be taken care of by a common superclass? Can you organize classes into clusters that are independent of each other? Finding class relationships and documenting them with diagrams is the topic of the next section.

14.3 Relationships between Classes

When designing a program, it is useful to document the relationships between classes. This helps you in a number of ways. For example, if you find classes with common behavior, you can save effort by placing the common behavior into a superclass. If you know that some classes are *not* related to each other, you can assign different programmers to implement each of them, without worrying that one of them has to wait for the other.

You have seen the inheritance relationship between classes many times in this book. Inheritance is a very important relationship between classes, but, as it turns out, it is not the only useful relationship, and it can be overused.

Inheritance is a relationship between a more general class (the superclass) and a more specialized class (the subclass). This relationship is often described as the *is-a* relationship. Every truck *is a* vehicle. Every savings account *is a* bank account. Every circle *is an* ellipse (with equal width and height).

Inheritance is sometimes abused, however. For example, consider a `Tire` class that describes a car tire. Should the class `Tire` be a subclass of `Circle`? It sounds convenient. There are quite a few useful methods in the `Circle` class—for example, you inherit the methods that tell you the width, height, and center point. All that should come in handy when drawing tire shapes. Yet though it may be convenient for the programmer, this arrangement makes no sense conceptually. It isn't true that every tire is a circle. Tires are car parts, whereas circles are geometric objects.

There is a relationship between tires and ellipses, though. A tire *has* a circle as its boundary. Java lets us model that relationship, too. Use an instance variable:

```
class Tire
{   ...
    private String rating;
    private Circle boundary;
}
```

The technical term for this relationship is *aggregation*. In Java, aggregation is implemented by using instance variables.

Here is another example. Every car *is a* vehicle. Every car *has a* tire (in fact, it has four or, if you count the spare, five). Thus, you would use inheritance from `Vehicle` and use aggregation of `Tire` objects:

```
class Car extends Vehicle
{   ...
    private Tire[] tires;
}
```

In this book, we use the UML notation for class diagrams. You have already seen many examples of the UML notation for inheritance—an arrow with an open triangle pointing to the superclass. In the UML notation, aggregation is denoted by a line with a diamond. The diamond is placed toward the aggregating class. Figure 6 shows a class diagram with an is-a and a has-a relationship.

The third useful relationship between classes is *dependency*. A class depends on another if one of its methods *uses* it in some way. This can happen in several ways:

◆   A method receives an object of the dependent class, either as a parameter or as the result of another method call.

◆   A method creates a new object of the dependent class.

◆   A method uses a static method or variable of the dependent class.

For example, all of our applet classes depend on the `Graphics` class, because they receive a `Graphics` object in the `paint` method. The console applications depend on the `System` class, because they use the static variable `System.out`.

Figure 6

UML Notation for Aggregation and Inheritance

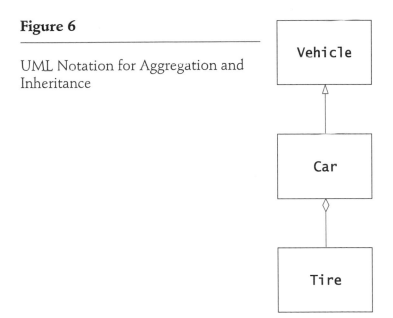

In the UML notation, dependency is denoted by a dashed line with an open arrow that points to the dependent class. See Figure 7 for an example.

Why does the dependency relationship matter? If the `Graphics` class changes in the next release of Java, all the classes that depend on it may be affected. If the change is drastic, the classes that use it must all be updated. These classes are said to be *coupled*. You analyze dependency so that you can *minimize* coupling (see Figure 8).

Finally, there is a useful notation to show that a class implements an interface. The interface is denoted by a circle, with the name of the interface next to it, and the class and interface are joined by a line (see Figure 9).

Sometimes it is useful to indicate class *attributes* and *methods* in a class diagram. An *attribute* is an externally observable property that objects of a class have. For example, `name` and `price` would be attributes of the `Product` class. Usually, attributes correspond to instance variables. But they don't have to—a class may have a different way of organizing its data. Consider the ellipse class from the Java library. Conceptually, it has attributes `center`, `width`, and `height`, but it doesn't actually store the center of the ellipse. Instead, it stores the top left corner and computes the center from it.

Figure 7

UML Notation for Dependency

Figure 8

Low and High Coupling

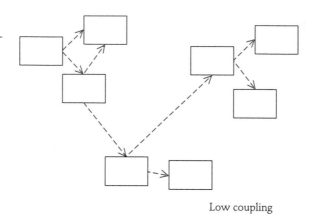

Low coupling

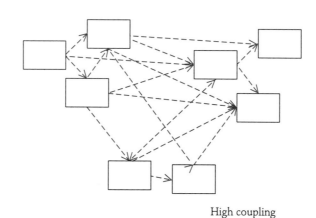

High coupling

Figure 9

UML Notation for
Interfaces

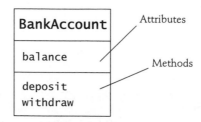

Figure 10

Compartments for Attributes and
Methods

You indicate attributes and methods by dividing a class rectangle into three compartments, with the class name in the top, attributes in the middle, and methods in the bottom (see Figure 10). You need not list *all* attributes and methods in a particular diagram. Just list the ones that are helpful to understand whatever point you are making with a particular diagram.

The final step for the design phase is to document the behavior of the methods. An excellent way to do that is to use the `javadoc` utility. Write Java source files with the classes, class comments, and only the signatures and comments of the key methods. Do not supply any implementation. Then run the `javadoc` utility to get formatted HTML documentation.

14.4 Example: Printing an Invoice

In this chapter, we suggest that you follow a five-part development process:

1. Gather requirements.
2. Use CRC cards to find classes, responsibilities, and collaborators.
3. Use UML diagrams to record class relationships, attributes, and methods.
4. Use `javadoc` to document method behavior.
5. Implement your program.

This process is particularly well suited for beginning programmers. There isn't a lot of notation to learn. The class diagrams are simple to draw. The deliverables of the design phase are obviously useful for the implementation phase—you simply take the source files and start adding the method code. Of course, as your projects get more complex, you will want to learn more about formal design methods. There are many techniques to describe object scenarios, call sequencing, the large-scale structure of programs, and so on, that are very beneficial even for relatively simple projects. The book [3] gives a good overview of these techniques.

In this section, we will walk through the object-oriented design technique with a very simple example. In this very simple case, the methodology will certainly feel overblown, but it is a good introduction to the mechanics of each step. You will then be better prepared for the more complex example that follows.

14.4.1 Requirements

The task of this program is to print out an *invoice*. We omit complexities such as dates, taxes, and invoice and customer numbers. The program simply prints the customer information, all items, and the amount due:

```
             I N V O I C E

Sam's Small Appliances
100 Main Street
Anytown, CA 98765

Item                    Qty Price    Total
Toaster                 3   29.95    89.85
Hair dryer              1   24.95    24.95
Car vacuum              2   19.99    39.98

AMOUNT DUE: $154.78
```

Also, in the interest of simplicity, we do not provide a user interface. The program will simply have a `main` method that adds items to the invoice and then prints it.

14.4.2 CRC Cards

First, you need to discover classes. Classes correspond to nouns in the problem description. In this problem, it is pretty obvious what the nouns are:

```
Invoice
Customer
Item
Quantity
Price
Total
Amount Due
```

(Of course, `Toaster` doesn't count—it is the name of an `Item` object, not the name of a class.)

Quantity and price are numbers, not classes. They are attributes of the `Item` class. The total and amount due are also numbers, but they are computed—not stored anywhere.

Thus, we are left with three candidates for classes:

```
Invoice
Customer
Item
```

Each of them represents a useful concept, so let's make them all into classes.

The purpose of the program is to print an invoice. Let's record that responsibility in a CRC card:

Invoice	
print	

How does an invoice print itself? It must print the customer, print all items, and then print the amount due. To print the customers and items, we can just add print methods to the **Customer** and **Item** classes:

Customer	
print	

Item	
print	

The **print** method of the **Invoice** class calls the **print** methods of **Customer** and **Item** objects. Whenever a method uses another class, you list that other class as a collaborator. In other words, `Customer` and `Item` are collaborators of `Invoice.print`:

Invoice	
print	Customer, Item

How do you generate the objects that this program manipulates? Of course, each class will have a constructor. We don't record them at this stage. However, the `Invoice` object can hold any number of `Item` objects, and a constructor won't be able to supply them all. Thus, the `Invoice` class needs an **add item** responsibility.

Finally, you need to be able to compute the amount due. That is a responsibility of the invoice. The invoice asks each item for its total, and then adds up all totals. Thus, **Item** is a collaborator, and **Item** needs a **get total price** responsibility:

Invoice	
print	Customer, Item
add item	Item
compute amount due	Item

Item	
print	
get total price	

That completes the CRC card process.

14.4.3 UML Diagrams

The aggregation relationships among the three classes in this example are simple: each invoice *has* items.

There is no inheritance in this example.

You get the dependency relationships from the collaboration column in the CRC cards. Each class depends on the classes with which it collaborates. In our example, the `Invoice` class collaborates with the `Customer` and `Item` classes.

However, if two classes are related by aggregation *and* dependency, then you only need to record aggregation, as the stronger relationship between the two. Since an invoice *has* items, we won't record the fact that it also uses the items. This keeps the diagram simpler.

Thus, in our example, there is one added dependency relationship. The `Invoice` class depends on the `Customer` class. Figure 11 shows the class relationships that we discovered.

Next, you add the methods. You can simply read them off from the CRC cards and add them to the diagram (see Figure 12).

The attributes require more work, because you cannot directly gather them from the CRC cards. Some attributes are straightforward. From the problem description, you know that an item has a name, quantity, and price.

To complete the search for attributes, you must *visit each method* and ask whether it depends on any attributes of its class. Consider the `print` method of the `Customer` class. It needs to print the name and address of the customer. Those are attributes of the `Customer` class.

You don't use an attribute if you already have aggregation. For example, is a customer an attribute of an invoice? No—you already recorded the fact that the `Invoice` class has a `Customer` object. In general, attributes tend to be numbers, strings, or other "small" objects such as date and time values.

Figure 13 shows the complete UML diagram for this example, with attributes and methods added.

Figure 11

The Relationships
between the
Invoice Classes

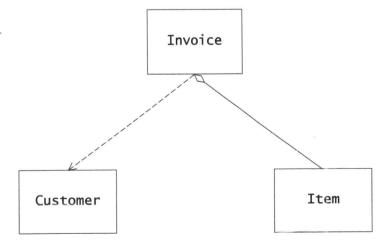

Figure 12

The Invoice Classes
and Their Methods

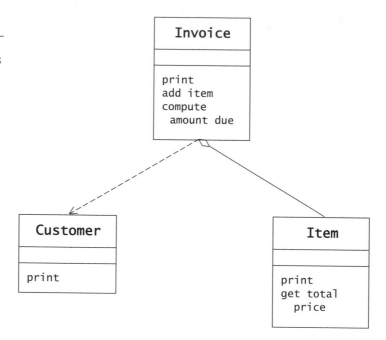

Figure 13

Attributes and
Methods
of the Invoice
Classes

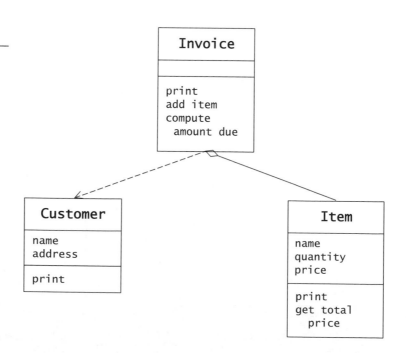

14.4.4 Method Documentation

The final step of the design phase is to write the documentation of the discovered classes and methods. Simply write a Java source file for each class, write the method comments for those methods that you have discovered, and leave the bodies of the methods blank.

```java
/**
    Describes an invoice for a set of purchased items.
*/

public class Invoice
{  /**
       Adds an item to this invoice.
       @param anItem the item to add
    */
    public void addItem(Item anItem)
    {
    }

    /**
       Prints the invoice.
    */
    public void print()
    {
    }

    /**
       Computes the total amount due.
       @return the amount due
    */
    public double getAmountDue()
    {
    }
}

/**
    Describes a customer with a mailing address.
*/

public class Customer
{  /**
       Prints the customer name and address.
    */
    public void print()
    {
    }
}
```

```
/**
    Describes a quantity of an article to purchase and its price.
*/

public class Item
{   /**
        Computes the total cost of this item.
        @return the total price (unit price * quantity)
    */
    public double getTotalPrice()
    {
    }

    /**
        Prints the item name, quantity, unit price, and total.
    */
    public void print()
    {
    }
}
```

Then run the **javadoc** program to obtain a prettily formatted version of your documentation in HTML format (see Figure 14).

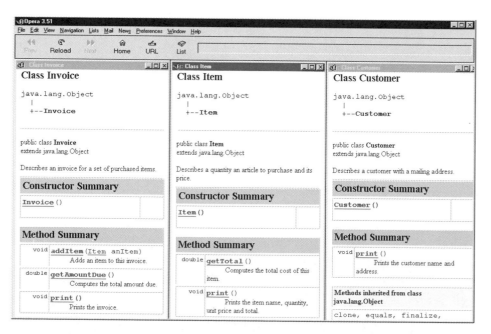

Figure 14

The Class Documentation in HTML
Format

This approach for documenting your classes has a number of advantages. You can share the HTML documentation with others if you work in a team. You use a format that is immediately useful—Java source files that you can carry into the implementation phase. And, most importantly, you supplied the comments of the key methods already—a task that less prepared programmers leave for later, and then often neglect for lack of time.

14.4.5 Implementation

Finally, you are ready to implement the classes.

You already have the method signatures and comments from the previous step. Now look at the UML diagram to add instance variables. Both aggregated classes and attributes yield instance variables. Start with the **Invoice** class. An invoice aggregates **Customer** and **Item**. Every invoice has one customer, but it can have many items. You could store them either as an array or as a vector. Let's say you don't want to deal with a partially filled array and therefore choose a vector. Now you have the instance variables of the **Invoice** class:

```
public class Invoice
{  . . .
   private Customer theCustomer;
   private Vector items;
}
```

As you can see from the UML diagram, the **Item** class does not aggregate any other classes. Instead, it has attributes name, quantity, and price. Make them into instance variables:

```
public class Item
{  . . .
   private String name;
   private int quantity;
   private double price;
}
```

The **Customer** class also has attributes: name and address:

```
public class Customer
{  . . .
   private String name;
   private String address;
}
```

The methods themselves are now very easy. Here is a typical example. You already know what the **Invoice.getAmountDue** needs to do—visit all items, ask them for their totals, and add them up:

```
/**
    Computes the total amount due.
    @return the amount due
*/
public double getAmountDue()
{   double amountDue = 0;
    for (int i = 0; i < items.size(); i++)
    {   Item nextItem = (Item)items.get(i);
        amountDue = amountDue + nextItem.getTotalPrice();
    }
    return amountDue;
}
```

We will not discuss the other methods in detail—they are equally straightforward.
Finally, you need to supply constructors, another routine task.

Here is the entire program. It is a good practice to go through it in detail and match up the classes and methods against the CRC cards and UML diagram.

Program InvoiceTest.java

```
import java.util.Vector;

public class InvoiceTest
{   public static void main(String[] args)
    {   Customer sam
            = new Customer("Sam's Small Appliances",
                "100 Main Street\nAnytown, CA 98765");

        Invoice samsInvoice = new Invoice(sam);
        samsInvoice.addItem(new Item("Toaster", 3, 29.95));
        samsInvoice.addItem(new Item("Hair dryer", 1, 24.95));
        samsInvoice.addItem(new Item("Car vacuum", 2, 19.99));
        samsInvoice.print();
    }
}

/**
    Describes an invoice for a set of purchased items.
*/

class Invoice
{   /**
        Constructs an invoice for a customer.
        @param c the customer
    */
    public Invoice(Customer c)
    {   theCustomer = c;
        items = new Vector();
    }
```

```
/**
    Adds an item to this invoice.
    @param anItem the item to add
*/
public void addItem(Item anItem)
{   items.add(anItem);
}

/**
    Prints the invoice.
*/
public void print()
{   System.out.println("                 I N V O I C E");
    System.out.println();

    theCustomer.print();
    System.out.println();

    System.out.print("Item                          ");
    System.out.println("Qty Price    Total");

    for (int i = 0; i < items.size(); i++)
    {   Item nextItem = (Item)items.get(i);
        nextItem.print();
    }

    System.out.println();
    System.out.println("AMOUNT DUE: $" + getAmountDue());
}

/**
    Computes the total amount due.
    @return the amount due
*/
public double getAmountDue()
{   double amountDue = 0;
    for (int i = 0; i < items.size(); i++)
    {   Item nextItem = (Item)items.get(i);
        amountDue = amountDue + nextItem.getTotalPrice();
    }
    return amountDue;
}

private Customer theCustomer;
private Vector items;
}

/**
    Describes a customer with a mailing address.
*/
```

```java
class Customer
{   /**
        Constructs a customer from the name and mailing
        address.
        @param aName the customer name
        @param anAddress the customer address
    */
    public Customer(String aName, String anAddress)
    {   name = aName;
        address = anAddress;
    }

    /**
        Prints the customer name and address.
    */
    public void print()
    {   System.out.println(name);
        System.out.println(address);
    }

    private String name;
    private String address;
}

/**
    Describes a quantity of an article to purchase and its price.
*/

class Item
{   /**
        Constructs an item from the name, quantity, and
        price.
        @param aName the item name
        @param aQuantity the item quantity
        @param aPrice the unit price
    */
    public Item(String aName, int aQuantity, double aPrice)
    {   name = aName;
        quantity = aQuantity;
        price = aPrice;
    }

    /**
        Computes the total price of this item.
        @return the total price (unit price × quantity)
    */
    public double getTotalPrice()
    {   return price * quantity;
    }
```

```
/**
    Prints the item name, quantity, unit price and total.
*/
public void print()
{  final int COLUMN_WIDTH = 30;

   System.out.print(name);

   // pad with spaces to fill column

   int pad = COLUMN_WIDTH - name.length();
   for (int i = 1; i <= pad; i++)
      System.out.print(" ");

   System.out.println(quantity + "    " + price
      + "    " + getTotal());
}

private String name;
private int quantity;
private double price;
}
```

14.5 Example: An Automatic Teller Machine

14.5.1 Requirements

The purpose of this project is to design a simulation of an automatic teller machine (ATM). The ATM has a keypad to enter numbers, a display to show messages, and a set of buttons, labeled A, B, and C, whose function depends on the state of the machine (see Figure 15).

The ATM is used by the customers of a bank. Each customer has two accounts: a checking account and a savings account. Each customer also has a customer number and a personal identification number (PIN). Both are required to gain access to the accounts. (In a real ATM, the customer number would be recorded on the magnetic strip of the ATM card. In this simulation, the customer will need to type it in.) With the ATM, customers can select an account (checking or savings). The balance of the selected account is displayed. Then the customer can deposit and withdraw money. This process is repeated until the customer chooses to exit.

Specifically, the user interaction is as follows. When the ATM starts up, it expects a user to enter a customer number. The display shows the following message:

```
Enter customer number
A = OK
```

Figure 15

The User
Interface of the
ATM

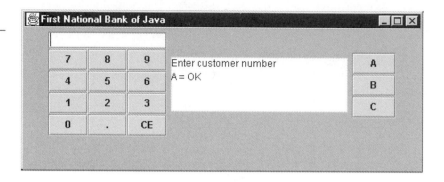

The user enters the customer number on the keypad and presses the A button. The display message changes to

```
Enter PIN
A = OK
```

Next, the user enters the PIN and presses the A button again. If the customer number and ID match one of the customers in the bank, then the customer can proceed. If not, the user is again prompted to enter the customer number.

If the customer has been authorized to use the system, then the display message changes to

```
Select Account
A = Checking
B = Savings
C = Exit
```

If the user presses the C button, the ATM reverts to its original state and asks the next user to enter a customer number.

If the user presses the A or B button, the ATM remembers the selected account and the display message changes to

```
Balance = balance of selected account
Enter amount and select transaction
A = Withdraw
B = Deposit
C = Cancel
```

If the user presses the A or B button, the value entered in the keypad is withdrawn from or deposited into the selected account. This is just a simulation, so no money is dispensed and no deposit is accepted. Afterwards, the ATM reverts to the preceding state, allowing the user to select another account or to exit.

If the user presses the C button, the ATM reverts to the preceding state without executing any transaction.

Since this is a simulation, the ATM does not actually communicate with a bank. It simply loads a set of customer numbers and PINs from a file that lists customer numbers and PINs. All accounts are initialized with a zero balance.

14.5.2 CRC Cards

We will again follow the recipe of Section 14.2 and show how to discover classes, responsibilities, and relationships and how to obtain a detailed design for the ATM program.

Recall that the first rule for finding classes is "look for nouns in the problem description". Here is a list of the nouns:

```
ATM
User
Keypad
Display
Display message
Button
State
Bank account
Checking account
Savings account
Customer
Customer number
PIN
Bank
```

Of course, not all of these nouns will become names of classes, and it is possible to discover the need for classes that aren't in this list, but it is a good start.

Let's start simply with a noncontroversial choice. A **Keypad** sounds like an excellent idea for a class. A keypad is a component with buttons and a text field that lets the user type in a value. What can we do with a keypad? There is one essential method: get the value the user entered. (Of course, the keypad will end up using one or more internal methods to track the button clicks, but we are not concerned with such an implementation detail now.) Here is the CRC card for the **Keypad** class:

Keypad	
get value	

On the other hand, there is already a good class for the display, namely **JTextArea**. Thus we won't need to create a separate **Display** class. Similarly, there is no need for a class to encapsulate display messages—we will just use strings. Also, we will use the existing **JButton** class for buttons.

Users and customers represent the same concept in this program. Let's use a class **Customer**. A customer has two bank accounts, and a customer object must be able to tell us the accounts. A customer also has a customer number and a PIN. We can, of course, require that a customer object give us the customer number and the PIN. But perhaps that isn't so secure. Instead, let us simply require that a customer object, when given a customer number and a PIN, will tell us whether it matches its own information or not.

Customer	
get account	BankAccount
match number and PIN	

A bank contains a collection of customers. When a user walks up to the ATM and enters customer number and PIN, it is the job of the bank to find the matching customer. How can the bank do this? It needs to check for each customer whether its customer number and PIN match. Thus, it needs to call the **match number and PIN** method of the **Customer** class that we just discovered. Because the **find customer** method calls a **Customer** method, it collaborates with the **Customer** class. We record that fact in the right-hand column of the CRC card.

When the simulation starts up, the bank must also be able to read a collection of customers and PINs. For this, the bank must also collaborate with the **Customer** class, because it must call the **Customer** constructor for each record that it reads in.

Bank	
find customer	Customer
read customers	Customer

The **BankAccount** class is our familiar class, with methods to get the balance and to deposit and withdraw money:

BankAccount	
get balance	
deposit	
withdraw	

In this program there is nothing that distinguishes checking and savings accounts. The ATM does not add interest or deduct fees. Therefore, we decide not to implement separate subclasses for checking and savings accounts.

Finally, we are left with the ATM class itself. An important notion of the ATM is the state. Whenever the state changes, the display needs to be updated, and the meaning of the buttons changes. There are four states:

1. START: Enter customer ID
2. PIN: Enter PIN
3. ACCOUNT: Select account
4. TRANSACT: Select transaction

To understand how to move from one state to the next, it is useful to draw a *state diagram* (Figure 16). The UML notation has standardized shapes for state diagrams. Draw states as rectangles with rounded corners. Draw state changes as arrows, with labels that indicate the reason for the change.

We will implement a `setState` method that sets the system to a new state and updates the display.

The user must type a valid customer number and PIN. Then the ATM can ask the bank to find the customer. This calls for a `select customer` method. It collaborates with the bank, asking the bank for the customer that matches the customer number and PIN. Next, there must be a `select account` method that asks the current customer for the checking or savings account. Finally, the deposit and withdraw methods carry out the selected transaction on the current account.

ATM	
set state	
select customer	Bank,Customer,KeyPad
select account	Customer,BankAccount
	KeyPad
withdraw	BankAccount, KeyPad
deposit	BankAccount, KeyPad

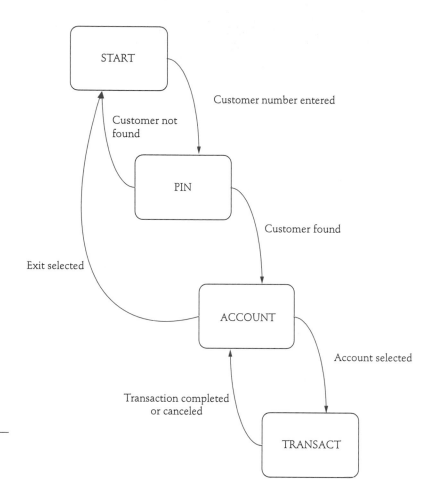

Figure 16

The States of
the ATM

Of course, discovering these classes and methods was not as neat and orderly as it appears from this discussion. When I designed these classes for this book, it took me several trials and tearing up of cards to come up with a satisfactory design. It is also important to remember that there is not necessarily one best design.

This design has several advantages. The classes describe clear concepts. The methods are sufficient to implement all necessary tasks. (I mentally walked through every ATM usage scenario to verify that.) There are not too many collaboration dependencies between the classes. Thus, I was satisfied with this design and proceeded to the next step.

14.5.3 UML Diagram

Figure 17 shows the relationship between these classes. It is easy to see the aggregation and inheritance relationships. A bank *has* customers. A customer *has* accounts. An ATM *has* a keypad. A keypad *is* a panel.

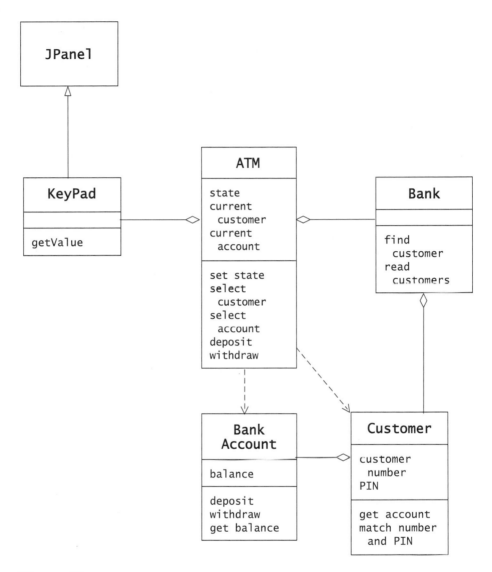

Figure 17

A UML Diagram for the ATM
Classes

Note that inheritance is not used heavily in this system. A keypad is a panel, so that we can add it to other containers. Otherwise, there are no inheritance relationships in this project.

To draw the dependencies, use the "collaborator" columns from the CRC cards. Looking at those columns, you find that the dependencies are as follows:

- ATM uses KeyPad, Bank, Customer, and BankAccount.
- Bank uses Customer.

However, since the Bank class already aggregates the Customer class, you record only the stronger aggregation relationship.

The class diagram is a good tool to visualize dependencies. Look at the Keypad class. It is completely independent from the rest of the ATM system—you could take out the Keypad class and use it in another application. Also, the Bank, BankAccount, and Customer classes, although dependent on each other, don't know anything about the ATM class. That makes sense—you can have banks without ATMs. As you can see, when you analyze dependency relationships, you look for the absence of relationships more than their presence.

Next, you can add the methods—just copy them from the CRC cards.

Finally, add the attributes. Some attributes are straightforward. From the problem description, you know that a customer has a customer number and a PIN. We also discovered that the ATM has a current state, an important attribute that affects its behavior.

To complete the search for attributes, visit each method. Consider the deposit method of the ATM class. It deposits money into a bank account. Into *which* account? The UML diagram shows that the ATM class does not directly aggregate bank accounts. The ATM has a bank, the bank has customers, and the customers have accounts. Thus the ATM needs a *current account* attribute—the account that determines the behavior of the deposit method.

Figure 17 shows the complete UML diagram for the ATM classes.

14.5.4 Method Documentation

Now you are ready for the final step of the design phase: to document the classes and methods that you discovered. Here is the documentation for the ATM class:

```
public class ATM
{  /**
       Gets PIN from keypad, finds customer in bank.
       If found sets state to ACCOUNT, else to START.
    */
    public void selectCustomer()
    {
    }

    /**
       Sets current account to checking or savings.
       Sets state to TRANSACT
       @param account one  of Customer.CHECKING_ACCOUNT
       or Customer.SAVINGS_ACCOUNT
    */
    public void selectAccount(int account)
    {
    }
```

```
/**
    Withdraws amount typed in keypad from current account.
    Sets state to ACCOUNT.
*/
public void withdraw()
{
}

/**
    Deposits amount typed in keypad to current account.
    Sets state to ACCOUNT.
*/

public void deposit()
{
}

/**
    Sets state and updates display message.
    @param state the next state
*/
public void setState(int newState)
{
}
}
```

Then run the `javadoc` utility to turn this documentation into HTML format.
For conciseness, we omit the documentation of the other classes.

14.5.5 Implementation

Finally, the time has come to implement the ATM simulator. You will find that the
implementation phase is very straightforward and should take *much less* time than
the design phase.

In order to implement the methods, you need to define the necessary instance
variables. From the class diagram, you can tell that the ATM has a keypad and a
bank object. They become instance variables of the class:

```
class ATM
{  . . .
   private Bank theBank;
   private Keypad pad;
   . . .
}
```

The attributes also turn into instance variables:

```
class ATM
{  . . .
   private Bank theBank;
   private Keypad pad;
```

```
private int state;
private Customer currentCustomer;
private BankAccount currentAccount;
. . .
}
```

Most methods are very straightforward to implement. Consider the `withdraw` method. From the design documentation, we have the description

```
/**
    Withdraws amount typed in keypad from current account.
    Sets state to ACCOUNT.
*/
```

This description can be almost literally translated to Java instructions:

```
public void withdraw()
{  currentAccount.withdraw(pad.getValue());
   setState(ACCOUNT_STATE);
}
```

Much of the remaining complexity in the ATM program results from the user interface. The ATM constructor has many statements to lay out components, and there are three button handlers that laboriously call the various ATM methods, depending on the state. This code is lengthy but straightforward.

We won't go through a method-by-method description of the ATM program. You should take some time and compare the actual implementation against the CRC cards and the UML diagram.

Program ATMSimulation.java

```
import java.awt.Container;
import java.awt.FlowLayout;
import java.awt.GridLayout;
import java.awt.event.ActionEvent;
import java.awt.event.ActionListener;
import java.awt.event.WindowEvent;
import java.awt.event.WindowAdapter;
import java.io.IOException;
import javax.swing.JButton;
import javax.swing.JFrame;
import javax.swing.JOptionPane;
import javax.swing.JPanel;
import javax.swing.JTextArea;

/**
    A simulation of an automatic teller machine
*/

public class ATMSimulation
{  public static void main(String[] args)
   {  ATM frame = new ATM();
```

```
         frame.setTitle("First National Bank of Java");
         frame.show();
      }
}

class ATM extends JFrame
{  /**
         Constructs the user interface of the ATM application.
      */
      public ATM()
      {  final int FRAME_WIDTH = 500;
         final int FRAME_HEIGHT = 200;
         setSize(FRAME_WIDTH, FRAME_HEIGHT);

         addWindowListener(new WindowCloser());

         // initialize bank and customers

         theBank = new Bank();
         try
         {  theBank.readCustomers("customers.txt");
         }
         catch(IOException e)
         {  JOptionPane.showMessageDialog
               (null, "Error opening accounts file.");
         }

         // construct components

         pad = new KeyPad();

         display = new JTextArea(4, 20);

         aButton = new JButton("  A  ");
         aButton.addActionListener(new AButtonListener());

         bButton = new JButton("  B  ");
         bButton.addActionListener(new BButtonListener());

         cButton = new JButton("  C  ");
         cButton.addActionListener(new CButtonListener());

         // add components to content pane

         JPanel buttonPanel = new JPanel();
         buttonPanel.setLayout(new GridLayout(3, 1));
         buttonPanel.add(aButton);
         buttonPanel.add(bButton);
         buttonPanel.add(cButton);
```

```
      Container contentPane = getContentPane();
      contentPane.setLayout(new FlowLayout());
      contentPane.add(pad);
      contentPane.add(display);
      contentPane.add(buttonPanel);

      setState(START_STATE);
   }

   /**
      Sets the current customer number to the keypad value
      and sets state to PIN.
   */
   public void setCustomerNumber()
   {  customerNumber = (int)pad.getValue();
      setState(PIN_STATE);
   }


   /**
      Gets PIN from keypad, finds customer in bank.
      If found, sets state to ACCOUNT, else to START.
   */
   public void selectCustomer()
   {  int pin = (int)pad.getValue();
      currentCustomer
         = theBank.findCustomer(customerNumber, pin);
      if (currentCustomer == null)
         setState(START_STATE);
      else
         setState(ACCOUNT_STATE);
   }


   /**
      Sets current account to checking or savings. Sets
      state to TRANSACT.
      @param account  one of  Customer.CHECKING_ACCOUNT
      or  Customer.SAVINGS_ACCOUNT
   */
   public void selectAccount(int account)
   {  currentAccount = currentCustomer.getAccount(account);
      setState(TRANSACT_STATE);
   }


   /**
      Withdraws amount typed in keypad from current account.
      Sets state to ACCOUNT.
   */
```

```java
public void withdraw()
{  currentAccount.withdraw(pad.getValue());
   setState(ACCOUNT_STATE);
}


/**
   Deposits amount typed in keypad to current account.
   Sets state to ACCOUNT.
*/
public void deposit()
{  currentAccount.deposit(pad.getValue());
   setState(ACCOUNT_STATE);
}


/**
   Sets state and updates display message.
   @param state the next state
*/
public void setState(int newState)
{  state = newState;
   pad.clear();
   if (state == START_STATE)
      display.setText("Enter customer number\nA = OK");
   else if (state == PIN_STATE)
      display.setText("Enter PIN\nA = OK");
   else if (state == ACCOUNT_STATE)
      display.setText("Select Account\n"
         + "A = Checking\nB = Savings\nC = Exit");
   else if (state == TRANSACT_STATE)
      display.setText("Balance = "
          + currentAccount.getBalance()
          + "\nEnter amount and select transaction\n"
          + "A = Withdraw\nB = Deposit\nC = Cancel");
}

private int state;
private int customerNumber;
private Customer currentCustomer;
private BankAccount currentAccount;
private Bank theBank;

private JButton aButton;
private JButton bButton;
private JButton cButton;

private KeyPad pad;
private JTextArea display;
```

```java
      private static final int START_STATE = 1;
      private static final int PIN_STATE = 2;
      private static final int ACCOUNT_STATE = 3;
      private static final int TRANSACT_STATE = 4;

      private class AButtonListener implements ActionListener
      {  public void actionPerformed(ActionEvent event)
         {  if (state == START_STATE)
               setCustomerNumber();
            else if (state == PIN_STATE)
               selectCustomer();
            else if (state == ACCOUNT_STATE)
               selectAccount(Customer.CHECKING_ACCOUNT);
            else if (state == TRANSACT_STATE)
               withdraw();
         }
      }

      private class BButtonListener implements ActionListener
      {  public void actionPerformed(ActionEvent event)
         {  if (state == ACCOUNT_STATE)
               selectAccount(Customer.SAVINGS_ACCOUNT);
            else if (state == TRANSACT_STATE)
               deposit();
         }
      }

      private class CButtonListener implements ActionListener
      {  public void actionPerformed(ActionEvent event)
         {  if (state == ACCOUNT_STATE)
               setState(START_STATE);
            else if (state == TRANSACT_STATE)
               setState(ACCOUNT_STATE);
         }
      }

      private class WindowCloser extends WindowAdapter
      {  public void windowClosing(WindowEvent event)
         {  System.exit(0);
         }
      }
   }
```

Class KeyPad.java

```java
import java.awt.BorderLayout;
import java.awt.GridLayout;
```

```java
import java.awt.event.ActionEvent;
import java.awt.event.ActionListener;
import javax.swing.JButton;
import javax.swing.JPanel;
import javax.swing.JTextField;

/**
    A component that lets the user enter a number, using
    a button pad labeled with digits
*/
public class KeyPad extends JPanel
{  public KeyPad()
   {  setLayout(new BorderLayout());

      // add display field

      display = new JTextField();
      add(display, "North");

      // make button panel

      buttonPanel = new JPanel();
      buttonPanel.setLayout(new GridLayout(4, 3));

      // add digit buttons

      ActionListener listener = new DigitButtonListener();
      addButton("7", listener);
      addButton("8", listener);
      addButton("9", listener);
      addButton("4", listener);
      addButton("5", listener);
      addButton("6", listener);
      addButton("1", listener);
      addButton("2", listener);
      addButton("3", listener);
      addButton("0", listener);
      addButton(".", listener);

      // add clear entry button

      clearButton = new JButton("CE");
      buttonPanel.add(clearButton);
      clearButton.addActionListener
         (new ClearButtonListener());

      add(buttonPanel, "Center");
   }
```

```
/**
    Gets the value that the user entered.
    @return the value in the text field of the keypad
*/
public double getValue()
{  return Double.parseDouble(display.getText());
}

/**
    Clears the display.
*/
public void clear()
{  display.setText("");
}

/**
    Adds a button to the button panel
    @param label the button label
    @param listener the button listener
*/
public void addButton(String label,
    ActionListener listener)
{  JButton button = new JButton(label);
    buttonPanel.add(button);
    button.addActionListener(listener);
}

private JPanel buttonPanel;
private JButton clearButton;
private JTextField display;

private class DigitButtonListener implements ActionListener
{  public void actionPerformed(ActionEvent event)
    {  // Get the button label
        // it is a digit or decimal point
        JButton source = (JButton)event.getSource();
        String label = source.getText();

        // don't add two decimal points
        if (label.equals(".")
            && display.getText().indexOf(".") != -1)
        return;

        display.setText(display.getText() + label);
    }
}

private class ClearButtonListener implements ActionListener
{  public void actionPerformed(ActionEvent event)
```

```
            {  clear();
            }
        }
    }
```

Class Bank.java

```java
import java.io.BufferedReader;
import java.io.FileReader;
import java.io.IOException;
import java.util.StringTokenizer;
import java.util.Vector;

public class Bank
{   /**
        Constructs a bank with no customers
    */
    public Bank()
    {   customers = new Vector();
    }

    /**
        Reads the customer numbers and PINs
        and initializes the bank accounts.
        @param filename the name of the customer file
    */
    public void readCustomers(String filename)
        throws IOException
    {   BufferedReader in = new BufferedReader
            (new FileReader(filename));
        boolean done = false;
        while (!done)
        {   String inputLine = in.readLine();
            if (inputLine == null) done = true;
            else
            {   StringTokenizer tokenizer
                    = new StringTokenizer(inputLine);
                int number
                    = Integer.parseInt(tokenizer.nextToken());
                int pin
                    = Integer.parseInt(tokenizer.nextToken());

                Customer c = new Customer(number, pin);
                addCustomer(c);
            }
        }
        in.close();
    }
```

```
/**
    Adds a customer to the bank.
    @param c the customer to add
*/
public void addCustomer(Customer c)
{  customers.add(c);
}

/**
    Finds a customer in the bank.
    @param aNumber a customer number
    @param aPin a personal identification number
    @return the matching customer, or null if no customer
    matches
*/
public Customer findCustomer(int aNumber, int aPin)
{  for (int i = 0; i < customers.size(); i++)
   {  Customer c = (Customer)customers.get(i);
      if (c.match(aNumber, aPin))
         return c;
   }
   return null;
}

private Vector customers;
}
```

Class Customer.java

```
/**
    A bank customer
*/

public class Customer
{  /**
       Constructs a customer with a given number and PIN.
       @param aNumber the customer number
       @param PIN the personal identification number
    */
   public Customer(int aNumber, int aPin)
   {  customerNumber = aNumber;
      pin = aPin;
      accounts = new BankAccount[2];
      accounts[CHECKING_ACCOUNT] = new BankAccount();
      accounts[SAVINGS_ACCOUNT] = new BankAccount();
   }

   /**
       Tests whether this customer matches a customer
       number and PIN.
```

```
    @param aNumber a customer number
    @param aPin a personal identification number
    @return true if the customer number and PIN match
*/
public boolean match(int aNumber, int aPin)
{   return customerNumber == aNumber && pin == aPin;
}


/**
    Gets an account of this customer.
    @param account one of Customer.CHECKING_ACCOUNT
    or Customer.SAVINGS_ACCOUNT
    @return the selected account, or null if account
    number not valid.
*/
public BankAccount getAccount(int a)
{   if (0 <= a && a < accounts.length)
        return accounts[a];
    else
        return null;
}

public static final int CHECKING_ACCOUNT = 0;
public static final int SAVINGS_ACCOUNT = 1;

private int customerNumber;
private int pin;
private BankAccount[] accounts;
}
```

In this chapter, you learned a *systematic* approach for building a relatively complex program. However, object-oriented design is definitely not a spectator sport. To really learn how to design and implement programs, you have to gain experience by repeating this process with your own projects. It is quite possible that you don't immediately home in on a good solution and that you need to go back and reorganize your classes and responsibilities. That is normal and only to be expected. The purpose of the object-oriented design process is to spot these problems in the design phase when they are still easy to rectify, instead of in the implementation phase when massive reorganization is more difficult and time-consuming.

Random Fact 14.2

Programming—Art or Science?

There has been a long discussion whether the discipline of computing is a science or not. We call the field "computer science", but that doesn't mean much. Except possibly for librarians and sociologists, few people believe that library science and social science are scientific endeavors.

A scientific discipline aims to discover certain fundamental principles dictated by the laws of nature. It operates on the *scientific method:* by posing hypotheses and testing them with experiments that are repeatable by other workers in the field. For example, a physicist may have a theory on the makeup of nuclear particles and attempt to verify or falsify that theory by running experiments in a particle collider. If an experiment cannot be verified, such as the "cold fusion" research in the early 1990s, then the theory dies a quick death.

Some programmers indeed run experiments. They try out various methods of computing certain results, or of configuring computer systems, and measure the differences in performance. However, their aim is not to discover laws of nature.

Some computer scientists discover fundamental principles. One class of fundamental results, for instance, states that it impossible to write certain kinds of computer programs, no matter how powerful the computing equipment is. For example, it is impossible to write a program that takes as its input any two Java program files and as its output prints whether or not these two programs always compute the same results. Such a program would be very handy for grading student homework, but nobody, no matter how clever, will ever be able to write one that works for all input files. The majority of programmers write programs, however, instead of researching the limits of computation.

Some people view programming as an *art* or *craft.* A programmer who writes elegant code that is easy to understand and runs with optimum efficiency can indeed be considered a good craftsman. Calling it an art is perhaps far-fetched, because an art object requires an audience to appreciate it, whereas the program code is generally hidden from the program user.

Others call computing an *engineering discipline.* Just as mechanical engineering is based on the fundamental mathematical principles of statics, computing has certain mathematical foundations. There is more to mechanical engineering than mathematics, though, such as knowledge of materials and of project planning. The same is true for computing.

In one somewhat worrisome aspect, computing does not have the same standing as other engineering disciplines. There is little agreement as to what constitutes professional conduct in the computer field. Unlike the scientist, whose main responsibility is the search for truth, the engineer must strive for the conflicting demands of quality, safety, and economy. Engineering disciplines have professional organizations that hold their members to standards of conduct. The computer field is so new that in many cases we simply don't know the correct method for achieving certain tasks. That makes it difficult to set professional standards.

What do you think? From your limited experience, do you consider the discipline of computing an art, a craft, a science, or an engineering activity?

Chapter Summary

1. Software construction can be divided into five phases: analysis, design, implementation, testing, and deployment. The *waterfall* model suggests that each phase should complete before the next one starts. However, in practice, that is not realistic. Controlled iteration and limited forward-looking activities, such as prototyping and unit testing, are modifications that address shortcomings of the waterfall model.

2. One source for class discovery is to look for the nouns in the requirements specification. Look for verbs to find methods, then find the classes that are responsible for carrying them out.

3. CRC cards are a good informal tool for discovering classes, responsibilities, and collaborators.

4. UML diagrams can record relationships between classes. Three relationships are particularly interesting: inheritance ("is"), aggregation ("has"), and dependency ("uses").

5. This chapter introduced an object-oriented design process that consists of three steps: (1) Use CRC cards to find classes; (2) use UML diagrams to record class relationships, attributes, and methods and; (3) use **javadoc** to prepare documentation for method behavior.

6. By spending time on a good design, the total time spent on a programming project is lowered.

Further Reading

[1] W. H. Sackmann, W.J. Erikson, and E.E. Grant, "Exploratory Experimental Studies Comparing Online and Offline Programming Performance", *Communications of the ACM,* vol. 11, no. 1 (January 1968), pp. 3–11.

[2] F. Brooks, *The Mythical Man-Month,* Addison-Wesley, 1975.

[3] Grady Booch, James Rumbaugh, and Ivar Jacobson, *The Unified Modeling Language User Guide*, Addison-Wesley, 1999.

Review Exercises

Exercise R14.1. What is the software life cycle?

Exercise R14.2. Explain the process of object-oriented design that this chapter recommends for student use.

Exercise R14.3. Give a rule of thumb for how to find classes when designing a program.

Exercise R14.4. Give a rule of thumb for how to find methods when designing a program.

Exercise R14.5. After discovering a method, why is it important to identify the object that is *responsible* for carrying out the action?

Exercise R14.6. What relationship is appropriate between the following classes: aggregation, inheritance, or neither?

```
University—Student
Student—TeachingAssistant
Student—Freshman
Student—Professor
Car—Door
Truck—Vehicle
Traffic—TrafficSign
TrafficSign—Color
```

Exercise R14.7. Every BMW is a car. Should a class BMW inherit from the class Car? BMW is a car manufacturer. Does that mean that the class BMW should inherit from the class CarManufacturer?

Exercise R14.8. Some books on object-oriented programming recommend deriving the class Circle from the class Point. Then the Circle class inherits the setLocation method from the Point superclass. Explain why the move method need not be redefined in the subclass. Why is it nevertheless not a good idea to have Circle inherit from Point? Conversely, would deriving Point from Circle fulfill the "is-a" rule? Would it be a good idea?

Exercise R14.9. Write CRC cards for the Coin and Purse classes of Chapter 3.

Exercise R14.10. Write CRC cards for the bank account classes in Chapter 9.

Exercise R14.11. Draw a UML diagram for the Coin and Purse classes of Chapter 3.

Exercise R14.12. Draw a UML diagram for the bank account classes in Chapter 9.

Exercise R14.13. Draw a UML diagram for the classes in the Eggs program in Chapter 10.

Exercise R14.14. Discover classes and methods for generating a student report card that lists all classes, grades, and the grade point average for a semester. Produce a set of javadoc comments.

Programming Exercises

Exercise P14.1. Implement a program to teach your baby sister to *read the clock*. In the game, present an analog clock such as the one in Figure 18. Generate random times and display the clock. Accept guesses from the player. Reward the player for

Figure 18

An Analog Clock

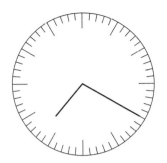

correct guesses. After two incorrect guesses, display the correct answer and make a new random time. Implement several levels of play. In level 1, only show full hours. In level 2, show quarter hours. In level 3, show five-minute multiples, and in level 4, show any number of minutes. After a player has achieved five correct guesses at one level, advance to the next level.

Exercise P14.2. Write a program that implements a different game, to teach arithmetic to your baby brother. The program tests addition and subtraction. In level 1 it tests only addition of numbers less than 10 whose sum is less than 10. In level 2 it tests addition of arbitrary one-digit numbers. In level 3 it tests subtraction of one-digit numbers with a nonnegative difference. Generate random problems and get the player input. The player gets up to two tries per problem. Advance from one level to the next when the player has achieved a score of five points. Your user interface can be text-based or graphical.

Exercise P14.3. Write a bumper car game with the following rules. Bumper cars are located in grid points (x, y), where x and y are integers between -10 and 10. A bumper car starts moving in a random direction, either left, right, up, or down. If it reaches a boundary (that is, x or y is 10 or -10), then it reverses direction. If it is about to bump into another bumper car, it reverses direction. Supply a user interface to add bumper cars, and to run the simulation. Use at least four classes in your program.

Exercise P14.4. Define a class Country that stores the name of the country, its population, and its area. Using that class, write a program that reads in a set of countries and prints

- The country with the largest area
- The country with the largest population
- The country with the largest population density (people per square kilometer)

Think through the problem that you need to solve. What methods will you need? Then design the class and implement the methods. Then write the program. Did you need to add methods later? Did you supply methods that you never needed?

Exercise P14.5. Write a program that can be used to design a suburban scene, with houses, streets, and cars. Users can add houses and cars of various colors to a street. Design a user interface that firms up the requirements, discover classes and methods, provide UML diagrams, and implement your program.

Exercise P14.6. Design a simple email messaging system. A message has a recipient, a sender, a time stamp, and a message text. A mailbox can store messages. Supply a number of mailboxes for different users and a user interface for users to log in, send messages to other users, read their own messages, and log out. Your user interface can be text-based or graphical. Follow the design process that was described in this chapter.

Exercise P14.7. Write a program that simulates a vending machine. Products can be purchased by inserting the correct number of coins into the machine. A user selects a product from a list of available products, adds coins, and either gets the product or gets the coins returned if insufficient money was supplied or if the product is sold out. Products can be restocked and money removed by an operator. Follow the design process that was described in this chapter.

Exercise P14.8. Write a program to design an appointment calendar. An appointment includes the starting time, ending time, and a description; for example,

```
Dentist 2001/10/1 17:30 18:30
CS1 class 2001/10/2 08:30 10:00
```

Supply a user interface to add appointments, remove canceled appointments, and print out a list of appointments for a particular day. Supply a printout of all *overlapping* appointments; for example,

```
Dentist 2001/10/1 12:30 13:30
CS1 class 2001/10/1 13:00 14:00
```

Your user interface can be text-based or graphical. Follow the design process that was described in this chapter.

Exercise P14.9. *Airline seating.* Write a program that assigns seats on an airplane. Assume the airplane has 20 seats in first class (5 rows of 4 seats each, separated by an aisle) and 180 seats in economy class (30 rows of 6 seats each, separated by an aisle). Your program should take three commands: add passengers, show seating, and quit. When passengers are added, ask for the class (first or economy), the number of passengers traveling together (1 or 2 in first class; 1 to 3 in economy), and the seating preference (aisle or window in first class; aisle, center, or window in economy). Then try to find a match and assign the seats. If no match exists, print a message. Your user interface can be text-based or graphical.Follow the design process that was described in this chapter.

Exercise P14.10. Write a simple graphics editor that allows users to add a mixture of shapes (ellipses, rectangles, lines, and text in different colors) to a panel. Supply commands to load and save the picture. For simplicity, you may use a single text size, and you don't have to fill any shapes. Design a user interface, discover classes, supply a UML diagram, and implement your program.

Exercise P14.11. Write a tic-tac-toe game that lets a human player play against the computer. Your program will play many turns against a human opponent, and it will learn. Process human inputs as in the preceding exercise. When it is the computer's turn, the computer randomly selects an empty field, except that it won't ever choose a losing combination. For that purpose, your program must keep an array of losing combinations. Whenever the human wins, the immediately preceding combination is stored as losing. For example, suppose that x = computer and o = human. Suppose the current combination is

```
 O | X | X
---+---+---
   | O |
---+---+---
   |   |
```

Now it is the human's turn, who will of course choose

```
 O | X | X
---+---+---
   | O |
---+---+---
   |   | O
```

The computer should then remember the preceding combination

```
 O | X | X
---+---+---
   | O |
---+---+---
   |   |
```

as a losing combination. As a result, the computer will never again choose that combination from

```
 O | X |
---+---+---
   | O |
---+---+---
   |   |
```

or

Discover classes and supply a UML diagram before you begin to program. *Hint:*
Make a class `Combination` that contains an `int[][]` array. Each element in that
two-dimensional array is EMPTY, FILLED_X, or FILLED_O. Write an `equals` method
that tests whether two combinations are identical.

Algorithms

Chapter Goals

- ◆ To study the selection sort, merge sort, linear search, and binary search algorithms

- ◆ To appreciate that algorithms for the same task can differ widely in performance

- ◆ To understand the big-Oh notation

- ◆ To learn how to estimate and compare the performance of algorithms

- ◆ To learn how to measure the running time of a program

- ◆ To understand when the use of recursion affects the efficiency of an algorithm

One of the most common tasks in data processing is sorting. For example, a collection of employees needs to be printed out in alphabetical order or sorted by salary. We will study several sorting methods in this chapter and compare their performance. This is by no means an exhaustive treatment on the subject of sorting. You will revisit this topic at a later time in your computer science studies. Reference [1] gives a good overview of the many sorting methods available.

Once a sequence of records is sorted, one can locate individual records rapidly. We will study the *binary search* algorithm that carries out this fast lookup.

The fast sorting and searching algorithms that we discuss in this chapter are recursive. However, not all recursive algorithms are fast. We end the chapter with a discussion of when recursion is appropriate.

15.1 Selection Sort

To keep the examples simple, we will discuss how to sort an array of integers before going on to sorting strings or employee data. Consider the following array a:

| 11 | 9 | 17 | 5 | 12 |

An obvious first step is to find the smallest element. In this case the smallest element is 5, stored in a[3]. We should move the 5 to the beginning of the array. Of course, there is already an element stored in a[0], namely 11. Therefore we cannot simply move a[3] into a[0] without moving the 11 somewhere else. We don't yet know where the 11 should end up, but we know for certain that it should not be in a[0]. We simply get it out of the way by *swapping* it with a[3].

Now the first element is in the correct place. In the foregoing figure, the color indicates the portion of the array that is already sorted from the unsorted remainder.

Next we take the minimum of the remaining entries a[1]...a[4]. That minimum value, 9, is already in the correct place. We don't need to do anything in this case and can simply extend the sorted area by one to the right:

We repeat the process. The minimum value of the unsorted region is 11, which needs to be swapped with the first value of the unsorted region, 17:

Now the unsorted region is only two elements long, but we keep to the same successful strategy. The minimum value is 12, and we swap it with the first value, 17.

That leaves us with an unprocessed region of length 1, but of course a region of length 1 is always sorted. We are done.

Let us program this algorithm. For this program as well as the other programs in this chapter, we will use a number of utility methods that we pack up in a class `ArrayUtil` so that we don't have to repeat them for every code example.

Program SelSortTest.java

```
public class SelSortTest
{  public static void main(String[] args)
   {  int[] a = ArrayUtil.randomIntArray(20, 100);

      ArrayUtil.print(a);
      SelSort.sort(a);
      ArrayUtil.print(a);
   }
}
```

Class SelSort.java

```
public class SelSort
   /**
      Finds the smallest element in an array range.
```

```
      @param a the array to search
      @param from the first position in a toompare
      @return the position of the smallest element in the
      range a[from]...a[a.length - 1]
   */
{  public static int minimumPosition(int[] a, int from)
   {  int minPos = from;
      for (int i = from + 1; i < a.length; i++)
         if (a[i] < a[minPos]) minPos = i;
      return minPos;
   }


   /**
      Sorts an array.
      @param a the array to sort
   */
   public static void sort(int[] a)
   {  for (int n = 0; n < a.length - 1; n++)
      {  int minPos = minimumPosition(a, n);
         if (minPos != n)
            ArrayUtil.swap(a, minPos, n);
      }
   }
}
```

Class ArrayUtil.java

```
import java.util.Random;


/**
   This class contains utility methods for array
   manipulation.
*/

public class ArrayUtil
{  /**
      Creates an array filled with random values.
      @param length the length of the array
      @param n the number of possible random values
      @return an array filled with length numbers between
      0 and n-1
   */
   public static int[] randomIntArray(int length, int n)
   {  int[] a = new int[length];
      Random generator = new Random();
      for (int i = 0; i < a.length; i++)
```

```
         a[i] = generator.nextInt(n);
      return a;
   }

   /**
      Swaps two elements in an array.
      @param a  the array with the elements to swap
      @param i  the index of one of the elements
      @param j  the index of the other element
   */
   public static void swap(int[] a, int i, int j)
   {  int temp = a[i];
      a[i] = a[j];
      a[j] = temp;
   }

   /**
      Prints all elements in an array.
      @param a  the array to print
   */
   public static void print(int[] a)
   {  for (int i = 0; i < a.length; i++)
         System.out.print(a[i] + " ");
      System.out.println();
   }
}
```

This algorithm will sort any array of integers. If speed were not an issue for us, or if there simply were no better sorting method available, we could stop the discussion of sorting right here. As the next section shows, however, this algorithm, while entirely correct, shows disappointing performance when run on a large data set.

15.2 Profiling the Selection Sort Algorithm

To measure the performance of a program, you could simply run it and measure how long it takes by using a stopwatch. However, most of our programs run very quickly, and it is not easy to time them accurately in this way. Furthermore, when a program does take a noticeable time to run, a certain amount of that time may simply be used for loading the program from disk into memory (for which we should not penalize it) or for screen output (whose speed depends on the computer model, even for computers with identical CPUs). We will instead create a StopWatch class. This class works just like a real stopwatch. You can start it, stop it and read out the elapsed time. The class uses the System.currentTimeMillis method, which returns the milliseconds that have elapsed since midnight at the start of January 1, 1970. Of course, you don't care about the absolute number of seconds since this historical moment, but the *difference* of two such counts gives us the number of milliseconds of a time interval. Here is the code for the StopWatch class:

Class StopWatch.java

```
/**
    A stopwatch accumulates time when it is running. You can
    repeatedly start and stop the stopwatch. You can use a
    stopwatch to measure the running time of a program.
*/

public class StopWatch
{  /**
        Constructs a stopwatch that is in the stopped state
        and has no time accumulated.
    */
    public StopWatch()
    {  reset();
    }

    /**
        Starts the stopwatch. Time starts accumulating now.
    */
    public void start()
    {  if (isRunning) return;
        isRunning = true;
        startTime = System.currentTimeMillis();
    }

    /**
        Stops the stopwatch. Time stops accumulating and
        is added to the elapsed time.
    */

    public void stop()
    {  if (!isRunning) return;
        isRunning = false;
        long endTime = System.currentTimeMillis();
        elapsedTime = elapsedTime + endTime - startTime;
    }
    /**
        Returns the total elapsed time.
        @return the total elapsed time
    */
    public long getElapsedTime()
    {  if (isRunning)
        {  long endTime = System.currentTimeMillis();
```

```
                    elapsedTime = elapsedTime + endTime - startTime;
                    startTime = endTime;
                }
                return elapsedTime;
            }


            /**
                Stops the watch and resets the elapsed time to 0.
            */
            public void reset()
            {   isRunning = false;
                elapsedTime = 0;
            }

            private long elapsedTime;
            private long startTime;
            private boolean isRunning;
        }
```

Here is how we will use the stopwatch to measure the performance of the sorting algorithm:

Program SelSortTime.java

```
public class SelSortTime
{   public static void main(String[] args)
    {   ConsoleReader console = new ConsoleReader(System.in);

        // construct random array

        System.out.println("Enter array size: ");
        int n = console.readInt();
        int[] a = ArrayUtil.randomIntArray(n, 100);

        // use stopwatch to time selection sort

        StopWatch timer = new StopWatch();

        timer.start();
        SelSort.sort(a);
        timer.stop();

        System.out.println("Elapsed time: "
            + timer.getElapsedTime() + " milliseconds");
    }
}
```

By measuring the time just before the sorting and stopping it just afterwards, you don't count the time it takes to initialize the array or the time during which the program waits for the user to type in n.

Figure 1

Time Taken by Selection Sort

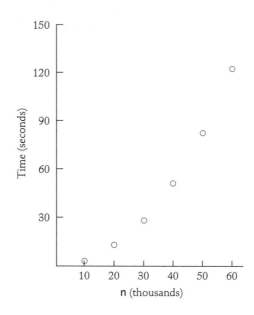

Here are the results of some sample runs:

n	Milliseconds
10,000	3,460
20,000	13,240
30,000	28,290
40,000	51,520
50,000	82,670
60,000	121,820

These measurements were obtained with a Pentium processor with a clock speed of 166 MHz, with 96MB of memory, and running Windows 98. On another computer the actual numbers will look different, but the relationship between the numbers will be the same. Figure 1 shows a plot of the measurements. As you can see, doubling the size of the data set more than doubles the time needed to sort it.

15.3 Analyzing the Performance of the Selection Sort Algorithm

Let us count the number of operations that the program must carry out to sort an array by the selection sort algorithm. Actually, we don't know how many machine operations are generated for each Java instruction or which of those instructions are more time-consuming than others, but we can make a simplification. We will simply count how often an array element is *visited*. Each visit requires about the same amount of work by other operations, such as incrementing subscripts and comparing values.

Let n be size of the array. First, we must find the smallest of n numbers. To achieve that, we must visit n array elements. Then we swap the elements, which takes 2 visits. (You may argue that there is a certain probability that we don't need to swap the values. That is true, and one can refine the computation to reflect that observation. As we will soon see, doing so would not affect the overall conclusion.) In the next step, we need to visit only $n - 1$ elements to find the minimum. In the following step, $n - 2$ elements are visited to find the minimum. The last step visits two elements to find the minimum. Each step requires 2 visits to swap the elements. Therefore, the total number of visits is

$$n + 2 + (n - 1) + 2 + \cdots + 2 + 2$$
$$= n + (n - 1) + \cdots + 2 + (n - 1) \cdot 2$$
$$= 2 + \cdots + (n - 1) + n + (n - 1) \cdot 2$$
$$= \frac{n \cdot (n + 1)}{2} - 1 + (n - 1) \cdot 2$$

because

$$1 + 2 + \cdots + (n - 1) + n = \frac{n \cdot (n + 1)}{2}$$

After multiplying out and collecting terms of n, we find that the number of visits is

$$\tfrac{1}{2}n^2 + \tfrac{5}{2}n - 3$$

We obtain a quadratic equation in n. That explains why the graph of Figure 1 looks approximately like a parabola.

Now let us simplify the analysis further. When you plug in a large value for n (for example, 1000 or 2000), then $\frac{1}{2}n^2$ is 500,000 or 2,000,000. The lower term, $\frac{5}{2}n - 3$, doesn't contribute much at all; it is just 2,497 or 4,997, a drop in the bucket compared to the hundreds of thousands or even millions of comparisons specified by the $\frac{1}{2}n^2$ term. We will just ignore these lower-level terms. Next, we will ignore the constant factor $\frac{1}{2}$. We are not interested in the actual count of visits for a single n. We want to compare the ratios of counts for different values of n. For example, we can say that sorting an array of 2000 numbers requires 4 times as many visits as sorting an array of 1000 numbers:

$$\left(\tfrac{1}{2} \times 2000^2 \right) / \left(\tfrac{1}{2} \times 1000^2 \right) = 4$$

The factor $\frac{1}{2}$ cancels out in comparisons of this kind. We will simply say, "The number of visits is of order n^2". That way, we can easily see that the number of comparisons increases fourfold when the size of the array doubles: $(2n)^2 = 4n^2$.

To indicate that the number of visits is of order n^2, computer scientists often use *big-Oh notation*: The number of visits is $O(n^2)$. This is a convenient shorthand.

To turn an exact expression like

$$\tfrac{1}{2}n^2 + \tfrac{5}{2}n - 3$$

into big-Oh notation, simply locate the fastest-growing term, n^2, and ignore the constant coefficient $\frac{1}{2}$.

We observed before that the actual number of machine operations, and the actual number of microseconds that the computer spends on them, is approximately proportional to the number of element visits. Maybe there are about 10 machine operations (increments, comparisons, memory loads and stores) for every element visit. The number of machine operations is then approximately $10 \times \frac{1}{2}n^2$. Again, we aren't interested in the coefficient and can say that the number of machine operations, and hence the time spent on the sorting, is of the order of n^2 or $O(n^2)$. The sad fact remains that doubling the size of the array causes a fourfold increase in the time required for sorting it. To sort an array of a million entries, for example to create a telephone directory, takes 10,000 times as long as sorting 10,000 entries. If 10,000 entries can be sorted in 3.5 seconds (as in our example), then a million entries require over 9 hours. That is a problem. We will see in the next section how one can dramatically improve the performance of the sorting process by choosing a more sophisticated algorithm.

15.4 Merge Sort

Suppose we have an array of 10 integers. Let us engage in a bit of wishful thinking and hope that the first half of the array is already perfectly sorted, and the second half is too, like this:

| 5 | 9 | 10 | 12 | 17 | | 1 | 8 | 11 | 20 | 32 |

Now it is an easy matter to *merge* the two sorted arrays into a sorted array, simply by taking a new element from either the first or the second subarray and choosing the smaller of the elements each time:

| 5 | 9 | 10 | 12 | 17 | 1̶ | 8 | 11 | 20 | 32 |

| 1 | | | | | | | | | |

| 5̶ | 9 | 10 | 12 | 17 | 1̶ | 8 | 11 | 20 | 32 |

| 1 | 5 | | | | | | | | |

| 5̶ | 9 | 10 | 12 | 17 | 1̶ | 8̶ | 11 | 20 | 32 |

| 1 | 5 | 8 | | | | | | | |

| 5̶ | 9̶ | 10 | 12 | 17 | 1̶ | 8̶ | 11 | 20 | 32 |

| 1 | 5 | 8 | 9 | | | | | | |

| 5̶ | 9̶ | 1̶0̶ | 12 | 17 | 1̶ | 8̶ | 11 | 20 | 32 |

| 1 | 5 | 8 | 9 | 10 | | | | | |

| 5̶ | 9̶ | 1̶0̶ | 12 | 17 | 1̶ | 8̶ | 1̶1̶ | 20 | 32 |

| 1 | 5 | 8 | 9 | 10 | 11 | | | | |

| 5̶ | 9̶ | 1̶0̶ | 1̶2̶ | 17 | 1̶ | 8̶ | 1̶1̶ | 20 | 32 |

| 1 | 5 | 8 | 9 | 10 | 11 | 12 | | | |

| 5̶ | 9̶ | 1̶0̶ | 1̶2̶ | 1̶7̶ | 1̶ | 8̶ | 1̶1̶ | 20 | 32 |

| 1 | 5 | 8 | 9 | 10 | 11 | 12 | 17 | | |

| 5̶ | 9̶ | 1̶0̶ | 1̶2̶ | 1̶7̶ | 1̶ | 8̶ | 1̶1̶ | 2̶0̶ | 32 |

| 1 | 5 | 8 | 9 | 10 | 11 | 12 | 17 | 20 | |

| 5̶ | 9̶ | 1̶0̶ | 1̶2̶ | 1̶7̶ | 1̶ | 8̶ | 1̶1̶ | 2̶0̶ | 3̶2̶ |

| 1 | 5 | 8 | 9 | 10 | 11 | 12 | 17 | 20 | 32 |

In fact, you probably performed this merging before when you and a friend had to sort a pile of papers. You and the friend split up the pile in the middle, each of you sorted your half, and then you merged the results together.

That is all good and well, but it doesn't seem to solve the problem for the computer. It still has to sort the first and the second half of the array, because it can't very well ask a few buddies to pitch in. As it turns out, though, if the computer keeps dividing the array into smaller and smaller subarrays, sorting each half and merging them back together, it carries out dramatically fewer steps than the selection sort requires.

Let us write a program that implements this idea. Because we will call the sort method multiple times to sort portions of the array, we will supply the range of elements that we would like to have sorted:

```
public static void mergeSort(int[] a, int from, int to)
{  if (from == to) return;
   int mid = (from + to) / 2;
   // sort the first and the second half
   mergeSort(a, from, mid);
   mergeSort(a, mid + 1, to);
   merge(a, from, mid, to);
}
```

The **merge** method is somewhat long but actually straightforward:

Program MergeSortTest.java

```
public class MergeSortTest
{  public static void main(String[] args)

   {  int[] a = ArrayUtil.randomIntArray(20, 100);
      ArrayUtil.print(a);
      MergeSort.sort(a);
      ArrayUtil.print(a);
   }
}
```

Class MergeSort.java

```
public class MergeSort
{  /**
      Merges two adjacent subranges of an array
      @param a  the array with entries to be merged
      @param from  the index of the first element of the first range
      @param mid  the index of the last element of the first range
      @param to  the index of the last element of the second range
   */
   public static void merge(int[] a,
      int from, int mid, int to)
   {  int n = to - from + 1;
         // size of the range to be merged

      // merge both halves into a temporary array b
      int[] b = new int[n];

      int i1 = from;
         // next element to consider in the first range
      int i2 = mid + 1;
         // next element to consider in the second range
      int j = 0;
         // next open position in b

      // as long as neither i1 nor i2 past the end, move
      // the smaller element into b
      while (i1 <= mid && i2 <= to)
      {  if (a[i1] < a[i2])
         {  b[j] = a[i1];
            i1++;
         }
         else
         {  b[j] = a[i2];
            i2++;
         }
```

```
      j++;
   }
   // note that only one of the two while loops
   // below is executed

   // copy any remaining entries of the first half
   while (i1 <= mid)
   {  b[j] = a[i1];
      i1++;
      j++;
   }

   // copy any remaining entries of the second half
   while (i2 <= to)
   {  b[j] = a[i2];
      i2++;
      j++;
   }

   // copy back from the temporary array
   for (j = 0; j < n; j++)
      a[from + j] = b[j];
}

/**
   Sorts a range of an array, using the merge sort
   algorithm.
   @param a the array to sort
   @param from the first index of the range to sort
   @param to the last index of the range to sort
*/
public static void MergeSort(int[] a, int from, int to)
{  if (from == to) return;
   int mid = (from + to) / 2;
   // sort the first and the second half
   mergeSort(a, from, mid);
   mergeSort(a, mid + 1, to);
   merge(a, from, mid, to);
}

/**
   Sorts an array, using the merge sort algorithm.
   @param a the array to sort
*/
public static void sort(int[] a)
{  mergeSort(a, 0, a.length - 1);
}
}
```

15.5 Analyzing the Merge Sort Algorithm

This algorithm looks a lot more complicated than the selection sort algorithm, and it appears that it may well take much longer to carry out these repeated subdivisions. However, the timing results for merge sort look much better than those for selection sort:

n	Merge sort (milliseconds)	Selection sort (milliseconds)
10,000	110	3 460
20,000	160	13,240
30,000	220	28,290
40,000	280	51,520
50,000	360	82,670
60,000	450	121,820

Figure 2 shows a graph comparing both performance data. That is a tremendous improvement. To understand why, let us estimate the number of array element visits that are required to sort an array with the merge sort algorithm. First, let us tackle the merge process that happens after the first and second half have been sorted.

Each step in the merge process adds one more element to **b**. There are **n** elements in **b**. That element may come from the first or second half, and in most cases the elements from the two halves must be compared to see which one to take. Let us count that as 3 visits (one for **b** and one each for the two halves of **a**) per element, or 3**n** visits total. Then we must copy back from **b** to **a**, yielding another 2**n** visits, for a total of 5**n**.

If we let $T(n)$ denote the number of visits required to sort a range of n elements through the merge sort process, then we obtain

$$T(n) = T\left(\frac{n}{2}\right) + T\left(\frac{n}{2}\right) + 5n$$

because sorting each half takes $T(n/2)$ visits. (Actually, if n is not even, then we have one subarray of size $(n-1)/2$ and one of size $(n+1)/2$. Although it turns out that this detail does not affect the outcome of the computation, we will nevertheless assume for now that n is a power of 2, say $n = 2^m$. That way, all subarrays can be evenly divided into two parts.)

Figure 2

Merge Sort Timing
(Rectangles) versus Selection
Sort (Circles)

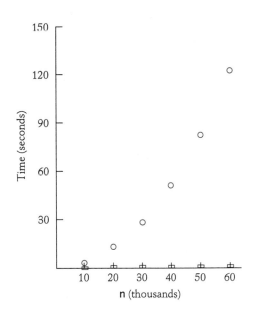

Unfortunately, the formula

$$T(n) = 2T\left(\frac{n}{2}\right) + 5n$$

does not clearly tell us the relationship between n and $T(n)$. To understand the relationship, let us evaluate $T(n/2)$, using the same formula:

$$T\left(\frac{n}{2}\right) = 2T\left(\frac{n}{4}\right) + 5\frac{n}{2}$$

Therefore

$$T(n) = 2 \times 2T\left(\frac{n}{4}\right) + 5n + 5n$$

Let us do that again:

$$T\left(\frac{n}{4}\right) = 2T\left(\frac{n}{8}\right) + 5\frac{n}{4}$$

hence

$$T(n) = 2 \times 2 \times 2T\left(\frac{n}{8}\right) + 5n + 5n + 5n$$

This generalizes from 2, 4, 8, to arbitrary powers of 2:

$$T(n) = 2^k T\left(\frac{n}{2^k}\right) + 5nk$$

Recall that we assume that $n = 2^m$; hence, for $k = m$,

$$T(n) = 2^m T\left(\frac{n}{2^m}\right) + 5nm$$

$$= nT(1) + 5nm$$

$$= n + 5n \log_2 n$$

(Because $n = 2^m$, we have $m = \log_2 n$.) To establish the growth order, we drop the lower-order term n and are left with $5n \log_2 n$. We drop the constant factor 5. It is also customary to drop the base of the logarithm, because all logarithms are related by a constant factor. For example,

$$\log_2 x = \log_{10} x / \log_{10} 2 \approx \log_{10} x \times 3.32193$$

Hence we say that merge sort is an $O(n \log n)$ algorithm.

Is the $O(n \log n)$ merge sort algorithm better than an $O(n^2)$ selection sort algorithm? You bet it is. Recall that it took $100^2 = 10{,}000$ times as long to sort a million records as it took to sort 10,000 records with the $O(n^2)$ algorithm. With the $O(n \log n)$ algorithm, the ratio is

$$\frac{1{,}000{,}000 \log 1{,}000{,}000}{10{,}000 \log 10{,}000} = 100 \left(\frac{6}{4}\right) \approx 150$$

Suppose for the moment that merge sort takes the same time as selection sort to sort an array of 10,000 integers, that is, 3.5 seconds on the test machine. (Actually, it is much faster than that.) Then it would take about 3.5×150 seconds, or about 9 minutes, to sort a million integers. Contrast that with selection sort, which would take over 9 hours for the same task. As you can see, even if it takes you nine hours to learn about a better algorithm, that can be time well spent.

In this chapter we have barely begun to scratch the surface of this interesting topic. There are many sorting algorithms, some with even better performance than the merge sort algorithm, and the analysis of these algorithms can be quite challenging. If you are a computer science major, you will revisit these important issues in a later computer science class.

Random Fact 15.1

The First Programmer

Before pocket calculators and personal computers existed, navigators and engineers used mechanical adding machines, slide rules, and tables of logarithms and trigonometric functions to speed up computations. Unfortunately, the tables—whose values had to be computed by hand—were notoriously inaccurate. The mathematician Charles Babbage (1791–1871) had the insight that if a machine could be constructed that produced printed tables automatically, both calculation and typesetting errors could be avoided. Babbage set out to develop a machine for this purpose, which he called a *Difference Engine* because it used successive differences to compute polynomials. For example, consider the function $f(x) = x^3$. Write down the values for $f(1)$, $f(2)$, $f(3)$, and so on. Then take the *differences* between successive values:

```
1
     7
8
     19
27
     37
64
     61
125
     91
216
```

Repeat the process, taking the difference of successive values in the second column, and then repeat once again:

```
1
     7
8         12
     19         6
27        18
     37         6
64        24
     61         6
125       30
     91
216
```

Now the differences are constant. You can retrieve the function values by a pattern of additions—you need to know the values at the fringe of the pattern and the constant difference. This method was very attractive, because mechanical addition machines had been known for some time. They consisted of cog wheels, with ten cogs per wheel, to represent digits, and mechanisms to handle the carry from one digit to the next. But mechanical multiplication machines were fragile and unreliable. Babbage built a successful prototype of the Difference Engine (see Figure 3) and, with his own money and government grants, proceeded to build the table-printing machine. However, because of funding problems and the difficulty of building the machine to the required precision, it was never completed.

While working on the Difference Engine, Babbage conceived of a much grander vision that he called the *Analytical Engine*. The Difference Engine was designed to carry out a limited set of computations—it was no smarter than a pocket calculator is today. But Babbage realized that such a machine could be made *programmable* by storing programs as well as data. The internal storage of the Analytical Engine was to consist of 1,000 registers of 50 decimal digits

Figure 3

Babbage's Difference Engine

each. Programs and constants were to be stored on punched cards—a technique that was at that time commonly used on looms for weaving patterned fabrics.

Ada Augusta, Countess of Lovelace (1815–1852), the only child of Lord Byron, was a friend and sponsor of Charles Babbage. Ada Lovelace was one of the first people to realize the potential of such a machine, not just for computing mathematical tables but for processing data that were not numbers. She is considered by many the world's first programmer. The Ada programming language, a language developed for use in U.S. Department of Defense projects (see Random Fact 10.1), was named in her honor.

15.6 Searching

Suppose you need to find the telephone number of your friend. You look up his name in the telephone book, and naturally you can find it quickly, because the telephone book is sorted alphabetically. Quite possibly, you may never have thought how important it is that the telephone book is sorted. To see that, think of the following problem: Suppose you have a telephone number and you must know to what party it belongs. You could of course call that number, but suppose nobody picks up on the other end, or you just get a recording. You could look through the telephone book, a number at a time, until you find the number. That would obviously be a tremendous amount of work, and you would have to be desperate to attempt that.

This thought experiment shows the difference between a search through an unsorted data set and a search through a sorted data set. The following two sections will analyze the difference formally.

If you want to find a number in a sequence of values that occur in arbitrary order, there is nothing you can do to speed up the search. You must simply look through all elements until you have found a match or until you reach the end. This is called a *linear* or *sequential* search.

Here is a method that performs a linear search through an array a of integers for the value v. The procedure then returns the index of the match, or -1 if v does not occur in a:

Program LinearSearch.java

```
public class LinearSearch
{  public static void main(String[] args)
   {  ConsoleReader console = new ConsoleReader(System.in);

      // construct random array

      int[] a = ArrayUtil.randomIntArray(20, 100);

      ArrayUtil.print(a);
      System.out.println("Enter number to search for:");
      int n = console.readInt();

      int j = search(a, n);
      System.out.println("Found in position " + j);
   }

   /**
      Finds a value in an array, using the linear search
      algorithm.
      @param a the array
      @param v the value to search
      @return the index at which the value occurs, or -1
      if it does not occur in the array
   */
   public static int search(int[] a, int v)
   {  for (int i = 0; i < a.length; i++)
```

```
    {  if (a[i] == v)
          return i;
    }
    return -1;
}
}
```

How long does a linear search take? If we assume that the element v is present in the array a, then the average search visits $n/2$ elements. If it is not present, then all n elements must be inspected to verify the absence. Either way, a linear search is an $O(n)$ algorithm.

15.7 Binary Search

Now let us search an item in a data sequence that had been previously sorted. Of course, we could still do a linear search, but it turns out we can do much better than that.

Consider the following example: The data set is

a[0]	a[1]	a[2]	a[3]	a[4]	a[5]	a[6]	a[7]
14	43	76	100	115	290	400	511

and we would like to see whether the value 123 is in the data set. The last point in the first half of the data set, a[3], is 100. It is smaller than the value we are looking for; hence, we should look in the second half of the data set for a match, that is, in the sequence

a[4]	a[5]	a[6]	a[7]
115	290	400	411

Now the last value of the first half of this sequence is 290; hence, the value must be located in the sequence

a[4]	a[5]
115	290

The last value of the first half of this very short sequence is 115, which is smaller than the value that we are searching, so we must look in the second half:

a[5]
290

It is trivial to see that we don't have a match, because 123 ≠ 290. If we wanted to insert 123 into the sequence, we would need to insert it just before a[5].

This search process is called a *binary search,* because we cut the size of the search in half in each step. That cutting in half works only because we know that the sequence of values is sorted.

The following method implements a binary search in a sorted array of integers. It returns the position of the match if the search succeeds, or −1 if a is not found in a:

Program BinarySearch.java

```
public class BinarySearch
{  public static void main(String[] args)
   {  ConsoleReader console = new ConsoleReader(System.in);

      // construct random array and sort it

      int[] v = ArrayUtil.randomIntArray(20, 100);
      SelSort.sort(v);

      ArrayUtil.print(v);
      System.out.println("Enter number to search for:");
      int n = console.readInt();

      int j = search(v, n);

      System.out.println("Found in position " + j);
   }

   /**
      Finds a value in a range of a sorted array, using the binary
      search algorithm.
      @param a the sorted array
      @param from the first index in the range to search
      @param to the last index in the range to search
      @param v the value to search
      @return the index at which the value occurs, or −1
      if it does not occur in the array
   */
   public static int binarySearch(int[] a,
      int from, int to, int v)
   {  if (from > to)
         return -1;

      int mid = (from + to) / 2;
      int diff = a[mid] - v;

      if (diff == 0) // a[mid] == v
         return mid;
      else if (diff < 0) // a[mid] < v
         return binarySearch(a, mid + 1, to, v);
      else
         return binarySearch(a, from, mid - 1, v);
   }
```

```
/**
    Finds a value in a sorted array, using the binary
    search algorithm.
    @param a  the sorted array
    @param v  the value to search
    @return  the index at which the value occurs, or -1
    if it does not occur in the array
*/
public static int search(int[] a, int v)
{   return binarySearch(a, 0, a.length -1, v);
}
}
```

Let us determine the number of visits of array elements required to carry out a search. We can use the same technique as in the analysis of merge sort and observe that

$$T(n) = T\left(\frac{n}{2}\right) + 1$$

since we look at the middle element, which counts as one comparison, and then search either the left or the right subarray. Using the same equation,

$$T\left(\frac{n}{2}\right) = T\left(\frac{n}{4}\right) + 1$$

and, by plugging it into the original equation, we get

$$T(n) = T\left(\frac{n}{4}\right) + 2$$

That generalizes to

$$T(n) = T\left(\frac{n}{2^k}\right) + k$$

As in the analysis of merge sort, we make the simplifying assumption that n is a power of 2, $n = 2^m$, where $m = \log_2 n$. Then we obtain

$$T(n) = 1 + \log_2 n$$

Therefore, binary search is an $O(\log n)$ algorithm.

That result makes intuitive sense. Suppose that n is 100. Then after each search, the size of the search range is cut in half, to 50, 25, 12, 6, 3, and 1. After seven comparisons we are done. This agrees with our formula, since $\log_2 100 \approx 6.64386$, and indeed the next larger power of 2 is $2^7 = 128$.

Since a binary search is so much faster than a linear search, is it worthwhile to sort an array first and then use a binary search? It depends. If you only search the array once, then it is more efficient to pay for an $O(n)$ linear search than for an $O(n \log n)$ sort and an $O(\log n)$ binary search. But if one makes a number of searches in the same array, then sorting it is definitely worthwhile.

15.8 Searching and Sorting Real Data

In this chapter, we have studied how to search and sort arrays of integers. Of course, in real programming there is rarely a need to search through a collection of integers. However, it is easy to modify these techniques to search through real data. Recall the `Comparable` interface that was mentioned in Chapter 9. A class can indicate that its objects can be compared with another by implementing the following interface:

```
public interface Comparable
{  int compareTo(Object other);
}
```

For example, to sort a collection of bank accounts, the `BankAccount` class would need to implement this interface. The `compareTo` method should return a negative integer if `this` is less than `other`, zero if they are equal, and a positive number if `this` is greater than `other`:

```
public class BankAccount
{  . . .
   public int compareTo(Object other)
   {  BankAccount otherAccount = (BankAccount)other;
      if (balance < otherAccount.balance) return -1;
      if (balance > otherAccount.balance) return 1;
      return 0;
   }
   . . .
}
```

Among the standard Java classes, the `String` class implements the `Comparable` interface. The following method carries out a binary search of an array of `Comparable` objects.

```
/**
   Finds a value in a range of a sorted array, using the binary
   search algorithm. The array objects must implement
   the Comparable interface.
   @param a the sorted array
   @param from the first index in the range to search
   @param to the last index in the range to search
   @param v the object to search
   @return the index at which the object occurs, or −1
   if it does not occur in the array
*/
```

```
public static int binarySearch(Comparable[] a,
   int from, int to, Comparable v)
{  if (from > to)
      return -1;
   int mid = (from + to) / 2;
   int diff = a[mid].compareTo(v);
   if (diff == 0) // a[mid] == v
      return mid;
   else if (diff < 0) // a[mid] < v
      return binarySearch(a, mid + 1, to, v);
   else
      return binarySearch(a, from, mid - 1, v);
}
```

The `Arrays` class implements both binary search and sorting for arrays of numbers as well as arrays of objects that implement the `Comparable` interface. In practice, when you want to carry out searching and sorting, you can call those methods rather than your own algorithms.

```
int[] a = . . .;
String[] staff = . . .;
Arrays.sort(a); // sorts int[] array
Arrays.sort(staff); // sorts Comparable[] array
int pos13 = Arrays.binarySearch(a, 13); // search sorted int[] array
int posHarry = Arrays.binarySearch(staff, "Harry"));
   // search sorted Comparable[] array
```

◆Random Fact 15.2

Cataloging Your Necktie Collection

People and companies use computers to organize just about every aspect of our lives. On the whole, computers are tremendously good for collecting and analyzing data. In fact, the power offered by computers and their software makes them seductive solutions for just about any organizational problem. It is easy to lose sight of the fact that using a computer is not always the best solution to a problem.

John Bear [2] describes a home computer user who wrote him to describe how he uses a personal computer. That user catalogs his necktie collection, putting descriptions of the ties into a database and generating reports that list them by color, price, or style. Hopefully that person had another use to justify the purchase of a piece of equipment worth several thousand dollars, but that application was so dear to his heart that he wanted to share it. Perhaps not surprisingly, few other users share that excitement, and you don't find the store shelves of your local software store lined with necktie-cataloging software.

The phenomenon of using technology for its own sake is quite widespread. A few years ago, several large corporations showed great enthusiasm for using computer networks to deliver movies to home viewers on demand. With today's technology, that is an expensive way of getting a movie to a person's home. Fast network connections and new receiving equipment are required. It sounds like a lot of trouble just to eliminate the trip to the video rental store. Indeed, initial field experiments were sobering. In these experiments, the network lines and computers are simulated by employees putting tapes into remote video tape players. Few customers were willing to pay a sufficient premium for this service to warrant the huge investments needed. At some point in the future it may be economical to send movies over computer networks, but today the $200 VCR and $3 rental tapes do a better job more cheaply.

At the time of this writing, many elementary schools are spending tremendous resources to bring computers and the Internet into the classroom. Indeed, it is easy to understand why teachers, school administrators, parents, and politicians are in favor of computers in classrooms. Isn't computer literacy absolutely essential for youngsters in the new millennium? Isn't it particularly important to give low-income kids, whose parents may not be able to afford a home computer, the opportunity to master computer skills? However, schools have found that computers are enormously expensive. The initial cost of purchasing the equipment, while substantial when compared to the cost of books and other teaching materials, is not beyond the budget of most schools. However, the *total cost of ownership*—that is, the initial cost plus the cost of keeping the computers in working order and of replacing them when they become outdated, all too quickly—is staggering. As schools purchased more equipment than could be maintained by occasional volunteers, they had to make hard choices—should they lay off librarians and art instructors to hire more computer technicians, or should they let the expensive equipment become useless? What *were* the educational benefits anyway? Interestingly, many schools were so caught up in the hype that they never asked themselves that question until after the computers arrived.

As computer programmers, we might like to program everything. As computer professionals, though, we owe it to our employers and clients to understand what problems they want to solve, and to deploy computers and software only where they add more value than cost.

15.9 The Efficiency of Recursion

As we have seen in this chapter, recursion can be a powerful tool to implement efficient algorithms. On the other hand, recursion can lead to algorithms that perform poorly. In this section, we will analyze the question of when recursion is beneficial and when it is inefficient.

Consider the Fibonacci sequence introduced in Chapter 5: a sequence of numbers defined by the equation

$$f_1 = 1$$
$$f_2 = 1$$
$$f_n = f_{n-1} + f_{n-2}$$

That is, each value of the sequence is the sum of the two preceding values. The first ten terms of the sequence are

$$1, \ 1, \ 2, \ 3, \ 5, \ 8, \ 13, \ 21, \ 34, \ 55$$

It is easy to extend this sequence indefinitely. Just keep appending the sum of the last two values of the sequence. For example, the next entry is $34 + 55 = 89$.

We would like to write a function that computes f_n for any value of n. Suppose we translate the definition directly into a recursive method:

Program FibTime.java

```
public class FibTime
{  public static void main(String[] args)
   {  ConsoleReader console = new ConsoleReader(System.in);
      System.out.println("Enter n: ");
      int n = console.readInt();

      // use stopwatch to time Fibonacci number computation

      StopWatch timer = new StopWatch();

      timer.start();
      int f = fib(n);
      timer.stop();

      System.out.println("fib(" + n + ") = " + f);
      System.out.println("Elapsed time = "
         + timer.getElapsedTime() + " milliseconds");
   }

   /**
      Computes a Fibonacci number.
      @param n an integer
      @return the  nth Fibonacci number
   */
   public static int fib(int n)
   {  if (n <= 2) return 1;
      else return fib(n - 1) + fib(n - 2);
   }
}
```

That is certainly simple, and the method will work correctly. However, consider the following timing data. They indicate that the method runs quite slowly, even for moderate values of n:

n	Seconds
30	3
31	4
32	7
33	12
34	21
35	33
36	53
37	85

That makes no sense. Armed with pencil, paper, and a pocket calculator you could calculate f_{37} in about a minute, so it shouldn't take the computer so long. (Try it out: Extend the sequence to its 37th term. It is 24,157,817.)

To find out the problem, let us insert trace messages into the method:

Program FibTrace.java

```
public class FibTrace
{  public static void main(String[] args)
    {  ConsoleReader console = new ConsoleReader(System.in);
       System.out.println("Enter n:");
       int n = console.readInt();

       int f = fib(n);

       System.out.println("fib(" + n + ") = " + f);
    }

    /**
       Computes a Fibonacci number.
       @param n  an integer
       @return the  nth Fibonacci number
    */
    public static int fib(int n)
    {  System.out.println("Entering fib: n = " + n);
       int f;
       if (n <= 2) f = 1;
       else f = fib(n - 1) + fib(n - 2);
       System.out.println("Exiting fib: n = " + n
          + " return value = " + f);
       return f;
    }
}
```

Following is the trace for computing `fib(7)`.

```
Entering fib: n = 7
Entering fib: n = 6
Entering fib: n = 5
Entering fib: n = 4
Entering fib: n = 3
Entering fib: n = 2
Exiting fib: n = 2 return value = 1
Entering fib: n = 1
Exiting fib: n = 1 return value = 1
Exiting fib: n = 3 return value = 2
Entering fib: n = 2
Exiting fib: n = 2 return value = 1
Exiting fib: n = 4 return value = 3
Entering fib: n = 3
Entering fib: n = 2
```

```
Exiting fib: n = 2 return value = 1
Entering fib: n = 1
Exiting fib: n = 1 return value = 1
Exiting fib: n = 3 return value = 2
Exiting fib: n = 5 return value = 5
Entering fib: n = 4
Entering fib: n = 3
Entering fib: n = 2
Exiting fib: n = 2 return value = 1
Entering fib: n = 1
Exiting fib: n = 1 return value = 1
Exiting fib: n = 3 return value = 2
Entering fib: n = 2
Exiting fib: n = 2 return value = 1
Exiting fib: n = 4 return value = 3
Exiting fib: n = 6 return value = 8
Entering fib: n = 5
Entering fib: n = 4
Entering fib: n = 3
Entering fib: n = 2
Exiting fib: n = 2 return value = 1
Entering fib: n = 1
Exiting fib: n = 1 return value = 1
Exiting fib: n = 3 return value = 2
Entering fib: n = 2
Exiting fib: n = 2 return value = 1
Exiting fib: n = 4 return value = 3
Entering fib: n = 3
Entering fib: n = 2
Exiting fib: n = 2 return value = 1
Entering fib: n = 1
Exiting fib: n = 1 return value = 1
Exiting fib: n = 3 return value = 2
Exiting fib: n = 5 return value = 5
Exiting fib: n = 7 return value = 13
```

Now it is becoming apparent why the function takes so long. It is computing the same values over and over. For example, the computation of `fib(7)` calls `fib(4)` three times and `fib(3)` five times. That is very different from the computation we would do with pencil and paper. There we would just write down the values as they were computed and add up the last two to get the next one until we reached the desired entry; no sequence value would ever be computed twice.

If we imitate the pencil-and-paper process, then we get the following program.

Program FibLoop.java

```
public class FibLoop
{  public static void main(String[] args)
    {  ConsoleReader console = new ConsoleReader(System.in);
        System.out.println("Enter n: ");
```

```
            int n = console.readInt();

            // use stopwatch to time Fibonacci number computation

            StopWatch timer = new StopWatch();

            timer.start();
            int f = fib(n);
            timer.stop();

            System.out.println("fib(" + n + ") = " + f);
            System.out.println("Elapsed time = "
                + timer.getElapsedTime() + " milliseconds");
         }

         /**
             Computes a Fibonacci number.
             @param n an integer
             @return the  nth Fibonacci number
         */
         public static int fib(int n)
         {  if (n <= 2) return 1;
            int fold = 1;
            int fold2 = 1;
            int fnew = 1;
            for (int i = 3; i <= n; i++)
            {  fnew = fold + fold2;
               fold2 = fold;
               fold = fnew;
            }
            return fnew;
         }
      }
```

This method runs *much* faster than the recursive version.

In this example of the **fib** method, the recursive solution was easy to program because it exactly followed the mathematical definition, but it ran far more slowly than the iterative solution, because it computed many intermediate results multiple times.

Let $T(n)$ denote the number of times the recursive **fib** method calls itself when computing the nth Fibonacci number. It can be shown that $T(n)$ is of the same order as f_n, and that f_n is equal to the integer closest to $g^n/\sqrt{5}$, where $g = (1 + \sqrt{5})/2$ is the so-called *golden ratio number*. (See [3] for a proof.) Hence the running time of the recursive **fib** method is $O(g^n)$. This is an example of *exponential growth*. When n gets larger, the exponential term g^n grows very rapidly—much more rapidly than a polynomial such as n^2.

It is not always true that the recursive solution to a problem is slower than a nonrecursive one. Frequently, the iterative and recursive solution have essentially the same performance. For example, the computation of $n!$ can be equally well performed with a recursive method,

```
public static int factorial(int n)
{   if (n <= 0) return 1;
    else return n * factorial(n - 1);
}
```

or a simple loop,

```
public static int factorial(int n)
{   int r = 1;
    int i;
    for (i = 1; i <= n; i++)
        r = r * i;
    return r;
}
```

There is a good reason to choose the loop over the recursion. Each method call takes a certain amount of processor time. Nested method calls also consume a small amount of space for the return address and the local variables of the nested methods. It is in principle possible to exhaust the space set aside for these data values (the so-called run-time stack).

Let us reconsider the binary search method from Section 15.7. Is it possible to remove the recursion? After we compare a with the middle element, we can just reset the boundaries of the range to the selected subrange and recompute its middle. This can be done in a loop.

```
public static int binary_search(int[] v, int a)
{   int from = 0;
    int to = v.length() - 1;
    while (from <= to)
    {   int mid = (from + to) / 2;
        int diff = v[mid] - a;
        if (diff == 0) /* v[mid] == a */

            return mid;
        else if (diff > 0) /* v[mid] > a */
            from = mid + 1;
        else
            to = mid - 1;
    }
    return -1;
}
```

Can we rewrite the merge sort algorithm in the same way? There is an essential difference between the recursive calls in binary search and merge sort. In binary search, the range was cut in half and only one of the two subranges was further considered. In merge sort, *both* subranges are again subdivided. There is no easy way to capture this in a simple loop. While it is possible to write a non-recursive version of merge sort, such a procedure would be more complex. In this situation, the recursive method is an example of the effective use of recursion.

Chapter Summary

1. Algorithms that perform the same task can have significant differences in performance. We analyzed two sorting algorithms: selection sort and merge sort. Both rearrange an array in sorted order, but merge sort is much faster on large data sets.

2. Computer scientists use big-Oh notation to give approximate descriptions of the efficiency of algorithms. In big-Oh notation only the fastest-growing term is important; constant factors are ignored. Selection sort is an $O(n^2)$ algorithm; merge sort is an $O(n \log n)$ algorithm.

3. Searching for a value in an unsorted data set requires $O(n)$ steps. If the data set are sorted, binary search can find the value in $O(\log n)$ steps.

4. Recursive algorithms are often more convenient to program, but they can be slower than iterative algorithms. Recursion is, however, useful for algorithms that cannot easily be expressed as an iteration.

Further Reading

[1] Michael T. Goodrich and Roberto Tamassia: *Data Structures and Algorithms in Java*, John Wiley & Sons, 1998.

[2] John Bear, *Computer Wimp*, Ten Speed Press, 1983.

[3] Donald E. Knuth, *The Art of Computer Programming, Vol. 1: Fundamental Algorithms*, Addison-Wesley, 1973.

Classes, Objects, and Methods Introduced in This Chapter

```
java.lang.System
   currentTimeMillis
java.util.Arrays
   binarySearch
   sort
```

Review Exercises

Exercise R15.1. *Checking against off-by-1 errors.* When writing the selection sort algorithm of Section 15.1, a programmer must make the usual choices of < against <=, a.length against a.length - 1, and next against next + 1. This is a fertile ground for off-by-1 errors. Make code walkthroughs of the algorithm with arrays of length 0, 1, 2, and 3 and check carefully that all index values are correct.

Exercise R15.2. What is the difference between searching and sorting?

Exercise R15.3. For the following expressions, what is the order of the growth of each?

$$n^2 + 2n + 1$$

$$n^{10} + 9n^9 + 20n^8 + 145n^7$$

$$(n + 1)^4$$

$$(n^2 + n)^2$$

$$n + 0.001n^3$$

$$n^3 - 1000n^2 + 10^9$$

$$n + \log n$$

$$n^2 + n \log n$$

$$2^n + n^2$$

$$(n^3 + 2n)/(n^2 + 0.75)$$

Exercise R15.4. We determined that the actual number of visits in the selection sort algorithm is

$$T(n) = \tfrac{1}{2}n^2 + \tfrac{5}{2}n - 3$$

We then characterized this method as having $O(n^2)$ growth. Compute the actual ratios

$$T(2000)/T(1000)$$

$$T(4000)/T(1000)$$

$$T(10000)/T(1000)$$

and compare them with

$$f(2000)/f(1000)$$

$$f(4000)/f(1000)$$

$$f(10000)/f(1000)$$

where $f(n) = n^2$.

Exercise R15.5. Suppose algorithm A takes 5 seconds to handle a data set of 1000 records. If the algorithm A is an $O(n)$ algorithm, how long will it take to handle a data set of 2000 records? Of 10,000 records?

Exercise R15.6. Suppose an algorithm takes 5 seconds to handle a data set of 1,000 records. Fill in the following table, which shows the approximate growth of the execution times depending on the complexity of the algorithm.

	$O(n)$	$O(n^2)$	$O(n^3)$	$O(n \log n)$	$O(2^n)$
1000	5	5	5	5	5
2000					
3000		45			
10000					

For example, since $3000^2/1000^2 = 9$, the algorithm would take 9 times as long, or 45 seconds, to handle a data set of 3000 records.

Exercise R15.7. Sort the following growth rates from slowest growth to fastest growth.

$$O(n)$$
$$O(n^3)$$
$$O(n^n)$$
$$O(\log n)$$
$$O(n^2 \log n)$$
$$O(n \log n)$$
$$O(2^n)$$
$$O(\sqrt{n})$$
$$O(n \sqrt{n})$$
$$O(n^{\log n})$$

Exercise R15.8. What is the growth rate of the standard algorithm to find the minimum value of an array? Of finding both the minimum and the maximum?

Exercise R15.9. What is the growth rate of the following method?

```
public static int count(int[] a, int c)
{  int i;
   int count = 0;
```

```
    for (i = 0; i < a.length; i++)
    {   if (a[i] == c) count++;
    }
    return count;
}
```

Exercise R15.10. Your task is to remove all duplicates from an array. For example, if the array has the values

4 7 11 4 9 5 11 7 3 5

then the array should be changed to

4 7 11 9 5 3

Here is a simple algorithm. Look at a[i]. Count how many times it occurs in a. If the count is larger than 1, remove it. What is the growth rate of the time required for this algorithm?

Exercise R15.11. Consider the following algorithm to remove all duplicates from an array. Sort the array. For each element in the array, look at its next neighbor to decide whether it is present more than once. If so, remove it. Is this a faster algorithm than the one in the preceding exercise?

Exercise R15.12. Develop a fast algorithm for removing duplicates from an array if the resulting array must have the same ordering as the original array.

Exercise R15.13. Consider the following sorting algorithm. To sort a, make a second array b of the same size. Then insert elements from a into b, keeping b in sorted order. For each element, call the binary search method of Exercise P15.7 to determine where it needs to be inserted. To insert an element into the middle of an array, you need to move all elements above the insert location up.

Is this an efficient algorithm? Estimate the number of array element visits in the sorting process. Assume that on average half of the elements of b need to be moved to insert a new element.

Programming Exercises

Exercise P15.1. Modify the selection sort algorithm to sort an array of integers in descending order.

Exercise P15.2. Modify the selection sort algorithm to sort an array of products by price.

Exercise P15.3. Write a program that generates the table of sample runs of the selection sort times automatically. The program should ask for the smallest and largest value of n and the number of measurements and then make all sample runs.

Exercise P15.4. Modify the merge sort algorithm to sort an array of products by price.

Exercise P15.5. Write a telephone lookup program. Read a data set of 1000 names and telephone numbers from a file that contains the numbers in random order. Handle lookups by name and also reverse lookups by phone number. Use a binary search for both lookups.

Exercise P15.6. Modify the binary search algorithm so that you can search the records stored in a *database file* without actually reading them into an array. Use the product database of Chapter 11, sort it by product name, and make lookups for products.

Exercise P15.7. Consider the `binarySearch` method in Section 15.7. If no match is found, the method returns -1. Modify the method so that if a is not found, the method returns the index of the next larger value instead, or to `v.length()` if a is larger than all the elements of the array.

Exercise P15.8. Use the modification of the binary search method of the preceding exercise to sort an array as described in Exercise R15.13. Implement this algorithm and measure its performance.

Exercise P15.9. Implement the `mergeSort` method without recursion, where the length of the array is a power of 2. First merge adjacent regions of size 1, then adjacent regions of size 2, then adjacent regions of size 4, and so on.

Exercise P15.10. Implement the `mergeSort` procedure without recursion, where the length of the array is an arbitrary number. *Hint:* Use a stack to keep track of which subarrays have been sorted.

Exercise P15.11. Give a *graphical animation* of selection sort as follows: Fill an array with a set of random numbers between 1 and 100. Set the window coordinate system to `a.length` by 100. Draw each array element as a stick, as in Figure 4. Whenever you change the array, clear the screen and redraw.

Exercise P15.12. Write a graphical animation of merge sort.

Exercise P15.13. Write a graphical animation of binary search. Highlight the currently inspected element and the current values of `from` and `to`.

Figure 4

Graphical Animation

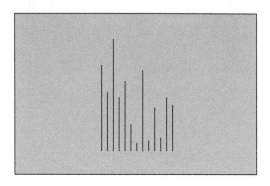

Exercise P15.14. Find out how often the recursive version of `fib` calls itself. Keep a global variable `fibCount` and increment it once in every call of `fib`. What is the relationship between `fib(n)` and `fibCount`?

Exercise P15.15. Write a program that keeps an appointment book. Make a class `Appointment` that stores a description of the appointment, the appointment day, the starting time, and the ending time. Your program should keep the appointments in a sorted vector. Users can add appointments and print out all appointments for a given day. When a new appointment is added, use binary search to find where it should be inserted in the vector. Do not add it if it conflicts with another appointment.

An Introduction to Data Structures

Chapter Goals

- ◆ To learn how to use linked lists provided in the standard library

- ◆ To understand the implementation of linked lists

- ◆ To be able to program insertion and removal of list elements

- ◆ To understand how to traverse the elements that are stored in lists

- ◆ To learn about binary trees

16.1 Using Linked Lists

Imagine a program that maintains an array of employee records, sorted by the last names of the employees. When a new employee is hired, a record needs to be inserted into the array. Unless the company happened to hire employees in dictionary order, the new record needs to be inserted into the middle of the array. Then all other employee records must be moved toward the end.

Conversely, if an employee leaves the company, the record must be removed and the hole in the sequence needs to be closed up by moving all employee records that come after it. Moving a large number of employee records can involve a substantial amount of computer time. We would like to discover a method that minimizes this cost.

To minimize movement of records, let us change the structure of the storage. Rather than storing the object references in an array, let us break up the array into a sequence of *links*. Each link stores an element and a reference to the next link in the sequence (see Figure 1). Such a data structure is called a *linked list*.

When you insert a new element into a linked list, only the neighboring link references need to be updated. The same is true when removing an element.

What's the catch? Linked lists allow speedy insertion and removal, but *element access* is slow. To locate the fifth element, you have to traverse the first four. This is a problem if you need to access the elements in random order. But if you mostly visit all elements in sequence (for example, to display or print the elements), the lack of random access is not a problem. You use linked lists when you are concerned about

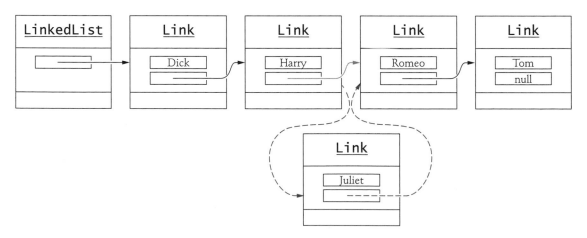

Figure 1

Inserting an Element Into a
Linked List

the efficiency of inserting or removing elements and you don't need element access in random order.

The Java library provides a linked-list class. In this section you will learn how to use this class. In the next section you will peek under the hood and see how some of its key methods are implemented.

The `LinkedList` class in the `java.util` package implements linked lists. This linked list remembers both the first and the last link in the list. You have easy access to both ends of the list with the methods

```
void addFirst(Object obj)
void addLast(Object obj)
Object getFirst()
Object getLast()
Object removeFirst()
Object removeLast()
```

How do you add and remove elements in the middle of the list? The list will not give you references to the links. If you had direct access to them and somehow messed them up, you would break the linked list. As you will see in the next section, where you implement some of the linked list operations yourself, keeping all links intact is not trivial. For your protection, the Java library supplies a `ListIterator` type. A list iterator encapsulates a position anywhere inside the linked list (see Figure 2).

Conceptually, you should think of the iterator as pointing between two links, just as the cursor in a word processor points between two characters (see Figure 3). In the conceptual view, think of each link element as being like a letter in a word processor, and think of the iterator as being like the blinking cursor between letters.

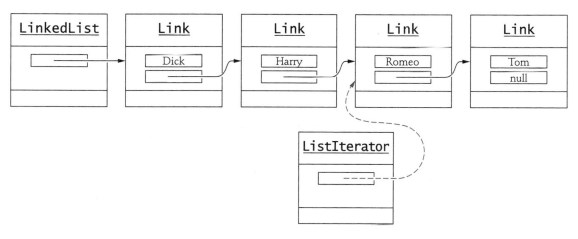

Figure 2

A List Iterator

Figure 3

A Conceptual View
of the List Iterator

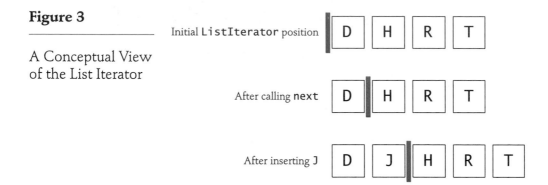

Initial ListIterator position

After calling next

After inserting J

You obtain a list iterator with the listIterator method of the LinkedList class:

```
LinkedList list = . . .;
ListIterator iterator = list.listIterator();
```

Initially, the iterator points before the first element. You can move the iterator position with the next method:

```
iterator.next();
```

The next method throws a NoSuchElementException if you are already past the end of the list. You should always call the method hasNext before calling next—it returns true if there is a next element.

```
if (iterator.hasNext())
    iterator.next();
```

The next method returns the object of the link that it is passing. Therefore, you can traverse all elements in a linked list with the following loop:

```
while (iterator.hasNext())
{  Object obj = iterator.next();
   do something with obj
}
```

Actually, the links of the LinkedList class store two links: one to the next element and one to the previous one. Such a list is called a *doubly linked list*. You can use the previous and hasPrevious methods of the iterator class to move the list position backwards.

The **add** method adds an object after the iterator, and then moves the iterator position past the new element.

```
iterator.add("Juliet");
```

You can visualize insertion to be like typing text in a word processor. Each character is inserted after the cursor, and then the cursor moves past the inserted character (see Figure 3). Most people never pay much attention to this—you may want to try it out and watch carefully how your word processor inserts characters.

The **remove** method removes and returns the object that was returned by the last call to **next** or **previous**. For example, the following loop removes all objects that fulfill a certain condition:

```
while (iterator.hasNext())
{  Object obj = iterator.next();
   if (obj fulfills condition)
      iterator.remove();
}
```

You have to be careful when calling **remove**. It can be called only once after calling **next** or **previous**, and you cannot call it immediately after a call to **add**. If you call the method improperly, it throws an **IllegalStateException**.

Here is a sample program that inserts elements into a list and then iterates through the list, adding and removing elements. Finally, the entire list is printed. The comments indicate the iterator position.

Program ListTest1.java

```
import java.util.LinkedList;
import java.util.ListIterator;

public class ListTest1
{  public static void main(String[] args)
   {  LinkedList staff = new LinkedList();
      staff.addLast("Dick");
      staff.addLast("Harry");
      staff.addLast("Romeo");
      staff.addLast("Tom");

      // | in the comments indicates the iterator position

      ListIterator iterator = staff.listIterator(); // |DHRT
      iterator.next(); // D|HRT
      iterator.next(); // DH|RT

      // add more elements after second element

      iterator.add("Juliet"); // DHJ|RT
      iterator.add("Nina"); // DHJN|RT

      iterator.next(); // DHJNR|T
      // remove last traversed element

      iterator.remove(); // DHJN|T

      // print all elements
```

```
            iterator = staff.listIterator();
            while (iterator.hasNext())
               System.out.println(iterator.next());
         }
      }
```

16.2 Implementing Linked Lists

In the last section you saw how to use the linked list class that is supplied by the Java library. In this section, we will look at the implementation of a simplified version of this class. This shows you how the list operations manipulate the links as the list is modified.

To keep this sample code simple, we will not implement all methods of the linked-list class. We will implement only a singly linked list, and the list class will supply direct access only to the first list element, not the last one. The result will be a fully functional list class that shows how the links are updated in the **add** and **remove** operations and how the iterator traverses the list.

A `Link` object stores an object and a reference to the next link. Because the methods of both the linked list class and the iterator class have frequent access to the `Link` instance variables, we do not make the instance variables private. Instead, we make `Link` a private inner class of the `LinkedList` class. Since none of the list methods returns a `Link` object, it is then safe to leave the instance variables public.

```
class LinkedList
{   . . .
   private class Link
   {   public Object data;
       public Link next;
   }
}
```

The `LinkedList` class holds a reference `first` to the first link (or `null`, if the list is completely empty).

```
class LinkedList
{   public LinkedList()
   {   first = null;
   }

   public Object getFirst()
   {   if (first == null)
          throw new NoSuchElementException();
       return first.data;
   }

       . . .
   private Link first;
}
```

Figure 4

Adding a Link
to the Head of a
Linked List

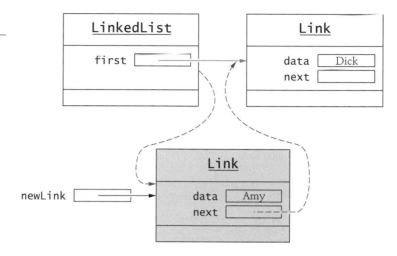

Now let us turn to the **addFirst** operation (see Figure 4). When a new link is added to the list, it becomes the head of the list, and the link that was the old list head becomes its next link:

```
class LinkedList
{  . . .
   public void addFirst(Object obj)
   {  Link newLink = new Link();
      newLink.data = obj;
      newLink.next = first;
      first = newLink;
   }
   . . .
}
```

Removing the first element of the list works as follows. The data of the first link is saved and later returned as the method result. The successor of the first link becomes the first link of the shorter list (see Figure 5). Then there are no further references to the old link, and the garbage collector will eventually recycle it.

```
class LinkedList
{  . . .
   public Object removeFirst()
   {  if (first == null)
         throw new NoSuchElementException();
      Object obj = first.data;
      first = first.next;
      return obj;
   }
   . . .
}
```

Next, let us turn to the iterator class. In the standard Java library, **ListIterator** is an interface and the **listIterator** method returns an object of an inner class

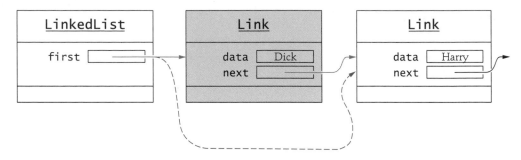

Figure 5

Removing a Link from the Head of a
Linked List

implementing it. For simplicity, we will follow a slightly different approach than the standard Java library and make **Iterator** a public inner class of the **LinkedList** class. Programs using this iterator need to refer to it as a **LinkedList.Iterator**. Because the iterator is an inner class, it has access to the private features of the **LinkedList** class—in particular, the private **Link** class.

```
class LinkedList
{   . . .
    public Iterator listIterator()
    {   return new Iterator();
    }

    public class Iterator
    {   public Iterator()
        {   position = null;
            previous = null;
        }

        . . .
        private Link position;
        private Link previous;
    }
    . . .
}
```

Each iterator object has a reference **position** to the last visited link. We also store a reference to the last link before that. We will need that reference to adjust the links properly in the **remove** operation.

The **next** method is simple. The **position** reference is advanced to **position.next**, and the old position is remembered in **previous**. There is a special case, however—if the iterator points before the first element of the list, then the old **position** is **null** and must be set to **first**.

```
public class Iterator
{  . . .
   public Object next()
   {  if (position == null)
      {  position = first;
         return getFirst();
      }
      else
      {  if (position.next == null)
            throw new NoSuchElementException();
         previous = position; // remember for remove
         position = position.next;
         return position.data;
      }
   }
   . . .
}
```

The next method is supposed to be called only when the iterator is not yet at the end of the list. The iterator is at the end if the list is empty (that is, first == null) or if there is no element after the current position (position.next == null).

```
public class Iterator
{  . . .
   public boolean hasNext()
   {  if (position == null)
         return first != null;
      else
         return position.next != null;
   }
   . . .
}
```

Removing an element from the middle of the list is more involved. If the previous reference is null, then this call to remove does not immediately follow a call to next, and we throw an IllegalStateException. Otherwise, we set the successor of the previous element to its successor, thereby eliminating it (see Figure 6).

```
public class Iterator
{  . . .
   public void remove()
   {  if (position == first)
         removeFirst();
      else
      {  if (previous == null)
            throw new IllegalStateException();
         previous.next = position.next;
         position = previous;
      }
```

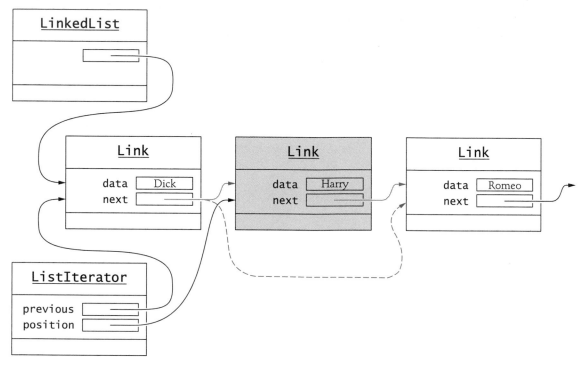

Figure 6

Removing a Link from the Middle of
a Linked List

```
            previous = null;
      }
        . . .
   }
```

According to the definition of the **remove** method, it is illegal to call **remove** twice
in a row. Therefore, the **remove** method sets the **previous** reference to **null**.

Finally, the most complex operation is the addition of a link. You insert the new
link after the current position, and set the successor of the new link to the successor
of the current position (see Figure 7).

```
public class Iterator
{  . . .
   public void add(Object obj)
   {  if (position == null)
         addFirst(obj);
      else
```

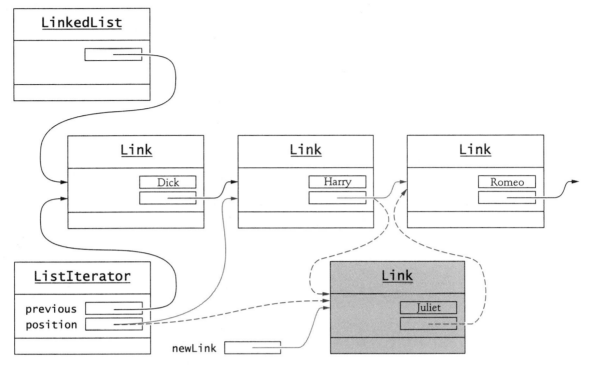

Figure 7

Adding a Link to the Middle of a
Linked List

```
    {  Link newLink = new Link();
       newLink.data = obj;
       newLink.next = position.next;
       position.next = newLink;
       position = newLink;
       previous = null;
    }
  }
    . . .
}
```

Here is a program that consists of the same test stub as in the previous section and
the complete implementation of our linked-list class.

Program ListTest2.java

```
import java.util.NoSuchElementException;

public class ListTest2
{  public static void main(String[] args)

   {  LinkedList staff = new LinkedList();
      staff.addFirst("Tom");
      staff.addFirst("Romeo");
      staff.addFirst("Harry");
      staff.addFirst("Dick");
      // | in the comments indicates the iterator position
      LinkedList.Iterator iterator
         = staff.listIterator(); // |DHRT
      iterator.next(); // D|HRT
      iterator.next(); // DH|RT
      // add more elements after second element
      iterator.add("Juliet"); // DHJ|RT
      iterator.add("Nina"); // DHJN|RT

      iterator.next(); // DHJNR|T
      // remove last traversed element

      iterator.remove(); // DHJN|T

      // print all elements

      iterator = staff.listIterator();
      while (iterator.hasNext())
         System.out.println(iterator.next());
   }
}

/**
    A linked list is a sequence of links with efficient
    element insertion and removal.
*/

class LinkedList
{  /**
       Constructs an empty linked list.
    */
    public LinkedList()
    {  first = null;
    }

    /**
        Returns the first element in the linked list.
        @return the first element in the linked list
    */
```

```
public Object getFirst()
{  if (first == null)
      throw new NoSuchElementException();
   return first.data;
}

/**
   Removes the first element in the linked list.
   @return the removed element
*/
public Object removeFirst()
{  if (first == null)
      throw new NoSuchElementException();
   Object obj = first.data;
   first = first.next;
   return obj;
}

/**
   Adds an element to the front of the linked list.
   @param obj the object to add
*/
public void addFirst(Object obj)
{  Link newLink = new Link();
   newLink.data = obj;
   newLink.next = first;
   first = newLink;
}

/**
   Returns an iterator for iterating through this list.
   @return an iterator for iterating through this list
*/
public Iterator listIterator()
{  return new Iterator();
}

private Link first;

private class Link
{  public Object data;
   public Link next;
}

public class Iterator
{  /**
      Constructs an iterator that points to the front
      of the linked list.
   */
```

```java
public Iterator()
{  position = null;
   previous = null;
}

/**
    Moves the iterator past the next element.
    @return the traversed element
*/
public Object next()
{  if (position == null)
   {  position = first;
      return getFirst();
   }
   else
   {  if (position.next == null)
         throw new NoSuchElementException();
      previous = position; // remember for remove
      position = position.next;
      return position.data;
   }
}
/**
    Tests whether there is an element after the iterator position.
    @return true if there is an element after the iterator position
*/
public boolean hasNext()
{  if (position == null)
      return first != null;
   else
      return position.next != null;
}

/**
    Adds an element before the iterator position
    and moves the iterator past the inserted element.
    @param obj the object to add
*/
public void add(Object obj)
{  if (position == null)
      addFirst(obj);
   else
   {  Link newLink = new Link();
      newLink.data = obj;
      newLink.next = position.next;
      position.next = newLink;
      position = newLink;
      previous = null;
   }
}
```

```
/**
    Removes the last traversed element. This method may
    be called only after a call to the next() method.
*/
public void remove()
{  if (position == first)
      removeFirst();
   else
   {  if (previous == null)
         throw new IllegalStateException();
      previous.next = position.next;
      position = previous;
   }
   previous = null;
}

private Link position;
private Link previous;
   }
}
```

This concludes our discussion about linked lists. You now know how to use the LinkedList class in the Java library, and you have had a peek "under the hood" to see how linked lists are implemented.

Advanced Topic 16.1

Static Inner Classes

You first saw the use of inner classes for event handlers. Inner classes are useful in that context because their methods have the privilege of accessing private data members of outer-class objects. The same is true for the Iterator inner class in the sample code for this section. The iterator needs to access the first instance variable of its linked list.

However, the Link inner class has no need to access the outer class. In fact, it has no methods. Thus, there is no need to store a reference to the outer list class with each Link object. To suppress the outer-class reference, you can declare the inner class as static:

```
class LinkedList
{  . . .
   private static class Link
   {  . . .
   }
}
```

The purpose of the keyword static in this context is to indicate that the inner-class objects do not depend on the outer-class objects that generate them. In particular, the methods of a static inner class cannot access the outer-class instance variables. Declaring the inner class static is more efficient, since its objects do not store an outer-class reference.

16.3 Binary Search Trees

When we moved from an array to a linked list, we gained the advantage of fast insertion and removal in the middle of the collection, but we lost one important algorithm: fast searching. Recall that binary search in an array of 1000 elements was able to locate an element in about 10 steps by cutting the size of the search interval in half in each step. That does not work for lists, which are not *random-access* data structures. To go to the middle of the list, you must start at the beginning and then go a link at a time. That makes the binary search algorithm meaningless. If you already have to traverse half the list to find its middle, that takes 500 steps for a list of 1000 elements. So you can't hope for an $O(\log n)$ algorithm.

In this section we will introduce the simplest of many *treelike* data structures that computer scientists have invented to overcome that problem. Binary search trees allow fast insertion and removal of elements, *and* they are specially designed for fast searching.

A linked list is a one-dimensional data structure. Every link has a reference to the next link. You can imagine that all links are arranged in line. In contrast, a *binary tree* is made of nodes with *two* references, called the *left* and *right children*. You should visualize it as a tree, except that it is traditional to draw the tree upside down, like a family tree or hierarchy chart (see Figure 8). In a binary tree, every node has at most two children, hence the name *binary*.

Finally, a *binary search tree* is carefully constructed to have the following important property:

> The data values of *all* descendants to the left of *any* node are less than the data value stored in that node, and *all* descendants to the right have greater data values.

The tree in Figure 8 has this property. To verify the binary search property, you must check each node. Consider the node "Juliet". All descendants to the left have data before "Juliet". All descendants on the right have data after "Juliet". Move on to "Eve". There is a single descendant to the left, with data "Adam" before "Eve", and a single descendant to the right, with data "Harry" after "Eve". Check the remaining nodes in the same way.

Figure 9 shows a binary tree that is not a binary search tree. Look carefully–the root node passes the test, but its two children do not.

Let us implement these tree classes. Just as you needed classes for lists and their links, you need a class for the tree, containing a reference to the *root node*, and a separate class for the nodes. Each node contains two references (to the left and right child node) and a data field. At the fringes of the tree, one or two of the child references are `null`. The data variable has type `Comparable`, not `Object`, because you must be able to compare the values in a binary search tree in order to place them into the correct position.

```
class Tree
{  public Tree(){ . . . }
   public void insert(Comparable obj) { . . . }
   public void print() { . . . }
```

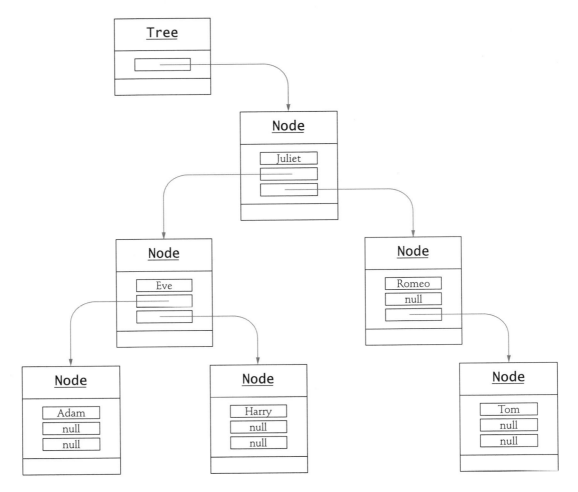

Figure 8

A Binary Search Tree

```
private Node root;

private class Node
{  public void insertNode(Node newNode) { . . . }
   public void printNodes() { . . . }

   public Comparable data;
   public Node left;
   public Node right;
}
}
```

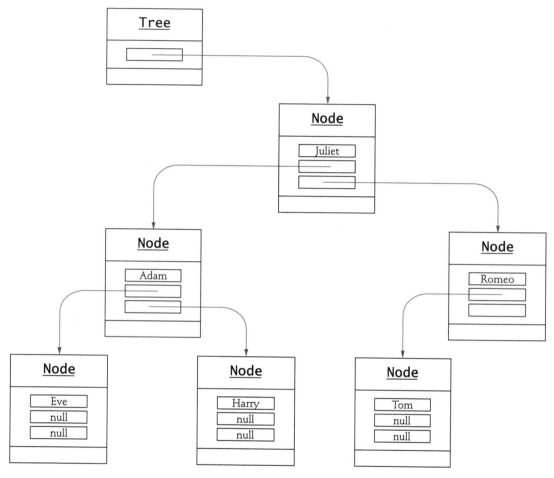

Figure 9

A Binary Tree That Is Not a Binary
Search Tree

To insert data into the tree, use the following algorithm:

◆ If you encounter a non-**null** node pointer, look at its data value. If the data value of that node is larger than the one you want to insert, continue the process with the left subtree. If the existing data value is smaller, continue the process with the right subtree.

◆ If you encounter a **null** node pointer, replace it with the new node.

For example, consider the tree in Figure 10. We want to insert a new element **Romeo** into it.

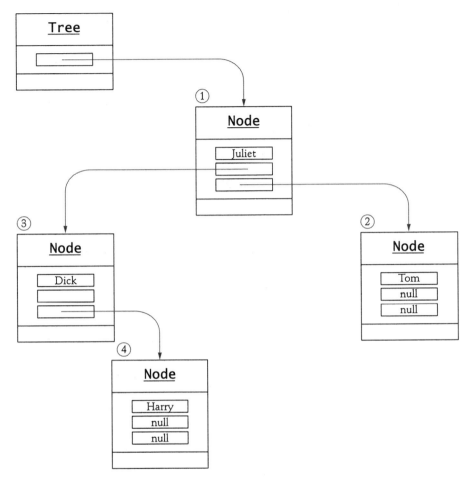

Figure 10

Binary Search Tree after Four
Insertions

Start with the root, Juliet. Romeo comes after Juliet, so you move to the right
subtree. You encounter the node Tom. Romeo comes before Tom, so you move to the
left subtree. But there is no left subtree. Hence you insert a new Romeo node as the
left child of Tom (see Figure 11).

You should convince yourself that the resulting tree is still a binary search tree.
When Romeo is inserted, it must end up as a right descendant of Juliet—that is
what the binary search tree condition means for the root node Juliet. The root
node doesn't care where in the right subtree the new node ends up. Moving along
to Tom, the right child of Juliet, all it cares about is that the new node Romeo ends up

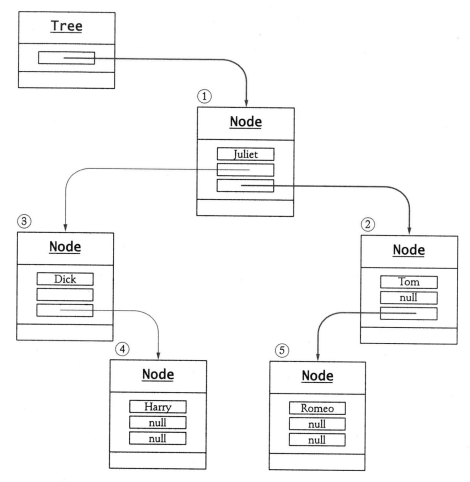

Figure 11

Binary Search Tree after Five
Insertions

somewhere on its left. There is nothing to its left, so **Romeo** becomes the new left
child, and the resulting tree is again a binary search tree.

Here is the code for the **insert** method of the **Tree** class:

```
class Tree
{ . . .
   public void insert(Comparable obj)
   { Node newNode = new Node();
     newNode.data = obj;
     newNode.left = null;
```

```
            newNode.right = null;
            if (root == null) root = newNode;
            else root.insertNode(newNode);
      }
      . . .
   }
```

If the tree is empty, simply set its root to the new node. Otherwise, you know that the new node must be inserted somewhere within the nodes, and you can ask the root node to perform the insertion. That node object calls the `insertNode` method of the **Node** class, which checks whether the new object is less than the object stored in the node. If so, the element is inserted in the left subtree; if not, it is inserted in the right subtree:

```
private class Node
{  . . .
   public void insertNode(Node newNode)
   {  if (newNode.data.compareTo(data) < 0)
      {  if (left == null) left = newNode;
         else left.insertNode(newNode);
      }
      else
      {  if (right == null) right = newNode;
         else right.insertNode(newNode);
      }
   }
   . . .
}
```

Let us trace the calls to `insertNode` when inserting **Romeo** into the tree in Figure 10. The first call to `insertNode` is

```
root.insertNode(newNode)
```

Since **root** points to **Juliet**, you compare **Juliet** with **Romeo** and find that you must call

```
root.right.insertNode(newNode)
```

root.right is **Tom**. Compare the data values again (**Tom** vs. **Romeo**) and find that you must now move to the left. Since **root.right.left** is **null**, set **root.right.left** to **newNode**, and the insertion is complete (see Figure 11).

Now that the data are inserted in the tree, what can you do with them? It turns out to be surprisingly simple to print all elements in sorted order. You *know* that all data in the left subtree of any node must come before the node and before all data in the right subtree. That is, the following algorithm will print the elements in sorted order:

1. Print the left subtree.
2. Print the data.
3. Print the right subtree.

Let's try this out with the tree in Figure 11. The algorithm tells us to

1.   Print the left subtree of `Juliet`; that is, `Dick` and children.
2.   Print `Juliet`.
3.   Print the right subtree of `Juliet`; that is, `Tom` and children.

How do you print the subtree starting at `Dick`?

1.   Print the left subtree of `Dick`. There is nothing to print.
2.   Print `Dick`.
3.   Print the right subtree of `Dick`, that is, `Harry`.

That is, the left subtree of `Juliet` is printed as

```
Dick
Harry
```

The right subtree of `Juliet` is the subtree starting at `Tom`. How is it printed? Again, using the same algorithm:

1.   Print the left subtree of `Tom`, that is, `Romeo`.
2.   Print `Tom`.
3.   Print the right subtree of `Tom`. There is nothing to print.

Thus, the right subtree of `Juliet` is printed as

```
Romeo
Tom
```

Now put it all together: the left subtree, `Juliet`, and the right subtree:

```
Dick
Harry
Juliet
Romeo
Tom
```

The tree is printed in sorted order.

Let us implement the `print` method. You need a worker method `printNodes` of the `Node` class:

```
private class Node
{  . . .
   public void printNodes()
   {  if (left != null)
         left.printNodes();
      System.out.println(data);
```

```
        if (right != null)
            right.printNodes();
    }
        . . .
}
```

To print the entire tree, start this recursive printing process at the root, with the following method of the Tree class.

```
class Tree
{   . . .
    public void print()
    {   if (root != null)
            root.printNodes();
    }
        . . .
}
```

Here is a complete program to insert data into a tree and to print them out in sorted order:

Program TreeTest.java

```
public class TreeTest
{   public static void main(String[] args)
    {   Tree staff = new Tree();
        staff.insert("Romeo");
        staff.insert("Juliet");
        staff.insert("Tom");
        staff.insert("Dick");
        staff.insert("Harry");

        staff.print();
    }
}

/**
    This class implements a binary search tree whose
    nodes hold objects that implement the Comparable
    interface.
*/

class Tree
{   /**
        Constructs an empty tree.
    */
    public Tree()
    {   root = null;
    }
```

```
/**
    Inserts a new node into the tree.
    @param obj  the object to insert
*/
public void insert(Comparable obj)
{  Node newNode = new Node();
   newNode.data = obj;
   newNode.left = null;
   newNode.right = null;
   if (root == null) root = newNode;
   else root.insertNode(newNode);
}


/**
    Prints the contents of the tree in sorted order.
*/
public void print()
{  if (root != null)
      root.printNodes();
}

private Node root;

private class Node
{  /**
       Inserts a new node as a descendant of this node.
       @param newNode  the node to insert
    */
   public void insertNode(Node newNode)
   {  if (newNode.data.compareTo(data) < 0)
      {  if (left == null) left = newNode;
         else left.insertNode(newNode);
      }
      else
      {  if (right == null) right = newNode;
         else right.insertNode(newNode);
      }
   }

   /**
       Prints this node and all of its descendants
       in sorted order.
    */
   public void printNodes()
   {  if (left != null)
         left.printNodes();
      System.out.println(data);
      if (right != null)
         right.printNodes();
   }
```

```
            public Comparable data;
            public Node left;
            public Node right;
        }
    }
```

Unlike a linked list or an array, a binary tree has no *insert positions*. You cannot select the position where you would like to insert an element into a binary search tree. The data structure is *self-organizing;* that is, each element finds its own place.

Deleting an element from a binary search tree is a little more complicated, because the children of the deleted node must be rearranged. We will leave that topic to a course on data structures.

Now that you have implemented this complex data structure, you may well wonder whether it is any good. Like links in a list, nodes are allocated one at a time. No existing elements need to be moved when a new element is inserted in the tree; that is an advantage. How fast insertion is, however, depends on the shape of the tree. If the tree is *balanced*—that is, if each node has approximately as many children on the left as on the right—then insertion is very fast, because about half of the nodes are eliminated in each step. On the other hand, if the tree happens to be *unbalanced,* then insertion can be slow—no faster than insertion into a linked list. (See Figure 12.)

If new elements are fairly random, the resulting tree is likely to be well balanced. However, if the incoming elements happen to be already in sorted order, then the resulting tree is completely unbalanced. Each new element is inserted at the end, and the entire tree must be traversed every time to find that end!

Binary search trees work well for random data, but if you suspect that the data in your application might be sorted or have long runs of sorted data, you should not use a binary search tree. There are more sophisticated tree structures whose methods keep trees balanced at all times. To learn more about those advanced data structures, you may want to enroll in a course about data structures.

◆ Random Fact 16.1

Software Piracy

As you read this, you have written a few computer programs, and you have experienced firsthand how much effort it takes to write even the humblest of programs. Writing a real software product, such as a financial application or a computer game, takes a lot of time and money. Few people, and fewer companies, are going to spend that kind of time and money if they don't have a reasonable chance to make more money from their effort. (Actually, some companies give away their software in the hope that users will upgrade to more elaborate paid versions. Other companies give away the software that enables users to read and use files but sell the software needed to create those files. Finally, there are individuals who donate their time, out of enthusiasm, and produce programs that you can copy freely.)

When selling software, a company must rely on the honesty of its customers. It is an easy matter for an unscrupulous person to make copies of computer programs without paying for

Figure 12

An Unbalanced Binary Search Tree

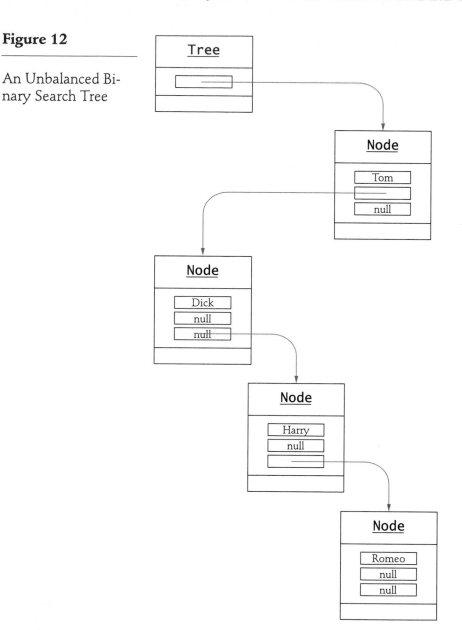

them. In most countries that is illegal. Most governments provide legal protection, such as copyright laws and patents, to encourage the development of new products. Countries that tolerate widespread piracy have found that they have an ample cheap supply of foreign software, but that no local manufacturer is stupid enough to design good software for their own citizens, such as word processors in the local script or financial programs adapted to the local tax laws.

When a mass market for software first appeared, vendors were enraged by the money they lost through piracy. They tried to fight back by various schemes to ensure that only the legitimate owner could use the software. Some manufacturers used *key disks:* floppy disks with a special pattern of holes burned in by a laser, which couldn't be copied. Others used *dongles:* devices that are attached between the computer and a printer port. Legitimate users hated these measures. They paid for the software, but they had to suffer through the inconvenience of inserting a key disk every time they started the software or having a meter's worth of dongles stick out from the back of their computer. In the United States, market pressures forced vendors to give up on these copy protection schemes, but they are still commonplace in other parts of the world.

Because it is so easy and inexpensive to pirate software, and the chance of being found out is minimal, you have to make a moral choice for yourself. If a package that you would really like to have is too expensive for your budget, do you steal it, or do you stay honest and get by with a more affordable product?

Chapter Summary

1. Linked lists permit faster insertion and removal in the middle of a data set than arrays and vectors do.

2. The links of a linked list are connected by *object references.* Each link contains a reference that either is `null` or specifies the location of the successor link.

3. Positions inside a linked list are specified with an iterator position.

4. Inserting and removing elements from a linked list involves rearranging the links of the surrounding elements.

5. Tree structures can significantly speed up the storage and retrieval of sorted data. The simplest of such tree structures is the binary search tree.

6. A binary search tree is a self-organizing data structure. You insert elements into the tree, not into a particular position. The insertion algorithm finds an appropriate position for the new element.

Classes, Objects, and Methods Introduced in This Chapter

```
java.util.AbstractList
    listIterator
java.util.LinkedList
    addFirst
    addLast
    getFirst
    getLast
```

```
      removeFirst
      removeLast
    java.util.ListIterator
      add
      hasNext
      next
      previous
      remove
```

Review Exercises

Exercise R16.1. Explain what the following code prints. Draw pictures of the linked list after each step. Just draw the forward links, as in Figure 1.

```java
LinkedList staff = new LinkedList();
staff.addFirst("Harry");
staff.addFirst("Dick");
staff.addFirst("Tom");
System.out.println(staff.removeFirst());
System.out.println(staff.removeFirst());
System.out.println(staff.removeFirst());
```

Exercise R16.2. Explain what the following code prints. Draw pictures of the linked list after each step. Just draw the forward links, as in Figure 1.

```java
LinkedList staff = new LinkedList();
staff.addFirst("Harry");
staff.addFirst("Dick");
staff.addFirst("Tom");
System.out.println(staff.removeLast());
System.out.println(staff.removeFirst());
System.out.println(staff.removeLast());
```

Exercise R16.3. Explain what the following code prints. Draw pictures of the linked list after each step. Just draw the forward links, as in Figure 1.

```java
LinkedList staff = new LinkedList();
staff.addFirst("Harry");
staff.addLast("Dick");
staff.addFirst("Tom");
System.out.println(staff.removeLast());
System.out.println(staff.removeFirst());
System.out.println(staff.removeLast());
```

Exercise R16.4. Explain what the following code prints. Draw pictures of the linked list and the iterator position after each step.

```
LinkedList staff = new LinkedList();
ListIterator iterator = staff.listIterator();
iterator.add("Tom");
iterator.add("Dick");
iterator.add("Harry");
iterator = staff.listIterator();
if (iterator.next().equals("Tom"))
    iterator.remove();
while (iterator.hasNext())
    System.out.println(iterator.next());
```

Exercise R16.5. Explain what the following code prints. Draw pictures of the linked list and the iterator position after each step.

```
LinkedList staff = new LinkedList();
ListIterator iterator = staff.listIterator();
iterator.add("Tom");
iterator.add("Dick");
iterator.add("Harry");
iterator = staff.listIterator();
iterator.next();
iterator.next();
iterator.add("Romeo");
iterator.next();
iterator.add("Juliet");
iterator = staff.listIterator();
iterator.next();
iterator.remove();
while (iterator.hasNext())
    System.out.println(iterator.next());
```

Exercise R16.6. The linked-list class in the Java library supports operations addLast and removeLast. To carry out these operations efficiently, the LinkedList class has an added reference last to the last node in the linked list. Draw a "before/after" diagram of the changes of the links in a linked list under the addLast and removeLast methods.

Exercise R16.7. The linked-list class in the Java library supports bidirectional iterators. To go backwards efficiently, each Link has an added reference, previous, to the predecessor node in the linked list. Draw a "before/after" diagram of the changes of the links in a linked list under the addFirst and removeFirst methods that shows how the previous links need to be updated.

Exercise R16.8. What advantages do lists have over arrays? What disadvantages do they have?

Exercise R16.9. Suppose you needed to organize a collection of telephone numbers for a company division. There are currently about 6,000 employees, and you know that the phone switch can handle at most 10,000 phone numbers. You expect several hundred lookups against the collection every day. Would you use an array or a linked list to store the information?

Exercise R16.10. Suppose you needed to keep a collection of appointments. Would you use a linked list or an array of **Appointment** objects?

Exercise R16.11. What is the difference between a binary tree and a binary search tree? Give examples of each.

Exercise R16.12. What is the difference between a balanced and an unbalanced tree? Give examples of each.

Exercise R16.13. The following elements are inserted into a binary search tree. Draw the resulting tree after each insertion.

Adam
Eve
Romeo
Juliet
Tom
Dick
Harry

Exercise R16.14. Insert the elements of the preceding exercise in opposite order. Then determine how the **Tree.print** method prints out both the tree from the preceding exercise and this tree. Explain how the printouts are related.

Exercise R16.15. Consider the following tree. In which order are the nodes printed by the **Tree.print** method?

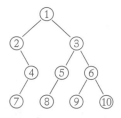

Programming Exercises

Exercise P16.1. Using just the public interface of the linked-list class, write a method

```
public static void downsize(LinkedList staff)
```

that removes every second employee from a linked-list.

Exercise P16.2. Using just the public interface of the linked list class, write a method

```
public static void reverse(LinkedList staff)
```

that reverses the entries in a linked list.

Exercise P16.3. Add a method `reverse()` to our implementation of the `LinkedList` class that reverses the links in a list. Implement this method by directly rerouting the links.

Exercise P16.4. Write a method `draw` to display a linked list graphically. Draw each element of the list as a box, and indicate the links with arrows.

Exercise P16.5. Add a method `size()` to our implementation of the `LinkedList` class that computes the number of elements in the list, by following links and counting the elements until the end of the list is reached.

Exercise P16.6. Add a `currentSize` field to our implementation of the `LinkedList` class. Modify the add and remove methods of both the linked list and the list iterator to update the `currentSize` field so that it always contains the correct size. Change the `size()` method of the preceding exercise to simply return the value of this instance variable.

Exercise P16.7. Write a class `Polynomial` that stores a polynomial such as

$$p(x) = 5x^{10} + 9x^7 - x - 10$$

Store it as a linked list of terms. A term contains the coefficient and the power of x. For example, you would store $p(x)$ as

$$(5, 10), (9, 7), (-1, 1), (-10, 0)$$

Supply methods to add, multiply, and print polynomials. For example, the polynomial p can be constructed as

```
Polynomial p = new Polynomial();
p.insert(-10, 0);
p.insert(-1, 1);
p.insert(9, 7);
p.insert(5, 10);
```

Then compute $p(x) \times p(x)$.

```
Polynomial q = p.multiply(p);
q.print();
```

Exercise P16.8. Design a data structure `Set` that can hold a set of integers. Hide the private implementation: a linked list of `Integer` objects. Provide the following methods:

◆ A constructor to make an empty set
◆ `add(int x)` to add x if it is not present
◆ `remove(int x)` to remove x if it is present
◆ `print()` to print all elements currently in the set

Exercise P16.9. Enhance the set class from the previous example by supplying an iterator object that supports *only* the `hasNext/next` methods.

```
SetIterator iterator = mySet.setIterator();
while (iterator.hasNext())
   System.out.println(iterator.next());
```

Note that the `next` method returns an `int`, not an object. For that reason, you cannot simply return a list iterator.

Exercise P16.10. Enhance the set class from the previous examples by supplying methods

```
Set union(Set other)
```

```
Set intersection(Set other)
```

that compute the union and intersection of two sets.

Exercise P16.11. Implement the *sieve of Eratosthenes:* a method for computing prime numbers, known to the ancient Greeks. Choose an n. This method will compute all prime numbers up to n. First insert all numbers from 2 to n into a set. Then erase all multiples of 2 (except 2); that is, 4, 6, 8, 10, 12, ... Erase all multiples of 3; that is, 6, 9, 12, 15, ... Go up to $\sqrt{n}$. The remaining numbers are all primes. Of course, you should use only the public interface of the set data structure.

Exercise P16.11. Implement the *sieve of Eratosthenes:* a method for computing prime numbers known to the ancient Greeks. Choose an n. This method will compute all prime numbers up to n. First insert all numbers from 1 to n into a set. Then erase all multiples of 2 (except 2); that is, 4, 6, 8, 10, 12, ... Erase all multiples of 3, that is, 6, 9, 12, 15, ... Go up to $\sqrt{n}$. The remaining numbers are all primes. Of course, you should use only the public interface of the set structure.

Exercise P16.12. Design an `IntTree` class that stores just integers, not objects. Support the same methods as the `Tree` class in the book.

Exercise R16.13. Write a method of the `Tree` class

```
Comparable smallest()
```

that returns the smallest element of a tree. You will also need to add a method to the `Node` class.

Exercise P16.14. Change the `print` method to print the tree as a tree shape. You can print the tree sideways. Extra credit if you instead display the tree graphically, with the root node centered on the top.

Exercise P16.15. The `print` method of the tree class prints a tree according to the following algorithm:

Print the left subtree
Print the current node
Print the right subtree

This is called *inorder traversal.* There are two other traversal schemes, namely *preorder traversal,*

Print the current node
Print the left subtree
Print the right subtree

and *postorder traversal,*

Print the left subtree
Print the right subtree
Print the current node

Write a program that builds a tree of strings from user input and then prints the user's choice of preorder, inorder, or postorder traversal.

Appendix  A1

Java Language Coding Guidelines

A1.1 Introduction

This coding style guide is a simplified version of one that has been used with good success both in industrial practice and for college courses.

A style guide is a set of mandatory requirements for layout and formatting. Uniform style makes it easier for you to read code from your instructor and classmates. You will really appreciate that if you do a team project. It is also easier for your instructor and your grader to grasp the essence of your programs quickly.

A style guide makes you a more productive programmer because it *reduces gratuitous choice.* If you don't have to make choices about trivial matters, you can spend your energy on the solution of real problems.

In these guidelines, several constructs are plainly outlawed. That doesn't mean that programmers using them are evil or incompetent. It does mean that the constructs are not essential and can be expressed just as well or even better with other language constructs.

If you already have programming experience, in Java or another language, you may be initially uncomfortable at giving up some fond habits. However, it is a sign of professionalism to set aside personal preferences in minor matters and to compromise for the benefit of your group.

These guidelines are necessarily somewhat dull. They also mention features that you may not yet have seen in class. Here are the most important highlights:

- ◆ Tabs are set every three spaces.
- ◆ Variable and method names are lowercase, with occasional upperCase characters in the middle.

- Class names start with an Uppercase letter
- Constant names are UPPERCASE, with an occasional UNDER_SCORE.
- There are spaces after keywords and surrounding binary operators.
- Braces must line up horizontally or vertically.
- No magic numbers may be used.
- Every method, except for `main` and overridden library methods, must have a comment.
- At most 30 lines of code may be used per method.
- No `continue` or `break` is allowed.
- All non-`final` variables must be private.

Note to the instructor: Of course, many programmers and organizations have strong feelings about coding style. If this style guide is incompatible with your own preferences or with local custom, please feel free to modify it. For that purpose, this coding style guide is available in electronic form from the author.

A1.2 Source Files

Each Java program is a collection of one or more source files. The executable program is obtained by compiling these files. Organize the material in each file as follows:

- `package` statement, if appropriate
- `import` statements
- A comment explaining the purpose of this file
- A `public` class
- Other classes, if appropriate

The comment explaining the purpose of this file should be in the format recognized by the `javadoc` utility. Start with a /**, and use the `@author` and `@version` tags:

```
/**
    COPYRIGHT (C) 1997 Harry Hacker. All Rights Reserved.
    Classes to manipulate widgets.
    Solves CS101 homework assignment #3
    @author Harry Hacker
    @version 1.01 1997/2/15
*/
```

A1.3 Classes

Each class should be preceded by a class comment explaining the purpose of the class.

List features in the following order:

- ◆ `public` instance methods
- ◆ `public static` methods
- ◆ `public static final` constants
- ◆ `private` instance methods
- ◆ `private static` methods
- ◆ `private` instance variables
- ◆ `private static final` constants
- ◆ `private static` variables (but see the last paragraph in this section)
- ◆ Inner classes

Leave a blank line after every method.

All non-`final` variables must be private. (However, instance variables of a `private` inner class may be public.) Methods and final variables can be either public or private, as appropriate.

All features must be tagged `public` or `private`. Do not use the default visibility (that is, package visibility) or the `protected` attribute.

Avoid static variables (except `final` ones) whenever possible. In the rare instance that you need static variables, you are permitted one static variable per file.

A1.4 Methods

Every method (except for `main`) starts with a comment in `javadoc` format.

```
/**
   Convert calendar date into Julian day.
   Note: This algorithm is from Press et al., Numerical Recipes
   in C, 2nd ed., Cambridge University Press, 1992
   @param day  day of the date to be converted
   @param month  month of the date to be converted
   @param year  year of the date to be converted
   @return  the Julian day number that begins at noon of the
   given calendar date.
*/
```

```
public static int dat2jul(int day, int month, int year)
{ . . .
}
```

Parameter names must be explicit, especially if they are integers or Boolean:

```
public Employee remove(int d, double s)
    // Huh?
public Employee remove(int department, double severancePay)
    // OK
```

Of course, for very generic methods, short parameter names may be very appropriate:

```
public static void sort(int[] a)
    // OK
```

Methods must have at most 30 lines of code. The method header, comments, blank lines, and lines containing only braces are not included in this count. Methods that consist of one long if/else or switch may be longer, provided each branch is 10 lines or fewer. This rule forces you to break up complex computations into separate methods.

A1.5 Variables and Constants

Do not define all variables at the beginning of a block:

```
public static double squareRoot(double a)
{  double xold; // Don't
   double xnew;
   boolean more;
   . . .
}
```

Define each variable just before it is used for the first time:

```
public static double squareRoot(double a)
{  . . .
   while (more)
   {  double xnew = (xold + a / xold) / 2;
      . . .
   }
   . . .
}
```

Do not define two variables on the same line:

```
int dimes = 0, nickels = 0; // Don't
```

In Java, constants must be defined with the keyword `final`. If the constant is used by multiple methods, declare it as `static final`. It is a good idea to define static final variables as `private` if no other class has an interest in them.

Do not use *magic numbers!* A magic number is a numeric constant embedded in code, without a constant definition. Any number except -1, 0, 1, and 2 is considered magic:

```
if (p.getX() < 300) // Don't
```

Use `final` variables instead:

```
final double WINDOW_WIDTH = 300;
. . .
if (p.getX() < WINDOW_WIDTH) // OK
```

Even the most reasonable cosmic constant is going to change one day. You think there are 365 days per year? Your customers on Mars are going to be pretty unhappy about your silly prejudice. Make a constant

```
public static final int DAYS_PER_YEAR = 365;
```

so that you can easily produce a Martian version without trying to find all the 365s, 364s, 366s, 367s, and so on, in your code.

A1.6 Control Flow

A1.6.1 The if Statement

Avoid the "if...if...else" trap. The code

```
if ( ... )
   if ( ... ) ...;
else ...;
```

will not do what the indentation level suggests, and it can take hours to find such a bug. Always use an extra pair of { ... } when dealing with "if...if...else":

```
if ( ... )
{  if ( ... ) ...;
} // {...} are necessary
else ...;

if ( ... )
{  if ( ... ) ...;
   else ...;
} // {...} not necessary, but they keep you out of trouble
```

A1.6.2 The for Statement

Use for loops only when a variable runs from somewhere to somewhere with some constant increment/decrement:

```
for (int i = 0; i < a.length; i++)
    System.out.println(a[i]);
```

Do not use the for loop for weird constructs such as

```
for (a = a / 2; count < ITERATIONS; System.out.println(xnew))
    // Don't
```

Make such a loop into a while loop. That way, the sequence of instructions is much clearer.

```
a = a / 2;
while (count < ITERATIONS) // OK
{  . . .
    System.out.println(xnew);
}
```

A1.6.3 Nonlinear Control Flow

We recommend that you not use the switch statement, because it is easy to fall through accidentally to an unwanted case. Use if/else instead.

We recommend that you not use the break or continue statements. Use another boolean variable to control the execution flow.

A1.6.4 Exceptions

Do not tag a method with an overly general exception specification:

```
Widget readWidget(Reader in)
    throws Exception // Bad
```

Instead, specifically declare any checked exceptions that your method may throw:

```
Widget readWidget(Reader in)
    throws IOException, MalformedWidgetException // Good
```

Do not "squelch" exceptions:

```
try
{  double price = in.readDouble();
}
catch (Exception e)
{} // Bad
```

Beginners often make this mistake "to keep the compiler happy". If the current method is not appropriate for handling the exception, simply use a throws specification and let one of its callers handle it.

A1.7 Lexical Issues

A1.7.1 Naming Convention

The following rules specify when to use upper- and lowercase letters in identifier names.

- All variable and method names and all data fields of classes are in lowercase (maybe with an occasional upperCase in the middle); for example, `firstPlayer`.
- All constants are in uppercase (maybe with an occasional UNDER_SCORE); for example, `CLOCK_RADIUS`.
- All class and interface names start with uppercase and are followed by lowercase letters (maybe with an occasional UpperCase letter); for example, `BankTeller`.

Names must be reasonably long and descriptive. Use `firstPlayer` instead of `fp`. No drppng f vwls. Local variables that are fairly routine can be short (`ch`, `i`) as long as they are really just boring holders for an input character, a loop counter, and so on. Also, do not use `ctr`, `c`, `cntr`, `cnt`, `c2` for variables in your method. Surely these variables all have specific purposes and can be named to remind the reader of them (for example, `current`, `next`, `previous`, `result`, ...).

A1.7.2 Indentation and White Space

Use tab stops every three columns. That means you will need to change the tab stop setting in your editor!

Use blank lines freely to separate parts of a method that are logically distinct.

Use a blank space around every binary operator:

```
x1 = (-b - Math.sqrt(b * b - 4 * a * c)) / (2 * a);   // Good
x1=(-b-Math.sqrt(b*b-4*a*c))/(2*a);//Bad
```

Leave a blank space after (and not before) each comma, semicolon, and keyword, but not after a method name:

```
if (x == 0) y = 0;
f(a, b[i]);
```

Every line must fit on 80 columns. If you must break a statement, add an indentation level for the continuation:

```
a[n] = ...........................................
   + .................;
```

Start the indented line with an operator (if possible).

If the condition in an `if` or `while` statement must be broken, be sure to brace the body in, *even if it consists of only one statement:*

```
if ( .......................................................
    && ..................
    || ......... )
{   . . .
}
```

If it weren't for the braces, it would be hard to separate the continuation of the condition visually from the statement to be executed.

A1.7.3 Braces

Opening and closing braces must line up, either horizontally or vertically:

```
while (i < n) { System.out.println(a[i]); i++; }
```

```
while (i < n)
{   System.out.println(a[i]);                    // OK
    i++;
}
```

Some programmers place the { in a line all by itself:

```
while (i < n)
{                                    // OK
    System.out.println(a[i]);
    i++;
}
```

That is fine, but it does take away a line of precious screen space. If you like the first approach (which is the one used in this book), be sure to type a tab after the opening brace.

Some programmers don't line up vertical braces but place the { behind the key word:

```
while (i < n) {                    // Don't
    System.out.println(a[i]);
    i++;
}
```

Doing so makes it hard to check that the braces match.

A1.7.4 Unstable Layout

Some programmers take great pride in lining up certain columns in their code:

```
firstRecord = in.readInt();
lastRecord  = in.readInt();
cutoff      = in.readDouble();
```

This is undeniably neat, but the layout is not *stable* under change. A new variable name that is longer than the preallotted number of columns requires that you move *all* entries around:

```
firstRecord        = in.readInt();
lastRecord         = in.readInt();
cutoff             = in.readDouble();
marginalFudgeFactor = in.readDouble();
```

This is just the kind of trap that makes you decide to use a short variable name like `mff` instead.

Do not use `//` comments for comments that extend for more than two lines. You don't want to have to move the `//` around when you edit the comment.

```
// comment — don't do this
// more  comment
// more  comment
```

Use `/* ... */` comments instead. When using `/* ... */` comments, don't "beautify" them with additional asterisks:

```
/* comment—don't do this
 * more  comment
 * more  comment
 */
```

It looks neat, but it is a major disincentive to update the comment. Some people have text editors that lay out comments. But even if you do, you don't know whether the next person who maintains your code has such an editor.

Instead, format long comments like this:

```
/*
   comment
   more  comment
   more  comment
*/
```

or this:

```
/*
comment
more  comment
more  comment
*/
```

These comments are easier to maintain as your program changes. If you have to choose between pretty but unmaintained comments and ugly comments that are up to date, truth wins over beauty.

Appendix A2

The Java Library

This appendix lists all classes and methods from the standard Java library that are used in this book.

In the following inheritance diagram, superclasses that are not used in this book are shown in gray. Some classes implement interfaces not covered in this book; they are omitted. Classes are sorted first by package, then alphabetically within a package.

```
java.lang.Object
    java.awt.Color implements Serializable
    java.awt.Component implements Serializable
        java.awt.Container
            javax.swing.JComponent
                javax.swing.AbstractButton
                    javax.swing.JButton
                    javax.swing.JMenuItem
                        javax.swing.JMenu
                    javax.swing.JToggleButton
                        javax.swing.JCheckBox
                        javax.swing.JRadioButton
                javax.swing.JComboBox
                javax.swing.JFileChooser
                javax.swing.JMenuBar
                javax.swing.JPanel
                javax.swing.JOptionPane
                javax.swing.JSlider
                javax.swing.text.JTextComponent
                    javax.swing.JTextArea
                    javax.swing.JTextField
            java.awt.Panel
                java.applet.Applet
                javax.swing.JApplet
```

```
        java.awt.Window
          java.awt.Frame
            javax.swing.JFrame
java.awt.FlowLayout implements Serializable
java.awt.Font implements Serializable
java.awt.Graphics
    java.awt.Graphics2D;
java.awt.GridLayout implements Serializable
java.awt.event.MouseAdapter implements MouseListener
java.awt.event.WindowAdapter implements WindowListener
java.awt.font.FontRenderContext
java.awt.font.TextLayout implements Cloneable
java.awt.geom.Line2D implements Cloneable, Shape
    java.awt.geom.Line2D.Double
java.awt.geom.Point2D implements Cloneable
    java.awt.geom.Point2D.Double
java.awt.geom.RectangularShape implements Cloneable, Shape
    java.awt.geom.Rectangle2D
        java.awt.Rectangle implements Serializable
        java.awt.Rectangle2D.Double
    java.awt.geom.Ellipse2D
        java.awt.geom.Ellipse2D.Double
java.io.File implements Comparable, Serializable
java.io.InputStream
    java.io.FileInputStream
    java.io.ObjectInputStream
java.io.OutputStream
    java.io.FileOutputStream
    java.io.ObjectOutputStream
java.io.RandomAccessFile
java.io.Reader
    java.io.BufferedReader
    java.io.InputStreamReader
        java.io.FileReader
java.io.Writer
    java.io.PrintWriter
    java.io.OutputStreamWriter
        java.io.FileWriter
java.lang.Boolean implements Serializable
java.lang.Math
java.lang.Number implements Serializable
    java.math.BigDecimal implements Comparable
    java.math.BigInteger implements Comparable
    java.lang.Double implements Comparable
    java.lang.Float implements Comparable
    java.lang.Integer implements Comparable
java.lang.String implements Comparable, Serializable
java.lang.System
java.lang.Throwable
```

```
            java.lang.Error
            java.lang.Exception
               java.lang.CloneNotSupportedException
               java.io.IOException
                  java.io.EOFException
                  java.io.FileNotFoundException
               java.lang.RuntimeException
                  java.lang.IllegalArgumentException
                     java.lang.NumberFormatException
                  java.lang.NullPointerException
      java.text.Format implements Cloneable, Serializable
         java.text.NumberFormat
      java.util.AbstractCollection
         java.util.AbstractList
            java.util.AbstractSequentialList
               java.util.LinkedList
      java.util.Arrays
      java.util.EventObject implements Serializable
         java.awt.AWTEvent
            java.awt.event.ActionEvent
            java.awt.event.ComponentEvent
               java.awt.event.InputEvent
                  java.awt.event.MouseEvent
               java.awt.event.WindowEvent
         javax.swing.event.ChangeEvent
      java.util.StringTokenizer
      java.util.Random implements Serializable
      java.util.Vector implements Cloneable, Serializable
      javax.swing.ButtonGroup implements Serializable
      javax.swing.ImageIcon implements Serializable
      javax.swing.border.AbstractBorder implements Serializable
         javax.swing.border.EtchedBorder
         javax.swing.border.TitledBorder
```

In the following descriptions, the phrase "this object" ("this component", "this container", and so forth) means the object (component, container, and so forth) on which the method is invoked (the implicit parameter, this).

A2.1 Package java.applet

Class java.applet.Applet

◆ void destroy()
This method is called when the applet is about to be terminated, after the last call to stop.

♦ `void init()`
This method is called when the applet has been loaded, before the first call to `start`. Applets override this method to carry out applet-specific initialization and to read applet parameters.

♦ `void start()`
This method is called after the `init` method and each time the applet is re-visited.

♦ `void stop()`
This method is called whenever the user has stopped watching this applet.

A2.2 Package `java.awt`

Class `java.awt.BorderLayout`

♦ `BorderLayout()`
This constructs a border layout. A border layout has five regions for adding components, called `"North"`, `"East"`, `"South"`, `"West"` and `"Center"`.

Class `java.awt.Color`

♦ `Color(float red, float green, float blue)`
This creates a color with the specified red, green, and blue values between `0.0F` and `1.0F`.
Parameters:
   `red`—The red component
   `green`—The green component
   `blue`—The blue component

Class `java.awt.Component`

♦ `int getHeight()`
This method gets the height of this component.
Returns: The height in pixels.

♦ `int getWidth()`
This method gets the width of this component.
Returns: The width in pixels.

♦ `void repaint()`
This method repaints this component by scheduling a call to the `paint` method.

Class `java.awt.Container`

◆ void add(Component c)

◆ void add(Component c, Object position)
These methods add a component to the end of this container. If a position is given, the layout manager is called to position the component.
Parameters:
  c—The component to be added
  position—An object expressing position information for the layout manager

◆ void paint(Graphics g)
This method is called when the surface of the container needs to be repainted.
Parameters:
  g—The graphics context

◆ void setLayout(LayoutManager manager)
This method sets the layout manager for this container.
Parameters:
  manager—A layout manager

◆ void setSize(int width, int height)
This method changes the size of this container.
Parameters:
  width—The new width
  height—The new height

Class `java.awt.FlowLayout`

◆ FlowLayout()
This constructs a new flow layout. A flow layout places as many components as possible in a row, without changing their size, and starts new rows when necessary.

Class `java.awt.Font`

◆ Font(String name, int style, int size)
This constructs a font object from the specified name, style, and point size.
Parameters:
  name—The font name, either a font face name or a logical font name, which must be one of "Dialog", "DialogInput", "Monospaced", "Serif", or "SansSerif"
  style—One of Font.PLAIN, Font.ITALIC, Font.BOLD, or

Font.ITALIC + Font.BOLD
  size—The point size of the font

Class java.awt.Frame

♦ void setTitle(String title)
This method sets the frame title.
Parameters:
  title—The title to be displayed in the border of the frame

Class java.awt.Graphics

♦ void setColor(Color c)
This method sets the current color. From now on, all graphics operations use this color.
Parameters:
  c—The new drawing color

♦ void setFont(Font font)
This method sets the current font. From now on, all text operations use this font.
Parameters:
  font—The font

Class java.awt.Graphics2D

♦ void draw(Shape s)
This method draws the outline of the given shape. Many classes—among them **Rectangle** and **Line2D.Double**—implement the **Shape** interface.
Parameters:
  s—The shape to be drawn

♦ void drawString(String s, int x, int y)

♦ void drawString(String s, float x, float y)
These methods draw a string in the current font.
Parameters:
  s—The string to draw
  x, y—The basepoint of the first character in the string

♦ void fill(Shape s)
This method draws the given shape and fills it with the current color.
Parameters:
  s—The shape to be filled

◆ FontRenderContext getFontRenderContext()
This method gets the font render context, an object that is used for measuring and drawing fonts.
Returns: The font render context.

Class java.awt.GridLayout

◆ GridLayout(int rows, int cols)
This constructor creates a grid layout with the specified number of rows and columns. The components in a grid layout are arranged in a grid with equal widths and heights. One, but not both, of rows and cols can be zero, in which case any number of objects can be placed in a row or in a column, respectively.
Parameters:
    rows—The number of rows in the grid
    cols—The number of columns in the grid

Class java.awt.Rectangle

◆ Rectangle()
This constructs a rectangle whose top left corner is at (0, 0) and whose width and height are both zero.

◆ Rectangle(int x, int y, int width, int height)
This constructs a rectangle with given top left corner and size.
Parameters:
    x, y—The upper left corner
    width—The width
    height—The height

◆ Rectangle intersection(Rectangle other)
This method computes the intersection of this rectangle with the specified rectangle.
Parameters:
    other—A rectangle
Returns: The largest rectangle contained in both this and other.

◆ void setLocation(int x, int y)
This method moves this rectangle to a new location.
Parameters:
    x, y—The new top left corner

◆ void setSize(int width, int height)
This method changes the size of this rectangle.
Parameters:
    width—The new width
    height—The new height

◆ `void translate(int dx, int dy)`
   This method moves this rectangle.
   Parameters:
       `dx`—The distance to move along the *x*-axis
       `dy`—The distance to move along the *y*-axis

◆ `Rectangle union(Rectangle other)`
   This method computes the union of this rectangle with the specified rectangle. This is not the set-theoretic union but the smallest rectangle that contains both `this` and `other`.
   Parameters:
       `other`—A rectangle
   Returns: The smallest rectangle containing both `this` and `other`.

Interface `java.awt.Shape`

The `Shape` interface describes shapes that can be drawn and filled by a `Graphics2D` object.

Class `java.awt.Window`

◆ `void addWindowListener(WindowListener listener)`
   This method adds a window listener. The window listener is notified whenever a window event originates from this window.
   Parameters:
       `listener`—The window listener to be added

◆ `void show()`
   This method makes the window visible and brings it to the front.

A2.3 Package `java.awt.event`

Class `java.awt.event.ActionEvent`

◆ `String getActionCommand()`
   This method returns a string describing this action event, such as the label of the button or menu that caused it. These strings are subject to change, so you should generally not use them to identify the event source.
   Returns: The action command string.

Interface `java.awt.event.ActionListener`

◆ `void actionPerformed(ActionEvent e)`
   The event source calls this method when an action occurs.

Class `java.awt.event.MouseAdapter`

- ◆ `void mouseClicked(MouseEvent e)`
  This method is called when the mouse has been clicked (that is, pressed and released in quick succession).
- ◆ `void mousePressed(MouseEvent e)`
  This method is called when a mouse button has been pressed.
- ◆ `void mouseReleased(MouseEvent e)`
  This method is called when a mouse button has been released.

Class `java.awt.event.MouseEvent`

- ◆ `int getX()`
  This method returns the horizontal position of the mouse when the event occurred
  Returns: The x-position of the mouse.
- ◆ `int getY()`
  This method returns the vertical position of the mouse when the event occurred
  Returns: The y-position of the mouse.

Interface `java.awt.event.MouseListener`

- ◆ `void mouseClicked(MouseEvent e)`
  This method is called when the mouse has been clicked (that is, pressed and released in quick succession).
- ◆ `void mousePressed(MouseEvent e)`
  This method is called when a mouse button has been pressed.
- ◆ `void mouseReleased(MouseEvent e)`
  This method is called when a mouse button has been released.

Class `java.awt.event.WindowAdapter`

- ◆ `void windowClosing(WindowEvent e)`
  This method is called when a window is in the process of being closed. Override this method if you want to exit the program when the window is closed.

Interface `java.awt.event.WindowListener`

- ◆ `void windowClosing(WindowEvent e)`
  This method is called when a window is in the process of being closed. Override this method if you want to exit the program when the window is closed.

A2.4 Package `java.awt.font`

Class `java.awt.font.FontRenderContext`

A font render context is an object that is used for measuring and drawing fonts. It is obtained by the `getFontRenderContext()` method of the `java.awt.Graphics2D` class and used by the `java.awt.font.TextLayout` constructor.

Class `java.awt.font.TextLayout`

◆ `TextLayout(String s, Font f, FontRenderContext context)`
This constructs a text layout to measure and draw a string in a particular font.
Parameters:
  `s`—The string to lay out
  `f`—The font to use
  `context`—The font render context of the output device

◆ `float getAdvance()`
This method gets the total width of the string laid out by this `TextLayout` object.
Returns: The advance (width in pixels) of the string.

◆ `float getAscent()`
This method gets the height above the base line of the string laid out by this `TextLayout` object.
Returns: The ascent of the string in pixels.

◆ `float getDescent()`
This method gets the depth below the base line of the string laid out by this `TextLayout` object.
Returns: The descent of the string in pixels.

◆ `float getLeading()`
This method gets the distance between two lines in the font used by this `TextLayout` object.
Returns: The leading of the font in pixels.

A2.5 Package `java.awt.geom`

Class `java.awt.geom.Ellipse2D.Double`

◆ `Ellipse2D.Double(double x, double y, double w, double h)`
This constructs an ellipse from the specified coordinates.

Parameters:
> x, y—The top left corner of the bounding rectangle
> w—The width of the bounding rectangle
> h—The height of the bounding rectangle

Class java.awt.geom.Line2D

◆ double getX1()

◆ double getX2()

◆ double getY1()

◆ double getY2()
These methods get the requested coordinate of an end point of this line.
Returns: The x- or y-coordinate of the first or second end point.

◆ void setLine(double x1, double y1, double x2, double y2)
This methods sets the end points of this line.
Parameters:
> x1, y1 A new end point of this line
> x2, y2—The other new end point

Class java.awt.geom.Line2D.Double

◆ Line2D.Double(double x1, double y1, double x2, double y2)
This constructs a line from the specified coordinates.
Parameters:
> x1, y1—One end point of the line
> x2, y2—The other end point

◆ Line2D.Double(Point2D p1, Point2D p2)
This constructs a line from the two end points.
Parameters:
> p1, p2—The end points of the line

Class java.awt.geom.Point2D

◆ double getX()

◆ double getY()
This method gets the requested coordinate of this point.
Returns: The x- or y-coordinate of this point.

◆ void setLocation(double x, double y)
This method sets the x- and y-coordinates of this point.
Parameters:
> x, y—The new location of this point

Class `java.awt.geom.Point2D.Double`

◆ `Point2D.Double(double x, double y)`
This constructs a point with the specified coordinates.
Parameters:
    `x, y`—The coordinates of the point

Class `java.awt.geom.Rectangle2D.Double`

◆ `Rectangle2D.Double(double x, double y, double w, double h)`
This constructs a rectangle.
Parameters:
    `x, y`—The upper left corner
    `w`—The width
    `h`—The height

Class `java.awt.geom.RectangularShape`

◆ `int getHeight()`
◆ `int getWidth()`
These methods get the height or width of the bounding rectangle of this rectangular shape.
Returns: The height or width, respectively.

◆ `double getCenterX()`
◆ `double getCenterY()`
◆ `double getMaxX()`
◆ `double getMaxY()`
◆ `double getMinX()`
◆ `double getMinY()`
These methods get the requested coordinate value of the corners or center of the bounding rectangle of this shape.
Returns: The minimum, center, or maximum x- and y-coordinates.

◆ `void setFrame(double x, double y, double w, double h)`
This method sets the bounding rectangle of this rectangular shape.
Parameters:
    `x, y`—The upper left corner
    `w`—The width
    `h`—The height

◆ `void setFrameFromDiagonal(double x1, double y1, double x2, double y2)`
This method sets the bounding rectangle of this rectangular shape.

Parameters:
> x1, y1—A corner point
> x2, y2—The diametrically opposite corner point

A2.6 Package java.io

Class java.io.BufferedReader

◆ BufferedReader(Reader in)
This constructs a buffered reader, an object that stores characters in a buffer for more efficient reading.
Parameters:
> in—A reader

◆ String readLine()
This method reads a line of input from this buffered reader.
Returns: The input line, or null if the end of input has been reached.

Class java.io.EOFException

◆ EOFException(String message)
This constructs an "end of file" exception object.
Parameters:
> message—The detail message

Class java.io.File

This class describes a disk file or directory. Objects of this class are returned by the getSelectedFile() method of the javax.swing.JFileChooser class.

Class java.io.FileInputStream

◆ FileInputStream(File f)
This constructs a file input stream and opens the chosen file. If the file cannot be opened for reading, a FileNotFoundException is thrown.
Parameters:
> f—The file to be opened for reading

◆ FileInputStream(String name)
This constructs a file input stream and opens the named file. If the file cannot be opened for reading, a FileNotFoundException is thrown.
Parameters:
> name—The name of the file to be opened for reading

Class `java.io.FileNotFoundException`

This exception is thrown when a file could not be opened.

Class `java.io.FileOutputStream`

◆ `FileOutputStream(File f)`
This constructs a file output stream and opens the chosen file. If the file cannot be opened for writing, a `FileNotFoundException` is thrown.
Parameters:
   f—The file to be opened for writing

◆ `FileOutputStream(String name)`
This constructs a file output stream and opens the named file. If the file cannot be opened for writing, a `FileNotFoundException` is thrown.
Parameters:
   name—The name of the file to be opened for writing

Class `java.io.FileReader`

◆ `FileReader(File f)`
This constructs a file reader and opens the chosen file. If the file cannot be opened for reading, a `FileNotFoundException` is thrown.
Parameters:
   f—The file to be opened for reading

◆ `FileReader(String name)`
This constructs a file reader and opens the named file. If the file cannot be opened for reading, a `FileNotFoundException` is thrown.
Parameters:
   name—The name of the file to be opened for reading

Class `java.io.FileWriter`

◆ `FileWriter(File f)`
This constructs a file writer and opens the chosen file. If the file cannot be opened for writing, a `FileNotFoundException` is thrown.
Parameters:
   f—The file to be opened for writing

◆ `FileWriter(String name)`
This constructs a file writer and opens the named file. If the file cannot be opened for writing, a `FileNotFoundException` is thrown.
Parameters:
   name—The name of the file to be opened for writing

Class `java.io.InputStream`

◆ `void close()`
This method closes this input stream (such as a `FileInputStream`) and releases any system resources associated with the stream.

◆ `int read()`
This method reads the next byte of data from this input stream.
Returns: The next byte of data, or −1 if the end of the stream is reached.

Class `java.io.InputStreamReader`

◆ `InputStreamReader(InputStream in)`
This constructs a reader from a specified input stream.
Parameters:
   `in`—The stream to read from

Class `java.io.IOException`

This type of exception is thrown when an input/output error is encountered.

Class java.io.ObjectInputStream

◆ `ObjectInputStream(InputStream in)`
This constructs an object input stream.
Parameters:
   `in`—The stream to read from

◆ `Object readObject()`
This method reads the next object from this object input stream.
Returns: The next object.

Class java.io.ObjectOutputStream

◆ `ObjectOutputStream(OutputStream out)`
This constructs an object output stream.
Parameters:
   `out`—The stream to write to

◆ `Object writeObject(Object obj)`
This method writes the next object to this object output stream.
Parameters:
   `obj`—The object to write

Class `java.io.OutputStream`

◆ `void close()`
This method closes this output stream (such as a `FileOutputStream`) and releases any system resources associated with this stream. A closed stream cannot perform output operations and cannot be reopened.

◆ `void write(int b)`
This method writes the lowest byte of b to this output stream.
Parameters:
   b—The integer whose lowest byte is written

Class `java.io.PrintStream`

◆ `void print(int x)`
◆ `void print(double x)`
◆ `void print(Object x)`
◆ `void print(String x)`
◆ `void println()`
◆ `void println(int x)`
◆ `void println(double x)`
◆ `void println(Object x)`
◆ `void println(String x)`
These methods print a value to this print stream. The `println` methods print a newline after the value. Objects are printed by converting them to strings with their `toString` method.
Parameters:
   x—The value to be printed

Class `java.io.PrintWriter`

◆ `PrintWriter(Writer out)`
This constructs a print writer from a specified writer (such as a `FileWriter`).
Parameters:
   out—The writer to write output to

◆ `void print(int x)`
◆ `void print(double x)`
◆ `void print(Object x)`
◆ `void print(String x)`
◆ `void println()`
◆ `void println(int x)`

◆ void println(double x)

◆ void println(Object x)

◆ void println(String x)
These methods print a value to this print writer. The println methods print a newline after the value. Objects are printed by converting them to strings with their toString method.
Parameters:
    x—The value to be printed

Class java.io.RandomAccessFile

◆ RandomAccessFile(String name, String mode)
This method opens a named random access file for reading or read/write access.
Parameters:
    name—The file name
    mode—"r" for reading or "rw" for read/write access

◆ long getFilePointer()
This method gets the current position in this file.
Returns: The current position for reading and writing.

◆ long length()
This method gets the length of this file.
Returns: The file length.

◆ char readChar()

◆ double readDouble()

◆ int readInt()
These methods read a value from the current position in this file.
Returns: The value that was read from the file.

◆ void seek(long position)
This method sets the position for reading and writing in this file.
Parameters:
    position—The new position

◆ void writeChar(int x)

◆ void writeChars(String x)

◆ void writeDouble(double x)

◆ void writeInt(int x)
These methods write a value to the current position in this file.
Parameters:
    x—The value to be written

Class java.io.Reader

◆ int read()
This method reads the next character from this reader (such as a FileReader).
Returns: The next character, or −1 if the end of the input is reached.

Interface java.io.Serializable

A class must implement this interface to enable its objects to be written to object streams.

Class java.io.Writer

◆ void write(int b)
This method writes the lowest two bytes of b to this writer (such as a FileWriter).
Parameters:
    b—The integer whose lowest two bytes are written

A2.7 Package java.lang

Class java.lang.Boolean

◆ Boolean(boolean value)
This constructs a wrapper object for a **boolean** value.
Parameters:
    value—The value to store in this object
◆ boolean booleanValue()
This method returns the **boolean** value stored in this **Boolean** object.
Returns: The Boolean value of this object.

Interface java.lang.Cloneable

A class implements this interface to indicate that the **Object.clone** method is allowed to make a shallow copy of its instance variables.

Class java.lang.CloneNotSupportedException

This exception is thrown when a program tries to use **Object.clone** to make a shallow copy of an object of a class that does not implement the **Cloneable** interface.

Interface java.lang.Comparable

◆ int compareTo(Object other)
This method compares this object with the **other** object.
Parameters:
   other—The object to be compared
Returns: A negative integer if this object is less than the other, zero if they are
equal, or a positive integer otherwise.

Class java.lang.Double

◆ Double(double value)
This constructs a wrapper object for a double-precision floating-point number.
Parameters:
   value—The value to store in this object
◆ double doubleValue()
This method returns the floating-point value stored in this **Double** wrapper
object.
Returns: The value stored in the object.
◆ static double parseDouble(String s)
This method returns the floating-point number that the string represents. If
the string cannot be interpreted as a number, a **NumberFormatException** is
thrown.
Parameters:
   s—The string to be parsed
Returns: The value represented by the string parameter.
◆ static String toString(double x)
This method converts a number to a string representation.
Parameters:
   x—The number to be converted
Returns: The string representing the number parameter.

Class java.lang.Error

This is the superclass for all unchecked system errors.

Class java.lang.Float

◆ static float parseFloat(String s)
This method returns the single-precision floating-point number that the
string represents. If the string cannot be interpreted as such a number, a
NumberFormatException is thrown.
Parameters:
   s—The string to be parsed
Returns: The value represented by the string parameter.

Class java.lang.IllegalArgumentException

◆ IllegalArgumentException()
This constructs an IllegalArgumentException with no detail message.

Class java.lang.Integer

◆ Integer(int value)
This constructs a wrapper object for an integer.
Parameters:
    value—The value to store in this object.

◆ int intValue()
This method returns the integer value stored in this wrapper object.
Returns: The value stored in the object.

◆ static int parseInt(String s)
This method returns the integer that the string represents. If the string cannot be interpreted as an integer, a NumberFormatException is thrown.
Parameters:
    s—The string to be parsed
Returns: The value represented by the string parameter.

◆ static Integer parseInt(String s, int base)
This method returns the integer value that the string represents in a given number system. If the string cannot be interpreted as an integer, a NumberFormat-Exception is thrown.
Parameters:
    s—The string to be parsed
    base—The base of the number system (such as 2 or 16)
Returns: The value represented by the string parameter.

◆ static String toString(int i)

◆ static String toString(int i, int base)
This method creates a string representation of an integer in a given number system. If no base is given, a decimal representation is created.
Parameters:
    i—An integer number
    base—The base of the number system (such as 2 or 16)
Returns: A string representation of the number parameter in the specified number system.

◆ static final int MAX_VALUE
This constant is the largest value of type int.

◆ static final int MIN_VALUE
This constant is the smallest (negative) value of type int.

Class `java.lang.Math`

◆ `static double abs(double x)`
This method returns the absolute value $|x|$.
Parameters:
  x—A floating-point value
Returns: The absolute value of the parameter.

◆ `static double acos(double x)`
This method returns the angle with the given cosine, $\cos^{-1} x \in [0, \pi]$.
Parameters:
  x—A floating-point value between -1 and 1
Returns: The arc cosine of the parameter, in radians.

◆ `static double asin(double x)`
This method returns the angle with the given sine, $\sin^{-1} x \in [-\pi/2, \pi/2]$.
Parameters:
  x—A floating-point value between -1 and 1
Returns: The arc sine of the parameter, in radians.

◆ `static double atan(double x)`
This method returns the angle with the given tangent, $\tan^{-1} x \in (-\pi/2, \pi/2)$.
Parameters:
  x—A floating-point value
Returns: The arc tangent of the parameter, in radians.

◆ `static double atan2(double y, double x)`
This method returns the arc tangent, $\tan^{-1}(y/x) \in (-\pi, \pi)$. If x can equal zero, or if it is necessary to distinguish "northwest" from "southeast" and "northeast" from "southwest", use this method instead of `atan(y/x)`.
Parameters:
  y, x—Two floating-point values
Returns: The angle, in radian, between the points $(0,0)$ and (x,y).

◆ `static double ceil(double x)`
This method returns the smallest integer $\geq x$ (as a `double`).
Parameters:
  x—A floating-point value
Returns: The "ceiling integer" of the parameter.

◆ `static double cos(double radians)`
This method returns the cosine of an angle given in radians.
Parameters:
  radians—An angle, in radians
Returns: The cosine of the parameter.

◆ `static double exp(double x)`
This method returns the value e^x, where e is the base of the natural logarithms.
Parameters:
  x—A floating-point value
Returns: e^x.

◆ `static double floor(double x)`
This method returns the largest integer $\leq x$ (as a `double`).
Parameters:
   x—A floating-point value
Returns: The "floor integer" of the parameter.

◆ `static double log(double x)`
This method returns the natural (base e) logarithm of x, $\ln x$.
Parameters:
   x—A number greater than 0.0.
Returns: The natural logarithm of the parameter.

◆ `static double pow(double x, double y)`
This method returns the value x^y ($x > 0$, or $x = 0$ and $y > 0$, or $x < 0$ and y
is an integer).
Parameters:
   x, y—Two floating-point values
Returns: The value of the first parameter raised to the power of the second
parameter.

◆ `static long round(double x)`
This method returns the closest `long` integer to the parameter.
Parameters:
   x—A floating-point value
Returns: The value of the parameter rounded to the nearest `long` value.

◆ `static double sin(double radians)`
This method returns the sine of an angle given in radians.
Parameters:
   radians—An angle, in radians
Returns: The sine of the parameter.

◆ `static double sqrt(double x)`
This method returns the square root of x, $\sqrt{x}$.
Parameters:
   x—A non-negative floating-point value
Returns: The square root of the parameter.

◆ `static double tan(double radians)`
This method returns the tangent of an angle given in radians.
Parameters:
   radians—An angle, in radians
Returns: The tangent of the parameter.

◆ `static double toDegrees(double radian)`
This method converts radians to degrees.
Parameters:
   radians—An angle, in radians
Returns: The angle in degrees.

◆ `static double toRadians(double degrees)`
This methods converts degrees to radians.

Parameters:
    degrees—An angle, in degrees
Returns: The angle in radians.

◆ `static final double E`
This constant is the value of *e*, the base of the natural logarithms.

◆ `static final double PI`
This constant is the value of π.

Class `java.lang.NullPointerException`

This exception is thrown when a program tries to use an object through a `null` reference.

Class `java.lang.NumberFormatException`

This exception is thrown when a program tries to parse the numerical value of a string that is not a number.

Class `java.lang.Object`

◆ `protected Object clone()`
This method constructs and returns a shallow copy of this object whose instance variables are copies of the instance variables of this object. If an instance variable of the object is an object reference itself, only the reference is copied, not the object itself. However, if the class does not implement the `Cloneable` interface, a `CloneNotSupportedException` is thrown. Subclasses should redefine this method to make a deep copy.
Returns: A copy of this object.

◆ `boolean equals(Object other)`
This method tests whether this and the other object are equal. This method tests only whether the object references are to the same object. Subclasses should redefine this method to compare the instance variables.
Parameters:
    other—The object with which to compare
Returns: `true` if the objects are equal, `false` otherwise.

◆ `String toString()`
This method returns a string representation of this object. This method produces only the class name and location of the objects. Subclasses should redefine this method to print the instance variables.
Returns: A string describing this object.

Class `java.lang.RuntimeException`

This is the superclass for all unchecked exceptions.

Class `java.lang.String`

- ◆ `int compareTo(String other)`
  This method compares this string and the other string lexicographically.
  Parameters:
      `other`—The other string to be compared
  Returns: A value less than 0 if this string is lexicographically less than the other, 0 if the strings are equal, and a value greater than 0 otherwise.

- ◆ `boolean equals(String other)`

- ◆ `boolean equalsIgnoreCase(String other)`
  These methods test whether two strings are equal, or whether they are equal when letter case is ignored.
  Parameters:
      `other`—The other string to be compared
  Returns: `true` if the strings are equal.

- ◆ `int length()`
  This method returns the length of this string.
  Returns: The count of characters in this string.

- ◆ `String substring(int begin)`

- ◆ `String substring(int begin, int pastEnd)`
  These methods return a new string that is a substring of this string, made up of all characters starting at position `begin` and up to either position `pastEnd - 1`, if `pastEnd` is given, or the end of the string.
  Parameters:
      `begin`—The beginning index, inclusive
      `pastEnd`—The ending index, exclusive
  Returns: The specified substring.

- ◆ `String toLowerCase()`
  This method returns a new string that consists of all characters in this string converted to lowercase.
  Returns: A string with all characters of this string converted to lowercase.

- ◆ `String toUpperCase()`
  This method returns a new string that consists of all characters in this string converted to uppercase.
  Returns: A string with all characters of this string converted to uppercase.

Class `java.lang.System`

- ◆ `static void arraycopy(Object from, int fromStart, Object to, int toStart, int count)`
  This method copies values from one array to the other. (The array parameters are of type `Object` because you can convert an array of numbers to an `Object` but not to an `Object[]`.)

Parameters:
>   from—The source array
>   fromStart—Start position in the source array
>   to—The destination array
>   toStart—Start position in the destination data
>   count—The number of array elements to be copied

◆ `static long currentTimeMillis()`
This method returns the difference, measured in milliseconds, between the current time and midnight, Universal Time, January 1, 1970.
Returns: the current time in milliseconds.

◆ `static void exit(int status)`
This method terminates the program.
Parameters:
>   status—exit status. A nonzero status code indicates abnormal termination.

◆ `static final InputStream in`
This object is the "standard input" stream. Reading from this stream typically reads keyboard input.

◆ `static final PrintStream out`
This object is the "standard output" stream. Printing to this stream typically sends output to the console window.

Class `java.lang.Throwable`

This is the superclass of exceptions and errors.

◆ `Throwable()`
This constructs a `Throwable` with no detail message.

◆ `void printStackTrace()`
This method prints a stack trace to the "standard error" stream. The stack trace contains a printout of this object and of all calls that were pending at the time it was created.

A2.8 Package `java.math`

Class `java.math.BigDecimal`

◆ `BigDecimal(String value)`
This constructs an arbitrary-precision floating-point number from the digits in the given string.
Parameters:
>   value—A string representing the floating-point number

◆ BigDecimal add(BigDecimal other)

◆ BigDecimal subtract(BigDecimal other)

◆ BigDecimal multiply(BigDecimal other)

◆ BigDecimal divide(BigDecimal other, int roundingMode)
These methods return a **BigDecimal** whose value is the sum, difference, product, or quotient of this number and the other.
Parameters:
   other—The other number.
   roundingMode—The Rounding mode to apply to division. Use **BigDecimal.ROUND_HALF_EVEN** for general-purpose calculations
Returns: The result of the arithmetic operation.

Class java.math.BigInteger

◆ BigInteger(String value)
This method constructs an arbitrary-precision integer from the digits in the given string.
Parameters:
   value—A string representing an arbitrary-precision integer

◆ BigInteger add(BigInteger other)

◆ BigInteger subtract(BigInteger other)

◆ BigInteger multiply(BigInteger other)

◆ BigInteger divide(BigInteger other)

◆ BigInteger mod(BigInteger other)
These methods return a **BigInteger** whose value is the sum, difference, product, quotient, or remainder of this number and the other.
Parameters:
   other—The other number
Returns: The result of the arithmetic operation.

A2.9 Package java.text

Class java.text.NumberFormat

◆ String format(double x)
This method formats a number according to the formatting rules of this object.
Parameters:
   x—The number to format
Returns: A string representing x.

◆ `static NumberFormat getCurrencyInstance()`
This method returns a currency formatter that formats numbers with a currency symbol and a fixed number of fractional digits.

◆ `static NumberFormat getNumberInstance()`
This method returns a number formatter that formats numbers with decimal separators and a user-selectable number of fractional digits.

◆ `void setMaximumFractionDigits(int digits)`
This method sets the maximum number of fraction digits used when formatting numbers. Numbers will be rounded if they have more digits.
Parameters:
 `digits`—The maximum number of to digits to use

◆ `void setMinimumFractionDigits(int digits)`
This method sets the minimum number of fraction digits used when formatting numbers. Formatted numbers are padded with trailing zeroes if they have fewer digits.
Parameters:
 `digits`—The minimum number of digits to use

A2.10 Package `java.util`

Class `java.util.AbstractList`

This is the superclass of other list classes such as `LinkedList`.

◆ `ListIterator listIterator()`
This method gets an iterator to visit the elements in this list.
Returns: An iterator that points before the first element in this list.

Class `java.util.Arrays`

◆ `static int binarySearch(Object[] a, Object key)`
This method searches the specified array for the specified object using the binary search algorithm. The array elements must implement the `Comparable` interface. The array must be sorted into ascending order.
Parameters:
 `a`—The array to be searched
 `key`—The value to be searched for
Returns: The position of the search key, if it is contained in the list; otherwise, $-index-$ 1, where *index* is the position where the element may be inserted.

◆ `static void sort(Object[] a)`
This method sorts the specified array of objects into ascending order. Its

elements must implement the **Comparable** interface.
Parameters:
　　a—The array to be sorted

Class `java.util.EventObject`

◆ `Object getSource()`
This method returns a reference to the object on which the event initially occurred.
Returns: The source of this event.

Class `java.util.ListIterator`

Objects of this class are created by the `listIterator` method of list classes.

◆ `void add(Object element)`
This method adds an element after the iterator position and moves the iterator after the new element.
Parameters:
　　`element`—The element to be added
◆ `boolean hasNext()`
This method checks whether the iterator is past the end of the list.
Returns: `true` if the iterator is not yet past the end of the list.
◆ `boolean hasPrevious()`
This method checks whether the iterator is before the first element of the list.
Returns: `true` if the iterator is not before the first element of the list.
◆ `Object next()`
This method moves the iterator over the next element in the linked list. This method throws an exception if the iterator is past the end of the list.
Returns: The object that was just skipped over.
◆ `Object previous()`
This method moves the iterator over the previous element in the linked list. This method throws an exception if the iterator is before the first element of the list.
Returns: The object that was just skipped over.
◆ `void remove()`
This method removes the element that was returned by the last call to **next** or **previous**. This method throws an exception if there was an **add** or **remove** operation after the last call to **next** or **previous**.

Class `java.util.LinkedList`

◆ `void addFirst(Object element)`
◆ `void addLast(Object element)`

These methods add an element before the first or after the last element in this list.
Parameters:
  element—The element to be added

◆ Object getFirst()

◆ Object getLast()
These methods return a reference to the specified element from this list.
Returns: The first or last element.

◆ Object removeFirst()

◆ Object removeLast()
These methods remove the specified element from this list.
Returns: A reference to the removed element.

Class java.util.Random

◆ Random()
This constructs a new random number generator.

◆ double nextDouble()
This method returns the next pseudorandom, uniformly distributed floating-point number between 0.0 (inclusive) and 1.0 (exclusive) from this random number generator's sequence.
Returns: The next pseudorandom floating-point number.

◆ int nextInt(int n)
This method returns the next pseudorandom, uniformly distributed integer between 0 (inclusive) and the specified value (exclusive) drawn from this random number generator's sequence.
Parameters:
  n—Number of values to draw from
Returns: The next pseudorandom integer.

Class java.util.StringTokenizer

◆ StringTokenizer(String s)
This method constructs a string tokenizer that breaks the specified string into tokens. Tokens are delimited by white space.
Parameters:
  s—The string to break up into tokens

◆ int countTokens()
This method counts the number of tokens in the string being processed by this tokenizer.
Returns: The token count.

◆ `boolean hasMoreTokens()`
This method checks whether all tokens in the string being processed by this tokenizer have been skipped over by `nextToken()`.
Returns: `true` if more tokens are available.

◆ `String nextToken()`
This method skips over and returns the next token in the string being processed by this tokenizer.
Returns: A string containing the token that was just skipped over.

Class `java.util.Vector`

◆ `Vector()`
This constructs an empty vector.

◆ `boolean add(Object element)`
This method appends an element to the end of this vector.
Parameters:
   `element`—The element to add
Returns: `true`. (This method returns a value because it overrides a method in the `List` interface.)

◆ `boolean add(int index, Object element)`
This method inserts an element into this vector.
Parameters:
   `index`—Insert position
   `element`—The element to insert
Returns: `true`.

◆ `void copyInto(Object[] array)`
This method copies the components of this vector into an array. The array must be big enough to hold all the objects in this vector.
Parameters:
   `array`—The array into which the components get copied

◆ `Object get(int index)`
This method gets a reference to the element at the specified position in this vector.
Parameters:
   `index`—Position of the element to return
Returns: The requested element.

◆ `Object remove(int index)`
This method removes the element at the specified position in this vector and returns a reference to it.
Parameters:
   `index`—Position of the element to remove
Returns: The removed element.

◆ `Object set(int index, Object element)`
This method replaces the element at a specified position in this vector.

Parameters:
   index—Position of element to replace
   element—Element to be stored at the specified position
Returns: The element previously at the specified position.

◆ `int size()`
This method returns the number of elements in this vector.
Returns: The number of elements in this vector.

A2.11 Package `javax.swing`

Class `javax.swing.AbstractButton`

◆ `void addActionListener(ActionListener listener)`
This method adds an action listener to the button.
Parameters:
   listener—The action listener to be added

◆ `boolean isSelected()`
This method returns the selection state of the button.
Returns: `true` if the button is selected.

◆ `void setSelected(boolean state)`
This method sets the selection state of the button. This method updates the button but does not trigger an action event.
Parameters:
   state—`true` to select, `false` to deselect.

Class `javax.swing.ButtonGroup`

◆ `void add(AbstractButton button)`
This method adds the button to the group.
   Parameters:
   button—The button to add

Class `javax.swing.ImageIcon`

◆ `ImageIcon(String filename)`
This constructs an image icon from the specified graphics file.
Parameters:
   filename—A string specifying a file name

Class `javax.swing.JApplet`

◆ `Container getContentPane()`
This method returns the content pane of this applet.
Returns: The content pane.

Class `javax.swing.JCheckBox`

◆ `JCheckBox(String text)`
This constructs a check box, having the given text, initially deselected. (Use
the `setSelected()` method to make the box selected; see the `javax.swing.`
`AbstractButton` class.)
Parameters:
     `text`—The text displayed next to the check box

Class `javax.swing.JComboBox`

◆ `JComboBox()`
This constructs a combo box with no items.

◆ `void addItem(Object item)`
This method adds an item to the item list of this combo box.
Parameters:
     `item`—The item to add

◆ `Object getSelectedItem()`
This method gets the currently selected item of this combo box.
Returns: The currently selected item.

◆ `boolean isEditable()`
This method checks whether the combo box is editable. An editable combo
box allows the user to type into the text field of the combo box.
Returns: `true` if the combo box is editable.

◆ `void setEditable(boolean state)`
This method is used to make the combo box editable or not.
Parameters:
     `state`—`true` to make editable, `false` to disable editing

Class `javax.swing.JComponent`

◆ `protected void paintComponent(Graphics g)`
Override this method to paint the surface of a component. Your method needs
to call `super.paintComponent(g)`.

Parameters:
> g—The graphics context used for drawing

◆ `void setBorder(Border b)`
This method sets the border of this component.
Parameters:
> b—The border to surround this component

◆ `void setFont(Font f)`
Sets the font used for the text in this component.
Parameters:
> f—A font

Class `javax.swing.JFileChooser`

◆ `JFileChooser()`
This constructs a file chooser.

◆ `File getSelectedFile()`
This method gets the selected file from this file chooser.
Returns: The selected file.

◆ `int showOpenDialog(Component parent)`
This method displays an "Open File" file chooser dialog.
Parameters:
> parent—The parent component or `null`

Returns: The return state of this file chooser after it has been closed by the user:
either `APPROVE_OPTION` or `CANCEL_OPTION`. If `APPROVE_OPTION` is returned,
call `getSelectedFile()` on this file chooser to get the file.

◆ `int showSaveDialog(Component parent)`
This method displays a "Save File" file chooser dialog.
Parameters:
> parent—The parent component or `null`

Returns: The return state of the file chooser after it has been closed by the user:
either `APPROVE_OPTION` or `CANCEL_OPTION`.

Class `javax.swing.JFrame`

◆ `Container getContentPane()`
This method returns the content pane of this frame.
Returns: The content pane.

◆ `void setJMenuBar(JMenuBar mb)`
This method sets the menu bar for this frame.
Parameters:
> mb—The menu bar. If `mb` is `null`, then the current menu bar is removed.

Class `javax.swing.JLabel`

◆ `JLabel(String text, int alignment)`
   This container creates a `JLabel` instance with the specified text and horizontal alignment.
   Parameters:
       `text`—The label text to be displayed by the label
       `alignment`—One of `SwingConstants.LEFT`, `SwingConstants.CENTER`, or `SwingConstants.RIGHT`

Class `javax.swing.JMenu`

◆ `JMenu()`
   This constructs a menu with no items.
◆ `JMenuItem add(JMenuItem menuItem)`
   This method appends a menu item to the end of this menu.
   Parameters:
       `menuItem`—The menu item to be added
   Returns: The menu item that was added.

Class `javax.swing.JMenuBar`

◆ `JMenuBar()`
   This constructs a menu bar with no menus.
◆ `JMenu add(JMenu menu)`
   This method appends a menu to the end of this menu bar.
   Parameters:
       `menu`—The menu to be added
   Returns: The menu that was added.

Class `javax.swing.JMenuItem`

◆ `JMenuItem(String text)`
   This constructs a menu item.
   Parameters:
       `text`—The text to appear in the menu item

Class `javax.swing.JOptionPane`

◆ `static String showInputDialog(Object prompt)`
   This method brings up a modal input dialog, which displays a prompt and

waits for the user to enter an input in a text field, preventing the user from doing anything else in this program.
Parameters:
    `prompt`—The prompt to display
Returns: The string that the user typed.

◆ `static void showMessageDialog(Component parent, Object message)`
This method brings up a confirmation dialog that displays a message and waits for the user to confirm it.
Parameters:
    `parent`—The parent component or `null`
    `message`—The message to display

Class `javax.swing.JPanel`

This class is a component without decorations. It can be used as an invisible container for other components. A subclass can implement its own `paintComponent` method.

Class `javax.swing.JRadioButton`

◆ `JRadioButton(String text)`
This constructs a radio button having the given text that is initially deselected. (Use the `setSelected()` method to select it, see the `javax.swing.AbstractButton` class.)
Parameters:
    `text`—The string displayed next to the radio button

Class `javax.swing.JSlider`

◆ `JSlider(int min, int max, int value)`
This constructor creates a horizontal slider using the specified minimum, maximum, and value.
Parameters:
    `min`—The smallest possible slider value
    `max`—The largest possible slider value
    `value`—The initial value of the slider

◆ `void addChangeListener(ChangeListener listener)`
This method adds a change listener to the slider.
Parameters:
    `listener`—The change listener to add

◆ `int getValue()`
This method returns the slider's value.
Returns: The current value of the slider.

Class `javax.swing.JTextArea`

◆ `JTextArea()`
This constructs an empty text area.

◆ `JTextArea(int columns)`
This constructs an empty text area with the specified number of rows and columns.
Parameters:
  `rows`—The number of rows
  `columns`—The number of columns

Class `javax.swing.JTextField`

◆ `JTextField()`
This constructs an empty text field.

◆ `JTextField(int columns)`
This constructs an empty text field with the specified number of columns.
Parameters:
  `columns`—The number of columns

◆ `void addActionListener(ActionListener listener)`
This method adds an action listener to be notified when the user hits the Enter key in this text field.
Parameters:
  `listener`—The action listener

A2.12 Package `javax.swing.border`

Class `javax.swing.border.EtchedBorder`

◆ `EtchedBorder()`
This constructor creates a lowered etched border.

Class `javax.swing.border.TitledBorder`

◆ `TitledBorder(Border b, String title)`
This constructor creates a titled border that adds a title to a given border.
Parameters:
  `b`—The border to which the title is added
  `title`—The title the border should display

A2.13 Package `javax.swing.event`

Class `javax.swing.event.ChangeEvent`

A slider emits change events when it is adjusted.

Class `javax.swing.event.ChangeListener`

◆ `void stateChanged(ChangeEvent e)`
This event is called when the event source has changed its state.
Parameters:
    `e`—A change event

A2.14 Package `javax.swing.text`

Class `javax.swing.text.JTextComponent`

◆ `String getText()`
This method returns the text contained in this text component.
Returns: The text

◆ `boolean isEditable()`
This method checks whether this text component is editable.
Returns: `true` if the component is editable.

◆ `void setEditable(boolean state)`
This method is used to make this text component editable or not.
Parameters:
    `state`—`true` to make editable, `false` to disable editing.

◆ `void setText(String text)`
This method sets the text of this text component to the specified text. If the text is empty, the old text is deleted.
Parameters:
    `text`—The new text to be set

Appendix A3

The Basic Latin and Latin-1 Subsets of Unicode

Table 1   The Basic Latin (ASCII) Subset of Unicode

Char.	Code	Dec.	Char.	Code	Dec.	Char.	Code	Dec.
			@	'\u0040'	64	'	'\u0060'	96
!	'\u0021'	33	A	'\u0041'	65	a	'\u0061'	97
"	'\u0022'	34	B	'\u0042'	66	b	'\u0062'	98
#	'\u0023'	35	C	'\u0043'	67	c	'\u0063'	99
$	'\u0024'	36	D	'\u0044'	68	d	'\u0064'	100
%	'\u0025'	37	E	'\u0045'	69	e	'\u0065'	101
&	'\u0026'	38	F	'\u0046'	70	f	'\u0066'	102
'	'\u0027'	39	G	'\u0047'	71	g	'\u0067'	103
(	'\u0028'	40	H	'\u0048'	72	h	'\u0068'	104
)	'\u0029'	41	I	'\u0049'	73	i	'\u0069'	105
*	'\u002A'	42	J	'\u004A'	74	j	'\u006A'	106
+	'\u002B'	43	K	'\u004B'	75	k	'\u006B'	107
,	'\u002C'	44	L	'\u004C'	76	l	'\u006C'	108
-	'\u002D'	45	M	'\u004D'	77	m	'\u006D'	109
.	'\u002E'	46	N	'\u004E'	78	n	'\u006E'	110
/	'\u002F'	47	O	'\u004F'	79	o	'\u006F'	111
0	'\u0030'	48	P	'\u0050'	80	p	'\u0070'	112
1	'\u0031'	49	Q	'\u0051'	81	q	'\u0071'	113
2	'\u0032'	50	R	'\u0052'	82	r	'\u0072'	114
3	'\u0033'	51	S	'\u0053'	83	s	'\u0073'	115
4	'\u0034'	52	T	'\u0054'	84	t	'\u0074'	116
5	'\u0035'	53	U	'\u0055'	85	u	'\u0075'	117
6	'\u0036'	54	V	'\u0056'	86	v	'\u0076'	118
7	'\u0037'	55	W	'\u0057'	87	w	'\u0077'	119
8	'\u0038'	56	X	'\u0058'	88	x	'\u0078'	120
9	'\u0039'	57	Y	'\u0059'	89	y	'\u0079'	121
:	'\u003A'	58	Z	'\u005A'	90	z	'\u007A'	122
;	'\u003B'	59	[	'\u005B'	91	{	'\u007B'	123
<	'\u003C'	60	\	'\u005C'	92	|	'\u007C'	124
=	'\u003D'	61	]	'\u005D'	93	}	'\u007D'	125
>	'\u003E'	62	^	'\u005E'	94	~	'\u007E'	126
?	'\u003F'	63	_	'\u005F'	95			

Table 2   The Latin-1 Subset of Unicode

Char.	Code	Dec.	Char.	Code	Dec.	Char.	Code	Dec.
			À	'\u00C0'	192	à	'\u00E0'	224
¡	'\u00A1'	161	Á	'\u00C1'	193	á	'\u00E1'	225
¢	'\u00A2'	162	Â	'\u00C2'	194	â	'\u00E2'	226
£	'\u00A3'	163	Ã	'\u00C3'	195	ã	'\u00E3'	227
¤	'\u00A4'	164	Ä	'\u00C4'	196	ä	'\u00E4'	228
¥	'\u00A5'	165	Å	'\u00C5'	197	å	'\u00E5'	229
¦	'\u00A6'	166	Æ	'\u00C6'	198	æ	'\u00E6'	230
§	'\u00A7'	167	Ç	'\u00C7'	199	ç	'\u00E7'	231
¨	'\u00A8'	168	È	'\u00C8'	200	è	'\u00E8'	232
©	'\u00A9'	169	É	'\u00C9'	201	é	'\u00E9'	233
ª	'\u00AA'	170	Ê	'\u00CA'	202	ê	'\u00EA'	234
«	'\u00AB'	171	Ë	'\u00CB'	203	ë	'\u00EB'	235
¬	'\u00AC'	172	Ì	'\u00CC'	204	ì	'\u00EC'	236
	'\u00AD'	173	Í	'\u00CD'	205	í	'\u00ED'	237
®	'\u00AE'	174	Î	'\u00CE'	206	î	'\u00EE'	238
¯	'\u00AF'	175	Ï	'\u00CF'	207	ï	'\u00EF'	239
°	'\u00B0'	176	Ð	'\u00D0'	208	ð	'\u00F0'	240
±	'\u00B1'	177	Ñ	'\u00D1'	209	ñ	'\u00F1'	241
²	'\u00B2'	178	Ò	'\u00D2'	210	ò	'\u00F2'	242
³	'\u00B3'	179	Ó	'\u00D3'	211	ó	'\u00F3'	243
´	'\u00B4'	180	Ô	'\u00D4'	212	ô	'\u00F4'	244
µ	'\u00B5'	181	Õ	'\u00D5'	213	õ	'\u00F5'	245
¶	'\u00B6'	182	Ö	'\u00D6'	214	ö	'\u00F6'	246
·	'\u00B7'	183	×	'\u00D7'	215	÷	'\u00F7'	247
¸	'\u00B8'	184	Ø	'\u00D8'	216	ø	'\u00F8'	248
¹	'\u00B9'	185	Ù	'\u00D9'	217	ù	'\u00F9'	249
º	'\u00BA'	186	Ú	'\u00DA'	218	ú	'\u00FA'	250
»	'\u00BB'	187	Û	'\u00DB'	219	û	'\u00FB'	251
¼	'\u00BC'	188	Ü	'\u00DC'	220	ü	'\u00FC'	252
½	'\u00BD'	189	Ý	'\u00DD'	221	ý	'\u00FD'	253
¾	'\u00BE'	190	Þ	'\u00DE'	222	þ	'\u00FE'	254
¿	'\u00BF'	191	ß	'\u00DF'	223	ÿ	'\u00FF'	255

Table 3   Selected
Control
Characters

Char.	Code	Dec.
Space	' '	32
Newline	'\n'	10
Return	'\r'	13
Tab	'\t'	9

Glossary

Abstract class A class that cannot be instantiated.

Abstract method A method with a name, parameter types, and return type, but without an implementation.

Accessor method A method that accesses an object but does not change it.

Actual parameter The expression supplied for a formal parameter of a method by the caller.

Aggregation The "has-a" relationship between classes.

Algorithm An unambiguous, executable, and terminating specification to solve a problem.

Applet A graphical Java program that executes inside a web browser or applet viewer.

Argument An actual parameter in a method call, or one of the values combined by an operator.

Array A collection of values of the same type stored in contiguous memory locations, each of which can be accessed by an integer index.

Assertion A claim that a certain condition holds in a particular program location.

Assignment Placing a new value into a variable.

Balanced tree A tree in which *each* subtree has the property that the number of descendants to the left is approximately the same as the number of descendants on the right.

Big-Oh notation The notation $g(n) = O(f(n))$, which denotes that the function g grows at the same rate with respect to n as the function f. For example, $10n^2 + 100n - 1000 = O(n^2)$.

Binary file A file in which values are stored in their binary representation and cannot be read as text.

Binary operator An operator that takes two arguments, for example $+$ in $x + y$.

Binary search A fast algorithm to find a value in a sorted array. It narrows the search down to half of the array in every step.

Binary search tree A binary tree in which *each* subtree has the property that all left descendants are smaller than the value stored in the root, and all right descendants are larger.

Binary tree A tree in which each node has at most two child nodes.

Bit Binary digit; the smallest unit of information, having two possible values: 0 and 1. A data element consisting of n bits has 2^n possible values.

Black box testing Testing methods without knowing their implementation.

Block A group of statements bracketed by {}.

Boolean operator $\longrightarrow$ **Logical operator**

Boolean type A type with two possible values: `true` and `false`.

Boundary test case A test case involving values that are at the outer boundary of the set of legal values. For example, if a function is expected to work for all nonnegative integers, then 0 is a boundary test case.

Bounds error Trying to access an array element that is outside the legal range.

Breakpoint A point in a program, specified in a debugger, at which it stops executing the program and lets the user inspect the program state.

`break` **statement** A statement that terminates a loop or `switch` statement.

Buffered input Input that is gathered in batches, for example, a line at a time.

Byte A number made up of eight bits. Essentially all currently manufactured computers use a byte as the smallest unit of storage in memory.

Bytecode Instructions for the Java virtual machine.

Call stack The set of all methods that currently have been called but not yet terminated, starting with the current method and ending with `main`.

Case-sensitive Distinguishing upper- and lowercase characters.

Cast Explicitly converting a value from one type to a different type. For example, the cast from a floating-point number `x` to an integer is expressed in Java by the cast notation `(int)x`.

Class A programmer-defined data type.

Class method A method with no implicit parameter. Class methods are defined with the keyword `static`.

Class variable A variable defined in a class that has only one value for the whole class, which can be accessed and changed by any method of that class. Class variables are defined with the keyword `static`.

Cloning Making a copy of an object whose state can be modified independently of the original object.

Command line The line you type when you start a program in a command window in DOS/Windows or UNIX. It consists of the program name and the command line arguments.

Comment An explanation to help the human reader understand a section of a program; ignored by the compiler.

Compiler A program that translates code in a high-level language (such as Java) to machine instructions (such as bytecode for the Java virtual machine).

Compile-time error An error that is detected when a program is compiled.

Compound statement A statement such as `if` or `while` that is made up of several parts such as a condition and a body.

Concatenation Placing one string after another to form a new string.

Console program A Java program that does not have a graphical window. A console program reads input from the keyboard and writes output to the terminal screen.

Constant A value that cannot be changed by a program. In Java, constants are defined with the keyword `final`.

Construction Setting a newly allocated object to an initial state.

Constructor A method that initializes a newly allocated object.

Container A user interface component that can hold other components and present them together to the user. Also, a data structure such as a linked list or a vector that can hold a collection of objects and present them individually to a program.

CPU (Central Processing Unit) The part of a computer that executes the machine instructions.

Debugger A program that lets a user run another program one or a few steps at a time, stop execution, and inspect the variables in order to analyze it for bugs.

Default constructor A constructor that is invoked with no parameters.

Dependency The "uses" relationship between classes, in which one class needs services provided by another class.

Dictionary ordering → **Lexicographic ordering**

Directory A structure on a disk that can hold files or other directories; also called a folder.

Dot notation for method calls The notation *object*.*method*(*parameters*) used to invoke a method on an object.

Doubly linked list A linked list in which each link has a reference to both its predecessor and successor links.

Early binding Choosing at compile time among several methods with the same name but different parameter types.

Encapsulation The hiding of implementation details.

End of file The condition that is true when all characters of a file have been read. Note that there is no special "end of file character". When composing a file on the keyboard, you may need to type a special character to tell the operating system to end the file, but that character is not part of the file.

Escape character A character in text that is not taken literally but has a special meaning when combined with the character or characters that follow it. The \ character is an escape character in Java strings.

Event class A class that contains information about an event, such as its source.

Event adapter A class that implements an event listener interface by defining all methods to do nothing.

Event listener An object that is notified by an event source when an event occurs.

Event source An object that can notify other classes of events.

Exception A class that signals a condition that prevents the program from continuing normally. When such a condition occurs, an object of the exception class is thrown.

Exception handler A sequence of statements that is given control when an exception of a particular type has been thrown and caught.

Explicit parameter A parameter of a method other than the object on which the method is invoked.

Expression A syntactical construct that is made up of constants, variables, method calls, and operators combining them.

Extension The last part of a file name, which specifies the file type. For example, the extension .java denotes a Java file.

Fibonacci numbers The sequence of numbers 1, 1, 2, 3, 5, 8, 13, . . . , in which every term is the sum of its two predecessors.

File A sequence of bytes that is stored on disk.

File pointer The position within a random-access file of the next byte to be read or written. It can be moved so as to access any byte in the file.

Floating-point number A number that can have a fractional part.

Folder → **Directory**

Formal parameter A variable in a method that is initialized with an actual parameter value when the method is called.

Frame A window with a border and a title bar.

Garbage collection Automatic reclamation of memory occupied by objects that are no longer referenced.

goto statement A statement that transfers control to some other statement, which is tagged with a label. Java does not have a **goto** statement.

grep The "generalized regular expression pattern" search program, useful for finding all strings matching a pattern in a set of files.

HTML Hypertext Markup Language, in which Web pages are described.

Implicit parameter The object on which a method is invoked. For example, in the call x.f(y), the object x is the implicit parameter of the method f.

Inheritance The "is-a" relationship between a more general superclass and a more specialized subclass.

Initialization Setting a variable to a well-defined value when it is created.

Inner class A class that is defined inside another class.

Instance method A method with an implicit parameter; that is, a method that is invoked on an instance of a class.

Instance of a class An object whose type is that class.

Instance variable A variable defined in a class for which every object of the class has its own value.

Instantiation of a class Constructing an object of that class.

Integer A number that cannot have a fractional part.

Integer division Taking the quotient of two integers, discarding the remainder. In Java the / symbol denotes integer division if both arguments are integers. For example, 11 / 4 is 2, not 2.75.

Interface A type with no instance variables and only abstract methods.

Iterator An object that can inspect all elements in a container such as a linked list.

Late binding Choosing at run time among several methods with the same name invoked on objects belonging to subclasses of the same superclass.

Layout manager A class that arranges user interface components inside a container.

Lexicographic ordering Ordering strings in the same order as in a dictionary, by skipping all matching characters and comparing the first nonmatching characters of both strings. For example, "orbit" comes before "orchid" in lexicographic ordering. Note that in Java, unlike a dictionary, the ordering is case-sensitive: Z comes before a.

Library A set of precompiled classes that can be included into programs.

Linear search Searching a container (such as an array, list, or vector) for an object by inspecting each element in turn.

Linked list A data structure that can hold an arbitrary number of objects, each of which is stored in a link object, which contains a pointer to the next link.

Local variable A variable whose scope is a block.

Logical operator An operator that can be applied to Boolean values. Java has three logical operators: &&, ||, and !.

Logic error An error in a syntactically correct program that causes it to act differently from its specification.

Loop A sequence of instructions that is executed repeatedly.

Loop and a half A loop whose termination decision is neither at the beginning nor at the end.

Loop invariant A statement about the program state that is preserved when the statements in the loop are executed once.

Machine code Instructions that can be executed directly by the CPU.

Magic number A number that appears in a program without explanation.

main **method** The method that is first called when a Java application executes.

Merge sort A sorting algorithm that first sorts two halves of a data structure and then merges the sorted subarrays together.

Method A sequence of statements that has a name, may have formal parameters, and may return a value. A method can be invoked any number of times, with different values for its parameters.

Method signature The name of a method and the types of its parameters.

Mutator method A method that changes the state of an object.

Name clash Accidentally using the same name to denote two program features in a way that cannot be resolved by the compiler.

Negative test case A test case that is expected to fail. For example, when testing a root-finding program, an attempt to compute the square root of -1 is a negative test case.

Nested block A block that is contained inside another block.

Newline The `'\n'` character, which indicates the end of a line.

new **operator** An operator that allocates new objects.

Null reference A reference that does not refer to any object.

Object A value of a class type.

Object-oriented design Designing a program by discovering objects, their properties, and their relationships.

Off-by-one error A common programming error in which a value is one larger or smaller than it should be.

Opening a file Preparing a file for reading or writing.

Operating system The software that launches application programs and provides services (such as a file system) for those programs.

Operator A symbol denoting a mathematical or logical operation, such as + or **&&**.

Operator associativity The rule that governs in which order operators of the same precedence are executed. For example, in Java the - operator is left-associative because a - b - c is interpreted as (a - b) - c, and = is right-associative because a = b = c is interpreted as a = (b = c).

Operator precedence The rule that governs which operator is evaluated first. For example, in Java the **&&** operator has a higher precedence than the || operator. Hence a || b **&&** c is interpreted as a || (b **&&** c).

Oracle A program that predicts how another program should behave.

Overloading Giving more than one meaning to a method name.

Overriding Redefining a method in a subclass.

Package A collection of related classes. The `import` statement is used to access one or more classes in a package.

Parallel arrays Arrays of the same length, in which corresponding elements are logically related.

Parameter An item of information that is specified to a method when the method is called. For example, in the call `System.out.println("Hello, World!")`, the parameters are the implicit parameter `System.out` and the explicit parameter `"Hello, World!"`.

Parameter passing Specifying expressions to be actual parameter values for a method when it is called.

Partially filled array An array that is not filled to capacity, together with a companion variable that indicates the number of elements actually stored.

Polymorphism Selecting a method among several methods that have the same name on the basis of the actual types of the implicit parameters.

Positive test case A test case that a method is expected to handle correctly.

Postfix operator A unary operator that is written after its argument.

Precondition A condition that must be true when a method is called if the method is to work correctly.

Predicate method A method that returns a Boolean value.

Prefix operator A unary operator that is written before its argument.

Project A collection of source files and their dependencies.

Prompt A string that tells the user to provide input.

RAM (random-access memory) Electronic circuits in a computer that can store code and data of running programs.

Random access The ability to access any value directly without having to read the values preceding it.

Recursive method A method that can call itself with simpler values. It must handle the simplest values without calling itself.

Redirection Linking the input or output of a program to a file instead of the keyboard or display.

Reference A variable that permits access to an object. A variable that is defined to be of a class type actually holds a reference to an object of that class, not the object itself.

Regression testing Keeping old test cases and testing every revision of a program against them.

Regular expression A pattern of characters that defines a set of strings according to their content. Each character position in a regular expression can be specified as an individual character; a set of characters such as `[abc]`; a range of characters such as `[a-z]`; a set of forbidden characters, such as `[^0-9]`; a repetition of one or more strings, such as `[0-9]*`; a set of alternative choices such as `+|-`; or a concatenation of other expressions.

Reserved word A word that has a special meaning in a programming language and therefore cannot be used as a name by the programmer.

Return value The value returned by a method through a `return` statement.

Roundoff error An error introduced by the fact that the computer can store only a finite number of digits of a floating-point number.

Run-time error $\longrightarrow$ **Logic error**

Run-time stack The data structure that stores the local variables of all called methods as a program runs.

Scope The part of a program in which a variable is defined.

Selection sort A sorting algorithm in which the smallest element is repeatedly found and removed until no elements remain.

Sentinel A value in input that is not to be used as an actual input value but to signal the end of input.

Sequential access Accessing values one after another without skipping over any of them.

Shadowing Hiding a variable by defining another one with the same name.

Shell A part of an operating system in which the user types commands to execute programs and manipulate files.

Shell script A file that contains commands for running programs and manipulating files. Typing the name of the shell script file on the command line causes those commands to be executed.

Side effect An effect of a method other than returning a value.

Signature $\longrightarrow$ **Method signature**

Simple statement A statement consisting only of an expression.

Single-stepping Executing a program in the debugger one statement at a time.

Source file A file containing instructions in a programming language such as Java.

Stack A data structure in which elements can be added and removed only at one location, called the top of the stack.

Statement A syntactical unit in a program. In Java a statement is either a simple statement, a compound statement, or a block.

Static method $\longrightarrow$ **Class method**

Static variable $\longrightarrow$ **Class variable**

Stream An abstraction for a sequence of bytes from which data can be read or to which data can be written.

String A sequence of characters.

Stub A method with no or minimal functionality.

Subclass A class that inherits variables and methods from a superclass but adds instance variables, adds methods, or redefines methods.

Superclass A general class from which a more specialized class (a subclass) inherits.

Syntax Rules that define how to form instructions in a particular programming language.

Syntax error An instruction that does not follow the programming language rules and is rejected by the compiler.

Tab character The '\t' character, which advances the next character on the line to the next one of a set of fixed positions known as tab stops.

Ternary operator An operator with three arguments. Java has one ternary operator, a ? b : c.

Test coverage The instructions of a program that are executed in a set of test cases.

Test harness A program that calls a function that needs to be tested, supplying parameters and analyzing the function's return value.

Test suite A set of test cases for a program.

Text field A user interface component that allows a user to provide text input.

Text file A file in which values are stored in their text representation.

Trace message A message that is printed during a program run for debugging purposes.

Two-dimensional array A tabular arrangement of elements in which an element is specified by a row and a column index.

Unary operator An operator with one argument.

Unicode A standard code that assigns code values consisting of two bytes to characters used in scripts around the world. Java stores the characters in all strings as their Unicode values.

Uninitialized variable A variable that has not been set to a particular value. In Java, using an uninitialized local variable is a syntax error.

Unit test A test of a method by itself, isolated from the remainder of the program.

User interface component A building block for a graphical user interface, such as a button or a text field. User interface components are used to present information to the user and allow the user to enter information to the program.

Value parameter A method parameter whose value is copied into a formal parameter of a method. If a variable is passed as a value parameter, changes made to the parameter inside the method do not affect the original variable outside the method. In Java, all parameters are value parameters. If a variable is an object reference and is passed to a method, the method cannot change which object the original variable refers to. However, the method can invoke methods to change the state of the object itself.

Variable A symbol in a program that identifies a storage location that can hold different values.

Vector A Java data structure that allows random access and that can grow to hold an arbitrary number of elements.

Virtual machine A program that simulates a CPU that can be implemented efficiently on a variety of actual machines. A given program in Java bytecode can be executed by any Java virtual machine, regardless of which CPU is used to run the virtual machine itself.

Visual programming Programming by arranging graphical elements on a form, setting program behavior by selecting properties for these elements, and writing only a small amount of "glue" code linking them.

void **keyword** A keyword indicating no type or an unknown type.

Watch window A window in a debugger that shows the current values of selected variables.

White-box testing Testing functions taking their implementation into account; for example, by selecting boundary test cases and ensuring that all branches of the code are covered by some test case.

White space Any sequence of only space, tab, and newline characters.

Photo Credits

Chapter 1

Figures 1 & 2: Courtesy Intel. *Figure 3:* Courtesy Lisa Passmore. *Figure 4:* Courtesy Seagate. *Figure 5:* Courtesy Iomega. *Figure 6:* Courtesy Toshiba/The Benjamin Group. *Figure 7:* Courtesy Maynard Electronics. *Figure 8.* Courtesy of International Business Machines Corporation. *Figure 9:* Courtesy Intel. *Figure 11:* Sperry Univac, Division of Sperry Corporation.

Chapter 3

Figure 4: Courtesy of International Business Machines Corporation.

Chapter 4:

Figure 13: Courtesy SAS Institute, Inc. *Figure 14:* Courtesy of Autodesk, Inc. *Figure 15:* M. Tchervkf/The Image Bank.

Chapter 5

Figure 5: Courtesy Digital Equipment Corporation, Corporate Photo Library. *Figure 6:* ©Sun Microsystems. *Page 198* ©1997 by Sidney Harris.

Chapter 8

Figure 2: Naval Surface Weapons Center.

Index